Praise for *America Aflame*

"Riveting, often heartbreaking . . . [A] masterly synthesis of political, social, economic and religious history . . . Goldfield's thought experiment in alternative history is provocative in the best sense. Most history books try to explain the past. The exceptional ones, of which *America Aflame* is a distinguished example, remind us that the past is ultimately as inscrutable as the future."
—**Andrew Delbanco**, *The New York Times Book Review*

"A sweeping, insightful and articulate new look at the war and the country it transformed."
—**Kasey S. Pipes**, *The Dallas Morning News*

"A riveting, comprehensive, and delightful piece of historical writing . . . [Goldfield] is a wonderful storyteller with a facile, compact prose style that transforms complex historical ingredients into a savory meal."
—**David Holahan**, *The Christian Science Monitor*

"A monumental new appraisal of the war."   —**Nick Owchar**, *Los Angeles Times*

"Fascinating . . . Meticulously researched, passionately argued."
—**Joan Walsh**, *Salon*

"This provocative new look at the era of Civil War and Reconstruction places evangelical religion at center stage. Northern evangelicals branded slavery a sin; southern theologians portrayed it as a positive good ordained by God. Political questions became a moral battle between good and evil."
—**James M. McPherson, author of** *Battle Cry of Freedom* **and**
Tried by War: Abraham Lincoln as Commander in Chief

"[*America Aflame*] is unusually striking as narrative . . . A particularly effective device that lends coherence to an otherwise sprawling canvas is frequent reference to how the entire period was experience by a select cast of notables. For all its other virtues, the book's best feature is its argument . . . with its forceful articulation and wealth of supporting evidence, it offers readers a gratifyingly clear statement about the war's encompassing significance."
—**Mark Noll**, *The American Interest* **magazine**

"In *America Aflame* David Goldfield offers a wonderful portrait of a nation scarred yet transformed by a war that in retrospect seems as unnecessary as it was destructive."   —**Doug Bandow**, *Forbes*

"Brilliant . . . [Goldfield's] persuasively argued and elegantly written synthesis of war historiography should find its way to every thoughtful American's bookshelf. By skillfully peeling away the veneer of righteousness from the North as well as putting the stain of the South's racial bondage in historical context, Goldfield reveals an America that all its citizens hoped it might someday become."
—**Gordon Berg**, *Civil War Times*

"Here is an extremely thoughtful, persuasively argued, beautifully written, and highly original look at the Civil War and its impact on the nation—both in the short and long term. This book should stir much healthy debate, challenging us to reconsider the fundamentals of the war we think we know so well."
—**Harold Holzer, author of *Lincoln President-Elect***

"*America Aflame* immediately invites comparison with classic works ranging from James Ford Rhodes to James McPherson . . . A most timely offering as the country enters the sesquicentennial of its great national trauma."
—**George C. Rable, *The Virginia Magazine of History and Biography***

"In *America Aflame*, distinguished historian David Goldfield turns an unflinching eye on a—if not the—central event in American history. The resulting narrative goes far toward correcting the popular tendency to romanticize the Civil War. Few histories of the war make its meaning and impact so central to their narratives."
—**Gaines M. Foster, author of *Ghosts of the Confederacy* and *Moral Reconstruction***

"[Goldfield] presents a superb, stylishly written historical synthesis that insightfully foregrounds ideology, faith, and public mood . . . An ambitious, engrossing interpretation with new things to say about a much-studied conflagration."
—***Publishers Weekly* (starred review)**

"A provocatively written, scrupulously researched, and well-framed consideration of evangelical religion's questionable role in the antebellum, Civil War, and Reconstruction periods of our history."   —***Library Journal* (starred review)**

"Readers who wonder if there's really much left to say about the Civil War and its impact on America will find their doubts evaporating only a few pages into this remarkable book. Although there is plenty of new information here, David Goldfield's greatest contribution may lie in showing us new ways to understand what we already know."
—**James C. Cobb, author of *Away Down South: A History of Southern Identity***

"This masterful synthesis of the Civil War is a stunning achievement. With fresh perspective and inspiring, often provocative ideas, Goldfield challenges some of the old narratives of sectional conflict, war, and Reconstruction. His examination of disparate, even divergent ways of thinking in the nineteenth century is brilliant, especially his exploration of the power of evangelical religion before and its diminished authority after the Civil War. A rich and vivid work, *America Aflame* is an extraordinary contribution to the historical understanding of our most defining war."   —**Orville Vernon Burton, author of *The Age of Lincoln***

AMERICA AFLAME

BY THE SAME AUTHOR

Southern Histories: Public, Personal, and Sacred
Still Fighting the Civil War: The American South and Southern History
American Dilemmas in the Twenty-First Century: Historical Perspectives
on Race, Religion, and Ethnicity
Region, Race, and Cities: Interpreting the Urban South
Black, White, and Southern: Race Relations and Southern Culture
Promised Land: The South since 1945
Cotton Fields and Skyscrapers: Southern City and Region, 1607–1980
Urban Growth in the Age of Sectionalism: Virginia, 1847–1861

EDITED AND CO-AUTHORED WORKS

The American Journey: A History of the United States (lead author)
Major Problems in the History of the American South, 2 vols. (co-editor)
The Encyclopedia of American Urban History, 2 vols. (editor)
Twentieth-Century America: A Social and Political History (lead author)
The South for New Southerners (co-author)
Urban America: A History (lead author)
The City in Southern History: The Growth of Urban Civilization in the
South (co-author)
The Enduring Ghetto: Sources and Readings (co-editor)

AMERICA AFLAME

. . .

HOW THE CIVIL WAR
CREATED A NATION

DAVID GOLDFIELD

BLOOMSBURY PRESS

NEW YORK · LONDON · NEW DELHI · SYDNEY

For Marie-Louise

Copyright © 2011 by David Goldfield

All rights reserved. No part of this book may be used or reproduced in any
manner whatsoever without written permission from the publisher except
in the case of brief quotations embodied in critical articles or reviews.
For information address Bloomsbury Press, 175 Fifth Avenue,
New York, NY 10010.

Published by Bloomsbury Press, New York

All papers used by Bloomsbury Press are natural, recyclable products made
from wood grown in well-managed forests. The manufacturing processes
conform to the environmental regulations of the country of origin.

LIBRARY OF CONGRESS CATALOGING-IN-PUBLICATION DATA

Goldfield, David R., 1944–
America aflame : how the Civil War created a nation / David Goldfield. — 1st U.S. ed.
p. cm.
Includes bibliographical references and index.
ISBN: 978-1-59691-702-6 (alk. paper hardcover)
1. United States—History—Civil War, 1861–1865—Influence.   2. United States—
History—Civil War, 1861–1865—Causes.   3. United States—History—Civil War,
1861–1865—Campaigns.   4. United States—History—Civil War, 1861–1865—
Social aspects.   5. National characteristics, American.   I. Title.
E468.9.G685 2011
973.7'11—dc22
2010025241

First published by Bloomsbury Press in 2011
This paperback edition published in 2012

Paperback ISBN: 978-1-60819-390-5

1 3 5 7 9 10 8 6 4 2

Typeset by Westchester Book Group

Printed in the United States of America by Quad/Graphics, Fairfield, Pennsylvania

CONTENTS

INTRODUCTION

A NATION REBORN

CAN ANYONE SAY ANYTHING new about the Civil War? In this book, the outcome of the conflict will be the same as in every other book on the war. That goes for the battles, too. My main concerns are how we got into the war, how the war transformed the men who fought, and how America came out of the war. These are also the itineraries of countless other authors. I hope, however, that my treatment of the war's origins, the conflict itself, and its aftermath will enable readers to view the Civil War from a new perspective. After the Revolutionary War, the Civil War is the defining event of American history. The Civil War not only tells us a great deal about Americans at that time, but it offers numerous insights into our nation today.

The Civil War was both the completion of the American Revolution and the beginning of a modern nation. The war proved America's resilience. If nothing else, holding a presidential election in the midst of the Civil War, as the Union did in 1864, was a testament to that strength. The war also transformed America in ways prefigured in the antebellum years but recognizable only after the nation went through the fire.

The Civil War is also America's greatest failure. The political system could not contain the passions stoked by the infusion of evangelical Christianity into the political process. Westward expansion, sectarian conflict, and above all slavery assumed moral dimensions that confounded political solutions. Violence became an acceptable alternative because it worked. It put the Catholics in their proper place and away from Protestant girls. It worked against the Native Americans and against the Mexicans. And it worked against the slaveholders. Antebellum America was a turbulent place—in cities, on the frontier, and at the ballot box. The violence took its toll. Gradually, the bonds of Union fell away: the national church polities, the national political parties, and the moderate politicians disappeared.

War was not inevitable. But the prevailing political culture made it difficult to solve issues peaceably. The failure is evident in the deaths of over 620,000 young men, the misery of their families and friends left to mourn their loss, the destruction of homes and personal property, the uprooting of households, and the scenes of war haunting those who managed to live through it. Without gainsaying the individual heroism of those who fought and died, it would have been a greater tribute to our nation had they lived.

The idea that a bumbling generation of politicians—the mediocrities who came after such giants as Daniel Webster, Henry Clay, and John C. Calhoun— led the nation into civil war is not a new idea. The concept dates as far back as the late nineteenth century. Avery Craven was perhaps its most gifted advocate. That might account for my attraction to the thesis, as I served as Professor Craven's graduate assistant at the University of Maryland in the late 1960s. Professor Craven had retired but had come to Maryland on a one-year appointment. He was eighty-four at the time, and his mind was still razor sharp.

My initial encounter with him did not go well. One of my professors invited me over to dinner in order to meet the legend I would be assisting that coming term. I was very excited about the prospect of working with such a great historian, whose graceful writing I had always admired, and doubly grateful because this would be a difficult semester for me, as I was studying for my comprehensive examinations. If you have ever been through that process you know that your brain is so cluttered with names of books and historians that only a periodic flushing allows you to keep your sanity. The purge takes numerous forms, one of which is to verbally disgorge at a breathless pace everything you know about a given school of historical thought to friends and family members. It accounted for the fact that my colleagues tended to avoid conversations with me on anything related to history. I also did not get invited to many parties that term.

So, I welcomed the dinner invitation. As we sat around the dinner table, I chatted with Professor Craven and his wife, Georgia. "I understand you are studying for your comprehensives," he announced suddenly. I could feel the sweat bead on my forehead. Without waiting for my response, he asked me what book I had read that had changed my view of a person or an era. Relieved that he had not requested a recitation on some obscure historical theory, I searched my cluttered mental file for an intelligent response. It would have been too precious to have cited one of Professor Craven's books, and besides, his work affirmed my views, which he already knew. Instead, I told him that C. Vann Woodward's *Tom Watson, Agrarian Rebel* (1938) profoundly altered my perception of both the Populist movement in the South and Tom Watson. I went on for the next ten minutes or so regaling the Cravens and the other guests about how Woodward accounted for the remarkable and sad transformation of the Georgia Populist from a champion of the poor, regardless of color, to a raving anti-Catholic, anti-Jewish, and anti-black demagogue.

When I had finished my speech, for that's what it was, the room was funeral-parlor quiet. My host nervously shuffled his knife and fork. Had I said something wrong? He cleared his throat and said, "David, perhaps Georgia here can provide another perspective on Tom Watson, as she is his granddaughter." It was one of those moments when you hope for a diversionary earthquake or a sudden gust of wind at, say, 150 miles an hour that peels off the roof. Georgia graciously waved it off, noting that her grandfather could be difficult at times. We all laughed, and that seemed to break the tension. We raised our wine-glasses and toasted the new term.

Professor Craven was wonderful to work for, and he and his wife, even after my gaffe, were extremely kind to me. What struck me most about him during our association was how much he hated war, the Civil War in particular. Some historians have associated Craven with a pro-southern analysis of the war's origins, and some might identify my narrative as compatible with that inter-pretation. My book is neither pro-southern nor pro-northern. It is anti-war, particularly the Civil War. More than bumbling politicians, however, I cite the invasion of evangelical Christianity into the political debate as an especially toxic factor in limiting the options of political leaders. Evangelicals never comprised a majority of the population, but their organization, wealth, use of technology and the media, and access to politicians, especially in the Republi-can Party, enabled them to infiltrate and influence the political process.

Evangelical Christianity polarized political debate. It is a perspective that Professor Craven did not discuss much, nor did most of the historians of his generation. But evangelical Christianity's influence was everywhere in the po-litical arena, in discussions about the West, about Roman Catholics, and espe-cially about slavery. What was troubling about this religious immersion was the blindness of its self-righteousness, its certitude, and its lack of humility to understand that those who disagree are not mortal sinners and those who subscribe to your views are not saints.

It is good, of course, to be righteous against slavery. I am not arguing that the death and destruction of the Civil War outweighed the good of abolition—rather, that there may have been other means to achieve that noble end. In fact, the United States was the only country to require a civil war in order to abolish slavery. The elevation of political issues into moral causes poisoned the democratic process. Just as evangelicals did not distinguish between the Catholic Church and Catholic immigrants, so they did not separate the sin of slavery from the slaveholder. In a crusade, the enemy is the infidel, and even-tually both sides viewed the other as apostates to God and the Constitution.

I tell this story mainly through the lives of the second post-Revolutionary generation that came of age in the 1830s. Though the cast of characters is large,

I focus especially on Harriet Beecher Stowe, Frederick Douglass, Abraham Lincoln, Alexander Stephens, and Walt Whitman. I do not claim that these individuals are surrogates for all Americans. I have selected them because they are interesting and have important things to say about events, many of which they influenced. Their stories inform the book's major episodes.

These individuals, and other Americans of that generation, were intensely aware of the Revolutionary legacy. They understood that the balance between individual liberty and collective stability was delicate and to err too far in either direction risked chaos or despotism. The one would invariably lead to the other. America was still an experiment, a lonely outpost of democratic government in a world dominated by autocracy and littered with failed attempts at self-government.

The greatest dangers lurked at home. The advance of the Roman Catholic Church in the form of more than a million immigrants menaced both individual liberty and the republican experiment. Slaveholders, as despotic as the Roman hierarchy, threatened to pollute the golden West with their black bondsmen and obstruct the national government with their selfish priorities. Alien cultures and nations intruded on the edges of settlement—Native Americans and Mexicans foremost—thwarting national destiny. These were the fears of white Protestant Americans, especially in the North.

The book opens with the destruction of the Ursuline convent in Charlestown, Massachusetts, by a Protestant mob in August 1834. The episode exposed the deep and growing resentment against the Catholic Church and its adherents, particularly among Protestant workingmen. It also highlighted the tolerance for violence as a tactic to intimidate or eliminate groups or institutions perceived as threats to prevailing religious and political ideals. The passions that fueled the convent fire would nearly immolate the nation in a ruinous civil war.

The anti-Catholic and anti-slavery movements shared some of the same personnel, rhetoric, and tactics. Lyman Beecher, a New England evangelical minister, moved his family to Cincinnati to save the West from the Catholic Church. His daughters Harriet and Catharine and his son Henry Ward would become prominent in the anti-slavery movement. Aided by technological innovations in printing, both anti-Catholic and anti-slavery advocates saturated the country with their literature. They employed similar apocalyptic rhetoric to energize faithful followers to action against both of these threats to the nation and God.

Both the anti-Catholic and anti-slavery movements flourished during a national religious revival known as the Second Great Awakening. The Awakening saved souls and spawned numerous reform movements but also indulged in bigotry and self-righteousness. In the North, it veered toward a general reform of society as a prelude for the Second Coming of Jesus Christ. Evangelical Protestantism in the South was more concerned with individual conversion, and its adherents looked with alarm on the mixture of religion and politics brewing toxic potions in the North. Nor did southerners join with northern evangelicals in the excoriation of their Catholic and immigrant populations.

For all of its concern about reforming society, the northern version of evangelical Christianity only rarely promoted the notion of racial equality. The expansion of white male suffrage occurred alongside the spread of evangelical Protestantism. Restrictions against free blacks in the North increased as well. A few states banned free blacks from entering altogether. That white and black liberty moved in opposite directions seemed to affirm the belief of white southerners that the existence of slavery for blacks guaranteed freedom for whites.

The energy unleashed by the Second Great Awakening affected America's westward movement, which began in earnest after 1840. The West encapsulated antebellum Americans' hopes and anxieties. It held a special place in American culture as a region of renewal. It was our geographic version of religious rebirth. The West was the place Americans could start over and the nation could fulfill its destiny as a democratic, Protestant beacon to inspire other peoples and nations. By conquering a continent with their people and ideals, Americans would conquer the world. John L. O'Sullivan, a Harvard-educated journalist, gave a name to this vision: "manifest destiny."

Fulfilling that destiny meant removing (or eliminating) those who stood in the way. The Mexican War was not a religious war; it was a conflict over territory. Even so, the Catholicism of the Mexicans was not a minor detail. Nor was the evangelical certitude that the conflict was justified as part of God's plan. The beginning of the Plains Indian Wars in 1854, which would flare sporadically over the next two decades, was not a religious controversy either. It, too, was a territorial conflict, but Americans also justified it in religious terms, denigrating the pagan "savages" who were poor stewards of God's creation and standing in the way of America's divine mission.

The religious fervor entered political campaigns with unprecedented vigor beginning with the 1844 presidential race. From then on, political parties paraded their religious bona fides and attacked opponents as infidels. The campaigns themselves came to resemble religious revivals as much as political exercises. Religion was not only an issue itself, it permeated other issues of the day, especially slavery.

Given the importance of both evangelical religion and the West during the

1840s, the exclusion of slaveholders from that promised land, first broached by David Wilmot, a Democratic congressman from Pennsylvania in 1846, was guaranteed to raise howls in the South. And it did. The issue of slavery had already unraveled the evangelical family by sundering the Methodists and Baptists along sectional lines. Now the disintegration of the nation no longer seemed far-fetched.

Decent men attempted to resolve the slavery controversy so the nation could get on with the business of economic expansion and promoting individual opportunity. America was at the beginning of a major economic transformation. Commerce, steam technology, the migration of Americans westward, immigration, and urbanization were all breaking down the isolation of the family farm and small town. People and goods were on the move, connecting with each other and with neighboring communities. Advances in printing technology created an explosion of newspapers, tracts, magazines, and dime novels devoured by a population high in literacy. The nation of the 1840s was very different from the thirteen states that hugged the Atlantic coast and formed a "more perfect Union" led by men of property and education. Would America survive? Would the Revolutionary legacy remain secure? The anxieties raised by these questions moved men to push for compromise.

The Compromise of 1850 represented a last heroic attempt by the first post-Revolutionary generation to save the Union for the second generation. Despite the best efforts of Kentucky's Henry Clay and Massachusetts senator Daniel Webster, the compromise quieted controversy only momentarily. The Fugitive Slave Law provision of the compromise drove a wider wedge between North and South. The law motivated Harriet Beecher Stowe to write *Uncle Tom's Cabin,* awakened northerners to the possibility of a Slave Power conspiracy to restrict the rights not only of slaves but also of white men, and left many southerners wondering whether mere laws could protect them and their property.

Defending his opposition to the fugitive slave provision of the compromise, Senator William H. Seward of New York declared, "There is a higher law than the Constitution." In a nation of laws, when political leaders advocate working outside those boundaries, especially invoking the deity as an authority, trouble can only follow. Abraham Lincoln urged, "Let every American, every lover of liberty . . . swear by the blood of the Revolution never to violate in the least particular the laws of the country, and never to tolerate their violation by others. . . . Reverence for the laws [should be] the *political religion* of the nation." He said that in 1838.

While disputes over laws inevitably arise in a republic, the Constitution has designated the judicial branch of government to adjudicate those conflicts. As for interpreting God, according to evangelical doctrine that is the individual's right and responsibility. The danger is that such a religious standard applied to politics makes each person a law unto himself.

Moderates still controlled the political apparatus in the early 1850s. The second generation was then more aware of the fragility of their experiment than at any other previous time in their memory. The European revolutions of 1848, greeted with great rejoicing in America, collapsed. The restored regimes were, in some cases, worse than those that provoked the rebellions in the first place. Americans interpreted the failed revolutions in three ways. First, the excess of the democratic forces contributed to their downfall. Second, despotism, not democracy, inevitably emerges from chaos. Finally, democratic institutions are fragile plants. They require constant nurturing, and even then their survival is not certain. America was a lonely outpost in an undemocratic world.

The survival of that outpost became more tenuous by the mid-1850s. A cascade of events increasingly polarized the nation. Rather than viewing these events as discrete episodes, both northerners and southerners perceived them as parts of a greater conspiracy to undermine the freedoms of the other. Senator Stephen A. Douglas, an Illinois Democrat and a fervent nationalist, hoped that his transcontinental railroad bill submitted in January 1854 would be just the thing to bind the nation together, literally and ideologically. It did not turn out that way. The resulting Kansas-Nebraska Act touched off a civil war in Kansas, led to an assault on a U.S. senator, and damaged the credibility of a presidential administration dedicated to removing slavery from public debate. A Supreme Court decision delivered with a similar objective in mind also had the opposite effect. The harder political leaders tried to render the slavery issue invisible, the more prominent it grew. And the larger its presence in the political arena, the greater the moral stake. Political parties disintegrated and new organizations formed, including an anti-Catholic party and a sectional antislavery party. The Democrats, the remaining national party, became increasingly dysfunctional between its northern and southern wings. The political center eroded, and the extremists on both sides captured the debate.

Reality fled. Northerners perceived Slave Power conspiracies infesting every issue, where none in fact existed. Southerners perceived northerners as intent on subjugating them while simultaneously instigating a race war, though few in the North had any such designs. A religious revival during a serious economic downturn over the winter of 1857–58 among middle-class urban men only added a sense of foreboding that something cataclysmic was afoot.

The Lincoln-Douglas debates during the late summer and early fall of 1858 in Illinois not only highlighted the differences between Republican and

Democrat, but they also reflected a growing messianic sentiment in Lincoln's views. When he accepted the Republican nomination for the U.S. Senate seat in Illinois in June 1858, Lincoln took his text from Matthew 12:25: "And Jesus knew their thoughts, and said unto them, Every kingdom divided against itself is brought to desolation; and every city or house divided against itself shall not stand." The "House Divided" speech, as it is known, implied an irreconcilable divide between North and South. Lincoln elaborated on the theme during his debates with Douglas. The slavery issue, Lincoln contended, was not merely a political question but a test of America's democratic and religious ideals: "It is the eternal struggle between these two principles—right and wrong— throughout the world." In this context, compromise would be difficult.

The 1860 presidential contest occurred in a politically poisonous atmosphere. By this time, southern evangelicals had assumed a millennial view similar to the North's. The shift had more to do with the anti-slavery evangelical assault on the slaveholder and his society than on a heartfelt doctrinal transformation, but it further polarized North and South at a critical time. The Democrats broke apart, opening the way for Lincoln's victory in the fall. By the time he took office in March 1861, seven southern states had left the Union to form the Confederate States of America. To evangelical Christians in the South, the Confederacy represented a rebirth, just as they had been reborn in Christ.

The seceded states sent emissaries to the slaveholding states still in the Union to convince them that remaining in a government led by Republicans was suicidal. The outcome would be a bloody race war and the ultimate subjugation of white southerners, they argued. There was no doubt in the minds of southern contemporaries that the Confederacy rested on the "cornerstone" of slavery.

Lincoln entered office assuring the South he meant no harm to slavery where it existed. He also vowed to uphold the Constitution and defend federal property. Secession, from Lincoln's perspective, presaged anarchy and therefore threatened democratic government and individual freedom. When he maneuvered Confederate president Jefferson Davis into foolishly firing the first shot at Fort Sumter, Lincoln noted, "They attacked Sumter. It fell and thus did more service than it otherwise would." The "service" was uniting a northern population heretofore skeptical of Lincoln's ability to lead and divided over policies to deal with secession. When he called for northern volunteers to put down the rebellion, four additional southern states seceded, and the war began.

The war lasted far longer and was far bloodier than almost anyone expected. Given the Union's significant advantages in men and materiel, it was not surprising that most predicted a short war. After the Battle of Shiloh in

April 1862, a narrow Union victory along the Tennessee-Mississippi border, the illusion of a quick, glorious end to the fighting fled. The carnage shocked even Union General William T. Sherman: "Who but a living witness can adequately portray those scenes on Shiloh's field, when our wounded men, mingled with rebels, charred and blackened by the burning tents and underbrush, were crawling about, begging for someone to end their misery?"

The slaughter spurred Lincoln to emancipate the slaves. He had always harbored a deep animus against slavery, for both moral and practical reasons. However, he loved the Union more than he hated slavery. As the war dragged on and with the outcome uncertain, he deployed the proclamation. It was a calculated risk. While a majority of white northerners supported banning slavery from the territories, abolishing the institution where it existed was another matter. Lincoln's concerns reflected the limited reservoir of goodwill in the North toward African Americans even in the midst of a civil war.

Lincoln also understood that he had raised the stakes of the war. The proclamation would only stiffen the Confederates' resolve to fight to the bitter end. When Lincoln dedicated the Union cemetery at Gettysburg in November 1863 he made it clear, however, that the war was not only about freedom for the unfree. Saving the Union meant securing freedom for everyone: "that this nation under God shall have a new birth of freedom; and that this government of the people, by the people, for the people, shall not perish from the earth."

America would be born again. But it would not be cleansed of sin. Victory in the Civil War did not make northerners chaste, though it chastened them. As it did white southerners, with the notable difference that the former Rebels believed Redemption—retaking control of their government and their former slaves—would deliver them to grace. Science and reason governed the North after the war along with an insatiable desire for progress. Neither the press nor Horatio Alger fabricated a land of opportunity: it was real. The national rebirth would be measured in economic and political terms, not as a moral absolution.

The South not only lost the war but also forfeited its place as a participant in forging the nation's future. While the rest of the nation hurtled toward the future, southerners created a past. For nearly a century after the war and until the rest of the nation could no longer ignore the anomaly of poverty, ignorance, segregation, and disfranchisement on its border, the South remained a regional outlier to the story of national success.

The new nation taking shape after the Civil War only included the South as a gauzy intermezzo to a dazzling show of economic development, ethnic diversity, alabaster cities, and technological innovation. As P. T. Barnum cranked up his Wild West shows to provide easterners with a stylized version of the

West, so minstrel shows and early film portrayed a magnolia-scented South that sealed racial stereotypes and preserved the region as "Old" in an America obsessed with the New, a feminized counterpoint to a masculine colossus.

Some of these changes were already evident during the war. When Walt Whitman took leave of his grueling hospital work in Washington, D.C., in November 1863 to recuperate in his Brooklyn home, the train trip northward was a revelation. It was scarcely possible to see that a war was going on. Passing through Baltimore, then Philadelphia, and alighting in Manhattan, he marveled, "It looks anything else but war, everybody well dressed, plenty of money, markets boundless & the best, factories all busy." The North was a hive of activity and innovation as the South was collapsing under spiraling inflation, severe manpower shortages, and the scarcity of basic necessities. Whitman was witnessing the birth of the modern state and of modern America.

The Republican Congress, free of the southern Democratic albatross, passed an array of economic and educational legislation that helped to establish the federal government as an important catalyst in creating a national economy. The small town and family farm still characterized the nation, but northern cities absorbed thousands of newcomers and large orders for war materiel.

A transformation was also occurring among the soldiers in the field. Although periodic religious revivals visited both camps, especially the Confederates during the last year of the war, the messianic tenor of correspondence from both sides subsided. The randomness of death regardless of piety and the general horror of the war transformed the soldiers' faith. They still believed, of course, but often without the certitude and self-righteousness that marked evangelical Christian perceptions on the eve of the war. The advancing perception was that, rather than the personal, interventionist God of evangelical Christianity, the war confirmed a Supreme Being who was more detached and more inscrutable. Soldiers maintained their personal piety as they grew increasingly skeptical of God's role in the war.

The outcome of the war was not inevitable, at least not until the last months. Regardless of the Union's advantages in men, materiel, and organization, the war would be won or lost on the battlefields. Many of the key battles that preceded Sherman's decisive march through Georgia, Sheridan's depredations in the Valley of Virginia, and Grant's relentless siege of Petersburg were narrow victories for Union troops. As late as the summer of 1864, northern public opinion was tilting decidedly toward a truce and peace with the Confederacy.

By the time of Lincoln's second inaugural in March 1865, the result of the war was not in doubt. His brief inaugural speech was a remarkable effort, a combination sermon and introspective rumination, not the triumphal declaration the assembled expected. The president talked about the limits of man, the inscrutability of God, and the nature of forgiveness—views that challenged prevailing evangelical Protestant beliefs nurtured by the Second Great Awakening.

Northerners rapidly left the war behind. Their quick embrace of reconciliation reflected less a recognition of the moral equivalency of Union and Confederate causes than a desire to move on. Southern whites, on the other hand, may have talked of reconciliation, but beneath the veneer of accommodation lay resentment. They did not move on; they moved back.

Wade Hampton III, a prominent South Carolina planter and Confederate general who lost both a son and a brother in the war, consistently counseled in favor of reconciliation. Yet his correspondence reveals that he was not reconciled to the verdict of the war. Hampton continued to believe secession was constitutionally legitimate, and he disputed the government's right to abolish slavery. He was willing to accept federal authority but little else. And his was a moderate position.

Reconstruction was doomed because white southerners had to account for their terrible loss, not only in lives but also in their patrimony. The acceptance of any Reconstruction policy short of none would have negated the cause for which they fought and for which many died. When Congress imposed a Reconstruction policy that included a modicum of black civil equality and black suffrage, most white southerners would not, could not accept the legitimacy of governments elected under such terms. The white South was never more solid than during the brief period of Congressional Reconstruction.

It was not coincidental that the white southerners who took back their governments from black and white Republicans were called Redeemers, nor that the process through which it occurred was called Redemption. The term "redemption" was, of course, in widespread use in America prior to the Civil War, especially among evangelicals. It referred to the process by which Jesus sacrificed His life to rescue sinful mankind from God's wrath. The term implied a new birth as those who come to Christ are cleansed of their sins and saved "unto a new life eternal."

Confederates talked of "redeeming" their states from Union control during the Civil War. After the war, the term usually implied a two-step process. Redemption would cleanse southern sins and therefore restore the Lord's blessing on the South that He had withdrawn, as evidenced by defeat. It would also remove "the yoke of Yankee and negro rule." Redemption, therefore, would secure for white southerners the victory denied to them in the Civil War. The process toward Redemption was clear. As an Alabama editor declared in 1871,

"The road to redemption is under the white banner." White southerners employed evangelical Protestantism to re-create an antebellum regime cleansed of sin. White religion in the South became the handmaiden of white supremacy.

Northerners focused their attention on the cornucopia of opportunity opened up by innovation, invention, and industrialization. The South was only a peripheral concern. And then it was not a concern at all. In fact, many northerners felt they understood the concerns of white southerners, with their allegedly incompetent and corrupt Republican governments. White northerners felt similarly burdened by incompetence and corruption, though in their case the culprits were immigrants and venal local politicians rather than blacks and white outsiders. The mutual empathy caused the northern press and citizens to underplay or even excuse the mounting violence against Republicans in the South. Just as the failed revolutions of 1848 gave many Americans pause concerning the potential for democratic movements to spin out of control and result in a greater despotism, so the news of the Paris Commune in 1871 affirmed the evils of too much democracy. Given the racial attitudes of most white northerners, such empathy was not difficult to come by. Also, the scientific wisdom of the period mandated a more cautious role for government in the affairs of men.

Science assumed the reputation of religion after the Civil War: infallible and ignored at one's own peril. Charles Darwin's *On the Origin of Species* (1859) became enormously popular in the United States, not only for its value in explaining the process of evolution but also because it seemed to offer a blueprint for ordering society—and order was a perennial concern of Americans. The popularization of scientific theories is not always a good thing, however. Subtleties become lost in translation. "Survival of the fittest," a term Darwin never used, became shorthand for natural selection.

Society, like the animal world, worked on immutable natural laws, Darwin's social interpreters claimed. Uninformed intervention in these natural processes was not only unwise but also potentially destructive. While it was appropriate for government to complement these processes by assisting lesser races in attaining their fullest potential, paternalism could only go so far. Legislatures and other policy-making institutions, public and private, must devise actions based on scientific data and facts. Research must displace intuition in the public sphere.

Americans also interpreted Darwin as positing a natural hierarchy. Darwin himself wrote of inferior races. These ideas circulated at a time when Americans were making major decisions on Indians and African Americans. For both the red and the black, the consensus was that sedentary farm work or simple mechanical labor in environments controlled by whites provided the best opportunities for these lesser races to reach their full, though limited, potentials.

Science replaced evangelical Protestantism as the nation's primary faith and policy arbiter. Science did not posit an end to government, but rather a public policy carefully calibrated to incorporate scientific evidence as the basis for legislation. In that respect, the advocates of a political science were more measured than their evangelical Christian predecessors, who wanted to use the government as an arm of the Lord. They wanted a Protestant constitution and a Protestant public policy to speed the millennial advent. Political scientists looked less to the millennium than to professional stewardship as their ultimate goal.

Evangelical Christianity did not disappear after the war. Rather, it was increasingly secular, a function of the prevailing postwar culture rather than the other way around. Dwight L. Moody packed his revivals with the simple message of eternal salvation and banned politics from his pulpit. He offered little in the way of theological exegesis. Most of his "sermons" took the form of secular stories sprinkled with treacly aphorisms much more than biblical texts. As the Wild West and minstrel shows made caricatures of Indians and blacks, Moody succeeded in making religion a spectacle. Many of his middle- and upper-class congregants came to see a show and to be part of an event. It was comfort religion, part of the culture of affluence and prosperity, a turn taken to its ultimate by Russell Conwell, whose sermon "Acres of Diamonds" unabashedly preached the Gospel of Money. The sermon stayed in print for over a century. When evangelicals ventured to influence public policy, such as the periodic attempts to impose a Christian amendment on the Constitution or to legislate against Catholic influence in the public schools, their efforts fell flat. Their great crusade became alcohol. Personal behavior rather than national sin became their focus.

Evangelical Protestantism became culture-bound in the South as well, though in a quite different form. "Redemption" retained its born-again connotation, but in the South after the Civil War, it was indelibly connected to the restoration of white supremacy. Religion became a prop of the Lost Cause for whites. For blacks, evangelical Christianity became their community. The focus was less on the hereafter than on the here-and-now.

Science suited the new era well. It was rational. America's Romantic Age had produced a civil war. The Age of Reason would offer up the telephone, the incandescent bulb, and the Brooklyn Bridge. Public policy would be rational, too. Cities were inefficient because experts and professionals were not in charge.

States in the South were ill governed because unqualified electorates ruled. Just as the second generation of Americans thought they could discern the will of God, so their postbellum offspring believed they could divine the secrets of science and apply them to their society. Both were wrong.

The North settled into prosperity. The Gospel of Money was apolitical, and it soothed the conscience by validating financial success as a calling unto itself. Entrepreneurs were the heroes. Industries blossomed that did not exist before the war, such as steel and oil, feeding the railroads, stoking home and commercial construction, and generating new white-collar jobs in accounting, insurance, finance, and managerial positions. Affluence and new technologies enabled families to move from congested inner cities to tranquil suburbs. Thomas Edison's successful experiments with electric lighting and the phonograph and Alexander Graham Bell's telephone were merely a few of the innovations that eased the lives of middle-class families, especially of women. Many of those women now had an array of employment opportunities open to them as well, including office work, education, and retail.

The transcontinental railroad completed in 1869 was a symbol of the innovative spirit and of the new role of government as a facilitator to the national economy. Stephen Douglas's railroad finally got built. It was a marvel, spanning the continent, conquering difficult terrain, enlisting over twenty thousand immigrant construction workers, and doing it all ahead of schedule. The railroad also accelerated confrontations with the Plains Indians. Here was some unfinished business, though now, instead of justifying Indian removal in terms of manifest destiny, the government rationalized it as a way to save the Indians and allow a superior civilization to develop the land to its fullest potential—a more scientific approach. By 1877, the last of the Plains tribes were entering reservations.

The African American fared little better. Like the Indian, he belonged to a subordinate race incapable of full equality with whites, so the prevailing scientific racial theories suggested. The Indians would fare best converted to sedentary farm life under the paternalistic protection of the federal government. The freedman would reach his full capacity as a worker for wages, on a farm preferably, under the supervision of whites. The aspirations of the freedman were not taken into account any more than the aspirations of the Plains tribes. The respective places of both races would serve each well, and together they would serve the country best.

The book concludes with the 1876 Centennial Exhibition celebrating the nation's hundredth birthday. The fair built an instant city of technological wonder. Here was the future, and the future of America lay in its cities. As a magnet for millions from small towns and farms, and from abroad, the city served as the nation's cultural crucible and economic engine. Americans would wax nostalgic over small towns and farms, but they invariably voted with their feet for the city. America's genius for invention and innovation, proudly displayed over the fairgrounds, took root and flourished in urban America after the war. That was the major story of the decade after the Civil War, not the persistent contention between black and white in the South, however heartbreaking that was. I hope this book restores a balance between what was happening in the South during this period we call Reconstruction and the beginnings of the industrial revolution and its accompanying transformations in demography, culture, and work in the urban North. The future of the country rested with the latter.

As in any economic transition, there were winners and losers. The fiction of an identity of interest between capital and labor crumbled under the weight of strikes and the reality of genuine suffering. Northerners recoiled against the deployment of troops to protect southern Republican regimes as a usurpation of federal power. They applauded, however, when President Rutherford B. Hayes rushed soldiers to put down the Great Railroad Strike of 1877. White southerners were merely ending the "unnatural" occupation of their government by mountebanks and incompetents. Workers, however, like the Paris communards, were sowing disorder that threatened the republic.

The second generation of Americans had succeeded in eliminating or neutralizing the threats the nation confronted beginning in the 1830s—Catholics, slaveholders, Mexicans, and Native Americans. Republicans still worried about the Catholics, but they would not think of burning convents to get their points across. They resurrected the slaveholder every four years as a reminder of the treason, though he was more a mascot than an imminent threat. And they tacked on a crusade against alcohol, as it reinforced their anti-immigrant base and added a nice alliterative quality to their campaigns against "Rum, Romanism, and Rebellion." African Americans and Native Americans were in their science-ordained places. The nation was now secure and indivisible.

The "new birth of freedom" Lincoln promised as the reward for so much sacrifice proved more elusive. The carnage did not translate into a universal application of the Declaration of Independence. The fates of the Indians, the African Americans, and the Chinese during and after the Reconstruction era testified to that serious shortcoming. Yet the folly of the second generation in exposing the great experiment of self-government to a bloody civil war had the redeeming feature of preserving the founding ideals for another day. Gradually, the excluded gender, races, and religions would find inclusion, even if incompletely. I believe that the political system established by the

Founders would have been resilient and resourceful enough to accommodate our great diversity sooner without the tragedy of a civil war. Of course, that is impossible to know. We *do* know that the transformative nature of the Civil War did not include liberty, equality, and justice for all. Lincoln's vision would wait at least a century, and it is yet a work in progress.

CHAPTER 1

CRUSADES

CONVENT LIFE NO LONGER SUITED Sister Mary John. Born Elizabeth Harrison in Philadelphia, she had converted to the Catholic faith and entered the Ursuline order at the age of eighteen in 1824. By all accounts, Sister Mary John was a gifted teacher and musician. Now, in this sweltering summer of 1834 at the order's convent school in Charlestown, Massachusetts, she walked out. The oppressive heat, teaching fourteen forty-five-minute lessons a day, conducting music classes, and attending to administrative duties as the Mother Assistant became overwhelming. She needed some time off.[1]

Sister Mary John appeared at the doorstep of a neighboring farmhouse sweating profusely, thinly clad, and incoherent. The following day, Benedict Fenwick, Boston's Roman Catholic bishop, came to retrieve the errant nun. She agreed to return to the convent. The matter might have ended there were it not for an unfortunate convergence of events.

The Ursulines had arrived in Boston from their mother convent in Quebec in 1819. They opened a modest school serving the city's growing Irish community. Bishop Fenwick, installed in 1829, had more grandiose plans for the Ursulines. The Church purchased land in nearby Charlestown to erect a convent. The new facility included a new mission. The school would educate Protestant girls from wealthy families, not the offspring of poor Irish immigrants, though the nuns would accept a few charity pupils.

The new convent occupied a hill, called Mount Benedict after the bishop. The main building, a barn, stables, an icehouse, a restored farmhouse, and gardens sprawled across twenty-four acres offering commanding views of the spires of nearby Boston and its harbor. The complex rose next to another Charlestown promontory, Bunker Hill, a sacred Revolutionary site to area residents.

Bishop Fenwick viewed his project as a fund-raising enterprise. He also hoped to ingratiate himself and his religion with prominent Protestant families at a time of increasing hostility to "Romanism." Perhaps that influence might leave a deeper impression. At least four of the six nuns who taught at the convent were converts to Catholicism, including Mary Anne Moffatt (Sister Mary St. George), the Mother Superior, and Elizabeth Harrison (Sister Mary John), the Mother Assistant.

The possibility of conversion did not weigh heavily among the up-and-coming Unitarian families who sent their daughters to the new convent school in Charlestown. What impressed them most was the rigor of the curriculum. This was no "finishing" school. In an era when girls' education was still haphazard—Boston did not allow girls to attend its public schools until 1827—the Ursuline course of study was unique. Reading, writing, math, history, geography, poetry, astronomy, philosophy, and language lessons filled the school day, which went from early morning to late afternoon. The school also included an excellent music program directed by Sister Mary John. Students learned to play instruments, compose, sing, and dance. Boston's Congregational churches—the dominant denomination in New England—alarmed at the success of the convent school, established a girls' academy in 1831, but enrollment was meager.

The Ursulines' success and the Congregationalists' struggles occurred in a context of growing religious antagonism in the Boston area. Protestant Americans had held suspicions about the Roman Catholic Church since the colonial era. They associated the Church with despotism, hierarchy, and orthodoxy, all enemies of American republican ideals forged in the blood of revolution. Most Protestants knew little about the rituals of the Church and understood their meaning even less. The secrecy surrounding convents and monasteries fueled imaginations already primed with suspicion.

The antagonism renewed in the late 1820s and the 1830s with immigration from Ireland and as the Second Great Awakening sparked an evangelical Protestant resurgence. In 1829, Protestant laborers stoned the dwellings of Irish Catholics on Broad Street in Boston. Protestants and Catholics clashed violently in Lowell, just north of Boston, in 1833. That same year, a sectarian brawl resulted in the death of an Irish worker in Charlestown. During that year, the convent's stable went up in flames under suspicious circumstances, and the convent's dog was shot and killed.

Charlestown's working-class Protestant population was especially prone to anti-Roman hysteria. Competition from Irish Catholic workers and the use of Irishmen to break strikes among Protestant brickmakers contributed to the animosity. Brickmakers and carpenters worked long hours for little pay and lived in squalid dormitories. Local politicians found that anti-Catholic diatribes garnered votes and diverted criticism from management, and the press knew that editorials denouncing encroaching "Popery" sold newspapers.

The Ursuline convent was a lightning rod for Protestant discontent. Run by celibate women in an era when society expected females to adhere to domestic roles revolving around childbearing and -rearing and deference to male decision-making, the convent invested women with administrative authority and demanded an unnatural sexuality. The Protestant girls in the school were of an impressionable age and subject to conversion. Once married, they would carry their new faith to their children, as mothers were responsible for the religious training of offspring. As one Protestant writer warned, "The sole object of all monastic institutions in America is merely to proselyte [sic] youth of the influential classes of society, and especially females as the Roman priests are conscious that by this means they shall silently but effectually attain the control of public affairs."[2]

The convent girls came from affluent families at a time when Protestant workingmen chafed under the growing gap in wealth, status, and living conditions in a region just on the cusp of an industrial revolution. The formation of a Workingman's Party in Boston in 1832 emphasized the class-consciousness of workers. The *Boston Recorder*, a prominent local newspaper, summarized Protestant fears of the convent in an 1830 editorial: that its students "may yet go forth, with their minds imbued with such principles which, if embraced by our descendents, will counteract every good for which our fathers fought." The editor hoped for the day "when all false religion shall be overthrown, and the true religion of Christ pervades the whole world."[3]

Few Congregational ministers feared the Catholic menace more than Lyman Beecher, pastor of the Park Street Church in Boston, whose fiery sermons had earned the church the reputation as the city's "Brimstone Corner." He attracted national attention with a series of sermons in 1830 denouncing the Catholic Church as a sworn enemy of the nation's republican ideals. Beecher practiced what he preached. He uprooted his large family from their comfortable New England home and moved to Cincinnati, then a raw frontier town, to establish a theological seminary. The purpose of this institution was to save the West, and especially its children, from the Catholic Church. To that end, he also encouraged his eldest daughter, Catharine, to open a school and dedicate her life to female children of "the rising generation in which Catholics and infidels have got the start of us."[4]

Resentment against Catholics and specifically the Mount Benedict convent grew through the early 1830s. The impressive school perched high above Charlestown was not the City on a Hill the Protestant burghers contemplated as the fulfillment of the Pilgrims' progress. A commemorative monument rising on adjacent Bunker Hill illuminated the perceived threat of the sprawling convent even more.

In the weeks before and after Sister Mary John's peregrination, an uncannily similar story circulated in the Boston area. Rebecca Reed, a Protestant girl, was the protagonist in this tale. She had allegedly fled the Mount Benedict convent to escape from a satanic environment. To silence her, Reed charged, the nuns plotted to carry her off to Canada. Mother Superior admitted that Reed had entered the convent in 1831 as a charity student but was dismissed after six months when she balked at the rigor of the curriculum. Sister Mary John's "escape," however, lent credence to Reed's story, conflating the two episodes in the primed minds of Yankee residents.

On August 8, a story appeared in a Boston newspaper headlined "Mysterious." It read: "We understand that a great excitement at present exists in Charlestown in consequence of the mysterious disappearance of a young lady at the Nunnery in that place. . . . [A] few days since, her friends called for her but she was not to be found, and much alarm is excited in consequence."[5]

The Charlestown selectmen who governed the community now rose to action. They marched over to the convent on Monday, August 11, and demanded to search the facility for the "missing" nun. Mother Superior obliged and presented Sister Mary John as their tour guide. The selectmen reported to the press that "Miss Harrison was entirely satisfied with her present situation, it being that of her own choice, and that she has no desire or wish to alter it."[6]

The retraction came too late to save the convent. Forces were already in motion that created a frenzy of hate and revenge beyond the control of local leaders. Lyman Beecher made a hasty return from Cincinnati to deliver three violent anti-Catholic sermons on August 10 exhorting congregations to action against "Popery." Beecher was not alone in his diatribes. Protestant ministers throughout the Boston area that Sabbath reminded churchgoers of their responsibility to fight for faith and country. Placards appeared all over Boston and Charlestown: "Go Ahead! To Arms!! To Arms!! Ye brave and free the Avenging Sword unshield!! Leave not one stone upon another of that curst Nunnery that prostitutes female virtue and liberty under the garb of holy Religion. When Bonaparte opened the Nunnerys in Europe he found cords of infant skulls!!!!!!"[7]

John R. Buzzell, a brawny six-foot-six brickmaker, required no such encouragement. A year earlier he had severely beaten the convent's Irish caretaker. He still harbored resentment over the use of Irish strikebreakers. The selectmen had scarcely departed Mount Benedict when Buzzell and a mob of sixty Protestant men marched toward the front gate shouting, "No Popery" and "Down with the Cross." Charlestown's lone police officer stood off at a discreet distance.[8]

Ursuline convent aflame.
(Harvard College Library, Widener Library)

Mother Superior came out to meet the mob. Seeing that her pleadings did not diminish the crowd's determination, she warned that "the Bishop has twenty thousand Irishmen at his command in Boston." That threat only stoked the mob's fury. The men battered in the front door and ransacked the main convent building, finding, to their dismay, nothing more incriminating than the books and clothing of the students and nuns who had already fled the premises. Within the hour, flames consumed the convent and its contents.[9]

Certain that dark secrets lay somewhere on the grounds, the mob turned to the small chapel behind the convent. A dozen men armed with clubs and pick-axes burst through the portal. They found a trapdoor, smashed it, and rushed down the stone steps to the crypt. Seven coffins lay in front of them. Here, they believed, were the remains of murdered Protestant girls. They pried open the coffin lids and pulled out the bodies. Arrayed before them were no defiled Protestant damsels but the corpses of seven nuns. One of the men clubbed a skull in frustration, sending its teeth skittering across the stone floor. The men picked up the teeth for souvenirs and moved on to other targets. By dawn, the school and all of the outbuildings lay in smoldering ruins.

The episode appalled some of Boston's leading citizens, including Harrison Gray Otis, a future U.S. senator, who told an audience in Faneuil Hall, "The destruction of property and danger of life caused thereby, calls loudly on all good citizens to express individually and collectively the abhorrence they feel of this high-handed violation of the laws." Lyman Beecher also condemned the violence, though he noted that preventing the conversion of innocent

Protestant girls represented a noble cause. He assured anxious civic leaders that "the excitement . . . had no relation whatever to religious opinions."[10]

The authorities rounded up thirteen rioters and tried them individually in December 1834, beginning with John R. Buzzell. It soon became clear, however, that the Catholic Church and not Buzzell was on trial. Witnesses for the prosecution were difficult to find, particularly after the posting of a warning on Charlestown Bridge, "All persons giving information in any shape or testifying in court against any one concerned in the late affair at Charlestown may expect assassination." Rebecca Reed was a star witness for the defense, spinning her fantasies to the delight of the packed galleries. After twenty hours of deliberation, the jury returned a verdict of not guilty. All of the subsequent trials found each of the defendants innocent of the charges, except for a sixteen-year-old boy who led a book-burning spree on the property. He received a life sentence. At the behest of Bishop Fenwick, the governor commuted the sentence and released the prisoner.[11]

Buzzell emerged from the trial a local hero. The citizens of Boston and Charlestown showered him with so many gifts he found it necessary to place a card of thanks in the Boston newspapers. Buzzell eventually moved to New Hampshire, where he entered politics. Mother Superior and Sister Mary John returned to the Ursuline convent in Quebec. Despite numerous lawsuits, the order never received any compensation for the loss of its property. The convent stood a charred ruin for nearly half a century before the town leveled the hill and used the soil as a landfill. Some bricks from the convent were spared in the final demolition and today form the arch in the front vestibule of the Cathedral of the Holy Cross in Boston. Only Bunker Hill rises above Charlestown now, along with its monument commemorating a nation's heroic stand against British oppression.

Rebecca Reed had a more colorful if brief career after the fire. Her "spiritual autobiography," *Six Months in a Convent* (1835), appeared several months after the trial and sold ten thousand copies in the Boston area alone during its first week in print. Reed recounted her "imprisonment" and how the nuns forced her to renounce the Protestant faith. Mother Superior published a sharp rejoinder a few months later, *An Answer to Six Months in a Convent Exposing Its Falsehoods and Manifold Absurdities* (1835), refuting all of Reed's allegations, noting that it was a strange prison that kept the front door unlocked. That book sold well, too.[12]

Reed's supporters responded to the Mother Superior's book with *Supplement to "Six Months in a Convent" Confirming the Narrative of Rebecca Reed . . . by the Testimony of More Than One Hundred Witnesses* (1835), a screed whose strongest appeal lay in its conclusion: "It [the convent] was wholly *foreign*; having been founded, in 1820, by two *foreigners*, who imported four Ursuline *for-eigners* into this country for that purpose, and . . . established [with] *foreign money*, collected by a Mr. John Thayer in Rome . . . who rejoiced in the American Revolution only as the means of accomplishing a 'much more happy revolution' in the supremacy of the Pope in America!"[13]

The vast evangelical network created by the Second Great Awakening and the steam printing press advertised Reed's books to a broad audience. Reed saw little of the profits; she died of tuberculosis, allegedly brought on by the rigors of convent life, shortly after the publication of the *Supplement*.

The popularity of Reed's books and the credulity of a public receptive to almost anything sensational about the Catholic Church inspired a more extraordinary tale. Maria Monk's problem was more immediate than Rebecca Reed's: she was pregnant in an era when unwed motherhood was decidedly unfashionable. The solution: write a book, a strategy concocted by a team of prominent evangelists and abolitionists, including Theodore Dwight, great-grandson of Jonathan Edwards, the leading light of the First Great Awakening. The result eclipsed the mild perturbations of Rebecca Reed. The book, *Awful Disclosures of the Hôtel Dieu Nunnery* (1836), sold more copies than any other book in America before the Civil War, with the exception of Harriet Beecher Stowe's *Uncle Tom's Cabin*.

Awful Disclosures, true to its title, chronicled the debauched life of nuns and priests in a Montreal convent. Mother Superior parceled out nuns to priests and issued orders for the murder of their babies. Licentious priests roamed the halls, feasting on young virgins at will. "Often they were in our beds before us," Maria wrote. Especially fascinating for readers were the detailed descriptions of the convent's Gothic rituals. The ceremony marking Maria's entrance into the novitiate required her to lie down in a coffin, after which three priests ravished her (accounting for her pregnancy). Mother Superior forced her to reveal her most secret thoughts and desires to priests in the confessional. Maria concludes her story with a tour of the convent for the reader, probing the secret recesses and passageways down into a subbasement where she discovers an enormous lime pit employed to devour the bodies of the murdered infants.[14]

All was fantasy. Contrary evidence poured in almost immediately. Maria's mother told a reporter that a Protestant minister had impregnated her daughter and had spun the tale to cover up the deed. A New York lawyer, William Stone, sympathetic to Maria, traveled to Montreal to inspect the ribald, murderous Hôtel Dieu Nunnery. Stone discovered only a placid religious community whose residents lived with "confidence, esteem, and harmony among each other."[15]

But these contradictions only confirmed the perfidy of the Catholic Church for convinced Protestants. The conspiracy of silence and secrecy confounded investigators. Further revelations that Maria was actually a prostitute did not erode the book's popularity, or that of a sequel. Like Rebecca, Maria gained little from her book's success. She died penniless on Welfare Island in New York in 1849.

The destruction of the Ursuline convent underscored the challenges facing the still new nation. Despite Lyman Beecher's disingenuous denial, religious discord played a major role in the conflagration. Irish Catholics were unwelcome in New England, especially in the Puritan Protestant strongholds in and around Boston. In the volatile religious marketplace of the era, Catholicism more than held its own. By the time Bishop Fenwick arrived in Boston, more than two thousand Protestants had converted to the Catholic faith.

The convent represented more than religious rivalry. It was an outpost for a religion deemed incompatible with Revolutionary ideals. The convent also subverted ideals of the family and gender; celibate women were training young Protestant girls into womanhood with an ambitious curriculum the equal or better of comparable boys' schools. Mount Benedict and Bunker Hill were more than two elevations in a Boston suburb. The elegant convent rising alongside the sacred hill provided a bricks-and-mortar threat to the Revolutionary legacy, a reminder that, perhaps, the future lay with Rome.

The Protestant brickmakers, truckmen, and carpenters also wondered about the future. Artisanal labor was beginning its long and precipitous decline from a worthy craft with the potential of entrepreneurial status to one of semiskilled drudgery with little prospect of advance. If the economy offered diminishing prospects for the Charlestown artisans, the convent and the Irish Catholic hierarchy that sponsored it represented a source of that declension.

This religious discord occurred as the second generation of Americans came of age. The passing of the Founders left the new generation with the responsibility of preserving and advancing the Revolutionary legacy, a difficulty compounded by the absence of a consensus on the specifics of that legacy. The second generation would both conserve and redefine the founding principles. America was still very much an experiment, and pundits, both abroad and at home, predicted its imminent demise from too much democracy, too much territory, or too much diversity.

Threats abounded, as did severe solutions. If Indians stood in the way of fulfilling the Revolutionary heritage of a free, democratic, and prosperous nation, remove them. If slaveholders mocked the founding principles of American government, restrict their movement, and ultimately their livelihood. If foreign nations encroached on soil rightfully American, negotiate if possible, make war if necessary. If Roman Catholics flooded American cities with their foreign allegiances, secretive ways, and despotic hierarchy, then convert them, or limit their rights.

Catholics menaced not only the Revolutionary legacy but also God's plan for the New World. One way of securing the national experiment was to link its cause with God. Evangelical Protestants believed that it was more than coincidence that the Reformation had followed closely upon the European discovery of America, more than coincidence that the world's first truly republican government based on the dignity and equality of men appeared on this soil. American Protestantism reinforced and complemented American republican government. The awakened cherished individuality, their personal decision to come to Jesus, their use of intuition and reason to determine the will of God, and the willingness to break with traditions and with the people and institutions that upheld those traditions. They cherished also their system of government, unique in the world, forged in blood, and dedicated to the self-evident truths of equality and government by consent of the governed. Catholics stood as the great historic threat, to both the Protestant God and the American nation. The rigid hierarchy of the Church denigrated individual reason, stifled dissent, and disdained democratic discourse. It was a despotic institution, accustomed to supporting like regimes in Europe.

The Catholic threat seemed real and imminent to American Protestants in the midst of a religious revival. The Holy See under Pope Gregory XVI (1831–46) was an expansionist institution, allied with conservative regimes and deeply suspicious of republican influences. Catholic leaders in the United States often favored confrontation over conciliation. New York's archbishop, John Hughes, boasted to Protestants, "Everyone should know that we have for our mission to convert the world—including the inhabitants of the United States." The Catholic Church clearly threatened America's destiny as God's Chosen Nation.[16]

So did slavery, at least according to abolitionists. The anti-slavery and anti-Catholic movements shared a number of common characteristics and some of the same personnel. Maria Monk's *Awful Disclosures* was frankly pornographic by the conventions of the era, though its authors always took care to frame lurid passages within the context of victimhood, demurely apologizing to the genteel reader while at the same time whetting his appetite. This was a technique that abolitionists would put to good use in promoting slave narratives: providing details of life in bondage guaranteed to shock the reader while making the larger point that slavery itself was a violent and pornographic institution, destructive of normal family life, faith, and republican sensibilities, just like the Roman Catholic Church. It was hardly surprising that the Beecher family stood in the forefront of both the crusade against Catholics and the crusade against slavery. Both institutions, in their view, condoned slavish adherence to false doctrines, imprisoned their victims and stripped them of their humanity, and conspired to subvert American ideals of self-government and free thought. They were old, outmoded traditions and now deserved to be vanquished by the righteous.

The anti-slavery and anti-Catholic movements both attained greater prominence during the 1830s as the Second Great Awakening peaked. The movements benefited from the print revolution and the persistent concerns about individual freedom as a threatened legacy from the Revolutionary era. Charles Grandison Finney, a New York lawyer who had heard the voice of God while researching a case and promptly dropped his law books for the Bible, reasoned that as long as evangelicals mailed Christian newspapers, sermons, and Bibles across the land, why not add anti-slavery tracts to the mailbag. Conversion to one cause might stimulate conversion to the other. While they were at it, why not employ the American entrepreneurial spirit and toss in anti-slavery kerchiefs, medals, and even wrappers around chocolate—build an anti-slavery franchise.[17]

The flurry of evangelical anti-slavery mail and gewgaws produced precious few conversions, but it infuriated residents in southern port cities. Charleston's mayor gathered the incendiary materials and lit a huge bonfire as a signal to the Yankee holier-than-thou preachers to stay the hell out of the South and stop mixing religion with politics. The southern reaction startled many northerners, including Lyman Beecher's daughter Harriet. Slaveholders, she thought, threatened free speech and thought as much as the Roman Catholic hierarchy. She signed her name on an anti-slavery petition to Congress calling for the abolition of slavery in the District of Columbia.[18]

Northern lawmakers dutifully unfolded the reams of paper petitions and brought Congress to a standstill. The lawmakers voted to receive the abolition petitions but table them immediately so they could conduct the country's business. Such a timesaving maneuver had occurred in the past, but this order was meant to last the entire session. Abolitionists called it a "gag rule" and declared that the issue now was not freedom for the slaves but freedom for all Americans. As William Jay, head of the New York Anti-Slavery Society, commented, "We commenced the present struggle to obtain the freedom of the slave; we are compelled to continue it to preserve our own." Abolitionists understood that as long as northerners perceived slavery as a black problem, the prospects for liberation were dim. They set about to show their neighbors that slavery was everyone's problem. They would receive significant and unexpected help from white southerners in this effort.[19]

The suppression of the petitions energized the evangelical faithful. By 1838, more than a hundred thousand citizens, half of them women, had distributed one million pieces of anti-slavery literature and an additional twenty thousand religious tracts directly to the South. Petitions bearing two million names descended upon Congress. The gag rule remained in force.

Abolitionists were yet a small and often despised group, and not only in the South. The same year that rioters destroyed the Ursuline convent, William Lloyd Garrison, the founder of the American Anti-Slavery Society, claimed that a "Reign of Terror" had descended upon fellow abolitionists. Citizens broke up meetings and at one point led Garrison through the streets of Boston with a rope around his neck. The objections against the abolitionists were manifold. They disrupted the public order by calling for an end to an institution clearly protected by the Constitution; they threatened the destruction of the Union with their incendiary rhetoric and publications; and they seemed oblivious to the dangers of unleashing four million freed slaves to migrate to the North to compete for jobs and live among whites.

Some northern whites feared the black migration was already under way. The black population in the North had grown faster than any other segment of the northern population between 1800 and 1830 to nearly 320,000. Restrictions on their civil liberties and employment accompanied this increase. States excluded them from basic rights of citizenship such as serving in state militias and voting. Laws and customs barred them from hotels and restaurants and relegated them to segregated schools. The pattern of segregation in the North extended to cemeteries, jails, and churches, where blacks sat in "nigger pews." Most states outlawed interracial marriage and prohibited blacks from testifying in court against whites. Employment options narrowed, especially after the 1830s when immigrants crowded into northern cities and competed with native-born whites and blacks for work. Even domestic service, long a preserve of black women, became less available as the growing urban middle class in the North found prestige in hiring Irish girls to cook and clean for them. Some states in the Midwest banned free blacks from entering altogether.

As voting restrictions for whites fell away, blacks found less room under the broadened canopy of democracy. Every new state from the 1820s onward restricted suffrage to white males only, and in New Jersey and Connecticut, lawmakers amended constitutions to limit suffrage to white men. Barred from jury service in most states, either by custom or law, free blacks comprised a disproportionate number of prisoners and suffered wildly disparate sentences from

whites for similar offenses. When the city of Worcester, Massachusetts, admitted black citizens to jury duty, the event became national news and elicited a
warning from an Indiana congressman that such a precedent "would allow a
white man to be accused of crime by a negro; to be arrested on the affidavit of
a negro, by a negro officer; to be prosecuted by a negro lawyer; testified against
by a negro witness; tried before a negro judge; convicted before a negro jury;
and executed by a negro executioner; and either one of these negroes might
become the husband of his widow or his daughter!"[20]

Although northern blacks organized and protested against these restrictions, only in Massachusetts did they achieve some success, as the legislature
in 1843 repealed the state's ban against interracial marriage and railroad companies abandoned segregated seating. An English traveler at the time, noting
the obstacles blacks confronted living in the North, concluded, "We see in effect, two nations—one white and another black—growing up together within
the same political circle, but never mingling on a principle of equality."[21]

African Americans' living conditions in the North reflected their limited
work and educational choices. Housed in sheds, stables, run-down tene-
ments, or not at all, dodging police who served more as tormentors than
protectors, and targets of periodic violence—black life in the urban North
may have been free, but it was not good. When southern whites countered
anti-slavery arguments by pointing out that blacks' living conditions in the
North proved their unfitness for freedom, they were half right.

Northern opposition to the gag rule and southern demands for a federal
ban on abolitionist literature (and the arrest and extradition to the South of
those responsible for the mailings) had much more to do with Revolutionary
principles as embodied in the Constitution than with liberating slaves. Southern
whites, in denying freedom for the black man, now threatened freedom for
whites. As one northern white argued, southerners must not "require of us a
course of conduct which would strike at the root of everything we have been
taught to consider sacred." The White Protestant Republic, as codified in the
Revolutionary documents and ordained by God, had no room for those who
threatened both the laws of God and those of man.[22]

The political process might have contained the sectarian and anti-slavery
conflicts, as it had in the past, were it not for the changing landscape of America. It was not happenstance that Lyman Beecher and Charles Grandison
Finney both left their eastern homes and sought converts in Ohio. Beecher
authored a blueprint for this crusade, A Plea for the West (1835). The book exposed the alleged Catholic conspiracy in the West to defile the virgin land,
working through the "dread confessional" to manipulate elections and "inflame and divide the nation, break the bond of our union, and throw down

our free institutions." The mission of America to guide the world to grace depended on "the religious and political destiny" of the West. And this destiny depended on capturing the West for Protestants and whites.[23]

Americans in the 1830s and 1840s were on the move—to the West, to the cities, to anyplace where they could pursue the main chance, a better life, more land, independence, or just a change of scenery. As God's rule knew no boundaries, so the American continent offered a limitless expanse of opportunity. Space, the ability to pursue it, get it, and own it, set the American apart from the European and from Europe, where land was the prerogative of the elite and often closed to certain classes, ethnic groups, and dissenting religions. Yet not all religions or races were welcome in the American West. Their exclusion would become a contentious political issue, a holy crusade, a cause to violence, and eventually a call to civil war.

The movement west seemed inexorable. Even the great contrarian Henry David Thoreau found himself drawn to a western route in meanderings from his home in Concord: "I must walk toward Oregon, and not toward Europe." For the awakened, the migration affirmed God's plan for America. The destiny of these transplanted Europeans lay in peopling a continent. They perceived this destiny as a fulfillment, not a conquest. "I always consider the settlement of America with reverence and wonder," wrote John Adams, "as the opening of a grand scene and design in Providence for the illumination of the ignorant, and the emancipation of the slavish part of mankind all over the earth." The West was more than a place; it was a sacred trust that God held until His Chosen People arrived to spread His faith and His government over the land.[24]

Migration meant more than moving from one place to another; it became a holy work to turn virgin soil and to grow republican ideals and Christian virtues. Many nineteenth-century Americans believed they could discern the will of Providence in daily events, and in these migrations they perceived a divine destiny. As Americans settled new land, they expiated old sins and edged closer to the day of the coming of the Lord. These sentiments blended the sacred with the secular and transcended the evangelical community to engage most Americans. Thomas Jefferson visualized the providential nature of migration with his proposal for the Great Seal of the United States, a portrait of "the children of Israel, led by a cloud by day and a pillar of fire by night"—the new nation inexorably moving toward Canaan.[25]

Moving also offered an opportunity to perfect America, to synthesize the best of the old settlements to create a new, more perfect Union. In this western crucible "pride and jealousy gave way to natural yearnings of the human heart for society. . . . Take the Virginian from his plantation or the Yankee from his boat and harpoon, . . . and place him in the wilderness, with an axe in his hand and rifle on this shoulders, and he soon becomes a different man; his national character will burst the chains of local habit." It was the process of casting off the provincialism of the past and becoming an American.[26]

John L. O'Sullivan, a Harvard-educated journalist, coined a phrase for this sense of geographic entitlement and providential oversight when he wrote in July 1845 of "our manifest destiny to overspread and to possess the whole of the continent allotted by Providence for the free development of our yearly multi-plying millions." He did not mean it in a belligerent way, but rather as a sacred responsibility to spread America's government and religion far and wide in order to save all mankind.[27]

The westward trek was odyssey, ordeal, and mission. The Mormons offered the best proof of just how distinctively American was this journey, though O'Sullivan and most other Americans would not have singled them out as representative of anything except trouble. The Mormons sought the ultimate West: the establishment of a new Zion, a literal heaven on earth. From the first New England settlements, the building of a perfect society, defying the Augustinian dictum about the city of God and the secular realm as distinctive spheres, had burrowed into the national consciousness through the churches, political discourse, and literature. The Mormons would realize this dream.[28]

Of all the varied movements in American society during the first half of the nineteenth century, the Mormons perhaps best embodied the culture of that era: deeply spiritual in a religious age, hardworking in a nation where the work ethic assumed the proportions of an Eleventh Commandment, and willing to endure hardship in pursuit of their dream. While they cherished the importance of the individual conversion, the Mormons believed strongly in the group as both a shield of protection and an engine of advancement, principles that new settlements west of the Appalachians had enshrined. It was a most optimistic faith in the most optimistic country; its founding story was America's story: the progressive triumph of God's power over evil, and the belief that America was the Lord's Zion, and that this Zion would be located somewhere in the western Eden. Yet this most American group was also among the most persecuted. They stretched Americans' tolerance in religious affairs, but their primary "sin" was carrying nineteenth-century American culture to its logical conclusion. At what point did hard work become obsession? How much should communal cohesion overwhelm individual choice? When did religious freedom slide into heresy?

Their secondary sin was success. Mid-nineteenth-century America was a crucible for all sorts of ideas and beliefs. Learned individuals measured and counted bumps on peoples' heads to determine their personality, and they called it science. Leading literary lights left their comfortable homes and villages to establish rural communes where members exchanged work roles, money, and each other's spouses, and they called it utopia. Physicians advocated immersions in hot and cold water, emulsions of mercury, and diets heavy on crackers as body-cleansing regimens, and they called it therapy. Some people believed that biblical numerology predicted the end of the world—the date shifted, but 1843 seemed to be most likely—and they called this revelation. All of these movements crashed, most sooner, some later. Just as personal failure reflected an individual character flaw, so the failure of movements indicated their shaky underpinnings. Such, most assumed, would be the case with the Latter-day Saints. But they did not fail; and their detractors expressed both wonder and anger at their persistence. If the Mormons succeeded, then there must be something to their theology. Just as failure was the measure of men, so too was success. Even more.

In the 1820s, across western Vermont, into adjacent New York State, and on the shores of the Great Lakes into the Middle West, the fires of religious enthusiasm stirred thousands of residents, who carried the flames with them as they migrated westward. The western part of New York State was so singed by the phenomenon that people called it the "burnt" district. In catching this spirit, young Joseph Smith was not unlike myriad other youngsters, wrestling with changes in their bodies and the assault of new ideas on their minds, the wild blending of the occult and the Christian. Daniel Hendrix, a neighbor, thought young Joe "was the most ragged, lazy fellow in the place, and that is saying a good deal." His very appearance portended failure: "I can see him now in my mind's eye," Hendrix related, "with his torn and patched trousers, his calico shirt as dirty and black as the earth, and his uncombed hair sticking through the holes in his old battered hat." In the dead of winter, young Joseph, so poor, or so oblivious, trudged through the snow and slush with paper-thin shoes. Yet he never seemed moody or resentful and made friends easily. Above all, everyone agreed, Joseph had "a fertile imagination. He never could tell a common occurrence in his daily life without embellishing the story with his imagination."[29]

The story he told of one day in 1820 was about his sudden conversion—not a unique experience in the overheated religious environment—and the appearance of two bright angels who told him that all existing religious beliefs were false: "I asked the personages who stood above me in the light, which of all the sects was right. . . . And which I should join. I was answered that I must join none of them, for they were all wrong, and . . . all their Creeds were an abomination in his sight." It was a feeling many spiritual Americans experienced, including Ralph Waldo Emerson, who, in his 1832 "Divinity School

Address," lamented the emptiness of the contemporary church. For Emerson, "God is, not was; ... He speaketh, not spake," and "the gleams which flash across my mind" were contemporary revelation. But when the fourteen-year-old Joseph confided his visions to a Methodist minister, "he treated my communication not only lightly but with great contempt, saying it was all of the Devil, that there was no such thing as visions or revelations in these days."[30]

The angel Moroni told young Joseph where to find a book written on gold plates accompanied by special stones that would enable him to translate the tablets. The prophet Mormon and his son Moroni, survivors of a lost tribe of Israel, had written on the plates. The plates revealed the history of the tribe and predicted the emergence of a new prophet, Joseph Smith.

The prophet began modestly, conducting healing ceremonies in the neighborhood and offering predictions about politics and souls. He forecast that the United States would eventually fall into a civil war that would begin in South Carolina. Smith and his followers, like Emerson, sought perfection—to live the life that God commanded; to live the life of Truth as detailed in the Book of Mormon, the Bible (numerous passages of which appeared in the Book of Mormon), and Smith's writings. In common with other movements at the time, Mormons abstained from alcohol and tobacco as part of the personal regimen of moving toward perfection. Smith believed that his mission was to build a new Zion in America where the thousand-year reign of Christ would begin: "We believe in the literal gathering of Israel and in the restoration of the Ten Tribes, that Zion will be built upon this [American] continent; that Christ

Joseph Smith discovering the Book of Mormon, 1827.
(Courtesy of Robert T. Barrett, Bringham Young University)

will reign personally upon the earth, and that the earth will be renewed and receive its paradisiacal glory." Only by being perfect could the Mormons realize this promise. It was a difficult task that required the utmost discipline and adherence to the faith.[31]

Smith moved west with his growing band of followers, men and women much like himself with dreams to do well and good, though not yet blessed with success at either. They went first to Kirtland, Ohio, where he created a utopian settlement based upon principles of common property, and then to Missouri, where the Saints established a town, the Land of Zion, near Independence. But in this slave state, the Mormons' equanimity toward Indians and blacks roused suspicion, and their zealous industriousness generated rumors of a plan to take over Missouri. In 1833, mobs pushed the Mormons back across the Mississippi River into Illinois, where they regrouped yet again and built a new community, Nauvoo, which by the early 1840s boasted fifteen thousand inhabitants, making it the largest city in the state.

Their success and their disdain for the false religions surrounding them did not earn the Mormons their neighbors' admiration, but the greater trouble came from within the Mormon camp. When Smith revealed that God condoned polygamy, a group of Saints denounced him in a rival newspaper. Smith ordered the destruction of the newspaper, an action that resulted in his being arrested and taken to jail in nearby Carthage. A few days later a mob of two hundred murdered Smith and his brother and unleashed mayhem on his followers. The reduced Mormon band could no longer stay in Illinois. The decision fell to the new leader, Brigham Young, to lead the Saints to a land as far away from settlement as possible. Young concluded that the Mormons could not live among Gentiles. Separation was the only way. They would build their Zion, and to the devil with everyone else.

Young was forty-three years old at the time and looked like an unprepossessing Quaker farmer, a fairly short, stocky man with poor posture and long light brown hair. Not a charismatic presence, but, like Smith, he had a vision, and unlike his predecessor, he would make it a reality in the West.

Like many travelers west, Young had read up avidly on the territories. It appeared that the area around the Great Salt Lake was precisely the isolated oasis that the Saints sought. Towering mountains bordered it to the east, and deserts extended west and south. Guidebooks alluded to streams, good soil, and grass in the valley.

On February 17, 1846, Brigham Young stood on a wagon outside Nauvoo and informed the Saints of his plan to depart for this distant valley in a series of small parties, the first of which he would lead. He urged his followers to maintain order and be peaceful with any peoples encountered along the way.

"If you do these things," Young promised, "faith will abide in your hearts; and the angels of God will go with you, even as they went with the children of Israel when Moses led them from the land of Egypt." Here on the flat plains of Illinois, the fulfillment of the dreams of Americans from John Winthrop forward would begin: the Chosen People going off to plant their City on a Hill.[32]

On the trail, they met up with mountain man Jim Bridger, who warned them that the Great Salt Lake rested not in a lush valley but in a desert. Bridger offered Young a thousand dollars for every bushel of corn he could grow there. Undaunted, an advance party arrived at the great valley on July 22, 1847. Their first glimpse of Zion was disappointing: "A broad and barren plain hemmed in by mountains, blistering in the burning rays of the midsummer sun. No waving fields, no swaying forests, no verdant meadows . . . but on all sides a seemingly interminable waste of sagebrush . . . the paradise of the lizard, the cricket and the rattlesnake." But Jim Bridger would lose his bet. Almost immediately, the Saints planted crops, built a dam across what they dubbed City Creek, and watched the rain fall. When the first wave of migration ended that autumn, eighteen hundred Saints called the Great Salt Lake home. On this site, Young would build a great city and, as at Jerusalem, a great temple.[33]

Brigham Young was the latest in a long line of American prophets who held fast to the faith of a distinctive national destiny: that the United States was a resurrected Israel whose fulfillment was only a matter of time and the hard work of God's servants. These ideas permeated American society long before Young's odyssey. But not until the 1840s did the connection between westward migration and national destiny become an integral part of popular culture. And not until that time did the United States understand itself as an exemplar of faith and liberty—what Thomas Jefferson called a "standing monument and example"—and move to a more active role. An evangelical religion spawned an evangelical democracy.[34]

The Latter-day Saints demonstrated the creative possibilities of the Second Great Awakening. The movement's energy, however, could unhinge as well as bind together peoples and places. Its destructive potential was evident in the breakup of the major evangelical Protestant denominations beginning in the 1840s, an ominous portent of a larger national disintegration.

The Methodists, meeting in New York in June 1844, ordered Bishop James O. Andrew of Georgia to relinquish his office or his slaves. The demand touched off a bitter debate not ultimately resolved until 1854, but it effectively sundered the largest evangelical denomination in the country.

The Methodist breakup was not amicable, as sporadic violence drove dissenting ministers from pulpits in Missouri, Maryland, and Virginia. Each side accused the other of heresy. Southern Methodists charged their northern counterparts with "preaching what Christ never preached" in opposing slavery. Northern Methodists, in turn, alleged that southerners walked away from the church "to breed slaves for the market, to separate husband and wife, parents and children, in the face of the laws of God and nature."[35]

The divorce of the Baptists resembled the breakup of the Methodists. The second-largest evangelical denomination foundered in 1844 when Georgia Baptists put forward the name of James Reeve, a slaveholder, as a missionary to the Indians. The Home Missionary Society rejected Reeve's nomination because he owned slaves. When the Baptist State Convention in Alabama demanded "the distinct, explicit avowal that slaveholders are eligible and entitled equally with nonslaveholders to all the privileges and immunities of their several unions," the mission board replied that it could "never be a party to any arrangement which would imply approbation of slavery." Southern Baptists, insulted by what they perceived as high-handed and un-Christian treatment, met in Augusta, Georgia, in May 1845 to create the Southern Baptist Convention. The other major evangelical Protestant denomination, the Presbyterians, split along sectional lines in stages, beginning as early as 1837 over a doctrinal dispute emanating from anti-slavery agitation among northern Presbyterians.[36]

For people of faith these internecine religious schisms were very troubling. If citizens could not get along within the fellowship of Christ, what did the future hold for the nation? South Carolina senator John C. Calhoun observed that the evangelical denominations "contributed greatly to strengthen the bonds of the Union." If all bonds are loosed, he worried, "nothing will be left to hold the States together except force." Kentucky senator Henry Clay wondered, "If our religious men cannot live together in peace, what can be expected of us politicians, very few of whom profess to be governed by the great principles of love?"[37]

The schism also ended the dialogue between sections. Former coreligionists split into hostile camps, each believing themselves the true bearer of the Gospel, and their former brethren its desecrator. Slavery, at the center of the denominational sundering, became the measure of all that differentiated North from South. For evangelical southerners, slavery was no sin and churches must not make social policy. For evangelical northerners, the belief in individual spiritual rights and personal religious activism made such involvement a Christian duty. Southerners now saw northern ministers and their churches as instruments of the abolition fiend, and northerners viewed southern clerics and their congregations as complicit in the sin of slavery. The sacred and secular were becoming much less distinct and poisoning each other.

It is difficult to measure the impact of the schisms across the body politic.

The awakened were a minority, though their rhetoric, publications, and beliefs had impact far beyond their numbers. Issues of slavery, sectarian strife, and territorial expansion had a distinctive moral dimension and, in a Chosen Nation, it was hard not to invest all political questions with moral weight.

The two major political parties, the Whigs and the Democrats, had revolved more around Andrew Jackson than Jesus Christ in the decade preceding the election of 1844. The Whigs were an ill-fitting (as it turned out) conglomeration united only in opposition to Jackson. If they had a philosophy, it was that of Kentuckian Henry Clay. Clay had an expansive vision for his country: to use the government and its wealth to enhance the nation's economy and strengthen the Union he dearly loved.

As Americans moved westward, Clay wondered, could democracy traverse a continent as easily as it had the eastern seaboard? As with most questions in the new nation, any answer was speculation. There were simply no precedents. But a country knitted together by internal improvements—canals and railroads—and by the commerce that would flow from such connections would have greater self-interest in staying intact. Clay called his program, appropriately, the American System, a scheme designed to make and maintain a nation.

Whigs described themselves as "sober, industrious, thrifty people." Their ranks swelled with the awakened, for whom self-improvement and self-discipline were crucial values. The Democrats were wary of national government power and more supportive of individual liberties and states' rights than the Whigs; they did not support federal aid for internal improvements until the 1850s. They fiercely protected the wall between church and state, while the Whigs blurred the distinction. More egalitarian, more secular, and more open to immigrants, the Democrats benefited from the advance of universal white male suffrage in the 1820s and 1830s.[38]

By 1844, both parties had gotten religion. The fissures among evangelicals, the conflicts between Protestants and Catholics, the slavery debates, and the settlement of the West placed religion at the forefront of American politics. Under normal circumstances, the Whigs, especially northern Whigs, would have been favored by most evangelicals. But Henry Clay, the Whig standard-bearer, was not the ideal presidential candidate for a time of evangelical agitation. Democrats seized on Clay's reputation as a duelist, gambler, imbiber of alcohol, and habitual violator of the Sabbath. According to Democratic sources, his "debaucheries and midnight revelries" were "too disgusting to report." The Whigs attempted to balance the ticket by nominating New Jersey's Theodore Frelinghuysen, a devout and abstemious Methodist, for vice president. The Whigs also reminded voters of the Democrats' close ties to Romanism. Although the Whigs could hardly portray Clay as Virtue Incarnate, they larded descriptions of their nominee with an array of religious metaphors implying that he walked with the saints, even if he was not of their number. One broadside vowed that Clay was "in form a man . . . [but] LOOKED A GOD" and would be "the *redeemer* of the country."[39]

James K. Polk, the Democratic presidential nominee, was not a religious man; his wife dragged him to church occasionally, but he never took membership. Polk's religion was work, and his work was to complete the continental empire begun by his idol, Thomas Jefferson, and advanced by his mentor, Andrew Jackson. Supporters, in fact, called him "Young Hickory." If the Whigs could resurrect the errant Clay as the nation's redemptive angel, the Democrats could shape James K. Polk into a moral paragon with supramortal qualities.

Democrats staged mock baptisms, anointing the faithful "in the name of Andrew JACKSON, the Father! James K. POLK, the Son!! and TEXAS, the Holy Ghost!!!"—typically followed with copious sprinklings of whiskey or hard cider. Democrats, well aware of the importance of women in bringing indifferent husbands to Christ, offered the example of Polk's wife, the very Presbyterian Sarah Childress. They confided that Sarah served as a mentor of faith to her husband and ensured that he was "strictly a temperance man in everything—in liquor, tobacco, in eating, and in all respects." Moreover, Polk found gambling abhorrent and was "an anti-duellist on Christian principles." This marked one of the first occasions in American politics where the wife of a candidate became an active part of the campaign, an indication of how evangelical Protestantism helped to extend women's influence beyond the home. Democrats hoped that Sarah Childress's example would inspire women to evangelize their husbands to vote for James K. Polk.[40]

While the Whigs and the Democrats wrapped their causes and candidates in the Shroud of Turin, the Liberty Party was the genuine article, America's first Christian political party. Its conventions resembled revivals, and its platform stressed the sacred obligation of state and national governments to promote equality and free labor. Its spokesmen urged citizens "to vote the Liberty ticket as a religious duty." One of its leaders recalled years later the excitement of the 1844 campaign: "The Liberty Party, unlike any other in history, was founded on moral principles—on the Bible, originating a contest not only against slavery but against atheistic politics from which Divine law was excluded." Others called the party "intolerant and denunciatory."[41]

The country was not ready for a major Christian political party, especially one with a partisan anti-slavery agenda. But after polling a paltry 7,000 votes in the 1840 presidential election, the Liberty Party won 62,300 votes in 1844 and peeled off enough disaffected Whigs in New York and Michigan to swing those states and the election to Polk. For increasing numbers of northern voters—but not yet a critical mass—the two major parties offered no purity on moral issues, especially on slavery. The Democrats and the Whigs invoked faith in campaigns but ignored it in governance. On the campaign trail, the whiskey flowed as freely as quotes from Scripture. The Liberty Party offered a salutary alternative to such hypocrisy.

The slavery issue, which provoked the denominational schisms, loomed over the 1844 election campaign for an even more salient reason: the proposed annexation by the United States of the Texas Republic, the Holy Ghost of the Democratic trinity. By 1844, the annexation of Texas seemed to many Americans like a natural progression of the country's territorial expansion, the God-inspired sweep of ideals and citizens across a continent. Those who led the revolt of the Texas province from the Mexican government in 1836 were former Americans, so annexation would complete the crusade to restore to them the blessings of democratic government and Protestant Christianity.[42]

Few Americans clamored for the annexation of Texas initially. The onset of a severe economic downturn in 1837 that lasted into the early 1840s focused Americans' attention on matters closer to home. The penny presses and pulp paperbacks regaled their growing audiences with tales of the Far West, not Texas. Besides, the Mexican government had never recognized Texas independence. The Mexicans had made it clear that they would perceive any move on the part of the United States to annex this province as an act of war. President Andrew Jackson, not one to shrink from a fight, nevertheless muttered a few platitudes about self-determination and let Texas alone, as did his successor, Martin Van Buren.

In the meantime, Texas president Sam Houston, like a boy hopping up and down at his school desk for attention, openly entertained proposals from Mexico and Great Britain. Mexico intimated that Texas could enjoy the status of a free state within a loose Mexican confederation. Rumors circulated that the British had promised to protect the independence of Texas in exchange for the compensated abolition of slavery, a plausible deal given Sam Houston's indifference to the institution. Houston did not seriously entertain the Mexican offer, and, although a British official visited Texas with such a scheme in mind, neither the British government nor Houston discussed it formally.

Houston was much less interested in striking dubious deals with foreign

governments than in raising the profile of the annexation issue in Washington. The Whigs had always been cool to annexation. They worried about the
expansion of the country beyond the means to govern it, and they worried
about the probability of a war with Mexico. The big Whig, President John
Tyler, was not really much of a Whig at all. Placed on the ticket as the vice
presidential candidate in 1840 as a sop to southerners whose major attraction
to Whig philosophy was that Andrew Jackson and Martin Van Buren were
Democrats, Tyler suddenly found himself president when William Henry
Harrison succumbed to the rigors of the job after only one month in office.
Tyler, a thin, sour-faced Virginian, was genial enough to intimates and held
the usual graces one associates with the Old Dominion. The fact that Tyler
was an accidental president bothered him not in the least, and he proceeded
to chart his own course, much to the dismay of mainstream Whigs.

As a nationalist, Tyler worried about Sam Houston's dalliances with the
Mexicans and especially with the British. So he sent Abel P. Upshur, his
secretary of state, to sound out Houston about a possible annexation treaty
in October 1843. However, while Upshur was inspecting a navy vessel, one
of its prize guns blew up, destroying a good deal of the ship and Upshur as
well. Tyler compounded the accident by appointing John C. Calhoun as his
new secretary of state. Calhoun was brilliant, but he was not a diplomat.
With a face and ideology seemingly chiseled from rock, Calhoun had the
appearance of an Old Testament prophet who should not be messed with.
Like Tyler, more a Whig by convenience than by conviction, Calhoun had
some specific ideas about how the United States should handle the annexation issue.

For Calhoun, annexation made sense only as a measure to save slavery
from destruction. History and prevailing wisdom dictated that the institution,
like a vampire, required periodic infusions of fresh blood—territory—to survive. Cotton cultivation depleted the soil. The abundance of fertile land lulled
planters into a security that abjured principles of conservation. The slave population, which, despite the closure of the overseas slave trade, increased twofold during the first half of the nineteenth century, would soon overrun the
white population. Too many slaves on too little land raised security concerns
and could ruin the value of a planter's investment, eventually destroying the
institution itself.

From Calhoun's political standpoint, the South had already lost the
national population competition by the early 1840s. Representatives from
nonslaveholding states easily outnumbered those where slavery yet existed.
The Senate was the South's last bastion of influence in the federal legislature.
Regardless of population, each state sent two senators to Washington. It did

not take a clairvoyant to see that the migration westward to the Pacific Coast would, eventually, result in an avalanche of free states that would make the South forever beholden, a slave if you will, to the power and whims of the free states.

Calhoun drafted an annexation treaty and laid it before the Senate in April 1844 with a cover letter urging passage because British abolitionists were poised to abolish slavery in Texas. That no such plot existed was beside the point. The association of slavery and annexation effectively doomed the measure, even among southerners who wondered why the slavery issue even entered the picture when an argument for annexation in the name of manifest destiny might have drawn a majority of the votes. But Calhoun hoped to educate Congress that annexation was a matter both of national patriotism—the British threat—and of southern equality within the Union, a cause to which he dedicated his life. Calhoun was no disunionist. What he worked for was a Union of equals. He raised the fundamental issue of a democratic society: how to protect the rights of a minority in a political system predicated on majority rule.[43]

Although Calhoun lost the vote, he gained an election issue. Northern vilification of Calhoun, the Tyler administration, and the South itself irritated southerners, especially in the Lower South, where slaveholding was more prevalent. If equality was a great principle of the Union, then why were northerners hell-bent on relegating the South to a permanent minority? All white southerners understood the implications of dependence, a term synonymous with slavery in the national lexicon.

The Democratic Party platform cannily linked Texas with Oregon (where the British and Americans held conflicting claims), rendering the acquisition of both a matter of national security and honor rather than sectional greed. Polk, despite his southern origins, perceived Texas as a way station on the road to his ultimate goal of a Pacific empire, not as a safety valve for excess slaves. The Whigs chose party loyalty over Texas, recognizing that advocacy for annexation would split the party irrevocably. Northern Whigs perceived annexation fever as a symptom of a larger disease, a conspiracy among slave states to undermine basic American ideals. Henry Clay focused on promoting his American System, fearing that agitation of the slavery issue threatened his beloved Union. But Texas and Oregon had gotten the patriotic juices flowing, and voters perceived Clay as soft on the foreign menaces and as hostile to the interests of slaveholders. He lost every Lower South state, barely broke even in the border states, and faltered in the North, where Polk and the Democrats convinced voters that the party wanted Oregon and California as badly as it longed for Texas.

John Tyler interpreted Polk's victory as a mandate for annexation. Three days from the end of his presidency, on March 1, 1845, Tyler signed the Texas annexation bill after it passed both the House and the Senate by narrow party-line votes. The Lone Star Republic entered the Union as a slave state. When Polk took office on March 4, he confronted two pressing issues: Mexico had made it clear that annexation meant war, and the British were girding for battle if Polk attempted to make good on his pledge to throw them out of Oregon. Destiny would not wait.

CHAPTER 2

EMPIRE

EMIGRANTS STREAMING TOWARD OREGON and California and settlers already established in Texas believed themselves agents of destiny. The British, Mexicans, and Indians who inhabited or claimed all or parts of these lands felt differently. President Polk hoped that a combination of negotiation, compensation, and the incessant flow of migrating Americans would convince these parties to withdraw gracefully. A well-placed threat was not out of order either.

The British blinked first. The facts on the ground—the daily arrival of American settlers—moved them to offer Oregon to the United States up to the 49th parallel. Polk rejected the deal outright. In his first message to Congress in December 1845, what today we call the State of the Union Address, Polk gave the British a geography lesson as to why the Oregon territory belonged to the United States all the way up to the 54th parallel. "Oregon is part of the North American Continent, to which, it is confidently affirmed, the title of the United States is the best now in existence. . . . The British proposition of compromise . . . can never for a moment be entertained by the United States."[1]

As crowds gathered around railroad depots in Baltimore, Philadelphia, and New York to see the message transmitted almost instantaneously by a remarkable new invention, the telegraph, a murmur and then a hurrah burst forth: "Jackson is alive again!" Back in March, when Andrew Jackson was still clinging to his first life, he had advised his protégé not to mind the British; they would protest giving up all of Oregon "to alarm us . . . and give strength to the traitors in our country. . . . England with all her boast dare not go to war."[2]

Steadfast against the British, Polk turned a sharp eye toward the Mexicans. In June, he ordered the United States Army under General Zachary Taylor to take up a position south of the Nueces River. The Mexicans considered the Nueces their northern boundary; the Americans and Texans claimed the Rio Grande, much further south, as the correct border. Sending General Taylor into disputed territory was obviously a provocation. The president felt a show of force would convince Mexicans of the rectitude of American geography. The Mexicans, however, were unimpressed and refused to hear what the president's minister, John Slidell, had to offer in the way of settlement. Slidell left Mexico in a snit, reporting to Polk, "Be assured that nothing is to be done with these people until they have been chastised." Mexicans, he said, were "ignorant Indians, debased by three centuries of worse than colonial vassalage . . . a semi-barbarous people."[3]

Zachary Taylor was a good soldier and expert farmer, owning a large plantation in Louisiana populated by over two hundred slaves. He had given a daughter to a young, well-connected Mississippi planter by the name of Jefferson Davis, but the daughter died shortly after the marriage, and the general never forgave his former son-in-law. Taylor's dual career as a farmer and a soldier spoke volumes about the regular army, only seven thousand strong scattered among various western outposts. Their major role to date had been moving Indians to barren lands and, occasionally, shooting them when they resisted. But politicians, not soldiers, make war.

Taylor hardly looked the part of a commander; he appeared as if he had just exited a cotton press and was only awaiting twine to be shipped to some textile mill up north. Squat, with a face that had more ridges than most mountain ranges, he rarely wore anything that would indicate his rank. One of his lieutenants, Ulysses S. Grant, hardly a fashion plate himself, commented, "In dress he was possibly too plain." More important to Grant, though, Taylor "was known to every soldier in his army, and was respected by all."[4]

The Mexicans and the British were part of the same problem, according to Polk. The British had negotiated with Sam Houston, president of Texas, trying to lure the Lone Star Republic away from the United States. Now the Mexicans were conspiring to give the British a stronger foothold in California. To counter that purported threat, the president, in October 1845, ordered United States Consul Thomas Larkin at Monterey, California, to take advantage of any unrest. Unrest conveniently materialized in the person of Captain John C. Frémont, who had explored the West on behalf of the U.S. Army. He now commanded a band of about sixty army irregulars; no one knew for certain if they were officially American soldiers or an assortment of mountain men looking for work and adventure. They rode into California supposedly scouting for better trails into that territory.

The movements in California and Texas (or Mexico, depending on one's perspective) received close attention in Mexico City. General Mariano Paredes, riding a wave of anti-American sentiment, led a group of army officers into the capital and deposed President Joaquín Herrera after firing a few perfunctory shots and coaxing the priests to ring the church bells. Paredes held the same view of Americans that many in the United States held of Mexicans: they were stupid and cowardly.

On January 13, 1846, Secretary of War William Marcy sent the following message to General Taylor at Corpus Christi: "Sir: I am directed by the President to instruct you to advance and occupy, with the troops under your command, positions on or near the east bank of the Rio del Norte [Rio Grande]. . . . You will not act merely on the defensive." Taylor dutifully broke camp and moved to the Rio Grande, but the last sentence of Marcy's order puzzled him.[5]

Three hundred yards across the Rio Grande, the citizens of Matamoros clambered to their rooftops, waving good-naturedly to the four thousand or so Yanks, who waved back. American soldiers enjoyed the view of the young, dark-skinned Mexican women who, without inhibition, disrobed along the riverbank and plunged in for a bath. Several soldiers waded into the river to get a closer look, but Mexican guards warned them away.

President Paredes made clear to the Polk administration that he considered the presence of American troops on the banks of the Rio Grande an act of war. To affirm his position, he refused to meet with John Slidell, the oft-rejected emissary from Washington who now hoped to arrange an agreement with the new and financially strapped Mexican government to buy New Mexico and northern California. But no Mexican government could sell those territories at any price and remain in power.

The Mexicans and the Americans watched each other warily across the river. The only troop movement occurred among some of Taylor's Irish Catholic soldiers. In the early spring of 1846, they began to cross over to the other side of the river, responding to Mexican pleas of religious brotherhood and a bounty of 320 acres. The Mexicans asked them to weigh the bigotry they encountered in American cities against the full citizenship and the grant of land they would enjoy in Mexico. After fourteen Irish Americans swam over one night, General Taylor issued shoot-to-kill orders. When two more attempted desertion shortly thereafter, they were shot. Desertions declined but not before at least two hundred Irish Catholics joined the Mexican army, forming the San Patricio Battalion.[6]

On the Matamoros shore one April morning, a solemn file of priests appeared, sprinkling holy water on the cannons aimed at American troops. When Colonel Truman Cross, the quartermaster, did not return from his usual morning horseback ride, Taylor sent out a patrol. The patrol encountered sixteen hundred Mexican soldiers, who easily overwhelmed them. That evening, an American soldier wrote home: "All idea of there being *no fight* has ceased. *War has commenced*, and we look for a conflict within a few days."

Taylor reported to the president in his usual terse style: "Hostilities may now be considered as commenced."[7]

No telegraph line existed between Texas and Washington, so it would be three weeks before the president submitted his message to Congress requesting a declaration of war. The message, like most of Polk's writings, was long and larded with legal jargon citing "grievous wrongs perpetrated upon our citizens throughout a long period of years." The United States had maintained a remarkable forbearance through these insults. But, with the Mexican invasion of American soil, the nation must defend itself. That Mexico claimed this territory and that the lengthy oppression of American citizens was an overwrought assertion did not faze the Congress. The House of Representatives took all of thirty minutes to debate Polk's message and then voted for war. It took a bit longer in the Senate—John C. Calhoun put forth the novel idea that perhaps it might be best to wait and see if the Mexican government would repudiate the ambushers—but who could vote against punishing Mexico for killing Americans?[8]

War fever erupted. Crowds thronged city streets shouting "Mexico or Death!" Posters plastered public buildings and businesses. In Illinois, three regiments were called for and fourteen regiments volunteered; Tennessee was forced to hold a lottery as thirty thousand men volunteered for three thousand places. The young editor of the *Brooklyn Daily Eagle*, Walt Whitman, joined the war whooping: "Mexico must be thoroughly chastised . . . with prompt and *effectual* hostilities. . . . Let our arms now be carried with a spirit which shall teach the world that, while we are not spoiling for a quarrel, America knows how to crush as well as how to expand."[9]

It was the idea of expansion that so intrigued the young editor, as it had motivated President Polk and tens of thousands of other Americans. Predestined, sanctified, and inevitable expansion. Celebrating the war declaration, Whitman wrote, "The daring, burrowing energies of the Nation will never rest till the whole of this northern section of the great West World is circled in the mighty Republic—there's no use denying that fact!" Like the Indian, the Mexican was no worthy steward of the New World: "What has miserable, inefficient Mexico," Whitman asked, "with her actual tyranny by the few over the many—what has she to do with the great mission of peopling the New World with a noble race?"[10]

Whitman spoke the unbounded optimism of youth. With his parents, he had joined the great migration to the cities, greater than that of the westward movement and enveloped in the same spirit of hope and success. What these emigrants, both to the West and to the cities, held in common was a faith in America, that they and the country were traveling on an unstoppable arc of progress. They identified with their country as they identified themselves. As a saga of empire unfolded on the Rio Grande, its underpinnings could be found on the trails to the Pacific and in the streets of the burgeoning cities.

When Whitman was a boy of six, in 1825, the marquis de Lafayette visited Brooklyn to lay the cornerstone for the Apprentices' Library Building. The young republic put great stock in education, for an educated populace was both a requisite for and guarantor of democratic government. A crowd of schoolchildren followed the French general's procession as he rode up Fulton Street in an open carriage. The construction site was a hole in the ground bounded by piles of dirt, and men lifted youngsters on their shoulders to take in the scene. The marquis descended from the carriage and waded through the crowd. Suddenly, young Walt found himself whisked into the general's arms for a better view. The encounter made a lasting impression on Whitman. The incident also underscored how close Americans were to the hallowed Revolutionary generation.[1]

Yet the Revolutionary generation was gone. A distance had set in. The living had to carry on and interpret a most uncommon legacy. George Bancroft, a historian, politician, and writer, set about to write the history of the United States in the 1830s. His task would take him ten volumes and forty years to complete. How presumptuous it seemed to Europeans that a country barely more than a half century old could think that it had a history. Bancroft's history was as unique as the nation he wrote about, a sweeping chronicle of providential will and virtuous statesmen coming together to create a unique experiment whose ultimate destiny still awaited. The Founders had become gods and the nation a new Israel.[2]

Whitman, like so many other Americans of that era, held a sense of obligation to that first generation, not only to honor their work and ideals but also to fulfill their vision. When Whitman assailed the Mexicans and trumpeted the destiny of America, it was not the bloody yawp of a mindless warmonger but an essay of belief that all of this, pain included, would make the world a better place.

Whitman believed, as did many other Americans, that almost anything was possible in this new land, just because it was new. As with the person, so with the country—work hard, overcome obstacles, and attain success even at a price. Such was the credo of Young America. In James K. Polk, Young America had a president, and Young America would soon have its poet. And Young America would have a war, and then an empire.

Polk had little in common with Whitman, but they both shared the optimism of a nation beyond history, a country that would reach the Pacific, build great cities, and lead the world to salvation. When Polk sent Zachary

Taylor and the "tan-faced children" of Tennessee, Kentucky, Arkansas, and Louisiana to that contested patch of ground, it was with the same confidence with which Whitman strode the streets of New York, that this was our land and by right it will be.

When word reached New York of Congress's declaration of war on Mexico in May 1846, a boisterous multitude filled the streets shouting hurrahs. The theme of '76 played across the land. For this generation of Americans, here was an opportunity to honor the Founders' legacy and extend the experiment across the continent. The United States Army was God's sword, whose "every cannon ball is a missionary; and every soldier is a Colporteur [a traveling salesman of religious literature]."[1 3]

To be sure, voices, especially in the Whig Party and in New England, spoke out against the war. A disgusted Whig editor in Georgia complained, "We have territory enough, especially if every province, like Texas, is to bring in its train war and debt and death." Some of the professional soldiers questioned the basis for going to war. Lieutenant Colonel Ethan Allen Hitchcock confided that "my heart is not in this business; I am against it from the bottom of my soul as a most unholy and unrighteous proceeding. It looks as if the government sent a small force on purpose to bring on a war, so as to have a pretext for taking California and as much of this country [Mexico] as possible."[1 4]

Some saw a foreboding in the conflict. Not one given to optimism in any case, now-Senator John C. Calhoun warned, "A deed has been done from which the country would not be able to recover for a long time, if ever." Ralph Waldo Emerson shared the senator's concern: "The United States will conquer Mexico but it will be as the man swallows the arsenic which brings him down in turn. Mexico will poison us."[1 5]

Nor did the evangelical Christian community line up with the Polk administration. Theodore Parker, among several New England evangelicals, intoned, "War is an utter violation of Christianity. If war be right, then Christianity is wrong, false, a lie." Invoking the spirit of '76 much as the war's proponents did, Parker continued: "Men will call us traitors; . . . That hurt nobody in '76. We are a rebellious nation; our whole history is treason; our blood was attainted before we were born; our creeds are infidelity to the mother church, our constitution treason to our fatherland. What of that? . . . Let God only be a master to control our conscience."[1 6]

Dissent from the war produced fine literature and poetry, inspirational sermons, and Henry David Thoreau's notable civil disobedience, but the wave of patriotism drowned these voices. The Bible included numerous examples of violence, often inflicted by God or His hosts, to further greater ends. The greater end was extending the American mission across a continent, saving souls from false religion, and planting the flag of democracy in the face of despotism. Mexico disdained democracy and exhibited the same pomposity as the regimes of the Old World. The disarray of its government attracted European interest and meddling. This had already occurred in Texas. With Great Britain and possibly France and Russia breathing down the Pacific Coast, where California hung on to its Mexican government by a thread and where Oregon was by no means yet secure, peace was a luxury. Americans must defend their experiment.

The boys signing up in droves spoke volumes against the dissenters. The early news from the war further dampened opposition. Even the Whig Party, which grumbled about the conflict and set strict conditions for its conduct, began to weigh the possibilities of riding Zachary Taylor's growing popularity into the White House in 1848. Taylor scored quick victories against courageous but disorganized Mexican troops at the Battles of Palo Alto and Resaca de la Palma in May 1846. Americans hailed him as the common man's Napoleon, "Old Rough and Ready," who spurned the trappings of his rank like a true democrat.

Polk was now the ringmaster of a three-ring circus: intrigue in California, staring down the British in Oregon, and war in Mexico. He moved quickly to defuse the Oregon standoff, retreating from his campaign promise of "54° 40' or Fight" and settling on the British offer of the 49th parallel. Northern Democrats, who had stood with Polk on Texas and Mexico, rebelled. He had promised them all of Oregon, a safety valve for their workers and dreamers, and now he had given part of it away. Maybe the Whigs were right that the Mexican War was just a plot to extend slavery and grab territory.

In August 1846, Polk asked Congress to appropriate $2 million for "extraordinary expenses" connected to the war. Many suspected the funds represented a down payment on land the United States would purchase from the Mexican government, already reeling from a series of military reverses. By this time, few lawmakers held to the fiction that the conflict with Mexico was simply a defensive war. The president had already dispatched expeditions to Santa Fe, New Mexico, and California to dislodge those provinces from Mexico. To be fair, although Polk hailed from a slave state, his territorial ambitions were primarily patriotic. A firm believer in manifest destiny, he just wanted to hurry the process along. Others, however, looked upon the president as a tool of the slaveholders. The Oregon betrayal was merely the latest in a line of devious deeds to add more slave territory.[17]

It was 7:00 P.M. on a fetid August evening in the Capitol when Pennsylvania congressman David Wilmot, a member of Polk's Democratic Party, rose to

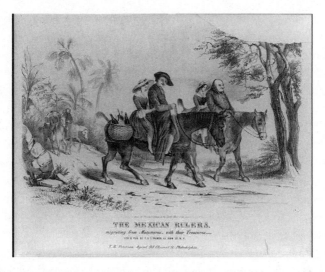

Manifest Destiny and anti-Catholic sentiment combine in this 1846 drawing mocking supposedly celibate priests retreating with their women from American forces at Matamoros. (Courtesy of the Library of Congress)

attach an amendment to the appropriations bill that for all the fuss about Polk's motives seemed destined for passage, especially since everyone wanted to go home and escape the cloying heat of Washington. Wilmot's amendment was a model of simplicity: "*Provided*: That as an express and fundamental condition to the acquisition of any territory from the Republic of Mexico by the United States, by virtue of any treaty which may be negotiated between them, and to the use by the Executive of the moneys herein appropriated, neither slavery nor involuntary servitude shall ever exist in any part of the said territory, except for crime, whereof the party shall first be duly convicted."

David Wilmot was not an abolitionist—as he put it, he had no "morbid sympathy for the slave"—but he detested slavery because he believed bonded black labor would compete unfairly with free white labor. In order to place his proviso within a conservative constitutional context, Wilmot had deliberately cribbed from the language of Thomas Jefferson's Northwest Ordinance of 1787 that prohibited slavery in those territories. All he wanted was to preserve the territories for "the sons of toil, of my own race and own color."[18]

Wilmot and his constituents, indeed most northern whites, couldn't have cared less about slavery where it existed. But the West as a place of personal and national redefinition and rebirth held a sacred place among American ideals. To defile the West with bonded labor, to nullify the hard work and perseverance of those migrants who sacrificed so much to make the journey, would be a crime of great enormity. Pennsylvanians were not about to debark for the West tomorrow, but many had moved from other places, and they would move again, and they wanted above all a fair chance. Slavery removed that possibility.

Party discipline collapsed as northern Democrats rallied behind the Wilmot Proviso and against the president, who was furious that his appropriations bill had become a vehicle for grandstanding on an extraneous and divisive issue. He considered the proviso "a Mischievous & foolish amendment." Polk wrote in his journal what he deeply believed: "What connection slavery had with making peace with Mexico it is difficult to conceive." Others found it much easier to make the connection. The *Boston Whig* summarized the impact precisely: "As if by magic, it brought to a head the great question which is about to divide the American people."[19]

Threats and recriminations flew. The rhetoric of the Congress ratcheted to a fever pitch. Ohio congressman Columbus Delano warned the South: "We will establish a cordon of free states that shall surround you; and then we will light up the fires of liberty on every side until they melt your present chains and render all your people *free*." Southerners responded in kind. Whig senator Robert Toombs of Georgia issued a warning: "I do not hesitate to avow before this House and the Country, and in the presence of the living God, that if, by your legislation, you seek to drive us from the territories of California and New Mexico, purchased by the common blood and treasure of the whole people . . . thereby attempting to fix a national degradation upon half the states of this Confederacy, *I am for Disunion*."[20]

The truth was that much of the territory, any territory, that could be gained from Mexico would likely remain free, proviso or no. Too many emigrants from the free states, too few slaveholders, and a climate and soil uncertain for the gang cultivation of crops necessary for slave labor to be profitable. But from August 1846 onward, reality scarcely made a demonstration in the Capitol. Symbols mattered. It mattered to the South when the rest of the nation did not respect its institutions. Pride, honor, face-saving, call it what you will, tinged every issue henceforth. And every issue seemed to touch on slavery. Missouri Democrat Thomas Hart Benton compared the slavery question with the plague of frogs that God had inflicted on the Egyptians to convince them to release the Hebrews from bondage: "You could not look upon the table but there were frogs, you could not go to the bridal couch and lift the sheets but there were frogs!" So it was with "this black question, forever on the table, on the nuptial couch, everywhere!"[21]

The House of Representatives would pass the Wilmot Proviso more than fifty times over the next four years, but it would always fail in the Senate. For those who loved the Union and what it stood for more than anything else, these were ominous times. The great mission of the nation to the world hung in the balance. Its new alabaster cities stretching now from the Atlantic to the Pacific, its productive farms and thriving small towns, and the deep and abiding faith in personal and national destiny must overcome this trial. America could not collapse back on itself.

While politicians wrangled, American soldiers fought, and fought better than anyone had hoped or expected. General Taylor's successes in northern Mexico, the fall of the venerable trading outpost of Santa Fe, and then the province of California, to the American forces, stoked the dreams of manifest destiny. Children in the streets of American cities sang, "Old Zack's at Monterrey / Bring out your Santa Anner; / For every time we raise a gun / Down goes a Mexicaner."[22]

The success of American forces, often outmanned, gave cause for more than children to burst into patriotic song. Mounting losses did not deter General Antonio López de Santa Anna, the target of children's ditties and American artillery. President Polk recognized that nothing short of capturing Mexico City would put a satisfactory end to this military exercise. General Winfield Scott, as officious and resplendent as Taylor was casual and crumpled, took his crisp uniforms and giant ego to Vera Cruz. After taking the port with an amphibious landing, he marched overland with fewer than nine thousand troops, most of who were unaccustomed to military discipline. Scott defied conventional military wisdom, cut his supply line, lived off the land, and fought his way into a capital guarded by a hundred thousand able-bodied men. Scott had two advantages over the Mexicans: light artillery expertly positioned and aimed, and a junior officer corps, each member of which was capable of making decisions in the field, including future luminaries George G. Meade, Ulysses S. Grant, Joseph E. Johnston, P. G. T. Beauregard, and Robert E. Lee. Despite spirited Mexican resistance, Scott prevailed, conquering the country in five months. At 7:00 A.M. on September 14, 1847, John Quitman, the president's emissary, raised the American flag above the Plaza de Armas in Mexico City, the first time the Stars and Stripes had flown over the capital of a conquered nation.

Now what? Immediately the cry of "All Mexico" went up, and President Polk began to rethink his modest objective of securing the Texas border and liberating New Mexico and California. Some southerners saw Scott's dash to victory as an opportunity to extend the slave empire and thereby save slavery as well as the souls and society of the liberated Mexicans. South Carolina novelist and poet William Gilmore Simms wrote excitedly to his senator James Henry Hammond that "slavery will be the medium & great agent for rescuing and recovering to freedom and civilization all the vast tracts of Texas, Mexico &c., and our sons ought to be fitted out as fast as they are ready to take the field, with an adequate provision in slaves and find their way in the yet unopened regions." Once the United States secured all of Mexico, it would ensure, Simms predicted, "the perpetuation of slavery for the next thousand years." Though many Americans and Mexicans would dispute the proposition that a thousand-year slave empire was necessary for their salvation, the argument resonated well in the South.[23]

As in Oregon, Polk settled for less. The high political risks and the idea of absorbing a large alien population persuaded the president to choose the more modest course. Modest was quite a bit. By the terms of the Treaty of Guadalupe Hidalgo, Mexico received $15 million in exchange for the Rio Grande boundary the Polk administration had claimed to begin with and the cession of both California and New Mexico. The Senate ratified the treaty 38 to 14 with four abstentions. The annexations of Texas and Oregon combined with the territories gained from the Mexican Cession comprised America's greatest expansion ever, as the nation's territory increased by 66 percent. The United States was now a continental empire, a status predicted, preached, and promoted for a generation. The Mexican and British obstacles dissolved. Only the Indians remained to challenge America's continental ambitions. It would not be long before the United States recouped the monetary cost of the war at least a thousandfold. The moral accounting would follow, and a greater threat to America's destiny would emerge. Quickly.

Both Democrats and Whigs retained enough discipline to convince their supporters to steer clear of the Wilmot Proviso in the election year of 1848 and support the results of the war in a general way. Most Whigs backed General Zachary Taylor. His major qualification was that he was electable. His enormous popularity, they hoped, would overcome sectional differences and unite the country. Whig congressman Abraham Lincoln urged the general to put himself above politics like a rough-hewn Washington and delegate to Congress the role of formulating and implementing legislation. It was not difficult for Taylor to follow Lincoln's advice. The general had never voted, and after forty years in the saddle, most of it out West, he was not a fount of erudition on the major issues of the day. Although he obviously had a stake in the debate as an owner of more than two hundred slaves, he made it clear that he would defer to Congress on that and other issues.

The Whigs resurrected some of their ribald campaign tactics from the Log Cabin and Hard Cider contest of 1840. They published a series of "Rough and Ready Songs" touting their candidate's innocence of politics and party: "The country's tired of party striving, / Which so retards our Nation's thriving, /

And hence she calls on *Zachary Taylor*, / Since nothing else can now avail her. / Get out of the way for Zachariar, / He's the White House purifier." The lyrics probably worked better with a musical accompaniment.[24]

The Democratic nominee for president, Senator Lewis Cass of Michigan, a War of 1812 veteran, hoped to unite both northern and southern wings of the party with his own solution to the deadlock over slavery in the territories. Cass advocated removing the federal government entirely from the slavery issue and handing responsibility for that decision to the territory's residents. Known as "popular sovereignty," it had the attraction of resolving the territorial issue in a democratic manner. But the term meant different things to northerners and southerners, and Cass was not about to disabuse anyone of whatever interpretation he might make. To northerners, popular sovereignty meant that territorial residents could ban slavery whenever they wanted to. Southerners believed that popular sovereignty gave settlers the right to abolish slavery only at the time the territory was about to become a state. Until that moment, the territorial government would protect slave property just as it would any other property.

For the third presidential election in a row, an anti-slavery party joined the field. The Free Soil Party cast a broader net than its predecessor, the Liberty Party. Free Soilers said little about slavery where it existed. Instead, they stood on the Wilmot Proviso and its prohibition of slavery in the territories. This position allowed the party to present itself as anti-slavery but not abolitionist, a white man's party, an organization dedicated to preserving the West for white men, a friend of the workingman who sought a better life in the territories. The new party's slogan, "Free Soil, Free Speech, Free Labor, and Free Men," perfectly captured its platform and appeal.

Like the Liberty Party, the Free Soilers tapped into the still-strong evangelical spirit in the North, staging a revival-style convention in Buffalo in August 1848. Speakers called for a "great moral revolution" founded on "the idea of right and justice and the truth of God." They entreated listeners to experience a spiritual rebirth, "to be baptized in the Free Soil principle," comparing David Wilmot to David of the Bible whom "God raised up . . . to slay the giant of Goth." The themes of spiritual rebirth and national rededication resonated throughout the hall. "God had determined to make the convention," one speaker assured the assemblage, "the medium of reviving . . . throughout this great . . . Nation, the pure principles of Free Government . . . ; and by founding here a real . . . Republic, to diffuse its light and truth to all Nations, until every member of the great human family shall know and rejoice in this great Salvation."

The Free Soil convention anointed former president Martin Van Buren with the nomination, after which they concluded their revival, joining hands to sing: "DAUGHTER OF ZION! from the dust, / Exalt thy fallen head; / Again in thy Redeemer trust, / He calls thee from the dead. / Awake! Awake!! put on thy strength / Thy beautiful array; / The day of Freedom dawns at length— / The Lord's appointed day!" The "freedom" in the hymn referred to the white man's freedom to pursue his personal manifest destiny. The born-again nation extolled in song was a White Republic. The enemy was less slavery than the slaveholder extending his evil institution to the Edenic West.[25]

Frederick Douglass attended the gathering in Buffalo and recognized both its limitations and its possibilities. He was realistic enough to understand that a straight-out abolition party would never make a political impact. Slavery, constricted to where it already existed, would eventually atrophy and die. Douglass and many others believed the Free Soil movement was a potential means to an end.

Zachary Taylor was enough of a slaveholder to triumph over the Democrats in the South and enough of a nonpartisan hero to overcome the Democrats in the North, some of who defected to the Free Soil movement. For all their revivalist fervor, Free Soilers polled only 14 percent of the vote in the North and probably did not sway the outcome in any one state. However, the party polled four times the vote of the Liberty Party in 1844. As long as the major parties remained mostly intact and as long as northern voters were leery of any party that attracted abolitionists, an anti-slavery political movement would remain on the political fringes.

Frederick Douglass reached this conclusion in the days after Taylor's victory, pouring out his despair in his abolitionist newspaper, the *North Star*. He scorned the religious and political hypocrisy of white voters who held selective views on freedom: "As a people you claim for yourselves a higher civilization—a purer morality—a deeper religious faith—a larger love of liberty, and a broader philanthropy, than any other nation on the globe." Yet Zachary Taylor, a slaveholder, won the presidency. "While Gen. Taylor is the well-known robber of three hundred human beings of all their hard earnings, and is coining their hard earnings into gold, you have conferred upon him an office worth twenty-five thousand dollars a year, and the highest honor within your power."[26]

What Douglass failed to understand was that Americans did indeed vote their ideals, both personal and national. General Taylor, the hero of a war that secured a continental empire, embodied the voters' faith in the nation's special mission and the imperative of routing those forces that stood in the way of its fulfillment. Because a man held slaves did not mean that he would elevate economic self-interest above the national weal. George Washington and Thomas Jefferson had pursued national ideals, not interest group politics; so would Zachary Taylor.

Two events, far apart in space but occurring close in time, would soon test Taylor and the nation. Neither event had anything to do with slavery, at least initially. The first was an offshoot of good old American entrepreneurial spirit, though its engine, John Sutter, was a Swiss immigrant. He had escaped his native land to avoid jail on a bankruptcy charge. Alighting in New York in 1834, he conned several merchants with tales of a noble background to secure letters of introduction enabling him to join the Santa Fe trade. Sutter made his way to California, where he used the letters to snag a huge land grant in the Sacramento Valley from the Mexican government. In 1843, he built an imposing fort to enclose a village of shops, homes, and small manufacturing enterprises. Sutter's Fort stood astride the terminus of the California Trail. From that advantageous location, Sutter earned a nice living selling supplies.[27]

As emigration grew, Sutter decided to erect a sawmill on his property to supply the newcomers with lumber to build their communities. With the rapidly flowing American River less than forty miles from his fort, Sutter had an ideal site for a water-powered sawmill, and he instructed another immigrant, James W. Marshall, to supervise the erection of a twelve-foot water wheel on a millrace carved from the riverbed. On the morning of January 24, 1848, Marshall noticed a glint of yellow in the millrace. He could not keep the secret. Sam Brannon, a prominent San Francisco merchant, heard the rumors and came out to see for himself. Hastening back to the city, he ran through its streets shouting, "Gold! Gold! Gold from the American River." Few would have paid much attention—men howling in the streets of the frontier town were not unknown—were it not for the fact that Brannon carried a bottle filled with gold dust in his hands. By mid-June, San Francisco was a ghost town. Signs proclaiming GONE TO THE DIGGINGS or OFF TO THE MINES adorned the shops and houses of the forlorn city.

Wild stories of instant riches accompanied the frenzy. Some were true. Two men prospecting in one canyon came away with $17,000 in gold dust and nuggets. A newspaper editor, touring the mining camps looking for stories, dipped his pan into a stream every now and then and earned $100 a day for his casual efforts. On average, miners in 1848 garnered about $20 worth of gold per day. The average daily wage back east was $1.

Back east, though, not many paid much attention when the news finally reached readers of the *New York Herald* in August. There were already so many outrageous claims about California floating about. Only when President Polk made a brief comment about the gold strike in his annual message to Congress in December 1848 did easterners realize the Golden West was more than a metaphor. "The accounts of the abundance of gold in that territory," Polk related, "are of such an extraordinary character as would scarcely command belief were they not corroborated by the authentic reports of officers in the public service." The arrival two days later of a tea caddy sent by the California territorial governor to the president convinced the remaining skeptics. More than 230 ounces of pure gold crammed the caddy.[28]

The gold rush lured several hundred thousand fortune hunters to California, with eighty thousand coming during the first full year (1849) alone. The future suddenly seemed truly golden. The tale of a man who discovered an 839-pound gold nugget and who was so afraid to leave his find that he offered $27,000 to a colleague to fetch him a plate of pork and beans sounded perfectly plausible. The West was the culmination of the American dream and the prophecy of greatness, and the gold rush was proof.

Western fever, which had never really broken, now reached an unprecedented pitch. Entrepreneurs, anxious to transport gold rushers to the fields quickly, concocted imaginative if unworkable vehicles. Rufus Porter, the founder of *Scientific American* magazine, devised a thousand-foot-long propeller-driven balloon airship powered by two steam engines to whisk eastern passengers on a swift three-day journey to San Francisco for a mere fifty dollars, "wines included." Porter never built his airship. Most forty-niners trekked west by covered wagon, though an increasing proportion came by the sea route over Panama. Since most gold rushers were single men with relatively few possessions, the sea route, despite delays and greater exposure to disease, was nearly as popular as the wagon route.

Though briefly emptied by the initial gold mania, San Francisco became an instant city, the Manhattan of the West. Prior to the gold rush, emigration had been steady enough for city fathers to call upon Jasper O'Farrell, a civil engineer, to lay out a town as quickly as possible, which he did, merely imposing the grid and some of the street names of Philadelphia (such as Market Street) on the California boom town. By fastening a grid on a very hilly site, O'Farrell unwittingly created breathtaking vistas and breathless climbs for pedestrians and horses alike and forever confined the business district to the base of the hills around Market Street.

The second test was much less redolent of manifest destiny. The year 1849 was also the time of cholera. One child among the many who succumbed during that summer of death would leave a lasting legacy. His name was Charley. He was a healthy baby, and therein lay the tragedy. The scourge of cholera swept through Cincinnati, Charley's home. The city's inattention to sanitation, even by the standards of the time, allowed the disease to flourish. The booming Ohio River port city thought more of commerce than cleanliness. In this, Cincinnatians resembled their colleagues in other western cities, where people

Daguerreotype of San Francisco Harbor, 1850 or 1851.
It was just a small village only a few years earlier; the Gold Rush created a boomtown,
the first great western city. (Courtesy of the Library of Congress)

moved in and out at dizzying rates and urban services were lax, if they existed
at all. Dirty water was a price of progress.[29]

But what a price. The cholera epidemic that summer carried off more than
8 percent of Cincinnati's population, and the city ran out of coffins. The disease
showed no respect for class or civic eminence. Cholera dispatched the weak
quickly, sometimes within hours of onset. The particular cruelty of the disease
was its slow, painful progress in strong and healthy bodies—the persistent diarrhea and vomiting, the excruciating pain of leg and stomach cramps, and then
the gradual failure of liver and kidneys. Young Charley suffered immensely.
His tiny body convulsed in pain; his cries pierced the hearts of his parents, who
were helpless to relieve his distress. The peace that often accompanies the last
breaths of life eluded Charley, who lingered for two weeks.

Harriet Beecher Stowe bore six other children, but Charley was special to
her. She had gone through bouts of uncertainty and loneliness, yet Charley,
baby though he was, provided solace for her troubled soul. She poured out

her grief in a letter to her husband, Calvin. "Never was he anything to me but a comfort. He has been my pride and joy. Many a heartache has he cured for me. Many an anxious night have I held him to my bosom and felt the sorrow and loneliness pass out of me with the touch of his little warm hands. Yet I have just seen him in his death agony, looked on his imploring face when I could not help nor soothe nor do one thing, not one, to mitigate his cruel suffering, do nothing but pray in my anguish that he might die soon."[30]

In the past, Harriet had worked through sorrows by writing. But her grief for Charley was so great that another short story or letter would hardly mend her broken heart. What could, what should she write that would restore her faith in God's ultimate goodness?

The sweep of evangelical religion and evangelical democracy had brought Americans to the shining sea. Yet their hold on both the continent and their system of government was tenuous. One million Irish Catholics were flooding into America. Slaveholders clamored for access to the new territorial bounty. Universal white male suffrage was becoming the norm rather than the exception. Evangelicals pursued politics as faithfully as eternal salvation and with equal righteousness. The nation had grown far beyond the borders of the original thirteen states. Would a continental America survive? Would the Revolutionary legacy remain secure?

Most second-generation Americans would have answered these questions affirmatively in 1849. They had brushed aside the Mexicans and stared down the British. They had gained a golden West. Americans were confident, yet wary. Their Revolutionary experiment was incomplete and constantly tested. Their government was a unique outpost in a hostile world. Historian George Bancroft had written of a God-blessed nation. The past and the future would be one. But history is not a compass. A gold rush and a mother's grief would converge in unforeseen ways. Americans would soon discover that they would need to plot a course through some very complex terrain over the next decade. They would lose their way. Only a bloody war would enable them to carve out a new path to a new nation. A Chosen Nation would confront its Revolutionary legacy and determine whether it would fulfill or destroy that sacred trust.

CHAPTER 3

REVOLUTIONS

THE QUICK VICTORY IN THE MEXICAN WAR confirmed Americans' view that they were unique in the world; that despite lurking dangers they had escaped history and were embarked on an inexorable progression to grace. Along the way, they would inspire other peoples by their example of Christian democracy. When Europe exploded in a series of popular uprisings beginning in February 1848, Americans took heart. Here was a sign of the universality of America's experiment, confirmation that the Revolutionary legacy remained secure.[1]

Americans rejoiced at the wonderful news from Paris. The French had forced Louis Philippe from the throne and had declared the Second Republic. Within a month, revolts against authoritarian regimes erupted all over the Continent. On March 3, the great Hungarian patriot Lajos Kossuth stood outside the Diet in Budapest and called for a representative government; two weeks later, revolution engulfed Vienna and Berlin, then the Papal States, including Milan and Venice. By spring, the revolutionary tide had swept the Hapsburg emperor from his throne and Pope Pius IX from the Vatican. The flames of representative government and nationalism had ignited all of Europe.

The uprisings caught the ruling governments off guard, and initially they appeared to accede to the citizens' demands for representative assemblies. Friedrich Wilhelm IV of Prussia promised a liberal constitution and allowed the election of a Prussian legislature, while an all-German parliament convened in Frankfurt. With the tacit support of the Prussian monarch, republican newspapers appeared throughout the German states.

The all-German parliament had such strong representation from the professoriate that locals called it the *Gelehrtenparlament* (parliament of scholars). As expected with such a composition, the body deliberated interminably and inconclusively from May to October 1848, giving the Prussian monarchy an opportunity to regain its balance and, ultimately, its power. Divisions between the moderate and more radical elements of the movement weakened the insurgency. By November 1848, Friedrich Wilhelm IV and his wealthy Prussian supporters, including future chancellor Otto von Bismarck, had sufficient military support to dissolve the Prussian legislature, thus ending the March Revolution.

By then, the forces of reaction had snuffed out the fires of freedom across Europe. In July 1848, Austrian troops overwhelmed Milan and the Italian Piedmont, restoring the pope to the Vatican and sending the Italian patriot Giuseppe Garibaldi into exile on Staten Island, New York, where he eked out a living as a candlemaker. The revolution in Paris had already collapsed. The coalition of workers and middle-class citizens that had toppled the monarchy split apart violently as the new bourgeois government, supported by the army, clashed with workers in the streets of Paris in June. The bloody "June Days" left more than fifteen hundred people killed in fighting, three thousand executed, and twelve thousand arrested. The disorder and violence sickened a good deal of France, and another Napoleon, Louis in this case, rode into Paris to rescue the country for the reactionaries.

Initially, the European revolutions galvanized American public opinion. Occurring at the end of America's successful war against an authoritarian Catholic regime, democratic movements across Europe seemed to vindicate the American experiment as an exportable model for all mankind. At a time when the slavery debate and persistent sectarian strife threatened that experiment, the European uprisings offered the hope that the good of self-government would overcome the evil of despotism and bigotry. It was a perspective on the future less grounded in history than in the faith that America had escaped history.

News that French revolutionaries had declared the Second Republic produced a rare consensus in a divided Congress, which voted overwhelmingly to "congratulate" the French people on their new government. A few weeks later, President Polk officially recognized the new French republic. Walt Whitman expressed the excitement coursing through the streets of New York: "One's blood races and grows hot within him the more he learns or thinks of this news from the continent of Europe!" The revolutions accomplished what the American political process could not: uniting both North and South in the common sentiment that the uprisings validated America's experiment. The *Richmond Enquirer* proclaimed, "American principles are triumphant! What a sublime spectacle does Europe present to the American patriot!" The *New York Tribune* noted portentously that the outbreak of the French uprising began on George Washington's birthday, and, carrying the democratic numerology further, the *Baptist Banner* of Louisville rejoiced that Italian nationalists had driven out Pope Pius IX on the anniversary of American independence. When Kossuth toured the United States to raise money and weapons for his cause, admirers created a huge traffic jam in Manhattan impounding his carriage for more than two hours and literally tearing the clothes off his back, so eager were they to see and touch the embodiment of American democratic principles in Europe.[2]

As the revolutionaries' success waned and violence overtook reform, public opinion in the United States shifted. The class divisions reflected in the differing revolutionary programs between moderates (mostly middle-class) and socialists (mostly working-class) concerned Americans who were at the beginning of a significant urban and industrial revolution of their own. Many Americans continued to believe that the interests of capital and labor were identical, that with education and hard work, workers could move up the social ladder. The European revolutions exposed both the inherent antagonism between capital and labor and the violent potential of that animosity. The failure of the revolutions also highlighted for many Americans the precious, precarious, and unique nature of their own democratic experiment.

By December 1848, the failure of the revolutionary movements, especially in France and the German states, became evident. President Polk, in his annual message to Congress, ruminated about the differences between America and Europe: "While the people of other countries struggle to establish free institutions under which man may govern himself, we are in actual enjoyment of them—a rich inheritance from our fathers."[3]

In accounting for the disappointing European revolutions, some Americans argued that the despotic history of the continent inhibited the growth of democratic institutions. The long-standing reigns of authoritarian church and state regimes provoked radical responses splitting the liberal opposition and undermining the initial good intentions of the revolutions. As historian George Bancroft explained in a volume of his *History of the United States* published in 1852, unlike in Europe, "In America, the influences of the time were molded by the creative force of reason, sentiment and nature. Its political edifice rose in lovely proportions, as if to melodies of the lyre.... The American Revolution ... was most radical in its character, yet achieved with such benign tranquility, that even conservatism hesitated to censure."[4]

Americans came to understand that theirs was a rare and lonely cause, that the flame of freedom could not burn in the stone-cold traditions of despotic Europe. The Mexican War had demonstrated the benefits of a proselytizing democracy. But one example was not enough. In the era of manifest destiny a more active role in spreading democratic institutions, not only over a continent but also around the world, would fulfill God's plan for America. The collapse of the popular movements in Europe and the ensuing reactionary resurgence also underscored the fragility of democratic institutions, how easily a national consensus could shatter from within. The unfortunate turn in Europe remained fresh in the minds of Americans as they began to grapple with a new crisis of their own.

California, its population swelled by gold rushers, clamored for statehood. The admission of California to the Union would push the number of free states to sixteen, while the slave state total remained at fifteen. Two decades earlier, southerners had slipped into the minority in the House of Representatives. They were about to lose the Senate. With two national parties interested in maintaining party discipline, perhaps political craftsmanship could overcome sectional tension. But Congress could not even organize itself to elect a Speaker, select committee chairs, and ratify basic rules, such was the contention in the chamber. Henry Clay stepped forward to mend the rent national unity. He had done so a generation earlier during the Missouri crisis, and he had dedicated his political life to promoting the Union above sectionalism.

It was a different country Clay sought to bring together as debate opened on the California petition in January 1850. A democratic revolution had occurred in the intervening thirty years. As property qualifications for the franchise dropped away, as new immigrants entered the political process, as political campaigns took on aspects of revivals, military reviews, and carnival hi-jinks, the electoral process exploded. A proliferation of print media including the penny press, magazines, and party newspapers jostled for readers, adding to the cacophony.

These changes were not contemplated by the Founding Fathers, who operated in a more exclusive and sedate environment. The California debate would bring together for the last time the great political lights of an earlier generation, Clay himself, Daniel Webster, the Whig senator from Massachusetts, and the ever-brilliant Calhoun. Within two years, they would all be dead, and the new men put into power by the new electorate would prove inadequate to saving the country.

For southerners, the issue of California statehood would portend their future in a nation increasingly obsessed with economic development and opening new territories to migration and enterprise. As a soon-to-be permanent minority in Congress, they wondered about appropriations, appointments, the use of the mails, and, above all, the future of their heavy investment in land and slaves.

Southerners wanted to participate in the national mission equally. It was irrelevant that slavery would not flourish in the arid Southwest, or that the laborers and farmers streaming westward from the East and Midwest would overwhelm any migration by slaveholders. Southerners were just as good as any other Americans, and they wanted to compete on an equal basis with everyone else. They were realistic enough to understand the long odds of extending slavery to some areas of the Mexican Cession. But it was the chance they were after, not the guarantee of success, at least not yet. Throughout the increasingly acrimonious debates of the 1850s, this was at the core of the South's concerns: to be treated equally in a confederation of equals.

Henry Clay offered a compromise bundling together a number of related issues hoping to banish slavery once and for all as a political issue. He proposed that Congress ratify the decision of California citizens to enter the Union as a free state as well as any future decisions made by residents of the other portions of the Mexican Cession, the Utah and New Mexico territories. Applying the popular sovereignty doctrine at the point of statehood, Clay believed, had the virtue of keeping the federal government out of the territories and leaving important constitutional decisions to the residents on the ground.[5]

In all likelihood, Clay's proposal would also keep slavery out of the Mexican Cession and deepen the South's minority status in the federal government. To secure the support of southern lawmakers on the territorial issue, Clay offered to strengthen the constitutional provision that stated that a person "held to Service or Labor in one state . . . escaping into another . . . shall be delivered upon Claim of the party to whom such Service or Labor may be due" (Article IV, Section 2) with a strong fugitive slave law.

Rounding out his compromise package, Clay would resolve a bitter border dispute between the state of Texas and New Mexico Territory to the latter's benefit. As compensation, the federal government would assume Texas's public debt. Clay next dealt with an issue that troubled many members of Congress, the presence of the slave trade in the District of Columbia. He proposed ending the slave trade outright, but also reaffirmed the right of slavery to exist as an institution in the District of Columbia unless the residents desired otherwise.

Clay's package had the benefit of addressing at one go several difficult issues related to the slavery question, each one of which could paralyze Congress. It also had the virtue of ignoring the Wilmot Proviso, which had become anathema to the South and destructive of party discipline. At the same time, the proposal probably guaranteed three additional free-soil states in California, New Mexico, and Utah. Clay's compromise ensured Wilmot's intentions without involving Congress in the territorial question.

The compromise faced an uphill battle. President Taylor indicated that he expected Congress to admit California and New Mexico as free states. Period. He would not sign a fugitive slave bill, nor would he entertain any monetary or border claims from Texas. If Texas resisted New Mexico's interpretation of where the appropriate border lay, he vowed, he would send in troops and lead them himself if necessary to force the Lone Star State's compliance. This was not the way southerners expected a slaveholding president to act.

Meanwhile, a great debate unfolded in the Senate. Since the late 1820s, Calhoun had attempted and failed to rally southern forces into a regional co-alition that would rise above party. Fearing the consequences of the South's decreasing presence in Congress, and pessimistic about mankind's ability to transcend self-interest for the good of the whole, Calhoun devised a gover-nance plan to address the problem of protecting minority rights in a system where the majority prevailed. He called it a "concurrent majority," where the majority of every important group (or section of the country) would need to pass legislation before it became law. Each group would, in effect, have a veto. In practice, the system might lead to gridlock. But if, as Calhoun believed, the role of government was to protect against not only outside threats but also enemies within, a mechanism to blunt the power of the majority seemed well worth an experiment.

The great interest Calhoun sought to protect from an aggressive majority was, of course, slavery. The battle over the extension of slavery into the ter-ritories had begun during the Missouri debates thirty years earlier. In Cal-houn's political lifetime, the institution had come under siege not only from fellow lawmakers but also from the press and the pulpit. The difficulty of or-ganizing a Congress where neither Whigs nor Democrats comprised a ma-jority of lawmakers, and Free Soilers held the balance, brought the enemy closer to power. He understood that slavery stood at the heart of southern society, and that without a mechanism to protect it for all time, the Union's days were numbered. "I fix its probable [breakup] within twelve years or three presidential terms. . . . The probability is it will explode in a presiden-tial election."[6]

On March 4, 1850, an ailing Calhoun entered the Senate chamber, helped to his chair by a colleague. He slumped down in his seat, a deathly pallor over his face, his hair hanging like wild strings from a head struggling to remain aloft. Too weak to deliver his speech, he passed it on to his South Carolina colleague, Andrew P. Butler, who, due to poor eyesight, handed it to Virginia's James M. Mason, who read Calhoun's words to a hushed chamber and packed gallery. Calhoun dismissed California statehood and the retrieval of runaway slaves as peripheral to the main issue of the North's permanent majority and its threat to the South from an inevitable abuse of power. He denied that he advocated disunion; in fact, quite the opposite. He was offering a way to save the Union from destruction.[7]

Not all southerners shared Calhoun's perspective on their future in the Union. They recoiled from the threats of secession and disunion attributed to Calhoun and his allies. The *New Orleans Bee* declared that the evils of the proviso were "a thousandfold more endurable" than the "unnumbered" woes of disunion. Others simply dismissed Calhoun as someone who had outlived his time. North Carolina's Whig senator George E. Badger thought that Calhoun "on anything concerning *niggers* [was] absolutely deranged." Badger for one would not even contemplate leaving the Union for the "privilege of carrying slaves to California or keeping up private jails for slave dealers" in the District of Columbia. The Union still represented an indelible bond of common destiny for many southerners.[8]

Daniel Webster took the Senate stage next. In declining health, but still a vigorous orator, the Whig senator from Massachusetts had stood down disunionists before. There was scarcely a person in the crammed galleries of the Senate chamber who did not recall his memorable speech during the Nullification Crisis of 1830: "When my eyes shall be turned to behold, for the last time, the sun in heaven, may I not see him shining on the broken and dishonored fragments of a once glorious Union. . . . Let their last feeble and lingering glance, rather, behold the gorgeous ensign of the republic, now known and honored throughout the earth, still full high advanced. . . . Liberty *and* Union, now and forever, one and inseparable!"[9]

This article of faith that the Union and liberty could not exist apart from each other propelled Daniel Webster to support Henry Clay's compromise, fugitive slave bill included. While he acknowledged that many of his constituents viewed human bondage as a sin, he also recognized that many in the South saw slavery as a benevolent institution sanctioned by the Bible. In any case, there was no good way southerners could "relieve themselves from this relation" without descending into economic ruin and social chaos, a situation that would eventually threaten all Americans. The best solution, he argued, lay in Clay's compromise: allow the people of the territory to solve the issue of slavery for themselves. Besides, it was unlikely that the new territories, by virtue of geography, climate, and soil, could support slavery.

Recognizing that the issue of slavery expansion had taken on a moral dimension, especially in New England, Webster warned against mixing "religious sentiments" with public policy, the result of which would be "a

*"Union." The Great Triumvirate together for the last time during
the debates over what became the Compromise of 1850: Henry Clay
(seated on the near left), John C. Calhoun, and Daniel Webster each with a hand on the
Constitution and surrounded by their colleagues. The Senate would dearly
miss their brilliance and civility.
(Courtesy of the Library of Congress)*

great degree of excitement" that would preclude an amicable settlement of differences. If politics was the art of compromise, religion, by its nature, allowed no ambiguity. Webster had believed in 1830 that defiance to southern extremism would save the Union; twenty years later, he felt that concessions to the South would produce the same result.[10]

New England was unforgiving. Daniel Webster, the conscience of a nation, had sold out to the Slave Power. His position broke apart the Whig Party in Massachusetts and led to his name becoming synonymous with "traitor" among the growing anti-slavery sentiment of New England. "Monster," "fallen angel," and "personification of all that is vile" were among the epithets that could be printed. An enraged and clearly overreaching William Lloyd Garrison accused the senator of maintaining a harem of "big black wenches as ugly and vulgar as Webster himself." The storm overwhelmed him, and he died two years later. John Greenleaf Whittier poured the bitterness of his section into the poem "Ichabod," Hebrew for "inglorious":

Of all we loved and honored, naught
  Save power remains—
A fallen angel's pride of thought,
  Still strong in chains.

All else is gone, from those great eyes
  The soul has fled;
When faith is lost, when honor dies,
  The man is dead![11]

It fell to William H. Seward, a fellow Whig from New York, to offer the rebuttal to Webster. Like Calhoun, Seward viewed Clay's compromise proposals as a symptom of a much larger problem. But unlike Webster, he did not think religious faith was irrelevant to the discussion. A Chosen Nation could not take its mission lightly nor adjudicate major questions without an abiding faith in God. Slavery was clearly a sin, and to compromise with sin was a greater evil. Seward was not a theocrat, but, like many Americans, he held a deep belief in God's particular benevolence to America. Whether necessity or the Constitution sanctioned slavery was quite beside the point. As Seward argued, "There is a higher law than the Constitution, which regulates our authority over this domain, and devotes it to the same noble purposes."[12]

Seward's "higher law" doctrine would be familiar to nineteenth-century American evangelicals who believed Peter's order "to obey God rather than men" (Acts 5:29). Americans cherished the Constitution, but it did not serve as the ultimate standard for personal action. Although God may have blessed the American government, "does it therefore follow that Congress may amend the ten commandments, or reverse the principles of Christ's Sermon on the Mount . . . ? Man could not, by any law, make right what God and his own conscience declared wrong."[13]

The Senate could not come to an agreement on what God or the Constitution said about Clay's proposals. Even if the Senate agreed on a bill, President Taylor was clearly not in a compromising mood and, despite his deep southern connections, seemed to move closer to Senator Seward's position with each passing day. As the Senate debate droned on, the president celebrated July 4, 1850, a very hot day, with the usual reception at the White House. He cooled off with copious amounts of cherries and milk. Five days later he was dead from gastroenteritis.

Taylor's death failed to break the Senate deadlock, and Henry Clay took the floor for the last time on July 22 to inspire his colleagues to support his compromise and save a nation he believed in great danger from splitting apart. The debate had generated so much acrimony and so many threats of disunion, especially from the southern members, that Clay believed only his compromise could put things rights again. Clay hoped that his proposal would perform a national "lustration"—an archaic term for a ceremony purifying people and places. The cleansing ritual would enable Americans to divest themselves "of all selfish, sinister, and sordid impurities, and think alone of our God, our country, our consciences, and our glorious Union; that Union without which we shall be torn into hostile fragments." Americans would be born again into patriots instead of self-interested individuals. Without the compromise the world's judgment on America would be harsh, Clay predicted. The United States would no longer be a beacon of hope to a world enveloped in the darkness of despotism. The failed revolutions of Europe would stand as a permanent monument to the futility of self-government, not just a temporary setback. "What will be the judgment of . . . that portion of mankind who are looking upon the progress of this scheme of self-government as being that which holds out the highest hopes and expectations of ameliorating the condition of mankind?" Clay's plea went unanswered. Despairing, he departed for home. Within eighteen months he was dead.[14]

Clay's compromise would experience a resurrection in another guise. New Yorker Millard Fillmore, who as vice president succeeded Taylor, signaled he was amenable to compromise. Along with Stephen A. Douglas, the Democratic senator from Illinois, Fillmore believed that they could construct a bipartisan coalition from the men of the Border South and the Old Northwest to provide a core group to pass each of Clay's proposals separately, first pairing with southern lawmakers on one part of the compromise, then with northerners on others. Such a strategy had forged the Missouri Compromise thirty years earlier. With Calhoun dead, Clay ailing at his home in Newport, Kentucky, and Webster now a member of President Fillmore's cabinet, the Senate passed the series of measures collectively known as the Compromise of 1850. The border men had carried the day.

Most Americans accepted the compromise as a whole, even if they did not like one or more of its constituent parts. The Union, they believed, and what it stood for—peace, prosperity, liberty, and the future of mankind—remained more important than sectional grievances. Many hoped with Stephen A. Douglas that the compromise represented the "final settlement" of the slavery issue. "Let us cease agitating," Douglas implored, "stop the debate, and drop the subject." His admonition was at once an order and a hope.[15]

George Templeton Strong, a New York attorney and devoted Whig, summarized the prevailing view on the compromise: "Extreme people on both sides must be disgusted with the result, but the great majority satisfied and relieved." Strong rejoiced to see "South Carolina spanked." As for the abolitionists, "They deserve to be scourged and pilloried for sedition or hanged for treason." Strong concluded his diary entry with an interesting confession, a point of view shared by many residents of the North: "My creed on [the slave] question is: That slave-holding is no sin. . . . That the slaves of the Southern States are happier and better off than the niggers of the North, . . . That the reasoning, the tone of feeling, the first principles, the practices, and the designs of Northern Abolitionists are very particularly false, foolish, wicked and unchristian." The key issue for most Americans was the preservation of the Union, not slavery.[16]

Northerners, even evangelicals, also drew back from Seward's "higher law" doctrine. If each individual could determine what laws to obey based on a particular interpretation of Scripture, then anarchy would ensue. "Higher lawism" tilted the balance too far toward individual discretion. The appeal to God's law also violated the separation of church and state. As Charles Hodge, a Philadelphia evangelical minister, noted, "Those who resist the magistrate, resist the ordinance of God, and . . . shall receive unto themselves damnation." Southern evangelicals held this view as a matter of course, that evangelical abolitionists violated the intent of the Founding Fathers to separate church and state, thereby threatening not only religious freedom but government as well.[17]

The Compromise of 1850 stifled disunionists in the South, except in South Carolina. More typical of southern sentiment was the "Georgia Platform" of December 1850. The platform avowed that the citizens of Georgia cherished their "beloved Union" and accepted the compromise in total as an effort to secure the national compact. But that acceptance, Georgians warned, required a reciprocal acknowledgment among northerners. Otherwise, Georgians would consider their options "even to the disruption of every tie binding Georgia to the Union." In the only state that held a referendum on the compromise, Georgians supported the pact overwhelmingly by nearly a two-to-one margin. Henry Clay, exhausted from his months-long ordeal in the Senate, rejoiced that the Georgia vote had "crushed the spirit of discord, disunion and Civil War." Elsewhere in the South, a special convention in Mississippi resoundingly endorsed the compromise, and pro-compromise candidates for office won handily in Alabama state elections.[18]

The Bible tells of Isaac and Ishmael, the one the offspring of Abraham and Sarah, the other of Abraham and a bondswoman. God looked upon Isaac as the future patriarch of His Chosen Nation. In order to secure that legacy, He banished Ishmael and his mother. For most Americans, the slave was an unworthy cause for which to risk the Union. To banish the slave from the political discourse, just as to banish the Indian and the Mexican from the land, was to preserve the Union. As a writer in the *Southern Literary Messenger* reasoned in January 1851, "Our nation is to enter Canaan as certainly as the Hebrew once did. . . . And shall any inferior nation stop us in our heaven-marked course? . . . Did the red men arrest us? . . . And who removed them from before our fathers, but the God who planted our fathers here?—the same God that has made us increase by the same manifest destiny by which he has made them wane and fade away. And shall the black man stop us? If one must yield, are we not right in saying—the son of the bondwoman shall not be heir with the son of the free? Does not God by his providence say so too?" The writer concluded, "*The dissolution of our Union, for the sake of a handful of bondmen,*" would be a "wicked disregard of God's word."[19]

As it turned out, the slavery debate did not dissolve and the Union did. It would take a civil war to banish the slave and the slaveholder, and yet another war to banish the "red men." Other Americans could not agree that a loving God would exorcise one of His children, even a black slave. It was not the slave, they believed, but slavery that blocked the road to Canaan. They argued that a Union with slavery was a thing not worth saving. The principles of the nation's founding and the destiny that God had designed for America stood in reproach to a Union without principle. The issue of slavery and the integrity of the Union could not be separated.

The problem was more than philosophical for Frederick Douglass. A former slave who had stolen his freedom a decade earlier, he had served the abolitionist cause as an effective orator and writer. After the compromise he feared for himself, his family, and his free black friends in the North who suddenly found themselves vulnerable to slave catchers. Three weeks after President Millard Fillmore signed the Fugitive Slave Law portion of the Compromise of 1850, an angry interracial gathering of five thousand in Boston's Faneuil Hall heard Douglass invoke the Revolutionary legacy and preach defiance of the law. "We one and all,—without the slightest hope of making successful resistance,—are resolved rather to die than to go back. If you are . . . prepared to see the streets of Boston flowing with innocent blood, . . . just give in . . . to the fugitive slave bill—you, who live on the street where the blood first spouted in defense of freedom."[20]

African Americans formed "leagues of freedom" to protect themselves and organize rescue from slave catchers if necessary. Some abandoned America altogether. More than three hundred African Americans from Pittsburgh resolved to migrate north of the border. Within ninety days of the law taking effect, more than three thousand free blacks left the northern states for Canada.

With the Fugitive Slave Law, the northern and southern extremes switched sides: the former now strong defenders of states' rights, particularly the right of a state to nullify federal laws, and the latter insisting on federal intervention. The reversed roles indicated that the debate centered on slavery, not on differing interpretations of the Constitution.

Several northern states—Massachusetts, Vermont, Ohio, Connecticut, Pennsylvania, and Rhode Island—had enacted personal liberty laws in the 1840s barring state officials from aiding in the arrest and detention of fugitive slaves. The Fugitive Slave Law voided these statutes, but lawmakers in several northern states called for either outright nullification or tacit nonenforcement of the federal law. Northerners, even those not particularly inclined toward anti-slavery politics, recoiled from the provision requiring them to actively participate in the capture, prosecution, and return of escaped slaves. Their involvement with slavery had heretofore been indirect: the clothes they wore, the profits they accumulated from the sale and manufacture of cotton, and the banks, railroads, and shipping companies that grew wealthy from the proceeds of human bondage and then shared those receipts with tens of thousands of workers and shareholders.

Few northerners thought about these connections. The Fugitive Slave Law, however, suddenly threw them into direct contact with one of the most unsavory aspects of the institution. It commanded citizens "to aid and assist in the prompt and efficient execution of this law, whenever their services may be required." Anyone caught providing food and shelter to an escaped slave, assuming northern whites could discern who was a runaway, would be subject to a fine of one thousand dollars and six months in prison. The law also suspended habeas corpus and the right to trial by jury for captured blacks. Judges received a hundred dollars for every slave returned to his or her owner, providing a monetary incentive for jurists to rule in favor of the slave catchers.

Congress's law had nationalized slavery. No black person was safe on American soil. The old division of free state/slave state had vanished, and with it Douglass's faith in the power of American ideals. Invited to give the Fourth of July address at a meeting of the Rochester (New York) Ladies' Anti-Slavery Society, Douglass declined. Instead, he gave his speech on July fifth because "I am not included within the pale of this glorious anniversary! The rich inheritance of justice, liberty, prosperity, and independence, bequeathed by your fathers, is shared by you, not by me. . . . This Fourth [of] July is yours, not mine."[21]

How could Americans rectify this hypocrisy? Douglass despaired of conventional means—persuasion and politics. "It is not light that is needed, but fire; it is not the gentle shower, but thunder. We need the storm, the whirlwind, and the earthquake." He put the situation in personal terms: "Cast one glance, if you please, upon that young mother, whose shoulders are bare to the scorching sun, her briny tears falling on the brow of the babe in her arms. See, too, that girl of thirteen, weeping, yes! weeping, as she thinks of the mother from whom she has been torn!"

These scenes were no longer part of only a southern tableau. "By an act of the American Congress . . . slavery has been nationalized in its most horrible and revolting form. By that act, Mason & Dixon's line has been obliterated; . . . and the power to hold, hunt, and sell men, women, and children as slaves remains no longer a mere state institution, but is now an institution of the whole United States."

The law exposed for Douglass the vast abyss between the nation's Christian and democratic ideals and the reality for African Americans. "You profess to believe 'that, of one blood, God made all nations of men to dwell on the face of all the earth,' and hath commanded all men, everywhere to love one another; yet you notoriously hate . . . all men whose skins are not colored like your own. You declare, before the world . . . that you 'hold these truths to be self evident, that all men are created equal; and are endowed by their Creator with certain inalienable rights; and that, among these are, life, liberty, and the pursuit of happiness'; and yet, you hold securely, in a bondage which, according to your own Thomas Jefferson, 'is worse than that which your fathers rose in rebellion to oppose,' a seventh part of the inhabitants of your country."

The Fugitive Slave Law radicalized Walt Whitman as well. He expressed his anger in "Blood-Money," a poem that foreshadowed his groundbreaking compilation *Leaves of Grass*. In "Blood-Money" Whitman used the common evangelical technique of applying biblical parables to contemporary events, echoing in literary form William H. Seward's "higher law" speech:

> *Of olden time, when it came to pass*
> *That the beautiful god, Jesus, should finish his work on*
>   *earth,*
> *Then went Judas, and sold the divine youth,*
> *And took pay for his body. . . .*
>
> *The cycles, with their long shadows, have stalk'd*
>   *silently forward*
> *Since those ancient days—many a pouch enwrapping*
>   *meanwhile*
> *Its fee, like that paid for the son of Mary.*

And still goes one, saying,
"What will ye give me, and I will deliver this man
unto you?"
And they make the covenant, and pay the pieces of
silver.[22]

It would fall to Harriet Beecher Stowe, though she could not know it yet, deep in her grief over Charley, to take the ideals expressed in the oratory of Douglass and the poetry of Whitman, take their admonishments to people of faith, take their shame over the rank hypocrisy of their fellow Americans, and take their belief that God placed America on this earth to do great things, and transform these expressions into a language both universal and personal.

Harriet took her grief and her family to Brunswick, Maine. Her husband, Calvin, had received a teaching position at Bowdoin College. Although packing up and leaving Charley was not easy, Harriet looked forward to the more healthful environment of New England, her home.[23]

Harriet set up a modest household for her family in Brunswick. She was well aware of her obligation to support her husband, take care of the children's moral upbringing, and create a comfortable home for her family. She was also aware of the growing feminist movement in the North, especially in the cities, where middle-class women enjoyed an array of consumer options, employment, and education. Some of those women were clamoring for the vote, wider educational opportunities, and property and marriage benefits on the same ground as men. Neither Harriet nor her sister Catharine, who was already making a name for herself as a promoter of women's education, was a feminist in the nineteenth-century sense of that word. They believed in separate though complementary roles for men and women and asserted that a woman's stewardship of her family's spiritual life exceeded any role men possessed in the larger society. The family and the home, woman's domain, were the foundations of that society. They did not support woman's suffrage, and they believed that a woman's place at home, what Harriet called the "site of perfect love on earth," afforded her significant power in shaping the future generation, in bringing family members to Christ, and in using that moral capital to support an array of causes from prison reform to temperance to the abolition of slavery. From Harriet's perspective, that was fulfillment enough.[24]

Harriet believed that even the most mundane household chores were worthy of a woman's attention. The domestic sphere, rather than being a confinement for women, held liberating possibilities: "even the small, frittering cares of women's life—the attention to buttons, trimmings, thread and sewing-silk—may be an expression of their patriotism and their religion." She complained about modern middle-class city women who hired "operators [to] stretch and exercise their inactive muscles," and extolled the women of bygone days who had "knowledge of all sorts of medicines, gargles, and alleviates . . . [and] perfect familiarity with every canon and law of good nursing. . . . To be really great in little things, to be truly noble and heroic in the insipid details of everyday life, is a virtue so rare as to be worthy of canonization."[25]

Harriet did not attend the historic meeting of women activists at Seneca Falls, New York, in July 1848; nor did she comment on its outcome. Elizabeth Cady Stanton, a leading organizer of the event, believed, contrary to Harriet and Catharine, that a woman's place in the home reflected her subordinate position in society and confined her to domestic duties that served "to destroy her confidence in her own powers, to lessen her self-respect, and to make her willing to lead a dependent and abject life." Stanton, like Frederick Douglass, appealed to the nation's origins, especially to the Declaration of Independence, which became the template for her "Declaration of Sentiments" presented at the Seneca Falls meeting. Frederick Douglass was one of the few males in attendance, and Stanton drew a direct parallel between women's dependence and that of the slave, a position neither Harriet nor her sister Catharine supported.[26]

Anti-slavery remained Harriet's great interest. By 1850, she had not yet embraced politics as a means to attack the institution. She believed in the power of moral persuasion, of using evangelical Christianity to open minds and touch hearts. She believed in her literary gifts. She wanted to write again, to salve her grief and, not incidentally, to add to Calvin's meager professorial income. Writing was one of the few acceptable ways a married woman with children could earn extra money for the household.

Harriet was not a stranger to writing. She shared her father's passion for expository literature, though she wrote much more politely. In Cincinnati, her first publication was a geography textbook. A very practical endeavor for a nation in motion hither and yon; even more practical as her sister Catharine, following their father's admonition to train up young Protestants, had opened a school. The textbook would be just the thing to familiarize recently arrived children—and everyone in those days was a newcomer to Cincinnati—with the West.

The research for the book provided an education for Harriet as well. Locating Cincinnati at the center of things was not only a device to engage her sister's pupils, but it also seemed appropriate in other ways. Her father taught that curiosity was a good thing; that inquiry and freedom complemented each other. Cincinnati stood astride a great river that separated freedom from slavery, and, as a New England girl, she knew little of the latter. So she crossed the river and visited a plantation in Kentucky. To her evolving thought, this institution seemed a more immanent threat than the pope.

When Harriet returned to Cincinnati, she walked the streets with new eyes, as sometimes happens to returning travelers awakened to new experiences. Here, a bustling slave market existed beneath her very eyes. For a place north of the Ohio River, Cincinnati was deeply southern on slavery. In that, Cincinnati differed little from many other northern cities. In New York, on July 4, 1834, a mob attacked a church service celebrating the emancipation of slaves in that state. The following year, several northern and border cities experienced anti-abolitionist violence. To Harriet, these episodes threatened the coming Kingdom of Christ more than the machinations of the Roman Catholic Church. Here was an institution—human bondage—that also destroyed the family, stifled free expression, and contradicted the nation's self-evident truths of equality and human dignity.[27]

She turned her pen from geography to gently prodding her neighbors on the subject of slavery. She was no firebrand, merely a pious young woman employing moral suasion and satire to stress the importance of airing unpopular views in order to better engage man's God-given reason. What was at stake for Harriet was not merely free speech, freedom of the press, or even freedom itself, but the very future of mankind. If America was to be the Redeemer Nation, then it must purge itself of sin.

The parlor of mid-nineteenth-century homes functioned as a gathering place for family, friends, and ideas. It was in such a setting that Harriet first shared her anti-slavery essays during her years in Cincinnati. Family members and perhaps a few guests would exchange news and discuss literature and the day's events. One of the most common parlor activities was to read letters from extended family members. In a mobile nation, letters connected far-flung families and friends, providing news and mutual support. One evening, sitting with her family in the parlor of her Brunswick home, Harriet opened a letter from her sister-in-law Isabella Jones Beecher. The writer, like those in the room, deeply regretted the recent passage of the Fugitive Slave Law. She concluded with a challenge to Harriet: "How, Hattie, if I could use a pen as you can, I would write something that would make this whole nation feel what an accursed thing slavery is." As she read that sentence, Harriet rose from her chair, crumpled the letter in her fist, and declared, "I will write something. I will if I live."[28]

The result of her determination was *Uncle Tom's Cabin*, which first appeared in serial form in the *National Era*, a Washington, D.C.–based anti-slavery newspaper with a national readership, beginning in June 1851. Harriet had been conducting research for this book for most of her adult life. The anti-slavery tracts she read, the narratives of former slaves, her correspondence with Frederick Douglass, who served as a valued consultant to the project, her brother George, who lived in New Orleans, her contact with a runaway slave in Cincinnati, and her brief time in Kentucky across the river from her Cincinnati home provided the sinews for her novel. She would pour her research, her faith, her grief, and her love for her family into the work. It was a personal novel and as such appealed to people generally unmoved by the slave or by slavery. It was a book about family, God, and redemption—surefire topics to attract a broad readership in mid-nineteenth-century America.

The novel's story took shape as Harriet sat in church one February morning in 1851. She experienced a vision: a white man wielding a whip onto an old slave, beating him until the black man died. The vision became Tom. The book became a retelling of the crucifixion in family terms.

It was not an anti-southern book. Slavery existed due not only to southern forbearance but to northern complicity as well. "Northern men, northern mothers, northern Christians, have something more to do than denounce their brethren at the South; they have to look to the evil among themselves," Harriet wrote in the "Concluding Remarks" that accompanied the novel.[29] The slaveholders who appear in the book are decent Christians for the most part, with the exception of Simon Legree, who is from Vermont. Harriet wanted to show that slavery perverted Christianity, that even good Christian masters succumbed to the institution's inherent evil. If northerners felt that the Fugitive Slave Law enrolled them into the service of slaveholders, *Uncle Tom's Cabin* told them they were already serving southern masters. In the book, a New York City creditor sells a young woman to Simon Legree to settle an estate. Ophelia St. Clare, a Vermont woman of evangelical rectitude, visiting her relatives in New Orleans, recoils from the presence of a black child, Topsy. She confesses: "I've always had a prejudice against negroes, . . . and it's a fact, I never could bear to have that child touch me." Northern lawmakers supported the institution through the Fugitive Slave Law. Referring to a northern senator, Harriet wrote, "He had never thought that a fugitive might be a hapless mother, a defenseless child." He had not realized that black people held the same sensibilities as whites. That they were people just like himself.[30]

What set *Uncle Tom's Cabin* apart from other less sophisticated anti-slavery literature was its relentless criticism of the North and northerners, its insistence that slavery was a national sin, not solely a southern problem. Harriet put the matter bluntly in her conclusion: "The people of the free states have defended, encouraged, and participated; and are more guilty for it, before God, than the south, in that they have *not* the apology of education or custom. . . . Northern men, northern mothers, northern Christians . . . have to look to the evil among themselves."[31]

Harriet, like Catharine, believed strongly in the power of education to convert Americans. Throughout the novel, she intrudes into the narrative with entreaties, biblical passages, and admonitions. Often, she uses irony to make her
point. On the interstate slave trade: "Trading negroes from Africa, dear reader,
is so horrid! But trading them from Kentucky,—that's quite another thing!" Biblical quotes abound in the novel, passages that readers would have found familiar, though the context in which they appeared was startlingly different. When
Legree beats Tom senseless, Harriet wrote, "Fear not them that kill the body,
and, after that, have no more that they can do," from Matthew 10:28, adding,
"And yet, oh my country! These things are done under the shadow of thy laws!
O, Christ! Thy church sees them, almost in silence." At which point Tom dies.[32]

Tom is one of the book's great teachers, along with Eva, the child of a New
Orleans slaveholding family. The powerful—men, ministers, legislators, the
Yankee schoolmarm, Ophelia, the Kentucky slaveholder's son George Shelby,
and all white Americans—are the students. The more Tom endures, his faith
strengthens—"He that dwelleth in love dwelleth in God, and God in him"
(1 John 4:16). Faith gives Tom comfort and strength as he confronts Legree in
the chapter titled "The Victory." A voice called out to him: "He that overcometh
shall sit down with me on my throne, even as I also overcame, and am set
down with my Father on his throne" (Revelation 3:21). When a fellow slave is
incredulous that Tom could love Legree, Tom assures her, "When we can love
and pray over all and through all, the battle's past, and the victory's come,—
glory be to God!" There is no other adult, white or black, in the novel that ap-
proaches the unalloyed goodness of Tom, whose ordeal has transformed him
from a slave to a man, then to a martyr.[33]

When the prospect of imminent financial ruin compels the good-
intentioned Shelbys of Kentucky to sell Tom to a slave trader, Tom is fortunate
to land in the New Orleans home of Augustine St. Clare. Before Augustine's
untimely death forces another sale, this time to the infamous Legree, Harriet
introduces the reader to Eva, the St. Clares' doomed child. The St. Clares love
Eva as Harriet loved Charley, and like Charley, Eva is a special child, too good
to survive in a world saturated with sin. Eva's innocence is the innocence of
Eve before the fall, as Tom radiates the goodness of Christ before the cross.
Like Tom, Eva is a teacher. "Eva was an uncommonly mature child," Harriet
wrote, "and the things that she had witnessed of the evils of the system under
which they were living had fallen, one by one, into the depths of her thoughtful, pondering heart. She had vague longings to do something for them—to
bless and save not only them, but all in their condition,—longings that contrasted sadly with the feebleness of her little frame." In a chapter titled "The
Little Evangelist," Eva helps Ophelia overcome her prejudice against the black

child Topsy, who is unruly because she has no family and therefore no love. When Topsy despairs of her condition, Ophelia cries out, "Topsy, you poor child, don't give up! *I* can love you, though I am not like that dear little child. I hope I've learnt something of the love of Christ from her."[34]

But like Tom, Eva must die for the sins of America. Eva confronts death with rapture and grace: "A bright, a glorious smile passed over her face, and she said, brokenly,—'O! love,—joy,—peace!' gave one sigh, and passed from death unto life!"[35]

In the concluding section of the novel, Harriet addresses the men and women of the South, "whose virtue, and magnanimity, and purity of character, are the greater for the severer trial it has encountered." She beseeches southerners to recognize that the system of slavery endows man with a "wholly irresponsible power." While some masters wield that power benevolently, even the most Christian masters, such as the Shelbys, cannot overcome the evil of an institution that sunders families and exposes the slave to brutality.[36]

Then she addresses the people of the North, especially the mothers. From Charley, his unconditional love, his unmerited suffering, and from her own helplessness and loss, Harriet imagined the agony of slave mothers. She asks her readers to extend such feelings from their own experience to slave mothers who hurt and love and grieve just like them. "And you, mothers . . . you, who have learned, by the cradles of your own children, to love and feel for all mankind, . . . I beseech you, pity the mother who has all your affections, and not one legal right to protect, guide, or educate, the child of her bosom! By the sick hour of your child; by those dying eyes, which you can never forget, by those last cries, that wrung your heart when you could neither help nor save; by the desolation of that empty cradle, that silent nursery,—I beseech you, pity those mothers that are constantly made childless by the American slave-trade!"[37]

What can the people of the North do to efface the sin of slavery, Harriet asked? First, personal conversion. Second, "you have another power; you can *pray!*" Finally, she entreats her readers to open northern schools, churches, and homes to their black neighbors. If instead they shrink away "from the helpless hand," then "the country will have reason to tremble, when it remembers that the fate of nations is in the hands of One who is very pitiful, and of tender compassion." A born-again faith, a change of heart, and the actions that naturally flow from such a transformation would redeem the nation.[38]

The consequence of not addressing this sin was the loss of God's favor, the casting down of America as the Lord's Chosen Nation, and a still worse fate. For evangelicals who believed in the immanence of the final battle before the coming of Christ's reign, the failure to expiate the sins of the world, especially human bondage, risked eternal damnation. "This is an age of the world when nations are trembling and convulsed," Harriet wrote. "A mighty influence is abroad, surging and heaving the world, as with an earthquake. And is America safe? Every nation that carries in its bosom great and unredressed injustice has in it the elements of this last convulsion."[39]

Harriet concluded with a sliver of hope. She understood well the compulsion of those who voted for slavery as a concession to the salvation of the Union. Her counter point was that the fate of the Union depended not on temporizing but on repenting and expiating the sin of slavery. "A day of grace is yet held out to us," she wrote encouragingly. "Both North and South have been guilty before God; and the *Christian church* has a heavy account to answer. Not by combining together to protect injustice and cruelty, and making a common capital of sin, is this Union to be saved,—but by repentance, justice and mercy; for, not surer is the eternal law by which the millstone sinks in the ocean than that stronger law, by which injustice and cruelty shall bring on nations the wrath of Almighty God!"[40]

Literary critics have dismissed *Uncle Tom's Cabin* as melodramatic—Eliza's escape over the ice of the Ohio River to freedom, Tom's improbable stoicism in the face of base brutality, and Eva's treacly goodness and untimely death. They have also complained about the novel's didactic passages and the frequent biblical references and digressions. But to the middle-class Americans in towns, in cities, and on prosperous farms in the 1850s, *Uncle Tom's Cabin* resonated deeply. They were romantics, deeply religious, viewing childhood as a time of innocence, and the family as the foundation of faith and society. Harriet touched all these chords of feeling, faith, and experience. Many of her readers had lost children; many of her readers experienced a crisis of faith; many strove to be better Christians; but most did not consider slavery or the slave as someone that bore an integral relationship to their own spiritual striving and family condition. The genius of *Uncle Tom's Cabin* was that it made the personal universal, and it made the personal political as well. For millions of readers, blacks became people.

Abraham Lincoln was only half-joking when he met Harriet at the White House in 1862 and exclaimed, "So you're the little woman who wrote the book that started this great war!" The book had a profound impact on northern public opinion. Relatively few northerners read the narratives of escaped slaves, and fewer still consumed abolitionist tracts or attended their rallies. But tens of thousands read *Uncle Tom's Cabin*. As one northern reader exclaimed, "What truth could not accomplish, fiction did, and Harriet Beecher Stowe has had the satisfaction of throwing a firebrand into the world."[41]

The last installment of *Uncle Tom's Cabin* appeared in the *National Era* on April 1, 1852. Shortly thereafter, John P. Jewett published the book version. On the first day in print, the book sold three thousand copies; by the end of the year, an unprecedented three hundred thousand copies had been sold. Only the Bible outsold *Uncle Tom's Cabin* that year. The book was translated into dozens of languages. In an era when spin-off products were unheard of, *Uncle Tom's Cabin* became a franchise, inspiring songs, theater performances, dolls, games, even wallpapers, spoons, and candlesticks.

Horace Greeley brought the book with him to read on the train from Boston to Washington, D.C. The tough-minded editor of the *New York Tribune* had supported the Compromise of 1850 and had little patience for abolitionists. Still, as the nation's most prominent journalist, he figured he should read this novel that everyone was talking about. Greeley opened the book as the train pulled out of Boston. By the time he reached Springfield, he was weeping so profusely that he had to get off the train and spend a night to compose himself.

Frederick Douglass read the book and found himself alternately moved and annoyed. Harriet had sought him out for information on plantation life from a slave's perspective as she wrote *Uncle Tom's Cabin*. In her characteristic straightforward manner, she also sparred with Douglass on the issues of religion and colonization. Douglass had attacked the Protestant churches for their silence; Harriet reminded him that most of the abolitionists were fervid evangelicals. She pointed out that her brothers and her father, ministers all, worked on behalf of "poor, oppressed, bleeding Africa." Harriet was convinced, she wrote to Douglass, that the anti-slavery movement "must and will become a purely religious one. The light will spread in churches, the tone of feeling will rise, Christians North and South will give up all connection with, and take up their testimony against slavery, and thus the work will be done." By the time Harriet wrote these lines to Douglass in July 1851, he had lost faith that evangelical witness could effect a revolution in public sentiment.[42]

Harriet's position on colonization troubled Douglass more. The prospect of freed slaves created a conundrum for Harriet. Like some other anti-slavery proponents, she believed that Africa offered the best solution. There, black men and women would reach their full potential, unencumbered by white interference or prejudice. At the end of *Uncle Tom's Cabin*, Harriet sends escaped slave George Harris and his family (now living in Canada beyond the grasp of the Fugitive Slave Law) to Liberia. In a pointed reply, Douglass informed Harriet, "The truth is, dear madam, we are *here*, and we are likely to remain. Individuals emigrate—nations never. We have grown up with this republic, and I see nothing in her character, or even in the character of the American people as yet, which compels the belief that we must leave the United States." Douglass, who had lost his faith both in the power of religious conversion to conquer slavery and in the political process to produce just laws, now placed his faith in the American people to live peaceably with free black men and women. Harriet was less optimistic. But Douglass's argument was so persuasive that she later told an anti-slavery society meeting "that if she were to write 'Uncle Tom' again, she would not send George Harris to Liberia."[43]

The colonization issue, a minor element in the novel, paled in comparison to the larger questions Harriet addressed. After visiting Harriet at home in March 1853, Douglass was impressed by her freedom "from the slightest tinge of affectation." Their cordial conversation and her willingness to rethink African colonization earned Douglass's respect. For here was a black man at a white woman's home discussing the major political questions of the day on an equal basis, a rarity in itself. He wrote of the encounter in his newspaper, in March 1853, where he called *Uncle Tom's Cabin* "the *master book* of the nineteenth century. . . . She who had walked with lighted candle, through the darkest and most obscure corners of the slave's soul, and had unfolded the secrets of the slave's lacerated heart, could not be a stranger to us; nor could we make ourselves such to her." An eloquent endorsement from one who knew of slavery well.[44]

Most southerners ignored Harriet's evenhanded treatment of their region. Slavery, after all, was the primary target of the novel, and slavery was primarily a southern institution. The immense popularity of the book caused southern states, even as far north as Maryland, to criminalize possession of a copy, which made the novel even more popular.

Maryland authorities, in April 1857, confiscated a copy of the book at the home of Samuel Green, a free black minister suspected of harboring runaways. They charged Green with "knowingly having in his possession a certain abolition pamphlet called 'Uncle Tom's Cabin,' of an inflammatory character and calculated to create discontent amongst the colored population of this State." Green was convicted and sentenced to ten years in prison. The conviction outraged many northerners, not all of them abolitionists, who barraged Maryland's governor, Thomas H. Hicks, with petitions for Green's release to no avail. Hicks's successor, Augustus W. Bradford, released and pardoned Green on the condition that he leave the state in sixty days. Green and his wife emigrated to Canada. Their daughter, Susan, remained enslaved in Missouri until the end of the Civil War. The Greens returned to Maryland after the war, where he taught at a black institution that later became Morgan State University. He died in Baltimore in 1877.[45]

Most southern responses to the book were less draconian but equally hostile. Southern literati produced "replies" to the book in novels, plays, and short stories. These works typically emphasized the paternalistic relationship between master and servant. None came close to matching the popularity of *Uncle Tom's Cabin*, which infuriated southerners all the more.

Southern critics adopted two strategies: one to attack Harriet personally, the other to question the veracity of the book (though it was a work of fiction). They criticized Harriet for broaching the subject of slavery and the related topics of miscegenation, rape, and pedophilia. They called her "Harriet 'Breeches' Stowe," as her discussion of such delicate topics had unsexed her. George Frederick Holmes, a prominent southern writer, composed a lengthy review of *Uncle Tom's Cabin* in the *Southern Literary Messenger*, the region's leading literary journal. Holmes explained the consequences of violating gender proscriptions: "Where a writer of the softer sex manifests . . . a shameless disregard of truth and of those amenities which so peculiarly belong to her sphere of life, we hold that she has forfeited the claim to be considered a lady, and with that claim all exemption from the utmost stringency of critical punishment."[46]

Holmes next turned to the book itself. He admitted that such men as Legree and Haley (a slave trader) existed in the South. But while Harriet attributed their character to the evil inherent in slavery, Holmes argued that such depraved people existed everywhere, regardless of slavery. "Slavery only furnishes the occasion and determines the forms of the brutality; it neither generates it, nor would its abolition extirpate it. . . . There are worse Haleys in the large cities than on the Ohio River." In fact, Holmes continued, "the evil assigned to slavery is equally or still more incident to societies where slavery does not exist."[47]

What exercised Holmes in particular was Harriet's use of Christianity to bind her characters and themes together. Holmes regretted that northerners used religion "as a common lure of deception to tempt the unreflecting favor of the populace to every scheme of anarchy or delusion." These false disciples "all claim to speak as the oracles of heaven, and as special messengers entrusted with the authority of Christ." Such assertions "may be legitimately regarded as presumptive evidence of unchristian motives and diabolical purposes."[48]

The international fame of the book also irked southerners and further isolated them from the humanitarian mainstream of the era. The *Southern Literary Messenger* confronted not only an unruly authoress but also a host of respected European publications that praised the novel and invariably used the occasion to condemn slavery and the South. As the *Messenger*'s editor complained in January 1853, "From the *Revue des Deux Mondes* and the *Allgemeine Zeitung* down to the most insignificant journal . . . this miserable tissue of falsehoods and abominations has been highly commended and American slaveholders have been denounced as monsters of oppression." The British reaction to the novel particularly cut the writer to the quick. If any journals should understand the role of deference and social hierarchy, it would be the high-toned British publications. But "in England, the assaults upon us have been peculiarly malignant. All classes and conditions of the English people— every shade of political sentiment and every tinge of religious faith—are found to agree to least in one thing—abhorrence, real or assumed, of negro slavery." The editor assigned this attitude to the desire of the British to break up the Union.[49]

Charley's death came to have a lengthy life beyond his tiny grave in Cincinnati. A mother could never get over the loss of a child; but Harriet possessed the talent to channel her grief into a cause greater than herself. As she wrote to a friend who had asked her how she came to write the novel, Harriet explained that she bore seven children, "the most beautiful and most loved of whom lies buried near my Cincinnati residence. It was at his dying bed and at his grave that I learned what a poor slave mother may feel when her child is torn away from her. In those depths of sorrow which seemed to me immeasurable, it was my only prayer to God that such anguish might not be suffered in vain. There were circumstances about his death of such peculiar bitterness, of what seemed almost cruel suffering that I felt I could never be consoled for it unless this crushing of my own heart might enable me to work out some great good to others."[50]

So it happened that a mother's grief became a nation's cause. *Uncle Tom's Cabin* did not cause the Civil War, but it touched the consciences of millions, and it put a face on slavery, and a soul on black people. The book did not transform northerners into abolitionists upon the reading. But it did cause people to think more deeply and more personally about the implications of slavery for family, society, and Christianity. The more southerners thrashed about trying to denounce, parody, or dismiss the book, the more impotent they seemed. The generation of southerners who grew to adulthood by the middle of the nineteenth century, who had inherited slavery from their grandfathers and fathers, who earned a substantial living from slavery, wondered how to protect an institution by which the world increasingly defined and judged them. Harriet had written that slavery was a national problem. But it was really the South that confronted the great dilemma of inheritance.

The failed revolutions of Europe provided an ominous background for the growing tensions over slavery. The agitation against the Fugitive Slave Law with states and citizens overriding its provisions, and the presumption of abolitionist ministers that individual interpretations of the Bible transcended the law of the land, resembled, to southerners, the Parisian mobs that turned promising republican movements into circuses of anarchy. Northerners increasingly viewed southerners as ancien régime despots intent on expanding their authoritarian reach and destroying the flame of individual liberty wherever it existed. Images, no matter how divergent from the reality of things, can quickly become facts, absent forces and events to the contrary.

The correct balance between individual freedom and collective order is the dilemma of democratic societies, of which the United States of America was then the world's sole representative. The brief and bloody revolutions of Europe failed to attain, let alone maintain, that balance. As the franchise in America expanded to include all white adult males in most states, and as an evangelical democracy and an evangelical religion spread across the land, some citizens wondered whether these centrifugal forces would ultimately tear apart the Union. In other nations, the institutions of Church and State held individual impulses in check. In America, these institutions existed, but their very nature encouraged individuality. Reading the popular literature of the era, including *Uncle Tom's Cabin*, Americans looked to the family as the basic building block in their democratic society. Morality, cooperation, and education received their foundation in the family setting. In a highly mobile society, however, where individual family members picked up and left with alacrity, the stress on family life was great.

What Harriet Beecher Stowe did not appreciate when she chastised Americans for loving the Union more than the slave was that for many of her fellow citizens, the Union symbolized not only the precious legacy of the Revolutionary era but also stability and safety in a rapidly changing society. The Union, in fact, was the only constant holding the expanding nation together. Many years before the present crisis, in 1838, the young lawyer Abraham Lincoln had wrestled with this dilemma of how to balance individual freedom and collective order, concluding that without the latter, the former could not exist. Living on the frontier and well aware of the rising religious and sectional strife, he believed that the Union and its sacred documents, the Declaration of Independence and the Constitution, must transcend individual preferences in order for the American experiment to survive. "Reverence for laws," he declared, should be "the *political religion* of the nation." Such reverence was the only prospect for securing the legacy of the Revolution: "Let every American, every lover of liberty, every well-wisher to his posterity swear by the blood of the Revolution never to violate in the least particular the laws of the country, and never to tolerate their violation by others."[51]

This perspective accounted for Lincoln's recoil from the abolitionists and his support for Henry Clay's Compromise of 1850, Fugitive Slave Law included. The law was the law, and any appeal to higher authority or secular intervention threatened the collective security of the Union. The failed European revolutions reinforced Lincoln's perspective on events closer to home. He read *Uncle Tom's Cabin* and wept at Tom's fate. He hated slavery; like his father, he always had. But he loved the Union more.

CHAPTER 4

Railroaded

THE REVOLUTIONS IN EUROPE caused Americans to look more closely at their own revolutionary legacy, to see how easily discord could undermine fragile democratic institutions. But America possessed something Europe did not: a vast western territory to absorb the hopeful and the hopeless, the farmer, the merchant, the laborer, and the immigrant. The West was the essential element that would hold America intact and preserve the legacy of its revolution.

The South did not want to be erased from this future; the North came to believe that only by excluding the South would there be a future for America. For Horace Greeley, the editor of the nation's most popular newspaper, the *New York Tribune,* and for many other northerners, the maintenance of the West as a bastion of white freedom secured freedom for everyone: "The freedom of the public lands to actual settlers . . . [is] vitally necessary to the ultimate emancipation of labor from thralldom and misery." Southerners would fight hard for the West because they were Americans too and because they also had a labor force that required room to migrate and settle new lands in order to survive.[1]

Carl Schurz came to America in 1852, to a nation both hopeful and guarded about its future. He had forsaken the cloistered life of a student in provincial Bonn four years earlier to join his classmates in revolution, only to flee for his life when the Prussian monarchy regrouped and routed the republican forces. Schurz had moved to London and joined the community of exiled revolutionaries that included Karl Marx, Giuseppe Mazzini, and Lajos Kossuth. He taught German to support himself. He fell in love with Margarethe Meyer, a dark-haired German beauty visiting London, whom he married in the summer of 1852. While Schurz was grateful for England's hospitality, he never felt totally at home. Like many other German "forty-eighters," he looked to America. Writing of his intentions to his future brother-in-law, Schurz placed the matter before him. "By and by I might have a good living here in England. But citizenship here, for the alien is merely formal. The stranger remains a stranger here. Under such circumstances I cannot feel at home. What I am looking for in America is not only personal freedom, but the chance to gain full legal citizenship. If I cannot be the citizen of a free Germany, at least I can be a citizen of free America." With his young bride, Schurz sailed into New York Harbor in September 1852, clutching a copy of the *Visitor's Handbook* to orient him to this strange metropolis.[2]

New York City in 1852 exuded a chaotic thrum of activity, one that inspired the poetry of Whitman and the prose of the pulp novelists and awed the young German immigrants. The Schurzes arrived in the midst of a listless presidential campaign. Both the Whigs and the Democrats had accepted the finality of the Compromise of 1850. With slavery in the territories off the table and with a general consensus on economic policy, there seemed little to distinguish the parties. But the debate over the compromise had fractured the Whig Party, irreparably as it turned out, with northern Whigs, many staunchly anti-slavery, supporting the candidacy of Mexican War hero Winfield Scott, a Virginian, and the pro-compromise faction, predominantly southern, promoting President Millard Fillmore. Scott received the nomination, and many southern Whigs stayed home. The Democrats proved the more disciplined group heading into the 1852 election, uniting behind New Hampshire's Franklin Pierce and fiercely embracing the Compromise of 1850 as the bedrock of its party platform. Pierce won a lopsided election, with Scott carrying only Tennessee and Kentucky in the South.

The schism of the Whig Party told only part of the election story. Since 1848 more than one million immigrants from Ireland and Germany had settled in the United States, primarily in the cities and towns of the Northeast and Midwest. Ireland was a tragedy-in-waiting long before the potato blight of 1845, especially in its Catholic south where absentee English landlords squeezed the land and the labor out of tenants. Disease accompanied poverty: in 1840 less than one fifth of the population lived beyond the age of forty. Gangs freely roamed the cities. Irish revolutionaries, Young Ireland, they called themselves—an alliance of liberal Protestants and Catholics—attempted to rally nationalist sentiment against the English.

Just when it seemed things in that troubled land could get no worse, they did. First came the potato blight and then the British repeal of the Corn Laws, which had protected Ireland's wheat farmers from foreign competition. The English landlords evicted their Irish tenants, throwing nearly a million people out of work. A general breakdown of law and order followed. An Englishman visiting a village in County Mayo in 1847 left this account: "Out of a population of 240 I found 13 already dead from want. The survivors were like walking skeletons." America offered a better alternative. By the mid-1850s,

Ireland had lost one quarter of its population to either famine or emigration. By the late 1850s, there were 1.6 million Irish-born immigrants in America, more than 20 percent of whom crowded into the three cities of New York, Philadelphia, and Boston. That these rural people typically settled in cities is hardly surprising given the association between farming and poverty in their native land.[3]

Poor, mostly illiterate, and Roman Catholic, the Irish arrivals faced a rocky reception. Irish neighborhoods became synonymous in the public mind with intemperance, prostitution, gambling, violence, and disease. Illnesses that some cities thought they had conquered, such as smallpox, reappeared in the Irish slums. Not all Irish immigrants fit this profile, but stereotypes would prove difficult to dispel. Unremarked at the time was the fact that hardworking Irish immigrants were remitting millions of dollars annually to the folks back home, a remarkable feat given the circumstances and recency of their arrival. These impressive sums underscored how much Irish labor pushed the urban economy. The Irish filled positions in the growing municipal services sector, heaved cargo on docks, built railroads, descended into mines, and manned looms in mills. In turn, many native-born young men and women moved into higher-paying occupations in the expanding urban economy. In tribute to the Irish immigration, Boston Unitarian clergyman Edward Everett Hale noted in 1852, "The consequence is that we are, all of us, the higher lifted because they are here."[4]

Carl Schurz, like many other German forty-eighters, differed from the majority of Irish immigrants in terms of education, skills, and wealth. Many Germans had arrived in America to escape the oppressions of the petty German princes, especially Jews, whose civil liberties were progressively eroded during this era. Others, like Schurz, arrived as failed revolutionaries or because of the same problems the Irish encountered: a potato blight in 1845, oppressive landlords, and a shortage of tillable land. Often traveling in groups, the Germans settled more diversely than the Irish, selecting midwestern farmland as well as cities from the Northeast to the Mississippi River. Nearly as numerous as the Irish, 1.3 million German immigrants had arrived in the United States by 1860.[5]

The Germans were builders: factories, refineries, distilleries, musical instruments, professions, and associations of all kinds. Henry Steinway, chafing under production restrictions established by his guild in Germany, migrated to New York in 1851. Together with his four sons, he began to manufacture pianos. Within eight years, he employed eight hundred workers turning out sixty pianos a week. Although most of the Germans were Protestants or Catholics, some ten thousand Bavarian Jews entered the migration stream in the 1840s. Mainly middle-class, they brought their mercantile skills and traditions of philanthropy and mutual assistance to American cities. One young Jewish German woman, Rebecca Gratz of Philadelphia, pioneered the profession of social work, and her good deeds so impressed Sir Walter Scott that he may have modeled the character of Rebecca in *Ivanhoe* after Miss Gratz.[6]

Ivanhoe and Scott were immensely popular throughout the country, not only in the South. Scott's works were among the most read across a broad geographic and social spectrum in the United States in the three decades prior to the publication of *Uncle Tom's Cabin*. In America's Romantic Age, chivalry, sacrifice, and the triumph of good over evil resonated widely. Fred Bailey, a young black runaway, changed his last name to Douglass in honor of Scott's epic poem *The Lady of the Lake*. The hero of the epic was Lord James of Douglas, who was willing to give up his life to avert a bloody civil war between highlanders and lowlanders. Bailey's black benefactor, Nathan Johnson of New Bedford, Massachusetts, suggested adding an extra *s* for good measure. Bailey would now be known as Frederick Douglass.[7]

The large Irish and German immigration of the late 1840s and 1850s did not meet with universal approbation, especially outside the Democratic Party. Never before or since has the proportion of immigrants coming to American shores been greater. Although the total number of immigrants arriving between 1845 and 1854—2.9 million—was considerably less than the 9.2 million who came between 1905 and 1914, they represented nearly 15 percent of the total population compared with the latter group, which comprised less than 11 percent of Americans living at that time. In some cities, especially the northeastern ports and the major midwestern cities, immigrants accounted for more than 50 percent of the total population in the 1850s. Southern cities also experienced an unprecedented influx of immigrants. The foreign-born in Richmond, for example, comprised 40 percent of the white workforce. While some reveled in the dizzying diversity of American cities, others looked upon the exploding foreign population with alarm. Already skittish about the potential of disorder to disrupt democracy, added to the always-present concern about an aggressive Roman Catholic Church, nativist sentiment flared anew in American cities, growing into a formidable political force.[8]

The presidential election of 1852 confirmed some of the nativists' fears. Most of the Irish and German immigrants voted Democratic. The party had forged this affiliation during the presidency of Andrew Jackson and had solidified the connection in the succeeding decades. Although evangelical Christians could be found in both political parties, those evangelicals who particularly feared the Catholic Church adhered to the Whig Party. That party's promotion of temperance and Sabbath legislation further alienated Irish and German immigrants, many of whom voted for the first time in 1852 and contributed to Pierce's victories in New York, Pennsylvania, and Ohio.[9]

With the slavery issue temporarily quieted and economic questions less salient, nativism filled the political void as former Whigs cast about for a viable party and cause. Political nativism had attracted some northern Whigs since the early 1840s as conflicts over school prayer, electoral fraud, and job competition erupted in the rapidly growing cities. One group, the Order of United Americans, combined a strong belief in free labor with an equally strong inclination to limit immigration and restrict the rights of foreigners already on American soil. The Order singled out Catholic immigrants in particular.

A new group, the Order of the Star-Spangled Banner, appeared in New York City in 1849, a nonpartisan secret organization promoting nativist candidates for elective office. The organization packaged an amalgam of traditional nativist ideas such as lengthening the period of naturalization from five to twenty-one years, limiting the political rights of foreigners and their sons unless they were educated in American schools, and prohibiting foreigners from holding elective office, along with traditional Whig principles favoring the construction of a Pacific railroad and a homestead act to provide western land for settlers. These retreaded Whigs named their organization the American Party, though more commonly called the Know Nothings because its members claimed ignorance of the party's existence. Secrecy, its supporters hoped, would veil the party's actual strength until election day.

Although the Know Nothings presented themselves as the advocates of a modern, industrial economy—super-Whigs promoting electoral reform, land for workers and the poor, the expansion of urban services, and city planning— their appeal rested on good old religious bigotry. As much as they qualified their proposals for restricting the political and civil rights of immigrants, their animus against foreigners, especially Catholics, drew a significant following. It was true that in some Democratic-controlled cities and precincts, registrars ushered immigrants into citizenship with remarkable alacrity. It was also true that Democrats spent freely on spirits and financial emoluments to ensure a good turnout at the polls. Both parties engaged in such chicanery, and there was no evidence that fraud ever swung a major election to one candidate or another. These complaints reflected more the fear of Roman Catholics as a threat to American democracy than a genuine effort to cleanse the electoral system. William Brownlow, a newspaper editor, expressed the raw prejudice behind the veneer of reform: "We can have no peace in this country until the CATHOLICS ARE EXTERMINATED."[10]

The Order's anti-Catholic position tapped into the broad evangelical Protestant movement that perceived the Roman Catholic Church as a threat both
to America's millennial aspirations and its democratic traditions. Immigration restriction, like anti-slavery, became a Bible-based political issue. Charles
Elliot, a noted evangelical minister, quoted the Book of Deuteronomy as justification for restrictive laws against the foreign-born: "The Almighty, in
conceding that Israel might choose a king, laid down the law that they must
not choose a *stranger*, but a Hebrew of their own nation."[11]

The immigrant diversity and energy that inspired Whitman repulsed Know
Nothings. New arrivals brought distinctive languages, cultures, and traditions
that challenged prevailing customs such as keeping the Sabbath. To many, they
represented the underside of the urban and economic transformation, a transformation that in itself concerned many Americans who grew up in small
towns or on farms and who believed in the Jeffersonian ideal that attachment
to the land guaranteed a republican government.

In the South, the Order muted its anti-Catholic rhetoric, given the long-
standing Catholic presence in places such as Mobile and New Orleans, emphasizing a broader xenophobia combined with devotion to the Union. Know
Nothings enjoyed some electoral success in the South, especially among former
Whigs in border cities, where immigrants comprised a growing percentage of

COMING TO AMERICA.   RETURNING FOR A VISIT.

"*Coming to America; Returning for a Visit.*" (*Picture Collection, the New York Public
Library, Astor, Lenox and Tilden Foundations*)

the white workforce, but religious bigotry generally did not fare well in southern politics. Many southerners agreed with Virginia governor Henry A. Wise (a Democrat) that "Knownothingism was the most impious and unprincipled affiliation of bad means, for bad ends, which ever seized upon large masses of men of every opinion and party, and swayed them for a brief period blindly." It was "a proscription of religions, for the demolition of some of the clearest standards of American liberty, and for a fanatical and sectional demolition of slavery." When the Know Nothings eventually folded as a national party, many of its members joined the new anti-slavery Republican Party, thus confirming Governor Wise's suspicions.[12]

The Know Nothings' secrecy and bigotry provided easy political targets for the opposition, Democrats and some Whigs. Abraham Lincoln had little use for the party and turned away a delegation that came to his Springfield law office soliciting his membership. Alexander Stephens, a nationalist Whig congressman from Georgia and good friend of Lincoln's, rejected their ideas as un-American, looking "not to *how* the country shall be governed, but *who* shall hold the offices." Besides, "I am utterly opposed to mingling religion with politics in any way whatever."[13]

It was not surprising that Stephens and Lincoln shared the same views on religion and politics. There were similarities in their backgrounds. Stephens's family had moved from Pennsylvania to farm the incredibly red loam of central Georgia, earning a modest living growing tobacco, Indian corn, and assorted grains. Then Eli Whitney came to Georgia and demonstrated a cotton gin, and soon everyone in the neighborhood discovered that green-seed upland cotton grew splendidly in the blood-red soil. By the time he was thirteen years of age, in 1826, both his mother and father had passed away. That death was a common occurrence in these frontier lands was little solace to the boy, and grief consumed him. A dark melancholy hung over him forever, not unlike that which periodically plagued his soon-to-be friend from Illinois. And as with Lincoln, such fatalism did not paralyze him; it energized his endeavors, as if he were constantly challenging his demons to throw what they had at him and he would return it double.[14]

Small for his age and bookish—he dazzled his classmates by memorizing huge chunks of the Old Testament—he often displayed a combativeness that belied his frailty. But it was his intellect that others noted, and a series of benefactors intervened and shipped him off to schools to prepare for the ministry. The Second Great Awakening did not, however, capture this slight college boy any more than it had moved Lincoln. The young Georgian liked the intellectual sparring of biblical debates but had little use for theology.

Stephens gave up the ministry for the law. Like Lincoln, he had discovered that the law afforded fellowship, income, and access to politics. In 1835, at the age of twenty-two, he was admitted to the Georgia bar. Like Lincoln, he was fascinated by railroads. He pronounced it "stupendous" when he whizzed through the countryside at fifteen miles per hour. And, like his Illinois friend, Stephens was gifted in court. Initially, it may have been low expectations that generated the good notices; for this five-foot-seven-inch ninety-seven-pound creature looked so frail and deathly pale that a cadaver would have appeared more lifelike. Then he began in a voice barely audible, almost feminine in its high pitch, and by the time he reached his crescendo he had the gallery and the jury and the judge enrapt.[15]

Stephens shared with Lincoln an unshakable belief in the rule of law. When abolitionist literature flooded his state during the 1830s, local postmasters meddled with the mail and terrorized dissenters. Though Stephens abhorred the material, the reaction of local officials left him cold. When he ran for his first political office, the Georgia House of Representatives in 1836, the state was in turmoil over the literature. To root out potential distributors of the materials, several counties mounted vigilante groups to deal summary justice to the offenders. Stephens opposed these measures from the stump, arguing that such matters belonged to the courts, not the mob. He won his election by a resounding two-to-one margin.

Once in the state legislature Stephens worked to keep the slavery issue off the floor. His main interest, like Lincoln's, was economic development, particularly railroads, and in his five years in the legislature, he promoted that interest day in and day out. Stephens was a nationalist. He believed that an economically vibrant South contributed to national strength and solidarity. And he believed that railroads, industry, scientific agriculture, and an educated citizenry would render that objective inevitable. By 1844, he was a successful candidate for Congress. After Lincoln won his seat from Illinois two years later, the two young congressmen became friends. They were Clay Whigs, intent on pursuing a nationalist agenda and opposing those issues that divided Americans.

From a political perspective, attacking the Catholic Church in the South made little sense to Stephens, as the Church had never attacked slavery. "No man can say as much of the New England Baptists, Presbyterians, or Methodists," Stephens pointed out. Most of all, he perceived the Know Nothings as assaulting the basic right of American suffrage, the right that separated the United States from many of those European nations so recently returned to oppression. Stephens believed that northern capitalists wanted cheap labor that could not vote, very much like slaves in the South. They "bought up" cargoes of foreigners from Europe. "The whole *sub stratum* of northern society will soon be filled up with a class who can work, and who, though *white*, cannot *vote*. . . .

It is a scheme . . . to get *white slaves* instead of black ones. No American *laborer*, or man seeking employment there, who has a *vote*, need to expect to be retained long when his place can be more cheaply filled by a *foreigner* who has *none*." Such was the hypocrisy of northern entrepreneurs.[16]

The Know Nothings also ran counter to America's growing self-identification as a nation of immigrants. The failed revolutions in Europe coincided with the massive wave of immigration. If America was a beacon of hope to a troubled world, then closing the doors snuffed the beacon's light. Newcomers would embrace the land of their liberation, not destroy it. As Henry Ward Beecher, the era's most influential evangelical minister, put it in terms everyone could understand, "When I eat chicken, I don't *become* chicken. *Chicken becomes me!*"[17]

Above all, the Know Nothings trampled on constitutional principles at a time when political leaders increasingly saw those ideals as holding the stretching fabric of American life together. Religious tests and the politicization of religion that the Know Nothings promoted challenged constitutional traditions. Horace Greeley articulated this sentiment when he wrote that "this whole broad assertion of a *'predominant* National Religion,' and that Religion not the Christian but the Protestant, and not the Protestant, but such Protestant sects as the majority pronounce 'Orthodox' or 'Evangelical' is fatally at variance with the fundamental principles of our Constitution."[18]

Still, the Order enjoyed electoral successes at the local level in 1853 and 1854. For some observers, this indicated that "Roman Catholicism is feared more than American slavery." That was a false perception. Slavery never lurked far from the surface of Know Nothing politics. Know Nothings in the Northeast were also likely to oppose slavery's expansion into the territories. Know Nothing candidates portrayed themselves as champions of native-born workingmen, advocating restricting the power of immigrants at home and of slaveholders out West. As one prominent Know Nothing explained, slavery was "a burden to the community in which it exists; . . . its influence is enervating of society; . . . wherever it goes it carries with it the corrosion of inactivity." Slavery defied America's enterprising spirit and, like the lowly Irish and other slavish followers of Rome, its presence inhibited the efficient progress of capital and labor. Though the Know Nothings did not appreciate the irony, they articulated the same racial superiority as pro-slavery advocates.[19]

Religious bigotry and ethnic exclusion were slender reeds upon which to build a political movement in mid-nineteenth-century America, even when packaged as a crusade for electoral virtue and efficiency amid the chaos of modern urban life. For a brief time, however, as one major political party imploded and the slavery issue seemed to fade into the background, the nativists ascended.

Carl and Margarethe Schurz moved westward, following the bands of German immigrants who set up shops, farms, and other enterprises in dozens of midwestern villages and cities. Milwaukee had become a center of German culture, and there the Schurzes decided to put down their bags, purchasing a farm in nearby Watertown. In 1853, American political life was, to put it mildly, in a state of transition. The multitude of voices and shifting alliances in the wake of the Whigs' disintegration (and internal divisions within the Democratic Party) dizzied the young immigrant. In his letters back to Germany he remarked that democracy was a wonderful if untidy process. As a revolutionary who failed to bring democratic government and unity to his native Germany, Schurz reveled in the open political system of his adopted land. He became a fervent nationalist in the process, opposing any threat to a national unity that he deemed essential for preserving democratic government.

Equally impressive to Schurz was the seemingly limitless economic opportunity west of the Appalachians. No old families, political hierarchies, or military establishments to hold a man down. Or a woman, for that matter, as he wrote to his friends. The freedom of movement and the opportunities to engage their minds and talents women enjoyed were in stark contrast to what they had in Europe.

Many in the German community knew Schurz's name through his revolutionary exploits, and those exploits became embellished over time. It was unlikely that he would settle down to life as an obscure Wisconsin farmer. Besides, as much as he immersed himself in American life, his heart ached for revolutionary Germany. Encouraged by the empathy for European revolutionary ideals, he traveled to Washington, D.C., to gauge the support of the Pierce administration for his German cause. Like most first-time visitors, Schurz found Washington disappointing, "rather dismal," he said. Equally disappointing were Schurz's meetings with various administration officials. He left with a positive impression of only one man, Secretary of War Jefferson Davis, whose dignity and erudition won Schurz's admiration, though he remained noncommittal on aid to the German nationalists. The energy of the administration seemed scattered in harebrained schemes and pointless aggression, with intrigue to dislodge Cuba from Spain and tacit support for ill-advised private ventures into Central America. As to why this state of affairs existed, Schurz, despite his favorable view of Davis, believed that slaveholders had captured the Democratic Party. Freedom frightened them. There would be no assistance for his German friends.[20]

Instead, Schurz immersed himself in local politics. If he could not save Germany, he would help Watertown. He became the town's commissioner for improvements, organized an insurance company, and studied law. Like any local booster, he touted Watertown to investors far and wide. No less than three railroad lines were under construction, he boasted. There he probably would have stayed were it not for Illinois senator Stephen A. Douglas, who not only rousted out Schurz from his life as a small-town entrepreneur and farmer but also stirred Abraham Lincoln from his lucrative law practice in Springfield. These career changes, it should be noted, were not what Senator Douglas had in mind when he submitted a railroad bill to the Senate in January 1854.

Douglas was a consummate nationalist. In some ways he resembled the railroads he represented in courts and promoted in the Senate. His mind ran straight to the horizon, where an ever-more glorious future awaited his clients and America. Railroads would connect the vast continental empire and preserve the nation's revolutionary ideals and democratic traditions. This vision was not much different from that held by Douglas's Illinois rival, Abraham Lincoln, who made his initial political reputation as a proponent of just the kind of internal improvements advocated by the Little Giant. Lincoln made his living, like Douglas, securing handsome fees from railroad companies. Both men supported the Compromise of 1850, the Fugitive Slave Law inclusive. They held differing views on slavery in the territories, with Lincoln much more the advocate of congressional intervention to prohibit it, Douglas supporting popular sovereignty. Both agreed, however, that the Union was paramount.

When Douglas submitted his railroad bill in January 1854, this was the consensus across America: citizens would agree to disagree on slavery in the territories, but all would rally to the cause of the Union to overcome those differences. Despite some well-publicized cases of resistance to the Fugitive Slave Law, northern states and their citizens adhered to the bargain for the most part. Although Harriet Beecher Stowe had touched northerners (and some in the South, when they could get their hands on the book) with her dramatic novel, its influence did not translate into political action. A frustrated Frederick Douglass saw the push for black civil rights in the North stall and even regress, while in the South slavery seemed as strong as ever as cotton prices soared. Religious intolerance and nativism, on the fringes of politics for twenty years, had entered the mainstream. It seemed, in fact, as if conservative reaction to the revolutionary movements in Europe had crossed the Atlantic.

Douglas hoped his railroad bill would not only keep the slavery issue quiescent but would also pull the nation together and open new territories to the farmers and townspeople of the East. A transcontinental railroad to tame the western "wilderness" had long been a dream of Douglas and many others.

Making land accessible to potential settlers and developing a lucrative commerce between the new territories and the East were the most certain methods of cementing his beloved Union and its democratic institutions. The railroad was the means to this glorious end. Douglas's own experience in Illinois, where Chicago grew from a raw frontier town to the major metropolis between the Appalachians and the Mississippi, confirmed his judgment. Railroads sealed Chicago's role as the commercial hub for prosperous midwestern farmers and eastern merchants and manufacturers.

Douglas was the voice of Young America: brash, assertive, and confident. That the land through which a Pacific railroad must pass was not a wilderness but a home to Indians did not concern the senator. Removing the "Indian barrier" and establishing white government, he asserted, were "first steps" toward the greater end of stimulating "a tide of emigration and civilization." He thought it absurd that parts of the Louisiana Purchase, American soil since 1803, remained unorganized and largely unsettled. "How are we to develop, cherish and protect our immense interests and possessions on the Pacific," he asked his Senate colleagues, "with a vast wilderness fifteen hundred miles in breadth, filled with hostile savages, and cutting off all direct communication?" The cure was simple: remove the "savages," pass a railroad bill, and organize the territories.[21]

Except, as Douglas well knew, it was not that simple. The Missouri Compromise of 1820 divided the Louisiana Purchase at 36° 30', prohibiting slavery above that line. The Nebraska Territory, which Douglas proposed to organize for the purpose of attracting settlers and building a railroad, lay above 36° 30'. Southern lawmakers would not support a bill that would further reduce their power in the Congress. Since the admission of California in 1850, the free states had, by 1854, almost double the number of representatives in the House, and held a majority in the Senate. Two, perhaps three states might be carved from the Nebraska Territory. By the provisions of the Missouri Compromise these would be free states. The territorial issue concerned not only southern slaveholders but also those farmers and workers in the South who might own slaves someday and migrate to the new lands. What seemed acceptable to southerners in 1820, with the rich soil of the Old Southwest newly opened to slavery, was much less attractive in the 1850s. What southerners found more palatable about Douglas's railroad bill was the railroad. A southern route for the Pacific railroad could secure economic independence for the South and provide a shield against political intrusions by the northern majority. As the *New Orleans Delta* explained, the Pacific Railroad was "the great panacea, which is to release the South from its bondage to the North."[22]

Douglas addressed southern desires in his Nebraska bill by providing for the construction of three railroads from the Mississippi River to the Pacific Ocean, one of which would traverse a southern route. None of these railroads would become reality until the Congress organized the Nebraska Territory so the government could grant lands for rights-of-way. Responding to southerners' objections to the Missouri Compromise prohibition, Douglas applied the language Congress employed in organizing the New Mexico and Utah territories as part of the Compromise of 1850. The Nebraska Territory, "when admitted as a State or States, . . . shall be received into the Union, with or without slavery, as their constitution may prescribe." It was Douglas's beloved principle of popular sovereignty, "the great fundamental principle of self-government upon which our republican institutions are predicated." The measure implicitly repealed the Missouri Compromise since residents could vote to sanction slavery in any new territory. But southerners asked Douglas to go further: to divide the Nebraska Territory into two entities, Nebraska and Kansas, and to make the repeal of the Missouri Compromise explicit. The tacit assumption was that Kansas, next door to slave state Missouri, would become a slave state and Nebraska would enter as a free state. Douglas, who had worked hard to ensure that his railroad bill would not revive the slavery controversy, reluctantly agreed, predicting that the revised bill would "raise a hell of a storm." He was right.[23]

No sooner had Douglas introduced his Nebraska bill to the Senate on January 23, 1854, than a manifesto, an "Appeal of the Independent Democrats," appeared in the *National Era*, the newspaper that had serialized *Uncle Tom's Cabin*. The bill, the authors declared, closed off opportunities both for immigrants from Europe and the native-born on the farms and the crowded cities of the East. The signers, mostly lawmakers from the Northeast and Midwest, saw the repeal as "a gross violation of a sacred pledge; as a criminal betrayal of precious rights; as part and parcel of an atrocious plot to exclude from a vast unoccupied region, emigrants from the Old World and free laborers from our own States, and convert it into a dreary regime of despotism." They attacked Douglas as a tool of "servile demagogues."[24]

The Missouri Compromise, which abolitionists despised as a pact with the devil, had suddenly assumed the trappings of holy writ. Congress had organized territories employing several principles including the outright prohibition of slavery (the Northwest Ordinance) and popular sovereignty (the Mexican Cession), as well as the geographically explicit Missouri Compromise. Lawmakers had demonstrated a flexible and accommodating spirit with respect to the issue of slavery in the territories, preferring the Union above all other principles. The Douglas bill did not guarantee slavery anywhere. The

Missouri Compromise, if anything, encouraged its existence within certain boundaries.

But 1854 was not 1820. In the interim, the Western world outside the United States had turned against slavery with a vengeance. Although few Americans identified with abolitionists, northerners increasingly opposed slavery's extension. Also, by the mid-1850s, American cities, especially those in the North, burst with newcomers, both from abroad and from the countryside. Perhaps all would fulfill their dreams in these hustling urban centers. But the era of small shops and artisanal work was passing, and the semiskilled labor force grew. Would opportunities continue to exist for all? At least there was the West. The West was much less important in the American imagination of 1820 than it was in 1854. Turning the West into plantation country implied, for many northerners, turning them away from the chance to prosper. But southerners felt the same way: keeping the West open for them meant keeping the dream of starting over or of growing greater alive.

Horace Greeley, from the moment Douglas introduced his bill, turned the pages of his *New York Tribune* into an anti-Nebraska newspaper. Greeley not only captured northern public sentiment but also shaped it with sharp editorials. In one editorial, he charged, "Not content within its own proper limits, . . . it now proposed to invade and overrun the soil of freedom, and to unroll the pall of its darkness over virgin territory whereon a slave has never stood. Freedom is to be elbowed out of its own home to make room for the leprous intruder. The free laborer is to be expelled that the slave may be brought in." It was all there: sex, class, and patriotism.[25]

The Douglas bill did not please all southerners initially either. Some dismissed the repeal of the Missouri Compromise as mere window-dressing to hide the fact that both Nebraska and Kansas would eventually enter the Union as free states anyway. Others expressed concern that an explicit repeal would unnecessarily inflame public opinion in the North. Senator John Bell of Tennessee predicted that the Nebraska bill would create in the North "a more decided and deep-rooted hostility to slavery and the whole South." If by some miracle slaveholders could actually capture a majority in Kansas, then anti-slavery sentiment would become "more widely diffused and more intense." In exchange for this heightened sectional animosity, the South would, in reality, gain nothing. Bell understood that the more populous North would win the migration race to Kansas.[26]

Yet southern lawmakers voted overwhelmingly in favor of a bill that offered so little to the South while generating so much northern ill will. Perhaps that was the point: to tweak the northern beast. The beast responded. It was a perfect example of how Newton's Third Law of Motion applied to politics in the 1850s. The Douglas bill produced such a sharp reaction in the North, and not just among the usual abolitionist contingent, that southerners reacted in kind, embracing a proposal that would have only marginal impact on their well-being. The northern response to the Nebraska bill gave the lie to the assumption that ethnicity and religion had eclipsed slavery as the nation's central political and moral issue.

The Kansas-Nebraska Act, like the toppling of the July monarchy in France, provoked a revolution of unintended consequences. The sectional response to the act destroyed what remained of the Second American Party System, splintering it into a kaleidoscope of parties and fusion groups so confusing that the *Congressional Globe*, the publication charged with matching lawmakers with their party affiliation, gave up the task following the 1854 congressional elections. Accompanying the disintegration of parties was the loss of the broad center in American politics, the Unionism of Henry Clay, Abraham Lincoln, Alexander Stephens, and Stephen A. Douglas. Lincoln, Stephens, and Douglas continued on, of course, but only Douglas could straddle the eroding national middle; Lincoln and Stephens found political homes in sectional causes and parties.

Reality, a rare commodity since the introduction of the Wilmot Proviso, became ever more elusive. Ghosts haunted Washington. Most northerners, especially those in the dynamic cities, wanted the opportunity to prosper, and increasingly viewed the South and slaveholders as obstacles to that end. Southerners wanted the same thing, and similarly viewed Yankees as barriers to their pursuit of happiness. Every political issue became a sign, a symbol confirming both views at the same time. Never mind that most of these issues worked little harm or benefit to either side. The reality, again, no longer mattered. In this atmosphere, demagogues prospered, and moderates faltered. Whoever could best convince his constituents of the perfidy of their common enemy achieved success. Politics became a religion, as religion had become politics: dogmatic, orthodox, and unflinching. America went to bed one night a moderate, accommodating nation and woke up the following morning ready for Armageddon. A railroad bill became a call to arms.

Abraham Lincoln answered the call. Out of politics and immersed in a successful law practice, Lincoln made no public comment on the Kansas-Nebraska Act in the months following its passage. He had spoken relatively little about slavery in a political career that extended back to the early 1830s. But Lincoln held a visceral dislike of slavery. The institution denied a man the right to improve himself. As a man devoted to the Constitution, however, he saw no way to interfere with slavery where it currently existed. The territories were another matter, though he was never in the forefront of those clamoring for the Wilmot Proviso, nor did he consider supporting anti-slavery parties. He was a Whig through and through, and a Clay Whig at that.

When Lincoln delivered a eulogy for his mentor in 1852, he stressed Clay's sense of duty, his elevation of the nation's interest above personal gain, and how he agonized over the institution of slavery, an inherited curse for which he could find no cure. Henry Clay, Lincoln explained, "did not perceive, that on a question of human right, the negroes were to be excepted from the human race." Consequently, "he ever was, on principle and in feeling, opposed to slavery." The great dilemma, for both Clay and Lincoln, was how to end slavery "without producing a greater evil." The dilemma led both Clay and Lincoln to support the American Colonization Society, which advocated transporting freed slaves, voluntarily, back to Africa. Such a plan, Lincoln believed, would succeed both "in freeing our land from the dangerous presence of slavery" and "in restoring a captive people to their long-lost father-land with bright prospects for the future."[27]

This was a pipe dream. The money to free four million slaves and transport them to Africa was beyond the capacity of any government or private group. The logistics of such an enterprise were daunting as well, even assuming enough vessels and crew existed to implement the plan. And what African nation could suddenly support millions of destitute freedmen who were as familiar with that continent as they were with the desolate steppes of Russia?

Lincoln's "curse" was Clay's, that they could not adopt the self-righteousness of northern evangelical abolitionists or southern slavery apologists. Instead, they appreciated the agony of the slave, the dilemma of the slaveholder, and the difficulty of reconciling the two short of revolution, which would bring horrors far beyond what the benefits of freedom were worth. Lincoln came to understand the flaws of colonization, even as he held on to the notion into his presidency. In October 1854, Lincoln admitted that, while he would like "to free all the slaves, and send them to Liberia . . . a moment's reflection would convince me, that whatever of high hope . . . there may be in this, in the long run, its sudden execution is impossible." He threw up his hands. "If all earthly power were given me, I should not know what to do, as to the existing institution" of slavery.[28]

But he knew very well what to do about slavery's extension. Lincoln acknowledged that the Kansas-Nebraska Act caught him and his fellow Illinois Whigs "by surprise—astounded us. . . . We were thunderstruck and stunned." It took Lincoln a while to find his voice, but, invigorated by the upcoming fall election campaign and the signs that Illinois was in full revolt against its favorite son, he responded in September 1854. Douglas had defended the act to his constituents as a democratic measure, leaving the fate of the territories in the hands of their settlers. For Lincoln, popular sovereignty was nothing less than a mask for dashing the opportunities of white middle- and working-class northerners. As he wrote, "The whole nation is interested that the best use shall be made of these territories. We want them for the homes of free white people. This they cannot be, to any considerable extent, if slavery shall be planted within them. New Free States are the places for poor people to go to and better their condition." It was a theme Lincoln returned to again and again over the next six years. For the territories to be a white man's country—an objective that resonated deeply with his constituents—slavery must be barred forever. The West must remain pure.[29]

The confrontation that transformed Lincoln's public position on slavery occurred at the Illinois State Fair in Springfield in October 1854. Douglas neither sought nor desired to debate Lincoln. He was worn out from defending his actions up and down the state since the late summer. In August 1854, shortly after Congress adjourned, he left Washington for his home in Chicago, to rest and mend political fences. He did not enjoy a pleasant journey home. "I could travel," he later recalled, ". . . by the light of my own effigy on every tree we passed." Arriving in Chicago, he addressed a large hostile crowd outside his hotel balcony. As he departed, he lost his temper and blurted, "It is now Sunday morning, I'll go to church, you can go to hell."[30]

Exhausted, yet adamant in his position, Douglas offered a spirited defense of popular sovereignty and a strong condemnation of Know Nothingism to the throng at the state fair. Lincoln responded the following day, with Douglas present. He believed with all his heart in the principle of government by the consent of the governed, and he agreed that residents of the territories knew best when framing the laws by which they would live. But protecting slavery was unlike any other legal question because it involved encumbering another human being. This is where Lincoln and Douglas parted ways. Douglas, Lincoln averred, "has no very vivid impression that the negro is a human; and consequently has no idea that there can be any moral question in legislating about him." The simple statement in the Declaration of Independence that "all men are created equal" included all men, regardless of race, capacity, or other limitation. "No man," Lincoln declared, "is good enough to govern another man, *without that other's consent*. I say this is the leading principle— the sheet anchor of American republicanism." To Lincoln, this was the real popular sovereignty, the right to govern one's self.[31]

Like many political leaders of the day, Lincoln blended religious and secular images in his speeches. Although he often struggled with his faith, Lincoln believed in the guiding hand of Providence even if he could not discern its meaning or existence. Explaining the intent of the Founding Fathers toward slavery four years later, Lincoln noted that in their "enlightened belief, nothing stamped with the Divine image and likeness was sent into this world to be . . . imbruted by its fellows." It is arguable whether this was an accurate account of the framers' intentions, but Lincoln believed it. Historians debate whether Lincoln was a religious man. He was. His religion was America, and that faith ran very deep.[32]

The Kansas-Nebraska Act was no longer a political issue for Lincoln; it was a moral cause. It was not enough to oppose the *extension* of slavery; it was time to express a moral outrage at the *existence* of slavery—a significant transformation of the public Lincoln, heretofore a moderate Clay Whig. It also marked Lincoln's reentry into the political arena. He talked now about "the monstrous injustice of slavery." "There can be no moral right in connection with one man's making a slave of another," and it followed that it was wrong to extend that immorality to the territories and "to every other part of the wide world, where men can be found inclined to take it."[33]

Lincoln's global perspective was not a rhetorical flourish. Like many other Americans, he believed in the nation's special mission to spread democracy and Christianity throughout the world. The failed revolutions in Europe set American democracy in bold relief as a distinctive and fragile experiment. Lincoln believed along with Clay "that the world's best hope depended on the continued Union of these States." And now, by permitting the extension of slavery, "we are proclaiming ourselves political hypocrites before the world, by thus fostering Human Slavery and proclaiming ourselves, at the same time, the sole friends of Human Freedom." It was this contradiction that troubled Lincoln most: the disconnect between American ideals and American reality.[34]

Frederick Douglass also viewed the Kansas-Nebraska Act as a transforming event. In a speech given to an abolitionist gathering in Chicago in October 1854, Douglass recounted the strengthening of the Slave Power since the annexation of Texas in 1845. The Fugitive Slave Law altered his view about the use of violence, though only in self-defense. Now, he wondered if more proactive measures would be necessary. Like a growing number of evangelicals, he saw in the pattern of southern power "the wisdom of that great God, who has promised to overrule the wickedness of men for His own glory." For Douglass, a war of liberation was inevitable.[35]

Horace Greeley issued a warning to the South following the passage of the Kansas-Nebraska Act. "If Slavery may encroach upon the domain of freemen," he wrote, "freemen may encroach upon the domain of Slavery. If slavery thinks this is a safe game to play at, let it be pursued as it has begun." The South would pick up the challenge, Senator David Atchison of Missouri vowed. As he wrote to his colleague Secretary of War Jefferson Davis, with more than a hint of glee, "We will be compelled to shoot, burn & hang, but the thing will soon be over. We intend to 'Mormonize' the Abolitionists," a reference to Missouri's earlier war to exterminate the Mormons. Within months, blood, not only white blood, would flow on the Plains, portending a broader confrontation with the Revolutionary legacy.[36]

CHAPTER 5

BLOOD ON THE PLAINS

ON A HOT AFTERNOON shortly after Congress passed the Kansas-Nebraska Act, a scraggly footsore cow wandered into Conquering Bear's camp near the North Platte River. Or maybe someone in Conquering Bear's camp "assisted" the cow's visit. A lean summer had followed a leaner winter. The trails to California and Oregon, carved out in the early 1840s, had become broad avenues, westbound traffic dispersing the buffalo into a wider arc until they disappeared altogether beyond the horizon. Now, after Douglas's railroad bill, the Sioux had become as expendable as the buffalo, more so because at least the hides and tongues of the animal still fetched handsome prices back east.[1]

There seemed no end to the white migration, or to the destruction of the Sioux land, the buffalo, the grasses, and the water. Only disease flourished. Some of the young Sioux talked resistance. But the elders knew that was futile. Some had gone to the white capital at Washington, D.C. They had traveled over iron rails, through small towns and large cities, had met the Great Father. They understood that challenging such wealth, power, and numbers could only end in extinction.

By the early 1850s, both the worsening plight of the Plains Indians and the mounting complaints of white migrants moved the federal government to act. Like the slaveholder and the Mexican, the Indian stood athwart the inexorable progress of a great nation chosen by God to spread His blessing to all mankind. It was the Native American's manifest destiny to succumb both to the superior race and the superior ideal. Perhaps democracy and evangelical Christianity could flourish among these people some day. In the meantime, they must step aside and defer to destiny. In February 1851, Congress passed the Indian Appropriation Act compensating Indians for their land and providing for their relocation and financial support during their transition to a sedentary agricultural lifestyle. In the mind of Congress, transforming a nomadic, marauding people into tillers of the soil not only protected white overlanders but also enabled the Indians to secure their own salvation, both in body and soul.

As the first step in this process of relocation and concentration, the government, in September 1851, invited the Plains Indians to a meeting at Horse Creek in what is today western Nebraska, thirty-five miles east of Fort Laramie on the Oregon Trail. The response was overwhelming—nearly ten thousand Plains Indians trekked to the site, the largest gathering of Indians ever on the Plains. The unprecedented response among the Native Americans, despite deep animosities within their own ranks, reflected burgeoning white traffic on the Oregon Trail and the consequent dispersion of the buffalo and the spread of disease among the tribes. The flood of whites onto Indian land had also generated sporadic violence between natives and the white migrants. Hungry, tired, and angry, the tribes readily responded to the government's invitation and its promise to "amply compensate for all the depredations of which they complain, on account of the destruction of game, timber, &c, by the passing of white men through their country."

Under a large tent, David D. Mitchell, representing the United States government, greeted headmen from various tribes, who arrived in their finest feather bonnets and colorful animal-hide shirts. Mitchell set out his terms: free and unmolested passage for overlanders on the Oregon Trail; an end to intertribal warfare, which had worsened as the buffalo disappeared; and the establishment of discrete boundaries for each tribe using natural topographic features such as mountains and rivers whenever possible. The tribes would also agree to recognize the right of the government to build roads and military posts along the trail. Mitchell assured the elders of the government's understanding and sincerity: "In times past you had plenty of buffalo and game to subsist upon, and your Great Father well knows that has always been your favorite amusement and pursuit. Your condition has changed, and your Great Father desires you will consider and prepare for the changes that await you." In return, Mitchell promised an annual payment of $50,000 in food and goods for the next fifty years to be shared among the tribes (the treaty did not specify how), permanent title to their new land, and eternal peace with the United States government. Mitchell believed that fifty years was sufficient "to give the experiment [of transforming the Indian from a hunter to a farmer] a fair trial, and solve the great problem whether or not an Indian can be made a civilized man."[2]

The assembled headmen reacted variously to the proposals, some not understanding the specifics, as it proved too difficult to translate the government's terms into the nine different languages represented. Even for those who grasped the full meaning of the offer, skepticism abounded. "Tell the wind to stop blowing" was the Lakota Sioux reaction to Mitchell's plea to end intertribal warfare. The demand to allow migrants to traverse the Plains unmolested also incurred mixed reviews. The Lakota derisively called the Oregon Trail the "Holy Road," for it obviously held sacred meaning for the white man. As for the geographic boundaries, such limits appeared on white men's maps but not in the Indians' minds. Hunger, disease, and warfare, however, had taken their toll on the Plains Indians. The large gathering itself underscored the Indians' willingness to reach an agreement that would secure their survival, even if they had to sacrifice their land and culture to achieve it.[3]

Following the negotiations, Mitchell provided a show for the assemblage, firing one of the army's big artillery pieces that shattered trees far distant into so many sticks of firewood. The Sioux warriors were not impressed. A few fast horsemen could kill the gunners before they had the chance to reload their machine, they thought.

In the end, the headmen watched their names etched on the document containing Mitchell's terms, which became the law of the land. Almost. Congress scaled back the annuity from fifty to fifteen years before ratifying Mitchell's work. The Indians moved closer to the forts to begin their new life protected by and dependent on the United States government. Not all the Indians, however. Many of the Lakota Sioux spurned the treaty, preferring to maintain their way of life, difficult though it was, rather than follow the promises of the white man. They resumed their hunting, their campaigns against other tribes, and their trading and confrontation with the white migrants. As the promised government annuities, food, and blankets arrived late and incomplete, the Lakota decision seemed prescient.

The whites kept coming. In 1852, the largest contingent of migrants in American history traveled west. From Council Bluffs in present-day western Iowa, wagons formed "an unbroken column fully 500 miles long." Observers called it "the greatest crowd of adventurers since the invasion of Rome by Goths[;] such a deluge of mortals had not been witnessed as was now pouring from the states . . . for the golden shores of California." To the Lakota Sioux, it did indeed seem like a barbarian invasion. One migrant likened the trail west from Fort Laramie to the crowds on Broadway. The same energy, determination, and hope roamed the streets of New York and the dusty summer trails of the West. Migration had consequences, however, as Stephen Douglas, the migrants themselves, and Americans everywhere would soon discover.[4]

Most Americans harbored the same dismissive view of Indians as Douglas. They held out little hope that the Indian could become a "civilized" race, federal policy notwithstanding. Prevailing scientific theories suggested that race, like other natural phenomena, reflected a hierarchy of order. Whether that hierarchy derived from God or from scientific principles, or both, remained open to discussion, but the variable abilities and potentials of the races attained the status of established fact. Mexicans, Indians, the Irish, and black people were clearly inferior, as their status, behavior, and culture confirmed. The superior race held a responsibility to help inferior races achieve their ultimate, though limited, potential. If these subordinate groups embraced such guidance, they would be saved both spiritually and physically. If not, they risked extinction.

Historians embraced the scientific view of race as well. William H. Prescott's histories of the Spanish conquest of Mexico and Peru (published in 1843 and 1847, respectively) distinguished the Spanish and Indian "races" and concluded that the "Anglo-Saxons" who settled to the North established a superior civilization. Francis Parkman espoused similar views in his epic book on the Oregon Trail (1849), and in other works narrating the struggle between the Anglo-Saxons and the "Celtic" French for control of North America. The Celts also fared poorly in John Lothrop Motley's book on the rise of the Dutch Republic (1856), with the Anglo-Saxon and Germanic races overcoming the inferior people. The Anglo-Saxon carried "in his blood a love of liberty, a spirit of individual enterprise and resourcefulness, and a capacity for practical and reasonable behavior," which the Celtic race lacked.[5]

It was perhaps ironic that slaveholders rarely evinced the degree of animosity toward the black that was found in press and policy statements about the Indian. The difference was, as Frederick Law Olmsted noted in his tour of the South, "Where the negro is a slave, natural antipathy of the white race to associate with him is lost." Slavery was the Africans' "natural" state, and in that position they would reach their highest potential, albeit well below the white man. Removal from Africa was a godsend. "Slavery has made the black man in America, in a few centuries," Virginia jurist William C. Daniell explained in 1852, "what thousands of years had failed to accomplish for him at home, cultivating the aptitudes of the negro race for civilization and Christianity."[6]

As Daniell's boast implied, it was incumbent upon white Americans, as part of their Christian duty, to rescue inferior races by offering instruction and the possibility of salvation. This was a key argument of white southerners for the institution of slavery, that it raised a downtrodden race from its primitive African origins to the possibility of salvation through Jesus Christ, inculcated discipline, and fashioned a family life unburdened by the need or concern for daily subsistence.

The Indians would also benefit from white civilization. The plan was simple, for the slave and for the Indian: work and live by the white man's standards, or die. But the Indians took poorly to farming, and a good many continued to roam the land convinced that freedom, however hard, was superior to an uncertain dependence on an unreliable government. Back east, sentiment grew that, regardless of federal ministrations, the Indian was congenitally committed to his destructive course. Horace Greeley recorded his observations of the Plains Indians after a trip out west. He noted their inability or unwillingness to work and improve themselves and their environment, a failing that guaranteed their extinction: "To the prosaic observer, the average Indian of the woods and prairies is a being who does little credit to human nature—a slave of appetite and sloth, never emancipated from the tyranny of one animal passion save by the more ravenous demands of another. As I passed over those magnificent bottoms of the Kansas . . . and saw their owners sitting around the doors of their lodges at the height of the planting season and in as good, bright planting weather as sun and soil ever made, I could not help saying, 'These people must die out—there is no help for them. God has given this earth to those who will subdue and cultivate it, and it is vain to struggle against His righteous decree.' "[7]

The impending disappearance of an unworthy race provided its own rationale for American migration and settlement. As undeserving stewards of God's bounty and heedless to the efforts of a higher civilization, the savages justly reaped the whirlwind of destruction. The transformation of the barren Plains into a garden would invariably follow. Now that Douglas's railroad bill had passed, these inevitables would accelerate. The Indians did not read these predictions of their demise, or if they did, they paid them little attention. In the meantime, they would not fade away.

The stray cow, or the stolen cow, quickly became dinner for Conquering Bear's camp, a welcome meal in a dry, hot season when dust had replaced the prairie grasses. Besides, the annuities promised by the government were late, and the four thousand Lakota Sioux in the camp were hungry. The cow had belonged to a group of Swedish Mormon emigrants traveling to Brigham Young's new city in the Utah territory. They reported the loss to Lieutenant Hugh B. Fleming at Fort Laramie, who questioned Conquering Bear about the animal. Since the cow's return was no longer possible, Conquering Bear offered a horse as compensation, a more than generous exchange. Ordinarily, the matter would have ended there, but Fleming had arbitrated a series of thefts since the overland season began in May 1854, and he determined to end the pilfering once and for all. Fleming rejected the offer, demanding that the chief turn over the young man who had dispatched the cow.[8]

The next day, Second Lieutenant John L. Grattan, fresh out of West Point, and eager for action, gathered troops and two large cannons mounted on wagons from Fort Laramie and rode to Conquering Bear's camp to enforce Lieutenant Fleming's order. Conquering Bear explained to Grattan that the offending Indian did not even belong to his tribe but was visiting from another

camp and had no intention of turning himself in. While the two sides continued their negotiations, the young warriors from a nearby Sioux camp streamed
quietly into Conquering Bear's settlement to join their colleagues in preparation for battle.

Lieutenant Grattan, sensing the futility of continued discussions, broke off
the negotiations and ordered his troops to fire on the settlement. Conquering
Bear fell wounded, but three hundred warriors rose from the dry creek bed
below the camp and swarmed over Grattan's twenty-nine soldiers, killing all
but one. When a party from the fort arrived to identify and collect the bodies,
they found Lieutenant Grattan with twenty-four arrows in his body. They
could identify him only by his watch. The Sioux, realizing they would probably not receive their annuities now, raided a nearby post for supplies and galloped out of the North Platte Valley for higher country. Conquering Bear,
transported on a travois, died of his wounds. Thus began the Plains Indian
Wars, a conflict that would not end until 1877.

News of Grattan's misfortune did not reach the public until about three
weeks later. The *Missouri Republican* broke the story under the headline
"Treacherous Slaughter of U. States Troops at Fort Laramie." Similar head-
lines soon appeared in the eastern press, led by "Troops Massacred by the
Indians" in Greeley's *New York Tribune*. Commanding General of the Army
Winfield Scott promised a "singular punishment" for the Sioux and dis-
patched General William S. Harney with six hundred men for that purpose.
Harney vowed, "By God, I'm for battle—no peace."[9]

Not everyone thirsted for revenge. Missouri Democratic congressman
Thomas Hart Benton believed there was more to the Grattan story than a
contrived ambush. If treachery occurred, the government and the migrants
shared in the deception. The death of Conquering Bear, who had resigned
himself to accommodation and who had promoted peace between the Sioux
and the white man, pained Benton in particular. He read the following tribute into the *Congressional Globe*:

> We knew him well, and a better friend the white man never had. He
> was brave, and gentle, and kind—a wise ruler, a skillful warrior, and
> respected chieftain. Even in accepting his position, assigned to him
> some four years ago at the treaty of Laramie, he only consented after
> much persuasion; and then remarked when he did so, that he gave
> his life to the Great Spirit. So far from any charge of treachery attach-
> ing to his conduct, his own fate is a sufficient proof of his fidelity; in
> recording it, we feel like inscribing a worthy memorial of one of the
> most high-toned and chivalric of all Indians we have known.[10]

The tribute fell on deaf ears. This was not a time of nuance, of mourning Grattan and his men yet understanding the circumstances that led to their deaths. It was a time for righteous retribution.

In the spring and early summer of 1855, the Lakota continued their raids on trading posts and migrants' livestock. Thomas Twiss, the federal Indian agent stationed at Fort Laramie, warned the Lakota about General Harney's mission and urged them to come to the fort to avoid certain destruction. Most Lakota warriors understood the long odds of fighting an army regiment, well armed and well provisioned. They heeded the warning and left for Fort Laramie. By August, Twiss could write to the secretary of the interior, "the Sioux difficulties have been magnified by false and malicious reports. There is not, as I can find, within this Agency, a hostile Indian. On the contrary, all are friendly." Three bands of Lakota Sioux, however, remained north of the Platte River, and beyond the protection of Fort Laramie. Little Thunder headed one of the bands. Though friendly to whites, Little Thunder had decided to remain in his camp to supervise and protect the women who were drying meat from the hunt.[11]

General Harney approached Little Thunder's camp and dismissed a request to negotiate: "As we had come for war and not for peace, we paid no attention to them." Cavalry blocked the band's retreat. Trapped, the Indians fell under withering rifle fire. Of the 250 Lakota, Harney killed 86 and captured 70. Most were women and children. Harney lost four men. Most of the soldiers did not realize that they were killing mainly women and children, though General Harney and some of the senior officers knew there were families in Little Thunder's camp.[12]

That evening, or maybe the next one, a young Lakota Sioux called Light Hair returned to Little Thunder's camp. As a boy, he and his friends had watched the long wagon trains stir up billowing clouds of dust as they passed along the Oregon Trail. When the trains had reached the far horizon, the boys scampered down from their ridge and collected items discarded by the migrants as they lightened their load for the tougher journey ahead. Slight of build, with wispy light brown hair, a rarity among the Sioux, Light Hair had overcome his unimposing physical stature to earn the respect of younger Lakota by the time he had reached the age of fifteen. On this occasion, Light Hair had been out hunting with several other young Sioux. The scene they found astonished them: acrid smoke rose from the camp; lodge poles lay broken and scattered over the terrain; bodies, now stiff, strewn about like sticks. Light Hair stumbled upon a woman; both of her breasts had been cut off. Almost all the bodies he encountered bore marks of mutilation. He covered the corpses as best he could. The Lakota Sioux chose a name for General Harney: Woman Killer.

The Black Hills of present-day South Dakota remain sacred to the Lakota Sioux. Deep in the interior of the hills, there is a high granite summit where the Sioux performed religious ceremonies and where warriors came for visions and courage. This holy place is now called Harney Peak.

In such a place, Light Hair went to dream. In his dream, a young man on horseback burst from the bottom of a lake and galloped across the plains, long hair flowing in the wind and a reddish brown stone tied behind his left ear. Blue hailstones adorned his bare chest, and a painted lightning bolt shot across one side of his face. The rider and his horse were running, running from an ominous rolling cloud filled with thunder and lightning that unleashed a relentless volley of bullets and arrows. Remarkably, the horse and rider remained unscathed, protected perhaps by a red-tailed hawk soaring above them. But then his own people suddenly appeared and surrounded the rider and pulled him from the horse. The dream ended.

Light Hair climbed down from the mountain, exhausted yet awed by the vision, a dream that occurred only to a chosen few of the Lakota Sioux. What it meant for him and for his people, he could not tell, except that the dark rolling cloud was coming closer.

By the terms of the Fort Laramie Treaty, the Plains Indians agreed to allow the government to build roads through their land. Douglas's railroad bill accelerated the road-building program by opening up the Kansas and Nebraska territories to settlement. Clashes between Indians and whites increased, as did the interventions of the United States Army. The Indians were demonstrating that they were indeed "obstacles" to white civilization, as Douglas had called them, but their removal or subjugation proved considerably more difficult than he had anticipated. As the Plains war lurched along in a cycle of Indian raids on wagon trains followed by retaliation from federal troops, which, in turn, inspired more Indian attacks, a conflict erupted among white settlers in Kansas.

Migrants came to Kansas to make a living and to fulfill a mission. Eli Thayer was one of those men whom only the nineteenth century could have produced, an individual typifying the unending curiosity and thirst for new things that characterized America at that time: an educator, inventor, founder of a colony of anti-slavery families in Virginia, and a politician. His latest enterprise was the Massachusetts Emigrant Aid Society, organized to subsidize anti-slavery settlers who wished to migrate to Kansas. He formed the society with the financial support of several wealthy New Englanders in April 1854. Although only 1,240 settlers took up Thayer's offer, the mere formation of such an organization raised the stakes of the contest. Speaking for the anti-slavery forces, William H. Seward declared in the Senate, "We will engage in competition for the virgin soil of Kansas, and God give this victory to the side which is strong in numbers as it is in right." South Carolina editor Robert Barnwell Rhett welcomed the challenge, urging fellow southerners to "send men to Kansas ready to cast in their lot with the proslavery party there and able to meet Abolitionism on its own issue, and with its own weapons." Especially promising from the southern perspective was the proximity of Missouri, a slave state, next door to Kansas. Missouri senator David Atchison, who had already vowed to "Mormonize" Thayer's minions, rallied his fellow Missourians to take the fight across the border to Kansas: "We are playing for a mighty stake; if we win we carry slavery to the Pacific Ocean, if we fail we lose Missouri, Arkansas, and Texas and all the territories."[13]

Not only did men from Missouri pour across the border to vote illegally in the first territorial legislature election in March 1855, but they harassed free-soilers passing through their state. In one such instance, Missourians attacked the Rev. William Moore, a Methodist preacher, forced alcohol down his throat, and threatened to kill him. In Missouri, pro-slavery mobs set upon anti-slavery ministers, occasionally tearing them from the pulpit, tarring, shooting, or other-wise abusing them. Such stories circulated widely in the evangelical press and further polarized northern and southern religious communities. Henry Ward Beecher raised money to purchase weapons for anti-slavery settlers in Kansas to defend themselves from the Missouri ruffians. "Beecher's Bibles" contrib-uted to a growing arms race in the territory that only fueled the violence.

Day-tripping Missourians, some twelve hundred of them, helped them-selves to ballots in neighboring Kansas on election day to cast five thousand votes (this is Missouri math) and, with anti-slavery forces boycotting what they considered a fraudulent process, succeeded in electing a pro-slavery ter-ritorial legislature. Roughly half the total votes cast were illegal. Strange ir-regularities appeared, such as one district that counted over six hundred votes though only twelve eligible voters resided there. The voting rolls of another district included names copied directly from the Cincinnati city directory.

The actions of the pro-slavery legislature confirmed the worst fears of those in the North who suspected a Slave Power conspiracy. Among the laws inscribed by Kansas lawmakers included a statute mandating the death pen-alty for aiding a fugitive slave, and another making it a felony to question slaveholding in Kansas. For good measure, the pro-slavery majority expelled the few free-staters elected to the assembly. In response, the free-staters es-tablished their own government in Topeka and vowed to make Kansas white.

By November 1855, Kansas had two territorial governments and a civil war. That beat Congress, which, when it convened in December 1855, could not agree on any government for Kansas. The House did not organize itself until February, confounded by the multitude of parties and factions. The contending parties in Kansas continued to spar with each other in isolated acts of violence through the early spring of 1856. On May 21, 1856, a group of pro-slavery men subjected the free-state stronghold of Lawrence to a heavy artillery barrage. No one was killed, but the town suffered substantial damage. The eastern press, monitoring the simmering contest unfolding in the new territory, transformed the episode into the beginning of Armageddon. The *New York Tribune* posted a banner headline: "Startling News from Kansas— The War Actually Begun—Triumph of the Border Ruffians—Lawrence in Ruins—Several Persons Slaughtered—Freedom Bloodily Subdued." The parts about the town's total destruction and the loss of life were palpably false, but they sold newspapers. The "sack of Lawrence" now took its place alongside the Visigoth hordes descending upon Rome.[14]

The disintegration of law and order on the Plains reminded many Americans of the failed European revolutions of 1848. The actions of the pro-slavery territorial legislature were especially troubling, and northern congressmen drew parallels between Kansas and the restoration of oppressive regimes in Europe. Indiana congressman Schuyler Colfax compared the territorial legislature's pro-slavery statutes, "dictated and enacted by usurpers and tyrants," to Louis Napoleon's wresting of democracy from the French people and confirming his ascension to power with a fraudulent plebiscite: "the mockery of the pretended freedom of elections . . . the shackles upon the freedom of speech; all . . . emanate from an autocrat who . . . governs France with a strong arm and an iron rule."[15]

For evangelicals, the desecration of democracy and the escalating violence in Kansas were mere preludes to a larger conflict to cleanse America, and the world, from sin. If the West held the brightest promise for the fulfillment of America's divine mission, then Kansas was now its vital center. "It is obvious . . . that the great conflict is . . . marshaling the two orders of civilization to a final encounter. . . . Kansas . . . the geographical centre of the western continent, is also the pivot of its most vital and determinative controversy. . . . [W]hat France is to Europe—this region of Kansas will be to the great valley of the west. It holds the key to . . . civilization. . . . [F]rom its capacious womb shall proceed the busy millions destined to redeem or to disgrace the extensive fields beyond." Would America lose or sustain its role as a light unto the world?[16]

Though the retreat from the rule of law in Kansas troubled Americans, violence per se no longer seemed a sinister subversion of democracy. Rather, more Americans believed that the fate of their institutions, and now their very lives, depended on meeting the enemy with force in kind. Violence as a solution to removing threats to American destiny, whether in Charlestown, Massachusetts, in Texas, or on the Great Plains, was nothing new. The enemy now, however, was not an alien religion or alien "races" but each other. Abolitionists, who, for all their rants against compromise, the Constitution, and the laws of the land, had rarely abandoned their pacifism, now advocated a strong-armed response. The swift restoration of reactionary regimes in Europe, the Fugitive Slave Law, and the Kansas-Nebraska Act had prepared them for this moment. But it was the blood on the Plains that stirred the fires of retaliation in the hearts of the righteous. They now associated cries for "law and order" with Europe's despots, not with democracy. Pennsylvania congressman Galusha Grow argued, "Law and order is the excuse of despotism the world over. . . . It was to preserve law and order that . . . the dungeon and the rack silenced the voice of patriotism in Hungary. To preserve law and order, the streets of Naples are crowded with chained gangs . . . guilty of no offence save that they hate oppression and love liberty."[17]

The peoples of Europe faced overwhelming odds in battling authoritarian regimes, but Americans had a vital revolutionary legacy, a tradition of baptizing democracy in blood. William H. Seward stood on the floor of the Senate and declared that he knew "the value of peace, and order, and tranquility. . . . But I know also the still greater value of Liberty. When you hear me justify the despotism of the Czar of Russia over the oppressed Poles, or the treachery by which Louis Napoleon rose to a throne on the ruins of the Republic in France, on the ground that he preserves domestic peace among his subjects, then you may expect me to vote supplies of men and money to the President . . . to execute the edicts of the Missouri borderers in the Territory of Kansas."[18]

Outrage and righteousness engulfed the Senate. A day before the sack of Lawrence, Massachusetts's Charles Sumner presented a lengthy speech on "The Crime Against Kansas." Sumner uncorked predictable perorations on the perfidy of the Slave Power and the rectitude of the free-staters. His stemwinder included the sexual imagery that northerners often employed in their depictions of the West, that pro-slavery settlers were committing "the rape of a virgin Territory, compelling it to the hateful embrace of slavery."[19]

Southerners had sat through these diatribes before, and, considering the source—a man who had repeatedly proposed repeal of the Fugitive Slave Law—they allowed the rant to proceed unmolested. However, at one point in the speech, Sumner singled out South Carolina senator Andrew P. Butler for particular attention. Butler had been a strong supporter of the territorial legislature and a critic of free-state activities in Kansas. Sumner portrayed Butler as a "Don Quixote who had chosen a mistress to whom he has made his vows, and who . . . though polluted in the sight of the world is chaste in his sight—I mean the harlot, slavery." The frequent imagery of sexual defilement was particularly noxious at the time. When directed at an individual who valued and protected the chastity of women above all else, it was unforgivable. Even in metaphor, Sumner's charge was a major slur. But Sumner did not stop there. Senator Butler was an elderly gentleman and, as a result of either a minor stroke or bad teeth, had difficulty controlling his saliva when he spoke so that, occasionally, he literally spit out his words. Sumner mimicked Butler's speech impediment, mocking his "loose expectoration."[20]

Regrettably, such a display of poor taste was no longer unusual in the United States Senate. But South Carolina congressman Preston Brooks, Butler's cousin, moved to defend his family's honor. The day after the sack of Lawrence, he entered a mostly empty Senate chamber—the Senate was not in session that day—and found Senator Sumner writing at his desk. Brooks carried a gutta-percha cane, and he struck Sumner some thirty blows to the head and shoulders in less than half a minute, as the Massachusetts senator could not get up from his seat to defend himself. Several lawmakers heard the commotion, but Brooks's colleague South Carolina representative Lawrence Keitt prevented them from coming to the senator's aid. The attack severely wounded Sumner. His seat in the Senate chamber stood empty for three years while he recovered; mute testimony to the wages of violence.

First "Bleeding Kansas," and now "Bleeding Sumner." To read the accounts of the incident in northern and southern newspapers was to measure the distance between two sides of an escalating conflict. The only question that seemed to remain was how far the breech would widen before the nation would crack. Horace Greeley and the *New York Tribune* fed the northern perception that the hallowed halls of Congress had now become an extension of Kansas, that the civil war in that territory had crossed a continent and spilled its blood on the nation's capital. The issue was no longer merely the extension of slavery in the territories but the enslavement of all Americans to the dictates of the Slave Power: "No meaner exhibition of Southern cowardice—generally miscalled Southern chivalry—was ever witnessed. . . . The reasons for the absence of collision between North and South—collision of sentiment and person—which existed a few years back, have ceased; and as the South has taken the oligarchic ground that Slavery ought to exist, irrespective of color . . . that Democracy is a delusion and a lie."[21]

Historians have written volumes about the concept of Southern Honor, about how the public image of a man required satisfaction if abused by a man of equal stature. Northerners cherished the concept of honor as well, though it may not have been as evident in their more urban, cosmopolitan society. If they perceived unwonted assaults on their liberties and leaders, however, they would act to uphold their honor, as decent men should.

Southerners swaggered to line up in support of Brooks. Sumner, they felt, was overdue for a severe chastisement. They showered Brooks with new canes, and, though the vote in the House of Representatives to expel him fell short of the required two-thirds majority, he resigned anyway and his constituents re-elected him in a landslide, a further insult to Sumner's defenders. A newspaper in Edgefield, South Carolina, Brooks's district, captured the sentiment in the Lower South: "Some say he [Sumner] received fifty stripes, yet we very much doubt if the Captain cared to exceed the legal number of thirty-nine, usually applied to scamps.... We feel that our Representative did exactly right; and we are sure his people will commend him highly for it.... [W]e have borne insult long enough, and now let the conflict come if it must."[22]

Georgia's Alexander Stephens had always lamented the loss of decorum and civility in Washington. But the northern reaction to the Kansas-Nebraska Act radicalized him and his constituents. His bemused endorsement of Brooks's actions and the stifling of free speech in democracy's forum indicated how far he had gone down the sectional road in just two years. "Brooks whipped Sumner the other day," he noted nonchalantly. "I have no objection to the liberty of speech when the liberty of the cudgel is left free to combat it." It was as if Sumner had behaved like a fractious slave and received an appropriate punishment, a connection that inflamed northern public opinion. Stephens's bemusement was palpable: "The Yankees seem greatly excited about the Sumner flogging. They are afraid the practice may become general & many of [their] heads already feel sore."[23]

One northerner determined to take the battle directly to the slaveholders. In 1848, Frederick Douglass received an invitation to visit a white man in Springfield, Massachusetts, known for his anti-slavery views. Douglass had met a number of such men since he had left bondage, but this person was different. In what he said and in how he looked, this man was a breed apart from the middle-class reformers Douglass had encountered, or from any other human being for that matter. The meeting so captivated Douglass that he set his impressions down immediately, describing the man, who stood "straight and symmetrical as a mountain pine. His bearing was singularly impressive.... His hair was coarse, strong, slightly gray, and closely trimmed, and grew low on his forehead. ... His eyes ... were full of light and fire."[24]

Douglass sat down at a spare pine table, and the man's wife and children waited on them. The white man looked older than his years, "lean, strong, and sinewy, ... built for times of trouble." What particularly struck Douglass was the ease with which the white man conversed with him, as an equal without affect or condescension. The white man unveiled a scheme to establish a black state in the Appalachian Mountains comprised of escaped slaves protected from recapture by an armed militia. How and when slaves would rise up and make their way to the mountains remained unclear, but the white man was convinced that a sign or a prophet would trigger the exodus. What Douglass thought of the plan remains unknown, but the man impressed him as a committed anti-slavery warrior willing to give his life to free his fellow man. They would meet again.[25]

Kansas stirred the white man's imagination. Here was a battleground where, unlike in the South, the slaveholder could not count on neighbors or government to protect his ill-begotten institution. So he went west with his sons. Connecticut native John Brown was fifty-six years old in May 1856, an age when most middle-class men in eastern cities were at the height of their business careers, engaged in civic activities, and doting on grandchildren. Brown had a family, a large family, but had not yet settled down to one particular occupation. He had a calling, though. He viewed himself as a liberator, and the chaos in Kansas afforded an opportunity to avenge the sin of slavery. The sack of Lawrence provided an immediate cause. At a small settlement along Pottawatomie Creek, Brown and his sons invaded the cabin of a pro-slavery family, dragged three men outside, shot the father through the head, and hacked and mutilated his two sons with broadswords. Ritual murders.

The eastern press, which had already inflated atrocities and inflamed public opinion on "Bleeding Kansas," at first dismissed stories of the murders. The *New York Tribune* went so far as to report that Comanche Indians had murdered the family, as evidenced by the mutilated corpses, something white men would never do. As the *Tribune* concluded with unintended irony, "Terrible stories have floated through the newspapers, distorted and misrepresented by those whose interest it was to misrepresent them." When it appeared that initial reports were proven correct, the *Tribune* placed Brown's actions within the larger context of "Bleeding Kansas." It was a civil war, after all, and bad things happened to both sides. In the meantime, Brown and his sons headed back east to raise money for a larger plan.[26]

The three incidents—the sack of Lawrence, the caning of Sumner, and John Brown's bloody foray to Pottawatomie Creek—occurred within days of each other. They blended together in the public mind and offered confirmation for the worst perspective of each section. If few northerners read southern newspapers and magazines and vice versa, northern and southern editors were certain to keep their readers informed. In September 1856, J. D. B. De Bow, a leading advocate for southern commercial and industrial development, and editor of the widely read magazine *De Bow's Review*, editorialized on "The War Against the South." It was less an editorial than a compilation of what the northern press and northern politicians were saying since the May incidents in Kansas and Washington, D.C. He collected the pieces with a sense of urgency as anti-slavery men were "coming nearer and nearer to the possession of the Federal power." The danger to the South and its institutions was no longer abstract, as the prayer of Ohio Republican congressman Joshua Giddings demonstrated: "I look forward to the day when there shall be a servile insurrection in the South, when the black man . . . shall assert his freedom, and wage a war of extermination against his master; when the torch of the incendiary shall light up the towns and cities of the South, and blot out the last vestige of slavery. And though I may not mock at their calamity, nor laugh when their fear cometh, yet I will hail it as the dawn of a political millennium." De Bow also quoted from Ralph Waldo Emerson's essay published in response to the assault on Senator Charles Sumner. Emerson concluded, as Greeley had, "I think we must get rid of slavery, or we must get rid of freedom." The nation could not persist as a whole with such disparate parts.[27]

Again referring to the Sumner assault, De Bow selected the following exegesis from the *Boston Chronicle.* The asterisks "supply the place of a sentence too infamous to be repeated." "Is it at all likely that animals * * * who tear little children from the arms of their mothers in order that they may be sold into everlasting bondage, is it at all likely, we ask, that such brutes would hesitate to murder the man who, in the discharge of his duty, has occasion to remind them of their crimes?"[28]

Without apparently realizing that his words confirmed the assertions of his northern antagonists, De Bow quoted approvingly from an item in the *Galveston News* about a Texas legislator who had criticized the pro-slavery faction in Kansas: "That your right in common with every other citizen, to free opinion, free discussion, and the largest liberty of self-defense, is fully recognized, and will be respected. But there is one subject connected with your course in the Legislature—that of slavery—on which neither you nor any one entertaining your views, will be permitted to appear before the community, in a public manner. . . . The entire subject of slavery, in all its connections, is forbidden ground, which you shall not invade."[29]

The events in Kansas energized the new Republican Party. Formed in several northern states in the aftermath of the Kansas-Nebraska Act, the party sought to broaden its base in advance of the 1856 presidential election. In particular, the Republicans hoped to attract former Whigs, such as Abraham Lincoln, who had feared that the new party's radicalism on the slavery issue endangered the Union. The Republicans also looked to disaffected northern

Know Nothings now as concerned about the threat of the Slave Power as with the threat of immigrants. There were Democrats as well, such as David Wilmot, who could no longer follow a party indifferent to the extension of slavery in the territories.

The Republicans represented themselves as the antidote to the Slave Power. Though they welcomed support in the South, they moved forward as an avowedly sectional party, attuned not only to northerners' opposition to slavery in the territories but to their economic interests as well: promoting a homestead act to open the territories to working men and women and their families; a higher tariff to protect the nascent industries of the Northeast and Midwest and the workers and entrepreneurs in those enterprises; and a vigorous program of internal improvements, especially a transcontinental railroad, to knit the far-flung western territories to the eastern seaboard facilitating migration and commerce. While former Know Nothings lent a nativist cast to some local races, by and large, the new party did not endorse anti-immigrant legislation. Instead, recognizing the growing influence of immigrants in American urban life, they appealed to their sense of fairness in keeping the territories white, and in maintaining an economic development program that would enhance opportunities for everyone.

"Bleeding Kansas" and "Bleeding Sumner" came at the beginning of the 1856 presidential campaign, a coincidence that only exacerbated sectional tension and further scrambled party affiliation. In northern states, leaders fashioned fusion tickets from the remnants of old parties. In the South, the Democratic Party presented itself as the protector of southern rights, and though the American, or Know Nothing, Party and the moribund Whigs continued to find adherents, especially in border cities, the Democrats increasingly cornered the political market in the cotton states. The fluidity of party politics that characterized the North was much less common in the South. Alexander Stephens abandoned two decades of hostility to the Democratic Party and joined his former enemies. The equality of the South in the Union meant more to him than any other issue. In fact, there really were no other issues; all derived from this basic principle.

The party switch was more agonizing for Abraham Lincoln. He had rebuffed Republican attempts to "unwhig him," as he put it in 1854, and he abhorred the nativism of the Know Nothings. But events in Kansas left Lincoln "ready to fuse with anyone who would unite with him to oppose the slave power." In May 1856, Lincoln took the plunge and attended the Illinois state convention of the Republican Party.[30]

Carl Schurz also faced a difficult decision. Most of his countrymen favored the Democratic Party. The Know Nothings were anathema, and the Whigs had dabbled around the fringes of nativism. Their combination in the new party did not endear the Republicans initially to the German community. But the strong anti-slavery orientation of the Republicans made forty-eighters listen. The party seemed to embody the principles of their revolution more than the political alternatives.

Walt Whitman was a lifelong Democrat, despite his flirtation with the Free Soilers. He had reveled in the Democrats' celebration of the individual and the party's inclusiveness. His poetry was the literary version of Democratic philosophy. The publication in 1855 of *Leaves of Grass* marked a major event in American literature, though, at the time, this was not apparent. What was obvious, however, was that *Leaves of Grass* was very different from anything that had come before. Unlike the formal rhymed and metered poetry of Henry Wadsworth Longfellow and John Greenleaf Whittier, Whitman's poems were improvisational and dealt with subjects such as the sensuality of the human body and the excesses of slavery in such vivid imagery that some reviewers condemned the work as obscene. Lincoln, an avid reader of American literature, carried around a dog-eared copy that he hid from his wife, Mary, who scorned it as perverted, though she had not read it.

What made the sectional divide especially troubling for Whitman was its threat to the Union and its divine mission. Whitman longed for a "Redeemer President," who would mend the separation and return the nation to its redemptive course. He was not certain if the Republicans could respond to that calling, but he was increasingly sure the Democrats could not.[31]

Harriet Beecher Stowe did not take long to throw herself headlong into the Republican cause. Here, at last, was a party dedicated to preserving the freedom of the territories. Even if party leaders equivocated on abolition, at least they were willing to stand up to the Slave Power's attacks on democracy. From December 1855 to September 1856—a time that spanned both the Kansas incidents and the presidential campaign—Harriet wrote a second anti-slavery novel, *Dred: A Tale of the Great Dismal Swamp*. Though less successful both artistically and financially than *Uncle Tom's Cabin*, the new novel reflected a shift in Harriet's perspective on slavery, as well as the impact of Kansas and the rise of the Republican Party on her writing.

Whereas Tom was saintly, Dred, an escaped slave and the purported son of Denmark Vesey, the former slave who led an abortive revolt in Charleston, South Carolina, in 1822, vows "a day of vengeance" against the slaveholders. Inspired by Old Testament parables of righteousness and revenge, Dred develops his plot. But Milly, a female slave, quoting pacifist passages from the New Testament, persuades Dred to drop his scheme. Dred's conversion is useless, as whites discover the plot and kill him. While Harriet took special care to depict the South and white southerners evenhandedly in *Uncle Tom's Cabin*, she is now extremely critical of southerners. Harriet also implies that martyrdom, however saintly, will neither impress slaveholders nor weaken slavery. More forceful strategies are necessary.[32]

The 1856 election campaign reflected the remarkable transformation that had changed not only American politics but also public opinion. The middle ground continued to shrink. Men such as Lincoln and Stephens sought out party affiliations that would cater to sectional interests even as they did so in the name of the Union. Both men still loved the Union but wondered if it could, or even should, survive in its present state. For Harriet Beecher Stowe, violence now seemed a viable and even necessary alternative. Her brother Henry Ward Beecher shipped guns to Kansas. Ministers and laymen north and south increasingly perceived violence as a policy option.

The upstart Republicans held their convention in Philadelphia in mid-July in a revivalist fervor reminiscent of the earlier Liberty and Free Soil party gatherings. The delegates framed a platform condemning the "twin relics of barbarism"—slavery and polygamy. It would be difficult to sustain an argument that polygamy represented a threat to the American body politic in the mid-1850s. There was no epidemic, current or pending, of men and women seeking multiple partners. As everyone at the time understood, however, the Mormons in Utah Territory espoused, though did not require, polygamy as part of their religious doctrine. Memories of Mormon settlements and the turmoil they generated remained fresh in the minds of midwesterners, a likely constituency for Republican votes. While anti-slavery sentiment varied, few voters were sympathetic to the Mormons.[33]

Polygamy was also a code word to mid-nineteenth-century Americans, especially to northerners and especially when paired with slavery. Polygamy attacked traditional family relations, as did slavery. Slavery and polygamy unleashed the same unbridled passions that would destroy religion, republican government, and the family, the basic institutions that held together far-flung Americans in the nineteenth century. Both reflected an absence of personal discipline. Linking slavery to a despised religious movement further discredited the institution and its supporters as beyond the pale of Christian democratic civilization. From there, it was but a few steps to read southerners out of America, as facile as dismissing Indians and Mexicans as vanishing relics of inferior civilizations.

The pairing of slavery and polygamy also highlighted the threat of both to a modern America, a nation devoted to progress, technology, and self-improvement. These "relics of barbarism" harked back to a dark (and Catholic) past when superstition and dependence bedeviled mankind. They were, in a word, un-American, at least the America posited by the new party and its followers.

The Republicans nominated Lieutenant Colonel John C. Frémont as their first presidential candidate, passing over more prominent names such as New York's William H. Seward and Ohio's Salmon P. Chase. Frémont's selection reflected both the fledgling party's attempt to broaden its appeal in the North and the tried-and-true Whig formula of nominating a military hero for the presidency. His lack of political experience—he was not a member of the party—placed him above the dirty fray of politics. Frémont's greatest asset was his wife, Jessie Benton Frémont, the daughter of Missouri's former Democratic senator and congressman Thomas Hart Benton. Lincoln later called her "quite a female politician." She managed her husband's campaign, ghostwrote his rare position papers, and advised the political novice not to say a word. Frémont, handsome and youthful, also represented the new party's appeal to the West, a region that held a special place in the American imagination. For a party focused on keeping the West white and free, a western candidate made sense. The Pathfinder, as Frémont was known, had helped create the West, both in image and in fact. Here was a new party with a new man from a new place to bring a new day to America.[34]

The Republican platform reflected the party's origins as an amalgam of anti-slavery Democrats, Whigs, and northern Know Nothings. The platform demanded the exclusion of slavery from the territories and the admission of Kansas as a free state, though in deference to conservative former Whigs, it did not call for the abolition of slavery in the District of Columbia.

The Democrats turned away from likely candidates out of necessity. The Kansas-Nebraska Act, followed closely by the clashes in Kansas and in the Senate, had alienated many northern Democrats against both President Pierce and Stephen A. Douglas. Facing a northern revolt and southern steadfastness against any candidate who would not support pro-slavery interests in the territories, the party turned to Pennsylvania's James Buchanan. His greatest virtue was that he had been out of the country the previous four years serving as ambassador to Great Britain. He had no established position on the slavery question. Southerners accepted him as electable. Northern Democrats hoped for the best. A blank slate was better than anyone tainted by either the Douglas bill or the war in Kansas. Buchanan was hardly a political novice, though. Unlike Frémont, Buchanan had been involved in politics for more than thirty years by the time of his nomination. He had cultivated a reputation as a friend of the South, and his closest friends were southerners. Tall and white-haired, he exuded an air of experience, though, according to one observer, he had the countenance of a "well-preserved mummy."[35]

The Know Nothing movement began to disintegrate as the slavery issue took precedence. The Know Nothings split into northern and southern factions, with many in the northern wing declaring for the Republican Party despite false rumors that Frémont was a Roman Catholic. It was a shocking denouement for a party that just one short year earlier had scored significant electoral successes in several major northern and border cities, trading on the immigration issue as a primary concern of native-born urbanites. All they could muster from their shattered convention was the nomination of former president Millard Fillmore, who, like his Republican counterpart, was not even a member of the party whose standard he carried.

With the Democratic Party as the only national political organization in the race, the presidential campaign of 1856 unfolded as a series of local and regional contests directed at specific audiences, primarily in the North and in the competitive border states. The Democrats would prevail overwhelmingly in the Lower South. In the North, the Democrats tried simultaneously to shore up their immigrant base by noting the connections between the Republicans and the erstwhile Know Nothings, and to appeal to evangelicals by intimating that Frémont had received a Catholic education, had studied for the priesthood, or was himself a secret Roman Catholic. Claims also surfaced alleging that Frémont and New York's Archbishop John Hughes had, on occasion, staggered drunkenly through the streets of the city at night on their way home from evening mass. The circumstantial evidence was sufficient for Democratic papers to cry out that Frémont was "*the instrument of vice, and the foe of God and of Freedom.*" Punning on the Republican declaration of "Free Soil and Frémont," Democratic editors quipped, "Free Love and Frémont."[36]

Democrats also denounced the meddling of evangelicals in politics. The party initiated a new publication, *Political Priestcraft Exposed,* to promote this connection and unfurled a large banner in lower Manhattan portraying a priest standing on a Bible with a revolver in one hand and a rifle in the other, bearing the caption "Beecher's Command—kill each other with Sharp's Rifles." It remains unknown what Lyman Beecher thought of his favorite son got up in the garb of a Roman Catholic priest.[37]

The Democrats played both sides of the religious aisle because the sectional crisis had energized northern churches, most of which had remained neutral over the issue of slavery, as a frustrated Harriet Beecher Stowe noted time and again in *Uncle Tom's Cabin.* But after the Kansas-Nebraska Act, and especially with events in Kansas and the caning of Senator Charles Sumner, more evangelical ministers began to speak out on political issues, justifying their position by emphasizing the moral questions these issues raised.

The Democrats also cast the election as a referendum on the Union, especially in the North. A Republican victory, they charged, would assuredly precipitate a secessionist movement in the South. Although the Republicans disavowed abolitionism, Democrats intimated that the party's radical fringe would have greater influence in a sectional crisis, further polarizing the nation and precipitating both a race war and a civil war. Widely circulated comments by southern Democrats confirmed this view. Virginia's Democratic governor, Henry A. Wise, declared that a Republican victory "would be an open, overt proclamation of public war." Georgia's Robert Toombs vowed that the "election of Frémont would be the end of the Union, and ought to be."[38]

The importance of evangelical imagery in the political campaigns of the major parties was especially evident among the Republicans, the heirs of the revivalist free-soil movement. A participant in the party convention allowed that the gathering resembled a "Methodist conference rather than a political convention," and another characterized the party platform as "God's revealed Word." Delegates concluded the convention with a rousing chorus of "The Frémont Crusader's Song": "We've truth on our side / We've God for our guide."[39]

The Republicans' campaign erased any line between religion and politics. Churches became party gathering places; ministers stumped for the party's candidates and even served as poll watchers. Frémont and his wife capped the campaign on election eve by attending the "Church of the Holy Rifles," as evangelicals proudly called Henry Ward Beecher's Plymouth Church in Brooklyn. The congregation gave the couple a rousing ovation.[40]

The ubiquity of religious rhetoric and imagery in the Republican campaign, however, further polarized an already divided Union. One minister depicted the upcoming election as "a decisive struggle . . . between freedom and Slavery, truth and falsehood, justice and oppression, God and the devil." The Republican faithful chimed in with an Election Day spiritual: "Think that God's eye is on you; / Let not your faith grow dim; / For each vote cast for Frémont / Is a vote cast for Him!"[41]

Away from the pulpit, Republican campaigners sometimes found tough going in the North. A portion of the northern electorate perceived the Republicans as a gilded version of the radical anti-slavery parties of the 1840s, promoting racial equality and emancipation to the detriment of the white population, an association the Democrats exploited. As Lincoln stumped for the ticket in Illinois, he confronted hecklers at numerous places throughout the state. The Democratic press charged him with "niggerism."[42]

Buchanan and the Democrats emerged victorious. The only national party had won a national election. Pennsylvania, New Jersey, Illinois, Indiana, and California voted for Buchanan, who swept the Lower South. Buchanan's victory, though, was narrow in these northern states; the Republicans performed remarkably well considering it was the first time they had fielded a presidential candidate. They had achieved a "victorious defeat" and eagerly looked forward to good prospects of prying at least Pennsylvania, Indiana, and Illinois from the Democratic column in 1860.[43]

The South had not yet lapsed into one-party politics. Fillmore garnered 40 percent of the popular vote in the South but won only the state of Maryland. He fared poorly in the Lower South. The states that had the greatest stake in slavery voted solidly Democratic.

Frémont and Fillmore combined outpolled Buchanan in the popular vote, 2.2 million votes to 1.8 million. The Democratic candidate achieved a majority in the electoral college, however, primarily as a result of his strong showing in the South. The results were not comforting for southerners. An upstart avowedly anti-slavery party had carried eleven free states.

The Republicans, except for a radical fringe, loved the Union as much as the Democrats did. The issue was never union or disunion but the nature of the national compact. The Republicans believed that the preservation of the Union was inseparable from the founding ideals and that those ideals were incompatible with the institution of slavery. They perceived a dynamic and prosperous nation and welcomed the changes that flowed all around them, from the settlement of the West to the peopling of the great cities of the East. They believed that slavery, and particularly slaveholders—the Slave Power— impeded both the operation of American ideals and the fulfillment of the nation's great potential. Republicans also agreed that the United States could never fulfill its role as a beacon to the world as long as it sustained the institution of slavery. Most Republicans were not abolitionists because they were constitutionalists. The law of the land was the law of the land. But the territories were another matter.

The Democrats, and more particularly the southern Democrats, cherished the Union as well. They perceived no contradiction between slavery and America's founding precepts. Many of the Founding Fathers, after all, had owned slaves, and although the word "slavery" never appears in the Constitution, the basis of representation and the return of fugitives clearly implied the Founders' tolerance of the institution. Besides, the nation had existed for nearly seventy years as a blend of free states and slave states, and during this time America had attained a continental empire, influence around the world, and untold prosperity. It would be an overstatement to declare that the Republicans looked to the Union of the future, and the Democrats, particularly the southern Democrats, perceived the Union from the perspective of the founding, but if northerners marched confidently into the future, southerners entered tomorrow with trepidation.

Abraham Lincoln retired to his law practice once again. Alexander Stephens, buoyed by the election of Buchanan, looked forward to working with the new administration and reducing sectional animosity in Congress and the nation. President-elect Buchanan spent the days before his inauguration settling his cabinet picks, a majority of whom were southerners, and in discussing various points of law with Supreme Court Chief Justice Roger B. Taney of Maryland.

Out on the Plains, Kansas remained on political tenterhooks, and bands of Lakota Sioux vowed to continue their way of life. The young warrior Light Hair became proficient with bow and arrow. One day, he joined his father on a routine raiding party against the Omaha, seizing livestock, an increasingly necessary activity as the buffalo dwindled. Light Hair claimed his first kill in the battle—a young Omaha woman—an act that earned him derision from his peers.

A year or so later, about the time James Buchanan took the oath of office as president, Light Hair killed two men in a raid on another tribe. In this skirmish he had demonstrated skill and courage, and soon all in camp talked about his bravery. Light Hair's father, a respected medicine man, decided it was time for his son to receive a name more in keeping with a Sioux warrior. In a brief but moving religious ceremony attended by the elders following a tradition as old as the wind that blew across the Plains, the tribe bestowed a new name on Light Hair. Henceforth, the land, his people, and his gods would know him as Crazy Horse.

CHAPTER 6

REVIVAL

THE MEN, somber-faced and silent, decked out in the urban middle-class uniform of black broadcloth and white shirts, ascended the wooden staircase to a large, sparsely furnished room. They stood or took the few chairs, opened their Bibles to pray, spoke of their conversion, and begged for forgiveness. They sang a hymn and went back down the stairs and out into the street crowded with lunchtime shoppers and businessmen purposefully headed somewhere. The worshipers had skipped lunch to read God's word and sing His praises in the fellowship of other men. It was autumn in New York, and the chill air hinted at winter's arrival.[1]

The streets seemed more crowded now than a week or a month ago: scruffy children with their hands out; beggars beseeching a penny or a piece of bread. An economic depression, called a "Panic," had halted prosperity with a thunderclap of vengeance. Wild speculation in western lands and railroads, the bane of frontier regions, had infested eastern financial centers. Rationality succumbed to the fever. Was not progress unending? Was not gold flowing from California? Never mind that the value of railroad stock reflected the hopes of promoters much more than the value of their railroads. A ship carrying millions in gold bullion from California to back the paper currency financing the fever sank. A bank failed. Then others, suddenly chastened, began to call in loans, and the call fell on deaf ears. British banks withdrew their funds from New York banks. Manufacturers could no longer fuel their expansion with borrowed capital as lenders closed their books, and then their doors. Inventories piled up; workers were dismissed; and the misery mounted with the cold weather. It had all happened so quickly: "in broad daylight and in fair weather, the blast came, in obedience to its own laws of existence and motion."[2]

The winter of 1857–58 would be hard. Already, children were dying in the squalid Irish warrens of lower Manhattan, and the poor in other cities would soon feel the harsh blast of a most miserable winter. Few could afford enough food, and fewer still coal to keep warm. Contemporary sources estimated that anywhere from 30,000 to 100,000 people lost their jobs in New York alone; 40,000 in Philadelphia; and 20,000 in Chicago. As the ripples of default spread out from Gotham, few escaped the Panic's impact. Carl Schurz's career as a real estate speculator and rising businessman in small-town Wisconsin came to an abrupt end. Facing severe financial embarrassment, the loss of his property, and even the ability to provide food for his family, Schurz took to the lecture circuit, eking out a living, studying law at night, hoping a career change would alter his fortunes. New York's *Journal of Commerce*, whose columns once touted new stock offerings, incredible inventions, and surefire advice on amassing fortunes, now proffered this poetic nostrum: "Steal awhile away from Wall Street and every worldly care / And spend an hour about mid-day in humble, hopeful prayer."[3]

That this should be happening in America's greatest city seemed all the more incredible. By 1857 Americans had come to understand the fragility of their democratic institutions; now they confronted the frailty of their dreams as embodied in the nation's burgeoning cities. The city was as much a destination for young men and women of ambition as the West. And like the West, the young nation's freewheeling spirit permeated the chock-a-block offices and residences of New York.

As America's cities transitioned from commercial entrepôts to diverse centers of trade, industry, and services in the 1840s, they forged a national economy that sustained unprecedented economic growth and energy. Walt Whitman, whose poetry mimicked the brashness of the city, liked nothing better than to stroll down Broadway, his hat cocked at a rakish angle, with a flower in his buttonhole and a cane swinging by his side, to revel in the myriad sights and sounds of a metropolis that seemingly changed before his eyes and ears: "The blab of the pave, tires of carts, sluff of boot-soles, talk of the promenaders, / The heavy omnibus, the driver with his interrogating thumb, the clank of the shod horses on the granite floor . . . / The hurrahs for popular favorites, the fury of the rous'd mobs."[4]

Such excitement was not for everyone, and the city began a geographic sorting-out process to shield those who could afford a quiet residence from those who could not, and to group like activities together for efficiency and profit—here a retail area, there an industrial enclave, and further away a middle-class residential neighborhood. The city characterized by eclectic land uses, a livery stable next to a dry goods shop, on top of which residences were located, was disappearing. A writer in *Harper's* in the 1850s complained that New York "is never the same city for a dozen years altogether," and that anyone born there forty years ago would "find nothing, absolutely nothing, of the New York he knew." New Yorkers swarmed up the narrow island as soon as and even faster than developers could plat lots. "How this city marches northward!" marveled attorney George Templeton Strong in 1850.[5]

New York's growth was nothing short of astonishing, not only by American but also by global standards. Between 1800 and 1850, Manhattan grew by 750 percent, the highest rate of urban growth in the world during that period. Immigrants from Germany and Ireland, raw farm boys like Walt Whitman, and hopeful girls and their families from small towns streamed into the nation's metropolis until New York came to be the synonym for a dynamic America: "the great city of New York wields more of the destinies of this great nation than five times the population of any other portion of the country."[6]

The rapid expansion of retail, banking, industry, and commerce spawned newer occupations in law, insurance, real estate, education, hotel and restaurant management, and financial services. Usually salaried positions, these occupations expanded the middle class—the readership for Greeley's *Tribune*, the patrons of the theater, the population for new subdivisions, and the consumers of things. This quintessential urban class was defined less by occupation and income—though obviously that counted—than by where they lived, how they spent their leisure time, the churches they went to, the books and magazines they read, and what they consumed.

Tales of the city fascinated other Americans just as the saga of the westward movement had captured their imagination. Many of these accounts made clear, however, that success in the city sometimes came at a price. Lurid titles such as George Foster's series *New York in Slices, New York by Gas-Light,* and *New York Naked* became best sellers. Rather than repelling readers, these stories rendered the city even more alluring. Foster was a guide of the city much as Frémont was a guide of the West, and negotiating the streets of New York at night could be just as exciting as riding through the Sioux country out west. If the West was redolent of a special freedom for Americans, so was the city. The city, like the West, represented a new beginning, a casting off of custom and tradition, a regeneration of the American experiment. Cities were "electric transformers" and "accelerators of all historical time."[7]

Foster told of liberated men and women enjoying the day- and nightlife of bustling, bawdy New York. The new urban woman was a particular delight to Foster's readers. Lize, a recurring character in his stories, "never feels herself at home but at the theater or the dance. . . . She is perfectly willing to work for a living, works hard and cheerfully, as any day laborer or journeyman mechanic of the other sex." Foster assures readers that Lize is not a housewife but an independent working woman: "She rises before the sun . . . swallows her frugal breakfast in a hurry, puts a still more frugal dinner in her little tin kettle . . . , and starts off to her daily labor. . . . From six to six o'clock she works steadily, with little gossip and no interruption save the hour from twelve to one, de-voted to dinner." This rigorous schedule—the hard work for which Americans were famous—does not dull Lize's demeanor or disposition. "Her very walk has a swing of mischief and defiance in it, and the tones of her voice are loud, hearty, and free."[8]

Lize exemplified what Americans found intriguing about the city. She en-joyed life, she played and worked hard, she was independent, and she flouted tradition. She was distinctive, as the city was distinctive, as America was dis-tinctive. To readers across the country, in small towns and farms—where most Americans still lived—these were the alluring aspects of urban life. They re-alized, as one magazine editor stated, that "the great things in history have not been done in the country. . . . If [a person] has talent and ambition, he will surely burst away from the relentless tedium of potatoes and corn, and earn more money in an hour by writing a paragraph exhorting people to go and hoe corn and potatoes, than he would by hoeing them for a day."[9]

While Americans found the city alluring, at least in literature, they also held reservations about the urban explosion. Much as some worried that a continental empire would stretch the democratic fabric to the breaking point, they expressed concern that cities and their diverse populations threatened the nation's future as well. "In the formation of a nation's education," wrote one woman at mid-century, "as of a national character, the country more than the city must control. The city becomes cosmopolitan; its people, blend-ing all nationalities, lose distinctive national characteristics, and . . . love of country as well."[10]

The rapid growth of evangelical Protestantism in the nineteenth century was fueled in part by a perception of urban godlessness. Roman Catholics concentrated in cities, and the city generally tended to erode Christian piety. The fact that New York City contained more than two hundred known houses of prostitution by the 1850s confirmed the erosion of faith. In such circum-stances, the task of ministers was clear. As Henry Ward Beecher declared from his pulpit in Brooklyn, "We must preach Him IN THE CITIES; for no-where else is the need of this greater, and nowhere else are the opportunities for doing it more numerous and inviting."[11]

Beecher also wrote "Lectures to Young Men," advising them on appropri-ate conduct in the new urban environment where temptations abounded. The Young Men's Christian Association (YMCA) appeared in Boston in 1851 and soon spread to other cities. Here was a place where young bank tellers, sales-men, attorneys, journalists, and clerks could expand their minds and protect their souls. These and like associations did not so much shield their charges from the city as they prepared them to cope with the challenges of urban living.

"This desire to press forward in the path of improvement, this ambition to excel," wrote one young member, "is one of the noblest attributes of the mind. . . . It is the power which, guided and directed by the grace of God, is destined to reform the world." Adherence to God and Christian virtues could harness the energy of the city to greater personal and national objectives.[12]

Just whose God reigned in the cities? The God of Abraham or the God of Mammon? As medieval urban dwellers had built cathedrals to express their faith, nineteenth-century city dwellers constructed department stores and brokerage houses as the palaces of their faith. Urban households enjoyed much larger disposable incomes than the rural families. City families in the mid-nineteenth century spent, on average, about three times as much per year as rural households. As advertisements cluttered the penny presses and new emporia sprang up to satisfy the demands of the burgeoning urban population, the city became a retail extravaganza.

Few establishments epitomized this urban affluence more than the department store. A. T. Stewart had arrived in New York from Belfast in 1825. He parlayed the savings and hard work from his dry goods business to open the aptly named "Marble Palace" department store in 1846. The glittering chandeliers, the wide aisles, the burnished mahogany counters, and the dazzling array of merchandise thrilled customers, who felt they were participating in an event merely by entering such an establishment. Many pressed their noses against the large plate-glass windows, and a new phrase— "window shopping"—was born. The stores became spaces for middle-class women, few of whom worked outside the home, but whose role was to decorate, purchase, and plan a household. The independence of the young, single working girl, exemplified by George Foster's Lize, percolated up the social ladder to middle-class women. But class was not the theme of the department store; here was a democratic space, where salesgirls, native-born or immigrant, and shoppers of all varieties mingled. A widely read book on urban etiquette published in the 1850s, *Miss Leslie's Behavior Book*, counseled readers about department-store protocol: "Testify no impatience if a servant-girl, making a six penny purchase, is served before you." In department stores, "the rule of 'first come, first served,' is rigidly observed."[13]

By the 1850s, all the major cities boasted these commercial palaces. Boston's Jordan Marsh, Philadelphia's Wanamaker and Brown, New York's Lord and Taylor, and Chicago's Marshall Field's were the marvels of their day as residents and tourists alike gaped at first sight of the latest innovations in retail establishments. The palaces were part of a new downtown, more exclusively given over to commercial and industrial uses. Those who could afford to do so moved uptown. They became commuters and, in some cases, suburbanites.[14]

Moving to the suburbs was a variation on the theme of westward movement. If abundance of land, the opportunity for work, and the possibility of success motivated the trekkers to the Pacific, they also accounted for the mobility to and from the cities of mid-nineteenth-century America. To own land and a home was a marker of success regardless of the geography. It represented less a rejection of the urban milieu than an opportunity to fulfill the American dream. Americans during this era learned to move easily from natural to man-made environments, remaking the natural to suit modern sensibilities and softening the artificial to remain connected to nature. A middle landscape, in other words, an ability to appreciate both places. It was the way Americans came to accept their urban civilization, despite misgivings, and take it for their own.

By the 1850s, the nation had gone too far in pursuit of urban life to turn back nostalgically to an earlier, more rural America. Cities had become the centers of innovation and wealth, and the egalitarian spirit flourished there contrary to fears that urban air would stifle democracy. Whatever problems accompanied urban life could be solved. This, after all, was America. If poverty existed, and it did, apply the new social science methodology, rationalize charity, and solve the problem. If crime and fire added to cities' growing pains, and they did, establish professional police and firefighting forces. If crowded cities generated health problems and epidemic diseases, and they did, provide cleaner drinking water, systematize public health services, and develop parks for esthetic and recreational pleasure. The American city stood on the cutting edge of a cutting-edge country. Some streets were paved, gas lighting adorned the thoroughfares, sewer systems flushed many city streets, water tasted more like a drink than a liquid menace, and all citizens could enjoy a stroll in the park on a Sunday afternoon.[15]

America's burgeoning cities inspired awe but no longer surprise. In fact, compared with Chicago's, Denver's, and San Francisco's, New York's growth seemed measured. Instant cities were the rage out West. As soon as migrants reached a likely place, down went streets and up went buildings. Immigrants from Europe and Asia eagerly sought these new places believing, correctly in most cases, that with everyone a newcomer, they stood about as good a chance at success as anyone.

Was there anything Americans could not accomplish, even turning crowded cities into airy gardens, solving the age-old scourges of disease and fire, and spreading wealth far and wide, not merely among a privileged elite but to anyone who would work hard? The ideals behind such achievements transcended the city or the farm. They were American principles of faith playing out in cities, on farms, and in the long wagon trains westward. Americans, those who came with hope to the new cities from near and very far, those who traveled westward with equal optimism, and even those who stayed put, pausing for a moment, a year, to persist here for the time being, and then maybe moving on if things did not work out right, or even if things did. All believed they were special, beyond Europe, beyond history; a new race of people, closer to God, and closer to His coming.

And each was as good as the other, a democracy of transcendence, Whitman wrote: "Come to us on equal terms. Only then can you understand us. We are not better than you. What we enclose you enclose. What we enjoy you may enjoy." Americans were all pioneers, trekking to uncharted territory and by the dint of hard work and faith creating a new nation, and ultimately a redeemed world. "All the past we leave behind," Whitman wrote. "We debouch upon a newer, mightier world, varied world, / Fresh and strong the world we seize, world of labor and the march, Pioneers! O pioneers!" Americans would conquer all obstacles: "We primeval forests felling, / We the rivers stemming, vexing we, and piercing deep the mines within; / We the surface broad surveying, we the virgin soil upheaving, Pioneers! O pioneers!"[16]

Americans stood apart from history. Other peoples and races were still bound to the historical inevitabilities of rise, fall, and extinction, be they Mexicans, Indians, or Africans. The chroniclers of America's new history, such as George Bancroft, projected a straight line of infinite progress watched over by Providence. Americans were new men and women connected to a new destiny. "Whenever a mind is simple," Emerson wrote, "and receives a divine wisdom, old things pass away—means, teachers, texts, temples fall; it lives now, and absorbs past and future into the present hour. . . . The centuries are conspirators against the sanity and authority of the soul. . . . [H]istory is an impertinence and an injury." Americans were "born with knives in their brains," Emerson declared, cutting through centuries of dead wisdom to sculpt a new individual and a new nation.[17]

Which is why the economic crash of 1857 sent city men to their knees. It was all so unexpected. What had they done to God to derail the nation from its divine mission? If the rush and the glitter of the mid-nineteenth-century city had made the poor invisible, the Panic revealed them and many more. The small-town, small-shop, small-farm American economy was transforming, and in such transitions many benefited, but some were left far behind. Fifty years earlier, the top 1 percent of income earners owned 12 percent of the wealth. By the late 1850s, they controlled nearly one-third of the nation's wealth. Artisanal work was disappearing, and laborers crowded a market of low wages and few benefits. The separation between manual and mental labor grew wider, as did the compensation for each.

The economic downturn not only cost jobs and deepened urban poverty, it

shattered the confidence of the flamboyant fifties when progress seemed limitless and when God appeared everywhere, on the street, within men, and
across the American continent ratifying the words and deeds of His Chosen
People; an era when steam engines conquered time and space, and when the
western rivers and rocks offered up untold treasures, and when a few dollars
down today would yield a fortune tomorrow. America transcended the western tribes, the contentious slaveholder, the culture-bound Catholic, the en-
crusted hierarchies of Old Europe. But the rising misery of the winter of
1857–58 sent stocks and confidence tumbling one after the other.

Walt Whitman, normally an ebullient drumbeater for his country and his
city, wondered if the Panic reflected a deeper disaffection that portended the
disintegration of American democracy. The prosperity and technological advances of the 1840s and 1850s and the extension of a continental empire had
concealed troubling fissures in American society. Whitman's meanderings
along the streets of New York distressed him, not only the squalor he encountered but also the gratuitous violence that flared from the bowels of the burgeoning tenement districts and occasionally spilled into nearby commercial
and residential districts.[18]

Clashes between sectarian gangs accelerated in the mid-1850s. The city's
Democratic political leadership, with its substantial Irish base, seemed uninterested in stemming the violence. The municipal police force was thoroughly
corrupt and merely added to the chaos. An exasperated state administration
formed the rival Metropolitan Police force in 1857 and ordered the city's force
disbanded. When the mayor refused to carry out the order, the two forces
joined battle in the streets. A court order succeeded in disbanding the city police on July 2, 1857. Two days later, the Irish "Dead Rabbits" and their Protestant
rivals, the "Bowery Boys," fought a pitched battle in Manhattan's "Bloody
Sixth" Ward, home to the notorious Five Points slum. The state-appointed police force stood by helplessly. Security was scarcely better in other cities. When
the Panic set in during the fall, worker demonstrations erupted across urban
America, most notably in New York, Philadelphia, Chicago, St. Louis, and
Louisville. Americans feared for their cities and their democracy.[19]

The Panic of 1857 did not invent urban disorder, but the increasing violence
did prompt the press and leading citizens to question the price of progress,
perhaps for the first time. The unalloyed boosterism of the early 1850s dissolved
into more sober reflection. In November 1858, a writer in *Harper's* catalogued
the "rowdyism and anarchy which obtain in New York. Riots and crimes
abound. Justice is not certain. The necessaries of life are notoriously and fatally
adulterated. The laws are neither obeyed by the people nor executed by the
magistracy." Little wonder that George Templeton Strong found a society in

*Gangs of New York: Paramilitary political gangs were not an invention of the
Reconstruction-era South. Throughout (mostly northern) cities, groups
of street gangs affiliated with rival political parties and divided by religious
differences clashed. On July 4, 1857, the "Bowery Boys," supporters of the Know Nothings,
fought a pitched battle with their Irish Catholic adversaries, the "Dead Rabbits."
(Courtesy of the Library of Congress)*

extremis: "We are a very sick people. The outward and visible signs of disease,
the cutaneous symptoms, are many." New York, or any other mid-nineteenth-
century American city, was neither as good as its boosters had declaimed nor as
rotten as the growing chorus of detractors feared. Whatever the reality, a shift
in perception had occurred. New evidence corroborated the view that disorder
was on the rise and that it threatened American democracy.[20]

The fledgling science of society—social science—and its penchant for statistical compilations indicated that the trend of urban crime matched popular perceptions. One study showed that in a four-year period between 1848
and 1852, violent crimes increased by 129 percent in New York, fueled by a
sixfold jump in murders. The press sensationalized the crime wave and undoubtedly contributed to the growing sense of urban lawlessness. The sensational became the routine: "Horrible murders, stabbings, and shootings, are
now looked for in the morning papers with as much regularity as we look for
our breakfast." Whitman's beloved city had become to him "crime-haunted
and dangerous," ruled by the revolver.[21]

None of this sudden awareness of urban lawlessness surprised southern
journalists, who had discussed the failure of "free" society for several years

prior to the Panic of 1857. A writer in *De Bow's Review* wondered, "What would be the result were the police force of one of our large cities withdrawn for a single night? . . . We would have life as in the streets of Byzantium when Mohammed the Turk poured his savage hordes through them." Such a result, the Virginian George Fitzhugh asserted, was the natural outcome of a society whose "whole moral code was every man for himself." The South, by contrast, was more humane and less troubled by disorder. The evils of "Pauperism, crime, and mortality" were decidedly less evident in southern cities than in the urban North.[22]

Southern publications now enlisted northern critics, heretofore rare, to make their argument as the economy worsened in 1857. The clash between capital and labor, hidden by the prosperity earlier in the decade, became more evident. *De Bow's Review* reprinted an editorial from a northern journal lamenting the loss of worker autonomy in the new market economy. "The capital which sustains mechanical business is not under the control of the operatives." The result, according to the editor, leaves "the operatives . . . helpless." The North was becoming more like Europe. Despotism would invariably follow disorder.[23]

Not only were northern publications making the southern argument, but the economic crisis seemed to spare the South from its worst consequences. Though white and black workers tangled in the streets of Baltimore and Richmond and sectarian gangs patrolled neighborhoods on election day in some southern cities, the degree of violence, or at least its publicity, seemed much less in the urban South. It was also true that southern enterprises that maintained close commercial and financial connections to northern cities suffered. But cotton retained a fair resiliency, and the low tariff Congress passed in 1857 aided exports. The lesson was obvious: the speculative mania and overweening pride that characterized the free labor North had not infected the South sufficiently to cause a similar economic dislocation. Where distress appeared, it resulted from dependence on northern banks and factors.

Governments, and the political parties connected to them, were both impotent and complicit in the crises that gripped the financial markets and the streets of urban America. New York reformer Thomas Low Nichols, looking back on these years from the not-too-distant perch of the early 1860s, commented that "it is a matter of world-wide notoriety that during the past ten years whole legislatures have been bribed; that the state and national treasuries have been despoiled of millions; that members of Congress have sold their votes in open market to the highest bidder."[24]

For a nation whose people expected virtue from their leaders, these allegations were distressing. If optimism turned to cynicism, the legitimacy of democratic government could crumble. While Americans were congenitally suspicious of party cabals, their governments seemed especially opaque and corrupt in the 1850s. Walt Whitman observed that the political process had served up "swarms of cringers, suckers, doughfaces, lice of politics, planners of sly involutions for their own preferment to city offices or state legislatures or the judiciary or congress or the presidency." Alexis de Tocqueville, ever the keen observer of American culture, seconded Whitman's judgment in 1857, connecting the speculative madness of the economy to a similar disposition in politics, where individuals "who lacked moderation, sometimes probity, above all education," seemed to have usurped the nation's democratic institutions.[25]

The economic distress placed political events in a new light. Just as the Panic of 1857 eroded the confidence of Americans in the inevitability of their progress and prosperity, the political events of that year eroded trust in their institutions of government. Political leaders would compromise two basic principles of American democracy: an independent judiciary and the sanctity of majority rule.

Roger B. Taney, a Marylander and a Roman Catholic, who had weathered the suspicion and prejudice elicited by his religion to attain the highest judicial post in the land—chief justice of the United States Supreme Court— believed he had a remedy for the growing sectional unrest that threatened his beloved Union. That judges were supposed to leave public policy to the politicians did not, apparently, trouble Chief Justice Taney. In fact, the chief justice saw nothing inappropriate in consulting with President-elect Buchanan on a case before him. In an era when legislators sat on railroad boards and then voted land grants to their partners with scarcely a raised eyebrow, the idea of a conflict of interest or, in this instance, the violation of the separation of powers probably did not enter the calculation of Chief Justice Taney.

Appointed by Andrew Jackson in 1836, Taney considered himself a nationalist who respected states' rights. He had served Jackson as both attorney general and secretary of the treasury and became one of the president's closest friends. Critics derided the appointment, characterizing the new chief justice as "stooped, sallow, ugly . . . [a] supple, cringing tool of Jacksonian power." Though a slaveholder, he disliked the institution and manumitted all of his slaves. Prior to his service in the Jackson administration he had defended a Methodist minister accused of inciting a slave insurrection. His opinions over the years were undistinguished and adhered closely to the facts at hand. As the sectional conflict heated up in the 1850s, the activities of abolitionists alarmed him. He feared that the contention over slavery could sunder the Union. The Dred Scott case provided an opportunity to put the issue to rest once and for all.[26]

The events surrounding the case dated back to the 1830s, when Dred Scott, a slave, traveled to Illinois, a free state, and then to Wisconsin, a free territory, in the company of his master, Dr. John Emerson, an army surgeon. When Dr. Emerson died in 1843, Scott sought to purchase his freedom, an offer that the doctor's widow refused. Scott sued for his freedom on the grounds that he had resided in a state and a territory where slavery was illegal by virtue of the Northwest Ordinance and Missouri Compromise, respectively. The case, *Dred Scott v. Sandford* (the executor of Dr. Emerson's estate), went to trial in Missouri in 1847. After a series of contradictory decisions and appeals, the case appeared before Taney's Supreme Court in 1856.[27]

President-elect Buchanan was anxious to resolve the slavery extension issue that had poisoned congressional debate and plagued administrations from James K. Polk forward. He perceived the Dred Scott case as an opportunity to settle the issue. In a bald violation of an independent judiciary, the president-elect corresponded with two associate justices of the Supreme Court and chatted with the chief justice to the effect that it would really be nice if they could put this problem to rest once and for all.

The Court's decision focused on two issues: was Dred Scott a citizen of the United States and therefore possessed of the standing to sue? Clearly, a slave was not a citizen. However, Scott's residence in Illinois and Wisconsin Territory, his lawyers contended, rendered him free and, therefore, a citizen. This first issue forced the justices to consider a second question: did Congress (or any other entity) have the right to prohibit slavery in the territories? If the Court answered in the negative, then Scott would be neither free nor a citizen and therefore barred from filing a lawsuit.

The Court rendered its decision on March 6, 1857, two days after Buchanan's inauguration. Buchanan knew what was coming, and he could not have been more delighted. Taney handed the administration a decision tailor-made to defuse the slavery issue, or so the collaborators thought.

Taney's majority opinion—two northern judges dissented—was more detailed and comprehensive than it had to be as a legal decision and employed dubious legal logic to emasculate a key provision of the Constitution. The decision was less an adjudication than a political remediation, and it failed at both duties. Taney concluded that Scott was not a citizen, not only because he was a slave but also because he was black, and even had he been free, Scott would have lacked standing in court by virtue of his race. To prove his point, Taney divined the sentiments of the Founding Fathers and their predecessors on this subject. Black people, he wrote, "had for more than a century before [1776] been regarded as beings of an inferior order, and altogether unfit to associate with the white race, either in social or political relations; and so far inferior that they had no rights which the white man was bound to respect; and that the negro might justly and lawfully be reduced to slavery for his benefit."[28]

As offensive as Taney's sociology appeared in a legal context, the bombshell was the Court's declaration that the law protected slave property as it did any other property, and, therefore, neither Congress nor a territorial or state legislature could ban slavery. Both the Northwest Ordinance and the Missouri Compromise, in this reading, were unconstitutional. This despite the clear intent of the Constitution in Article IV, Section 2, which states that Congress has the power to make "all needful rules and regulations respecting the territory or other property belonging to the United States." It was only the second time in American history that a court had rendered a congressional statute unconstitutional. In one decision, the U.S. Supreme Court provided the legal standing for a White Republic, undercut the major issue of the Republican Party, and threw Stephen A. Douglas's popular sovereignty into constitutional purgatory. For good measure, the Court's ruling contributed to the collapse of railroad stocks and the economic depression later that year by scaring off potential settlers (and their train fares) from the territories. Who knew if the Kansas war would be reprised across the West?

That it would not quell the slavery extension controversy became apparent before the ink was dry on the decision. The Court had essentially resurrected John C. Calhoun's argument that slaveholders could carry their property anywhere in the United States and its territories and enjoy the protection of the government. The Constitution was a slave code—protecting the slaveholders' property regardless of state or federal intent to the contrary. From this reading, slavery was legal everywhere and could exist in Massachusetts as well as Mississippi.

The southern press interpreted the decision in precisely the terms that Chief Justice Taney hoped the nation would embrace—that it put to rest a momentous "politico-legal question," as the *Richmond Enquirer* put it. The editor went on to say that the decision favored "the advocates and supporters of the Constitution and the Union, the equality of the States and the rights of the South . . . and that too by a tribunal of jurists, as learned, impartial and unprejudiced as perhaps the world has ever seen. . . . The *nation* has achieved a triumph, *sectionalism* has been rebuked, and abolitionism has been staggered and stunned."[29]

Northerners viewed the decision in much less sanguine terms. The Slave

Power conspiracy had now infected all branches of government, and the disease seemed to be spreading across the land. William Seward dramatically articulated the conspiratorial thesis: "the day of inauguration came—the first one among all the celebrations of that great national pageant that was to be desecrated by a coalition between the executive and the judicial departments to undermine the national legislature and the liberties of the people."[30]

Once a grand collusion is established, the fantastic becomes the plausible. The impression grew in the North that the decision not only protected slavery where it existed but also protected it where it did not yet, but now could, exist. As Horace Greeley reasoned in the *New York Tribune*, the decision established "that fact that *Slavery is National.*" If that was the case, Greeley concluded, it would be possible to buy and sell slaves in New York City. "At this moment, indeed, any wealthy New York jobber connected with the Southern trade can put in his next orders: 'Send me a negro cook, at the lowest market value! Buy me a waiter! Balance my account with two chambermaids and a truckman!' . . . The free hills of Vermont, the lakes of Maine, the valleys of Connecticut . . . may be traversed by the gangs of the negro-driver, and enriched by the legitimate commerce of the slave-pen." As if caught short by the absurdity of the scene, Greeley admitted that public opinion in the North prevented such scenarios for the time being, but the Constitution now did not.[31]

Greeley, despite the hyperbole, hit upon the issue that troubled increasing numbers of northerners: that slavery was no longer a local matter, a peculiarity of the southern states. The Fugitive Slave Law had implied as much, but its impact among whites was negligible. Now, however, "wherever the stars and stripes wave they protect Slavery and represent Slavery. The black and cursed stain is thick on our hands also. . . . The Star of Freedom and the stripes of bondage are henceforth one. American Republicanism and American Slavery are for the future synonymous. . . . In this all the labors of our statesmen, the blood of our heroes, the life-long cares and toils of our forefathers, the aspirations of our scholars, the prayers of good men, have finally ended! America the slavebreeder and slaveholder!"[32]

Northern evangelicals, who had begun to see signs of an approaching Armageddon in the rising sectional strife over slavery and the sectarian, class, and racial turmoil in the cities, viewed the Dred Scott decision within this broader context. Chief Justice Taney had essentially denied the basic humanity of the slave, an unconscionable position among mid-nineteenth-century evangelicals, even in the South. John Dixon Long, a Methodist minister in Philadelphia, condemned Taney's characterization, referring to the half-million free blacks in the North as "our brethren in Christ, and ambassadors from the Court of Heaven to sinful men." Another minister denounced "the corruptions of . . . the *tawny* decision—crushing out a whole race, and at one dash of his pro-slavery pen reducing men to mere chattels."[33]

Indeed, if a higher law than the Constitution existed, as these churchmen believed, it was time to invoke that law in the place of that now-sullied document. To a packed crowd of three thousand worshipers in his Plymouth Church, Henry Ward Beecher declared, "If the people obey this decision, they disobey God." Americans already held a dim view of the corruption of governments, parties, and politicians. Now it appeared that the independent judiciary was part of this foul process. It would be too much to say that the Dred Scott decision caused increasing numbers of northerners to lose faith in their government. But it would not be inaccurate to state they were losing patience with those who operated in its name. The Court's interpretation of the Constitution clashed with basic American principles of a common humanity and of government by the consent of the governed.[34]

The Dred Scott decision further eroded the middle ground. Now that neither Congress nor the people of a territory could decide the fate of slavery, the extreme positions—that slavery was a protected national institution or that the courts and Constitution be damned—moved closer to the mainstream. The Court, rather than excising the slavery issue from the body politic, added mightily to the festering wound of sectional strife.

The Dred Scott decision was especially troubling to the tens of thousands of free blacks in the South. The Court, in stripping their citizenship, made them vulnerable to reenslavement or expulsion. Southern states feared the collaboration of the mostly urban free black population with slaves, and white workers chafed at the competition for jobs. Virginia, North Carolina, and Missouri in 1858 debated offering free blacks the "choice" of expulsion or enslavement. Nothing came of these proposals, but the mere possibility caused numerous free blacks to leave the South for Canada. More generally, the Dred Scott case accelerated the restrictions on the southern free black population, as the legal recourse of that population vanished with the decision. Several cities, including Charleston, experimented with requirements that free blacks purchase and wear badges identifying them as free. Other southern cities barred their free black workers from certain occupations or facilitated white takeover of previously black occupations such as carting and barbering.

The loss of citizenship weighed heavily on free African Americans everywhere. The Fugitive Slave Law attacked the security of northern free blacks, but in actual operation it affected relatively few. The Dred Scott decision was another matter. It cast doubt on the free status of every African American regardless of residence. In April 1857, free blacks in northern cities crowded into churches and meeting halls to vent their anguish and sense of betrayal. A meeting in Philadelphia resolved "That the only duty the colored man owes to a constitution under which he is declared to be an inferior and degraded being . . . is to denounce and repudiate it, and to do what he can by all proper means to bring it into contempt."[35]

For African Americans, the enemy was no longer the slaveholder but the very government from which they had hoped for redress. As the State Convention of Ohio Colored Men concluded in 1858, "If the Dred Scott dictum be the true exposition of the law of the land, then are the founders of the American Republic convicted by their descendants of base hypocrisy, and colored men absolved from all allegiance to a government which withdraws all protection."[36]

A few addenda to the case: John Sandford, the executor of Dr. Emerson's estate, died in an insane asylum shortly after the decision. Dr. Emerson's widow, the woman who refused to allow Dred Scott to purchase his freedom, moved to Massachusetts, married an anti-slavery congressman, and transferred ownership of Scott to the son of his original owner, who promptly manumitted both Scott and his wife on May 26, 1857. Dred Scott died one year later.

The northern reaction to the Dred Scott decision dashed President Buchanan's hopes for a smooth beginning to his administration. Things would get worse. Again, Old Buck had good intentions. In May, he dispatched his friend Mississippi senator Robert J. Walker to clean out the mess in Kansas and oversee a convention that would frame a constitution for congressional approval as a precursor to statehood. Walker, a Pennsylvanian by birth, seemed as if he would expire at the first gust of wind. Less than five and a half feet tall and weighing ninety-five pounds, he looked sickly when he was well, and deathly when he was not. A journey to the Kansas Territory was hardly what the doctor ordered, though he was probably anxious to get out of Washington, where he had managed to anger the sensitive southern coterie around the president by noting offhandedly that he did not expect Kansas to enter the Union as a slave state.

Walker oversaw two elections during his embattled six-month tenure. One was an election to the constitutional convention boycotted by free-staters who feared fraud, intimidation, and gerrymandering. Another was a vote for the territorial legislature in which, at Walker's urging, free-state residents participated. The latter election validated the free-staters' skepticism about the manner of conducting political contests in Kansas. The pro-slavery forces' recurrent creative math produced sleepy towns that had suddenly become bustling metropolises with voter rolls to match. Walker threw out the suspect ballots, allowing free-staters to claim a majority in the legislature. Predictably, the constitutional convention at Lecompton, elected by pro-slavery voters, framed a pro-slavery constitution and submitted the document to voters in a rigged election that Walker termed a "vile fraud, a base counterfeit." Walker left Kansas for Washington in disgust to advise President Buchanan to throw out the Lecompton document. The legislature meanwhile, with its free-state majority, called for its own referendum, and voters overwhelmingly rejected the Lecompton Constitution. The message from this political circus, and one that Walker shared with anyone who would listen, was that free-state voters formed a solid majority in Kansas. If the Democratic Party was serious about its support for popular sovereignty, then rejecting the Lecompton Constitution was the only conscionable option.[37]

Buchanan had strong personal and political ties with southern politicians dating from the Andrew Jackson administration. His interventions in the Scott case had shown that these ties overwhelmed sound judgment. Buchanan dismissed the advice of his own emissary and decided to push the Lecompton Constitution through the Congress, much to the delight of his southern friends and to the dismay of almost everyone else. The president's message to the House on Lecompton touched off a twelve-hour donnybrook in February 1858. Alexander Stephens, seeing tempers rise and civility fall, pressed for an adjournment to no avail. Sometime past midnight, South Carolina's Lawrence Keitt lunged at Pennsylvania's Republican congressman Galusha Grow after a purported insult, and the fight was on. While the Speaker's gavel vainly pounded for order, about fifty congressmen in various states of inebriation tangled with each other on the House floor. Representative James B. Clay of Kentucky, a Democrat, implored his colleagues, "Gentlemen, remember where you are!" which only incited the lawmakers even more. The rumble subsided only when Mississippi congressman William Barksdale tackled an unidentified assailant as the latter snatched his toupee and waved it about like a captured flag. Barksdale finally retrieved his own scalp and plopped it on his head wrong side out, the absurdity of the scene giving the combatants pause. Stephens, a waif of ninety-seven pounds, witnessed all this from a safe corner of the chamber. He despaired that "all things here are tending to bring my mind to the conclusion that this Government can not or will not last long."[38]

Still, Stephens was not willing to give up on his beloved Union. Taking a page from his late and revered colleague Henry Clay, Stephens sought a compromise and enlisted two northerners, Republican William A. Howard of Michigan and William H. English of Indiana, a Democrat, in his cause. Stephens's efforts confronted a harsh reality: how does one compromise with fraud? This was the view not only of the Republicans but also of many northern Democrats, especially one of the most powerful and popular politicians, Stephen A. Douglas, who, in an unprecedented action, openly broke with the administration of his own party, a move that earned the permanent enmity of the president. He denounced the Lecompton document as a "flagrant violation of popular rights in Kansas" that he would "resist to the last." Douglas cared less whether Kansas entered the Union as a free state or a slave state than whether the process of popular sovereignty ran its course. The Lecompton Constitution fell far short of satisfying that process. When President Buchanan warned Douglas to hew to the party line or face the kind of discipline Andrew Jackson applied to wayward Democrats, the Illinois senator shot back: "Mr. President, I wish you to remember that General Jackson is dead." And soon General Jackson's party would join its founder.[39]

Stephens had no more faith in Lecompton than Douglas, despite its proslavery orientation. He admitted that "we all [knew] that the Lecompton constitution was procured by fraud." Yet Stephens was willing to forgo principle for the sake of salvaging a symbolic victory for the South, even though it was clear to the Georgian that Kansas would never become a slave state. Yet again, symbolism triumphed over reality. The Fugitive Slave Law would restore precious few slaves to their rightful owners; the Kansas-Nebraska Act would not create more slave states; and the Dred Scott decision would not secure the institution of slavery. These events did not substantively help the South in any way; but they did create a constituency of hostility far beyond the small minority of abolitionists who had raised up a lonely cant against the South for more than two decades before many more northerners joined the chorus. It was not the abolitionists, however, who grew the opposition. It was a perceived southern persistence at supporting measures that tortured the principles of fairness and democratic rule.[40]

By now, Stephens was thoroughly disillusioned with the political process and what it was doing to the country. He resolved to leave the Congress at the end of his term and return to Georgia to farm and practice law. But he wanted to resolve the Lecompton issue somehow. The result was a measure called the English Bill, a convoluted attempt to save face in a bad situation. The bill asked the voters of Kansas to determine whether they wanted statehood now with a modest federal land grant (considerably less than the Lecompton document requested), or statehood at some later time when the territory's population reached ninety thousand inhabitants. If voters supported the former proposition, they would ratify the Lecompton Constitution; if not, then presumably citizens would need to frame a new document at some unspecified future date. The English Bill was an ingenious measure that made no mention of slavery; its proponents called it a land grant bill and presented it to the voters as such, though scarcely a soul did not understand that the referendum would be an up or down vote on slavery. In the fair election that followed, Kansas voters decided to postpone statehood, thereby rendering the Lecompton Constitution moot. Kansas would enter the Union as a free state in 1861.

The crisis was over, but the damage was done. Coming on the heels of the Dred Scott decision, the Lecompton debacle further eroded northern faith in the federal government in its apparent vassalage to southern slaveholders. Southerners, confronted with a growing sentiment against them, even among moderate politicians and press, felt more estranged than ever from their fellow countrymen. The rapid ascendancy of the Republican Party, a purely sectional political organization, raised the specter of an administration hostile to southern interests at some not too distant point in time. The Democratic Party, with its strong southern base, no longer seemed the rock-solid upholder of those interests, as one of its most prominent leaders, Stephen A. Douglas, openly defied the president, a member of his own party, and took several other prominent northern Democrats into opposition with him.

Little wonder that the men in New York and other cities during the hard winter of 1857–58 filed into cold rooms or church pews to pray. The collapsing economy, the worsening sectional crisis, and the apparent escalation of social disorder created a sense of foreboding that drove these men to seek solace from God. In an increasingly evangelical nation, the suspicion that an epic struggle loomed took firmer root during these dark months, a sense that events were occurring that "may bring together the hosts of evil in one concentrated effort to crush the nation, whatever that nation be, which keepeth the truth."[41]

Many of these men were newcomers to the city, a fast-paced, anonymous, even alien environment so different from the family-oriented, self-contained life of small towns and farms that provided the major stream of urban migration during the first half of the nineteenth century. It was not so much a turn toward religion—these were already pious men for the most part—as an opportunity for personal rededication and spiritual fellowship at a time of growing strife. The urban economy and the principles of democracy and evangelical Protestantism had exalted the sovereignty of the individual: to work hard and achieve prosperity and independence, to support a political system that protected the rights of individuals, and to cultivate a personal relationship with God that would result in a spiritual rebirth and the absolution of sin. Walt Whitman sang about individual sovereignty in "Song of Myself," a paean to the transcendent power of the individual to be anything and everything, even to aspire to God Himself.

Somewhere along the way to individual omnipotence, the progression halted. This came as no surprise to southern writers who had warned of the folly of unbridled individualism, how it defied both history and heaven. The lesson of the Garden of Eden—that man had limits—seemed lost on the go-getters of the North. The financial panic brought on by unchecked speculation was a consequence of unchecked impulse. The North had transformed from the God-centered society of the Puritans to the man-centered society of Wall Street. Northerners had lost respect for order and exchanged it for the belief that "the individual man was ... of higher worth than any system of polity," and had strayed from the Calvinist view that man's nature is flawed to a new belief in "attainable perfection." Had reliance on self replaced reliance on God? Had sanctifying reason—that the intellect could solve any problem and overcome the forces of nature—created a false pride in human infallibility? Had pride caused Americans to assume they could transcend history itself?[42]

Southerners offered these critiques of northern urban society almost always within the context of the pro-slavery argument. Northerners mostly dismissed them as cynical propaganda. The connection between these southern indictments and the pro-slavery cause muffled similar critiques in the North, as most northerners smugly condemned human bondage in the South and ignored human misery outside their door. The reluctance to engage southern arguments on their own terms caused northerners to exaggerate the contented status of laborers in their midst, even during the Panic of 1857, and the freedoms of blacks and immigrants, despite the violence directed at them. Not all northerners were uncritical of their society. The Rev. Nathan Bangs of New York warned, "It is very danderous [sic] to exalt human reason so as to abuse revelation. Has it not a tendency to engender pride?" Historian Richard Hildreth cautioned against each individual appealing "to his own particular Reason, his own particular conscience, his own particular moral sentiment, as the ultimate tribunal." Such an appeal invited anarchy. But in the context of contending civilizations—North and South—the northern press and political leaders continued to adopt an uncritical stance to the growing problems of a modern urban society.[43]

The religious revival of 1857–58, occurring at the confluence of despairing events and scenes, especially in the North, represented an important time of reflection, a drawing away from the headlong rush of progress. But it was very much part of the urban, commercial culture from which it sprang. The revival came with a significant boost from the urban penny press tired of the bad news of economic doldrums and political missteps. Here was a new story with an unusual twist as the minions of monetary greed suddenly rediscovered their faith. The newspapers called it "The Great Revival," "the event of the century," and "our American awakening." More modest testimonials hailed the revival as the Third Great Awakening. It was none of these; but it was the first religious revival promoted by the secular press, prefiguring the media frenzy that would greet the mass revivals of Dwight L. Moody (a participant in the 1857–58 revival) in the postwar era. That the movement received its first and longest-lasting boost in New York City reflected the central role the metropolis now occupied in the nation's culture, economy, and communications. Although a national event, the revival centered primarily in the cities of the Northeast and Midwest. The South had escaped the brunt of the economic depression, and its need for such a middle-class expression of rededication was less.[44]

None of this is to diminish the significance of the event, especially for the businessmen involved. These were prayer meetings, with the emphasis on prayer. No sermons, typically, perhaps a hymn or two, but mostly reflections on God and the Bible and pledges to repent of sin. While the press generally treated these lunchtime retreats with generosity and approbation, they did not escape the scathing pen of James Gordon Bennett of the Democratic *New York Herald*. Bennett, and many other Democrats, loathed the do-goodism of evangelical Protestants, which they dismissed as little more than sectarian hypocrisy since most of their reform efforts seemed to center on getting immigrants out of taverns and off the voting rolls. The economic depression exacerbated these class and sectarian tensions, which Bennett, a consummate promoter like his rival Horace Greeley, exploited in the columns of his newspaper.

Under the heading of "A Religious Revolution," Bennett described the revival in satiric terms as a movement of "merchants, bankers, politicians, financiers [making] oral confession that they have done those things which they ought not to have done, and left undone those things which they ought to have done." Perhaps, he suggested, these devoted servants of God could repent their attempts "to drive the working class to church on their only day of rest," in reference to the Sabbatarian laws evangelicals promoted to control the Sunday behavior of Irish and German immigrants. The *Herald* offered frequent tallies of those who attended revival meetings and those who patronized the city's theaters, with the latter attendance always more than twofold the former. As Bennett gleefully concluded, "It would seem that Satan still has the majority."[45]

While Bennett poked fun, Greeley captured the essence of the revival as an exercise in self-discipline at a time when restraint and humility seemed in short supply. He congratulated the men on their high "moral tone . . . great sobriety, and a commendable freedom from undue excess." Greeley's *Tribune* was filled with stories of miraculous conversions and of a nation transformed. But the participants looked much more to themselves than to the nation. The revival was notable for its apolitical aspect. In fact, posted notices outside the rooms and buildings where these lunchtime meetings occurred specifically forbade discussion of politics. Revivalists boasted of their nonpartisan and nonsectarian services. Politics had become so corrupt and divisive that it had defiled religion.[46]

There was also an absence of women, especially in prominent and visible roles. At some meetings about the city, men expressly barred women from attending, or asked them to remain silent during the service. When Maggie Van Cott, who would go on to become the first female Methodist minister, stood up and spoke about "the power of Christ to save," several men informed her after the meeting that this was "strictly a men's meeting" and that there were "plenty of places elsewhere where women can speak."[47]

The masculinization of evangelical Protestantism represented by the revival countered a decades-long trend of female church leadership. Despite the high profile of ministers such as Charles Grandison Finney and Henry Ward Beecher, middle-class urban women had played a significant role in spreading the gospel of evangelical Christianity from the 1830s onward. They wrote for church tracts and journals, and they emphasized the importance of the family in establishing a Christian community and nation, and the mother's fundamental role in that process. But for the young men who came to cities in the 1850s, this feminized, family-centered Christianity proved insufficient as a bulwark against the anomie of modern urban life. The YMCA played a major role in publicizing and promoting the revival of 1857–58, and reinforced the anti-clerical, ecumenical Protestant nature of the movement. "Y" members touted a more muscular Christianity, stressing physical fitness and equating probity in business affairs with "manliness."

The economic crisis did not cause businessmen to reject the work ethic or question their faith. Commerce and religion mixed well and repeatedly at the lunchtime meetings. Evangelical Protestantism looked upon financial success as a correlate of spiritual worth. The Panic of 1857 was a not-so-gentle reminder that the urban commercial world had strayed from these connections. The revival was a means to resurrect the partnership between God and Mammon. As one participant noted, "We trust that since prayer has once entered the counting-room it will never leave it; and that the ledger, . . . the blotting-book, the pen and kin, will all be consecrated by a heavenly presence." That Dwight L. Moody moved from selling shoes to saving souls as a full-time urban evangelist, and that John Wanamaker left his YMCA executive post for a successful retail career, reflected the mutual accessibility of business and religion. Both employed similar promotional techniques, and both emphasized a strong work ethic with the promise of ultimate rewards for faithful service.[48]

If the revival was, in part, a response to the unbridled individualism of the 1850s, it was also, ironically, limited by that same individualism. The indifference to community needs, particularly those of the poor, now so visible as a result of the economic collapse, and the plight of working men and women were major failures of the evangelical revival. This lent some credibility to the charges of hypocrisy cast by southern critics who saw northerners as a collection of self-absorbed, hedonistic, and shallow individuals, blind to the misery in their midst, and self-righteous toward everyone else.

The hope proved elusive that the revival would generate a nationwide ecumenical Protestant movement away from sectional divisiveness and toward the one God. A religious publication, the *New York Christian Observer,* rejoiced that the revival had created an "era of good feelings between Christians who had forgotten all past alienations and distractions." But the emphasis on individual salvation did not dissolve the political sensibilities of the revivalists. To the contrary, it seemed to imbue even more the great political issues with moral import.[49]

As the spring of 1858 turned to summer, the economy slowly began to rebound, and the stream of men marching purposefully to lunchtime prayer meetings diminished to a trickle. The press turned to other phenomena. The men had prayed themselves and the economy back to health. The outpouring of religious sentiment, though fleeting, would leave a lasting impression, especially on the young men who had now found a soul in the city and a group of like-minded fellows as friends. The scripted prayer meetings fell away, but the spiritual rebirth did not. Religion provided not only solace but also explanations for a time beset by increasing uncertainty. The revival did not change society dramatically any more than it pushed the nation out of the economic doldrums. But now with each turn in the political arena many more people, not only the fervent evangelicals, came to understand that mere events could hold transcendent meaning.

Alexander Stephens merely wanted to transcend his foul mood. Leaving Washington disgusted, he traveled to his home state of Georgia. Loath to sweat through the usual stifling southern summer, he convinced his half-brother Linton to accompany him on a meandering journey across the Ohio Valley to Illinois. Now, Illinois was not, in those days, a prime destination for a summer vacation. The state boasted few natural springs or cool mountain retreats to attract well-heeled vacationers. But Stephens missed politics, even if he did not miss Washington. He came to Illinois to look up two of his friends, one his new fellow Democrat, Stephen A. Douglas, and the other his old crony from Whig Party days, Abe Lincoln. Douglas and Lincoln were locked in a battle for the United States Senate. When a reporter asked Stephens to handicap the race, the Georgian said he hoped Douglas would win, adding that he thought President Buchanan's animus against the Illinois senator for his opposition to the Lecompton Constitution was "wickedly foolish." Stephens's comments shocked his southern constituents, who had vigorously supported the Lecompton document. But now that he had set his mind on retirement,

Stephens did not feel obliged to follow sectional orthodoxy; he could return to principle. Principle also prevented him from supporting his old friend Lincoln, for Stephens feared that the sectional nature of the Republican Party threatened the Union, a point that Douglas would echo repeatedly in the unfolding Senate campaign.[50]

Lincoln and Douglas had been adversaries in Illinois since the late 1830s. When Douglas learned that Lincoln would be his opponent for the Senate seat, he remarked to a reporter, "I shall have my hands full." Illinois, like many of the other states carved from the old Northwest Ordinance, reflected the politics of the areas from which its settlers came, with the southern part of the state staunchly pro-southern and Democratic, and the northern part increasingly anti-slavery and Republican. Abolitionist sentiment existed in and around Chicago, but it was a decidedly minor political factor. Most Illinoisans believed in a White Republic, and if they harbored any abolitionist sentiment, they expected that upon emancipation the freed blacks would go someplace far away. Illinois Republicans were a diverse group, mixing anti-slavery politics, Whig economics, evangelical religion, and Know Nothing nativism. The state party's rallying cry in 1858—"The Two Despotisms—Catholicism and Slavery—Their Union and Identity"—reflected this amalgam. Setting out what they identified as the nation's two great threats to democracy, and with the recent evangelical Protestant revival fresh in people's minds, Illinois Republicans charged that their Democratic opponents were sinners twice over, a threat both to individual souls and the national polity.[51]

Abraham Lincoln did not quite fit the mold of a typical Republican, if there was such a thing. The new party was still a work in progress, and Lincoln considered himself an heir to Whig icon Henry Clay, a man willing to compromise on the issue of slavery for the sake of the Union and hostile to nativism. But over the years, and especially since the Kansas-Nebraska Act of 1854, Lincoln's speeches had assumed more of a messianic tone and more awareness of the nation's global destiny. He had good political sense, understanding what his fellow Americans were thinking and feeling, and then articulating those sentiments. When he gave his acceptance speech for the Illinois Republican senatorial nomination in June 1858, after Dred Scott and Lecompton, and just as the economic depression and the religious revival were winding down, he captured the reverent but troubled mood of his Illinois neighbors. The optimism of the 1840s and early 1850s had wavered in the political and economic crises. The utopian communities, the myriad reform movements, in fact all schemes, it seemed, to improve mankind had stalled by the late 1850s, including the once-promising democratic revolutions in Europe. These trends troubled Lincoln, normally an optimist when it came to his country and its institutions. Just as the religious revival represented a personal rebirth for its participants, perhaps the nation required a similar rededication for its salvation.

Lincoln took his text from Matthew 12:25: "And Jesus knew their thoughts, and said unto them, Every kingdom divided against itself is brought to desolation; and every city or house divided against itself shall not stand." He had visited this verse several times in the past as his conviction grew that America could not fulfill its mission nor preserve its precious and fragile institutions if the nation persisted half slave and half free. It must be one or the other. This was not a Union-loving compromiser talking; the mounting political crisis had convinced him that the battle must be joined, probably sooner rather than later. The speech implied that Lincoln opposed not only the extension of slavery but the institution itself; that he would promote or favor policies designed to prevent its extension and erode its presence where it already existed.[52]

Lincoln argued that support for the Republican Party (and therefore for himself) guaranteed a free nation; support for the Democrats and Douglas affirmed the nationalization of slavery, a process already begun with the Dred Scott decision and Douglas's complicitous role in voiding the Missouri Compromise with the Kansas-Nebraska Act. Though the prospect that Stephen A. Douglas was part of a Slave Power conspiracy was far-fetched—Douglas, after all, had a very public and politically damaging split with the administration— the allegations played well in a state determined to remain white. Just ten years earlier, 70 percent of Illinois voters favored a constitutional amendment to exclude African Americans from the state. Douglas, seizing on this sentiment, would emphasize that Lincoln was a dangerous radical, a lover of black people (often put in more inelegant language), and an advocate of the unnatural mingling of the races.[53]

Initially, Lincoln had difficulty getting his message across. Less well known than the popular Douglas, he followed the Little Giant around the state responding to his speeches. It was not an effective strategy, as it enabled Douglas to set the tone and agenda of the campaign. So Lincoln challenged Douglas to a series of debates up and down the state. Douglas understood that such face-to-face contests would only give his opponent the recognition, publicity, and audience that he could not attract on his own. However, if Douglas declined, the electorate might take it as a sign of fear in the face of a manly challenge. Douglas agreed, though he set ground rules on venues and the order of speaking that favored him. In the seven debates that followed throughout Illinois in the late summer and early fall of 1858, some stark contrasts emerged. If each side had hoped to use the debates to clarify its views and distinguish itself from the other, the affairs were smashing successes. But they offered positions, not solutions, and in that, they highlighted the increasingly irreconcilable nature of the current political crisis and how much the spiritual had entered the public discourse.

Citizens came in their wagons, families with picnic baskets and children in tow, by canal boats, on horseback, and on foot, townspeople, farmers, merchants, laborers, and housewives, a cross-section of mid-nineteenth-century America, to make a day or maybe two days of it, doing a little shopping in town, greeting old friends and family, and enjoying the communal culinary concoctions and the liquid refreshments that always accompanied such events. Not quite a circus, more than a political event, not as lengthy or as earnest as a religious revival, and more elevating than a county fair sideshow, the debates included all of these elements and then some. They were entertainment, education, and spiritual enlightenment.

Not least, there were the visual and aural contrasts—the unlikely sonorous voice emanating from the small, impeccably attired Democrat, and the squeaky Kentucky drawl of the Republican, so tall that his breeches never seemed long enough, and so awkward that his arms flailed about as he spoke, as if he were trying to find the right swimming stroke instead of the correct phrase. Douglas traveled to the venues in a private train, while Lincoln arrived rumpled from squeezing into uncomfortable public conveyances. Carl Schurz, who witnessed some of the debates, and who was not a paragon of fashion himself, noted with some pain that Lincoln dressed in a "rusty black frock-coat with sleeves that should have been longer" and black trousers that "permitted a very full view of his large feet." If Lincoln wanted to appear as a man of the people, he succeeded. Douglas, on the other hand, projected the aura of a statesman.[54]

The debates drew interest not only from the locals but also from well beyond the state. The *New York Times*, a Republican newspaper, noted that Illinois was "the most interesting political battle-ground in the Union." Few in Illinois would disagree. The debates attracted huge throngs, aided by the coincidence of the contests with lay-by time on the farm. At the first debate in Ottawa, some eighty miles southwest of Chicago, ten thousand people turned up, though the town contained a population of less than nine thousand.[55]

Douglas hammered on the Lincoln-as-radical theme. Lincoln's "House Divided" speech provided fodder for Douglas's charge that Republicans and Lincoln would sacrifice the Union to destroy slavery. Once emancipation occurred, Douglas asserted, freed slaves would flood Illinois to "cover your prairies with black settlements" and "turn this beautiful state into a free negro colony." He was not above more primitive race baiting. Warming up the crowd at the debate in Freeport, Douglas related that he had spotted Frederick Douglass a while earlier on the edge of the gathering in a "carriage—and a magnificent one

it was . . . a beautiful young lady was sitting on the box-seat, whilst Fred Douglass and her mother reclined inside, and the owner of the carriage acted as
driver." While laughter rippled through the crowd, a Lincoln backer yelled out,
"What of it?" Douglas replied, "All I have to say is if you, Black Republicans,
think that the negro ought to ride in a carriage with your wife, whilst you drive
the team, you have a perfect right to do so."[56]

The charges threw Lincoln on the defensive. He initially tried to match
Douglas's racial views and reassure his audiences that there would be no
black republic in Illinois or anywhere else on his watch. Lincoln also argued
that Republicans, not Democrats, would keep the territories white, since, in
the wake of the Dred Scott decision, popular sovereignty could no longer
guarantee that protection. But Douglas replied that the people of a territory
could exclude slavery prior to the formation of a state constitution simply by
not enacting legislation to protect it. By doing nothing, the territory's inhabitants complied with the letter of Dred Scott while at the same time effectively
excluding slaveholders. Since slavery could not exist anywhere without specific protective legislation, that would discourage slaveholders from bringing
their chattel into the territory.

This so-called Freeport Doctrine undercut Lincoln's attempt to connect
Douglas to an alleged Slave Power conspiracy. But Douglas's response did
longer-term damage to his political future and that of the Democratic Party. It
widened the breach between himself and President Buchanan, who believed
that the Dred Scott decision killed popular sovereignty. It further isolated
Douglas and like-minded northern Democrats from the Buchanan administration, and from southern Democrats.

In the meantime, Douglas was having the best of the debates. At the fourth
debate, in Charleston, Illinois, Lincoln encountered a mocking banner raised
by Democrats, captioned "Negro Equality," depicting a white man beside a
black woman with a mulatto boy in the background. Though Lincoln's supporters ripped down the banner before the debate began, he felt obliged to
address his views on race again: "I am not, nor ever have been, in favor of
bringing about in any way the social and political equality of the white and
black races. I am not nor ever have been in favor of making voters or jurors of
negroes, nor of qualifying them to hold office, nor to intermarry with white
people." He based his position on the belief that "there is a physical difference
between the white and black races which I believe will forever forbid the two
races living together on terms of social and political equality."[57]

Did Lincoln really believe what he said at Charleston, or was it merely a
question of tailoring the message to suit the crowd? It was not unusual for politicians conducting statewide campaigns to say different things at different ven-

Lincoln responding to Stephen A. Douglas (seated to his right) during their debate at Charleston, Illinois, September 18, 1858. Douglas repeatedly used race-baiting as a tactic, especially in this debate. Lincoln responded here by denying he favored social and political equality for blacks. (Abraham Lincoln Presidential Library and Museum)

ues, even to the point of appearing to contradict themselves. Few voters in downstate Illinois knew what Lincoln or Douglas had said in Chicago, and vice versa. In Chicago, Lincoln had expressed a general belief in black equality. But he had always expressed ambivalence about the ability of blacks and whites to live together in peace and harmony. Abraham Lincoln held the sensibilities of a nineteenth-century white man. What distinguished him, however, was that he believed deeply in the humanity of African Americans and in their equality before God.

It was not until the fifth debate, at Galesburg in the more friendly environs of northern Illinois, that Lincoln took to the offensive and presented his differences with Douglas in moral terms. "I confess myself as belonging to that class in the country that believes slavery to be a moral and political wrong. . . . I believe that slavery is wrong, and in a policy springing from that belief that looks to the prevention of the enlargement of that wrong, and that looks at some time to there being an end of that wrong. The other sentiment is that it is not wrong, and the policy springing from it that there is no wrong in its becoming bigger, and that there never will be any end of it. There is the difference between Judge Douglas and his friends and the Republican party."[58]

Unlike Douglas, Lincoln also believed that America's sacred founding documents were inclusive of all races. Changing the tone of the debate from expressions of racial orthodoxy to the meaning and legacy of America's democratic experiment, Lincoln elevated the dialogue and deepened the importance of the contest. He challenged Douglas directly on the origins of the republic, a subject under much discussion during these troubling years. Though most of these probings concluded predictably with one side or the other claiming that it best represented the nation's birthright, the exercise involved an important definition, or redefinition of America for this second generation.

Lincoln was unequivocal on that legacy. "The entire records of the world, from the date of the Declaration of Independence up to within three years ago, may be searched in vain for one single affirmation, from one single man, that the negro was not included in the Declaration of Independence." He squared that view with his earlier statements endorsing social and political racial inequality by explaining that "the inferior races" were equal in their right to life, liberty, and the pursuit of happiness.[59]

Lincoln placed his differences with Douglas into this broader moral context so his listeners might understand the high stakes involved, that the slavery issue was not merely a political question like, say, the tariff or the transcontinental railroad but a test of America's democratic and religious ideals: "It is the eternal struggle between these two principles—right and wrong—throughout the world. They are the two principles that have stood face to face from the beginning of time; and will ever continue to struggle. The one is the common right of humanity and the other the divine right of kings." In these few sentences, Lincoln related how the slavery issue connected to principles that transcended both time and space. He linked the anti-slavery cause to the nation's democratic legacy and its global mission.[60]

Lincoln held a universal perspective on the American experiment. His immersion in the writings of the founding generation, the abortive revolutions of 1848, and the anguish of America's friends over the nation's struggle with slavery convinced him that more was at stake than the integrity of the Union. After the election of James Buchanan, Alexis de Tocqueville wrote to a friend wondering if the event signaled a campaign to extend slavery to the territories. If that were the case, Tocqueville worried, then Europeans would view it as "one of the greatest crimes that men can commit against the general cause of humanity." Several months later, after Dred Scott and Lecompton, Tocqueville prayed for the integrity of the Union, identifying America with the cause "of liberty across the world."[61]

Lincoln not only identified the cause of the Republican Party with the forces of liberty and freedom all over the world but also framed the debate as a contest between good and evil. Evangelical rhetoric had pervaded political discourse at least since the early 1840s. But coming on the heels of a national religious revival, Lincoln's assertion reinforced the perception that the nation was approaching a battle that could determine the future of mankind for eternity: "As I view the contest, it is not less than a contest for the advancement of the kingdom of Heaven or the kingdom of Satan." The difficulty with raising the stakes so high was that it threatened to polarize the electorate so that one side or the other could find the results of a democratic election totally unacceptable. For how do you compromise with evil?[62]

The revival that began in the despair and disorder of New York City in the winter of 1857–58 now gave way to a broader revival. To save the Union and what it stood for in the world, Lincoln implied, it might be necessary to destroy it, to have it reborn in a form more consonant with its sacred founding documents and the sainted men who framed them.

CHAPTER 7

THE BOATMAN

ISAAC SMITH BOUGHT A FARM in Maryland. It was good land in this country of gently rolling hills. Perhaps Smith would grow corn, oats, wheat, and carve out a small patch for tobacco. That is what his neighbors did in this part of Maryland, so different from the plantation agriculture of the Eastern Shore where Frederick Douglass spent his early days. Only Smith was not a farmer. He was not even Isaac Smith. His name was John Brown.

Peace in Kansas had left Brown out of work but not out of ideas. The growing belief in the North of a Slave Power conspiracy inspired the patriarch to look up some of his old friends back east. He had nurtured a plan of liberation for a decade, waiting for the right time to implement it. God told him this was that time.

Not God but Frederick Douglass visited John Brown. They sat on a rock, and the white man unfolded his plan before the incredulous black man. Twenty-two men would seize the federal arsenal at Harpers Ferry and liberate Virginia's slaves. Brown wanted Douglass to join his righteous army. "I want you for a special purpose," Brown informed his guest. "When I strike, the bees will begin to swarm, and I want you to help hive them." Douglass liked neither his purported role as some black Queen Bee nor the plan. He urged Brown to revisit his idea of creating a mountain enclave for runaway slaves. When the white man demurred, Douglass thanked his host, quit the rock, and left Brown to his own devices.[1]

Brown financed the purchase of the farm and his small "army" with funds from some of New England's leading white abolitionists, known as the "Secret Six." Their support for Brown, though, was hardly clandestine. In the South, their names would become synonyms for perfidy: Gerrit Smith, Thomas Wentworth Higginson, Theodore Parker, George Stearns, Franklin Sanborn, and Samuel Gridley Howe—all from prominent New England families and most with close ties to evangelical Protestantism. These were more than armchair revolutionaries. They had defied the law by harboring escaped slaves and believed in the concept of righteous violence.

Although Frederick Douglass declined the role of accomplice, fellow black abolitionist Harriet Tubman proved more receptive to the plot. Tubman, like Douglass a native of Maryland's Eastern Shore, had become a legendary liberator by the late 1850s. After escaping from bondage in 1849, Tubman served as a powerful voice for abolition and women's rights. Her fame derived less from what she said than from what she did. At great personal peril, she ventured back into the South nearly a dozen times during the 1850s to spirit out slaves through the Underground Railroad. From 1852 until the beginning of the Civil War, Tubman made one, sometimes two trips a year into Maryland or Virginia to rescue ten or more slaves at a time. In an era when one slave could reveal a plot in exchange for a privilege, the volume of Tubman's nocturnal raids, and the fact that all of her charges (and herself) made it safely to freedom, were incredible.[2]

Tubman's feats proved to Brown that a vast slave population awaited the opportunity to liberate themselves and join the army of freedom. Brown determined to provide that opportunity and sought Tubman's help. She offered detailed information on the topography of western Virginia and agreed to enlist black recruits from Canada. Tubman proved much more successful in the first endeavor than in the second. Former slaves were willing to help their fellows in bondage but did not relish martyrdom as a probable consequence of such actions. Still, Brown was ecstatic at Tubman's endorsement and assistance. He wrote, "I am succeeding to all appearance beyond my expectation. . . . Harriet Tubman hooked on . . . at once. He is the most of a man naturally, that I ever met with." Brown did not confuse Tubman's gender; her actions and bravery seemed so masculine to nineteenth-century men that Brown un-self-consciously referred to her in this manner. Brown was not the only abolitionist who made this allusion. Thomas Wentworth Higginson simply called her "Moses."[3]

More than a Moses was necessary to pull off Brown's harebrained scheme. The secrecy of his operation was no more secure than the identities of his white abolitionist benefactors. He left a detailed paper trail at his Maryland farm. His small band (now down to eighteen men) departed for Virginia with only one day's rations. While the federal arsenal at Harpers Ferry was a logical target if one hoped to secure arms, it was not an ideal location from which to foment a slave rebellion. Situated in the northwestern part of Virginia, a region of small slaveholdings, Harpers Ferry lay a considerable distance from the main centers of plantation slavery in Southside Virginia where, nearly a generation earlier, Nat Turner launched his bloody but futile rebellion. Although Brown and his band would take the arsenal with deceptive ease, nary a slave rallied to their banner. But the United States Marines under the command of Colonel Robert E. Lee did, putting an inglorious end to the plot.[4]

Governor Henry A. Wise charged Brown with treason against the state of Virginia, a curious accusation since Brown was not a resident of Virginia and owed no allegiance to the state. The wounded warrior, carried into court on a stretcher, maintained a stoic defiance throughout the brief trial, at the end of which he was allowed to make a five-minute speech. His was the eloquence of a man just short of the gallows and long convinced of his righteousness. Brown's brief statement emphasized the basic contradiction between slavery and America's democratic Christianity. Men who loved God and who believed God loved them could not allow the institution to exist:

> This Court acknowledges, too, as I suppose, the validity of the law of God. I see a book kissed, which I suppose to be the Bible, or at least the New Testament, which teaches me that all things whatsoever I would that men should do to me, I should do even so to them. It teaches me, further, to remember them that are in bonds as bound with them. I endeavored to act up to that instruction. I say I am yet too young to understand that God is any respecter of persons. I believe that to have interfered as I have done ... in behalf of His despised poor, is no wrong, but right. Now, if it is deemed necessary that I should forfeit my life for the furtherance of the ends of justice and mingle my blood further with the blood of my children and with the blood of millions in this slave country whose rights are disregarded by wicked, cruel, and unjust enactments, I say let it be done.[5]

On December 1, 1859, John Brown wrote his last words before the escort came to his cramped cell: "I ... am now quite certain that the crime of this guilty land will never be purged away but with blood." Still suffering from his wounds, he slowly mounted the scaffold, ramrod straight. As he ascended he could look above and through the now-barren trees of impending winter to a church steeple. The bells were tolling.[6]

The bells tolled in New England, too. John Brown accomplished more in death than in life. He did not cause the nation to disintegrate or the bloody civil war that followed. But his death illuminated the growing estrangement of North and South perhaps more than any other previous incident, coming as it did on top of an accumulation of perceived wrongs, insults, and aggressions from both sides. George Templeton Strong, who, like many of his fellow northerners, condemned the raid but recognized the controlling influence of Brown's legacy, wrote in his diary: "Old John Brown was hanged this morning; justly, say I, but his name may be a word of power for the next half century." Strong underestimated that legacy. Sixty years later, in his poem "John

Brown," Edwin Arlington Robinson has the old man vowing, "I shall have more to say when I am dead."[7]

Most northerners denounced the deed even as they admired Brown's stoicism. His martyrdom did not create a groundswell for the abolitionist cause; nor did it provide a boost for the Republican Party. Northerners recoiled from the raid's implications: a slave insurrection and disunion. *Harper's Weekly,* a new and influential nonpartisan magazine, editorialized that "though the leading Republican politicians and papers may and do repudiate the acts of Brown and his associates, it is likely that a large section of the people of this country will hold them responsible for what has happened."[8]

Abraham Lincoln recognized the danger in just such an association, particularly after authorities discovered the cache of correspondence between Brown and various white and black New England abolitionists, some with ties to the Republican Party. Lincoln's opposition to Brown's Raid derived not from political expediency but from his genuine regard for the rule of law and his concern that such acts, however well intentioned, could set back the anti-slavery cause. He explained that Brown's plot was "wrong for two reasons. It was a violation of law and it was, as all such attacks must be, futile as far as any effect it might have on the extinction of a great evil." Lincoln admired Brown's "great courage [and] rare unselfishness" but diagnosed the old man as "insane," concluding with the wry comment that the raid was "an attempt by white men to get up a revolt among slaves, in which the slaves refused to participate."[9]

African Americans living in the North held a different perspective. For many, the idea that a white person would give up his life and the lives of his sons for their cause was a novel thought. White anti-slavery martyrs existed, such as Elijah Lovejoy, but these individuals used words; Brown took action and carried the fight to the South, and gave his life for that effort. Harriet Tubman, who knew about bravery, noted, "When I think how he gave up his life for our people, and how he never flinched, but was so brave to the end, it's clear to me it wasn't mortal man, it was God in him."[10]

Southerners dismissed northern disclaimers as self-serving. They read about the church bells tolling all over New England at the hour of Brown's execution. They recalled William H. Seward's comment about an "irrepressible conflict" and how that suddenly sprang to life in western Virginia. They saw the widely broadcast comments of prominent abolitionists whom they had come to invest with considerably more influence than they actually enjoyed—part of the process of each section believing the worst about the other and convincing themselves that the worst was the norm.

The event confirmed for southerners that the Republican Party was "organized on the basis of making war" against the South. Others mocked the demonstrations of piety and moral outrage, especially in New England, a region "built up and sustained by the products of negro slave labor." The solemn processions of mourning and the tableaux depicting the martyred Brown doubtless broke the cold, gray monotony of a Boston December. "It is a pity that they haven't a witch or two to drown or burn, by way of variety."[11]

That the Slave Power had created a martyr, abolitionists did not doubt. Some southerners agreed. A Kentucky editor predicted that "if old John Brown is executed, there will be thousands to dip their handkerchiefs in his blood; relics of the martyr will be paraded throughout the North." Though the journalist overestimated the procession, several prominent northern writers compared John Brown's execution with the crucifixion. Ralph Waldo Emerson predicted that Brown would "make the gallows as glorious as the cross." Thoreau, on the day of Brown's execution, wrote, "Some 1800 years ago Christ was crucified; this morning . . . Captain Brown was hung. These are the two ends of a chain which is not without its links. He is not Old Brown any longer; he is an angel of light."[12]

Such expressions of grief gave heart to southern disunionists. Since the Jackson administration, a small but expanding group of southern leaders dreamed of a unified region. The moderation of the Upper South, the discipline of party, and the influence of southern politicians in the federal government muted nationalist movements in the South. John C. Calhoun labored long and hard during the 1830s and 1840s to develop a regional unity that transcended party, to little avail. Occasionally, southerners came together in commercial conventions to lessen their dependence on northern trade, manufacturing, and finance. But concerted political efforts floundered. The flashpoints of the 1850s all seemed to break the South's way—the Fugitive Slave Law, the repeal of the Missouri Compromise, and Dred Scott. Yet the region had little to show for these "triumphs."

Brown's Raid was another matter: a bold if farcical invasion of the South compounded by an outpouring of grief and invective from the North. Perhaps southerners could see now the true beliefs of their adversaries. A South Carolina editor enthused, "Never before, since the Declaration of Independence, has the South been more united in sentiment." "Recent events have wrought almost a complete revolution in the sentiments, the thoughts, the hopes, of the oldest and steadiest conservatives in all the southern states," the *Richmond Whig* rejoiced. The *Whig* counted "thousands upon . . . thousands of men in our midst who, a month ago, scoffed at the idea of a dissolution of the Union as a madman's dream, but who now hold the opinion that its days are numbered, its glory perished."[13]

Southerners now had their own version of the Slave Power conspiracy. The

Charleston Mercury, ever in the forefront of disunion sentiment, admitted that Brown's insurrection "has been silly and abortive." But, the editor claimed, the raid was a small part of a "wide-spread scheme . . . maturing at the North for insurrections throughout the South." It was clear to the *Mercury* that "the great source of the evil is that we are under one government with these people." John Brown's Raid provided southern extremists with a patina of credibility. After more than a decade of preaching that the sky was falling, here was an overt act that seemed to corroborate their predictions.[14]

The fears themselves were all the more unsettling because they contradicted the basis of pro-slavery propaganda, that the institution was a positive good. Slavery rested on a tower of illogic that rendered the South increasingly defensive, for what is defended more fiercely than the indefensible: an institution of bondage in a land founded for freedom; evangelicals claimed slaves had souls, yet masters typically considered them property; slaveholders argued that the African possessed a limited intellect, yet slaves worked a variety of skilled occupations, and a few managed plantations; pro-slavery advocates maintained that the institution civilized the African, yet they emphasized the indelible primitive nature of his culture; and they asserted that the institution's basic benevolence created happy workers, yet feared their homicidal retribution.

Such introspection did not characterize southern public discourse in the 1850s. Protecting the institution of slavery remained foremost on the agenda of southern leaders as the Congress gathered three days after John Brown's execution. For the next two months, Republicans and Democrats hurled insults across the aisle until the Republicans, holding a scant majority of eight members, managed to elect the new Speaker of the House. South Carolina senator James H. Hammond commented wryly, "The only persons who do not have a revolver and a knife are those who have two revolvers." Reporters noted that even those in the gallery carried weapons.[15]

Republicans stood little chance of passing their favorite bills with a slim majority in the House, a Democratic majority in the Senate, and a Democratic administration. Measures such as a western homestead bill to attract eastern workers and farmers to the territories, federal assistance to a transcontinental railroad, and a higher tariff to protect industries and their workers all went down to defeat, either by the Senate or with President Buchanan's veto. Southern Democrats fought these proposals fiercely: 160-acre homesteads precluded plantation agriculture; a Republican-sponsored transcontinental railroad would invariably bypass the South; and the tariff threatened the South's booming cotton economy—all good reasons for opposition. But without a countervailing program other than the slave code, Democratic opposition appeared obstructionist, a collective vote against progress, against the workingman, against the settling of the West; in short, against everything Americans had dreamed of, fought for, and uprooted their lives to achieve over the past generation.

Southerners had dreams, too. They resented the implication that the North was synonymous with America. They resented any intimation that they were retrograde and opposed to progress, technology, and innovation. They rejected any suggestion of inferiority—moral, political, or economic. The fight over the extension of slavery into the territories touched on all three. The Republicans had made that extension a moral issue—Lincoln had stated as much during his debates with Douglas. The loss of access to the territories would seal the South's position as a perpetual political minority. If the Republicans, an avowedly sectional party, attained power, the consequences for the South and slavery could be dire.

Walt Whitman, ever the nationalist, groped for a way of uniting North and South on some common ground, of bypassing the self-serving politicians and poseurs. He envisioned a "healthy-bodied, middle-aged, beard-faced American blacksmith or boatman," who will "come down from the West across the Alleghenies, and walk into the Presidency." If the West embodied America's future, it also represented its salvation.[16]

Abraham Lincoln had considered the blacksmith's trade and had piloted various craft on the western waters, though he would claim neither as a vocation. He dared not think of himself as presidential timber either, joking in October 1858, "Just think of such a sucker as me as President." If Lincoln did not think much of the idea, other men did. Some viewed his relatively brief career in Washington as an attribute: an outsider unsullied by corruption and unseemly behavior; a fine orator conversant with the basic moral and religious principles that informed the beliefs of many Americans; and a man who, in the age of the common man, seemed genuinely common.[17]

Lincoln had distinguished himself in his losing battle against Stephen A. Douglas and in speeches throughout the Midwest during the latter part of 1859. Easterners began to notice, and a group of them supporting Ohio senator Salmon P. Chase for the Republican presidential nomination and seeking to upset the bandwagon for the front-runner, New York's William H. Seward, arranged an invitation through Horace Greeley for Lincoln to deliver a speech at Henry Ward Beecher's Plymouth Church in Brooklyn early in 1860. It was a difficult time for Republicans, as many Americans associated the party with Brown's Raid and the Union-threatening agitation of the slavery question. Lincoln's trip east represented not only an effort to overshadow

Seward's popularity in his home state but also an attempt to bring a fresh face and voice to eastern Republicans.[18]

The trip east was a big deal for Lincoln. He bought a new suit; he visited Mathew Brady's photographic studio to take a serious portrait; and he labored over his Plymouth speech more than he had over any other address—a labor he performed twice over as the venue for his presentation changed from Beecher's church to the decidedly more political forum of the Cooper Union in Manhattan. Greeley wanted a broader platform for his new western star.

Lincoln did not disappoint his eastern promoters. More than fifteen hundred people braved a driving snowstorm to listen to this strange-looking and -sounding westerner. Maybe the surprise of hearing eloquence emanating from such an ungainly form with a voice to match accounted for the enthusiasm, but there was no gainsaying that the western star had become an eastern phenomenon. The reviews gushed unstinting praise. Greeley's *Tribune* exclaimed, "He's the greatest man since St. Paul." Major Republican organs around the country picked up the speech and published it as a pamphlet, and venues throughout the Northeast clamored for Lincoln to speak.[19]

Lincoln did not expound any new ideas in his Cooper Union speech. But he had a knack throughout his political career of articulating what his audience was thinking with such eloquence that it appeared as a proclamation from the gods. He elevated not only his sentiments but also his listeners, imparting an importance to their mutual journey to a greater end. In February 1860, the nation wondered about the insurgent Republican Party, a sectional organization hostile to the South and, therefore, a threat to the integrity of the Union. John Brown's ascension to martyrdom, supported by select Republicans, damaged the party's profile in the North. Several southern leaders stated flatly that a Republican victory in the upcoming presidential election would end the Union. The front-runner for the Republican nomination, William H. Seward, concerned northerners with his confrontational rhetoric—the appeal to a "higher law," and the "irrepressible conflict" that he foresaw.

Two months earlier, just a few weeks after John Brown's execution, a Unionist rally drew a crowd of ten thousand to lower Manhattan in bitter weather. Five thousand of these citizens squeezed into the Academy of Music to hear patriotic speeches. Banners festooned the hall bearing famous Unionist quotes headed by George Washington's declaration, "Indignantly frowning upon the first dawning of every attempt to alienate any portion of our country from the rest, or to enfeeble the sacred ties which now link together the various parts." A thirty-two-gun salute punctuated the orations. New York brooked no patience with those who agitated the slavery question. Should the Republicans pull back to a position of conciliation and compromise?[20]

Abraham Lincoln's Cooper Union speech offered a resounding "no" and revived Republican morale by emphasizing the party's basic reason for existence: its political and moral opposition to the extension of slavery in the territories. Neither bullied by southern threats of disunion nor discouraged by the weakening of northern resolve, Lincoln refocused the attention on the party's primary objective, a position he believed appealed to a broad cross-section of northerners and threatened no malice to the South or to slavery where it currently existed. "Neither let us be slandered from our duty by false accusations against us, nor frightened from it by menaces of destruction to the Government nor of dungeons to ourselves," Lincoln counseled his audience. The Republican Party would not attack slavery where it existed but would "stand by our duty fearlessly and effectively" to prevent its extension. He concluded with a stirring call to carry forward the party's first principles with pride and purpose: "Let us have faith that right makes might, and in that faith, let us, to the end, dare to do our duty as we understand it." It was a classic Lincoln speech, steeped in morality and moderation, strong but not aggressive.[21]

The new voice from the West warmed to the reception. Lincoln allowed himself to entertain thoughts of the presidency. "The taste *is* in my mouth a little," he admitted. By the time the Republicans convened in Chicago in May 1860 to nominate their presidential candidate, Lincoln was not a long shot for the prize. He was almost everyone's second choice—acceptable as an alternative to the Seward men, to the supporters of Senator Salmon P. Chase, and to those who favored conservative former Whig Edward Bates of Missouri. He was, in effect, the least objectionable man at the convention. If any of the other candidates faltered, Lincoln would be the logical beneficiary.[22]

Lincoln also benefited from the location of the convention in his home state of Illinois. His reputation as the most moderate of the candidates, save for the colorless Bates, impressed delegates convinced that only a moderate nominee had a chance to carry the states of the lower North. The Republicans could win the presidency without the South, but they needed Pennsylvania, Ohio, and Indiana if they wanted to achieve that victory. Lincoln, more than Seward, could appeal to conservative former Whigs in these states.

Lincoln's campaign managers deftly portrayed the Illinois lawyer as a Republican Andrew Jackson, a man born in a log cabin who enjoyed splitting rails and plowing dirt, though in truth he abhorred any serious labor connected with rural life. The image harked back to the successful "Log Cabin and Hard Cider" Whig campaign of 1840, an association the Republicans hoped to cultivate among former Whigs. Lincoln was now the "Rail Splitter," as Andrew Jackson was "Old Hickory," a rough-hewn westerner, a striking evocation of the incorruptible and indomitable common man. What better individual to lead the nation out of sin and toward redemption than someone fresh out of the West, America's dream region.

The platform that Lincoln would run on—and party faithful paid much more attention to the specifics of these documents than we do today—expressed this promise. Although the Republicans did not abandon their strong opposition to the extension of slavery in the territories, they did not duplicate the defiant tone of the 1856 party platform that contained a specific denunciation of the Slave Power. The platform was a western document offering homesteads on the frontier, federal aid to improve rivers and harbors, and a slight increase in the tariff to stimulate the region's industrial base and appeal also to the older manufacturing districts of the East. The platform avoided offending immigrants, despite the party's vigorous Know Nothing contingent, calling for "full and efficient protection to the rights of all classes of citizens, whether native or naturalized, both at home and abroad."[23]

The revival-like unity of the Republicans reflected a growing confidence in the party's prospects, especially given the disarray of the Democratic Party after its nominating convention in Charleston, South Carolina, a few weeks earlier. A worse venue for a party that desperately needed to come together could not have been imagined. The idea was that if the Democrats could come out of this southern nationalist stronghold as a unified party, the most difficult part of the campaign would be behind them. But from the outset, Charleston proved an unfortunate choice. The city lacked the hotel space to accommodate the crush of delegates, and the oppressive April heat rendered the packed hall a cauldron of quick tempers and short wits. Southern delegates competed with each other as to who could elicit the most raucous cheers from the packed partisan galleries. If those delegates had followed through on their threats, the Democratic Party would have declared war on the United States by the midpoint of the convention. Incendiary rhetoric left the Democratic Party in ashes.

Southern delegates were much more intent on making a point than on nominating a presidential candidate. The posturing that southerners had exhibited in the current congressional session carried over into the convention's deliberations. When the platform committee called for a federal slave code in the territories, northern Democrats, in the majority, defeated the proposal, prompting a walkout by delegates from Alabama, South Carolina, Georgia, Florida, Mississippi, Louisiana, and Texas, thus depriving the likely nominee, Stephen A. Douglas, of the required two-thirds majority. The convention voted to reconvene in Baltimore in June.

The political landscape had darkened for the Democrats by June. The

Republicans were already fanning out over the North to spread their gospel of progress, prosperity, and national union. Rival delegations from the Lower South states arrived in Baltimore, one side pledged to Douglas and the other to obstruction. When the convention voted for the Douglas delegations, the spurned delegates walked out, this time joined by colleagues from the Upper South. The remaining delegates nominated Douglas for president and Herschel V. Johnson, of Georgia—one of the few southerners remaining in the hall—for vice president. Southern delegates convened to nominate sitting vice president John C. Breckinridge of Kentucky as their presidential candidate and Senator Joseph Lane of Oregon as vice president. The breakup of the last national party was complete.

Alexander Stephens, who stood with Douglas to the last, despaired, not only for his party but for his country: "There is a tendency everywhere, not only at the North, but at the South, to strife, dissension, disorder, and anarchy." The chaos that his friend Abraham Lincoln had warned against two decades earlier now seemed imminent. The southern bolters achieved their objectives: they denied Douglas the nomination of a unified party, and they crafted a platform brimming with a "full measure of Southern rights." Yet, by fracturing the Democratic Party, the southern delegates rendered it more likely that a party hostile to those rights would assume power. Perhaps that was their intention.[24]

A month before the Democratic Party reconvened to die, a group of former Whigs, mainly from northern and southern border states, gathered in Baltimore as the Constitutional Union Party and selected John Bell of Tennessee as its presidential candidate, with Edward Everett of Massachusetts as his running mate. The party platform was simple: for the Constitution and for the Union.

With four presidential candidates in the field, the 1860 presidential campaign unfolded in three distinct campaigns: Douglas against Lincoln in the North; Breckinridge versus Bell in the South; and Douglas contesting Bell in the border states, with Lincoln and Breckinridge hoping for some support there as well.

The Republicans left Chicago with the campaign initiative that they never relinquished. They used their congressional investigations into the corruption of the Buchanan administration—the first such hearings in the nation's history—and the southern Democratic obstruction of their programs to aid workers and farmers with land in the West, and the homespun nature of their presidential candidate to broaden the party's appeal in the key border states of the North.

Republican rallies exuded an evangelical fervor that blended religious and military pageantry much in the manner of the Free Soil Party, though on a grander scale. They performed before a more receptive audience, as anti-slavery and, especially anti-southern sentiment had grown in the North since 1848. The "Wide-Awakes," the party's shock troops of younger voters, four hundred thousand strong by one estimate, paraded in black oilcloth capes and red shirts after the fashion of the Paris revolutionaries of 1848. Even into the Democratic stronghold of New York City they marched, holding their torches high through the narrow streets of lower Manhattan preceded by booming military bands, and cheered on by thousands of partisan onlookers who sang out the "Freedom Battle Hymn," entreating citizens to march "On for free-dom, God, our country, and the right." The rally culminated at Broadway and Tenth Street at midnight in a shower of Roman candles. Wherever the Wide-Awakes went during that campaign season, their parades and the accompany-ing din of music and fireworks lent an impression of an inexorable tide changing the political landscape of America for all time. Here was not merely a political rally; here was a movement.[25]

Wide-Awakes marching through lower Manhattan, October 3, 1860.
Though not a paramilitary organization, the Wide-Awakes wore uniforms and
marched in precision order through northern streets supporting the candidacy of
Abraham Lincoln, lending a martial atmosphere to Republican rallies during
the 1860 election campaign. (Courtesy of the Library of Congress)

The Republicans flaunted their youthful exuberance and their righteousness. Morality was a major theme at these events, conveniently bundling the issues of slavery, Roman Catholicism, prohibition, and political corruption. Wide-Awakes were fond of chanting the doggerel "Little Doug [liked] lots of drink in his jug," while portraying Lincoln as a paragon of virtue—abstemious in alcohol, tobacco, and swearing—that was at least two-thirds accurate. Lincoln, moreover, was "religiously honest." "Honest Abe" would restore probity and purity to the White House. Not a politician but a statesman, a man who had only a brief stay in Washington before returning to toil humbly for his people.[26]

Despite the Republican Party platform's silence on religion and Lincoln's rejection of nativism, former Know Nothings grasped the evangelical fervor of the campaign to pursue their attacks on the Catholic Church. One Republican newspaper, blending anti-slavery and nativist rhetoric, alleged that "Roman Catholics, whose consciences are enslaved . . . regard the King of Rome—the Pope—as the depository of all authority." Another editor forged the same connection, charging that Irish Catholics "were sots and bums who crawled out of their 'rotten nests of filth' on elections to cast ignorant ballots for the candidates of the slaveocracy." Republicans distilled the Democrats to an unholy trinity of "the Pope, a whisky barrel, and a nigger driver." Little wonder that Catholics responded to this barrage by voting in unprecedented numbers for Democratic candidates. The nativist calculation that linking Catholics and slaveholders would attract rather than repel voters in key northern states proved correct, however. The Republicans' support of nativist policies in northern cities proved more compelling to some voters than the slavery issue.[27]

Stephen A. Douglas had no army drilling for him, though several northern cities managed spirited rallies for the Little Giant. Reviled by a substantial wing of his own party, Douglas took to the hustings, an unprecedented move for a major presidential candidate of that era. He crisscrossed the North and a good portion of the South, including a speaking tour in Georgia at the invitation of Alexander Stephens. He promoted popular sovereignty, exalted the Union, and warned against extremism.

In the South, the surrogates for Breckinridge and Bell carried on mannerly campaigns, with the former stressing the importance of protecting southern rights though not threatening disunion, and the latter hewing closely to the name of the party. Breckinridge's strong professions for the Union undercut Douglas's strategy to command the center position between anti-slavery and disunion. While there was plenty of disunion talk in the South, none of it came from Breckinridge.

The southern press and politicians devoted considerable space to these candidacies and, in the Upper South, to Douglas as well. They also reserved a good many column inches for a candidate whose name and party would not even appear on the ballots in ten southern states. A relative unknown in the South at the outset of the campaign—one Alabama newspaper referred to him as Gabriel Lincoln—he came to be known by many southerners as a subhuman creature whose political party existed primarily to destroy the South. The Republican candidate, according to one description, was a "horrid-looking wretch . . . sooty and scoundrelly in aspect; a cross between the nutmeg dealer, the horse-swapper, and the nightman."[28]

As "sooty" implied, southern journalists and politicians employed race to denigrate the Republicans. One editor claimed falsely that Lincoln's running mate, Hannibal Hamlin, "had negro blood in his veins and . . . one of his children had kinky hair." It was clear that the party stood for "one dogma— the equality of races, white and black." The amount of ink and rhetoric marshaled to excoriate Lincoln and the Republicans far exceeded their scant prospects for electoral success in the South. Rather, it seemed as if southern nationalists wished to educate the voters less about the election than about its aftermath should the Republicans win.[29]

Lincoln's frequent professions that Republicans bore no ill will toward the South or its institutions struck many in the South as disingenuous. After all, who would appoint the postmasters, the judges, and the customs agents, and who would control the military in a Republican administration? Southerners predicted a Republican administration's policies could wipe out "four hundred and thirty millions of dollars" of capital investment in slaves. "They know that they can plunder and pillage the South, as long as they are in the same Union with us, by . . . every other possible mode of injustice and peculation. They know that in the Union they can steal southern property in slaves." While Lincoln and Douglas sparred as to who best would promote the progress and prosperity of the nation, southerners viewed the election as a referendum on themselves—whether other parts of the Union valued their comity sufficiently to reject the Republican Party and accede to southern demands for protection.[30]

Lincoln did not say much during the campaign. "My published speeches contain nearly all I could willingly say." He did change his appearance, a source of constant comment by both his supporters and detractors. Several colleagues told him that he "would be much improved in appearance" if he cultivated "whiskers." When eleven-year-old Grace Bedell suggested during a campaign appearance that "you would look a great deal better" if he grew a beard, "for your face is so thin," he finally gave in and allowed hair to sprout and soften his sunken cheekbones.[31]

Alexander Stephens watched the campaign unfold from his Georgia residence and felt a rising sadness. The slanders against Lincoln pained him especially. Stephens believed that a Lincoln administration would run the government "just as safely for the South and honest and faithfully *in every particular*" as Buchanan had. "I know the man well," he emphasized. "He is not a bad man." Stephens feared the growing influence of disunionists in the South more than he feared the Republicans. If the future of slavery depended on conservative policies and leaders, then southern extremists played into the enemies' hands. Stephens stumped loyally for Douglas. He respected Breckin-ridge but worried about some of his supporters, noting that "those who begin revolutions seldom end them." By the fall, the extremists seemed ascendant. Stephens confided to a correspondent of the *New York Herald*, "I hold revolu-tion and civil war to be inevitable. The demagogues have raised a whirlwind they cannot control."[32]

Stephens's pessimism was justified. In those days, several northern states held statewide elections weeks before the presidential balloting, and the Re-publicans swept those races, portending their success in November. Douglas, sensing the inevitable, abruptly broke off his campaign and hurried to the South to plead with leaders and voters that the Union, above all, must be pre-served; that the legacy of the Founders transcended the election of one man. It was an extraordinary display of selfless patriotism and personal courage at a time when posturing passed for statesmanship. That it was a fool's errand, he could not know. Douglas knew only the Union.

Douglas fought a growing perception in the South that two nations already existed, a perspective shared by increasing numbers of northerners as well. The religious schism of the 1840s fueled these views initially. Southerners under-stood the implications of their increasingly minority status within the govern-ment and the nation. "Northern" and "American" now seemed interchangeable terms. Technology, fashion, finance, immigration, and the most widely read newspapers and magazines all congregated at the North and extended their influence throughout the nation. The fact that northern advances rested in part on the labor of four million slaves galled many southerners. They believed that without the South, the North would be a much lesser region.

Objectively, northerners and southerners shared many things. They both believed in the American dream that hard work brought financial well-being and independence. Both regions harbored aspiring urban middle classes that looked to investments in their families and their communities as down pay-ments on a rosy future. Northerners and southerners chased after railroads, canals, harbor improvements, and real estate. But for all the urban hubbub, the hiss of steam engines, and the click-click of the telegraph, America was still a nation of family farms and small shops, regardless of section. Ameri-cans prayed in similar ways; theirs was a personal God, and they reached for heaven with the same fervor with which they sought out the main chance of financial success. Northerners and southerners interpreted the world around them through their evangelical theology, that God had a purpose for them and their country, and that events fit into a larger divine plan.

North and South shared a revolutionary heritage, what Abraham Lincoln would call the "mystic chords of memory." They struggled to interpret that legacy, live up to it, and preserve it. Historical societies formed in profusion during the 1840s and 1850s in both sections. Northerners and southerners both prized the West, not only as the newest land but also as the American dream-scape, a place of renewal and redemption.[33]

Such similarities might have overcome political differences, were it not for slavery. The institution transformed common bonds into bitter differences. The technologies that drew a vast continent together—the steam railroad, the steamboat, and the telegraph—also transmitted news and information. Partisan political journals, magazines, sectarian publications, popular literature, and published speeches flooded homes, offices, and churches. An ink war erupted long before Fort Sumter. Citizens north and south exaggerated their mutual animosity. A claim from a southern journalist in 1860 that "nine-tenths" of northerners were abolitionists was preposterous, but the leading dailies and magazines in the South offered no contradiction. With every escalating event of the 1850s, "Slave Power" and "abolitionist" seemed as appropriate as "slave state" and "free state" as sectional descriptors.

The similar economic aspirations of North and South also foundered on the institution of slavery. If southerners could not carry their slaves westward or count on evenhanded economic development policies from the federal government, then their dependence was sealed and slavery doomed. By the late 1850s, southern political leaders looked to Mexico and the Caribbean, and the reopening of the African slave trade, to counter the immigrant population boom fueling northern political and economic power and leaving the South further behind.

Northerners and southerners may have prayed to the same God and espoused similar evangelical Protestant principles, but slavery inspired vastly different professions of faith. From the southern perspective, the Bible sanctioned slavery while northerners disregarded the holy book and the tradition of keeping religion out of politics. To one southern minister, the divide was simple. Northerners were "atheists, infidels, communists, free-lovers, rationalists, Bible haters, anti-christian levelers, and anarchists." Southerners, on the other hand, were "God-fearing and Christ-loving, conscientious people . . . that . . . have a zeal for God, and seek his glory and the good of man."[34]

Northern ministers preached that slavery violated the Golden Rule and threatened both individual souls and America's unique compact with God. Israel's downfall confirmed the truth that "righteousness exalteth a nation; but sin is a reproach." Expiating the sin of slavery was a Bible-based imperative for America. As for mixing religion and politics, slavery touched the core of personal and national morality. How could Christians remain silent?[35]

Southern writers and politicians believed that the anti-slavery spirit in the North derived not only from a very loose interpretation of the Bible but also from an excess of democracy. What a writer in *De Bow's Review* called the "no property masses" were ascendant in the North and would eventually unleash their hostility against property in the South. The writer drastically miscast the Republican Party as the repository of property-hating men, but the identity of Republicans and disorder in the southern mind obscured the reality. The affinity of propertyless men for the Republican Party was the "surest means of striking down the largest body of property holders in the country . . . as is the fact with the slave-owners of the South." The class struggle had spread from revolutionary Europe to northern cities, prompting cynical northern politicians to use the territories as a safety valve while retaining the migrants' allegiance in the West.[36]

The North represented to southerners the unfortunate conclusion of the democratic revolution in American politics during the first half of the nineteenth century, a revolution in which the South participated. From the 1820s onward, the newer states of the Lower South installed white male suffrage without property qualifications. In the older parts of the South, new constitutions afforded greater representation for western portions of those states and broadened the suffrage basis. Anxiety among the large property holders, who were also, of course, the large slaveholders, accompanied this process. Associating anti-slavery with propertyless masses in the North, the slaveholders projected their own fears onto northern society.

The restraint that characterized a society based on slavery was absent in the free North. Slavery, not freedom, best ensured republican government, an argument advanced by the editor of the *Southern Literary Messenger* in July 1860: "The defense of slavery is the defense not of the South alone . . . but a defense of republican institutions. The welfare of the Union and all the hopes of humanity that repose upon its maintenance, are inseparably bound up with slavery. With slavery and with the liberty to extend itself wherever it may, the Republic stands, without this liberty, it falls." Another southern editor, contemplating the likely election of Abraham Lincoln, put the matter bluntly: "Slavery cannot share a government with democracy."[37]

The democratic principle that most rankled the South was majority rule.

John C. Calhoun spent the better part of his political career devising schemes to ensure the protection of minority, i.e., southern, rights. In 1859, Louisiana's governor declared that "the Republican [Party] appears to foster the idea that . . . the majority of the voices in the whole United States . . . ought to rule." Few northerners would find that exceptional, but the idea frightened southerners. The result of majority rule had dire consequences for the South, matching even the worst excesses of European mass uprisings. South Carolina's Lawrence Keitt worried that "the concentration of absolute power in the hands of the North will develop the wildest democracy ever seen on this earth—unless it should have been matched in Paris in 1789."[38]

Southern concerns about the northern perversion of republican principles were well taken. The nation of the Founders no longer existed. The ethnic and religious diversity, the spread of universal white male suffrage, and the geographic expanse of the nation differed markedly from the conditions extant at the founding. These changes strained the orderly and balanced system of government established by the Constitution. "The worst of all possible forms of government," the Rev. James Henley Thornwell of South Carolina argued, was "democratic absolutism." On another occasion he wrote, "I am afraid that the tendency of things in this country is to corrupt a *representative* into a *democratic* government; and to make the State the mere creature of popular caprice."[39]

Southern references to the founding had to confront the inconvenient language of the Declaration of Independence, the self-evident truth that all men are created equal. Southerners asserted that Thomas Jefferson could only have been referring to white men or to Anglo-Saxon men, but his words stood as a shining rebuke to a society grounded on slavery. In 1855, Henry A. Washington, a law professor at William and Mary, delivered an address that summarized changing southern attitudes about that document. It proved so popular that the *Southern Literary Messenger* reprinted the speech in its April 1860 edition. After a "scientific" discussion on racial differences, Washington acknowledged that the concept of human equality "stands in the very front of the Declaration of Independence. It is there announced as a self-evident truth that all men are by nature equal." According to Washington, however, Jefferson's notion was both scientifically and morally incorrect and resulted "in many of the most mischievous errors of our times." It was incontrovertible that "the white races *are* superior to the brown, and the brown to the black."[40]

Most northerners would have agreed with southerners on the issue of white racial superiority. The cases of the Native American and the African "proved" white preeminence. However, others, including Lincoln, argued that the appropriate qualification to Jefferson's statement was that all men are created equal "to attain their respective capacities." Slavery was an institution that defied both God's law of creation and the nation's founding documents by inhibiting the African's proper evolution.

Southerners understood that the world and their country were changing, and they were being marginalized. From a purely statistical perspective, readily available in *De Bow's Review*, any literate southerner could trace the declining port revenues of New Orleans and Charleston, the burgeoning economies of Cincinnati, Chicago, and New York, and the pace of urbanization in the West. All foretold not only change but a deepening minority status. While De Bow continued to boost southern industrial and urban development, others imagined a graceful, agricultural South set off from the aggressive, materialistic, industrial North. Such a stark distinction was fanciful, but by 1860 it was easier to imagine difference.[41]

Slavery stood at the center of these perceived economic distinctions between North and South. Writers at the South told of the inexorable conflict between capital and labor in the North, a battle absent in the slaveholding South, where no white man could ever be subordinate or exploited, and where the slave is contented and cared for. "The dread *conflict* between *capital* and *labour . . . only finds a peaceful solution in slavery.*" As opposed to the tawdry, competitive, and chaotic society of the North, the South promoted the ascendancy of the "agricultural interest," which created "a highly refined state of society," true to its religion, the family, and the worker. These attributes "rest mainly upon the institution of slavery."[42]

Turning away from the dynamic example of the North also implied a rejection of northern reform closely connected to the abolition movement. The softening of property proscriptions against married women, the expansion of employment and educational options for women, and the trend toward universal public education received cool receptions in the South. A writer in *De Bow's Review* boasted that in the South, "the true position of woman in society [is] recognized and guarded—not the right to be unsexed, to brawl in political assemblies. . . . Beautiful by the heart—beautiful at the domestic board—beautiful in her ministering of charity . . . who would substitute for her—so soft, so lovely, so cherished and adored in the innermost heart of man—that modern Amazonian creation . . . of a 'Woman's Rights Convention.'"[43]

By 1860, some southerners were willing to believe that the differences between North and South were apparent from the beginning of European settlement. A correspondent in the *Southern Literary Messenger* wondered: "What attraction could exist between Puritan and Cavalier, between Rev. Cotton Mather and Capt. John Smith?" It was as if two separate races had somehow found themselves occupying the same contiguous geographic area and agreed to coalesce for convenience rather than on common cultural or racial grounds. Another writer summarized this argument in June 1860, just as the presidential campaign began. "A contest of races exists at present between the people of this government," the writer explained, "the native dissimilarities which . . . combined, form what is called the American people." The southern people, the writer asserted, derived from "that branch of the human race which . . . controls all the enlightened nations of the earth." Northerners, on the other hand, were "more immediately descended of the English Puritans . . . the common people of England."[44]

Thus was planted the fanciful notion that North and South represented the descendants of the Roundheads and the Cavaliers, respectively, and that each section's distinctive racial traits derived from this ethnic difference. Georgian Thomas Cobb concluded about northerners in 1860, "They are *different* people from us . . . and *there is no love* between us." The slavery controversy, brewing for more than three decades, boiled over to a realization that North and South not only had different interests but were, in fact, different peoples.[45]

Most northerners did not feel compelled to justify their "civilization," if indeed they stopped to distinguish northern life from American life generally. Some believed that southerners, as slaveholders, were more prone to violence, more of a threat to democratic institutions, and more hostile to progress in general than northerners. The Fugitive Slave Law, the repeal of the Missouri Compromise, the caning of Massachusetts senator Charles Sumner, the Dred Scott decision, and the Lecompton fraud convinced many northerners that slave society bred despotism. Much as southerners believed that slavery provided the foundation for a superior civilization, northerners saw the institution as a detriment to the spiritual and economic progress of the nation. In a society dedicated to progress, the future would always be more compelling.

The central flaw in southern society, many northerners were coming to believe, was slavery. In rhetoric reminiscent of Horace Greeley's lamentations about how the Indians' forlorn land reflected their lack of enterprise, William H. Seward noted that slavery undermined "intelligence, vigor, and energy" in southern blacks and whites. It produced "an exhausted soil, old and decaying towns, wretchedly-neglected roads . . . [and] an absence of enterprise and improvement," rendering the institution "incompatible with all . . . the elements of the security, welfare, and greatness of nations." Hinton Rowan Helper, a North Carolinian, corroborated these charges in *The Impending Crisis of the South: How to Meet It* (1857), a book on the debilitating impact of slavery on the South in general and on southern whites in particular. It became a popular Republican Party campaign document.[46]

When Stephen A. Douglas abandoned his campaign and headed south, he understood the stakes. Threats of disunion had escalated during the campaign. Many in the North, including most Republicans, dismissed these warnings. Southerners had threatened secession periodically since the Nullification Crisis of the early 1830s, and these tantrums had always dissipated. Horace Greeley quipped that "the South could no more unite upon a scheme of secession than a company of lunatics could conspire to break out of bedlam," and Lincoln confided to a friend that southern talk of disunion was "a sort of political game of bluff . . . meant solely to frighten the North." But a generation of invective and the events of the 1850s had taken their toll on Americans. The prospect of a sectional party assuming power in Washington alarmed most southerners. While a majority of southerners did not want to leave the Union, they were not unconditional Unionists; they wanted guarantees that if the Republicans won the election, this sectional, anti-slavery party would not undermine their civilization.[47]

Abraham Lincoln captured the 1860 presidential election by winning the North. He carried the four northern border states—Illinois, Indiana, New Jersey, and Pennsylvania—that John C. Frémont lost in 1856. He won these states by positioning himself in the conservative wing of the Republican Party, pledging to keep the territories free for white men and disavowing any hostility toward the states in which slavery existed. As one of his Pennsylvania supporters explained, Lincoln ran as "a consistent Whig." The people "think he is conservative, and will, if elected, carry out the principles & policies of Henry Clay." There was no deception in this position: Lincoln admired Clay greatly, and his staunch Unionism trumped his own moral misgivings about slavery. But, as a westerner, and as a Republican, his opposition to slavery in the territories was steadfast. He had stated on numerous occasions that the West was reserved "for homes of free white people." It was "God-given for that purpose." The sentiment resonated not only in Pennsylvania but also and especially in the West.[48]

John C. Breckinridge carried most of the southern states, as expected. However, John Bell and Stephen A. Douglas combined for 55 percent of the popular vote in the South, confirming northern beliefs on the weakness of disunion sentiment there. Yet Douglas, who could lay claim to being the only national candidate, won the electoral vote of just one state, Missouri, an ominous indicator of polarization.

Lincoln would be a minority president—he garnered just under 40 percent of the popular vote. Even had the three other candidates combined against him, Lincoln still would have received a majority of the electoral votes, a sure sign of the North's new dominance in national politics. The outcome was clear to southerners: a party had ascended to national power with scarcely a southern vote.

In a dingy slave cabin in western Virginia, a young boy awoke to find his mother praying for the election of Abraham Lincoln. It was one of the earliest memories of the boy, Booker T. Washington. At his home in Rochester, Frederick Douglass rejoiced that Lincoln's election would break the "exacting, haughty and imperious slave oligarchy."[49]

Hundreds of miles away in southern Georgia, a young girl stooped in her parents' garden gathering loose rose leaves to scatter among her clothes, a fall ritual repeated all over the South as the long hot summer blended into the brilliant southern autumn. Further away still, the boatman in Illinois gathered his belongings for the longest journey he would ever make.

CHAPTER 8

THE TUG COMES

WALT WHITMAN SAT ATOP his omnibus on Broadway despite the frigid February weather. The conveyance, pulled by a team of horses, normally lurched along at a top speed of three miles per hour, a bit slower than a fast walker. Even at that modest pace, the ride over the city's uneven cobblestones left a bone-jarring impression on passengers. Today, though, Walt was going nowhere. People, carts, wagons, carriages, and hacks competed on the city's busiest thoroughfare in a contest that counted few winners. Thirty thousand people clogged Broadway between Vesey and Barclay streets, five thousand of whom congregated near the entrance to the Astor House, New York's most elegant hotel, rising to a then-impressive height of six stories in Greek Revival splendor.

The focus of this throng pulled up to the hotel in a modest hack, stepped out, dressed in black from head to toe, and walked slowly but purposefully up the steps of the hotel entrance. He paused for a moment, looked at the crowd, turned sharply on his heel and disappeared into the lobby. Walt Whitman had known New York for many years and had reveled in its eccentricities and dynamism, but he had never witnessed such an odd scene. The spectators had stood in sullen silence, except for a few enthusiasts who braved reproof by applauding the stranger as he entered the hotel. Some had come out of curiosity to see this odd-looking man from the West whom they knew primarily from withering caricature and whose election had precipitated a national crisis. It was Whitman's first encounter with the president-elect, Abraham Lincoln. The date was February 19, 1861, and the nation was disintegrating. Already, the seven departing states of the Lower South had established a separate government in Montgomery, Alabama, calling itself the Confederate States of America. The man many New Yorkers regarded as the immediate cause of this catastrophe had just checked into the Astor House.

Lincoln had received only 35 percent of the city's vote. New York's Democratic mayor, Fernando Wood, did not even deign to greet the president-elect and, in fact, was plotting to take the city out of the Union to form an independent city-state called Tri-Insula. New York's economy depended heavily on the cotton trade, now disrupted because of this man's election. The city's large Catholic population had additional reasons to distrust an incoming administration that included within its ranks individuals hostile to their religion. Whitman reported that many in the crowd carried weapons and stood ready to use them "as soon as break and riot came." Lincoln seemed unperturbed by the surly reception. He locked eyes with the crowd for a long moment, demonstrating a fearlessness that dissolved much of the tension. Here was a different kind of leader, Whitman acknowledged.[1]

At the time, leadership of any kind would have been a welcome novelty. President James Buchanan, abandoned by his southern Democratic colleagues, wandered the White House bereft of friends and ideas. Although he considered secession illegal, his public comments seemed to justify it. He placed the blame for the current crisis squarely on a partisan northern electorate and its "incessant and violent agitation of the slavery question . . . for the last quarter of a century." Buchanan claimed, though without more evidence than what his erstwhile southern colleagues fed him, that the election had a "malign influence on the slaves and inspired them with vague notions of freedom." What the South required was security, he argued. He favored calling a constitutional convention to frame an amendment to guarantee protection for slavery in the territories, a proposal soundly rejected by a majority of voters in the recent presidential election. The president also prayed a lot. Alexander Stephens, watching Buchanan's dithering in the months after the November election, concluded that the crisis was "past praying, I fear. Mr. Buchanan has ruined the country. His appeal to heaven was made too late." While the president sought divine intervention, leaders in the Lower South forged a new nation.[2]

At least Buchanan understood the core of the sectional problem. It was not the tariff, states' rights, railroads, federal patronage, the territories, or religious differences. It was all of these things connected to one thing: slavery. It had always been thus. With the election of Abraham Lincoln and a Republican administration, the destiny of the South in the American Union now resided in hostile hands. In December 1860, the editor of the *Southern Literary Messenger* marked off "the last hours of the United States of America," an inglorious end to a noble experiment, precipitated by "the election to the Presidency of a candidate pledged to the ultimate extinction of a domestic institution which is the foundation stone of southern society."[3]

William D. Holcombe, a Mississippi physician and writer, disabused those who attributed the national breakup to causes other than slavery. "He has not analyzed this subject aright nor probed it to the bottom, who supposes that the real quarrel between the North and the South is about the Territories, or the decision of the Supreme Court, or even the constitution itself. . . . Opposition to slavery, to its existence, its extension and its perpetuation, is the sole cohesive element of the triumphant faction. . . . The only alternative left us is this: *a separate nationality or the Africanization of the South."*[4]

A South Carolina convention voted for secession on December 20, 1860, precipitating a procession of Lower South states out of the Union. The delegates defended their decision as necessary to protect both the institution of slavery and themselves. The state's "Declaration of the Immediate Causes Which Induce and Justify Secession" affirmed that northern states "have encouraged and assisted thousands of our slaves to leave their homes; and those who remain have been incited by emissaries, books and pictures to servile insurrection." The delegates warned that once Lincoln took office on March 4, 1861, "a war must be waged against slavery until it shall cease throughout the United States."[5]

To persuade other southern states to follow the path of secession, the early seceding states of the Lower South dispatched "commissioners" to plead the case for disunion in other slaveholding states. Their arguments centered on slavery. When Mississippi's commissioner, William L. Harris, appeared before the Georgia legislature in late December 1860, he noted that a Republican administration promised "freedom to the slave, but eternal degradation for you and for us." He elaborated: "Our fathers made this a government for the white man, rejecting the negro, as an ignorant, inferior, barbarian race, incapable of self-government, and not, therefore, entitled to be associated with the white man upon terms of civil, political, or social equality." The choice for the South was clear: "This *new union* with Lincoln Black Republicans and free negroes, *without slavery*; or, slavery under our old constitutional bond of union, *without* Lincoln Black Republicans, or free negroes either, to molest us."[6]

The commissioners pressed to get their message across forcefully and quickly. Compromise plans were afoot that would potentially abort the secession movement. Senator John J. Crittenden of Kentucky, a former Whig and disciple of the Great Compromiser, Henry Clay, and a man trusted by northerners, submitted a plan to the U.S. Senate on January 3, 1861, requesting a national plebiscite on several constitutional amendments. The most important of these advocated reviving and extending the Missouri Compromise line to the Pacific Coast, prohibiting slavery above the line, and not only allowing but guaranteeing federal protection for slavery below the line. Although the Senate could not agree on the constitutionality of a referendum, the plan caught the imagination of an American public hopeful of resolving the sectional crisis. Petitions supporting the Crittenden compromise poured into Congress. William H. Seward presented a petition from New York City with thirty-eight thousand signatures. Simon Cameron, a Republican from Pennsylvania, reported receiving "daily, by every mail, a large number of letters . . . all sustaining the proposition of the Senator from Kentucky." Horace Greeley believed that the plan would win a majority of votes in the North.[7]

Nothing happened. Although some Republicans favored Crittenden's proposals, the president-elect did not. The principles of his party and his interpretation of the Constitution informed Lincoln's opposition. Crittenden's plan canceled the Republican Party's central tenet: the exclusion of slavery from the territories. The plan also defied the wishes of voters who had cast their ballots for a party pledged to keep the territories white. Several weeks before Crittenden submitted his plan to the Senate, Lincoln wrote to Republican senator Lyman Trumbull of Illinois in unequivocal terms: "Let there be no compromise on the question of extending slavery. If there be, all our labor is lost, and ere long, must be done again." The Crittenden compromise failed in the House in January 1861, and in the Senate in March.[8]

Former president John Tyler tried one last effort to resolve the crisis. The elderly Tyler, in comfortable retirement at his Virginia estate, felt called to duty by the country that he had served two decades earlier. It was a selfless act that would exhaust and eventually kill him. But given the Republicans' intransigence, Buchanan's indecisiveness, and accelerating secession, it was worth a last chance. Tyler's Peace Conference, composed of delegates from the Border South and most of the northern states, met in Washington, D.C., in February. They crafted a seven-point proposal differing little from the Crittenden plan. It suffered the same fate. Republicans could not abide any proposition that eviscerated the major reason for the party's existence, its unalterable opposition to slavery in the territories. Even had the Republicans supported these plans, it was doubtful that the seven seceded states would have rejoined the Union on the dubious promise of more slave states in the territories. The real fears of the secessionists were that the Republicans would use every means within their power to undermine the institution where it existed, thereby unleashing an economic and social catastrophe.

The secessionists were as skeptical as the president-elect about the viability of compromise. They and their states moved quickly to leave the Union and establish their new nation. On January 21, Senator David Levy Yulee of Florida stood and delivered an emotional farewell to his colleagues, followed by senators from Alabama and Mississippi. Jefferson Davis of Mississippi was the last to speak. He had been ill, suffering from painful neuralgia, and the drama of the moment did little to ease his discomfort. As he spoke his farewell, thinking back to his years in government work, his gallant service to his country in the Mexican War, as a cabinet member, and now as a United States senator, his voice cracked. For a man of steadfast loyalty to his country and his state, this was a heart-rending time. At the end of this difficult speech, he spoke to his northern colleagues. "I am sure there is not one of you, whatever sharp discussion there may have been between us, to whom I cannot now say, in the presence of my God, I wish you well." With that, the gallery erupted into cheers, applause, and cries of anguish. Senator Yulee stood up again, and the five other senators followed him out of the chamber, single file. An observer reported, "There was everywhere a feeling of suspense as if, visibly, the pillars of the temple were being withdrawn and the great Government structure was tottering."[9]

Alexander Stephens saw the unfolding tragedy after Lincoln's election and spoke out to his fellow Georgians at the state capital in Milledgeville in November 1860. Like his friend Lincoln, Stephens held the utmost faith in the Constitution as a safeguard of southern interests. He argued that constitutional checks would render Lincoln "powerless to do any great mischief." Stephens employed biblical imagery to emphasize the perils of disunion to his audience. He warned that the dissolution of the Union would endanger "this Eden of the world," that "instead of becoming gods, we shall become demons, and at no distant day commence cutting one another's throats." He begged his state, and the South, to "wait for the act of aggression." Do not allow history to condemn the South for striking the first blow in response to a constitutional election, he urged. Stephens's speech received widespread coverage, appearing in the *London Times* almost in its entirety.[10]

Stephens's words evoked little enthusiasm at home. The secessionists were on the ascendant in the Lower South. Younger, vigorous, well organized, and armed with an activist plan, they easily outshone cautious conservatives. Waiting is rarely a flashy alternative, especially if others equate delay with submission or, worse, destruction. The failure of compromise proposals further eroded southerners' confidence in the efficacy of inaction.

Hence Alexander Stephens's pessimism. He had watched helplessly as Georgia seceded, giving a perfunctory speech at the convention urging delegates to wait, saying that the "point of resistance should be the point of aggression," but this was a weak argument compared to the clear-cut predictions of doom offered up by secessionists. Georgians rewarded his years of service by selecting him to represent the state in the new government now forming in Montgomery. Torn between his love of the Union and responsibility to his state, he consented only on the condition that the convention support his resolution that any government created in Montgomery must be based on the United States Constitution.[11]

Stephens journeyed to Montgomery in February more out of duty than out of conviction. He distrusted the hotspurs who had taken the seven Lower South states out of the Union, and, as he confided to a friend, he believed that war was "almost certain." It was not the so-called fire-eaters who controlled the formation of the new Confederate States of America, however. Some of the older political leaders stepped to the fore. They realized that their appeals had to reach three audiences: the reluctant and skeptical populations of the Border South, the citizens of the northern states, and the European powers. To win over these constituencies would require skill and tact. Radicalism would suit the revolutionary spirit but doom the revolution.[12]

The delegates elected Jefferson Davis to a six-year term as the first president of the Confederate States of America. A strong choice, given Davis's extensive military and political background. Even his ramrod-straight bearing made him look presidential. But colleagues found him aloof as if, at times, he were staring beyond them at something far distant, perhaps his own fate. Davis was also inclined to equate compromise with weakness and interpret opposition as a personal attack. Self-righteous at times and without a sense of humor always, Davis's character did not suit his position as a leader of a new nation, even if his professional credentials said otherwise. Even his wife, Varina Howell Davis, admitted, "He did not know the arts of the politician, and would not practice them if understood."[13]

Despite his distance from the radicals, Davis had supported secession from the time of Lincoln's election. He had led the Buchanan administration's charge against fellow Democrat Stephen A. Douglas. Robert E. Lee admired Davis's forthrightness but added that he was "of course, one of the extremist politicians."[14]

In an effort to appeal to the conservative sentiment both in and out of the Confederate government, the delegates turned to Alexander Stephens for vice president. So here he was, a prisoner of his sense of duty, not only supporting but also playing a leading role in a government he had fought to prevent. Perhaps he felt, along with fellow Unionist James Alcorn of Mississippi, that he could "seize the wild and maddened steed by the mane" and apply a brake to the hotspurs' course, thereby saving the South from certain ruin. In the meantime, he would speak his mind, as he always did.[15]

Jefferson Davis had delivered a lofty inaugural address meant for worldwide consumption. He stressed the constitutional bases of the new government and depicted secession as a conservative movement designed to preserve the founding principles of the American nation. A month later, on March 21, 1861, his vice president delivered a more candid and more memorable speech. Historians still quote it today. Yet Stephens did not believe he had said anything momentous on that evening of March 21, 1861. He merely reiterated what southerners had been saying and writing about their society since the sectional conflict flared in the 1850s: that slavery and southern civilization were synonymous. Stephens praised the new Confederate constitution that "put at rest *forever* all the agitating questions relating to . . . the proper status of the negro in our form of civilization." While many secessionists wrapped themselves in the cloak of the Founding Fathers and their ideals, Stephens, the realist, would have none of that. The Founders had believed "that the enslavement of the African was in violation of the laws of nature; that it was wrong in principle, socially, morally, and politically. Those ideas, however, were fundamentally wrong. They rested upon the assumption of the equality of races. This was an error."

Whether Stephens rendered the Founders' views on slavery accurately is beside the point. The Confederate States of America would remove any ambiguity about the permanent status and stature of the African. "Our new government," Stephens informed the audience, "is founded upon exactly the opposite idea: its foundations are laid, its cornerstone rests, upon the great truth that the negro is not equal to the white man; that slavery, subordination to the superior race, is his natural and moral condition."[16]

Stephens's "Cornerstone" speech attained a national notoriety that surprised him. Anyone who had read southern publications over the previous five years would find little new or startling in the address. Yet coming as the new Confederate nation was attempting to establish its legitimacy, such ideas were bound to achieve a wide circulation. Jefferson Davis was furious with his vice president. The speech jeopardized the careful work of building the case for his country on the issue of state versus national sovereignty. Northerners and Europeans roundly condemned the speech, though Stephens's words confirmed for many northerners the Republican charge that the Confederate States of America was nothing more than a slave republic. As one Republican editor wrote, the speech "was of incalculable value to us."[17]

Davis himself subscribed to Stephens's views. Many southerners did. In a speech to the Confederate Congress just after the war began, and with little national or international coverage, Davis placed the crisis squarely on the northern majority in Congress and its "persistent and organized system of hostile measures against the rights of the owners of slaves in the Southern States." He praised slavery as an institution in which "a superior race" transformed "brutal savages into docile, intelligent, and civilized agricultural laborers. With interests of such overwhelming magnitude imperiled, the people of the Southern States were driven by the conduct of the North to the adoption of some course of action to avert the danger with which they were openly menaced."[18]

Again, nothing new. Yet it seemed curious to identify slavery and the South as one and inseparable in order to forge a new nation and rally all southerners behind the government, given that a majority of white southerners did not own slaves. Plus, constitutional reforms in the southern states had increased the political power of the nonslaveholding majority. It would have seemed politic to broaden the appeal of secession. What benefits would disunion bestow on this large class of men and their families? Would a Republican administration tap into nonslaveholders' discontents—articulated in great detail by North Carolinian Hinton Rowan Helper—and offer patronage positions in exchange for their support? Perhaps the growing immigrant population in southern cities would combine with native-born nonslaveholding whites to oppose secession. Or, the fiercely independent yeomen farmers and their families in the southern mountains—the Appalachians and the Ozarks—might disdain following their "betters" out of the Union.

Except for South Carolina, secession was not a certain thing. Even in the Palmetto State divisions existed that worried Low Country planters. James H. Hammond, the governor and former senator, warned fire-eaters to tone down their rhetoric for fear of alienating upcountry nonslaveholding farmers and townsmen who did not share their zeal for disunion. In Georgia, the secessionist governor, Joseph E. Brown, was so concerned about opposition to leaving the Union that he suppressed the statewide vote totals for delegates to the special convention called in January 1861. Not until 1972, when historian Michael Johnson uncovered the tally, did we learn that secessionist candidates carried the state by a very narrow margin, though Brown had reported the result as a "clear majority."[19]

In convention delegate votes across the Lower South, secessionist candidates averaged fewer than 55 percent of the total vote, a majority but not an overwhelming mandate. These figures were unimpressive considering that the secessionists presented a clear program and controlled the press and much of the wealth and political power of their states, while their opponents divided on the conditions of cooperation with the federal government. Only one of the seven states that seceded by early February 1861—Texas—submitted its ordinance of secession to a popular vote. Across the Lower South, secessionists were strongest in those districts where plantation slavery predominated, a confirmation of the connection between the Confederate States of America and slavery, but also perhaps of the tenuous loyalty of the nonslaveholders.

It was easier to profess pro-Union sentiment in the Upper South. The situation in Virginia, North Carolina, Tennessee, and Arkansas presented a great problem for Davis's fledgling government, not to mention the border slave states of Delaware, Maryland, Kentucky, and Missouri. Without the states of the Upper South, particularly Virginia, the Confederacy could prove stillborn. Public expressions of contempt for secession and secessionists abounded in North Carolina and Virginia. Responding to South Carolina's secession ordinance, a Wilmington, North Carolina, editor asked readers, "Are you *submissionists* to the dictation of South Carolina . . . are you to be called cowards because you do not follow the crazy lead of that crazy state?" A Charlottesville, Virginia, editor declared that he "hated South Carolina for precipitating secession." When Virginia voted for its convention to meet in mid-February, only 32 of the 152 delegates identified themselves as secessionists. Tennessee went the Old Dominion one better by voting not to call a convention at all. On February 18, as Jefferson Davis prepared to take his oath of office, Arkansas voters elected to their convention a strong majority of Unionists. North Carolinians concluded the rout at the end of the month by joining Tennesseans in refusing to call a convention.[20]

The border states proved even less cooperative. A special session of the Kentucky state legislature voted decisively not to call a convention and promptly adjourned. In Maryland, Governor Thomas H. Hicks did not even bother to call a special session of the legislature on the subject. A unanimous vote in Delaware's lower house expressed "unqualified disapproval" of secession. Missouri decided to hold a convention, but voters elected nary a secessionist to serve.[21]

The very arguments mobilized by secessionists—protection of slavery, economic independence, political sovereignty, and security—found life on the other side of the debate. James Robb, a New Orleans entrepreneur, wondered if secession would merely result in trading a northern master for a European master, as British industry would overwhelm nascent southern enterprises. Businessmen in Upper South cities were as concerned about competition from Charleston, Mobile, and New Orleans as from Boston, New York, and Philadelphia. Merchants who had cultivated commercial and financial connections with northerners opposed secession. Some slaveholders feared for their property more out of the Union than in it. Others worried that war and violence would inevitably accompany secession. A Presbyterian minister in Richmond warned that secession would precipitate "a horrible civil war," and a fellow Presbyterian in Kentucky advised, "If we desire to perish, all we have to do is to leap onto this vortex of disunion."[22]

Northerners followed developments in the Upper South closely. The squabbling reinforced the Republicans' intransigence to compromise. Even the press in the seceding states expressed doubt about the secession of additional slave states by late February. "Virginia would never secede now," a Charleston editor lamented. An excited Republican colleague wrote to William H. Seward,

"We have scarcely left a vestige of secession in the western part of Virginia, and very little indeed in any part of the state. . . . The Gulf Confederacy can count Virginia out of their little family arrangement—*she will never* join them."[23]

The optimism was misplaced. Northerners and Republicans in particular overestimated the strength of Unionist sentiment throughout the South and underestimated the attraction of slavery to a broad swath of the white population. In the Lower South, slaveholding households ranged from 49 percent of total white households in South Carolina to 27 percent in Texas. In South Carolina and Mississippi, the first two states to leave the Union, nearly half of all white households owned slaves. In those states in particular, what debate existed revolved around how best to protect the institution of slavery and avert economic disaster and racial warfare. Those who opposed secession were almost always those who held out for a constitutional settlement or compromise. Few white citizens in those states wanted to remain in the Union under Republican rule without new constitutional protections.

The opposition to immediate secession in the Upper South reflected in part the lower percentages of white slaveholding families in those states, typically less than 20 percent. But even in states such as Virginia, North Carolina, and Tennessee, the Unionist position was rarely unconditional. The votes and decisions thwarting secession in those states occurred before the various compromise plans failed. Many there assumed that their continued adherence to the Union could serve as leverage to broker a compromise between the incoming administration and the seceding states of the Lower South. Only a handful of Upper South Unionists would countenance military action against the Confederate states.

Abraham Lincoln had heard about Alexander Stephens's pro-Union speech in Milledgeville in December and wrote to his old friend for a copy. Stephens complied but warned the president-elect that even Unionists would not tolerate interference with slavery where it already existed. Lincoln responded with surprise: "I wish to assure you, as once friend, and still, I hope, not an enemy, that there is no cause for such fears." Stephens pressed the issue further in his reply: "We both have an earnest desire to preserve and maintain the Union" provided the administration followed the principles upon which that Union was founded. The great fear of the South and even of Unionists such as himself, Stephens explained, was Lincoln's party, whose "leading object" was "to put the institutions of nearly half the States under the ban of public opinion and national condemnation." He begged Lincoln to understand that the "Union under the Constitution" could not be maintained by force. At that point, the entire South, Unionists included, would join the battle.[24]

Stephens understood, if northerners did not, that every white person in the South, slaveholder or not, had a stake in the institution. The existence of slavery, its proponents had argued for more than two decades, benefited all white southerners. Slavery protected the South from the incipient class warfare brewing in the North between capital and labor. African slavery created a permanent working class laboring in the most menial positions. The system liberated whites to pursue higher occupations and opportunities for economic independence. As members of the superior race, all whites were masters. Race was the new class: no white was inferior to another white as long as Africans remained in bondage. In January 1861, J. D. B. De Bow summarized the racial appeal of the pro-slavery argument to nonslaveholders. *"The non-slaveholder of the South preserves the status of the white man, and is not regarded as an inferior or a dependant."* Slavery also guaranteed republican government by conferring a broad equality on all whites. The South was a White Republic, and secessionists argued that only by leaving the Union and establishing a slaveholding nation could they preserve the political rights, the economic independence, and the superiority of all white southerners.[25]

The Republicans also threatened slavery where it existed, despite their protests to the contrary. They closed off the possibility of improvement by barring slaveholders from the territories. Secessionists emphasized how blocking the institution's expansion could create a racial explosion. With Republican control of government agencies and the expansion of the number of free states, the South would be helpless to protect slavery. The Republicans' alleged insistence on racial equality would remove the white man's special status, wreck the South's republican form of government with Negro rule, and precipitate racial conflict if not an all-out race war. As De Bow explained in January 1861, "In Northern communities, where the free negro is one in a hundred of the total population, he is recognized and acknowledged often as a pest. . . . What would be the case in many of our States, where every other inhabitant is a negro?" The end of the White Republic in the South meant the end of white liberty and equality.[26]

The secessionists' oft-repeated threat of race war and insurrection registered throughout the white South, not as some hysterical rant but as a likely outcome of a Republican administration. Just as whiteness conferred automatic superiority on all whites, it would become the target of a racial conflagration. John Brown's Raid, despite its bungled execution, had a significant impact on the white South. Coupled with the election of Abraham Lincoln, it signaled that northerners were insensitive to the political and racial vulnerability of white southerners. The testimony of former slaves indicated that the

Republican victory in November 1860 resounded in the quarters. "It all dif-frunt," one slave reported after the election. Slaves noticed that the easy access into the Big House became less so, and masters, mistresses, and overseers became more guarded. An untoward glance, a sullen gesture, a slower gait became preludes to rebellion in the minds of some whites, whose peace of mind could only be assuaged by a quarantine of northern people, opinions, and government.[27]

Religion, as well as race, connected white southerners to each other. Secession was a cleansing operation removing the South and slavery from the contamination of northerners infected with the virus of abolition. The Rev. William O. Prentiss of South Carolina explained his state's impending secession in December 1860: "We cannot coalesce with men whose society will eventually corrupt our own, and bring down upon us the awful doom which awaits them."[28]

The cleansing metaphor proved especially powerful from southern pulpits. White southerners practiced an evangelical Protestant religion that had grown more insular following the church schisms in the 1840s. The clergy had rallied to slavery's defense in the 1850s and now blessed secession. The Confederate States of America would aspire to be a Christian civilization of the highest order. While New England pulpits resonated with the righteousness of anti-slavery ministers, southern divines mobilized their influence for what they believed to be a holy cause.

To evangelical Christians in the South, the Confederacy represented a rebirth as they had been reborn in Christ. In early April 1861, Alabama minister T. L. DeVeaux blessed the new nation: "She will arise from her position cleansed from these sins, and clothed in the strength of God, manfully vindicate the right, and rescue it from the hands of destroyers." The very motto of the new nation—*Deo Vindice* (God will vindicate)—proclaimed it as such. It was a new country assuming the missionary calling cast down by the old nation.[29]

The Rev. Benjamin M. Palmer offered the most compelling case for the divinity of the Confederate cause in his Thanksgiving sermon, weeks after the Republican victory. Palmer's sermon received wide coverage throughout the South and helped to further the cause of secession, especially among those not yet convinced of the propriety of such action. At the same time, he indelibly connected the cause of slavery to the secession movement, and both to divine blessing. As one of the South's most prominent Presbyterian clergymen, Palmer carried considerable influence among southern evangelicals, who read accounts of his sermons in both the religious and secular press.

Palmer was a native South Carolinian who received his divinity degree at

Columbia (S.C.) Theological Seminary and spent fifteen years in the South Carolina capital pastoring the First Presbyterian Church. Although he supported slavery and southern rights, his sermons focused on theological issues. His political views, when they emerged, were more moderate than much of the prevailing opinion in South Carolina during the two decades prior to 1860. His reputation as a moving preacher of the Gospel spread throughout the South, and in 1856 he accepted a call to one of the region's most prestigious Presbyterian churches, the First Presbyterian Church of New Orleans, housed in a commanding Gothic structure and boasting a membership that included most of the city's Protestant elite, a number of whom were transplants from northern cities. As the reputation of his oratorical presence grew, the church began drawing non-Protestants and visitors from other parts of the country and the world. He preached to overflow crowds on numerous occasions. With the nation in crisis in November 1860, more than two thousand worshipers crowded into his church to hear a sermon that he titled "Slavery a Divine Trust: Duty of the South to Preserve and Perpetuate It."[30]

The sermon touched on every major secession argument and also eloquently summarized more than two decades of southern nationalist thought. These included the essential incompatibility between North and South and that slavery enjoyed God's blessing and served as the bedrock of southern civilization. Palmer told his congregation that the recent election confirmed that the North and the South had grown into two separate peoples, making their conflict indeed "irrepressible." Slavery lay at the core of these differences. To southerners, slavery was a divinely sanctioned institution; to northerners, it was a damning sin. The South, Palmer preached, was fulfilling God's command "*to conserve and to perpetuate the institution of slavery as now existing.*" As a blessed institution, slavery had become the South: "It has fashioned our modes of life, and determined all our habits of thought and feeling, and molded the very type of our civilization." The North would destroy this institution, spurred on by an abolitionist movement that was "undeniably atheistic." With "labor and capital grinding against each other like the upper and nether millstones; with labor cheapened and displaced by new mechanical inventions, bursting more asunder the bonds of brotherhood," the North received the sympathy of the South, but attacked it in return to divert attention from its own deep problems.

Perhaps the most egregious sin committed by northerners was their substitution of God with man, the overweening pride of believing that they were beyond history, beyond sin, and beyond judgment. Yankee reformers presumed to strike every blot on earth. "The Most High, knowing his own power, which is infinite, and his own wisdom, which is unfathomable, can afford to be patient. But these self-constituted reformers must quicken the activity of Jehovah or compel his abdication. . . . It is time to reproduce the obsolete idea that Providence must govern man, and not that man shall control Providence." The alternative was rampant individualism and unbridled democracy, both unchristian and untenable. Evoking the spirit of the French Revolution, Palmer declared, "Its banner-cry rings out already upon the air— 'liberty, equality, fraternity,' which simply interpreted means bondage, confiscation, and massacre."

In a stirring conclusion, Palmer argued that only independence could fulfill the South's "providential trust": the duty *"to ourselves, to our slaves, to the world, and to Almighty God . . . to preserve and transmit our existing system of domestic servitude, with the right, unchallenged by man, to go and root itself wherever Providence and nature may carry it."* The sermon stunned the congregation with its candor and eloquent justification for a reviled civilization under siege. No longer shunned prophets in their own land, they were God's Chosen Nation. Thirty thousand copies of the sermon blanketed the South, creating "a very great sensation." One southerner, years later, noted that Palmer had done more than "any other non-combatant in the South to promote rebellion." Union General Benjamin F. Butler agreed, placing a bounty on Palmer's head when his troops occupied New Orleans in 1862.[31]

Northerners were uncertain how to react to secession. Some uttered "good riddance"; others prayed for compromise; still others talked of coercion. If the president-elect had wanted to take the pulse of the northern public to help him determine a course of action, his findings would have been hard to interpret.

The editors of *Harper's* magazine, a bellwether of moderate northern public opinion, hoped for a rapid reconciliation, less for the sake of the departing Lower South states than for the northern economy, which stood to lose cotton exports valued at more than $180 million. *Harper's* solution was to allow secession to run its course and hope for a compromise to restore the Union. The editors supported almost any plan that raised that promise. They presented their own "Cornerstone" speech: "Our Government, like all other Governments, . . . rests upon the corner-stone of COMPROMISE—the yielding by each component part of something for the general good." The editors were optimistic that in this advanced age something could be worked out: "It is not possible that in the present day of enlightenment, civilization, progress, and commerce these obvious truths [of the value of compromise] should be ignored."[32]

Northern moderates received the selection of Davis as president of the Confederacy as an encouraging sign of reason in the new government. Alexander

Expulsion of black and white abolitionists from Tremont Temple,
Boston, December 3, 1860. (Picture Collection, the New York Public Library, Astor,
Lenox and Tilden Foundations)

Stephens's elevation to the vice presidency provided more optimism, as many northerners viewed him as "the most emphatic enemy of disunion." The Confederate Constitution, an almost verbatim copy of the United States Constitution, generated hope that grounds for reconciliation existed. In the meantime, many northerners cautioned, "the enterprise of holding the Union together by force would ultimately prove futile." Coercion would dash hopes for compromise and precipitate an economic debacle at a time when the financial panic of 1857–58 remained fresh in memory. Already southerners were canceling orders for northern goods; northern factories cut wages as demand dropped; and workers at several New England mills went out on strike, raising the specter of social unrest.[33]

Many abolitionists abjured compromise with the devil and rejoiced to be rid of the southern scourge. They not only agreed with moderates who dismissed coercion as an option but also argued for total disengagement. It was a curious position. Was slavery less of a sin if the South separated itself from the Union? Was abolition no longer a priority if the institution suddenly belonged to another country? Noted abolitionist Wendell Phillips declared in March 1861, "Every man who possesses his soul in patience, sees that disunion is gain, disunion is *peace*, disunion is virtue." Much as secessionists perceived their action to be an atonement and a rebirth as a new and pristine nation, these advocates of letting go saw the opportunity of a reconstituted United States to at last justify its promise as a Chosen Nation, now rid of slavery and reborn cleansed of that awful sin.[34]

Some northern clergy supported this view, though unlike in the South, the secession crisis did not create a consensus in northern pulpits. Joseph Bittinger, an evangelical minister from Cleveland, observed, "The feeling is gaining ground [among Christians] that it would be good riddance if the South went out. . . . God's people . . . favor . . . secession rather than . . . any more political compromise with slavery." Some Republican politicians, recalling how southern collusion had shredded their legislative agenda in the previous Congress, now looked forward to a friendlier body. Others began to plan for life without the South, including moving the capital to a more appropriate northern location. *Harper's* offered New York City as a possibility, but Philadelphia, Cincinnati, and Chicago received support as well.[35]

A good many northerners, especially those with close business and political ties to the South, clung to the hope of compromise even if they believed that secession was illegal and ill advised. The enthusiastic northern response to the Crittenden proposals reflected a reservoir of support for a peaceful resolution. It also indicated a willingness to bend to southern demands that heretofore many had deemed unacceptable.

While most northerners, regardless of political leaning, opposed coercion initially, a minority believed that the integrity of the Union was essential to fulfill the nation's destiny as God's Chosen Nation. Disunion would terminate America's noble experiment in spreading the ideals of a progressive Christian democracy across a continent and around the world. It would throw the globe into a downward spiral of chaos. The bloody aftermath of the failed European revolutions and sectarian violence and crime at home were harbingers of the social disintegration to come.

The northerners who considered coercion a viable option believed that allowing some states to leave the compact provided other states with the precedent to do the same at some later time. For these northerners, the issue was not states' rights—the states retained all of the rights bestowed on them by the Constitution. Secession was not one of these rights. The sacred documents were the foundations of law and order; secession, as a violation of the principles of Union articulated in these documents, threatened that stability. With that threat, the future of immutable progress and the order that supported it appeared doubtful. The Union, in other words, was a prerequisite for national greatness.

To defend the Union and the principle of law, and to avoid anarchy, Abraham Lincoln refused to rule out force as an option. Since the late 1830s he had warned against the dangers of internal dissension and the necessity of placing reason over impulse and of law over anarchy. From his reading of the Constitution, secession was illegal. The states derived their status from membership in the Union; they possessed no legal status apart from the Union. "By conquest, or purchase," Lincoln explained, "the Union gave each of them whatever of independence and liberty it has. The Union is older than any of the States; and, in fact, it created them as States."[36]

Lincoln believed that dismemberment presaged destruction. "The principle itself [of secession] is one of disintegration, and upon which no government can possibly endure." Much as southerners feared a slave insurrection in the wake of a Republican administration, so Lincoln saw chaos as the result of disunion. "Plainly," he argued, "the central idea of secession is the essence of anarchy."[37]

In February 1861, as he prepared for his journey from Springfield, Illinois, to Washington, D.C., Abraham Lincoln's views on compromise and secession were clear and unyielding. As he told his secretary John Nicolay, "The right of a State to secede is not an open or debatable question. It is the duty of a President to execute the laws and maintain the existing Government. He cannot entertain any proposition for dissolution or dismemberment."[38]

By the time Lincoln packed for his travel eastward, however, even some of his staunchest Republican allies were exploring possible grounds for compromise. They watched the deepening economic disruption and feared the consequences of armed conflict. Colleagues urged Lincoln to make conciliatory statements to the South as a "means of strengthening our friends" there. There was talk of resurrecting Stephen A. Douglas's popular sovereignty doctrine, previously a sacrilege to Republicans, as a basis for compromise. This plan had the virtue of avoiding specific safeguards for slavery while still holding open the possibility of its extension into the territories. Whether that doctrine held any interest in the seceding states was doubtful. It might give Upper South states some pause and bolster Union sentiment there. Lincoln remained unimpressed. The president-elect urged Republicans to "stand firm. The tug has to come, and better now, than any time hereafter."[39]

Abraham Lincoln departed Springfield for Washington, D.C., on February 11, 1861. He ordered his law partner, William Herndon, to keep the shingle, Lincoln & Herndon, "undisturbed" in front of their law office. "If I live I'm coming back some time, and then we'll go right on practicing law as if nothing had ever happened." He struck out on a meandering journey that lasted twelve days. Although the country's railroad mileage was more extensive in 1861 than it had been when Lincoln left the Congress in 1849, it was less a network than a kaleidoscope of short- and long-haul companies competing for freight and passenger traffic. The president-elect had to change trains seventeen times to reach his appointed destination, doubtless reinforcing his support for a seamless transcontinental railroad.[40]

The route took him to Indianapolis, Cincinnati, Columbus, Pittsburgh, Cleveland, Buffalo, Albany, New York City, Trenton, Philadelphia, Harrisburg, and numerous smaller places in between, before depositing him at the nation's capital on February 23. Mostly friendly, often curious crowds greeted his appearance, except in New York City, where Walt Whitman witnessed the tense scene outside the Astor House. Lincoln had undertaken this trip less as a triumphal tour than as an opportunity to generate support for the Union and instill confidence among troubled northerners regardless of party. The purposeful rail journey afforded Lincoln a chance to meet his new constituents and vice versa. As he told a crowd at a stop in Indiana, "While some of us may differ in political opinions, still we are all united in one feeling for the Union. We all believe in the maintenance of the Union, of every star and every stripe of the glorious flag."[41]

While he preached consensus to northern crowds, he offered no conciliation to the South. Some writers have argued that Lincoln did not appreciate the depth of southern animosity toward an impending Republican regime, implying that had he been aware of such sentiments he might have been more amenable to compromise. That was hardly the case. While he joshed about the innumerable southern threats of disunion prior to the election, the swift secession of the Lower South states convinced him that the crisis was real and required immediate attention. In his farewell speech to his neighbors in Springfield, he acknowledged that the challenge that awaited him was "greater than that which rested upon Washington." He would not back away from what he saw as his constitutional duty and his love for the Union. He denied that such a position implied coercion: would it be coercion if the government "simply insists upon holding its own forts, or retaking those forts which belong to it, . . . or . . . the collection of duties upon foreign importations, . . . or even the withdrawal of the mails from those portions of the country where the mails themselves are habitually violated?" He quickly added that he had not yet reached a decision on these issues, but, clearly, the statement itself implied the possibility of confrontation. As he told the New Jersey legislature in Trenton, "It may be necessary to put the foot down firmly."[42]

The most moving stop occurred at Philadelphia on February 22, the birthday of George Washington. The crowd at storied Independence Hall that day was decidedly friendlier than the one he had encountered in New York City. The atmosphere was still tense, however, as death threats had followed Lincoln's train. Outside this hallowed hall, the president-elect grasped a rope and hoisted a large Star-Spangled Banner. As he pulled on the halyards the flag rose, slowly unfurling in the gentle wind, revealing the colors radiant in the brilliant sunshine. A crescendo of cheers followed the flag upward as if the ascending standard embodied the enduring strength of their beloved Union, and the hope that everything and everyone would be saved. When the flag reached the summit, a band burst into a lively rendition of "The Star-Spangled Banner," and the cannon assembled in the square boomed a deafening affirmation.

Inside the hall, Lincoln spoke of the document framed within its walls and what it meant to Americans and to people around the world. "I have never had a feeling politically that did not spring from the sentiments embodied in the Declaration of Independence," he acknowledged. There was "something in that Declaration giving liberty, not alone to the people of this country, but hope to the world for all future time. It was that which gave promise that in due time the weights should be lifted from the shoulders of all men, and that *all* should have an equal chance." Even the lowly slave. It was this global vision of America offering hope to men everywhere that sustained Lincoln's love for the Union and the Constitution upon which it rested.[43]

That the president-elect had to clandestinely change trains in Baltimore at three in the morning on February 23 attested both to the hostility of this slave-holding city and to the precarious nature of the crisis he was about to inherit. Washington, D.C., was also a southern city. Confederate agents, spies, slaves, and slave traders occupied various precincts even if many southern lawmakers had officially abandoned the federal government. Intrigue and rumor were the prime currencies and trading cheaply. The city landscape remained incomplete, with vast distances connected by muddy thoroughfares populated by indifferent structures punctuated here and there by a stately residence or an imposing federal building. Scaffolding covered the Capitol dome, part of a building project sixty-three years old and still counting, a symbol of how fragile the nation seemed at the moment. As one reporter noted, "If the Union is preserved, and Washington remains the Capital, a hundred years hence the original scheme may be carried out."[44]

The extraordinary crisis called for extraordinary statesmanship. How the president-elect put together his cabinet provided some insight into his character and conviction. He collected some of his most bitter political rivals and critics and rewarded them with plum positions. A cynic might say he shrewdly co-opted his enemies, but these were men—Secretary of War Edwin M. Stanton, Secretary of the Treasury Salmon P. Chase, and Secretary of State William H. Seward—who would not be readily flattered by an individual for whom they held little respect. He explained his unorthodox choices: "We needed the strongest men of the party in the Cabinet. . . . I had no right to deprive the country of their service." Though Stanton and Seward eventu-

ally warmed to the president, Chase never did. Lincoln rewarded the obstrep-
erous Chase with a promotion to chief justice of the U.S. Supreme Court. All
would prove exemplary in their respective roles, made infinitely more difficult by the necessities of war and reconstruction.[45]

The composition of his cabinet revealed that Lincoln bore no grudges
against his enemies; that the interests of his country prevailed over his personal ego. Would he go that far with the South? His inaugural address on
March 4, 1861, was the most important speech he had ever delivered. With the
Union hanging in the balance, a new nation already up and running hard on
its borders, a brace of compromises fallen by the wayside, and Unionist sentiment becoming ever more precarious in the remaining slave states, he stepped
to the podium at the East Portico of the Capitol on a cool, clear March day to
take his oath of office from none other than Chief Justice Roger B. Taney.
Stephen A. Douglas sat in the front row. He was holding the president-elect's
hat. A fractured nation and many parts of the world waited anxiously for
Lincoln's words.

Preparing his address, Lincoln studied three texts: Andrew Jackson's proclamation against Nullification and the speeches of the two greatest Whig
luminaries, Henry Clay and Daniel Webster. From Clay, Lincoln chose his
speech on behalf of the Compromise of 1850, and from Webster, his renowned
speech against Nullification in 1830, a speech he had committed to memory
and had used numerous times in the past.

Lincoln's inaugural address was not a great speech, especially compared
with his earlier and later orations, though such comparisons may be unfair. It
was a walking-on-eggshells speech balancing his own conviction of the sanctity and destiny of the federal Union with the nation's desire to resolve the
current crisis peacefully.

He tried to address southern fears by reiterating what he had said in
countless speeches prior to 1861: "I have no purpose, directly or indirectly, to
interfere with the institution of slavery in the States where it exists. I believe I
have no lawful right to do so, and I have no inclination to do so." He also
pledged to uphold the Fugitive Slave Law. Much of the remainder of the
speech took the form of a detailed legal brief denying the constitutionality of
secession and coupling this denial with a vow to uphold his oath "to hold, occupy, and possess the property and places belonging to the Government."
Once again, he equated secession with "anarchy." While the government was
protective of minority rights, majority rule must prevail. "The rule of a minority, as a permanent arrangement, is wholly inadmissible; so that, rejecting
the majority principle, anarchy or despotism in some form is all that is left."

Time and again, Lincoln reminded listeners of his constitutional duty, "the most solemn one to 'preserve, protect, and defend'" the government and the country. Lincoln closed with the only stirring lines of the day, urging southerners to abandon "passion" and "think calmly and *well* upon the whole subject," so that "the mystic chords of memory, stretching from every battle-field, and patriot grave, to every living heart and hearthstone, all over this broad land, will yet swell the chorus of the Union."[46]

None of this left southerners, in or out of the Confederacy, with the warm feeling of conciliation. Lincoln's eloquent appeal to a common past only provided southerners with a painful reminder of their current diminished position in the Union compared with their formative role in the nation's founding. The new president's evocation of the Constitution and the Declaration of Independence did not resonate among a people schooled to doubt that those documents protected them and their institutions. Southerners did not need a history lesson; they required ironclad guarantees and explicitly conciliatory rhetoric. They got neither.

While some Republicans praised the "firmness" of the speech, and Douglas called it a "peace offering," Lincoln's failure to address the issue of coercion in relation to federal property in the Confederate states, particularly those few properties still in the government's possession, troubled many both north and south. An Ohio journalist believed Lincoln intended to "stain the soil and color the waters of the entire continent" with blood. A southerner echoed the sentiment: "This means war."[47]

Another factor aside from his constitutional scruples constrained Lincoln's ability to placate southerners. He did not wish to limit his policy options with respect to the status of federal property in the seceded states. Lincoln understood that this was one issue he would have to address immediately.

In November 1860, President Buchanan had ordered Major Robert Anderson to take command of Fort Moultrie, one of three federal fortifications surrounding Charleston Harbor; aside from Fort Pickens at Pensacola, Florida, these were the only remaining major federal installations not yet in the hands of the Confederate government. Anderson, a Kentuckian, a slaveholder, and a Democrat, received a promise from Buchanan that his role in Charleston was as a caretaker, not as a provocateur. Whatever Anderson's political leanings, he was a career military officer and believed that "neither slavery nor any thing else should stand in the way of the preservation of the Union." Arriving at Moultrie, he was appalled by the weakness of the fort's position and fortifications. He requested more troops, arguing that Moultrie's vulnerability invited a takeover by Confederate authorities. Buchanan denied the request.

Seeing no alternative, Anderson, on the night of December 26, spiked Moultrie's guns and stole away to the better-fortified though unfinished Fort Sumter, an installation that stood astride the harbor with a strategic view of the mainland. Major Anderson had salvaged the flag that had flown over Moultrie, and on December 27 he raised it over Fort Sumter to the accompaniment of an army band playing "Hail, Columbia." The soldiers cheered lustily for their banner, and, a reporter noted, "if South Carolina had at that moment attacked the fort, there would have been no hesitation on the part of any man within it about defending that flag."[48]

Charlestonians were furious. They considered Major Anderson's movement from Moultrie to Sumter a provocation and immediately took possession of Moultrie and surrounded Sumter with a battery of guns. When, on January 9, President Buchanan dispatched a supply ship, the *Star of the West*, to restock Major Anderson's declining provisions at the fort, the batteries opened fire, forcing the supply vessel to retreat. On February 28, Major Anderson wrote to President Buchanan that he had only six weeks' provisions remaining. Outgoing secretary of war Joseph Holt hand-delivered Major Anderson's letter to President Lincoln the day after his inauguration. The problem was now Lincoln's.

The issue was simple, though the choices were difficult: do not provision Fort Sumter and the garrison would fall to the Confederate government; provision the fort and risk a military confrontation, as the Confederate authorities would perceive such action as an act of war. Lincoln had vowed in his inaugural address to uphold the Constitution and to "protect and defend" the country's interests; yet he had also promised that he would not make any aggressive movements against the South.

The new president was determined to keep the flag flying in Charleston Harbor. He authorized a former naval officer, Gustavus Vasa Fox, to organize a relief expedition to Fort Sumter but did not order its dispatch. Commanding General of the Army Winfield Scott advised Lincoln to order Major Anderson to withdraw from Fort Sumter. Lincoln weighed this advice, his concern about how the states of the Upper South would react, and his own conflicting emotions as March turned into April. The northern press fumed at the president, contrasting the quiet heroism of Anderson and the resolve of the Confederate government with Lincoln's indecision. The *New York Times*, a Republican newspaper, in a testy editorial on April 3, under the heading of "Wanted—A Policy!" observed that the Confederate government was conducting itself with a "degree of vigor, intelligence, and success" absent in Washington, D.C.[49]

Surrendering Fort Sumter was never an option for Lincoln, given his constitutional responsibilities. Secretary of the Navy Gideon Welles recalled his conversation with the president as he contemplated sending the Fox relief expedition to Charleston. Lincoln "could not consistently with his conviction of his duty, and with the policy he had enunciated in his inaugural, order the evacuation of Sumter, and it would be inhuman on his part to permit the heroic garrison to be starved into a surrender without an attempt to relieve it."[50]

Provisioning Major Anderson would require the utmost diplomacy with an administration the president did not formally recognize. Lincoln dispatched a messenger to Charleston on April 6 notifying Governor Francis W. Pickens of South Carolina that "an attempt will be made to supply Fort Sumpter [sic] with provisions only, and that, if such an attempt be not resisted, no effort to throw in men, arms, or ammunition, will be made, without further notice, or in case of an attack on the Fort."[51]

Mary Boykin Chesnut, a witty, bright, and dedicated diarist, had a front-row seat at the proceedings. She and her husband, James, a Confederate senator, owned a home in Charleston near the Battery, where residents strolled in the early evening to escape the oppressive heat further inland. The Battery looked out onto Charleston Harbor and the drama that unfolded between land and sea. In early April, as a sense of impending confrontation gripped the city, Mary recorded the bellicose declarations of citizens thirsting for a confrontation. Everyone, it seemed, deemed war inevitable. One of her closest friends related that "the only feeling she had about the War was pity for those who could not get here."[52]

Governor Pickens forwarded Lincoln's message on April 8 to General P. G. T. Beauregard, commanding general of Confederate forces in Charleston, who, in turn, telegraphed President Davis in Montgomery for instructions. Beauregard received orders on April 10 to demand the evacuation of Fort Sumter and to attack the federal garrison there if Major Anderson refused to surrender. Major Anderson contacted General Beauregard and asked him what the hurry was about. He would run out of food by April 15 and then withdraw his troops. President Davis, with this new information, instructed Beauregard to wait, but countermanded his own order when Fox's federal relief expedition suddenly materialized in Charleston Harbor at three in the morning on April 12.

Georgia's Robert Toombs, the Confederate secretary of state, pleaded with Davis that an attack on the federal provision fleet "at this time . . . is suicide, murder, and will lose us every friend at the North. You will wantonly strike a hornet's nest which extends from mountains to ocean, and legions, now quiet, will swarm out and sting us to death. It is unnecessary; it puts us in the wrong; it is fatal." The cabinet sustained the president's decision. Beauregard issued the ultimatum to Anderson, who refused to surrender. At 5:00 A.M. on April 12, 1861, the Confederate forces launched a general bombardment of Fort Sumter.[53]

Residents of Charleston along the Battery clamored to the rooftops to witness the pyrotechnics, much as the citizens of Matamoros gaped at American troops across the Rio Grande fifteen years earlier awaiting a similar military display. After thirty-three hours and the explosion of nearly five thousand artillery shells, Major Anderson surrendered. General Beauregard allowed Fox's vessels, which had remained at a discreet distance from Confederate artillery, to transport Major Anderson and his men out of the harbor and back to the North. Despite the fierce bombardment, neither side experienced any fatalities, a deceptive start to what would become the bloodiest war in American history. Fort Sumter was now in the hands of the Confederate States of America.

Lincoln greeted the news from Sumter almost with a sense of relief. The Confederacy had fired the first shot: "They attacked Sumter. It fell and thus did more service than it otherwise would." Lincoln did not want war, but only the surrender of the fort, something he would not countenance, would have mollified the Confederate authorities. The attack on Fort Sumter did more than begin the Civil War. General Beauregard and President Davis had accomplished something Lincoln could not: unifying the North against the Confederate States of America.[54]

A great drama unfolds in the Book of Revelation as angels, demons, and mortals fight cataclysmic battles. The human race, in John's vision, is divided into the redeemed and the condemned. They are no mere spectators to this cosmic conflict, but are active participants in a war where good or evil will triumph. Revelation's view of history is progressive, with a series of victories for the forces of good over evil. But the final battle is the fiercest, as Satan rallies his minions to fight the armies of the Lord at a place called Armageddon. God's forces triumph ushering in the millennium, a thousand years of peace at the end of which Satan emerges from exile and "fire from heaven" destroys him and his followers once and for all. A "new heaven and a new earth" created by God appears, sheltering the righteous. In the spring of 1861, two nations claimed the mantle of God's Chosen Nation. He would choose only one.[55]

Walt Whitman sauntered down Broadway at midnight on April 13, the street still thrumming with people and vehicles in this city that never slept. He had just witnessed a fine performance of Giuseppe Verdi's new opera, *A Masked Ball*, about the assassination of Swedish monarch Gustav III. What differed on this particular night was that newsboys, rarely about at this hour, were excitedly hawking extra editions of their newspapers. Whitman bought a copy and walked over to a circle of lamplight to read about what had caused the commotion. The sidewalk was crowded with like-minded readers, and one of them read the news aloud: "Southern forces in Charleston, South Carolina, had bombarded Fort Sumter." The tug had come.[56]

CHAPTER 9

JUST CAUSES

WAR ENERGIZED WALT WHITMAN. An uncharacteristic pessimism had settled in the poet as the sectional crisis worsened. The firing on Fort Sumter and Lincoln's call for troops revived him. He took a bath, a baptism for a new birth. He went on a new diet. "I have this day, this hour, resolved to inaugurate for myself a pure, perfect, sweet, clean-blooded robust body . . . a great body, a purged, cleansed, spiritualized, invigorated body." He rejoiced:

> *War! an arm'd race is advancing! the welcome for*
> *battle, no turning away;*
> *War! be it weeks, months, or years, an arm'd race is*
> *advancing to welcome it.*[1]

His city celebrated with him. A fog had lifted; the way was now clear. Ambiguity and uncertainty had dissipated. Major Anderson's quiet heroism and the firing on the American flag had dissolved partisan discord. "It seems as if we never were alive till now; never had a country till now," a New Yorker exclaimed. People poured into the streets, even in such southern-leaning places as New York City and Cincinnati, to proclaim their patriotism. George Ticknor, a Boston educator, marveled to an English friend, "The whole population, men, women, and children, seem to be in the streets with Union favours and flags. . . . Civil war is freely accepted everywhere . . . by all, anarchy being the obvious, and perhaps the only alternative." Pacifists who had rejected violence, even in support of righteous causes, turned bellicose. Ralph Waldo Emerson enthused, "Sometimes gunpowder smells good."[2]

War had become a magic elixir to speed America's millennial march, no longer the destroyer of lives or the waster of lands. New England theologian Orestes Brownson likened the war to a "thunderstorm that purifies the moral and political atmosphere."[3]

Peace had feminized and anesthetized northerners. Peace had allowed the scramble for wealth and place to transcend piety and patriotism. An editorial in *Harper's Weekly* in October 1861 predicted that war would reorder America's priorities. "Peace enervates and corrupts society; war strengthens and purifies. . . . [M]oney has grown to be the sole idol worshiped by the bulk of our people. . . . If this evil can be cured, . . . this a war will do." Enthusiasm enveloped northerners. Otherwise sober publications extolled the war in terms better suited to advance publicity for a P. T. Barnum circus than to a deadly conflict. *Scientific American* promised "thrilling scenes . . . sublime daring, heroic achievement and grim horrors." Step right up.[4]

A similar frenzy gripped the South. Young men rushed to arms fearful that by the time they left their farms and small towns, the war would be over. A correspondent for the *London Times* reported immense throngs of people with "flushed faces, wild eyes, screaming mouths," cascading through southern city streets, rushing to Armageddon, while bands played spirited renditions of "Dixie" over and over again. Everyone was "full of zeal and patriotism!"[5]

Like their northern counterparts, southerners rejoiced in the prospect of war. "Thank God the war is open," a grateful South Carolina governor Francis Pickens declared. The war promised a spiritual rebirth. Virginia governor Henry A. Wise exulted, "I rejoice in this war. . . . It is a war of purification. You want war, fire, blood to purify you; and the Lord of Hosts has demanded that you should walk through fire and blood."[6]

The men and women who celebrated the war believed they were worthy of it. This second generation of Americans and their offspring carried the legacy of the American Revolution. Northerners saw the opportunity to extend and protect the Revolutionary legacy, to transform an experiment into a permanent, indivisible country. An Ohio recruit resolved, "Our Fathers made this country, we, their children are to save it." Southerners sought to duplicate the work of the rebels of '76 and found a new nation. Ivy Duggan, a Georgia recruit, read the Revolution as teaching "us . . . to resist oppression, to declare and maintain independence, to govern ourselves as we think best."[7]

Young men went off to war for reasons other than God and country, especially in the Confederacy, where the concept of "country" was not yet fully formed. Some enlisted for personal reasons—to protect their homes and families, to experience something meaningful—or just because they had nothing else better to do. One reluctant Alabamian hastened to join when his girlfriend mailed a dress to him and suggested that he wear it if he would not enlist. Then there was the case of Sam Clemens of Hannibal, Missouri, who did not want to fight, nor did he favor one side over the other, but who joined a Confederate regiment because his friends did. Given his weak sense of commitment, it was not surprising that, after two weeks in camp fighting mosquitoes instead of Yankees, he lit out for Nevada Territory. Clemens spent the war out West safely spinning yarns, searching for gold, and writing news-paper columns about life on the frontier, some of which were true.[8]

What is striking about the diaries and letters of the young men and of the families that they left behind is how much they had absorbed the cultural ide-als of their generation. Each side persisted in the belief that the other threat-ened liberty and the Lord, and that only the fire of battle could save these ideals for now and for all time. The Civil War was not about territory per se; nor was it about wealth; nor was it about forms of government—remarkably few southerners mentioned states' rights at all in their correspondence. Rather, the war was about God and the fulfillment of His plan to complete the American Revolution. Some likened the conflict to Armageddon or iden-tified it as Armageddon itself. This perspective presaged a brutal and lengthy war, for the stakes were as high as heaven.

Both sides claimed the Revolutionary mantle and the filial responsibility to emulate and protect it. One side fought to honor those ideals by reuniting the old Union, the other by establishing a new nation. Northerners worried that disunion would doom America's global destiny as a force for self-government worldwide. Abraham Lincoln emphasized America's global mission as "the last best hope of earth." Northern recruits believed with their president that the future of self-government for mankind depended on the outcome of the war. "I do feel that the liberty of the world is placed in our hands to defend," a Massachusetts soldier wrote to his wife, "and if we are overcome then farewell to freedom." Well into the war, even soldiers worn by the strain of battle vowed to fight on "for the great principles of liberty and self government at stake, for should we fail, the onward march of Liberty in the Old World will be retarded at least a century."[9]

Americans were also children of the Second Great Awakening. They had grown up believing in an omnipresent God who touched their lives and guided their country's destiny. He would take sides in the coming battle. In protecting the Revolutionary ideals, northerners would preserve God's plan to extend democracy and Christianity across an unbroken continent and around the world. Southerners welcomed a war to create a nation more per-fect in its fealty to God than the one they left.

The war was a religious conflict for many evangelicals, a contest to save both souls and nations. A Louisiana woman wrote to her bishop, "We are fighting the Battle of the Cross against the Modern Barbarians who would rob a Christian people of Country, Liberty, and life." Northern evangelicals believed that southerners, like the Indians and Mexicans, wallowed in a "hea-thenish condition." One minister rejoiced, "What a wide field will soon be opened for Christian labor."[10]

The holy war inevitably engaged the issue of slavery. Both northerners and southerners recognized slavery as the immediate cause of the war. Soldiers from both sides connected the institution to the broader ideals of freedom and faith. A young Iowa man, explaining his reasons for volunteering, cited "duty to my country and my *God*," to crush a rebellion instigated "to secure the extension of that blighting curse—*slavery*—o'er our fair land." White southerners, regardless of whether they held slaves or not, believed in the "divine right of slaveholding." They equated black slavery with white freedom. Northerners, in a mirror image, believed that defeat would speed their own enslavement. A Wisconsin recruit explained, "Home is sweet and friends are dear, but what would they all be to let the country go to ruin, and be a slave." Not literally, of course, but these young northerners had grown up in a time when the U.S. Supreme Court and the U.S. Congress had, in effect, nationalized slavery.[11]

For African Americans, the war for freedom was more than a metaphor. The war represented Exodus and Armageddon rolled into one glorious cause. Frederick Douglass rejoiced that "the keen knife of liberty" hurtled at white southern throats. In a speech in June 1861, Douglass called the conflict a "war in heaven" between the archangel Michael and the dragon, and when it was over "not a slave should be left a slave in the returning footprints of the American army gone to put down this slaveholding rebellion."[12]

Northern religious rhetoric often focused on slavery. In November 1861, Boston abolitionist Julia Ward Howe penned the words to a song that became a surrogate anthem for the Union army during the war. "The Battle Hymn of the Republic" was the Rebel yell set to music, a bloodthirsty cry hurling wrath and sword against a profligate enemy. "Let the hero born of woman crush the serpent with his heel." Howe encouraged the young Union soldiers to Christ-like martyrdom: "As he died to make men holy, let us die to make men free." Howe had an epiphany after the war and became a pacifist.

Harriet Beecher Stowe believed she was witnessing the unfolding of the Book of Revelation. The Civil War was a millennial war, she and many fellow evangelicals believed, "the *last* struggle for liberty" that would precede the coming of the Lord. "God's just wrath shall be wreaked on a giant wrong." Her brother Henry Ward Beecher related the familiar story of Exodus to his congregation, how Moses led the children of Israel out of Egypt to the Red Sea, and how the sea parted and allowed the Chosen People to escape while burying their pursuers. "And now our turn has come," he exclaimed. "Right before us lies the Red Sea of War." And God was ready; foretelling Julia Ward Howe's famous lines, "that awful wine-press of the Wrath of Almighty God" would come down from the heavens and bury the South.[13]

The causes of God and country blended together as the young men marched off to war, just as they had merged in the political crises of the 1850s. It was a natural conflation: a nation apart from history, sanctified by God, and a prelude to His coming. Political leaders spoke in biblical cadences and verses. And citizens believed in their country's divine destiny as much as in the salvation of their souls. When the young men wrote their first letters home or confided their thoughts to a diary, they wrote of how much they missed their loved ones, yet of how they felt themselves drawn to a cause greater than themselves. A diary entry from a twenty-three-year-old Iowa soldier: "Tuesday, July 9, 1861: I have volunteered to fight in this war for the Union and *a government*. I have left the peaceful walks of life and 'buckled on the harness of war' not from any feeling of enthusiasm, nor incited by any hopes of honor [or] glory, but because I believe that duty to my country and my *God*, bid me assist in crushing this wicked rebellion against our government."[14]

Confederate soldiers expressed their secular reasons for fighting less in terms of country than in terms of self-determination or self-government and, most of all, home and family. Like the Union soldiers, they naturally blended the sacred and the secular in their writing. A Mississippian claimed he and his compatriots fought "for a sacred principle—for the right of self-government, for the protection of their homes, and their families and their altars."[15]

In the beginning, faith reinforced the romance of war. "The men first gathered to defend the borders were men . . . in whom the love of an abstract principle became, not a religion, but a romantic passion." There were also men who responded skeptically to the call for a crusade, believing that to employ Christianity to kill represented less a sacred mission than a grave sacrilege. And there were men who saw through the charade of faith parading as patriotism. "All wars are sacred," Rhett Butler scoffed, "to those who have to fight them. If the people who started wars didn't make them sacred, who would be foolish enough to fight?" Butler is fictional, of course; it would be difficult to find some contemporary to express such thoughts. Margaret Mitchell had the benefit of hindsight.[16]

God may have authored the war, but men would have to fight it. The Confederate States of America faced, by far, the more difficult task. The list of challenges confronting President Jefferson Davis and the Confederate Congress was daunting: create a nation and develop an attachment to it among a citizenry deeply suspicious of central government; overcome class, political, and geographic divisions to rally around a common cause; establish a financial system to run government and pay for war; erect factories to supply an army not yet raised; and direct farms and plantations to produce adequate food supplies for both civilian and military needs. Jefferson Davis was capable, but he was not a magician.

The wives of Confederate leaders cheered the transfer of the rebel capital from Montgomery to Richmond. From a strategic standpoint, Richmond's proximity to enemy territory may have been a disadvantage, but its location also lured Union forces into numerous ill-fated confrontations. "On to Richmond!" became less a battle cry than a punch line. From an esthetic standpoint, Richmond was a hands-down winner. Montgomery's muddy main street had once swallowed an oxen team whole after a particularly heavy rain. At the city's two hotels, the mosquitoes were the only guests that ate well. Many have portrayed the move to Richmond as a bow to Virginia's power, but Confederate congressmen could not wait to pack their bags. Besides, Richmond's seven hills gave Rebel leaders the illusion they shared something with Rome.

Rome was not built in a day, but the Confederacy had to be. Davis recognized that adherence to states' rights conflicted with the needs of the new nation. He created a centralized administration that managed the cultivation of food crops for the military, forcibly commandeered both men and materiel, created a national currency, tax, and financial system, passed the first conscription act in American history (a year before the North instituted its draft), engaged in a vigorous international diplomacy, and planned military strategy. The Davis administration built a federal bureaucracy of seventy thousand workers, more than its counterpart in Washington. If the South was truly fighting for states' rights, it lost in spirit almost immediately.

Many of Davis's contemporaries gave him little credit until postwar historians rewrote the history of the war. Richmond harbored nests of spies, squads of soldiers, refugees from the countryside, office seekers, con men, and politicians and bureaucrats of varying competence. Some liked Davis; most did not. His belief that the new nation required a strong central government to make war and secure independence was, however, correct. His policies elicited such strong opposition from states'-rights advocates that Davis bitterly offered "Died of a Theory" as the Confederacy's epitaph. The Confederacy, though, died not from too much government or too little but on the battlefield.[17]

Davis's aloofness shielded him against an incompetent Congress and a mediocre cabinet. The Congress often met in secret session, a fact Vice President Alexander Stephens applauded, since that "kept from the public some of the most disgraceful scenes ever enacted by a legislative body." Unbound by any party discipline—there were no parties—the members often demonstrated no discipline at all, erupting into mayhem and even murder on one occasion. They saved their worst behavior for the president. A cabinet member snarled that Davis was a "false and hypocritical wretch." Linton Stephens, half brother of the vice president, collected a basket of adjectives to describe

Davis as a "*little, conceited, hypocritical, sniveling, canting, malicious, ambitious, dogged* knave and fool." Little wonder that Mary Chesnut in October
1861 reported the false rumor that Davis had fled to a farm with his doctor to
escape his Richmond critics.[18]

The sniping at Davis reflected a microcosm of the Confederacy. Divisions
and dissension abounded, waxing and waning with military fortunes. Some of
these divisions existed prior to the war, among Unionists opposed to secession,
white yeomen farmers resentful over planter hegemony, and most of the four
million slaves representing nearly one third of the total population. The opposition did not dissolve with war, and in some cases grew. If white southerners had
supported the war wholeheartedly, there would have been no need for the draft
in February 1862 and for subsequent conscription measures. Terms added to
the popular lexicon such as "before-breakfast secessionists" and "bomb-proofs"
denoted those who waved the flag and then sought shelter in exempted occupations or property-ownership brackets. North Carolina journalist and future
governor W. W. Holden, commenting on the numerous exemptions included
in the 1862 conscription act, charged that the conflict had become a "rich man's
war and a poor man's fight," an allegation echoed around military campfires
throughout the war.[19]

The so-called twenty-nigger law, which exempted those owning twenty
slaves or more, fueled resentment, especially since the loss of able-bodied men
on nonslaveholding farms could have a devastating economic impact on
families and localities. A Confederate congressman unsuccessfully seeking
the law's repeal argued, "Its influence upon the poor is most calamitous."
Fighting against starvation, wives and daughters encouraged desertion at the
risk of severe punishment. Mary Chesnut reported witnessing an impressment officer carting off a man as his wife cried, "You desert again, quick as
you kin. Come back to your wife and children."[20]

The mountains of western North Carolina and east Tennessee, the hills of
northern Alabama, and the German districts of Texas harbored Unionists opposed, sometimes violently so, to Confederate authorities. Geographic and
class divisions abounded, especially in the Appalachian South. North Carolina governor Zebulon B. Vance reported "an astonishing amount of disloyalty" to the Confederacy in the mountain counties of western North Carolina.
A farmer in Winston County in northern Alabama summarized the attitude
of these dissenters: "All tha want is to git you . . . to fight for their infurnal
negroes and after you do their fightin you may kiss their hine parts for a tha
care."[21]

Victories on the battlefield could overcome these divisions. The plan of
the Davis administration to create those victories contradicted conventional

military wisdom. Offensive tactics won wars. A defensive war seemed more sensible, however, for a new nation encompassing 750,000 square miles, or roughly twice the size of the thirteen colonies. Confederate leaders made frequent analogies to the Revolutionary War and how the ill-equipped and outmanned Continental Army had held off superior British forces. The great Napoleon faltered before the vastness of Russia. The South's wooded and hilly terrain, traversed by rivers difficult to ford, and the logistical problems presented by the Appalachian barrier made invasion difficult. The more territory the invading army seized, the more soldiers would be taken out of battle to perform the duties of occupation.

The Confederacy, though, could not wage a purely defensive war. Defensive wars are hard on the land and the people. They take time, which is part of the strategy: the enemy will eventually run out of patience and negotiate. At some point, however, time becomes the enemy as well, especially as shortages of manpower and materiel worsen the longer the war progresses. The Confederacy could not win a war of attrition.

The South instead adopted a hybrid approach, defending when necessary and selectively launching offensives when the opportunity arose. Southern armies were the first military forces in the world to take advantage of railroads to move and mass troops, overcoming topography and distance. The Confederacy also had the advantage of fighting on its own terrain and among a friendly population. Any offensive movements, however, carried with them new dangers as a result of improved weaponry. Rifled, as opposed to smoothbore, muskets increased the range and accuracy of minié balls from one hundred to upwards of four hundred yards. This pushed back artillery, rendering it less effective. Cavalry charges against massed infantry, however romantic, would be futile.[22]

West Point manuals counseled concentrated offensive charges against defensive positions. By the time defenders had a chance to reload—a process involving nine separate steps—the offensive troops would be on them with bayonets. Not so with rifles, where soldiers holding defensive positions could pull off three rounds before a charging enemy closed. Defensive wars conserved armies; offensive tactics could destroy them. The Confederacy would employ offensive tactics sparingly; the key was timing.

Washington, D.C., was not surrounded by seven hills, though some of its architecture possessed Classical pretenses. It was a creature of the swamp, fetid in summer and bone-chillingly damp in the winter. Foreign diplomats considered a posting there a punishment. It was a slave city, odd for the headquarters of a government fighting against slavery. It was a southern city, and Confederate spies and sympathizers abounded. By 1861, many northern cities had made rudimentary attempts to clean and pave their streets and improve the water supply and waste disposal. Washington was impervious to these salutary trends, with many of its streets muddy quagmires—a Union soldier reported watching a mule, albeit a small mule, disappear into the mud up to his ears one morning. Drainage ditches oozed with sewage and dead animals. Pigs rooted in the streets, and droves of cattle marched down thoroughfares as if the city were some displaced Kansas stockyard. At night, fires from the military camps blotted out the stars, and residents slumbered to the incessant roll of drums. A startled visitor from Maine concluded that he had come to "a squalid, unattractive, unsanitary country town infested by malaria, mosquitoes, cockroaches, bed bugs, lice and outdoor backhouses . . . and no end of houses of ill-fame."[23]

In this inauspicious place, the Lincoln administration took the war in hand. It faced many of the same problems confronting its Confederate counterpart—raising an army, financing a war, developing industry, dealing with dissent and divisions, and formulating a military strategy—though it possessed certain significant advantages. The North manufactured more than 90 percent of the nation's goods. The greatest differences existed in those industries most pertinent to waging war. Northern factories turned out seventeen times more textiles, thirty times as many shoes and boots, thirteen times more iron, thirty-two times as many firearms, and eleven times as many ships and boats as southern establishments. The South owned some vessels, but not a navy, a great problem with lengthy Atlantic and Gulf coastlines to defend. Of armories the South possessed none at the start of the war. Scarce specie went abroad to purchase weapons. The North possessed twenty thousand miles of railroad track, the South ten thousand miles. Northern tracks formed a system, too, while southern rails were unconnected. The maddening variety of gauges on southern railroad tracks impeded the smooth transfer of people and goods.[24]

The Republican Party, true to its Whig parentage, embodied the North's enterprising spirit, and it would build on these advantages. Lincoln's political idol, Henry Clay, would have heartily approved the Republicans' interest in using government to promote private enterprise. Democrats, believing the Constitution prohibited such measures, stymied Republican attempts to subsidize economic development. The Republicans hoped to use subsidies, tax breaks, and land sales to knit the nation together with a telegraph system and a transcontinental railroad. They would use government policy to help fulfill America's destiny as a continental empire. The war and the Republican majority in Congress—grown larger with the departure of southern Democrats—provided the opportunity to develop not only a more centralized federal government but also a nation.

With a Republican in the White House and a comfortable Republican majority in the Congress, it would seem likely that the Lincoln administration would not experience the dysfunction of the Richmond government. To an extent, that is true. Lincoln never generated the volume of enemies that tormented Jefferson Davis, but he attracted vocal opponents who made his life harder than it might have been. Most people, even his detractors, liked him, and unlike Davis, he had a deprecating sense of humor that often defused tense situations. The most common charge against him, especially when the war went badly, was that he lacked the intellect to lead. His own attorney general, Edward Bates, complained that the president lacked "*will* and *purpose*" and "has not *the power to command*." A fellow Republican predicted "the administration of Abraham Lincoln will stand even worse . . . with posterity than that of James Buchanan." Secretary of State William H. Seward was probably his closest confidant in government, but his cabinet, the "Team of Rivals," rarely met as a group. Considering the oil-and-water nature of their personalities, that may have been a good thing. Besides, Lincoln rarely consulted them. As a friend related, "They all disagreed so much he would not ask them—he depended on himself—always." Though his office was open to an eclectic assortment of job seekers, petitioners, old friends, and crackpot inventors, he rarely sought out opinions, but listened and then made up his own mind. Lincoln's cabinet appointments demonstrated his level of comfort with his own judgment, and his decision to hold few meetings with them reflected even better judgment.[25]

Charges that the president violated constitutional guarantees of civil liberties probably annoyed Lincoln more than any other criticism. He prided himself on both his knowledge of and adherence to the Constitution. He lectured one prominent Democrat, "The Constitution is not, in its application, in all respects the same, in cases of rebellion. . . . I can no more be persuaded that the Government can constitutionally take no strong measures in time of rebellion . . . than I can be persuaded that a particular drug is not good medicine for a sick man, because it can be shown not to be good food for a well one."[26]

While Lincoln struggled with his reputation among his political peers, he gradually won the affection of the people. His homespun humor and absence of affectation contributed to a common image. He had the knack of articulating what the people were feeling in a simple eloquence that captured the spirit of the moment. The president rendered the abstract concept of "Union" concrete. The Union, for Lincoln, was essential to secure equality of opportunity for all Americans. As he explained to a group of Ohio soldiers visiting the White House in 1864, saving the Union would ensure "an open field and a fair chance for your industry, enterprise and intelligence, that you may all have equal privileges in the race of life."[27]

Lincoln took this simple notion of fighting a war to preserve equal opportunity and enlarged it with a global perspective that transcended social class. In a July 1861 message to Congress, he declared, "This is essentially a People's contest. On the side of the Union, it is a struggle for maintaining in the world, that form, and substance of government, whose leading object is, to elevate the condition of men . . . to afford all an unfettered start and a fair chance in the race of life." Radical Republicans chafed that he dwelled upon the Union without addressing slavery. For Lincoln, however, equality of opportunity, not only within the United States but also throughout the world, would be impossible without first preserving the Union.[28]

The Lincoln administration must win the war to accomplish this objective. Both sides believed the war would be short, and neither held the opposing army in much esteem. A Virginian could not think of even one prominent northern-born soldier in American history save for Benedict Arnold. But the superintendent of a military academy in Louisiana, William Tecumseh Sherman, thought otherwise: "I think it is to be a long war—very long—much longer than any politician thinks."[29]

Lincoln shared the common assumption that the war would be over quickly. His initial call for seventy-five thousand troops for a three-month enlistment in mid-April reflected that judgment. By July, however, his view was changing. Congress applauded Lincoln's request for $400 million to raise an additional four hundred thousand volunteers with a three-year commitment. The lawmakers not only met his proposal but raised him to a total of $500 million for five hundred thousand men. The Union did not need to resort to conscripts until more than a year after the Confederacy passed the first American draft. It also benefited from a population at least three times the size of the South's. The federal force remained primarily a volunteer army organized by individual states to the end of the war. More than two million men served in the Union ranks.[30]

But in 1861, the regular army consisted of fewer than sixteen thousand soldiers, most posted in the West. Although the great majority of these men threw in with the Union, Lincoln lost one third of the officer corps, including some of the most experienced and highest-ranking officers. Civilian armies would fight the Civil War.

Both armies, consequently, were unprepared for battle. With no pension, army officers usually stayed in the saddle until they died. Of the nine highest-ranking officers in the Union army, eight were veterans of the War of 1812. The general-in-chief, Winfield Scott, at age seventy-four—a very old age in

those days—required an entourage to help him mount his horse. State militias would supply the earliest volunteers, but these soldiers were more accustomed to partying than training. Fortunately, a cadre of professional soldiers
with leadership skills and logistical expertise existed to create an effective
fighting force.

The nonnegotiable objectives of the two sides made a longer war more
likely. The North would not stop its armies short of reunion, and the South
would not cease the fight until it secured its independence and preserved
slavery. When the Union later added emancipation to its war objectives, a
negotiated truce or compromise became even more improbable.

The Mexican War had seasoned many Civil War officers, including the
leading general officers, Robert E. Lee and Ulysses S. Grant, but that was another war. General Scott's brilliant lightning march of eighteen weeks from
Vera Cruz to the gates of Mexico City over rough terrain benefited from the
creativity of engineer Lee and a series of bold offensives against good but
poorly led Mexican troops. After raising the American flag over Mexico City,
the troops left, the politicians negotiated, a compromise was struck in the
Americans' favor, and Mexico resumed its sovereignty. Quick victories, limited objectives, and a political solution would not characterize the Civil War.

The Lincoln administration understood that Union armies must take the
offensive to put down the rebellion. The message only partially registered
with General Scott, who proposed to surround the Confederacy with a naval
blockade along the Atlantic and Gulf coasts and establish defensive lines on
the Ohio and Potomac rivers. He would dispatch eighty-five thousand troops
down the Mississippi River, taking control of the South's major commercial
highway. The plan had the virtue of threatening the Confederacy from several points. Critics, though, derided Scott's proposal as the "Anaconda Plan":
instead of beating the enemy on the field of battle, squeeze it to death. Also, it
was doubtful that a hundred thousand Confederate troops in Virginia would
rest on their guns while Union forces attacked their comrades out west. The
naval blockade made sense, however, and it proved effective over time. In
1861, the Union blockade intercepted only one of ten Confederate vessels.
By 1865, the U.S. Navy stopped one of two ships.[31]

A young former regular army officer from Ohio, George B. McClellan, had
a bolder plan: invade western Virginia from his Ohio base, strike into Kentucky and Tennessee, and thence to the Gulf of Mexico. To prove how easily
he could implement the strategy, he led his Ohio troops into western Virginia
in May 1861, sent a small Confederate force into retreat, and enabled local
Unionists to organize a government that eventually became the state of West
Virginia.

Lincoln's greatest concern during the war's first few months was keeping the Border South—Maryland, Kentucky, and Missouri—in the Union. Maryland surrounded Washington, D.C., on three sides; Virginia, already a Confederate state, completed the encirclement. A crowd of Baltimore residents had already expressed their sentiment during the first week of the war when they attacked a Massachusetts regiment bound for Washington. The soldiers responded by firing into the mob and killing eleven of the rioters, touching off a three-day rampage as roaming gangs destroyed federal property and tore up rail lines to block the transit of Yankee troops to the southern front. General Scott ordered sandbags for federal buildings in Washington so troops could protect the government if the mob rolled south.

The Lincoln administration solved the problem of Maryland by a show of force. General Benjamin Butler, leading another Massachusetts regiment, marched to the state capital at Annapolis, placed the city under martial law, dispatched troops to Baltimore, planted artillery on Federal Hill, and promised to blast the city to smithereens if residents impeded federal troops making transit southward. The threat worked. The Maryland legislature voted against secession, and Union soldiers never again encountered violence in Baltimore. By the end of May, Maryland was secure for the Union, if grudgingly so. The state gained one benefit from the crisis. The federals' massive response so incensed poet James Ryder Randall that he dashed off lyrics to a song he titled "Maryland, My Maryland," including the line "The despot's heel is on thy shore," to remind future generations of the state's duress.[32]

The Democrats, though a minority in Congress, vigorously opposed the president's actions in Maryland and other curtailment of civil liberties. Lincoln believed he had constitutional authority in time of war to suspend habeas corpus, muzzle the press, and arrest those actively aiding the enemy. He summarized his philosophy with one of his folksy analogies: "Often a limb must be amputated to save a life; but a life is never wisely given to save a limb." Lincoln did not manufacture conspiracies where none existed. Confederate sympathizers were common in the southern parts of Ohio, Indiana, and Illinois, settled by families like Lincoln's own. Sentiment is not a crime, of course, but organizing secret societies to sabotage or murder endangered the Union war effort. During the course of the war, military and political authorities arrested more than thirteen thousand individuals in the North, revoked their right of habeas corpus, and remanded them for military trial.[33]

Some Republicans, on the other hand, believed the president did not go far enough. *Harper's* stated, "The most convenient government for a nation at war is a despotic monarchy; the most inconvenient—according to general opinion—a democratic republic." The editor suggested banning the Democratic *New*

York Herald for its criticism of General Scott. While both the Lincoln and Davis administrations erred occasionally in limiting civil liberties, on the whole, they preserved the basic essence of democratic government during a bloody civil war.[34]

Lincoln had to tread more carefully with respect to his home state of Kentucky than he had with Maryland. If Kentucky joined the Confederacy, the enemy would be on the banks of the Ohio River with easy access to the Old Northwest. Kentucky captured Lincoln's heart and attention. It was the state of his birth; his closest friends and his wife were Kentuckians, as was his political mentor and idol, Henry Clay. Lincoln hoped to have God on his side, but he had to have Kentucky. He adopted a gingerly approach. Federal troops steered clear of the state, and Lincoln reassured residents that their property was secure, indeed more secure in the Union than out of it. Kentucky announced its neutrality, but in September 1861 Confederate troops, attempting to preempt a possible advance by Federals across the Ohio under the command of Ulysses S. Grant, invaded the state. The Unionist legislature invited Grant to come in and clear out the Confederates, and he gladly complied. Eventually, eighty-five thousand Kentuckians fought for the Union; thirty-five thousand men joined Confederate forces. Officially neutral, its manpower and resources were under Union control throughout the war.

Missouri remained a problem through most of the war, as it was in the battle over Kansas. Internecine warfare began almost immediately after Sumter. Federal missteps compounded the problem when General John C. Frémont entered the state in August 1861. His incompetence as a military leader matched his poor political judgment. He placed the state under martial law, threatened the execution of any Missourian who aided secessionists, and issued an emancipation proclamation. Even Republicans in the state were aghast at Frémont's tactless measures. They feared the fallout from Frémont's antislavery activities could tip both Missouri and Kentucky to the Confederates. A Kentucky friend of Lincoln's warned him that the general's edict could "crush out every vistage [*sic*] of a union party in the state." Lincoln rescinded the emancipation edict and eventually dismissed his errant general. The Confederate national flag included stars for both Kentucky and Missouri. Their presence was strictly symbolic.[35]

As Lincoln monitored the situation in the border states, he was hopeful that a quick strike into Virginia and the Confederate capital at Richmond would end the rebellion quickly. Tens of thousands of green civilian Union recruits were camped along the Potomac waiting for that opportunity. They included Sullivan Ballou, a thirty-two-year-old Rhode Island lawyer well into his career with a wife and two young children. He could have remained at home, as volunteers filled the state's quota quickly. He would not stand down, though, and watch men younger than him go off to defend the Union and what it stood for. Joining the 2nd Regiment, Rhode Island Volunteers, Ballou deployed to Washington, D.C. Along with other recruits in that swollen city, he drilled and waited in stifling summer heat, longing for his family and for the cool sea breezes of his native state. On July 14, 1861, rumors darted through the camp that he and his fellow soldiers would finally see the war. He sat down by a tree and wrote to share the news with his wife, Sarah. Like so many other citizen soldiers, he wrote of God and country, of love and of thoughts of death, and of how to sort these conflicting feelings at a time of great peril. This is what he wrote:

> The indications are very strong that we shall move in a few days, per-haps tomorrow. And lest I should not be able to write you again I feel impelled to write a few lines that may fall under your eye when I am no more. . . . "Not my will but thine O God be done." If it is necessary that I should fall on the battle-field for my Country I am ready. . . . I know how American Civilization now leans upon the triumph of the government and how great a debt we owe to those who went before us through the blood and suffering of the Revolution. And I am will-ing, perfectly willing, to lay down all my joys in this life, to help maintain this government, and to pay that debt. But my dear wife, when I know that with my own joys I lay down nearly all of yours, . . . is it weak or dishonorable that while the banner of my purpose floats calmly and proudly in the breeze, underneath, my unbounded love for you my darling wife and children should struggle in fierce though useless contest with my love of country? . . .
>
> If I do not [return], my dear Sarah, never forget how much I loved you, nor that when my last breath escapes me on the battle-field, it will whisper your name.[36]

At two o'clock in the afternoon on the following day, July 15, General Irvin McDowell issued an order to all the division and brigade commanders from his headquarters at Arlington Heights overlooking the city of Washington. The officers informed Ballou and his comrades at parade that evening. They were to move out at two o'clock the next afternoon and carry three days' worth of rations. They would move south toward Richmond. The troops greeted the news with deafening cheers.

McDowell's headquarters had been the home of Colonel Robert E. Lee, late of the federal army. Lee had resigned his commission and cast his lot with the Confederacy. His home held both strategic and symbolic value for the federal government, which promptly seized the property. McDowell had recently advanced to commander of the Union armies as a surrogate for General Scott, who was too infirm to take the field. A West Pointer and a veteran of the Mexican War, McDowell had a strong military background but had never commanded troops in combat. He worried that his green troops were not yet ready to engage an enemy. Lincoln dismissed the concern: "You are green, it is true, but they are green, also; you are all green alike." The mounting pressure from both the general public and the Lincoln administration to strike at Richmond and quickly end the war forced McDowell to set aside his concerns and move his army south. The *New York Tribune* blared in large headlines every day for a week in late June, "FORWARD TO RICHMOND! FORWARD TO RICHMOND!" Other newspapers took up the chant. "Forward to Richmond!" became the nation's war cry. The fact that the three-month enlistment period was coming due for thousands of soldiers also factored into Lincoln's order to McDowell.[37]

Sullivan Ballou marched south with his Rhode Island neighbors and thirty-five thousand other young men to face combat for the first time. As the West Point manual prescribed, one regiment of skirmishers preceded the army to draw the first enemy contact and guard against an ambush. One regiment of infantry followed, then the artillery, and two infantry regiments completed the brigade. Another brigade followed. Baggage wagons brought up the rear. Up and down the rolling hills of northern Virginia they marched, bayonets glistening in the sun and the artillery rumbling along as if heralding a thunderstorm. The procession took several hours to pass a given point. Residents along the line of march either fled in fright or watched the scene sullenly. A few paid no attention and kept on tending their fields.[38]

Confederate General P. G. T. Beauregard, the hero of Fort Sumter, congregated his twenty-thousand-man force on the south bank of a stream called Bull Run near Manassas, an important railroad junction about twenty-five miles south of Washington and seventy miles north of Richmond. His orders were to turn around the federal advance on Richmond. A classmate of McDowell's at West Point, Beauregard confidently awaited the arrival of his former colleague. A Confederate force of twelve thousand under the command of General Joseph E. Johnston, the highest-ranking federal officer to resign, guarded the entrance to the Shenandoah Valley at Winchester. General Robert F. Patterson, one of the Union army's War of 1812 veterans, was charged to keep Johnston pinned down in the valley to prevent him from reinforcing Beauregard. Instead, while Patterson watched the road, Johnston took the railroad. McDowell's ponderous march from Washington allowed Johnston's army to arrive at the battlefield in time to bring the Confederate armies to roughly equal strength with the enemy. Johnston knew exactly where and when to deposit his men from the information President Davis conveyed via Rose O'Neal Greenhow, a Confederate spy in Washington, D.C. She and about one thousand other Washingtonians knew precisely the route and movements of McDowell's troops.

Although the first federal soldiers had arrived in the area as early as July 18, it was not until Sunday, July 21, that McDowell had his novice troops fully in place. By that time, General Johnston's men had almost completed their train trip from the valley. It would not be the last time that tardiness played a role in a battle's outcome.

The opposing armies marched into the valley of Bull Run on an idyllic early Sabbath morning preparing to send shot, shell, and shrapnel into each other's bodies. A group of congressmen, reporters, and other curious residents of Washington packed picnic lunches and drove out in an assortment of conveyances to watch the festivities. A Union shell crashed into the kitchen of the McLean house, where General Beauregard was eating his breakfast. The battle had begun.

As the West Point manual directed, both sides opened up with booming artillery along a line that extended for five miles. The Union infantry advanced smartly on the Confederate batteries, forced the Rebels back, and threatened to collapse their left flank, leaving the center and right exposed. General Barnard Bee, commanding the Confederate left with his South Carolina troops, shouted for reinforcements under the command of Virginian Thomas J. Jackson, whose reserves moved up quickly and halted the Yankee advance. General Bee rallied his troops, shouting, "Look, men! There is Jackson standing like a stone wall! Let us determine to die here and we will conquer!" Though General Bee fell mortally wounded, he had given his new nation a legend. Fresh troops led by Jubal A. Early and Edmund Kirby Smith boosted the wilting Confederate forces, and they mounted one final charge into the Union battle line, accompanying their thrust with a high-pitched curdling scream—the Rebel yell—that startled the raw Union soldiers.[39]

The spirited Confederate onslaught unnerved the exhausted federal troops who were so close to victory just hours earlier. They retreated. In the rear of the Union lines, army teamsters and spectators panicked and dashed toward Washington. The contagion spread to some of the retreating soldiers, who threw down guns, knapsacks, canteens, and blankets. Artillery gunners cut horses loose from the guns and escaped as fast as they could, leaving behind valuable arms for the Confederates.

In Richmond, the absence of news was maddening. Jefferson Davis lost patience and rode out to the battlefield, joining his troops just as the federal retreat became a rout. The rest of Richmond waited, fearing that Union forces would be upon the city momentarily. Confederate officials milled about Mechanics Hall, the temporary headquarters for the War Department. Suddenly, Judah P. Benjamin, the attorney general, burst into the hall with news that President Davis had sent a telegram from the front: "We have won a glorious but dear-bought victory; the night closed with the enemy in full flight, pursued by our troops." The hall erupted in celebration. The new nation was now a reality. The *Richmond Examiner* expressed the feelings of the city: "This blow will shake the Northern Union in every bone; the echo will reverberate round the globe. It secures the independence of the Southern Confederacy. The churches of this city should be open to-day and its inhabitants should render God their thanks for a special providence in their behalf."[40]

President Davis and others wondered why Beauregard did not pursue the scampering Federals back to Washington. The answer was simple, and it was a response that would figure time and again during the war. The Confederates were just as green and just as exhausted as their Union counterparts. As night fell, so did a heavy rain, turning the roads back to the capital into mud pits.

Bull Run confirmed for many southerners the idea that the Confederacy was God's Chosen Nation. In a sermon delivered a week after the battle, the Rev. Stephen Elliott of Georgia compared the southern triumph to the deliverance of the Jewish people from Egypt: "It was the crowning token of his love—the most wonderful of all the manifestations of his divine presence with us." The victory recalled Isaiah 37:26. Though the Confederate soldiers did not turn "defended cities into ruinous heaps" in a literal sense, they had defeated a mightier foe.[41]

Southerners assumed too much when they asserted, "By the work of Sunday we have broken the backbone of invasion and utterly broken the spirit of the North." Embarrassment, despair, but ultimately determination characterized the reaction of northerners to their defeat at Bull Run. New York attorney George Templeton Strong confided to his diary the day after the battle, "Today will be known as BLACK MONDAY." Lincoln, who had ordered the advance, sighed to a colleague, "If hell is any worse than this, it has no terror for me." Those in the North who had demanded action now conceded the Union attack was ill timed: "Hereafter our generals must not be hurried into premature demonstrations." Excuses abounded: ignorance of local topography, the elaborate construction of trenches by the enemy, and the superior training and experience of Confederate soldiers.[42]

In the North, the Battle of Bull Run refuted the notion of a quick and easy war, but it did not kindle a movement for peace. An essayist in *Harper's* sent a warning: "From the fearful day at Bull Run dates war. Not polite war, not incredulous war, not conciliatory war, but war that breaks hearts and blights homes; war that by bloody and terrible blows teaches causeless rebellion that it shall suffer in mind, body, and estate, and that wherever it can be harmed there the blow shall fall, until, in absolute submission, it shall sue for peace." This was the war that lay ahead. An illustration of Rebel soldiers bayoneting the Union wounded on the battlefield at Bull Run accompanied the piece. Whether this occurred or not was beside the point. The message to readers was clear: draw no quarter against the enemy.[43]

The Battle of Bull Run was a limited affair, with no strategic advantage gained or lost and with both armies remaining intact. It was, however, the first major engagement of the war, the first significant test of theories and presumptions. Union forces came away with the idea that much work remained to be done, but giving up the fight was not an option. The Confederacy concluded that its independence was secure or at least near at hand, that foreign governments would rush to recognize the new nation, and that Yankee troops would run at the first glint of southern steel. It would be another year before the South won a second major victory.

The toll from Bull Run stood at 481 dead on the Union side and 387 Confederates killed in battle. The numbers shocked citizens on both sides. President Davis's telegram noting a "dear-bought victory" accurately reflected the people's sentiment. These numbers would prove very modest compared to the casualties in the months and years to come, a mere five to ten minutes' worth of fighting in some battles. Sullivan Ballou would be spared the horror ahead; he died by the bank of Bull Run on July 21, 1861. For God and country.

CHAPTER 10

SHILOH AWAKENING

SHILOH WAS A BIBLICAL CITY. Its name means "tranquil." The Children of Israel gathered there to protect the Ark of the Covenant containing the two stone tablets of the Ten Commandments. The Children, however, slipped in their devotion to God. The Philistines delivered a crushing defeat and carried off the Ark. Eventually, Shiloh was destroyed.

Shiloh gave its name to several evangelical Christian churches in America. Congregants hoped to emulate the tranquility and sanctity of the biblical place, while admonishing each other to remain righteous unto the Lord. Such was the hope of Shiloh Chapel in southwest Tennessee. On April 6 and 7, 1862, two American armies fought each other near this church in the bloodiest battle in the nation's history up to that time. The outcome was indecisive and strategically ambiguous. The victors did not carry any priceless religious artifacts from the field. The church survived. How American soldiers and civilians viewed the civil war in their midst, however, changed for all time. And with that altered vision, the nation changed as well.

The protagonist of this bloody drama hardly seemed the heroic type. As a young man, Ulysses S. Grant wanted to be a high school math teacher but deferred to his father's wishes that he remain at West Point. He resigned from the army in 1854 after a mediocre military career punctuated by bouts of excessive drinking. Still a relatively young man, at age thirty-two, he returned to his family farm near St. Louis, working it with slaves borrowed from his father-in-law. Farming did not pan out for Grant, nor did a job as a bill collector in St. Louis. By 1860, he was working in his father's leather shop in Galena, Illinois. He took a perfunctory interest in politics, supporting Democrat Stephen A. Douglas in that year's presidential race, though he did not bother to vote.[1]

When Lincoln called for troops following the Fort Sumter bombardment, Grant offered his services to the governor of Illinois, who authorized him to recruit and train volunteers. He received the commission of colonel and the command of the 21st Illinois Infantry. Deployed to Missouri, it was probably

Colonel Grant's movements toward a Confederate camp rather than the mosquitoes that convinced young Sam Clemens to hightail it to the West. Grant moved up the command ladder quickly, to the rank of brigadier general by the end of July 1861, and soon seized the strategic Ohio River town of Paducah, Kentucky, from Confederate forces.

Grant looked more like a mathematician than an army officer. Plain, his brown hair and beard streaked with gray, he often appeared to have slept in his uniform, a younger and more unkempt version of his hero, Zachary Taylor. People underestimated his intelligence, sniped at his drinking, and questioned his strategy. Yet Ulysses S. Grant was that rare Union general: he fought.

As the new year of 1862 unfolded, citizens on both sides wondered if they were really at war. There had not been a major battle since Bull Run in July 1861. Lincoln ordered Union troops under the command of General McClellan to advance toward Richmond on February 22. That date came and went with the Federals marching to and fro but not in any particular direction. President Davis, on the other hand, was in no hurry to engage the enemy. He knew that as long as Confederate independence remained an open idea, it would, by and by, become a reality.

Out west, the story was different. By the new year, the Confederates had lost Kentucky and were perilously close to losing Tennessee. Grant, supported by his naval counterpart, Admiral Andrew H. Foote, launched an amphibious assault up the Tennessee and Cumberland rivers. The objectives were to open the way for Union troops to occupy Nashville, cut an important rail line, and deprive the Confederacy of a rich source of meat and grain. Two forts, twelve miles apart, just south of the Kentucky-Tennessee border, guarded the rivers. The first, Fort Henry on the Tennessee River, fell to the Union team in three hours. Confederates put up a more spirited fight at Fort Donelson on the west bank of the Cumberland River. Rebel sharpshooters hid behind rocks and tree stumps and in trenches above the fort picking off the enemy. This was not warfare from the West Point manual. Some considered such tactics barbaric, but it was well suited to the wooded, sloping terrain, and to the weaponry of the era. Union troops charged entrenched Confederate positions and, predictably, suffered heavy casualties.

Soldiers bit off cartridge caps at a furious pace to load and fire their weapons, splaying black powder on their sweaty faces. The sight of suddenly blackened troops startled the new recruits, who did not understand the cause. Ignorance was, initially, bliss. One green soldier marveled, "We discovered that as we moved on, the air was full of objects that flew like birds, and seemed to whisper softly as they went." It eventually occurred to this young man that these "birds" were Rebel bullets.[2]

The costly Union assault paid dividends, as Confederate officers failed to grasp the heavy casualties suffered by the enemy and lost their nerve at the fury of the onslaught. The two most senior Confederate officers absconded with several thousand troops in the middle of the night, leaving a subordinate officer to request surrender terms from Grant, to which the Union general famously replied: "Yours of this date, proposing armistice and appointment of commissioners to settle terms of capitulation, is just received. No terms except unconditional and immediate surrender can be accepted. I propose to move immediately upon your works." The Rebels, having no realistic choice, surrendered the fort, along with 11,500 men and forty guns. The loss of Fort Donelson forced Confederate General Albert Sidney Johnston to abandon Nashville to Union troops. Grant's army moved to control the entire Tennessee Valley and its rich grain and livestock resources. By the end of March, his Union forces had reached Pittsburg Landing, a few miles from the Mississippi border. They set up camp at a place some three miles distant, around the small church known in the neighborhood as Shiloh Chapel.[3]

The fall of Forts Henry and Donelson was the first in a string of late-winter successes for the western Union armies. On March 6, at the seemingly inconsequential crossroads of Elkhorn Tavern, Arkansas, seventeen thousand Confederate troops under the direction of General Earl Van Dorn attacked eleven thousand Union soldiers led by General Samuel R. Curtis. It was one of the few occasions during the war when Union forces were outnumbered. It didn't matter. Curtis routed the Rebels on the second day of fighting at what became known as the Battle of Pea Ridge. The Union victory was notable for two reasons. First, the Confederate force included thirty-five hundred mounted Indians led by Colonel Stand Watie, a Cherokee, who achieved one of the rare Rebel triumphs during the two-day battle. The Cherokees joined the Confederate cause in the hopes of securing a better deal than they had received from Washington. Curtis's report praised the bravery and skill of "the hordes of Indians . . . that were arrayed against us."[4]

The decisive Union victory at Pea Ridge also secured Missouri and northern Arkansas for federal forces, further diminishing Confederate influence in the Upper South. It enabled federal troops to invade Indian Territory (present-day Oklahoma) and dislodge the Indians from their Confederate allegiances. President Lincoln endorsed the invasion, asserting, "It is believed that upon the repossession of the country by the federal forces, the Indians will readily cease all hostile demonstrations, and resume their former relations to the government." To ensure a return to "former relations," Union forces laid waste to their settlements. The Confederacy never again seriously challenged federal forces in the trans-Mississippi West.[5]

Further west, the Confederates had designs on California gold to support their rapidly inflating paper currency. In February, Confederate Brigadier General Henry H. Sibley led four thousand Texans into New Mexico Territory with the vague goal of marching on to California and separating the state from the Union. Sibley's expedition went well at first, as the Texans took Albuquerque and Santa Fe, and chased off a federal force at Glorieta Pass on March 28. Though the Union troops did not defeat Sibley's modest band, they managed to destroy the group's supplies, ending the Confederate threat, such as it was, to the Southwest and California. The Battle of Glorieta Pass makes it into most Civil War books primarily because readers in the Southwest and California want to be included in this great American drama. So here it is. But the battle was meaningless. The Confederacy's designs on California were far-fetched and ill conceived.

The good news from the West in early 1862 dramatically changed the depressive mood in the North. Franklin Dick, a former federal official in Missouri, who had moved back home to Philadelphia, had despaired of ever seeing the Union reunited. In late January, in an angry burst at federal inaction, he confessed his "utter disgust with Lincoln. . . . He is in my opinion a paltry coward." On hearing the news from Fort Donelson three weeks later, he celebrated: "This has been the day of days—a great day of rejoicing & hope & thankfulness to the Lord God Almighty. . . . It looks now as if the rebellion could suddenly crumble away."[6]

The northern press concurred. The war had been in progress less than one year, but editors had become military pundits. *Harper's* informed readers that the surrender of Fort Donelson "is probably the culminating point in the struggle between the United States Government and the malcontents." Veteran Tennessee Unionist editor William Brownlow crowed, "Secession is well-nigh played out—the dog is dead." In Washington, a grateful president elevated Grant to the rank of major general. Lincoln's rising spirits crashed on February 20, when his beloved son Willie died of "bilious fever," most likely typhoid contracted from the White House water supply fouled by the excrement of thousands of troops camped along the Potomac.[7]

The northern jubilation was not entirely misplaced. Years later, General Grant argued that had he been in command of all the western armies, he would have proceeded swiftly to the south and west after the victories at Forts Henry and Donelson before Confederate troops could reorganize. He would have taken control of all of the Mississippi River and the rail lines leading to the Lower South, and overrun Chattanooga, opening the road to Georgia. All of that would happen for Union forces, but it would take years, not months, to realize.[8]

By late March, spring was well under way in southwestern Tennessee. Peach blossoms dotted the rolling countryside near the river, and torrential rains turned the road to Corinth, Mississippi, an important rail center twenty miles from Pittsburg Landing, into a branch of the Tennessee. Two Union armies, one led by Grant and the other by William T. Sherman, recently returned to military duty after suffering a mental breakdown, waited for the arrival of Don Carlos Buell's Army of the Ohio from Nashville to augment federal forces.

General Albert Sidney Johnston, still smarting from the loss of the river forts and Nashville, commanded Rebel troops of roughly equal strength located somewhere in the mud between Corinth and Pittsburg Landing. Johnston, a West Pointer to whom Lincoln had offered the second-highest command in the Union army, counted on the inexperience of Union troops and Grant's overconfidence after his relatively easy victories in his river campaigns. Over six feet tall, dark, and handsome, Johnston seemed born to command. Grant seemed more suited to the leather business.

Grant had finished near the bottom of his class at West Point, and his position at Pittsburg Landing confirmed it. The Tennessee River was at his back, which meant that in retreat, his army would have no place to go. It is easy to say that Grant never planned to retreat, that had Buell moved with more alacrity the issue of location would never have arisen, but any good general looks for a way out while devising the way in. While Grant waited for Buell, Johnston did not. Johnston formulated a bold, if risky, offensive plan to destroy the Union forces at Shiloh, crush Buell's army coming down from Nashville, retake Kentucky, and push his army to the banks of the Ohio River.

The Confederates suddenly bolted out of the woods in the early Sabbath morning of April 6, surprising the raw federal recruits and their officers, who should have known better. Grant would insist later that his troops were not surprised, but his was a lonely opinion. Besides, he was seven miles away from where the initial Confederate offensive occurred.

The Rebels pushed the shorthanded Federals back toward the river. General Johnston's prophecy before the morning assault, "Tonight we'll water our horses in the Tennessee River," was near fulfillment. As one Union soldier recorded in a letter to his family, "There were three things to do, surrender, swim the river, or fight to the death." The Confederate attack was uncoordinated, however, typical in an era when verbal commands traveled only so far and often became garbled in the heat of battle. Numerous Rebel soldiers wasted time gaping at and plundering the camp of the better-equipped Union soldiers. Knapsacks, food, rain gear, bedding, blankets, guns, ammunition, and even tents were much more engaging than the frightened federal troops backed up to the river.[9]

Those Confederate troops involved in the task at hand—fighting the Federals—discovered that their enemies acquitted themselves courageously considering their lack of preparation for an assault. Rebels could not take advantage of their position. At about two o'clock in the afternoon, a bullet severed an artery in General Johnston's leg. He refused medical attention, remaining in the saddle until he bled to death. Toward evening, another spring downpour halted military operations, though additional fighting was unlikely as the men on both sides approached sheer exhaustion. Union forces hung on by a thread.

William T. Sherman recalled meeting Grant around midnight. The ever-rumpled general was standing under a tree, sheltered from the rain, puffing on a cigar. Sherman, thinking that a stealthy retreat across the river was the only possible alternative, mumbled something about how badly the day's fighting had gone. Grant nodded, puffed some more, and replied, "Yes. Beat 'em in the morning, though."[10]

The greater part of Don Carlos Buell's army arrived during that stormy night. The next day, these fresh soldiers marched into battle singing "Dixie," of all things. Whether it was a taunt or they genuinely liked the song (as President Lincoln did), their enthusiasm energized Grant's shaken and sodden troops. By midmorning the Federals had retaken most of the ground they had lost the previous day, though the Confederates, now commanded by General P. G. T. Beauregard, contested every inch of ground fiercely. The Rebels hoped to keep the battle going long enough for General Earl Van Dorn to arrive with his army from Arkansas. When Beauregard learned that Van Dorn could not come in time, and now outnumbered with the arrival of Buell's troops, sixty-two thousand to forty thousand, he broke off the battle and retreated through the mud toward Corinth. The battle ended with both armies occupying pretty much the same ground as they had prior to the fighting. Since the Confederates left the field, however, the Battle of Shiloh was a Union victory.

The toll for this no contest was unprecedented in American annals: roughly thirty-five hundred killed, equally divided between Confederate and Union forces, with more than sixteen thousand soldiers wounded on both sides. Henry W. Halleck, commander of all Union forces in the West and known as "Old Brains" for his erudite textbooks on strategy, blamed Grant for the high casualties and urged his dismissal. Lincoln demurred, "I can't spare this man; he fights." A Union soldier put a poetic coda on the battle: "Gentle winds of Springtime seem a sighing over a thousand new made graves."[11]

Nearly two months later, on May 30, General Beauregard quietly abandoned Corinth and escaped with his army while a large federal army under the command of "Old Brains" camped nearby unaware. The subsequent federal occupation of Corinth cut a vital east-west rail link for the Confederacy and doomed Memphis. Loss of towns and cities hurt the Confederacy, but their armies remained intact, and until the South could not field a credible fighting force, the war would continue.

Battles can have an importance far beyond their strategic implications. Shiloh advanced the Union cause only marginally, but it changed the nature of the war in the minds of both soldiers and citizens on both sides forever. These were not grizzled veterans who took the field on successive spring mornings; most were new recruits, unaccustomed to battle, yet eager for combat, and armed with strong convictions about God, country, family, and home. They had spent most of their military lives in camp, not in combat. They cheered lustily when bugles sounded the assembly, signaling the order to line up and march out to fight. In the next moments they would find out a great deal about themselves. They would see and hear things they had never seen or heard before. No stories from those few who had experienced combat could replicate a battle. It would change them, or kill them.

Shiloh, General Sherman noted, "would have cured anybody of war." The one battle had doubled all of the casualties of the war up to that point. Most of the young men engaged in the battle would have agreed with the soldier who wrote, "I had no idea of war until then, and would have given anything in the world if I could have been away." A Confederate soldier who retreated with Beauregard to Corinth now cursed the war he had once welcomed: "Oh! What suffering, what misery, what untold agony this horrid hell-begotten war has caused." Any romantic notions of war had fled. He admitted that he was "awful tired of being a soldier."[12]

At Shiloh, soldiers witnessed the destructive potential of modern weaponry. The serene landscape had become a grisly tableau. Stretches of meadow puddled with blood and rainwater; in the woods, trees bursting with the buds of spring now appeared fractured, with large branches broken off or sundered altogether with just trunks remaining. Scarcely a tree did not exhibit bullet holes up and down its trunk; shrapnel protruded from the mud like abstract sculptures; and strewn all about, the detritus of things left behind: sardine boxes, soggy biscuits, belts, hats, canteens, and rucksacks. Dead horses and mules lay prostrate at random intervals. And the sea of dead men. Worse, those yet barely alive, breathing in spurts, a frothy saliva dripping creamily from their mouths down to their ears, strings of matter from their brains swaying in the breeze.

Over there, an Illinois regiment partially buried in ashes, victims of a brush fire kindled by dead leaves, stems, and hot projectiles on the first day of battle before the rains came. Those not reduced to ashes were bloated and blackened beyond recognition. Some held out their hands in a clawlike position as if grasping for something in their last moments.[13]

At a makeshift Confederate hospital, a former hotel in Corinth, nurse Kate Cumming gasped when the wounded flooded in "mutilated in every imaginable way." On the Tennessee River, supply boats served as floating Union hospitals, with wounded men "mangled in every conceivable way, the dead and dying lying in masses, some with arms, legs, and even their jaws shot off, bleeding to death, and no one to wait upon them or dress their wounds."[14]

At Shiloh, every moment threw someone into a profound moral dilemma that neither the Bible nor conventional ethics addressed back home. A young soldier sent to the rear to restock his company's ammunition supply came upon a severely wounded boy who begged for help to be carried out of harm's way. But the young soldier could not lift the boy and left him to die.[15]

Combat at Shiloh and thereafter was at once a group experience—marching and firing as a unit and forging a bond of brotherhood with comrades—and a very individual encounter, where certain sights and sounds became indelible, and others went unnoticed. The smoke and noise added to the confusion, and the numerous incidents of "friendly fire" lent the "fog of war" considerable credence. Sam Watkins, a private in Johnston's army at Shiloh, observed that he was so busy loading and shooting his rifle that he saw little of the battle, but remembered vividly a comrade who stepped out of the ranks and shot his finger off to avoid the fight. Whatever romance Watkins associated with war, Shiloh cleansed for all time. He ridiculed the "pomp and circumstance of the thing called glorious war," as he looked across the battlefield at "the dead lying with their eyes wide open [and] the wounded begging piteously for help."[16]

Tens of thousands of young men now understood the transformative nature of combat. The real battle was often not against the enemy but against oneself. The recruit must cope with fear; some did with an excessive bravado; others sweated profusely or shook; many went silent; a few shot off parts of their hands or feet. Some found a ditch or a gully where they hid while the battle raged. The sensations of sound, light, and smell were so overwhelming that some soldiers forgot fear entirely. When they engaged the enemy, this thought was common: "I didn't know it was like this." On the first sight of wounded soldiers, "Why, they're no better than mangled rabbits—I didn't know it was like this." The smell of battle, the dizzying mixture of oil, smoke, blood, and sweat, combined with the fear caused some men to vomit. The reassuring voice of an officer: "The best, of the worst of it, is that after the first fight it comes easy, my boy, it comes too easy." After the battle, the new recruit experienced "a new birth. . . . He could never be the same again; something was altered in him forever." A soldier wrote to his mother after his first battle, in June 1862, "I don't believe I am the same being I was two weeks ago."[17]

It was futile of these young men to think they could calibrate their emotions and will their fate. In truth, the private soldier controlled nothing. Like "the youth" in Stephen Crane's *The Red Badge of Courage* (1895), he could run at the first sight of fire, receive an accidental head wound from a comrade, and blindly stagger back into battle, where he becomes wildly aggressive and emerges a hero. Only his desertion is willful; the other occurrences are pure chance, and yet these are deeds for which his comrades praise him. Such logic as existed in battle often resulted in the opposite of what one would expect. Yet the experience of war was transformative. The hope was that all of this dying would transform a nation, but as future president James A. Garfield exclaimed, "My God, what a costly sacrifice!"[18]

Self-knowledge was sometimes the only discernment during a battle. At Shiloh, the smoke, the woods, and uneven terrain obscured the fight. A Union soldier swore that after two major battles he had yet to actually see a live Rebel. Sound more than sight guided the soldier to the direction of the battle. At Gettysburg, a Union soldier shouted to a colleague, "Which are the rebels and which are our men?" His companion shouted back, "You pays your money and you takes your choice." They could only hope that their rifles fired into the smoke found their appointed targets.[19]

The sounds occasionally obscured more than they helped. The roar and thunder of sixty-four-pound howitzers echoed off hillsides and, combined with relentless rifle fire, could render a soldier temporarily deaf. At other times, the sense of sound became acute. Veterans could tell the differences in bullet calibers; "some of them come with a sharp 'clit,' like striking a cabbage leaf with a whip lash, others come with a sort of screech. . . . Then there are others . . . that whistle on a much higher key, and snap against a tree." Artillery rattled against trees "like a handful of pebbles against the side of a building." And sometimes, the soldiers themselves provided sound effects, shouting to relieve tension or giving the famous Rebel yell to strike fear into the enemy. The moans and shrieks of the wounded added to the cacophony of battle.[20]

Now and then, the soldier could see a blue sky, the pink of a cherry tree in bloom, and the green of a meadow. Armies fought in the spring, summer, and fall mainly, and the South of the rolling countryside, shaded woods, and meandering streams and creeks put on a dazzling natural display. Nature's calm beauty contrasted with the tragedy unfolding before the soldier, and it momentarily startled him that such harmony could exist amidst such horror.

The bigger reasons for being there, the reasons for the war, scarcely entered a soldier's mind in the midst of chaos and death. He might muse on the theological and metaphysical nature of the conflict in letters home or in confessions to his diary, but never in battle. In combat he fought for himself and his comrades. That was all that mattered. To infuse the soldier with noble purpose in the midst of incoherence is to overlay implausibility on a reality. He was a machine, more properly a cog in the larger machine of war. His movements were not his own; the enemy, his officers, his comrades, the weather, the terrain determined where he went and what he did. In the most mechanized war fought up to that time, he was part of the industrial process that aimed to kill the enemy in the most efficient manner. "Like an automaton, I kept loading and firing, oblivious of everything about me except that musket and my duty to load and fire it," a Union private wrote at Antietam. As much as the sight of death sickened, it also elicited a sense of accomplishment, a job well done. Confederate artillery officer Osmun Latrobe rode over the grisly fields of Antietam and remarked with satisfaction, "I . . . enjoyed the sight of hundred[s] of dead Yankees. Saw much of the work I had done in the way of several limbs, decapitated bodies, and mutilated remains of all kinds."[21]

Could such misery produce a greater end? Are we doing the work of God or the devil? Joseph Hopkins Twichell, a Congregational minister who believed in the righteousness of the Union cause, asked these questions after his first battle in May 1862: "It was a sight too piteous for speech. It seemed as if the universe would stop with the horror of it. I could only cry to my own leaded heart, 'It costs too much.'"[22]

Shiloh separated the soldier from his civilian life, a breach that only time and peace could close, and sometimes nothing could. "I know that no one staying at home," a Union soldier wrote, "can have any idea of what this army has been through." The soldiers viewed with increasing disdain the civilians' insatiable desire for war news, for action, for concrete results, none of which, of course, could be had without considerable cost. A Union soldier wrote sarcastically, "We aren't doing much just now, but hope in a few days to satisfy the public taste with our usual Fall Spectacle—forty per cent of us knocked over." The loopholes in both northern and southern conscription laws fueled some of the animosity, but soldiers knew that the gap between what they saw and experienced and what civilians read and believed was unbridgeable.[23]

Soldiers often questioned civilians' capacity for sacrifice. Residents of Nashville and Confederate General Nathan Bedford Forrest's cavalry clashed in the streets when the soldiers attempted to burn bridges and supplies before the advancing Union army in February 1862. When Memphis fell the following month, an embittered Rebel soldier noted that the city's residents "are lukewarm in the southern cause and if the Yankees will protect their cowardly carcasses and save their property, they would give up the Southern cause without striking a blow." Several months later, another Confederate soldier gave this accounting: "God seems to have consigned one-half of our people to death at the hands of the enemy, and the other half to affluence and wealth realized by preying upon the necessities of those who are thus sacrificed."[24]

While understandable, these complaints did not account for the suffering of families who coped without a breadwinner, or worse, with his death. It did not account for the refugee families in the South who fled in advance of Union troops. Nor did it account for the daily worry about losing a loved one. War is that way. It creates an estrangement compounded by unknowing.

The soldiers tried as best they could to describe the war in their letters and diaries, but the unimaginable often proved impossible to convey. And the unimaginable stayed in the imagination forever. "A battle is indescribable," a Union chaplain wrote in December 1862, "but once seen it haunts a man till the day of his death." The scenes brutalized them and, to a point, inured them. Shiloh made them question God, man's inhumanity, and their own salvation. William T. Sherman, a man rarely given to sentimental musings, found Shiloh a deeply unsettling experience:

> Who but a living witness can adequately portray those scenes on Shiloh's field, when our wounded men, mingled with rebels, charred and blackened by the burning tents and underbrush, were crawling about, begging for someone to end their misery? Who can describe the plunging shot shattering the strong oak as with a thunderbolt, and beating down horse and rider to the ground? Who but one who has heard them can describe the peculiar sizzling of the minie ball, or the crash and roar of a volley fire? Who can describe the last look of the stricken soldier as he appeals for help that no man can give or describe the dread scene of the surgeon's work, or the burial trench?[25]

The slaughter at Shiloh shocked Grant into believing that the rebellion would end quickly. The Confederacy, he thought, could not sustain such losses and remain in the field much longer. Shiloh, coupled with the victories earlier in the year, gave Grant hope of an early peace. He realized soon after Shiloh, however, that the South could yet field vast armies. At that point, "I gave up all idea of saving the Union except by complete conquest." The general's body servant, who remained with him throughout the war, recalled "only one time when he [Grant] appeared troubled in his mind. That was ... after the battle of Shiloh. He used to walk his room all night."[26]

The press could not get out news of Shiloh fast enough. Civilians crowded telegraph offices to hear the latest from the front, and newspapers sold out as soon as they landed in newsboys' hands. One enterprising fifteen-year-old Michigan lad who sold newspapers on trains passing through his town, knowing that news from Shiloh would sell out his stock quickly, arranged for a line of credit to buy large numbers of newspapers, which he hawked at higher prices. Using the profits from such sales, he founded his own newspaper and set himself to learn the art and science of telegraphy. Thomas Edison went on to work for Western Union during the later years of the Civil War, where he experimented with improvements to telegraphic communications, launching his career as an inventor.[27]

The carnage at Shiloh created a dilemma for religious Americans on both sides. Evangelical Protestantism had defined the major political issues of the 1850s and influenced the sectional crisis and the war that followed. Each side had cloaked itself in righteousness. Yet, if the evangelical God was just and benevolent, how could He countenance the continuation of a bloody war? How could He approve of Christians killing each other? "How," in the words of one troubled Christian, "does God have the heart to allow it?"[28]

Abraham Lincoln wrestled with this question, especially after the death of his son Willie in February 1862 and mounting casualties on the battlefields. God was not, for Lincoln, the intimate deity of the evangelicals, but an inscrutable presence whose ultimate purpose was unknowable. Lincoln's view of a predestinarian God and the limits of man's ability to mold events harked back to the Calvinism of his father rather than the optimistic free will proponents of early nineteenth-century evangelical Protestantism. The war had taken turns beyond any man's expectations. "God's purpose is something different from the purpose of either party," he wrote in September 1862. "God wills this contest, and wills that it shall not end yet."[29]

As the war buffeted Lincoln's faith, it transformed those on the battlefield. Religion offered an understanding and a rationalization of the death and destruction surrounding these young men. Their chaplains reassured them that death was but a midpoint between life and the glorious hereafter. They heard about the exalted nature of their sacrifices, that "the rivers of blood" had "hallowed" their nation. Elevating the war as a tale of suffering and redemption enabled soldiers to make sense of death. Or, it did not. Herman Melville's poem "Shiloh: A Requiem" proclaims, "What like a bullet can undeceive!"[30]

Faith did not die on the battlefield, but the war shook it. Melville predicted the war would resemble "an upheaval affecting the basis of things," and he was right. Tales circulated of how a pocket Bible stopped a bullet and saved a private's life. As the war progressed, the veteran soldier learned that a deck of cards did just as well. A Confederate soldier summarized the view of many of his comrades: "The soldiers naturally distrusted the efficacy of prayer when they found that the most devout Christians were as liable to be shot as the most hardened sinner."[31]

Religious organizations on both sides rushed to shore up a faltering faith. Bibles, tracts, and sermons flooded camps. Ministers led revivals. Presidents Lincoln and Davis called for public fast days and prayer. Pocket songsters included tunes that urged piety and sobriety. These periodic paroxysms of religious fervor gained some converts, but they did nothing to ameliorate the war and may have prolonged it, for who could walk away from a crusade? Sacrifice required a great cause, but what kind of God would demand bloodletting on such a scale?

A sense of betrayal gripped some of the young men. The nobility of serving a just cause the politicians had promised had proved elusive. They expected a Walter Scott novel, a quick victory, a bloodless conquest, and young women throwing rose petals at their homecoming. Many never came home, and few experienced the war as a romantic adventure. Ashley Wilkes, in Margaret Mitchell's *Gone with the Wind* (1936), thought the war would be an extension of his chivalrous life in the Old South. It wasn't, as he wrote to Melanie from his Virginia camp: "I see too clearly that we have been betrayed, betrayed by our arrogant Southern selves, believing that one of us could whip a dozen Yankees, believing that King Cotton could rule the world." What was left for Ashley Wilkes and his Confederate comrades was to fight and die for home and family, which would never have been in peril in the first place were it not for the betrayal.[32]

Home and family rendered the threat of death and dying especially poignant. Most of these young men had never ventured beyond a few miles from home. They came from small towns and farms, generally, and they lived among extended family relations. They rarely met people from other parts of the country. Now, Georgia farm boys found themselves in Virginia camps, and Illinois clerks slogged through the mud of Mississippi. The shreds of familiarity in their lives were the letters to and from home. The correspondence documented that a reality existed outside the insanity of war. They complained when loved ones did not send replies quickly; they doted on information about young children; and they wept at the deaths they could not attend.

When they closed their eyes, they saw home, they heard the tapping of tree-tops against the roof, they felt the breeze, and "the sweet-smelling meadow." Long after the war was over, soldiers remembered how the visions of home sustained them. "Above the smoke of battle," a former Iowa soldier wrote in 1892, "in the clear empyrean, arose the vision of the American soldier's home, secure to him and his loved ones." Such visions supported the men in their camps and on the battlefields, but not always. Longing for home also produced homesickness, which, more than fear, contributed to desertion on both sides. The worry over crops or businesses, or over illness, or just plain missing someone, a lover, a child, a mother, could compromise a soldier's willingness to fight.[33]

Women recognized how important they were to the attitude of the troops. "Don't worry; all of us are fine" did more to boost a soldier's morale than the most inspired sermon. Complaints, tales of woe, and entreaties to come home had the opposite affect, and women, north and south, received copious advice on their roles as morale boosters, moral sentries, and sounding boards for their men in uniform. This was especially so in the South, where white women occupied a specific and prescribed role as secondary figures with primary roles as supporters of their men. They received unstinting praise for their work, as in poet Henry Timrod's salute "Two Armies," praising women and their "thousand peaceful deeds," satisfying "a struggling nation's needs." Newspapers set out their importance, that women held the "principal creation and direction" of Confederate public opinion "in their hands."[34]

These statements were as much warnings as endorsements. As the war progressed and battles produced more casualties, troop morale was ever more important. The press stepped up its admonitions to women: "The maid who binds her warrior's sash / And smiling, all her pain dissembles." "The mother who conceals her grief" had "shed as sacred blood as e'er / was poured upon the plain of battle." More bluntly, a Huntsville, Alabama, newspaper warned women in bold headlines, "DON'T WRITE GLOOMY LETTERS." Still, it was difficult, and time and again soldiers wrote home, "Be cheerful and do the best you can."[35]

Alabama writer Augusta Jane Evans published a popular novel, *Macaria; or, Altars of Sacrifice* (1864), based on the Greek mythological figure in the title who sacrificed herself on the altar of the gods in order to save Athens from defeat. The story's modern-day heroine gives up both her father and her lover to the Confederate cause and lives a life of "Womanly Usefulness," laboring in "God's great vineyard." Evans wrote approvingly of mothers who "closed their lips firmly to repress a wail of sorrow as they buckled on the swords of their first-born." Yet Evans did not follow her own advice, sending sharply critical letters to General Beauregard and Confederate congressmen on military strategy and the class bias of the draft, and complaining that women's talents were going wasted.[36]

Mary Chesnut, wife of a prominent Confederate official, shared Evans's frustration, confiding to her diary: "I think *these* times make all women feel their humiliation in the affairs of the world. With *men* it is on to the field— 'glory, honour, praise, &c., power.' Women can only stay at home—& every paper reminds us that women are to be *violated*—ravished & all manner of humiliation. How are the daughters of Eve punished."[37]

Most of all, it was difficult to reconcile grief and patriotism, and grief be- came ever more common in the years after Shiloh. Widows lay in darkened rooms day after day clutching pictures of their lovers. Well-intentioned neighbors and family came to express their sympathies, but "O God . . . if they only knew the misery I feel." Women in the North also sent their men into battle with smiles, forced or otherwise. By the time of the Civil War, however, northern women faced fewer strictures on maintaining a subordi- nate role. Their leadership in evangelical and anti-slavery causes, their nu- merous publications, and their organizing activities and political campaigning had primed society to accept a more diverse role for women during the war. It was not surprising, for example, that northern women quickly took up the nursing profession, while southern women debated its propriety.[38]

Few northern families suffered the dislocations southerners did; with hardly any exceptions, they did not cope with the destruction of land and livestock and the loss of family fortune. In the more dense and more urban North, isola- tion was less common, news more frequent, the mail more reliable, and the economy stronger. The war engaged a much higher percentage of southern men. Pleading letters to come home and save the family farm came less fre- quently from northern women. The war strengthened some northern women as they warmed to the task of self-reliance. An Iowa woman whose husband went off to war wrote that "the whole responsibility" of keeping the family farm running "rested with myself and the children"—a girl of thirteen, two boys, ten and eight, and a baby girl. "They were my only assistance and com- panions . . . and it was wonderful what enthusiasm and helpfulness those four dear children manifested all the time. They seemed enthused with the spirit of the times."[39]

Both sides shared a common grief. That less chaotic circumstances sur- rounded northern women and their families provided little solace for the loss of a life's partner. George Norris, a future senator from Nebraska, recalled his childhood in Ohio during the war when his older brother, John, died fighting in Georgia. Four months later, his father died. Thereafter, "I never heard a song upon the lips of my mother. I never even heard her hum a tune. . . . The war ended, and the young men came back, but John slept in a soldier's grave in the blackened southern countryside. There were times when it seemed that the heartache over her son never would pass."[40]

War was death, and death was war. How to deal with its possibility as a soldier, and how to process its reality if you were a friend or a family member? How do you die when you are lying helpless in the woods and the fire is about to consume you, or a wild pig is tearing at your entrails, or you have lost your legs to an artillery shell and you know you will bleed to death? Do you think about the Union? States' rights? God? Your family? Or, do you plead for someone to shoot you? Is it better to die as your comrade did this morning as you sat eating breakfast together and a minié ball crashed into his brain and splattered it over your plate? How do you die if you are stretched out on a hospital bed, sweating from fever and infection, while a young woman wipes your face with a cold cloth and you ask her if you are going to die and you do not hear her answer? Or, if you are moving in and out of consciousness, catching your breath at every draw, and gasping "water," and maybe your nurse hears "Jesus," because that is what she writes to your family. How do you respond when you receive a black-rimmed envelope bearing an official seal from Richmond? How do you respond when you are handed a letter from a stranger, a nurse, a comrade, assuring you that your husband or father or son died nobly for his country? Do you thank God?

Yet the manner of dying was important, particularly for the living. This was Victorian America, and sentiment and form counted a great deal. If the dying soldier in his pain and delirium could not think of a grand cause, of the angels who awaited his ascension, or of love of family, others could. Some soldiers composed farewell letters before the fact and requested comrades to forward them to loved ones in the event of death. William McKinley, a future president, wrote the following two days before he saw his first action in the war: "This record I want left behind, that I not only fell as a soldier for my Country, but also a Soldier of Jesus." The fear of an anonymous death was almost as great as the fear of battle, and sometimes greater.[41]

These letters told of deathbed conversions and of heartfelt expressions of love for God and country, sentiments that would have surprised the deceased's friends at home, but that consoled his family in their grief that, at last, he was saved. The wounded who could speak beseeched their comrades, "Won't you write to my folks that I died a soldier?" Parents appreciated these reassurances about their sons, that the war had not debased them. The parents of a dead Union soldier expressed their appreciation to the nurse who wrote about their son's last moments: "You wrote you thought he was praising God. It was the greatest comfort to us of anything." It was kind and very necessary for that nurse to pick out a prayer from her patient's incoherence. Not to die in vain, to die nobly and honorably, with words of faith and family on one's lips did not remove grief, but made it more bearable.[42]

It often fell to comrades to write a letter to the family and enclose a cherished possession of the deceased and perhaps a lock of his hair, always to reassure the loved ones that their son, husband, and brother died a meaningful death. Marion Hill Fitzpatrick, a Georgian in the Army of Northern Virginia, fell at Petersburg toward the end of the war. His comrade wrote the following to his mother: "I am happy to say he died happy and I certainly think that he is now better off. A few minutes before he breathed his last he sang Jesus can make a dying bed as soft as downy pillows are & he said he would of liked to of seen you before he died. He said that the Lord's will be done and for you to meet him in heaven." It was a sentiment many southern evangelical women would have understood, especially the lines referring to Jesus, which came from an 1844 Sacred Harp hymnal.[43]

Sometimes, words were all a family received. In an era when formal burial services were essential passages to heaven, their absence rode especially hard. Fortunate families received the remains of their soldiers. Most did not. More than half of the Union war dead, and a considerably larger percentage of Confederate casualties, were not even identified, let alone given proper burial in the soil of their birth. Battles reduced remains to ashes or mud, forever obliterating any remnant of a human being. A shocked Confederate soldier on his way to the battlefield at Shiloh on the second day of fighting reported, "The first dead soldier we saw had fallen in the road; our artillery had crushed and mangled his limbs, and ground him into the mire. He lay a bloody, loathsome mass, the scraps of his blue uniform furnishing the only distinguishable evidence that a hero there had died."[44]

Burials in the South occurred quickly, or as quickly as possible, and hopefully before the stench permeated the landscape for miles and before bloated bodies, human and animal, burst, and animals carried away or ate remains. Common graves and the absence of a formal religious service reflected the hastiness with which armies worked to bury the dead. Early in the war, Richmond staged elaborate funerals for the Confederate dead. The mounting death toll soon made those rituals impractical. There were 3,600 casualties at Bull Run in July 1861, 20,000 at Shiloh. And more wasteful battles were yet to come. Not to have the physical remains, the lock of hair, the swatch of cloth, the last look before the clods of dirt fell on the coffin, deepened the loss. Abraham Lincoln exhumed the coffin of his son Willie twice to gaze upon his

Proper burial of the battlefield dead became increasingly difficult, especially once Grant initiated his relentless spring 1864 offensive in Virginia. The burial party here is laying to rest the remains of federal soldiers—and "remains" is the operative word—at Cold Harbor in April 1865. The battle occurred ten months earlier. (Courtesy of the Library of Congress)

face; no one thought that was unusual. Soldiers may have felt estranged from civilian life from time to time, but both soldier and civilian shared the bond of death.

The randomness of it all. A Confederate soldier at Fredericksburg in December 1862, with shot coming thick and heavy, made ready to discard his blanket to move more quickly; at the last moment, he felt the winter chill and rolled the blanket and tied it around his shoulder at the precise instant a Yankee bullet hurtled toward his neck only to be buried harmlessly in the cloth. Or another seemingly lucky young man, a bullet grazing his arm, a superficial wound; only now he lies in a home, a makeshift hospital and morgue in the Tennessee countryside, with his arm crimson, swollen, and blistered, swathed in filthy bandages and emitting a stench so foul, no one can bear to tend him. He will lose the arm certainly, and his life probably.[45]

Medical knowledge was an oxymoron. A visit to a field hospital confirmed it. Sam Watkins, the young Tennessee private in Albert Sidney Johnston's army, decided to see a wounded friend near his camp. The field hospital was not difficult to find; just follow the penetrating odor caused by gangrene and sepsis, conditions that were rampant. And much more preventable had the overworked doctors and the caring nurses known what general practice would know in another decade or two. The evidence of this ignorance lay in the rear of the building in the form of rotting arms and legs taken from these young men to save their lives. Amputation was the first course of treatment. Watkins stumbled on his friend James Galbreath, who had received a severe wound several days earlier yet was still alive. Watkins gave the wounded soldier some water and promised to write to his family. He asked his comrade how he felt, and Galbreath pulled down his cover. "The lower part of his body was hanging to the upper part by a shred, and all of his entrails were lying on the cot with him, the bile and other excrements exuding from them, and they full of maggots." Watkins pulled the blanket back up. "I then kissed him on his lips and forehead, and left."[46]

The young men could not help but wonder when their turn would come, and how it would be for them. A New Yorker on the way to his first engagement came across a wounded Confederate soldier, lying by the road "with a sabre cut in the side of his head four inches long, and his brains were running out on to his coat. O! How sick I felt. . . . I thought to myself, if I got sick at the sight of one dead man what would I do on a battle field." Another New York recruit, coming up to replace a decimated unit at Fredericksburg in Decem-

Dead federal soldier, Petersburg, April 1865.
(Courtesy of the Library of Congress)

Dead Confederate soldier, Petersburg, April 1865.
(Courtesy of the Library of Congress)

A federal soldier disemboweled during the Battle of Gettysburg,
July 1863. (Courtesy of the Library of Congress)

ber 1862, hard-pressed to avoid stepping on mangled blue-clad corpses, saw "their ghastly gaping death wounds" and wondered if they predicted "what might be in store for us."[47]

Another soldier came upon a small group of severely wounded men moving on their hands and knees and led by a fellow whose face lacked a lower jaw, now replaced by weirdly angled shards of bone and flesh. The men crawled to a creek to drink its water, but lacked the strength to back away or keep their heads up. They drowned.[48]

Sometimes a young soldier envied the wounded with their red badges of courage; sometimes there was thankfulness that your wound was not as bad as another fellow's. Sam Watkins, shot in the arm, retreated to a field hospital. Along the road he encountered a comrade whose left arm was completely gone. Looking closer, he exclaimed "'Great God!' for I could see his heart throb, and the respiration of his lungs." The man soon collapsed and died.[49]

The longer you lived, the worse you felt. Death sundered the bond you had formed with the comrade who marched with you, shared your hardtack, sang songs, and talked about home and love and family. And suddenly, he was gone, just as the one before and perhaps the one after. The only permanency was the killing. You went through this because you believed you fought for a finer thing, an idea, a faith, a loved one. You wondered at times whether these were enough, whether anything would be enough to cover the broken hearts, the shattered bodies, and the lives ended.

In the meantime, the war would go on for three more bloody years. For Abraham Lincoln, God had obviously willed the war to continue, as no side appeared to gain a conspicuous advantage. Although it was not possible yet to discern God's plan for America, He must have a purpose in perpetuating the conflict. While waiting for God to decide, Union soldiers transformed Shiloh Chapel into a field hospital and ripped up the wooden floorboards to make coffins for their dead.

CHAPTER 11

BORN IN A DAY

FANNY BURDOCK RECALLED THE TIME she saw him. "We been picking
in the field when my brother he point to the road then we seen Marse Abe
coming all dusty and on foot." President Lincoln himself was making his way
down that hot Georgia road. Burdock and her brother ran to the fence where
a water bucket rested. "We give him nice cool water from the dipper. Then he
nodded and set off."[1]

Abraham Lincoln never set foot in Georgia, but so powerful and personal
were the memories of him among former slaves that his presence in their
lives assumed a literal meaning. It is fashionable now among some historians
to downplay Lincoln's role as the "Great Emancipator." The main story line is
that slaves stole their own freedom, and the Emancipation Proclamation, effective on January 1, 1863, did not free any slave in practical terms. Both assertions are generally correct. Tens of thousands of slaves flooded into Union
camps. Without a Union victory and a corresponding federal legal sanction,
their liberation would have been short-lived. Lincoln's proclamation placed
the power of the U.S. Constitution (and by war's end it became part of that
document in the form of the Thirteenth Amendment) behind the slaves' exodus and provided cover for thousands more who would leave bondage in the
remaining two years of the war. Emancipation also hastened the Confederacy's
defeat by removing a large portion of its work force and by placing 150,000
freedmen under Union arms. Even if the document freed few slaves in actu-
ality, it stands as an affirmation of the objectives for which Union forces
fought to save their country. It brought the full faith of the U.S. government
to secure the right of all Americans to be free.

Most northerners agreed that the war would somehow alter the institution
of slavery, perhaps even end it. Few, however, believed that the federal government should intervene to formally abolish slavery. Concerns about racial
strife, constitutional issues, the fear of thousands of freed blacks streaming
north, and just plain racism accounted for these views. Lincoln balanced
these views with pressure from more radical members of his own party. He

hoped for the abolition of slavery, called it immoral, but believed he lacked the constitutional authority to abolish it where it existed. Saving the Union remained paramount in Lincoln's thinking; that was the best chance for slavery's demise.

The vast majority of federal soldiers entered the war assuming they were fighting to preserve the Union of their fathers and the freedoms—personal and national—it stood for. Few looked upon the conflict as a war against slavery. Abolitionists remained a small minority in the North. The sentiment toward slavery among the Union soldiers began to change once they ventured south. They witnessed slaves stealing their own freedom, streaming into Union lines, offering to work for their keep. The Federals benefited from "black dispatches"— news of Confederate troop strength and movements delivered by fugitive slaves. As soon as the war began, slaves knew "the Union was 'IT', and we were all 'Yankees,'" one recalled. One slave in northern Virginia had a wife who washed and cooked for a group of Robert E. Lee's officers. She signaled the direction of Confederate troop movements by moving colored garments up and down a clothesline, a color for each corps commander.[2]

Robert Smalls, an escaped slave, pirated the Confederate gunboat *Planter* out of Charleston Harbor at three in the morning in June 1862, with a crew of fellow freedmen and their wives and children. According to Union military authorities, the *Planter* "was the most valuable war vessel the Confederates had at Charleston." An incoming tide slowed their progress, and daybreak found them beneath Rebel guns at Fort Sumter. Smalls, a veteran pilot, knew the signal for safe passage and slipped out of the harbor unmolested. Once outside of the range of Confederate guns, he hoisted a white flag and steamed for the federal blockade ship the *Augusta*.[3]

Union soldiers also saw how much slaves aided the Confederate cause, repairing railroads, digging trenches, ferrying supplies, and working the plantations to feed the armies and enable white men to go off and fight. In October 1861, a Wisconsin soldier reported to a newspaper in his state, "The rebellion is abolitionizing the whole army." Now that they had seen slavery, "men of all parties seem unanimous in the belief that to permanently establish the Union, is to first wipe [out] the institution" of slavery.[4]

This rising sentiment against slavery did not imply a more egalitarian attitude toward African Americans. As one Union soldier put it, "I have a good degree of sympathy for the *slave*, but I like the *Negro* the farther off the better." These were military, not moral, calculations, though some soldiers saw the contradiction of fighting in the name of freedom while four million human beings remained in bondage.[5]

Lincoln's thinking moved with the troops, though privately. During the

In May 1862 Robert Smalls (1839–1915), a slave, hijacked the Confederate transport boat the Planter *and sailed it through Charleston Harbor past Rebel batteries to Yankee lines, liberating himself to the bargain. Smalls became a Republican congressman from South Carolina after the war.*
(Courtesy of the Library of Congress)

early months of the war, he worked to keep the border states within the Union. Any step to legalize the informal acceptance of runaway slaves into Union lines risked losing the slave states of Kentucky and Missouri. Some Union officers obeyed the letter of the law and returned the runaway slaves to their masters. Others acted differently, such as Frémont in Missouri and General David Hunter on the Sea Islands off the coast of South Carolina. Lincoln dismissed Frémont and revoked Hunter's edict. The president stated his position clearly in September 1861: "We didn't go into the war to put down slavery, but to put the flag back, and to act differently at this moment, would, I have no doubt, not only weaken our cause but smack of bad faith." Of Lincoln's attitude, Radical Republican Benjamin Wade of Ohio sneered that it was all that could be expected "of one, born of 'poor white trash' and educated in a slave State."[6]

Lincoln correctly assessed the precarious nature of the border states and, more important, of northern public opinion on slavery. An editorial in *Harper's* in August 1861 reflected the thinking of many northerners on the slavery issue. The writer believed "that negro slavery will come out of this war unscathed is impossible." Slavery would fall because of the slaves who would take leave of their bondage at the first opportunity. Given this "natural" disintegration of slavery, "the hour of battle is not the time for the emancipation of four millions of slaves." Such a proclamation would overlook loyal slaveholders and run the risk of "servile wars and wholesale massacres." Better that slavery should dissipate gradually with the advance of Union armies.[7]

Congress nudged the "natural" process along by passing two confiscation acts in August 1861 and July 1862, which followed the letter of the Constitution by declaring slaves "contraband," that is, property seized from rebellious citizens. The first act called for the seizure of all property in aid of rebellion— including slaves. The legislators made it clear that only those owners in defiance of the government stood to lose their slaves. The second, bolder act provided for the confiscation of all property of those in rebellion against the United States *and* the emancipation of their slaves.

Lincoln continued to address the slavery issue within his view of constitutional limits and political realities. In November 1861, he drew up a plan for compensated emancipation for a Delaware legislator to introduce in that state. In March 1862, Congress endorsed Lincoln's plan for national compensated emancipation, though it did not provide any funding; and in July 1862, the president drafted a bill for Congress that included funding for national compensated emancipation. No slave state legislature stepped forward to consider compensated emancipation. Lincoln hesitated to act further: "The general government sets up no claim of a right, by federal authority, to interfere with slavery within state limits." He also feared that uncompensated emancipation would face a severe test in a Supreme Court still presided over by Roger B. Taney.[8]

Lincoln took the British example of West Indian emancipation in 1833 as a model. There, emancipation occurred gradually with compensation and the grudging support of the islands' white leadership. Lincoln did not view the compensation offered to planters as a federal giveaway but rather as seed money to ease the transition to a wage-labor system. The states most likely to accede to this plan—Delaware, Maryland, and Kentucky, where the institution was weakest—did not express interest in any form of compensated emancipation. Delaware's refusal came as a particular blow. Lincoln correctly surmised the reason. As a resident of the state explained, white citizens "look upon slavery as a curse; [they] also look upon freedom possessed by a negro, except in a very few cases, as a greater curse." Congress did pass a compensated emancipation bill in the one jurisdiction the federal government controlled— Washington, D.C. Lincoln signed it on April 16, 1862.[9]

By the time of the Second Confiscation Act, however, slaves increasingly took the war into their own hands and simply left their owners. Northern religious groups, most famously the American Missionary Association, were already sending teachers and supplies to the temporary villages and camps that sprouted wherever the Union army settled. The fact of freedom preceded the law of emancipation. And saving the Union still trumped the liberation of four million slaves.

General George B. McClellan conceived of himself as the blue-eyed salvation of the Union. His men loved him as they would love no other commander throughout the war, despite a fatal flaw: he did not like to fight. Or maybe because of that flaw. There is no gainsaying his brilliance in taking a broken army after the Bull Run disaster in July 1861 and drilling it into an effective fighting force. As much as his men loved him, McClellan loved them back. With all that love, sending them to battle proved too much.

By March 1862, Union forces appeared poised to deliver a knockout blow to the Confederacy. The Rebels had not won an important engagement since Bull Run in July 1861. The federal armies in the West had racked up impressive victories. It remained for McClellan's 130,000-man army to move in the East against Confederate General Joseph Johnston. Destroy Johnston's army, capture Richmond, end the rebellion.

On April 4, McClellan and his Army of the Potomac began their march up the peninsula formed by the York and James rivers. Their objective was Richmond. Secretary of War Edwin Stanton, so confident that the demise of the Confederacy was imminent, closed his department's recruiting offices. Standing between McClellan and Richmond were fifteen thousand Confederate troops protected in part by "Quaker guns"—logs painted black to resemble cannon. The sight of these "weapons" spooked McClellan into believing a much more substantial Confederate force lurked somewhere in the vicinity, so he proceeded cautiously, as if a Rebel regiment hid behind every tree between the coast and Richmond. In a month's time, he had made it only as far as Williamsburg, all the time pleading for more troops to confront an impossibly huge Confederate war machine.

Lincoln noted sarcastically that if he increased McClellan's force by an additional three hundred thousand men, the Confederate army would suddenly triple in size in the general's estimate. He implored his general: "I think it is the precise time for you to strike a blow. By delay the enemy will relatively gain upon you—that is, he will gain faster, by *fortifications* and *reinforcements*, than you can by reinforcements alone." McClellan continued to stall. In the meantime, Jefferson Davis ordered the first draft in American history. McClellan continued to move ponderously up the peninsula toward Richmond like Hannibal's elephants crossing the Alps. Spring rains turned the roads to mud, sometimes up to soldiers' knees, and sank heavy artillery. While McClellan waded, Confederate General Joseph Johnston's army grew to ninety thousand men.[10]

Walker Freeman, a private in Johnston's army, sat in a downpour outside of Richmond waiting orders to move on fortified Union positions. His brother had been killed at Bull Run. Walker took up the cause for his family. He wanted to end the war as badly as any soldier on the other side. Destroy Mc-Clellan's army and he would go home in peace, a citizen of a new nation. He would get that chance. Two corps of McClellan's troops had crept to within five miles of the Confederate capital. President Davis decided that was close enough and ordered Johnston, who was as reluctant as McClellan to engage his enemy, to attack before federal forces had an opportunity to consolidate.

The Confederate assault at Seven Pines might have had greater success had not the mud and swollen rivers upset plans for a coordinated attack. Private Freeman and his colleagues had to wade through seventeen hundred yards of muck to reach Union defenders protected by log breastworks and artillery. Two bullets struck his right leg and he fell into the mire, where he stuck until hoisted out by retreating comrades. Union forces blunted the Confederate assault, but McClellan's advance was checked. Freeman's brigade of two thousand men suffered 50 percent casualties. Overall, the Confederates lost six thousand men at Seven Pines, the Union, five thousand men.[11]

Joseph Johnston received a severe wound at Seven Pines, and President Davis turned over the Army of Northern Virginia to his military adviser, Robert E. Lee. McClellan's troops prepared for an all-out assault on the Confederate capital, confident that the new Rebel commander was "*too* cautious and weak under grave responsibility—personally brave and energetic . . . yet . . . wanting in moral firmness when pressed by heavy responsibility and . . . likely to be timid and irresolute in action." McClellan painted a more accurate portrait of himself than of his opponent.[12]

Robert E. Lee kept three books on his writing desk: his Bible, the Book of Common Prayer, and *Meditations* by the Stoic Roman emperor Marcus Aurelius. He had marked these lines from the Stoic: "Erase fancy, curb impulse, quench desire, let sovereign reason have the mastery." Compensating for his profligate father, the tarnished Revolutionary War hero Light Horse Harry Lee, the son valued order and duty. A brilliant engineer who had blazed Winfield Scott's path to Mexico City in the Mexican War, he had opposed secession, yet turned down command of Union forces for a lesser role in the new Confederate States of America. His fealty to his native state of Virginia superseded his loyalty to the Union.[13]

Lee cited duty to both state and family as the main reasons for his decision. Yet other members of the Lee family, citing those same responsibilities, sided with the Union. Lee was not a tragic figure any more than the Confederacy was a tragic attempt at sovereignty. Tragedy requires unmerited suffering. What we have in Robert E. Lee, and in the Confederacy, was a series of bad decisions, some startlingly impulsive, given Lee's embrace of reason, that led to predictable but not tragic destruction. We also have in Lee a bold, sometimes brilliant commander who seemed at once to relish and abhor combat and its consequences. His exterior reserve masked a gambler's soul. In the end, Lee would prove an enigma. The poet Stephen Vincent Benét captured him well:

> *A figure lost to flesh and blood and bones,*
> *Frozen into a legend out of life,*
> *A blank-verse statue— . . .*
> *For here was someone who lived all his life*
> *In the most fierce and open light of the sun . . .*
> *And kept his heart a secret to the end*
> *From all the picklocks of biographers.*[14]

The secession crisis found Lee in Texas. He wept when the Texas convention voted to leave the Union. He vowed to protect federal property from Lone Star partisans. Like Lincoln, Lee believed that secession invited "anarchy." Though he had little use for the Lincoln administration, he hoped Virginia would remain in the Union. When he left Texas for his native state, an officer called out to him, "Colonel, do you intend to go South or remain North?" Lee's reply reflected his internal conflict: "I shall never bear arms against the United States—but it may be necessary for me to carry a musket in defence of my native State, Virginia." After he arrived in the Old Dominion, Lee's confusion continued: "While I wish to do what is right, I am unwilling to do what is not, either at the bidding of the South or the North."[15]

Stopping off in Washington, Lee accepted President Lincoln's promotion to the rank of full colonel of the 1st Regiment of Cavalry. When the president inquired after Lee's loyalty, fellow Virginian General Winfield Scott replied, "He is true as steel, sir, true as steel!" Lincoln would offer Lee command of the Union army.[16]

The firing on Fort Sumter and Lincoln's troop call-up pushed Lee to a decision. In an emotional interview with Scott, Lee offered to sit out the conflict, which the older soldier dismissed outright. Lee then stated his intention to resign, to which Scott replied, "Lee, you have made the greatest mistake of your life." The two men grasped hands tightly, both "too full of feeling to find utterance for one word." The interview was over, and so was Colonel Lee's career in the U.S. Army. After the war, Lee claimed the situation presented him with no option but to go with Virginia. Yet roughly 40 percent of the Virginia-born officers in the Union army, including Scott, remained with the Federals. For these soldiers, their oath of allegiance to their country took precedence over their place of birth.[17]

Lee was never flamboyant or ostentatious, and rarely eloquent. His strength as a leader was his being. Sam Watkins recalled Lee's visit to his camp early in the war, likening the general to "some good boy's grandpa." Lee had "a calm and collected air about him, his voice was kind and tender, and his eye was as gentle as a dove's." Without so much as a gesture or a word, he possessed a "soothing magnetism" that "drew every one to him and made them love, respect, and honor him." Watkins confessed, "I fell in love with the old gentleman and felt like going home with him."[18]

Lee did not distinguish himself in his early campaigns in western Virginia and along the South Atlantic coast, though, like most generals, he blamed some of his difficulties on the lack of adequate troop strength. He immediately saw the Confederacy's great tactical problem: the number of troops necessary to defend Richmond from every direction would soon reduce the South to the perimeter around the capital. The remainder of the troops would be too widely dispersed to withstand Union assaults elsewhere. While Lee understood the basic defensive posture of the Confederacy, he counseled a more aggressive strategy that could relieve the mass of troops in Virginia for important service elsewhere: "We must decide between the positive loss of inactivity and the risk of action."[19]

Lee found a ready disciple in Thomas "Stonewall" Jackson who had launched a merry escapade in the Valley of Virginia—seventeen thousand Confederate troops toying with three federal armies totaling sixty-four thousand men. Jackson's mission in the spring of 1862: keep the federal forces occupied and prevent them from reinforcing McClellan's large Union army bearing down on Richmond to the east. The sickly, nearsighted, partially deaf math professor from the Virginia Military Institute found his calling in combat. He delighted in playing tag with assorted Union forces that could never quite catch up to him. Jackson carried on an incessant dialogue with God, not unusual among nineteenth-century evangelicals, except that God always answered back. Before a battle, Jackson paced his tent engaging his Mentor. He had lost nearly everyone he had loved in his life; God was, literally, all he had left. The depth of his penetrating pale blue eyes seemed to envelop at once an overwhelming sadness and a steadfast purpose. In appearance and background, he was the opposite of Lee. In his generalship, he was equally brilliant.

Believing he acted as God's sword, Jackson pressed his troops to uncommon exertions on long, fast marches and lightning strikes against the enemy, impervious to weather, terrain, or exhaustion. Between May 8 and June 9, Jackson and his foot cavalry raced four hundred miles up and down the Valley of Virginia, using the Massanutten mountain range as a shield and darting through the gaps to surprise Union forces, capturing huge supplies of arms and ammunition and enemy soldiers equal to the size of his army. Moving northward through the valley, Jackson gave the impression that Washington, D.C., was his ultimate goal. This false reading pinned down sixty thousand federal troops in the valley and prevented Lincoln from reinforcing the anxious McClellan. Jackson's quick strikes and withdrawals exhausted his troops, but they respected him. No long waits and brief skirmishes with Jackson; no futile charges in front of withering fire. Just hurtle forward, fall back, and then press on again. He exulted to fellow officers after a victory, "He who does not see the hand of God in this is blind, sir, blind!"[20]

Jackson, with God's help, drove the Federals crazy, inflicting seven thousand casualties while suffering less than half that number. "God has been our shield, and to His name be all the glory," he declared, as he prepared to depart from the valley and bring his "army of the living God" to Richmond. There he would join with Lee, to put an end to McClellan's campaign.[21]

Lee's initial move was to send his dashing cavalry commander, twenty-nine-year-old James Ewell Brown (J. E. B.) Stuart, and his twelve hundred Confederate cavalrymen on a ride around McClellan's army. Stuart disrupted communications and supplies, took prisoners, and eluded inept attempts by Union cavalry to chase them down. He lost all of one man in the escapade. The bold raid also gave Lee the intelligence that the Union's right flank was "in the air," that is, not anchored by a strong feature of terrain such as a hill or river, nor curled back in the form of a defensive perimeter. Lee ordered Jackson back from the valley while he engaged McClellan in a minor contest on June 25, beginning what became known as the Seven Days' Battles. With Jackson in place on the twenty-sixth, Lee launched an uncoordinated and largely ineffectual attack. Jackson was uncharacteristically lethargic, and Lee exercised little command over his troop movements. Whatever McClellan's personal shortcomings, his expert training was evident in the stiff resistance his men put up throughout the Seven Days. Lee mounted another assault on the twenty-seventh that broke one Union line, but again the lack of coordination produced little strategic advantage.

McClellan had seen enough. Already spooked by Stuart's dramatic ride and Lee's persistent if mostly ineffectual attacks, he concluded that he faced a larger and more formidable force than even his initial inflated estimates assumed. He began to withdraw down the peninsula, what one Rebel soldier called "the great skedaddle." McClellan fired off an angry telegram to President Lincoln: "I have lost this battle because my force was too small."[22]

Lee continued to harass McClellan, who successfully parried these attacks in a series of minor encounters over the next three days. Growing impatient, Lee decided on an all-out assault to destroy McClellan's army on July 1.

Union forces, however, occupied a strong defensive position on Malvern Hill and repulsed the attack, allowing McClellan to continue his withdrawal in relative peace.

So many things had gone wrong for Lee—poor intelligence, faulty maps, uncoordinated movements, and sluggish generals—that he viewed the Seven Days as a singularly frustrating episode. "Under ordinary circumstances," he told President Davis, "the Federal army should have been destroyed." The threat to Richmond was over, though at a frightful toll. Twenty thousand Confederates lay dead or wounded, nearly one fourth of Lee's army, sixteen thousand on the Union side. The Shiloh war had come east. Northern journalist Frederick Law Olmsted, horrified at the sight of battlefield dead, pronounced it a "republic of suffering." The battles were among the earliest demonstrations of the effectiveness of rifled muskets in the hands of well-trained defenders. Lee's aggressive tactics had saved Richmond, but many more such successes would leave him without an army. Still, McClellan's retreat gave southerners their first opportunity to exhale in many months, especially after the bad news from the West. The boost to morale was much needed. Lee proposed to push the advantage.[23]

The news of McClellan's retreat sorely tested President Lincoln's patience. He took the unusual step of traveling to the Virginia coast to meet with his general to find out what had happened and ponder the next step in an increasingly frustrating war. McClellan was unapologetic, blaming the weather, the lack of sufficient troops (though at no time did he engage his entire force), and even Lincoln's war aims. The president brushed aside these excuses, vowing to continue the contest "until successful, or till I die, or am conquered, or my term expires, or Congress or the country forsakes me." He replaced McClellan with John Pope, combined McClellan's Army of the Potomac with Pope's Army of Virginia, and ordered a new offensive against Richmond.[24]

Pope had enjoyed some success in the West and, unlike McClellan, was a Republican. Some Republicans attributed McClellan's reluctance to fight to his Democratic politics. His unhappiness with Lincoln was well known. Union Quartermaster General Montgomery C. Meigs was shocked to overhear several of McClellan's officers threaten "a march on Washington to clear out those fellows." Whether high-ranking officers ever discussed a coup, except in idle talk, is unknown, but it is clear that these were dangerous days for the administration, with increasingly hostile northern public opinion and a rank-and-file soldiery loyal to a dismissed commander.[25]

McClellan maintained popularity among his men. And why not? Retreating down the peninsula he made a point of being the last federal soldier to abandon camp or cross a bridge, though he also steered well clear of the fighting. He lived his creed, citing as his first responsibility "the lives of my men." As McClellan pictured the unfolding Peninsula Campaign in his mind's eye, it would be a relatively bloodless affair, capped by a Union victory: "I do not expect to lose many men, but to do the work mainly with artillery, and so avoid much loss of life." Nor did he countenance vandalism of Rebel property. The pity was that his war was over, if it ever existed. A new war had exploded in early 1862, and he could not adjust.[26]

McClellan left for Washington in early August with a token force. Many of his troops moved from the peninsula to Pope's command in northern Virginia. Sensing that the Union's Army of Virginia was in a state of flux and had a new commander few officers and fewer enlisted men liked, Lee was determined to destroy the Union army. It was a result that had evaded him during the Seven Days' Battles. Moving swiftly before McClellan's men could reinforce Pope, and dividing his army—a risk he took because he believed Pope would not take advantage—he sent Stonewall Jackson forward on a wide flanking movement around Pope to seize his supplies at a familiar place, Manassas Junction, on August 27. Pope took the bait and engaged Jackson while James B. Longstreet launched a smashing attack against the bewildered Union forces. Pope's greatest maneuver of the day was an effective retreat across Bull Run to Washington. As Robert Frost put it eloquently many years later, Lee's two great divisions under Jackson and Longstreet "were like pistols in his two hands, so perfectly could he handle them."[27]

The contest was almost a replay of the First Battle of Bull Run, though befitting the new ferocity of the war the casualties were greater. The 5th New York suffered three hundred deaths in ten minutes. For all his success, Lee's attack proved costly again, as he lost 19 percent of his force compared with 13 percent for the Federals, even though Union casualties were greater in absolute terms. Despite the casualties, the growing belief on both sides in the invincibility of Lee and the incompetence of Union officers and politicians was bolstered. Toward the end of June, Union forces had glimpsed the spires of Richmond. By the end of August, Rebel troops menaced Washington. Two days after the second Union debacle at Bull Run, President Lincoln relieved Pope of his command and reinstalled McClellan as commander of the consolidated Army of the Potomac.

The war in the East changed the men as much as the western war had altered the lives of its combatants. The Peninsula Campaign and Second Bull Run transformed them from wide-eyed recruits to hardened veterans. "I have changed much in my feelings," Marion Hill Fitzpatrick wrote a day after Second Bull Run. "The bombs and balls excite me but little and a battlefield strewed with dead and wounded is an every day consequence."[28]

The Peninsula debacle followed by the Bull Run disaster plunged President Lincoln into despair. The turn in the war after such a promising start to the new year altered his spiritual perspective on the conflict. The uncertainty of God's purpose gnawed at Lincoln. He waited for a sign.

The summer successes encouraged Robert E. Lee to gamble on continued federal incompetence. On September 4, 1862, the Army of Northern Virginia crossed the Potomac into western Maryland, a mere thirty-five miles from Washington. Lee had saved Richmond and sent Pope's army packing, but he had not destroyed the enemy's will or capability to fight. He knew his was a risky maneuver, but he felt he had no choice. With a force inferior in numbers and materiel, he must take advantage of every physical and psychological situation that favored his troops. Now was such a moment. Take the war to the enemy's territory. His plan was to move into Pennsylvania, capture the state capital at Harrisburg, sever railroad connections with the Northwest, and put himself in a position to threaten Philadelphia and Washington. At the least, it would take the pressure off Richmond. At most, he could destroy the North's resolve and end the war.

In a letter to President Davis just before he crossed into Maryland, Lee admitted that his army, now reduced to fifty thousand able-bodied men, was "not properly equipped for an invasion of an enemy's territory. It lacks much of the material of war, is feeble in transportation . . . and the men are poorly provided with clothes, and in thousands of instances are destitute of shoes. Still we cannot afford to be idle, [we] must endeavor to harass, if we cannot destroy them." He would carry still fewer troops into battle, as some could no longer walk on the gravel roads barefoot, and others sickened on a diet of green corn and green apples as the army marched beyond its supply lines. McClellan, of course, believed Lee had at least a hundred thousand men marching into Maryland.[29]

Lee's troops hoped for a friendly reception in Maryland. They struck up a popular song:

> I hear the distant thunder hum
> The Old Lines' bugle, fife and drum;
> She is not dead, nor deaf, nor dumb—
> Hazza—she breathes, she burns, she'll come!
>   Maryland! My Maryland!

The farmers and townspeople ignored the footsore soldiers. There would be no popular uprising. No flowers strewn across the army's path; just stones and dust.

McClellan moved at his usual snail's pace to intercept Lee's army. On September 13, two Union soldiers found a piece of paper wrapped around three cigars near Frederick, Maryland. The paper contained Lee's campaign orders, fallen from the pocket of a careless Rebel officer. The orders confirmed intelligence McClellan had already received about the division of Lee's army and where the forces were located. The orders also indicated that Union forces far outnumbered Lee's. McClellan clutched the document and cried, "If I cannot whip Bobbie Lee, I will be willing to go home." Despite the huge advantage, McClellan still took his time marching westward, allowing Stonewall Jackson's troops to come up and join Lee's army for a combined force of forty thousand men against McClellan's seventy-five thousand. The delay also allowed Lee to learn of the intelligence leak and plan accordingly. Had McClellan moved swiftly and attacked, he would have enjoyed a four-to-one advantage in troop strength. Lee decided to hold defensive positions along a creek called Antietam. With the Potomac behind him, Lee's only options were to fight or retreat. Despite inferior numbers, he had come too far to go home. Besides, Lee had great confidence his men could defeat McClellan. Lincoln hoped otherwise. He wired his general, "Destroy the rebel army, if possible."[30]

Antietam Creek runs through the Catoctin Valley "like a poem in blue and gold," covered with patches of woods, sunlit fields, ripe orchards, and mountains gently rolling on the near horizon. The trees were just beginning to show their autumn colors. The valley had not one level spot. The depressions between the hills offered cover for infantry against artillery. Though most of these depressions were dry, some had creeks meandering through. Such was Antietam Creek, whose crooked course was typical. The fields were fat with corn and deep-green clover.[31]

Although McClellan waited almost two days to initiate the battle, he still had a considerable edge in troop strength. Many Rebel soldiers were hobbled with feet bleeding from the rocky Maryland roads, and they struggled to join the main force. McClellan had more than twice as many soldiers ready for combat. Had his planned three attacks on the left, center, and right of the Confederate line occurred together, McClellan would have prevailed. Lack of coordination and poor communication, which plagued both armies at crucial moments throughout the war, thwarted those plans.

At dawn on Wednesday, September 17, Union General Joe Hooker attacked Jackson's corps on the Confederate left, advancing in a long line through David Miller's cornfield, bayonets flashing just above the stalks, and into the woods, where they found the enemy. Hooker's men pushed the Confederates back to the German Baptist Church (now known as the Dunkard Church) and a sunken road (now called, appropriately, Bloody Lane). The Union advance continued in severe combat until Hooker was wounded. The Rebels, under Texan John Bell Hood, pushed the Federals back over the same ground so dearly gained during the morning. By noon, the battle ended with thirteen thousand men lying dead or wounded and the two armies at virtually the same place where they began the day. After the fighting, a fellow officer asked Hood where his division was. The Texan responded, "Dead on the field." Sixty percent of his soldiers were gone.[32]

Union General Ambrose E. Burnside struck the Confederate right at midday and pushed the Rebels back across the Stone Bridge (today known as Burnside Bridge) over Antietam Creek and down toward the Potomac. How Burnside's men took this bridge astonishes because a steep bank rises from the creek, a perfect elevation from which to guard the bridge. Yet Burnside's men waded through the Rebel fusillade and pushed the Confederates back. He could not hold it. Reinforcements never came.

The Confederates were more fortunate. A. P. Hill's division, the last of Stonewall Jackson's corps to arrive, appeared just in time, setting off jubilation among the Rebels and confusion in federal ranks, as they wore captured blue uniforms. Hill waved his sword aloft to rally his men, who retook the bridge and saved the day and the war for the Confederacy. Years later, as Lee lay on his deathbed, his last words were "Tell Hill he must come up," recalling when the fate of his army and of his country hung in the balance.[33]

The day should have belonged to the Union army. McClellan's attacks were hopelessly uncoordinated, and he failed at crucial moments to bring up reserves that he never used. The Confederates fought ferociously, but had a more astute and aware commander been at the Union helm, Lee's army might very well have been destroyed.

The bloodiest day of the Civil War was over: thirteen thousand Confederate troops dead or wounded and twelve thousand Union casualties; twice as many Americans killed in that single day than in every other nineteenth-century American war combined. A survey of the field revealed the democracy of death. A boy of fifteen hugged in the death embrace of the veteran of fifty—"the greasy blouse of the common soldier here pressing the starred shoulder of the Brigadier," a boy from Georgia and another from Pennsylvania, their arms outstretched to each other as if seeking a last embrace. A Pennsylvania soldier expressed the feelings of many of his comrades on both sides when he walked over the battlefield at dusk: "No tongue can tell, no mind conceive, no pen portray the horrible sights I witnessed this morning. God grant these things may soon end and peace be restored. Of this war I am heartily sick and tired."[34]

The battle was a tactical draw, but a technical victory for the Union as the Confederates vacated the field, crossing the Potomac while McClellan congratulated himself on "saving the Union." The Army of the Potomac allowed Lee to escape without pursuit. McClellan's army was exhausted. The day was exceedingly hot, and the close combat blanketed the battlefield with smoke, making breathing difficult. Many soldiers had temporarily lost all or part of their hearing. The artillery fire rumbled down from the hills like peals of thunder that never ceased. The powdery smoke, laced with saltpeter, burned the noses, throats, and eyes of the soldiers, who left the field, if they could, with tears streaming down their faces. The soldiers themselves did not know the outcome. A Union soldier wrote, "So terrible has been the day; so rapid and confused the events, that I find it impossible to separate them, so as to give, or even to form for myself any clear idea of what I have seen."[35]

Lincoln was incredulous that McClellan had allowed Lee to cross back into Virginia, his army intact. McClellan and his army were still encamped near Antietam when the president visited on October 1, two weeks after the battle. From a high vantage point, Lincoln looked out over the valley and the Union camp. "What is all this?" he asked his guide. "Why, Mr. Lincoln, this is the Army of the Potomac." The president paused and declared, "No . . . This is *General McClellan's body-guard.*" While McClellan rested, J. E. B. Stuart's cavalry conducted raids into Maryland and Pennsylvania, virtually unopposed. Though of little strategic importance, these forays added to the embarrassment. Lincoln had had enough and relieved McClellan of his command, replacing him with Ambrose E. Burnside, whose troops had given a good account of themselves on that bloody day at the bridge.[36]

Lee's successful escape allowed him and his officers to put the best face on a failed invasion. He would fight another day. As he wrote to his daughter on September 23, "We . . . did not consider ourselves beaten as our enemies supposed. We were greatly outnumbered and opposed by double if not treble our strength and yet we repulsed all their attacks, held our ground and retired when it suited our convenience."[37]

The afterlife of Antietam far exceeded its meager strategic results. By September 1862, civilians on both sides had become uneasily accustomed to the high casualty accounts. Families of servicemen had received letters describing the carnage of war in gory detail. Newspapers sensationalized the brutality of battle and the heroic exploits of martyrs to their cause. Words painted vivid pictures, but the images were imagined.

Mathew Brady, already a noted photographer, sent two colleagues, Alexander Gardner and James Gibson, to record the Antietam battlefield a day after the bloody contest. They snapped photos of bloated corpses, bodies lying like cordwood in a ditch, and remnants of horses strewn across the field. The photographers may have taken a little artistic license in rearranging some

bodies for mass effect, but the pictures offered an accurate portrait of what
the war had become. They went on display in New York City in October, and
the response was electric. The *New York Times* reported, "Mr. Brady has done
something to bring home to us the terrible reality and earnestness of war. If
he has not brought bodies and laid them in our door-yards and along
streets, he has done something very like it." The reporter was sensitive enough
to recognize that behind the photographs lay "widows and orphans, torn from
the bosom of their natural protectors. . . . Hearts cannot be photographed."[38]

Antietam also held off European recognition of the Confederacy and any
attempt by the British to offer mediation. During the spring and summer of
Rebel triumphs, French and British diplomats had seriously discussed these
possibilities.

The Union victory at Antietam, narrow though it was, enabled President

Dead Confederate soldiers in a ditch at Antietam, September 1862.
Modern weaponry and traditional tactics produced horrific casualties
on both sides. Photo by noted war photographer Alexander Gardner (1821–1882),
who worked for Mathew Brady. (Courtesy of the Library of Congress)

Lincoln to push forward with an initiative he had undertaken several months earlier. Lincoln introduced the "First Draft" of his Emancipation Proclamation to the cabinet on July 22, 1862, a few weeks after the failed Peninsula Campaign. The proclamation was clearly a military document. Lincoln confided to Secretary of the Navy Gideon Welles that he had given emancipation "much thought and had about come to the conclusion that it was a military necessity absolutely essential for the salvation of the Union." As a military measure, it would satisfy Lincoln's constitutional conscience, since it could legitimately fall under the "war powers" granted to a president in a time of national emergency. The proclamation did not apply to those areas under Union control (the border states in particular). But in the rebellious parts of the South slaves were henceforth free. In practical terms, the document did not free any slave. Masters in those areas beyond the Union armies could safely ignore the edict, though their slaves would not. The document, however, represented a symbolic landmark for the nation that purported to live by the words of the Declaration of Independence, "We hold these truths to be self-evident, that all men are created equal." The slaves welcomed the symbolism and continued their flight to freedom.[39]

Lincoln's caution reflected both his constitutional scruples and his desire to keep the North united behind the single objective of saving the Union. At heart, however, he was an emancipationist well before the war started. Joshua Speed, his closest friend, stated, "My own opinion of the history of the emancipation proclamation is, that Mr. Lincoln foresaw the necessity for it long before he issued it." Lincoln himself confirmed Speed's judgment in 1865: "I have always thought that all men should be free." Still, knowing the racial sentiments of northerners, the president worried about the proclamation's reception. "When I issued that proclamation," he told a friend, "I was in great doubt about it myself. I did not think that the people had been quite educated up to it, and I feared its effects upon the border states."[40]

Secretary of State William H. Seward urged the president to wait for a Union military victory so the proclamation did not appear as an act of desperation. In the meantime, Lincoln leaked news of the proclamation to friendly sources, and to several Radical Republicans who had pestered him on abolition since before he took the oath of office. Horace Greeley, the editor of the influential *New York Tribune*, had been lobbying the president to issue such an order for months. In August 1862, Greeley penned an editorial, "The Prayer of Twenty Millions," urging emancipation. Lincoln responded, holding fast to his priorities: "My paramount object in this struggle is to save the Union, and is *not* either to save or to destroy slavery. If I could save the Union without freeing any slaves I would do it, and if I could save it by freeing all slaves I would do it."

Lincoln had already presented his preliminary proclamation to the cabinet, as he hinted privately to Greeley. The deft manipulation of the media would build public sentiment for emancipation so the president would appear to endorse that sentiment rather than being ahead of it.[41]

Antietam provided the opening the administration required. The latest draft of the proclamation Lincoln presented included a provision protecting the freed status of all those slaves who had stolen their freedom and had come to Union lines. He recognized that this simple document would make the cruel war that much more cruel. "The character of the war will be changed," he noted to a friend. "It will be one of subjugation and extermination."[42]

Although initially presented as a military measure, the proclamation also reflected Lincoln's deep moral commitment to ending slavery. Secretary of the Navy Gideon Welles took notes on the cabinet meeting that followed Antietam. According to Welles, the president made little reference to military strategy. Instead, Lincoln explained that he "had made a vow, a covenant, that if God gave us the victory in the approaching battle, he would consider it an indication of Divine will, and that it was his duty to move forward in the cause of emancipation. . . . God had decided this question in favor of the slaves." If God's purpose in continuing the war remained unknown to the president, the persistence of slavery may have held a clue. Lincoln, at last, had his sign.[43]

As news reached the army of Lincoln's intentions, the reaction was mixed. An Ohio private, Chauncey Welton, assured his father, "I can tell you we don't think mutch of [the Emancipation Proclamation] hear in the army for we did not enlist to fight for the negro and I can tell you that we neer shall or many of us anyhow no never." The 20th Massachusetts, a unit from the most radical state in the North, seemed equally intransigent, according to Henry Livermore Abbott, who wrote to his aunt, "The president's proclamation is of course received with universal disgust."[44]

Others greeted the news as an affirmation of the ideals for which they fought. At last, a Union soldier sighed, the American flag "shall triumphantly wave over a free land, which it has never done yet." An Illinois soldier expressed the most general feeling in the army when he noted that he and many of his fellow soldiers "like the Negro no better now than we did then but we hate his master worse and I tell you when Old Abe carries out his Proclamation he kills this Rebellion and not before." Emancipation stood a better chance of receiving the approbation of the Union soldier as a military necessity rather than as a moral imperative.[45]

The civilian press, especially Republican papers, lauded the Emancipation Proclamation. *Harper's*, which only a few months earlier had cautioned against abolition, reflected the evolving opinion in the North. The proclamation "clears the individual conscience and the national escutcheon. It is an invocation of the spirit of the Constitution to save its form. . . . For America does not say that all men are equal in any thing but right. But it does say, and, please God, will forever say and maintain, that all men . . . are men, and therefore are born with a natural equality of right to life, liberty, and the pursuit of happiness." Some Democratic papers were hostile to the notion of abolition and warned that freedom did not imply equality for blacks. The *Cincinnati Enquirer* lamented, "Slavery is dead, the negro is not, there is the misfortune."[46]

Southerners responded with fury. They accused the Lincoln administration of inciting racial warfare. For those who had doubted the fire-eaters' warnings that a Lincoln presidency doomed slavery, the proclamation confirmed the worst. President Davis warned that any blacks captured during Rebel forays into northern territory would be summarily sent south into slavery. He concluded with bravado, "The day is not distant when the old Union will be restored with slavery nationally declared to be the proper condition of all of African descent."[47]

Lincoln arrived at a different conclusion in his annual message to Congress on December 1, 1862. "In *giving* freedom to the *slave*, we *assure* freedom to the *free*—honorable alike in which we give, and what we preserve." The fulfillment of this vision, or of President Davis's, depended on battlefield results. Lincoln knew he had raised the stakes even higher: "We shall nobly save, or meanly lose, the last best hope of earth."[48]

Two weeks later, saving the Union seemed more elusive than ever. Ambrose E. Burnside was famous for his whiskers, "sideburns," as they came to be called. He was long on facial hair and short on military acumen. Burnside protested that he was unfit when Lincoln offered him command of the Army of the Potomac, and he was right. An Indiana native and West Pointer (1847), he resigned his commission in 1853 to concentrate on manufacturing rifles in Rhode Island. The enterprise failed. Like Grant, Burnside offered his services to his state when the Civil War began. He was an early supporter of the president, who enjoyed his friendship. Burnside rose to the rank of brigadier general in late 1861 after successful operations along the coast of North Carolina. Following McClellan's failure in the Peninsula Campaign, Lincoln offered Burnside the command, which he refused. When Lee routed Pope at Bull Run, the president again turned to Burnside and received the same negative response. After Antietam, a desperate Lincoln prevailed upon a reluctant Burnside to take command.

Lincoln, frustrated by McClellan's failure to follow Lee across the Potomac after Antietam, ordered Burnside to destroy Lee's army in Virginia. At least,

Lincoln reasoned, Burnside would fight. Yet again, cries of "On to Richmond!" filled the columns of the northern press. The southern press responded with derision, and a popular song, "Richmond Is a Hard Road to Travel," dedicated to General Burnside, made the rounds of Confederate camps. Never mind; Burnside's superior numbers would overwhelm the Rebels in one huge coordinated assault, and the war would be over by Christmas.[49]

On November 20, Burnside's army of 114,000 men was ready to cross the Rappahannock at Fredericksburg and place themselves between the Rebel forces and Richmond before Lee could gather his dispersed army and Jackson could join him from the valley. By the time the pontoons to cross the river arrived in early December, Lee's two pistols, James Longstreet and Stonewall Jackson, had joined him to constitute a force of 72,500 men enabling the Virginian to unfold a plan of his own.

Lee ceded Fredericksburg to Union forces on December 11 with only token resistance. The Confederates withdrew to Marye's Heights above the town. Lee's infantry dug in at the base of the Heights, protected by entrenchments and a stone wall. Above the infantry, Lee arrayed his artillery and reserve troops. Burnside's general officers counseled against an attack, but he was adamant. Lincoln had ordered Burnside to make a direct assault, and the general followed his orders. On the morning of December 13, federal forces emerged from the fog to attack the hills above the city.

Instead of a coordinated attack, Union soldiers attempted to scale the Heights in twelve successive waves across an open field raked by Rebel artillery. When each assault failed and the troops broke and ran, Rebel infantry, no longer fearing return fire, poured volley after volley against the retreating soldiers. Not one Union soldier reached the stone wall. A Union soldier compared the charge to "a great slaughter pen . . . they might as well have tried to take Hell." By dusk, 12,600 Federals lay killed or wounded, with some of their comrades taking cover behind corpses against withering Rebel fire. In contrast, Confederates suffered 5,300 casualties. The field had changed colors: brown before the fight, blue covered with Union dead, then white after Rebel soldiers, many without shoes or proper clothing against the cold, stripped the corpses, and then red. Only blood and skin remained. From one of the hills above the city, Lee watched the close-ordered ranks of Union soldiers, banners flying, marching double-quick to their deaths, and remarked to Longstreet, "It is well that war is so terrible—we should grow too fond of it."[50]

Yet Lee hoped to continue the battle. He expected Burnside to regroup and come at him again. When the Union forces slipped back across the river, breaking off the engagement, Lee expressed his disappointment to his wife: "After all their boasting and preparation . . . they came as they went, in the night. They suffered heavily as far as the battle went, but it did not go far enough to satisfy me." Lee did not press his own tired and cold men to pursue the retreating Federals, who still vastly outnumbered his own troops. He wired President Davis, "The enemy had disappeared from [my] front." Richmond was saved, again.[51]

Burnside wanted to renew the attack the following day, but this time his officers talked him out of it. The general waited for two additional days before requesting a flag of truce to collect the dead and wounded from the battlefield. Wounded Union soldiers spent fifty hours exposed to the freezing cold, and many had joined the ranks of the dead by the time burial parties arrived. Many corpses were stiff as marble slabs from the cold, and lay "in every conceivable position, some on their backs with gaping jaws, some with eyes as large as walnuts, protruding with glassy stare, some doubled up like a contortionist." Over there, one without legs, nearby, a head and legs without a trunk, and "every horrible expression, fear, rage, agony, madness, torture, lying in pools of blood . . . with fragments of shell sticking in oozing brains, with bullet holes all over the puffed limbs."[52]

The gruesome scene reflected the heroism of the soldier as much as the foolhardiness of the officers. Fredericksburg, though a devastating defeat for the Union, stood as a symbol of Yankee bravery. A colonel of the 77th New York wrote: "None were ever more brave or more desirous to test their valor. The heroic deeds of those who did advance against the enemy will ever redound to the glory of our arms." Walt Whitman, who had traveled hastily to Fredericksburg in search of his wounded brother, asserted, "Never did mortal man in an aggregate fight better than our troops at Fredericksburg. In the highest sense, it was no failure." Even the Confederates expressed admiration for the enemy's courage. General George E. Pickett, who would come to know the consequences of charging a well-entrenched enemy at its center, marveled in a letter to his wife at the heroism of the Union's Irish Brigade: "Your soldier's heart almost stood still as he watched those sons of Erin fearlessly rush to their death. The brilliant assault . . . was beyond description."[53]

Better to be an admiring spectator on the Confederate side than reaping the laurels of certain death in a futile charge. Henry Livermore Abbott, of the 20th Massachusetts, led one of the unsuccessful charges and was withering in his assessment of the battle and the war. "The whole army is demoralized," he wrote to a friend the day after the battle. "The strongest peace party is the army. . . . The men who ordered the crossing of the river are responsible to God for murder." Abbott reported mutinous talk among the soldiers against "those blood stained scoundrels in the government."[54]

Most northerners focused on the results of the battle, not the bravery of the troops. By now, the northern public was inured to casualty figures, but the lopsided result at Fredericksburg threw citizens across the North into the worst despair of the war. Even those who normally supported the administration now turned against it. The Republicans, already reeling from serious losses in the November midterm elections they blamed on military reverses and the impending emancipation decree, ripped into the administration. An editorial in *Harper's* reported that the events at Fredericksburg filled "the heart of the loyal North with sickness, disgust, and despair." The writer charged that "the Government is unfit for its office, and . . . the most gallant efforts ever made by a cruelly tried people are being neutralized by the obstinacy and incapacity of their leaders." He wondered aloud if "matters are rapidly ripening for a military dictatorship." Lincoln especially received scorn and ridicule. A popular illustration of the time depicted Columbia angrily asking the president, "Where are my 15,000 sons—murdered at Fredericksburg?" to which Lincoln replies, "This reminds me of a little Joke." Columbia cuts him off: "Go tell your Joke at Springfield!" Lincoln assessed his position accurately: "If there is a worse place than Hell, I am in it."[55]

Confederates were relieved but subdued. Their military situation in the West continued to slip, inflation gnawed at civilians, the death toll had mounted precipitously during the preceding year, and a major Union force still menaced in Virginia. Fredericksburg lifted southern spirits, though. Jefferson Davis told a cheering crowd in Richmond shortly after the new year that their Confederacy was the last hope "for the perpetuation of that system of government which our forefathers founded—the asylum of the oppressed and the home of true representative liberty." It was a speech Lincoln could have given. Preserving the last hope would not be easy, Davis averred. "Every crime which could characterize the course of demons has marked the course of the invader."[56]

Captain Oliver Wendell Holmes did not fight at Fredericksburg; dysentery disabled him before he could take the field with his regiment. It was a disease that would kill more than forty-four thousand men during the war. Holmes survived, but the loss of comrades at Fredericksburg "to certain and useless death," as he put it, had a profound effect on him. The battle persuaded him that the war, "in which the boldest are the likeliest to die, was a hideous human waste." The Cause, any cause, paled before the fact that the best men experienced a senseless death. A week later, in a letter to his father, Holmes summarized his new feelings that peace rather than war offered the best chance for the abolition of slavery: "But if it is true that we represent civilization, which is in its nature, as well as slavery, diffusive & aggressive, and if civilization & progress are the better things why they will conquer in the long run . . . and will stand a better chance in their proper province—peace—than in war, the brother of slavery—brother—it is slavery's parent, child and sustainer at once."[57]

On the evening of January 1, 1863, Frederick Douglass and three thousand of his friends gathered at Tremont Temple in Boston to await the arrival of the news that President Lincoln had signed the Emancipation Proclamation. Three crucial differences from the preliminary emancipation document of September 22 appeared. The latest version made no mention of colonization, muted the preservation of the Union as the primary motivation for the proclamation, and recommended that able-bodied freedmen be "received into the armed service." It was a radical proposal. Messengers waited at the telegraph office to bring the joyful news to the temple. The throng listened to inspirational speeches and Beethoven's "Ode to Joy," but by 11:00 P.M., no messengers had appeared. Near midnight, Judge Thomas Russell rushed into the temple waving a paper, which he read: "I do order and declare that all persons held as slaves within said designated States and ports of States are, and henceforward shall be, free." Douglass recalled, "I never saw Joy before. Men, women, young and old, were up; hats and bonnets were in the air." In North Carolina, a newly freed slave thought, "These are the times foretold by the Prophets, 'When a Nation shall be born in a day.'"[58]

CHAPTER 12

BLOOD AND
TRANSCENDENCE

WALT WHITMAN FOUGHT in another war. His war was deadlier than the one on the battlefield. Everyone was a hero in his war, all were comrades, and the enemy was invisible. Whitman fought against death as a nurse in Washington hospitals. He lost many battles, but he persisted and thanked God for small victories. For surely it was God and not the science of the day that accounted for the daily miracles of survival among the sick and wounded. In a cruel and senseless war, the hospitals were the cruelest places. They were also places of grace.

Whitman caught a train from New York the moment he heard his brother George was wounded at Fredericksburg. He searched frantically through forty hospitals and homes in Washington, D.C., to no avail. Learning of a field hospital in Falmouth, Virginia, Whitman located his brother lying in a tent with a nonthreatening shrapnel wound in his cheek. Yet the poet could not leave. Here, death was as common as the morning. He saw three dead men lying on stretchers outside a tent, untended, each with a brown woolen blanket covering them. The poet wrote,

> Then to the second I step—And who are you my child
>   and darling?
> Who are you, sweet boy, with cheeks yet blooming?
> Then to the third—a face nor child, nor old, very calm,
>   as of beautiful yellow-white ivory;
> Young man, I think I know you—I think this face of
>   yours is the face of the Christ himself,
> Dead and divine, and brother of all, and here again he
>   lies.[1]

The wounded lay in flimsy tents, often on the frozen ground, with only a blanket against the late December frost. He held their hands to comfort them. They would not let go. Far from home, far from family, they had made him their kin. He had found his life's new work. At the end of December, he accompanied a contingent of the wounded to Washington, D.C., serving as a scribe for the disabled soldiers writing messages to their families, and they returned his kindness tenfold. He stayed in Washington, found a job in the army paymaster's office, and, after work, dashed off to hospitals bearing gifts and solace for the soldiers.

Death had become so commonplace it bred indifference. Surgeons were careless in their amputations and unmindful of even the limited sanitary knowledge of the time. Attendants flung naked corpses onto a nearby field to await mass burial. Whitman never succumbed to the routine of death; it heightened his compassion and love. The sheer force of his being, Whitman believed, held healing powers. Over six feet tall, nearly two hundred pounds, with a ruddy complexion and a long gray beard, he was a commanding presence striding down hospital wards. He read stories and poems to the soldiers, changed dressings, cooled fevered brows, and wrote his verses, so different from the celebratory stanzas when the war began:

> From the stump of the arm, the amputated hand,
> I undo the clotted lint, remove the slough, wash off the
>   matter and blood,
> Back on his pillow the soldier bends with curv'd neck
>   and side-falling head,
> His eyes are closed, his face is pale, he dares not look
>   on the bloody stump,
> And has not yet looked on it.[2]

It was in one of these hospital wards that Whitman encountered the young soldier John A. Holmes. The Massachusetts private suffered from diarrhea, an affliction that struck 54 percent of Union soldiers and an incredible 99 percent of Confederates. Excrement and offal fouled the drinking water at military camps, spreading disease rapidly. By the end of the war, a hundred thousand soldiers had died from the disease, representing roughly 15 percent of all deaths.[3]

Holmes, who could not hold down food, was evacuated from Fredericksburg in an open rail car to a field hospital in Aquia Creek, Virginia. He lay on the ground, unattended, for several days without anything to eat or drink. The army shipped him on a steamer with other sick and wounded to Washington, D.C. Lying on an open deck in frigid winter weather, he was too weak to draw his blanket over him for a semblance of warmth. Despite requests, nobody came to his aid. Dropped off at the wharf in Washington, he caught a ride to a hospital and immediately fell onto an open bed only to be rousted out and admonished that he could not lie down with his clothes on. He complied, and now naked he was ushered into a bathroom where attendants scrubbed him down with cold water. He collapsed into unconsciousness.

Whitman saw a glassy-eyed, pale, and despairing face on his way out of the ward one evening. It was clear that the man was dying, so he stopped but received no response at first. "I sat down by him without any fuss; talked a little; soon saw that it did him good; led him to talk a little himself; got him somewhat interested; wrote a letter for him to his folks . . . soothed him down . . . gave him some small gifts and told him I should come again soon." Holmes asked the poet for a few pennies to buy milk from the woman who came through the ward in the morning. When Whitman pulled the change out of his pocket, the dying soldier wept uncontrollably.

Whitman visited Holmes the next day and the next, expecting on each visit to find an empty bed or another unfortunate soldier in his place. He followed this routine for several weeks, and, to his surprise, Holmes got stronger and eventually rejoined his unit. As he left the hospital, Holmes told Whitman that he had saved his life that first day he sat on the soldier's bed. "I can testify," the poet asserted later, "that friendship has literally cured a fever, and the medicine of daily affection a bad wound."[4]

Patients like Holmes resided in the same ward as wounded soldiers, a good prescription for spreading disease, only one source of the deadly infections that plagued the wounded on both sides. Field hospitals were especially noxious. At Antietam, Union surgeons set up a field hospital in a stable ankle-deep in manure. Physicians operated clad in blood- or pus-stained coats, wielded instruments and sponges rinsed off with water after being used on previous patients, and sharpened their surgical knives on the soles of their boots. They moistened thread with saliva to facilitate its placement in needles for sutures and wrapped wounds in any cloth available.

If they survived the operating table, recuperating soldiers contended with the groans and screams of comrades, the indifference of hospital personnel, and incessant visits from ministers trying to save their souls. When the young men wrote home about such visits, they typically expressed exasperation. They had seen war and its consequences. If God was omnipotent, why would he allow such carnage and the accompanying misery for families across the land? Most soldiers retained their religious beliefs, but the war shook their faith. A wounded Ohio soldier recalled ministers "who would come into my ward and preach and pray and sing to us, while we were swearing to ourselves all the time and wishing the blamed old fools would go away." One of the many reasons why Whitman's soldiers welcomed his presence was that, as one wounded private noted, he "didn't bring any tracts or Bibles; he didn't ask if you loved the Lord, and didn't seem to care whether you did or not."[5]

Whitman, the individualist, did not fit in well with the increasingly institutionalized methods of care promoted by the U.S. Sanitary Commission. The commission, established by the government but funded privately, gathered supplies, recruited nurses, organized hospitals, and grasped the connection between sanitation and health. While its efforts improved the delivery of health care among Union soldiers significantly—no comparable group existed in the Confederacy—the approach was more bureaucratic than caring. As one official advised nurses, "Put away feelings. Do all you can and be a machine— that's the way to act; the only way." Maintaining an emotional distance between nurse and patient became a paramount tenet of professionalism, which Whitman detested. He took every death personally and knew the signs of death, the delirium, the eyes turning back, the shallow breathing, as he walked through the wards. He would retrace his steps and see now a white sheet covering a form, another sacrifice, for what and for whom?[6]

The poet's disdain for bureaucratic care found resonance with a young Massachusetts woman whom he met in the days after Fredericksburg. Clara Barton, like Whitman, worked as a copyist in Washington, D.C., only for the U.S. Patent Office, the first woman to draw her salary from the U.S. government. A diminutive (not quite five feet tall), dark-haired woman of inestimable energy—she described herself as "athletic," a decidedly unfeminine characterization for the era—she had moved to the capital in 1854 for health reasons. Barton was probably the only resident of the city who migrated there for its climate. She wanted to settle further south but feared a single woman would not be safe in the land below the Potomac.[7]

When the war began, Barton brought little gifts to soldiers stationed in the city. She preferred the single life and the independence accompanying it. Not that she embraced celibacy. As a friend explained, "She was so much stronger a character than any of the men who made love to her that I do not think she was ever seriously tempted to marry any of them." During the war, she had a "tempestuous" affair with a married Union colonel. None of these biographical details were conventional for a middle-class New England woman, which hints at her greater destiny. Like Whitman, she moved to the front lines of the other war and made a lasting impact.[8]

The wounded soldiers returning from First Bull Run startled Barton. They were in horrible shape, bounced over rutted roads on transports and receiving little care. She collected three warehouses full of food and supplies for soldiers and resolved to deliver the goods in person. Barton played the tearful female to the quartermaster and received a pass to go into Virginia "for the comfort of the sick and wounded." The surgeons had few supplies when Barton suddenly turned up at the field hospitals with her wagonload of goods. A surgeon recalled, "I thought that night, if heaven ever sent out a homely angel, she must be one, her assistance was so timely." She also ministered to wounded Confederates at a nearby hospital, something Whitman would do as well. These angels knew no distinction among combatants, only the quality of mercy.[9]

The other war generated ghastly scenes, such as those Barton came across after Second Bull Run. The field hospital was, literally, a field on a hillside, where sick and wounded Union soldiers baked under an unforgiving sun, the fortunate resting on straw, the others on the bare ground, and almost all without food or water for two days. Barton distributed her supplies and tended to many soldiers personally. She resolved to accompany the army on its next campaign so the wounded would receive immediate treatment. Barton and four supply wagons joined the procession of McClellan's army into Maryland.

The carnage at Antietam overwhelmed even Barton's store of supplies. She resorted to applying green corn leaves to wounds in the place of bandages. As male surgical assistants fled Rebel artillery fire, Barton remained on the field, oblivious to the shells and bullets, aiding fallen soldiers as best she could. A surgeon proclaimed, "In my feeble estimation, General McClellan, with all his laurels, sinks into insignificance beside the true heroine of the age, *the angel of the battlefield.*" The 21st Massachusetts made her a daughter of the regiment. Much as Whitman had found his calling in the hospital wards of Washington, Barton was at home traveling with the army: "I am a U.S. soldier you know and therefore not supposed to be susceptible to fear."[10]

Fredericksburg nearly undid her. The sheer volume of casualties and the lack of space as the wounded crammed into private homes in the city and lay on floors slicked with blood, even on china cupboards, astounded Barton. In one house, twelve hundred men lay wounded. "I wrung the blood from the bottom of my clothing, before I could step." Barton returned to Washington on New Year's Eve. Too exhausted to see in the new year, she collapsed on the floor of her one-room flat and sobbed herself to sleep.[11]

Whitman's and Barton's other war raged in the South as well. There, angels of mercy had many more obstacles to overcome. The percentage of Confederate soldiers killed by disease was twice that of Union soldiers. The Confederacy suffered from chronic shortages of medicines and bandages, the absence of organizations such as the U.S. Sanitary Commission to coordinate giving and train nurses, and the general prejudice among male physicians against women as nurses. Traveling to Corinth after terrible Shiloh, Kate Cumming, a

A federal field hospital, Savage Station, Virginia, June 1862,
during the Seven Days' Battles. Makeshift field hospitals,
overcrowded and providing only straw on the bare ground for
comfort, offered little sanitation or care for
wounded soldiers. (Courtesy of the Library of Congress)

Scots immigrant who had settled in Mobile, Alabama, complained, "The surgeons entertain great prejudice against admitting ladies into the hospital in the capacity of nurses." Cumming prevailed, however, and entered a hotel, now serving as a hospital that included the wounded and sick from both sides. They lay strewn all over the floor, rendering her passage nearly impossible. Her thoughts cried out, "O, if the authors of this cruel and unnatural war could but see what I saw there, they would try and put a stop of it!"[12]

Like Whitman and Barton, Cumming had little patience for sanctimony. When southern women hesitated to enter the nursing ranks, she shot back: "Not respectable! And who has made it so? If the Christian, high-toned and educated women of our land shirk their duty, why others have to do it for them." Her heart broke to see the young men come in with rags for clothes, barefooted, and exhausted. She deeply resented the attitude of surgeons who dismissed any good idea she had. "I ask but one thing from any surgeon, and that is, to be treated with the same respect due to men in their own sphere of life."[13]

Cumming traveled to where she was needed, and she was needed everywhere. The southern built landscape became a hospital. Homes, churches, schools, stores, public buildings, hotels, and railroad depots served as repositories for the sick and wounded. The line between civilian and combatant in the South blurred as war came, literally, to southerners' doorsteps.

In early 1863, the end of the war was unimaginable. At dinner parties, in offices, and on the streets of cities and towns in the North, talk of a negotiated

"Our Women and the War," 1862, attributed to Winslow Homer (1836–1910).
Both northern and southern society expected women to fulfill various
supportive roles. (Smithsonian American Art Museum / Art Resource, NY)

peace flourished in the first month of the new year. The legislature in Lincoln's home state, Illinois, debated a resolution to call a Peace Convention. New Jersey legislators considered proposals to send commissioners south to treat with the Davis administration to determine on what terms the Confederate states might rejoin the Union.

General Burnside, armed with new orders from President Lincoln to destroy Lee's army, prepared to cross the Rappahannock in mid-January and redress the December disaster. By the time he acted, a series of winter storms had slammed into Virginia, turning the roads to mud. The mire trapped and killed draft animals, prevented artillery and supply wagons from moving, and created an army of soaked, mutinous, and dispirited soldiers. General Lee and his men remained safe and dry. *Harper's* asked plaintively, "Have We a General Among Us?"[14]

The West hardly looked better than the East for Union fortunes that bitter January. Lincoln directed General William S. Rosecrans to move against Confederate General Braxton Bragg and take Chattanooga. Rosecrans cited impassable roads and remained idle. Worse yet, Ulysses S. Grant had failed to capture Vicksburg, the important Mississippi River port and rail junction. The city sat on bluffs two hundred feet above the river, an excellent defensive promontory. Grant ordered General William T. Sherman to attack the bluffs on December 29. The assault was a disaster reminiscent of Fredericksburg. Grant, one newspaper wrote, "is a jackass in the original package. He is a poor drunken imbecile. He is a poor stick sober, and he is most of the time more than half drunk, and much of the time idiotically drunk."[15]

Volunteer totals plummeted for the Union armies. Growing public sentiment of incompetence among the civilian and military high commands, as well as opposition to emancipation as a war aim, reduced enthusiasm for service. The situation forced the administration to institute its first general draft in March 1863, for all males between the ages of twenty and forty-five. These individuals would enter a lottery, with names drawn until the army met its quota. A controversial provision allowed draftees to buy an exemption for three hundred dollars, an inconceivable sum for members of the working class.

Talk of a peace settlement became so general in the North that Republican leaders and the press felt compelled to remind citizens of the stakes involved. In an article headlined "No Surrender!" *Harper's* initiated the media's reeducation campaign, recycling arguments articulated at the start of the war: allowing the separate existence of the southern states would encourage other states to do the same, resulting in constant friction, warfare, and, ultimately the anarchy of "feeble, jarring States, exhausting their strength in internecine conflicts." The only acceptable result of the conflict was the creation of a strong central government untrammeled by dissenting factions. "There will be but one nation, but one Government, but one Union upon our domain," and its constituent parts would owe "absolute obedience to the lawful supreme national authority."[16]

The press not only warned of the consequences of peace but also wrote of the nobility of war. "No such war as ours has ever been waged since the Crusades." In a variation of the "House Divided" rationale, *Harper's* rallied northern citizens to fight "the battle of Democracy against Aristocracy—labor against capital—manhood against privilege. . . . A nation must be governed by the one or by the other. Both can not coexist."[17]

Lincoln understood that lack of civilian support could cripple the war effort. On January 26, 1863, he dismissed Burnside and appointed Joseph Hooker to lead the Army of the Potomac. "Fighting Joe" looked like a general—tall, handsome, and a commanding presence in the saddle or out. He had earned his nickname accidentally, as a newspaper typesetter omitted

a comma after "Fighting," in an article on an early battle. Hooker had a reputation for drinking and womanizing. Slang for both a shot of whiskey and a
prostitute allegedly derived from his last name.[18]

At Antietam, Hooker had demonstrated good leadership skills and bravery. His outsized ego, though, infuriated colleagues. Known for brash talk, he
once declared that the country would benefit from a military dictator. Lincoln, desperate for a soldier who not only fought but won, overlooked these
shortcomings. Besides, unlike Burnside, Hooker had earned the affection
and respect of his men. Taking command, he ordered fresh fruits and vegetables for his dispirited troops, granted generous furloughs, and set about to
train his 138,000-man army for the spring campaign against Robert E. Lee.

As the war closed in on the two-year mark, the Confederacy should have
gained in confidence. Its armies in the East and West remained intact; the
naval blockade, while annoying, had not closed down commerce; its forces
had thwarted an attack on the vital port of Vicksburg; Lee had pinned a ruinous defeat on a larger force at Fredericksburg. Dissension had grown in the
North, and hopes for peace bloomed in the South as a result.

Yet all was not well in Dixie. The two-year toll on men and materiel, both
in much shorter supply in the South than in the North, began to gnaw at the
resolve of southerners. Shortages and inflation forced civilians to make hard
choices in their lives, especially those who lived in towns and did not grow
their own food. Union soldiers commented on the threadbare appearance
of Rebel captives. While northern factories hummed at full speed, southern
manufacturing stumbled, plagued by manpower shortages, worn-out machinery, and an increasingly devalued currency. Foreign recognition, which
would have provided loans, munitions, and consumer goods, remained elusive. Since most of the fighting had occurred in the South, the destruction of
roads, bridges, livestock, and housing added to the discomfort for civilians.
"Refugeeing" women and children escaping advancing Union armies created
a large dislocated population with little means of support. The hardships led
to a growing peace sentiment in the South that would become more formidable as the year progressed.

Both the Davis administration and the press attempted to counter the
peace party with reminders of Yankee barbarity and the certainty of subjugation if peace were achieved on the North's terms. The Emancipation Proclamation revived the martial spirit for many throughout the South. The
Richmond Examiner called the document "the most startling political crime,
the most stupid political blunder, yet known in American history. . . . Southern
people have now only to choose between victory and death."[19]

Given those options, the Confederacy would fight on. If desertion rates and draft evasion were any measures, however, soldiers were the greatest advocates for peace. The inability to protect their families, especially women and children, the need for their labor on farms, and the sheer brutality and inconclusiveness of the war to date left most Rebel soldiers praying for peace. In early January, a Confederate private in Tennessee wrote in despair, "I am sick and tired of this war, and, I can see no prospects of having peace for a long time to come, I don't think it ever will be stopped by fighting, the Yankees cant whip us and we can never whip them."[20]

In less troubled times, Americans looked forward to the end of winter. Not so this year. Spring no longer meant soft fragrances, bright colors, freshly turned earth, and days bountiful in sunshine yet cool. A Confederate soldier wrote home, "Never before has returning spring brought with it such feelings of sorrow & regret. Regret because a winter so suitable for making peace should have passed and nothing done & sorrow at the thoughts of so many bloody battles this coming spring we'll be called upon to witness, and the many family circles that will have to mourn the loss of one or perhaps more of its members."[21]

As winter turned to spring across the South, neither side seemed anxious to renew the battle. In the West, Confederate Lieutenant General John C. Pemberton, a West Pointer and a Philadelphian with a wife from Virginia, still held Vicksburg with a modest force of twenty-nine thousand men. Grant had yet to figure out a way to capture the well-fortified city. Rosecrans and Bragg were content to stare at each other in southeastern Tennessee. In the East, Lee waited for Hooker while the latter continued to drill and discipline his army. Marion Hill Fitzpatrick of the 27th Georgia saw the lull as a promising sign of impending peace. He wrote home, "The boys . . . think we will have peace soon. We whipped the yanks last Summer. They gained nothing the past winter, a great many of their soldiers' times is up the first of May. . . . All these reasons I think bring at least a glimmering ray of hope for peace."[22]

The pace quickened in April. Grant moved south of Vicksburg, crossed the river, and marched overland to the state capital at Jackson, cut Pemberton's supply lines and attacked the river city from the east. In the East, Hooker forded the Rappahannock, boasting, "I have the finest army the sun ever shone on. My plans are perfect, and when I start to carry them out, may God have mercy on General Lee, for I will have none." After smashing Lee's army, Hooker planned to march into Richmond and end the war.[23]

On May 1, Hooker bore down on Lee's left flank with seventy-three thousand men, having left forty thousand men behind to mind Fredericksburg. Encountering resistance, he hesitated and then withdrew to form a defensive line at the crossroads town of Chancellorsville in an area of heavy underbrush and woods known, appropriately, as the Wilderness. The decision amazed his fellow officers, who felt the campaign was proceeding well. Hooker's hesitation allowed Lee to recover. The terrain mitigated Hooker's two-to-one advantage in troops and made judging the course of the battle nearly impossible, a major factor in Hooker's misapprehension of Confederate strength and position.[24]

Lee discovered that Hooker's right flank was "in the air," without solid defensive ground to anchor it, and boldly divided his army, sending Stonewall Jackson on a brilliant maneuver through the Wilderness to fall upon the exposed flank. Late in the afternoon of May 2, some Federals noticed frightened deer and rabbits fleeing the woods. Jackson's foot cavalry burst out of the cover with Rebel yells and blazing rifles to rout the immobile Union right. Jackson hoped to continue the assault through the night, taking advantage of the moonlight. But in the process of reconnoitering the enemy's defenses, Jackson was wounded by his own troops. Hooker, fearing for the destruction of his army, withdrew back across the Rappahannock. The Army of the Potomac had suffered seventeen thousand casualties, a greater defeat than the debacle at Fredericksburg five months earlier. The Confederates counted thirteen thousand casualties, a considerably higher percentage than the Federals, 22 percent to 13 percent.

The news devastated Lincoln, who had only recently recovered from Fredericksburg. A colleague reported that he had never seen the president "so broken, dispirited, and so ghostlike." He paced back and forth in a room at the White House muttering, "My God! My God! What will the country say! What will the country say!"[25]

Robert E. Lee derived the wrong lesson from his smashing victory at Chancellorsville: it fed his growing sense of invincibility. It was a conclusion seconded by the southern press, numerous northern newspapers, and a good many civilians on both sides. In his official report of the battle, Lee wrote, "The conduct of the troops cannot be too highly praised. Attacking largely superior numbers in strongly entrenched positions, their heroic courage overcame every obstacle of nature and art and achieved a triumph." Lee displayed strategic brilliance at Chancellorsville, but Hooker's incompetence and Jackson's discovery of a hidden farm road through the dense Wilderness played significant roles in the victory. Against a more competent opponent and with a little less luck, the outcome might have been different.[26]

Good fortune lasted only a short while for Lee. A bullet had shattered the bone in Stonewall Jackson's left arm just below the shoulder. There were no medical treatments for shattered bones at the time other than amputation. Lee remarked presciently, "He has lost his left arm, but I my right arm." Jackson endured a bone-jarring twenty-seven-mile wagon ride to a safe location.

Pneumonia settled in, another condition for which the medical practice of the time had no cure. On May 10, the general repeated the words of a favorite hymn, "Let us cross over the river and rest under the trees." Moments later, he died. May 10 was a Sunday. With the master of the daring flanking movement gone, a grief-stricken Lee wept, "I know not how to replace him."[27]

The Holy Cause had a Holy Martyr. For a nation still groping for a national identity, the martyrdom of Stonewall Jackson provided an opportunity to build sentiment for a common purpose and destiny. Sara Pryor, a Richmond resident, wrote, "On May 10 the General died, and we were all plunged into the deepest grief. By every man, woman, and child in the Confederacy this good man and great general was mourned as never man was mourned before." Jackson had assumed a legendary character even before his death, with his lightning raids, brilliant tactical maneuvers, and uncanny stealth. At a memorial service, a piece called "Stonewall's Requiem" declared him to be "the Martyr of our country's cause." On the fourth Sunday in May, ministers across the Confederacy began their sermons with 2 Samuel 3:38: "Know ye not that there is a prince and a great man fallen this day in Israel?"[28]

Even northerners stopped to praise their fallen adversary. Henry Ward Beecher, the abolitionist preacher, announced Jackson's death from his pulpit: "A brave and honest foe has fallen." Herman Melville expressed the ambivalence of many northerners with his elegiac poem "Stonewall Jackson," admiring the man but not the cause.

> *The Man who fiercest charged in fight*
> *Whose sword and prayer were long—*
> *Stonewall!*
> *Even him who stoutly stood for Wrong,*
> *How can we praise? Yet coming days*
> *Shall not forget him with this song.*[29]

Stonewall Jackson combined piety with valor. In an increasingly bloody war where success was measured in body counts, it was easy to lose sight of basic values and transcending causes. Jackson's death brought those values and causes to the fore. To what end remained unclear. The certitude of a holy cause that greeted the war's onset slid into doubt, the same doubt about God's intentions that Lincoln had expressed. How to understand why the best of men, "such men as Jackson[,] are cut down in the zenith of their glory?" Kate Cumming learned about Jackson's death while at her post in a Chattanooga hospital. "How unsearchable are His judgments, and His ways are past finding out" she wrote. "For who hath known the mind of the Lord." It was difficult, especially for evangelical Christians, to reconcile the death of a good and pious man with God's everlasting love.[30]

In late May, Union General Nathaniel Banks launched an assault on Confederate fortifications at Port Hudson, Louisiana, on the Mississippi River. The attack was part of a larger plan to open up the river for Union navigation. The battle marked one of the first deployments of black troops in combat. Though the assault failed to dislodge the Rebels, the troops, many of whom were free people of color from Louisiana, gave a good account of themselves. Banks noted in his report, "Whatever doubt may have existed heretofore as to the efficiency of Negro regiments, the history of the day proves conclusively to those who were in condition to observe the conduct of these regiments that the Government will find in the class of troops effective supporters and defenders."[31]

The decision to deploy black troops was not an easy one for the Lincoln administration. Many high-ranking Union officers and government officials remained convinced that African Americans were best suited for menial support occupations or tilling the soil at abandoned plantations. While many soldiers approved of emancipation in the abstract, fighting alongside black troops was quite another matter. Blacks, however, were anxious to fight for their own freedom, and numerous African Americans in the North lobbied the president to open recruiting for colored regiments.

In August 1862, Secretary of War Edwin Stanton approved the enlistment of five thousand black troops in South Carolina. Lincoln allowed the order to stand. The final draft of the Emancipation Proclamation authorized the recruitment of black troops. With emancipation a fact and the war going badly, Lincoln became a devoted convert to the idea: "The bare sight of 50,000 armed and drilled black soldiers on the banks of the Mississippi would end the rebellion at once." To the contrary. The prospect of armed black men threw Confederates into a murderous frenzy.[32]

The Davis administration warned that the army would consider captured black soldiers as "slaves captured in arms," not as prisoners of war, and therefore subject to execution. Lincoln advised the Richmond government that he would match man for man the death of captive black soldiers. The Confederacy never carried out this edict formally, though Rebel troops, on several occasions, killed black soldiers after they had surrendered. At Fort Pillow, Tennessee, in April 1864, Confederate General Nathan Bedford Forrest's troops murdered three hundred black prisoners, many of whom had begged for mercy. A Confederate soldier described the scene at Fort Pillow following the executions: "Human blood stood about in pools and brains could have been gathered up in any quantity." Another Rebel soldier stated flatly, "It was understood among us that

"A Shell in the Rebel Trenches," Winslow Homer, 1863. Yes, blacks did "fight"
for the Confederacy, but rarely voluntarily, and here is one of many reasons why.
The army used slaves to dig trenches and for other menial chores. It was dangerous
work, as this sketch indicates. The help slaves provided for the Confederate cause
supported the case for their enlistment in the Union armies.
(The New York Public Library / Art Resource, NY)

we take no negro prisoners." After capturing several black soldiers during the
assault on Fort Wagner near Charleston Harbor in July 1863, a Georgia soldier
reported with satisfaction that the prisoners were "literally shot down while on
their knees begging for quarters and mercy." Union officials found these incidents difficult to corroborate. Only later did sources confirm these murders.[33]

Union troops generally did not greet black comrades with equanimity.
Harper's reported that white Union soldiers stationed in Baton Rouge, Louisiana, mutinied when a black regiment camped nearby in February 1863. White
officers assigned to black troops experienced the opprobrium of fellow officers.
When Frederick Douglass noted that soldiering was an important step toward
full citizenship and equality for blacks, he confirmed the fears of many white
northerners who shuddered at the thought of racial equality. As a northern
editor explained, an "aversion to the negro is deeply ingrained" among "a large
number of our Northern troops."[34]

There were enough reported incidents (and likely many more unreported)
to substantiate racism among northern soldiers. Union soldiers in Kentucky
fired on a black church for no particular reason. Another soldier murdered a

black man in Louisiana and escaped punishment because, as a colleague admitted, "a negroes life is little more regarded than that of a dog." At the siege of Petersburg beginning in the summer of 1864, Confederate and Union pickets agreed they would not fire upon each other. As part of the agreement, the Yanks would alert the Rebels when black pickets took their positions. At those times, the agreement was off.[35]

These views were not unanimous. Some Union soldiers believed with a young Illinois soldier that "the nation will be purified" and "God will accomplish his vast designs" because "prejudice against color is fast going away." Some white soldiers never forgot the cheers and tears of African Americans who greeted them on wharves, along streets, and at country crossroads throughout the South. Nor the obvious pride of blacks as they put on the blue uniform and shouldered a rifle for the first time. Eventually, black soldiers would comprise 10 percent of the Union army, nearly 150,000 men.[36]

The exhilaration of fighting for one's freedom or liberating an enslaved population could come with considerable costs for black recruits, especially those from the South. They not only had to navigate the deep prejudices of white officers and troops, they feared for the safety of the families they left behind, and for their own lives should Confederates capture them. Sometimes families accompanied the soldiers to Union camps, but often they remained behind on farms and plantations where masters could retaliate against them. One slave woman in Missouri wrote to her soldier husband in December 1863, "I have had nothing but trouble since you left. . . . They abuse me because you went & say they will not take care of our children & do nothing but quarrel with me all the time and beat me scandalously the day before yesterday." She begged him to come home.[37]

For northern blacks, to fight for the freedom of their brothers and sisters in the South was a matter of honor that would earn the respect of whites. Self-help mattered more than self-preservation. In April 1863, Henry Gooding, a young black sergeant from Massachusetts, sent a letter to the editor of the *New Bedford* (Mass.) *Mercury* urging his fellow black citizens to enlist despite the great dangers they would face. "As one of the race, I beseech you not to trust to a fancied security, laying in your minds, that our condition will be bettered because slavery must die . . . [If we] allow that slavery will die without the aid of our race to kill it—language cannot depict the indignity, the scorn, and perhaps violence, that will be heaped upon us."[38]

Frederick Douglass threw himself into the recruiting effort and managed to enlist a hundred African American men in upstate New York for the 54th Massachusetts under the command of a young white officer, Robert Gould Shaw. Douglass gave two of his sons to the unit. The film *Glory* chronicled the exploits of the 54th Massachusetts, and a sculpture of Shaw and his men adorns Boston Common. On May 28, 1863, the 54th paraded through the streets of Boston en route to the Sea Islands of South Carolina. Just nine years earlier, federal marshals had dragged former slave Anthony Burns through the same streets to return him to his master. Now these black men marched as heroes, off to defend their country and to secure their own rights and privileges under the Constitution.

The 54th Massachusetts distinguished itself in the assault on Fort Wagner in Charleston Harbor in July, though in a losing cause. Shaw fell mortally wounded. When his father requested Rebel officials to ship his body to Massachusetts, a courtesy both sides attempted to honor for high-ranking officers, they informed him that they had thrown his body into a pit with "his niggers." Yet even some Union soldiers interpreted Shaw's death as proof of black incompetence, despite evidence to the contrary. Major Henry Abbott of the 20th Massachusetts wrote to his mother, "Poor Shaw. He was too good a fellow to be sacrificed for an experiment, & an experiment I think that has demonstrated niggers won't fight as they ought."[39]

If only the Confederacy could manufacture 150,000 recruits in a few months. Robert E. Lee was a fine engineer. He understood the math. The rate of attrition through casualties and desertions, the deteriorating standard of living among civilians, and the growing challenges of provisioning the armies added up to impending crisis. Lee wrote an earnest letter to Jefferson Davis after Chancellorsville detailing the difficulties of sustaining the war with diminishing resources. He urged Davis to cultivate the "peace party" in the North as "the most effectual mode of accomplishing [peace]." Alexander Stephens, the vice president of the Confederacy, endorsed Lee's analysis and told Davis, "Were I in conference with the authorities at Washington . . . I am not without hopes, that *indirectly*, I could now turn attention to a general adjustment upon such a basis as might ultimately be acceptable to both parties." The timing, Stephens argued, after the South's victories at Fredericksburg and Chancellorsville, was right.[40]

While the Davis administration mulled over the prospects for peace, Lee took the matter into his own hands. A decisive and dramatic military blow against the North would encourage northern peace advocates and force the Lincoln administration to the bargaining table. For the second time in less than a year, he decided to take the war to the North. Leading the Army of Northern Virginia into Pennsylvania would also relieve Virginia from the devastating warfare that had disrupted the state economy, prevented spring planting, and created a large number of refugees.

On June 16, the Army of Northern Virginia began to cross the Potomac, hoping to reach the Pennsylvania state capital in Harrisburg. A journalist in that city reported a "perfect panic" with citizens fleeing northward on packed trains. The state legislature boxed up everything they could and closed shop. The eroding confidence in the Union cause was apparent, as relatively few Pennsylvanians answered the call to enlist and fight the invading army. They demonstrated much more alacrity in running off their livestock out of Confederate reach.

Lincoln replaced Hooker with Major General George G. Meade. Meade, a tall, scholarly, bespectacled man who looked like "a good sort of a family doctor," was a classmate of Lee's at West Point and had fought alongside Lee during the Mexican War. Lee had counted on Hooker as his opponent. Meade, he noted to an aide, "will commit no blunder in my front." He then added, "And if I make one he will make haste to take advantage of it."[41]

The Confederates marched through Pennsylvania "requisitioning" food, clothing, and precious shoes, as well as greenbacks from local residents. Lee had issued an order forbidding plundering and attacks on civilians, but Confederates issued receipts for the requisitioned items in a currency that was worthless in the North. The Confederate bounty was substantial and included twenty-six thousand cattle and twenty thousand sheep promptly driven into Virginia. A Virginian wrote that he was capturing "horses and cattle by the hundreds" and plucking "anything we wanted in the eating line" from the farms along the way. Confederates also scoured the countryside for blacks, capturing those they found, with no distinction as to whether they were free or runaway slaves. One observer recalled a wagon full of captured blacks, mostly women and children, being driven to Virginia.[42]

In some towns, women jeered at the passing soldiers, held their noses to signify their stench, sang Union songs, waved Old Glory, and remarked how the Confederates resembled Pharaoh's army marching to the Red Sea. The women's conduct shocked officers. "They were not ladies in the Southern acceptation of the word," noted one officer. "They are a very different race from the Southerner."[43]

Meade and the Army of the Potomac moved swiftly through Maryland into Pennsylvania pursuing Lee's scattered forces. When Lee learned of Meade's movements, he ordered three corps to depart for Cashtown on June 29. That the greatest battle of the war would occur at nearby Gettysburg was an accident. The footsore Confederates needed shoes, and a Rebel infantry brigade marched to Gettysburg for that purpose. On July 1, they ran into Union cavalry, who engaged the Confederates while each side sent out couriers for reinforcements. The Rebels pushed the Union troops back through the town.

The Federals took positions outside the town on the high ground of Cemetery Hill, the most prominent feature of the area.

On the morning of July 2, both sides had drawn their battle lines: the Federals' line, in the shape of a fishhook running north to south, extended from Culp's Hill to Cemetery Hill along Cemetery Ridge, which sloped downward and then rose to Little Round Top and Big Round Top. These positions afforded Union officers a panoramic view over the surrounding fields. The Confederates massed about a mile away on a lower promontory, Seminary Ridge, directly across from the Federals, and through the town, a line about four miles in length, compared to the three-mile long Union line, an advantage for the Federals, who could communicate and move troops more quickly over a shorter distance. Lee ordered Longstreet to attack the federal left, the Round Tops, a plan Longstreet opposed. He would rather have gone around the Union left and cut Meade's communications with Washington. Lee remained steadfast in his belief that he must stand and fight at Gettysburg.

Generations of historians have debated whether Longstreet's opposition to the order led him to delay his attack and thus thwart the plan. Delays were common in most major Civil War battles, resulting from poor communication among officers or the difficulty of organizing and massing large numbers of troops on uneven terrain. There is no evidence that Longstreet deliberately dallied, and, in fact, he nearly pulled off a stunning victory. Longstreet's Republican politics after the war, and the desire to deflect criticism from Lee, account for some of the criticism.[44]

The Rebels might have taken Little Round Top were it not for the heroism of the 20th Maine commanded by Joshua L. Chamberlain. Running low on ammunition, the Union soldiers charged down the hill at their startled opponents, who retreated and left the key landmark in federal hands. Two hours later, General Richard S. Ewell attacked the Union right and nearly seized Cemetery Hill before Union troops repulsed the assault. The second day of battle closed with both armies essentially back where they began. Better coordination between Longstreet and Ewell might have resulted in a different outcome. Also, Lee's orders left considerable discretion to his corps commanders, a practice that had worked well with Stonewall Jackson, but less so with Longstreet and Ewell. The absence of J. E. B. Stuart and his cavalry, "the eyes of the army," limited Lee's intelligence on federal troop strength and movement. Stuart had taken off to ride around the Army of the Potomac, as he had the previous year. While he frightened a few Federals and destroyed some supplies, he did not appear at Gettysburg until July 2, almost too late to assist the Confederate cause.

Lee had failed to budge the Union left and right flanks. Believing that the concentration of Union troops on their flanks had weakened the center, he decided to attack there. Lee proposed to throw fifteen thousand Rebels, commanded by Major General George E. Pickett of Longstreet's corps, against the Union center on Cemetery Ridge. Stuart's cavalry would attack the center from the rear. At a midnight meeting with his generals, Meade predicted, "[Lee] has made attacks on both our flanks and failed and if he concludes to try it again, it will be on our center."[45]

At 1:00 P.M., July 3, another hot, cloudless day, Confederate artillery opened up on Union positions. Federal batteries responded in kind. The duel lasted nearly two hours until the federal guns suddenly fell silent. Thinking their artillery had weakened the Union line, the Rebels prepared their assault. Longstreet gave the order at 3:00 P.M., and Pickett and his men marched out of the woods in a line extending a mile and a half. For a moment the Union infantry, now flat on their stomachs, watched in awe as Pickett's men moved forward in perfect formation, their bright red battle flags waving gently in the summer breeze, while the faint strains of "Dixie" wafted down from Seminary Ridge. Two hundred pieces of Union artillery boomed out, cutting huge holes in the Rebel lines, yet still Pickett's men advanced, filling in the gaps and holding their line. Union infantry, protected by a stone wall, one portion of which jutted out at an angle (henceforth known as the Bloody Angle), opened fire. Pickett's men continued forward, now on double-quick through the hail of bullets, balls, and shells, returning the fire.[46]

Union soldiers, watching the destruction before them, cheered wildly and shouted, "Fredericksburg! Fredericksburg!" Some of Pickett's men got close enough to see the sooty faces of the federal infantrymen, and a few breached the wall to engage the enemy in desperate hand-to-hand combat. Federal reserves, however, closed in on the insurgents and pushed them back into full retreat while Union artillery and infantry fire continued to pound the Confederates. In the rear, Stuart never got close to his target. Union cavalry led by twenty-three-year-old General George Armstrong Custer repulsed his attack. The charge cost Pickett two thirds of his army, including every senior officer. Looking across the field of dead Confederate soldiers, Lee muttered, "All this has been my fault." The Battle of Gettysburg was over. Major Henry Abbott of the 20th Massachusetts summarized the feelings of his comrades: "By jove, it was worth all our defeats." On July 4, the remainder of the Army of Northern Virginia filed down from Seminary Ridge and headed for the Potomac, unmolested by Meade's drained troops.[47]

The casualty figures were astonishing, even after Antietam and Chancellorsville. Of the eighty-five thousand federal troops in the battle, there were twenty-three thousand casualties. The Confederacy put sixty-five thousand men onto the field and suffered twenty-eight thousand casualties. The meadow below Cemetery Hill was so strewn with Confederate dead that, as a Union soldier noted, you "could have walked across it without putting foot upon the ground." One soldier tried after an all-night rain. "I was going so fast that when I fell on my face I slid the whole length of this dead body, and a sort of slimy matter peeled off and stuck to my face." Arms, legs, and body parts were scattered across the landscape, with entrails, flesh, brains, and hair sticking to rocks and tree trunks. It took four to five days after the battle to bury the dead. Summer heat bloated bodies and turned them black, emitting a stench that wafted over Gettysburg for days. There was no time for proper interments. Burial parties dug trenches and placed bodies one on top of another. The corpses sometimes ruptured during these maneuvers, worsening the stench. Or they just disintegrated when crews moved them. Identification was often impossible, which is why American soldiers began wearing dog tags in World War I.[48]

Gettysburg, a town of twenty-four hundred residents, now dealt with twenty-two thousand wounded soldiers. A Union nurse described the streets of the town in the days after the battle. "It seemed impossible to tread the streets without walking over maimed men. . . . They lay on the bloody ground, sick with the poisons of wounds, grim with the dust of long marches and the smoke and powder of battle, looking up with wild haggard faces imploringly for succor." Flies, smells, and polluted wells plagued Gettysburg residents until the first frost in October. An estimated six million pounds of human and animal carcasses baked in the summer sun. Relatives of dead soldiers descended on the battlefield in the weeks following the conflict, digging up graves to find their loved ones. Their actions, though understandable, added to the foul conditions in the area. Death also touched the civilian population. Twenty-year-old Jennie Wade was kneading dough to make bread for wounded soldiers when a bullet tore through her front door, and then through her head.[49]

Gettysburg residents attempted to make sense of the carnage through their faith. A Presbyterian minister sermonized that the "bloodstained fields" would inspire everyone to "have their patriotism and gratitude to God kindled anew." For many northerners, the hand of God in the battle was obvious. "Who shall ever stand on these heights which marked the highest tide of the invasion," the *Cincinnati Gazette* wrote of Pickett's failed charge, "without hearing the voice of the Lord, sounding above the din of the well remembered battle, saying: 'Hitherto shalt thou come, but no further.' "[50]

In hindsight, always a better vantage point, Lee had few options at Gettysburg. His army was living off the countryside. Either he had to engage in battle quickly or withdraw. Union forces had superior defensive positions, and frontal assaults against rifled muskets reduced the chances of an attacking army. Even had the Confederates taken Little Round Top or Cemetery Hill, the fighting so decimated their ranks and reserves were so distant that fresh Union troops would have likely overwhelmed the Rebels in a counterattack. Meade, unlike Hooker, gave Lee no opportunity for a flanking maneuver. While Lee regretted the losses, he did not regret the strategy. He wrote to Jefferson Davis at the end of July, "I still think if all things could have worked together it [Pickett's assault] would have been accomplished."[51]

Some officers noted later that Lee looked fatigued at Gettysburg. He confided to Jefferson Davis after the battle, "I sensibly feel the growing failure of my bodily strength. I am becoming more and more incapable of exertion, and am thus prevented from making the personal examinations and giving the personal supervision to the operation in the field which I feel to be necessary." The cocky optimism that followed Chancellorsville had fled. "I believed my men were invincible," he said of his decision to attack Meade's center.[52]

On August 21, the day Jefferson Davis had set aside as a national day of fasting, humiliation, and prayer, Lee issued a proclamation to his troops. He placed the defeat in a theological context as both an explanation and an inspiration to continue the fight: "Soldiers! We have sinned against Almighty God. . . . We have not remembered that the defenders of a just cause should be pure in His eyes, that 'our times are in his hands,' and we have relied too much on our own arms for the achievement of our independence. God is our only refuge and our strength. Let us humble ourselves before him."[53]

For many northerners, the end of the rebellion seemed more imminent now than at any time since the first few months of the war when a false euphoria gripped the North. A new nation would emerge from the conflict, ordained by God. A Baptist minister, preaching in Philadelphia after Gettysburg, connected Revelation to a reborn America. He saw the time coming that the Founding Fathers "pictured and dreamed about, and prayed for. It will come with blessing, and be greeted with Hallelujahs, it will be the Millennium of political glory, the Sabbath of Liberty, the Jubilee of humanity." God and nation were one.[54]

Despite the Union victory at Gettysburg, Lincoln was furious with Meade, who, like McClellan before him, had allowed Lee to escape across the Potomac. "If I had gone up there, I could have whipped them myself," the frustrated president howled. "Our army held the war in the hollow of their hand and they could not close it." Robert Lincoln, home from Harvard, stopped by his father's office and found him "leaning upon the desk in front of him, and when he raised his head there were evidences of tears upon his face." Lincoln dashed off a pointed letter to Meade. Though congratulating him on his "magnificent success," he scolded, "My dear general, I do not believe you appreciate the magnitude of the misfortune involved in Lee's escape. He was within your easy grasp, and to have closed upon him would, in connection with our late successes, have ended the war. As it is, the war will be prolonged indefinitely. . . . Your golden opportunity is gone, and I am distressed immeasurably because of it." Lincoln placed the letter in his desk drawer. He never sent it.[55]

Meade might well have destroyed Lee's army and ended the war if he had pursued the retreating Confederates. Consider, though, that Meade had only recently assumed command of the Army of the Potomac. He was still learning about his corps commanders and officers. His army, after intense fighting in summer heat, was utterly exhausted. As was Meade. He wrote to his wife on July 8, "Now over ten days, I have not changed my clothes have not had a regular night's rest, and many nights not a wink of sleep, and for several days did not even wash my face and hands, no regular food, and all the time in a great state of mental anxiety."[56]

Lincoln's unsent letter to General Meade referred to "our late successes." One day after Pickett's fateful charge, Vicksburg fell to the Federals, dealing a double blow to the Confederacy. On May 14, Grant swept aside General Joseph Johnston's small (twelve thousand men) army at Jackson, destroyed the city's factories and cotton reserves, and bore down on Vicksburg. Pemberton established a ring of forts around the city that provided his troops with strong defensive positions from which they repulsed two attacks by Grant. The Union general then laid siege to Vicksburg, bombarding the city day and night, denying sleep or rest either to the soldiers defending it or its inhabitants. The Federals hurled six thousand shells into Vicksburg every twenty-four hours and an additional four thousand onto Rebel lines. Amazingly, only three civilians were killed during the siege.

To relieve tensions, soldiers on both sides occasionally hailed each other from their entrenchments. "Well, Yank, when are you coming into town?" a Rebel picket would call. In reply, "We propose to celebrate the Fourth of July there." Confederates exchanged tobacco for hard bread. The soldiers engaged in a game of hot potato, lobbing unarmed grenades back and forth to each other. These lighter moments between Americans temporarily alleviated the serious and tragic business of war.[57]

Reinforcements swelled Grant's army to seventy-one thousand men. With such a numerical advantage, Grant would have intercepted any attempt of Pemberton's force to leave the city. Living conditions deteriorated in Vicksburg during the siege, with residents, many of them women and children, taking refuge in caves gouged out from the bluffs and eating rats, dogs, and mules to avoid starvation. The soldiers were no better off and sent Pemberton a petition on June 28 stating, "If you can't feed us, you had better surrender." Pemberton and Grant met on July 3 to arrange the surrender of troops and the city. On July 4, the Rebels marched out and stacked their arms. Union soldiers shared their rations with the starving Rebels. There was no celebration in front of the Confederate troops, just "a feeling of sadness . . . in the breast of most of the Union soldiers," Grant noted, "at seeing the dejection of their late antago- nists." Lincoln, however, permitted himself an exaltation, "The Father of Waters again goes unvexed to the sea." He added, "Grant is my man."[58]

The Confederacy had lacked a coherent strategy for the western theater. Their adoption of a passive defense saved troops but lost key territory. And, whenever a Rebel force ventured an attack, it usually suffered heavy casualties. The loss of Forts Donelson and Henry (and, therefore, of Ken- tucky), the fall of Memphis and New Orleans, and the losses at Shiloh and Corinth cost the Confederates dearly in men, access to the Mississippi River, supplies, and food. Vicksburg was essential to Confederate fortunes in the West. Holding on to Vicksburg kept the Federals out of a major stretch of the river and the Gulf of Mexico and shut off the Old Northwest from using the river as a commercial outlet. The economic impact on the Old Northwest was severe enough that some political leaders there had discussed the possibility of a separate peace with the Confederacy.

Amid the celebrations over Gettysburg and Vicksburg, Lieutenant Quincy Campbell of the 5th Iowa expressed a more sober and, as it turned out, a more accurate view. These Union victories did not prefigure "the fall of the Confed- eracy. Many hard battles are yet to be fought, and months, perhaps years, of fighting stand between us and peace." The war would continue because "the chastisements of the Almighty are not yet ended . . . [T]he nation has not yet been brought down into the dust of humility and will not *let the oppressors go free*. . . . [T]he Almighty has taken up the cause of the oppressed and . . . he will deny us peace until we 'break every yoke' and sweep every vestige of the cursed institution from our land." It would be a sentiment that others, includ- ing Abraham Lincoln, would express during the next two years. Until God was satisfied that the blood had washed away the sin of slavery, the war would continue.[59]

The dual losses threw the Confederacy into the same despair northerners had experienced after Chancellorsville. Deeper, considering the optimism after Lee's great victory over Hooker. As one Confederate official lamented, "Yesterday, we rode on the pinnacle of success. Today absolute ruin seems our portion. The Confederacy totters to its destruction." Across the South crowds congregated at railroad depots and telegraph offices, anxious for news from Gettysburg and Vicksburg, understanding that the war's outcome likely hung in the balance. When the news finally arrived, disbelief mingled with despair. Both peace and independence seemed far off now. A Rebel private captured at Vicksburg wrote, "I see no prospect now of the South ever sustaining itself." And a North Carolina woman wrote to her husband, "The people is all turning Union here since the Yankees has got Vicksburg. I want you to come home as soon as you can." President Davis admitted, "We are now in the darkest hour of our political existence."[60]

As disheartening as the turn of events was for the Confederacy, it did not diminish the will to fight. The prospect of subjugation by the Yankees and the economic and racial consequences that would follow spurred southerners to continue the fight. Private Marion Fitzpatrick of Georgia allowed that the defeats "just fire me up to fight the harder."[61]

While northerners rejoiced, the largest civil insurrection in American history broke out in their midst. The implementation of the March conscription law was the immediate cause of the disturbance on July 13 in New York City. Few working-class New Yorkers, least of all the city's large Irish Catholic population, could afford the three-hundred-dollar exemption fee. The draft was tinder to racial and religious tensions that had simmered in northern cities for years. New York City was a Democratic Party stronghold. Its citizens supported the Union war effort up to a point. They opposed Republican incursions on civil liberties, the party's abolition policy, and its anti-Catholic fringe. The Emancipation Proclamation and the new draft law occurred only months apart. It was one thing to lay one's life on the line for the Union; quite another to liberate blacks who would come north to "steal the work and the bread of the honest Irish." Shippers on the city's docks had employed black strikebreakers the year before, triggering violence. New York's Democratic leaders used the draft and the sagging Union military fortunes in the spring to whip up public sentiment against the Republican administration.[62]

On the morning of July 13, hundreds of workers from the city's docks and construction sites beat copper kettles in front of the provost marshal's office, protesting the draft lottery scheduled to take place that day. A volunteer fire company arrived and obligingly set the office ablaze. That their grievances transcended the draft became apparent when the assaults spread to the homes of Republican politicians and to factories producing war materiel. The rioters burned the building housing the nation's leading Republican newspaper, the *New York Tribune*. The most concentrated and vicious violence occurred against the city's black population. The mob burned the Colored Orphans Asylum to the ground, home to over two hundred orphans, after looting the furniture and supplies. Miraculously, the children escaped without loss of life.

The mob had grown to a small army of thousands of men, women, and children by the afternoon. They attacked, murdered, or lynched any African American they encountered. As younger boys marked black houses by throwing rocks through windows, older boys and men followed, assaulting the residents. Sixteen-year-old Patrick Butler became a mob hero when he helped to lynch a crippled black coachman and then, as the crowd cheered, dragged the body through the streets by the genitals. They threw a black child from a fourth-story window, instantly killing him. A woman cradling an infant no more than a few hours old was set upon and savagely beaten. Several children were torn from their mothers' embrace and their brains blown out. The rioters also killed a sixteen-year-old Irish girl who had protested the violence.

Twenty thousand Union troops fresh from Gettysburg fired howitzers into the crowd, ending the riot, after the mob had its way with the city for three days. The toll included 119 dead, 18 of whom were black (most of the rest were Irish), $5 million worth of property damage, and 3,000 citizens left homeless. The Democratic city council appropriated funds to buy exemptions for all of the city's draftees. Most citizens, though, condemned the mob, often using the same rhetoric as the mob employed against blacks. Jeff Whitman told his brother Walt he was sorry Union troops "did not kill enough" of the Irish. "I am perfectly rabid on an irishman. I hate them worse than I thought I could hate anything."[63]

Resistance to the draft occurred throughout the North, in parts of Ohio, upstate New York, Newark, New Jersey, Chicago, and the mining districts of Pennsylvania. Only in New York City, however, did the protests turn deadly. White southerners took some solace from the riot. In a month of bad news, the insurrection in Manhattan looked like a silver lining. "I see one bright ray in these dark times," Marion Fitzpatrick wrote hopefully. "There was a general insurrection in New York a short time ago, caused by trying to enforce the draft. . . . Now if the Yankees will fight among themselves and let us alone it will please me the best in the world."[64]

The Republican press dismissed the mob as a small number of "thieves, incendiaries, and assassins," ignoring the deep class, racial, and religious divisions that the riot laid bare. Editors painted a halcyon portrait of the working class, noting that the "generally intelligent and industrious, from the laborer of yesterday who is the rich man of to-day to the laborer of to-day who is to-morrow the rich man . . . the true 'bone and sinew'" did not join with the mob. Whether the trajectory of the city's working class ever resembled this saga is questionable. Many Americans, though, including Abraham Lincoln, whose own career reflected these ideals, believed in the story. The disconnection between myth and reality, as the riot demonstrated, was growing and would fracture in the new nation birthed by the Civil War.[65]

The riots also fixed in the minds of many northerners the image of the disloyal and violent Irishman, despite the bravery of the Union's Irish brigade at Fredericksburg and Gettysburg. Some felt that once the Union won the war against slavery, the next conflict would be against the Roman Catholic population. A Union soldier expressed the views of many, writing that Catholics, like slaveholders, were opponents of American values; in fact, "they are the next thing to Slavery."[66]

By late fall, war news had supplanted stories of urban insurrection. The governor of Pennsylvania directed David Wills, a landscape architect, to lay out a formal cemetery for the "fallen heroes" of Gettysburg. Wills invited President Lincoln to make a few remarks at the cemetery's dedication. Edward Everett, former governor of Massachusetts and a silver-tongued orator, delivered the main address. Everett gave a masterful speech on the battle of Gettysburg lasting more than two and a half hours and moving his audience to tears. The president's comments, which followed, contained 272 words. The crowd applauded politely and left the grounds.[67]

Since the 1850s, Lincoln had viewed the conflict between North and South, slave and free, as a moral contest above all. Constitutional issues were important, but the integrity of the Union as a beacon to the world took precedence. The global mission was predicated on the nation's unique grounding in the ideals of the Declaration of Independence. Slavery was the great obstacle in fulfilling the nation's destiny. The Gettysburg Address, simple as it was, articulated the North's moral stake in the war.

The address adopted a biblical cadence, evident from the opening, "Four score and seven years ago." The Founders "brought forth on this continent a new nation, conceived in liberty," recalling the woman of St. John's Revelation who "brought forth a man child who was to rule all nations." Lincoln connected the young men who sacrificed their lives four months earlier "to the proposition that all men are created equal." The Civil War was the ultimate test to determine whether "any nation so conceived, and so dedicated, can long endure." The words of the Declaration of Independence were at the core of the contest. And the men who sacrificed their lives would bring forth a new nation shorn of sin and true at last to the propositions of the founders. Only then would the American experiment be secure.

The men who died on the battlefield had consecrated the ground. What was the task of the living? "That we here highly resolve that these dead shall not have died in vain; that this nation under God shall have a new birth of freedom; and that this government of the people, by the people, for the people, shall not perish from the earth." The "new birth of freedom" derived from evangelical Protestant culture. A nation born again, cleansed of sin.

Lincoln made his case for the sacrifice succinctly. The war was not only about freedom for the unfree, but even more about securing freedom for everyone by saving the only kind of government compatible with equality. He never mentioned the battle, the cemetery, the Confederacy, or the future prospects for the war. The common thread that bound Americans was the national idea dedicated to the unique proposition that all men are created equal. The address was transcendent. It gave meaning to the war and to the sacrifices in its name.[68]

One month later, during the Christmas season, Charles J. and Isaac Tyson placed an ad in a Gettysburg newspaper: "BATTLEFIELD VIEWS: A full set of our Photographic Views of the Battle-field of Gettysburg, form a splendid gift for the Holidays." They were among many engravers, artists, and photographers who sought to capitalize on the Gettysburg name during the Christmas shopping season.[69]

Walt Whitman had seen enough. One day in the fall of 1863, he viewed a line of Confederate prisoners passing up Pennsylvania Avenue under armed guard. He wrote to his mother, "Poor fellows, many of them mere lads—it brought the tears; they seemed our flesh and blood too, some wounded, all miserable in clothing." He could no longer countenance the war no matter what the cause. Whitman's experience had taught him that war was "about nine hundred and ninety-nine parts diarrhea to one part glory; the people who like the wars should be compelled to fight them." One night, at the home of friends, he cried out, "I say stop this war, this horrible massacre of men." William Henry Channing, a Unitarian minister, tried to calm him down. "You are sick; the daily contact with these poor maimed and suffering men has made you sick; don't you see that the war cannot be stopped now?" When another friend added, "The issues are not settled yet; slavery is not [everywhere] abolished," Whitman flew into a rage. "I don't care for the niggers in comparison with all this suffering and the dismemberment of the Union." Whitman took temporary leave from his hospital and government posts and went home to Brooklyn.[70]

The tens of thousands of young men who died on the battlefields and in the hospitals did consecrate a new nation. It remained to be seen whether that new nation would be dedicated to the proposition that all men are created equal, thereby transcending the sectarian and racial prejudices of white Americans, as Lincoln hoped, or whether America reborn would assume a different character. The senselessness of war drove men to rationalize it in religious or political terms. Those who worked in the hospitals, fought on the battlefield, and grieved at home believed they worked, fought, and grieved for a cause greater than themselves. Was there a point, or a time, when the blood would overwhelm the rationalization? Walt Whitman had reached that point by the fall of 1863. So had many other Americans.

Abraham Lincoln had hoped that the blood would enable Americans to transcend their differences, that they would now unite in a nation reborn, under God, indivisible, and grounded in the truths of the founding. That time had not arrived in the fall of 1863. The New York City draft riots, the mixed responses of Union soldiers and civilians to emancipation and to the recruitment of African American troops, and the feeling among many, especially, though not exclusively, in the South, that the black man was somehow responsible for all this misery indicated that transcendence was still elusive. The words of the Declaration of Independence remained an ideal. God had not yet decided to end the conflict. The war would go on.

CHAPTER 13

A NEW NATION

RICHMOND, THE CITY OF SEVEN HILLS, had fallen into a valley of despair. The downward spiral of Confederate military fortunes infected the capital's mood and appearance. The city government, strapped for money and overwhelmed with needs, could not keep up with basic maintenance. Infrastructure crumbled, crime escalated, the homeless population grew, prices soared, and want walked everywhere. Richmond's leading industry was health care. Every spare building became a hospital. The largest hospital, Chimborazo, named after a volcano in Ecuador for an unknown reason, sprawled over forty acres on one of Richmond's hills. Hollywood Cemetery, the city's largest burial ground, perched on another hill. Frequent discourse occurred between the two. In the early months of the war, solemn military funeral processions made their way up to Hollywood, accompanied by a brass band deserving of dead heroes. By the second year of the war, deaths escalated and the ritual ceased.

Civility, for which the Old South was allegedly famous, became another casualty of war in the Confederate capital. Consumers charged that merchants hoarded goods to drive up prices; merchants blamed currency inflation and the deteriorating distribution system; and everyone blamed the government. Confederate impressment policies exacerbated the problem as farmers hid food crops or grew less. A Louisiana farmer confessed he preferred "seeing the Yankees to seeing our cavalry." Regardless of fault, there was genuine distress in Richmond, especially among the working class. A Richmond diarist recorded this conversation. "A poor woman yesterday applied to a merchant in Carey Street to purchase a barrel of flour. The price he demanded was $70. 'My God!' exclaimed she, 'how can I pay such prices? I have seven children; what shall I do?' 'I don't know, madam,' said he, coolly, 'unless you eat your children.'"[1]

Deferential women, another southern staple, could no longer defer starvation. Living without men meant living without livelihood for many women. On the morning of April 2, 1863, a group of working-class women met at a

Baptist church in Richmond. Unable to feed their families, they resolved to march to the governor's mansion to seek redress. Their numbers grew as they walked, joined also by men and boys. A Richmond woman happened on the procession and asked a young girl, "Is there some celebration?" "There is," the girl replied. "We celebrate our right to live. We are starving. As soon as enough of us get together we are going to the bakeries and each of us will take a loaf of bread. This is little enough for the government to give us after it has taken all our men."[2]

The governor met with the women, expressed his sympathy, and wished them a good day. Dissatisfied with the interview, the women produced knives, hatchets, and pistols from their pocketbooks and skirts and proceeded to ransack shops within a ten-square-block area of the capitol. The women then turned their attention to the city marketplace, where a group of reserve Confederate soldiers confronted them. The rioters pulled a wagon across the street as a barricade against a possible assault from the troops. A tall, balding man in a black suit appeared and climbed onto the wagon, tossing all the coins he had into the crowd to get their attention.

Jefferson Davis glanced at the soldiers behind him and turned to the women. "We do not desire to injure anyone, but this lawlessness must stop. I will give you five minutes to disperse, otherwise you will be fired upon." The crowd froze. After a minute or two, the captain of the reserve guard gave the order, "Load!" The women slowly left. Davis ordered the newspapers and telegraph operators to remain silent about the disturbance. The Richmond city council blamed the riot on "outsiders," though the episode prompted them to initiate a program to provide food for the poor at the city's expense.[3]

"Bread riots" spread to cities across the Confederacy from the spring through the fall of 1863. When rumors of impending trouble surfaced in Mobile in September, the local newspaper assured, "There is enough food to carry army and people through to the next harvest." Two days later, a mob surged through the streets of the city bearing signs demanding "bread or blood" and looting shops along the way.[4]

The desperation of the women was evident and understandable. After Greensboro, North Carolina, authorities arrested twenty armed women about to descend on city shops, Nancy Mangum, a member of the group, wrote to Governor Zebulon Vance, "A crowd of we Poor women went to Greenesborough yesterday for something to eat as we had not a mouthful meet nor bread in my house what did they do but put us in gail—I have 6 little children and my husband in the armey and what am I to do?" Other women of higher social standing understood the dilemma. Anne Morehead, relative of a former governor of the state, wrote, "I do not see how our poor women & children are to be fed, & we have so many whose husbands are now in this unholy war, & no hope of its ending shortly."[5]

Poor women, it turned out, had leverage to reduce the Confederacy's ability to wage "this unholy war." As Nancy Mangum put it to Governor Vance, "We wimen will write for our husbans to come home and help us we cant stand it." A Georgia woman watching her daughter growing thinner and thinner, and her son crying out in hunger, wrote to her husband serving in the Army of Northern Virginia, "My dear Edward—I have always been proud of you. . . . I would not have you do anything wrong for the world, but before God, Edward unless yo come hom we must die." Edward came home.[6]

Most letters to the front did not put the choice so starkly. Southern women were aware of society's expectations of them as uncomplaining supporters of their men regardless of the hardships they endured. They could not, however, conceal their emotions or the reality of their situation for long. Marion Fitzpatrick's wife wrote that their children went without shoes and her spinning wheel had broken down with no spare parts available. She tried to make ends meet by killing a hog, but how much of it she should sell, and when, she was uncertain. Her husband could not help. "I am at a loss how to advise you about anything now. Just do the best you can." When she wrote of her loneliness and of how difficult it was to manage a household and a farm, he replied, "You must cheer up and hope for brighter days." The letters gnawed at him. He was helpless. As a man, he should be there to support his family. And he missed them terribly. When his wife wrote that their young son cried out for him, he wept.[7]

Most rural southern women, regardless of class, lived with a sense of foreboding as the war progressed. Deserters and Union armies raided farms. Despite all the brave talk about loyal slaves, women on plantations worried about their safety. Mary Chesnut wrote of her butler, "He looks over my head—he scents freedom in the air." As for the other slaves, "They go about in their black masks, not a ripple or an emotion showing—and yet on all other subjects except the war they are the most excitable of all races." Another plantation mistress admitted she was "always thankful, when morning comes, that the house has not been fired during the night."[8]

The volume of correspondence from southern women encouraging desertion increased as the Confederate war effort faltered and their own misery increased. Several weeks after the fall of Richmond in April 1865, a young man came across a bag in the city's post office crammed with undelivered letters. The vast majority of the correspondence came from women urging men to desert.[9]

The Union army experienced desertion as well. The difference, however, was that the Federals could easily replace a departed soldier. Soldiers extended their furloughs, disappeared, walked home, or were simply unaccounted for among the numerous anonymous battlefield and hospital deaths. The number accelerated in 1863. An estimated hundred thousand Rebel soldiers were absent without official leave by the end of the war. In Alabama, ten thousand armed deserters roamed the northern part of the state. Similar groups existed in Tennessee and North Carolina. Slaves hid deserters, as did wives and extended families. Confederate authorities resorted to brutal interrogations to pry information on the whereabouts of deserters. In North Carolina, Colonel Alfred Pike described the treatment he visited upon one suspect wife, tying "her thumbs together behind her back & suspending her with a cord tied to her two thumbs thus fastened behind her to a limb so that her toes could just touch the ground. . . . I think [then] she told some truth." So much for chivalry.[10]

Women responded to shortages and inflation in ways other than violence. A vigorous barter system emerged. Sorghum substituted for molasses and sugar. Rye, wheat, and peanuts comprised a coffee substitute. Women learned to cure bacon with ashes instead of salt. In an unintentional upgrade, families replaced calomel (basically mercury) as a standard medicine with roots and herbs from the forests. Straw and palmetto became raw materials for hats. As the weather turned colder in the fall of 1863, women lined their old dresses with rags and newspapers to keep the wind out.

Creativity could only go so far. Middle-class women did not typically participate in the bread riots, but everywhere in the urban South, merchants reported an alarming rise in shoplifting. Others sought to drown out the deprivation and death by partying. Kate Cumming reported that her brother, on furlough in Mobile for a week in early 1864, attended a party every night. The *Richmond Enquirer* in February 1864 noted disapprovingly that the city seemed to be a "carnival of unhallowed pleasure" and condemned these "shameful displays of indifference to national calamity." The festivities could only mask the reality temporarily. In early 1864, a Confederate official informed Jefferson Davis that civilian "deaths from starvation have absolutely occurred."[11]

Not all southern women turned away from the war. Phoebe Yates Pember, a young widow from a prominent southern Jewish family, served as chief matron for Richmond's vast Chimborazo Hospital. She wrote to her sister Eugenia, "The feeling here against Yankees exceeds anything I could imagine." She related the conversation at an evening gathering of women. "One lady said she had a pile of Yankee bones lying around her pump so that the first glance on opening her eyes would rest upon them. Another begged me to get her a Yankee skull to keep her toilette trinkets in." Pember told the women she was fortunate "at being born of a nation and a religion that did not enjoin forgiveness on its enemies, that enjoyed the blessed privilege of praying for an eye for an eye. . . . I proposed that till the war is over they should all join the Jewish Church, let forgiveness and peace and good will alone, and put their trust in the sword of the Lord and Gideon."[12]

By early 1864, there were fewer signs of bravado among southern civilians. A woman wrote to the *Montgomery* (Ala.) *Advertiser* in June 1864 that during the early months of the war women had rivaled "the other sex in patriotic devotion," but "Oh what a falling off is there! . . . The Aid Societies have died away. . . . The self-sacrifice has vanished; wives and maidens now labor only to exempt husbands and lovers from the perils of service." "The Confederacy!" Emily Harris confided to her diary in 1864, "I almost hate the word."[13]

Life was different in the North. Walt Whitman had spent the better part of eighteen months shuttling from his office to hospitals in Washington. Heading back to Brooklyn in November 1863 on his self-imposed furlough, he quickly left the war behind. Passing through Baltimore and Philadelphia, he marveled at the scenes out his train window. "It looks anything else but war, everybody well dressed, plenty of money, markets boundless & the best, factories all busy."[14]

When Whitman stepped out of his rail car in Manhattan, the pace of the city nearly overwhelmed him. Southerners had predicted that the loss of the cotton trade would beggar New York. The city scarcely missed a beat. Shipyards boomed, building vessels for the naval blockade. Local contractors and manufacturers supplied the army. Brooks Brothers, a Manhattan clothier already notable for its ready-made clothing, won a contract to provide twelve thousand blue uniforms at $19.20 apiece in four sizes for the state's soldiers. The sewing machines of Elias Howe and Isaac Singer mechanized the garment trade. Shoemaking machines allowed manufacturers to produce several hundred shoes a day instead of the few finished by hand. The city's railroad companies handled record shipments of grain from the West, sending manufactured goods back in the other direction. Crop failures in Europe and the feeding of one million soldiers spurred a lively grain trade. New York became the export center for petroleum, a new industry that emerged after the discovery of oil at Titusville, Pennsylvania, in 1859. Thousands of northern families lit their homes with kerosene lamps during the war, a marked improvement over other forms of illumination such as candles and whale oil. "There never was a time in the history of New York when business prosperity was more general," the *New York Sun* boasted in early 1865.[15]

Cyrus McCormick, the Virginian who revolutionized wheat harvests with his mechanical reaper, moved his factory to Chicago before the war. Taking advantage of greater proximity to wheat and the skilled labor and technology to build his machines, he could not turn out reapers fast enough once the war began. Farmers all over the Midwest, buoyed by the high prices of grains and short of labor, mechanized their operations, gaining efficiency and volume. The nation, including the South, produced 173 million bushels of wheat in 1859. In 1862, the northern states alone exceeded that total.

Had Whitman visited Chicago, he would have seen the western version of New York's energy. The crop bonanza, the need to feed a large army—the beginning of the city's reputation as "hog butcher of the world"—and the line of boxcars heading east generated a construction boom. Chicago shipped twice as much grain and meat east in 1862 as it did in 1860. The *Chicago Tribune* reported, "On every street and avenue one sees new building going up: immense stone, brick, and iron business blocks, marble palaces and new residences everywhere. . . . The unmistakable signs of active, thriving trade are everywhere manifest." Men became wealthy overnight. One enterprising young man, Philip Armour, became a millionaire selling pork to the army.[16]

In the Far West, gold and silver generated an economic surge. The Pike's Peak gold rush of 1859 set off a stampede to Colorado. Two years later, Congress granted Colorado territorial status, and Denver was the nation's newest instant city, a raucous boomtown where every fifth building was a saloon. In Nevada, the Comstock silver strike in 1859 touched off another wave of migration. Nevada became a state in 1864. By then, silver mines had produced $43 million for the U.S. Treasury. Gold flowed from Montana, Idaho, and the Dakotas as well, all benefiting the Union cause.

Quartermaster General Montgomery C. Meigs, a West Pointer and a talented engineer, orchestrated the procurement of government contracts that helped to generate such wealth. Meigs assumed the position when his predecessor, Joseph E. Johnston, joined the Confederacy. The Lincoln administration could not have hoped for a more efficient and honest official to organize a system that dealt with hundreds of firms, large and small, transportation logistics involving trains, ships, and wagons, and attending to quality control and financial issues. By the end of the war, Meigs's department had distributed over $1 billion dollars in U.S. Treasury funds, accounting for over 90 percent of all government spending. Lincoln remarked of his quartermaster general, "I do not know one who combines the qualities of masculine intellect, learning and experience of the right sort, and physical power of labor and endurance as well as he."[17]

Meigs drew on established firms for many of the army's needs. New

England, for example, led the world in small-arms technology. Supplementing the U.S. government's Springfield Arsenal in Massachusetts were the factories of Colt and Sharps in Hartford, Connecticut. For gunpowder, Meigs relied heavily on the Delaware-based firm DuPont. When these companies could not supply weapons fast enough, the quartermaster's office purchased guns from abroad, a vanishing option for the Confederate government, with its devalued currency. The South had few established firms for military ordnance and lacked the technology employed by northern factories. The Davis administration had to build from scratch, a difficult and expensive strategy. The output of the Tredegar Iron Works in Richmond and the artillery firms in Selma, Alabama, was remarkable given the limited resources. But time and money were not on the Confederacy's side. Machines lacked parts, and distribution became increasingly difficult.

The federal government was a willing and enabling partner in many of these enterprises. The Republican-dominated Congress passed a series of measures that transformed the nation's economic landscape for all time. The weakness of the northern Democratic minority and the defection of southern lawmakers enabled Republicans to enact a legislative agenda that significantly expanded the role and financial reach of the government and helped to create a national economy that dwarfed its predecessor both in scale and in wealth.

When Lincoln took office, the main role of the federal government was to deliver the mail. The government also conducted foreign policy, defended the frontier with a small army, and collected import duties, but primarily, Washington was a post office. By the end of the Civil War, the government supported an army of a million men, carried a national debt of $2.5 billion, distributed public lands, printed a national currency, and collected an array of internal taxes. This transformation in national power was not the "new birth of freedom" Lincoln envisioned at Gettysburg, but it overshadowed the liberation of four million slaves in terms of its long-range impact on all Americans.

The Republicans did not set out to establish a strong national state or to facilitate the industrial revolution. They believed strongly in the American dream of hard work and upward mobility. They saw no contradiction between capital and labor, between wealth accumulation and equality. Even in the exigencies of war, they directed their legislation to their political base, the farmers and the small-town merchants. Their vision assumed the virtue of rural and small-town America. The majority of Republicans who enacted the legislation grew up on farms. Yet they created an industrial juggernaut that flung railroads across the continent and grew great cities from seaboard to seaboard that attracted thousands from those small towns and farms. These results must be counted among the most sterling examples of unintended consequences in American history.[18]

The 1862–63 congressional session was among the most productive ever. A number of Republican leaders (including Lincoln) had benefited from western migration. They transformed their personal stories into the Homestead Act that offered 160-acre tracts of public land for a twelve-dollar registration and filing fee. If a homesteader lived on it for five years, built a house, and farmed, he owed an additional six dollars. Owen Lovejoy of Illinois, the "Farmer Congressman," as his constituents called him, introduced the bill. Over time, the act helped to settle 10 percent of the entire land area of the continental United States. Prior to the Civil War, Americans mainly lived east of the Mississippi with outposts along the Pacific Coast. The Homestead Act helped to "fill in" some of the spaces between the Mississippi and the Pacific, knitting a nation together, providing passenger and freight traffic for the coming transcontinental railroad, contributing to the abundance of food for the rising cities, and running off the Indians. Western settlement also stoked the federal treasury. Horace Greeley, the editor who had supposedly offered the famous advice "Go West, young man," wrote, "Every smoke rising from a new opening in the wilderness marks the foundation of a new feeder to Commerce and the Revenue."[19]

The war sparked an interest in science. Lincoln was the first president to hold a patent for an invention. He received a patent in 1849 for devising a series of bellows located in a ship's hold to be deployed to loft the boat over shoals or other obstructions in river beds. The purpose of the invention was to enable new and larger cargo vessels to navigate rivers further upstream than accustomed, thereby reviving the prosperity of river towns. Lincoln built a model to secure his patent but could not raise the funding for a prototype. The telegraph, the sewing machine, vulcanized rubber, the mechanization of agriculture, and the introduction of ready-made clothing and shoes fueled the widespread impression that this was the age of invention. Science and scientific inquiry, efficiency, and professionalism all received boosts from the war effort. Venerable Harvard modified its classical education and introduced the nation's first science curriculum before the war ended.[20]

The Union became a synonym for "modern," and a ready counterpoint to the "unmodern" South. Slavery was not a progressive institution. It was a relic from a bygone era that strangled man's ambition. Herbert Spencer, the British philosopher who would coin the phrase "survival of the fittest," believed that slavery's elimination was emblematic of man's progress. An American admirer wrote to him in affirmation in 1864, "The great slave system . . . had well nigh paralyzed the mind of the nation, but the war has broken the spell." Like the Indian, slavery and the slaveholder were stale mementos from a primitive past that must be eliminated if mankind were to progress.[21]

Congress passed the Morrill Land Grant Act, another measure designed to further science and efficiency. The federal government granted public lands to the states to finance colleges that would offer training in scientific agriculture and the mechanical arts. Justin S. Morrill, a Vermont congressman who had been too poor to attend college, spoke of the bill's benefits in economic terms: "Science, working unobtrusively, produces larger annual returns and constantly increases fixed capital, while ignorance routinely produces exactly the reverse."[22]

Creating the Department of Agriculture fulfilled scientific objectives, too. Lincoln hoped that such a department would generate statistics and publicize best practices that would help not only the farmer but merchants and manufacturers as well. As the *Philadelphia Inquirer* noted in support of the legislation, armed with statistics, the government could reduce social theories "to a certainty. A nation . . . with such analytic self-inspection at periodic intervals might mould its growth, and forecast its future with a knowledge of all the resources and all the forces operating to shape its destiny." Scientific agriculture would also increase crop production to feed the rapidly growing population.[23]

The Lincoln administration employed lavish grants of public lands to finance a transcontinental railroad. Many Americans had dreamed of a railroad spanning the country. Stephen A. Douglas had acted on that dream with disastrous political consequences for himself and the country. With southerners absent from Washington and slavery no longer a sticking point, Republicans resurrected the vision in the Pacific Railway Act of 1862. The Union Pacific Railroad could not afford to build across the vast and lightly populated Plains unless the government subsidized the project with land grants. Republicans viewed the railroad as a military necessity to move troops quickly against the Indians and secure the West for the Union, as well as to stimulate commerce with Asia. The railroad never realized the Asian trade, but it helped settle the West and, like the telegraph, created a country more closely resembling a national state than a series of disparate regions. As one of its congressional advocates observed, "Unless the relations between the East and the West shall be the most perfect and most intimate which can be established," the American "empire" would risk "breaking on the crest of the Rocky mountains." The railroad was part of a broader Republican effort to remake America in the image of the North. "The cultivated valley, the peaceful village, the church, the schoolhouse, and thronging cities"—key elements of northern culture—would spread west, making America "the greatest nation of the earth." The Lincoln administration gave away 158 million acres to railroads during the war.[24]

Giving away land, the federal government had to rely on tariffs and taxes for revenue. In wartime, however, these streams were insufficient. *Harper's* put the matter succinctly in May 1861. "In modern warfare . . . success is won not so much by numbers as by money. The longest purse, in the long-run, infallibly wins the day." While the war on the battlefield tilted toward the Union by the end of 1863, victory was not assured. In finance, however, the federal government was winning handily, as both the ragged Confederate soldiers and the protesting southern women attested.[25]

Among the ways the Republican administration raised money was the passage for the first time in American history of a progressive income tax, raising $55 million during the war. The government also floated large bond issues, sold not to banks but to the general public. The bonds not only raised money to wage the war but also drew northerners closer to the Union cause by giving them a financial stake in victory.[26]

The Treasury Department hired Jay Cooke, a Philadelphia banker, to market $500 million worth of bonds at 6 percent interest to the public. The bonds were redeemable after five years and matured after twenty. The so-called five-twenties were wildly successful thanks to Cooke's effective advertising and his army of agents. At one point, Cooke was selling a million dollars' worth of bonds per day. One out of four northern households invested in the instruments. The bonds, however, were not enough to cover the war's mounting expenses. The army spent over $1 million a month just on forage for its horses, or more than the cumulative federal budget for the first two decades of the nineteenth century.

The Lincoln administration resorted to the printing press and churned out $150 million in "greenbacks" (they were printed on green paper). To heighten confidence in the paper money, the government made them convertible to the five-twenties. The increased flow of gold and silver from the West also helped public confidence. After Gettysburg and Vicksburg, there was such a run on the five-twenties that the Treasury Department had to close the sale. By the end of the war, the Lincoln administration had run up a national debt of $2.5 billion, much of it absorbed by northern citizens.

The National Bank Act of 1863 resurrected the Hamiltonian idea of a national banking system. It established a national currency and permitted the creation of a network of national banks. The banks issued federal greenbacks as well as their own "national" banknotes, driving out the confusing array of state-issued money and increasing the stability of financial markets. Lincoln heartily approved these measures, predicting accurately, "Finance will rule the country for the next fifty years."[27]

All told, the war's direct costs amounted to $6.7 billion. If, upon Lincoln's inauguration, the government had purchased the freedom of four million slaves and granted a forty-acre farm to each slave family, the total cost would have been $3.1 billion, leaving $3.6 billion for reparations to make up for a century of lost wages. And not a single life would have been lost. No one, of course, foresaw the enormous cost of the war in dollars and lives in 1861. Based on the refusal of several border states to agree to a compensation program during the war's early years, it was also doubtful the Lincoln administration would have found willing partners for such a proposal in other parts of the South.[28]

With all this money injected into the marketplace, and contracts for clothing, shoes, food, horses, weapons, ammunition, and transportation let at a dizzying pace, several entrepreneurs launched spectacular careers as financial and industrial moguls. John D. Rockefeller was twenty-one years old when he cast his first presidential ballot for Abraham Lincoln in 1860. At that young age he was already a partner in a lucrative commodity business in Cleveland, Ohio. Mature beyond his years, he had assumed responsibility for his family, as his father disappeared for long periods of time. He sold grain, meat, and other foodstuffs, items that soared in price after the war began. When the war shut down the Mississippi River as an artery of commerce for the Old Northwest, the Great Lakes and the railroads became commercial lifelines for the region. By 1862, Rockefeller's profits topped seventeen thousand dollars annually, a large sum for a small commodity house.

Rockefeller was anxious to invest his profits in other parts of the war-heated economy. Cleveland's proximity by rail to the Pennsylvania oil fields caught his attention. He invested four thousand dollars in a new refining venture, "a little side issue," he called it. The war had stimulated numerous uses for oil. Kerosene lit lamps, physicians applied it to wounds, and the Union army used oil as a substitute for turpentine when the South cut off supplies. Kerosene gained in popularity among Union officers when a reporter noted that General Grant drafted his dispatches by the light of a kerosene lamp in his tent. Kerosene generated a bright light that extended daylight in cities and on farms. Manufacturers of arms, ammunition, and heavy machinery discovered that oil served as an excellent lubricant. In 1865, Congressman and former Union officer James A. Garfield remarked to a colleague, "Oil, not cotton, is King now in the world of commerce." The new greenback currency and the national banking system allowed banks to offer generous credit during the war. Rockefeller took advantage and secured a loan to expand his oil business. By the beginning of 1865, Rockefeller had built Cleveland's biggest oil refinery, one of the largest such facilities in the world.[29]

The artisan shop and the small factory employing a dozen or so operatives were characteristic of manufacturing in antebellum America. The war

Triumph Hill, near Tidioute, Pennsylvania (ca. 1870), was at the center of the oil boom that John D. Rockefeller parlayed into the Standard Oil Company. The photo shows buildings, derricks, and storage tanks.
(Courtesy of the Library of Congress)

demanded volume and speed, which privileged size and technology. Machinery was more important than artisanal skill, and uniformity more prized than individual handicraft. The Civil War did not create the industrial revolution in America; it accelerated it and gave it the shape of what was to come: large, mechanized factories manned by low-skilled workers turning out products for both domestic and foreign markets.

The war also expanded the white-collar middle class: managers, salesmen and clerks to run the railroads, distribute goods, solicit orders, maintain account books, and analyze price trends. The professions, especially medicine and engineering, profited significantly from the war, adding considerably to the knowledge of bridge and railroad construction, surgical practice, and nursing. Union engineers constructed a bridge over the Chattahoochee River near Atlanta more than 740 feet long and 90 feet high in just four days, facilitating General Sherman's capture of that city in September 1864.

The federal government was an active partner with private enterprise in expanding the economy and generating wealth. Government contracts, generous land grants, financial legislation and policy, and tax and tariff legislation contributed greatly to the economic expansion and to the Union war effort. John D. Rockefeller's Cleveland office became an important gathering point for colleagues during the war, and not only to receive the latest news from the front off the telegraph. Rockefeller had installed a telegraph connection in order to react quickly to price changes in oil, commodities, and transportation. The federal government helped Western Union string telegraph wires across America, facilitating contact with armies in the field, and also enabling entrepreneurs like Rockefeller to receive timely information to make their businesses more efficient and profitable.

The working class did not benefit from the wartime economic boom. Labor shortages resulted in rising wages, but not enough to keep up with inflation. Prices rose nearly 80 percent in the North during the war years, wages less than two thirds of that figure. The change in scale and the resort to machinery mitigated labor shortages and reduced dependence on skilled operatives. Women whose husbands were in the service and immigrants suffered hardships during the war. The New York City draft riot originated in part from widespread labor discontent among the Irish immigrant working class. The Lincoln administration brooked no opposition from striking workers, dispatching federal troops to quell labor disturbances in a number of locations. When troops broke up a strike in the Parrott cannon factory at Cold Spring, New York, the administration tossed labor leaders into a military prison. Several states enacted anti-union legislation to prevent workers from organizing.

Despite the general prosperity, it is probable that the condition of working-class Americans was worse at the end of the war than at the beginning. Republicans, including Lincoln, believed in the dream of easy upward mobility and of the harmony of interests between capital and labor. Many Republican leaders had experienced that mobility, but they attained adulthood in a different era. Karl Marx hailed the Union war effort as a "matchless struggle for . . . the reconstruction of a social world." He may have been correct, but not in the way he intended. Northerners pondered the addition of workers, especially immigrant workers, to the list of those, like the Indian and the slaveholder, who stood in the way of inevitable progress.[30]

The economic rush fomented by the war had its seedy side, besides the suppression of labor. Corruption and cronyism had existed before the Civil War, but the stakes were relatively low. With sums of money never seen before flowing to contractors, the temptations were great. Quartermaster General Meigs was an individual of impeccable integrity, but he relied on field officers scattered across the country, some of whom developed cozy relationships with contractors.

It is not surprising that the word "shoddy" made its initial appearance in the American lexicon during the Civil War. The term migrated from England, where it described the adulteration of wool textiles with other materials to reduce costs. Americans employed it during the war to denote both inferior goods and shady military contractors. The first appearance of the term came in connection with federal uniforms that disintegrated in the rain in the summer of 1861. The term became a rallying cry for war critics. A popular poem, "Song of the Shoddy," cited "Coats too large and coats too little / Coats not fitting any body / Jackets, overcoats, and trowsers, / Made of cheap and shameful Shoddy." Critics referred to the manufacturers who perpetrated such frauds as "the shoddy aristocracy." A popular novel published in 1863, *The Days of Shoddy: A Novel of the Great Rebellion in 1861*, by Henry Morford, warned, "The leech has fastened upon the blood of the nation, and it will not let go its hold until the victim has the last drop of blood sucked away. . . . Every swindling shoddy contractor . . . has been a national murderer." The strong language seemed disproportionate to the crime, but the contrast between young men laying down their lives for the Union and merchants profiting exorbitantly from clothing, feeding, and arming those soldiers with inferior goods incensed the public.[31]

The fabulous wealth and ostentation of some of these contractors also contrasted sharply with the struggles of working-class northerners. Seamstresses who made uniforms for the army worked at low wages and endured difficult working conditions. In 1864, Mary Pratt, a leader of Philadelphia seamstresses, declared, "Shoddy has been set on horseback, and fast as he can do so, shoddy is riding to the devil. In order to get there he must ride over our heads. The only way to save ourselves is to stand erect and maintain our rights." The sense of injustice was widespread, and even the Republican press remarked pointedly on the contrast between dying and profiting, as if injecting millions of dollars into the American economy should produce a collection of selfless individuals who peddled sterling products with a profit margin sufficient to sustain only a modest lifestyle. Partying and profiting while men were dying for a holy cause did not seem right, as *Harper's* suggested:

> It is in our large cities especially where this boasted insensibility to the havoc of war is found. It is there in the market-place and exchange, where large fortunes are being made with such marvelous rapidity, and in the haunts of pleasure, where they are spent with such wanton extravagance, that *they don't feel this war.* They are at a banquet of abundance and delight, from which they are not to be unseated, though the ghosts of the hundreds of thousands of their slaughtered countrymen shake their gory locks at them.[32]

Editors proposed draconian measures to deal with these criminals. The *Chicago Tribune*, a Republican newspaper, suggested having "robbery of the army and navy made a capital offence." The *Newark Daily Advertiser* concluded, "The people everywhere demand that the punishment of all offenders in this direction shall be summary and severe." Lawmakers heard the outcry, and Congress passed legislation enabling the government to haul cheating contractors before military rather than civilian tribunals. Between 1863 and 1865, at least a dozen contractors found themselves in these courts.[33]

The outrage far exceeded the reality. Contractors faced tight deadlines, often working at an unprecedented scale, dependent on a workforce subject to high turnover, and at the mercy of suppliers for raw materials. It was undeniable that some contractors made enormous profits and some produced "shoddy" goods. The system worked well for the most part, however, thanks to Quartermaster General Meigs and his staff. The Union army was the best-fed and best-equipped army the world had ever seen up to that time. The civilian population generally prospered, especially the expanding urban middle class and market-oriented farmers. The North fought a war and thrived at the same time. Corruption was hardly a new outcropping on the American landscape. The phrase "spoils system" had a lengthy lineage in the United States. The stuffers of ballot boxes in city elections and on the Plains of Kansas, and the "Buchaneers" of the Buchanan administration who made sweetheart land deals with cronies, were more threatening to democratic institutions than the alleged defalcations of "Honest Abe's" administration.[34]

The source of the outrage lay less in the reality of widespread profiteering than in the rapid economic change that disoriented northern civilians and their assumptions about the egalitarian nature of American society: of the relationship between capital and labor; and of the shared community of interest in prosecuting a holy war in a holy manner. The war, its horribly bloody toll on the battlefield, and the huge profits cascading into boardrooms seemed starkly at odds with the exalted goal of a nation reborn. A nation that prided itself on individual initiative and freedom now confronted the results of that pride. Corruption and outrageous fortunes made for good political theater. It would have many curtain calls in the coming Gilded Age. The reality, though, was much less sinister than the imagined ravishing of Columbia. The reality was that a new nation was emerging and Americans did not know quite yet of what to make of it.

This new nation would not have existed were it not for the Union victory on the battlefield. By the end of 1863, the growing confidence in the North supported bond issues, booming factories, and military enlistments. The draft, which had caused so many problems during the spring and summer, became less relevant. Through the remaining months of the war, volunteers exceeded draftees. In the end, only fifty thousand soldiers entered the Union army via conscription. Gettysburg and Vicksburg had an enormously positive psychological impact on the North at a time when the war was going badly for Union forces. In late fall, another significant Union victory emerged from the mountain fog of southeastern Tennessee.[35]

In late June, after much prodding from Lincoln, William S. Rosecrans moved his Army of the Cumberland against Braxton Bragg's Army of Tennessee, pushing the Confederates back to Chattanooga on July 7. After the victories at Gettysburg and Vicksburg, the campaign in southeastern Tennessee now assumed priority in the Lincoln administration. Defeating Bragg's army and occupying Chattanooga would open the way to the South's last and greatest rail center, Atlanta. And beyond Atlanta lay the rich farmlands of central Georgia, the breadbasket of the Confederacy. Rosecrans did not, however, press the attack against the Rebels. Prodded again, Rosecrans swung around Chattanooga into northwest Georgia, threatening Bragg's supply and communications lines and forcing the Confederates to abandon Chattanooga to protect their lines. Rosecrans took control of the city with a small force.

Bragg may have given up the city, but not the fight. His army attacked Rosecrans at Chickamauga Creek on September 19. According to legend, two Indian tribes had fought a desperate battle at the same place centuries earlier, with great slaughter on both sides. The survivors named the creek Chickamauga, or River of Death. In a reprise of the carnage from the distant past, General James B. Longstreet smashed through the right center of the federal line and seemed poised to destroy Rosecrans's army, most of which retreated toward Chattanooga, but could not budge the remaining federal corps under General George H. Thomas. Thomas's men, running low on ammunition, resorted to clubbed muskets and bayonets to fend off Longstreet's charges, earning their general fame as the "Rock of Chickamauga." That night, Thomas retreated to Chattanooga, where the remaining units of Rosecrans's army hunkered down for a siege. The Confederates for once outnumbered Union forces, sixty-six thousand to fifty-eight thousand men. Both armies suffered losses amounting to 28 percent of each fighting force, losses that the Confederacy could not sustain much longer.

Bragg secured a commanding position above the city on Lookout Mountain and Missionary Ridge, holding Rosecrans's Army of the Cumberland prisoner in Chattanooga. It was Vicksburg in reverse. Rosecrans would either starve or surrender. Within weeks, ten thousand horses had succumbed to starvation. Soldiers dined on hard bread. The weather grew colder, and Rose-crans's men lacked shoes and clothing suitable to the season.

The Union had too many resources to allow the Army of the Cumberland to wither away. Ulysses S. Grant, now commander of all Union forces from the Mississippi River to the Appalachians, dispatched four divisions to rescue Rosecrans. Two corps from the East under the command of a rehabilitated Fighting Joe Hooker also repaired to Tennessee. Grant forged a precarious lifeline into Chattanooga along the Tennessee River and provisioned the city. Bragg waited on his mountain. Down below, a Union soldier watching the bluecoats pour into camp struck up a popular tune, and soon a chorus of thousands joined him: "We'll rally round the flag, boys, we'll rally once again / Shouting the battle cry of Freedom." The October woods were golden, and now, suddenly, so were Union fortunes.[36]

With Bragg content to roost on his perch, and Union forces growing daily below, Grant took some time one day to reconnoiter along Chattanooga Creek. Confederate and Union pickets faced each other across the creek, periodically conversed, and often met on a log thrown across the creek from which both sides drew water. When Grant rode up, a Union picket called out, "Turn out the guard for the commanding general." A while later, a Confederate picket shouted, "Turn out the guard for General Grant," and saluted him. Grant rode up to the log, where he engaged a blue-clad soldier, asking him whose corps he belonged to. The lad, touching his cap in respect, replied politely, "General Longstreet's corps, sir." By this point in the war, Confederates wore any decent garments they could get their hands on, regardless of color.[37]

With the situation in Tennessee stabilized for the moment, and the fall elections going favorably for the Republicans, Lincoln took some time off on the evening of November 9 to indulge in his beloved pastime, the theater. He saw The Marble Heart, starring one of his favorite actors, John Wilkes Booth. The president was so taken with Booth's performance that he invited him to dinner at the White House. Booth declined.

Jefferson Davis, concerned about the concentration of federal troops near Chattanooga, visited Bragg. The president suggested that Bragg send Long-street to attack Ambrose Burnside at Knoxville to regain east Tennessee for the Confederacy while also diverting some of Grant's troops from Chatta-nooga. Grant, however, was too wily to go off chasing Longstreet. On November 24, Grant decided it was time to break the siege of Chattanooga. He sent Hooker to attack the Rebel positions on Lookout Mountain, but Fighting Joe and his men quickly disappeared into a heavy morning fog. All that the commanders on both sides could see of the battle was flashes of red light. When

Westward the Course of Empire Takes Its Way, by Emanuel Leutze (1818–1868). (Also known as "Westward Ho!") The German-born American painter completed this composition in 1861 on the eve of the Civil War. It is the apotheosis of Manifest Destiny, depicting the westward advance of European Americans across the continent as a divinely inspired mission. Note Moses and the Israelites on the painting's borders emphasizing this point. *(Smithsonian American Art Museum/Art Resource, NY)*

The popularity of *Uncle Tom's Cabin* transcended the sale of books to include plays, prints, and memorabilia. Here Eva, perhaps the book's most beloved character because of her innocence and goodness, confesses to Topsy, "I love you because you haven't had any Father, or Mother, or Friends.—because you've been a poor abused child!" The book resonated with people around the world precisely because it presented the issue of slavery within the context of family, a context everyone understood. *(Library of Congress)*

Fate of the Rebel Flag, c. 1861. Artists often used fire to depict apocalyptic events, either as a destructive or as a cleansing force. Here the mast and riggings of a sinking ship are aflame in the pattern of the Confederate national flag. *(Library of Congress)*

The Uprising of the North, by Thomas Nast (1840–1902), c. 1867. Though painted after the war, the image replicates northern feeling at the outset that the conflict was a crusade—note the soldiers are dressed as medieval knights. Here Nast uses flames to illuminate Liberty and as beacons to guide the way to the West and, ultimately, to a cathedral-like Capitol building lighting up the night sky. *(Library of Congress)*

Pickett's Charge as depicted in the Gettysburg Cyclorama, a massive 360-degree, three-dimensional painting by French artist Paul Philippoteaux (1846–1923) first displayed at the battlefield in 1884. The work captures the spectacle but little of the horror of the ill-fated Confederate assault. *(Gettysburg Foundation)*

The Rival Sunday Shows in Brooklyn, 1878, by Joseph F. Keppler (1838–1894), a popular Austrian-American cartoonist of the era. This cartoon would have been unthinkable before the Civil War. By the 1870s, Henry Ward Beecher's homilies had become so devoid of spirituality that they became a caricature, reflecting the reduced currency of evangelical Protestant religious fervor. On the left, Thomas DeWitt Talmage, a Brooklyn entrepreneur, is trying to entice customers toward his Museum of Monstrosities. On the other side, Beecher holds up a sign, "Here you are! Solid junks of religion." Keppler was as skeptical about what passed for science as what passed for religion. *(Library of Congress)*

The World's Greatest Railroad Scene, 1882. Despite the devastating fire of 1871, Chicago rebounded quickly and used its strategic location as a transportation and communication hub to capture the growing abundance of the West and ship it to the markets of the East. The Illinois Central Railroad logo and routes are superimposed on a global map of the United States. *(Library of Congress)*

Broadway looking north from Fulton Street, New York City, 1875. New York was the great American postwar metropolis—the center of commerce, finance, and innovation. It drew newcomers from across the country and the globe and epitomized the boisterous optimism after the Civil War that opportunity in the new nation was boundless. *(New York Public Library)*

Bicycling, 1887. By the 1870s, the growing urban middle class had sufficient time to take up leisure activities, especially those connected with athletics and the outdoors. These activities typically included women and children, as well as men, and cycling became one of the most popular family athletic pursuits. Note, however, in this print, the woman rides the three-wheeler while the men have what were called "high-wheelers." *(Library of Congress)*

The Great East River Suspension Bridge, 1877. What we now call in more pedestrian fashion the Brooklyn Bridge became an icon for the age of steel, architectural innovation and beauty, and the ability of technology to conquer nature. *(Library of Congress)*

The Lost Cause, attributed to Henry Mosler (1841–1920), 1868. Here a broken Confederate veteran returns home and discovers his house in ruins and his family gone. Around such melancholy scenes and memories, the myth of the Lost Cause took root. *(The Johnson Collection, Spartanburg, SC)*

From the Plantation to the Senate, 1883. Although only a few of the black political leaders depicted here actually served in the U.S. Senate, and fewer still jumped from plantation slavery to high political office, the point is the remarkable strides made by African Americans as a result of the ballot. By the time this lithograph appeared, however, southern laws and customs had stopped those strides dead in their tracks. (*Library of Congress*)

American Progress, by George A. Crofutt, 1873, based on John Gast's original painting of 1872. The title of this painting highlights the shift in American perceptions of the West after the Civil War as not only the fulfillment of God's plan but also as a triumph of technology and democracy. Note the railroads and the telegraph poles, the Indians conveniently moving out of the picture on the left, and the woman known variously as "Liberty" and "America" holding a Bible in one hand and stringing the transcontinental telegraph system and guiding the procession from above with the other. As another hallmark of the era, Crofutt used this painting to promote his overland tour business. *(Library of Congress)*

The Sunny South, 1883. This lithograph presents the South as an idyllic environment enveloped in harmony and productivity. The scene could have come from a time before the Civil War, which is how white Americans came to view the South in the decades after the war, despite the reality to the contrary. *(Library of Congress)*

the fog dissipated in the afternoon, the sunlight shone on a scene of retreating Rebels and pursuing Federals in what came to be known as the Battle Above the Clouds. Hooker's men planted the American flag atop the mountain, and a band played "The Star-Spangled Banner." The victory cleared the way for the main federal assault on Missionary Ridge.[38]

General William T. Sherman and the Army of Tennessee attacked the Ridge on November 25, marching against Bragg's right flank. The depleted Rebels held their ground. Grant ordered four divisions of the Army of the Cumberland, now commanded by George Thomas, to mount a diversionary attack on Confederate rifle pits at the base of the ridge to relieve pressure on Sherman's forces. Thomas's divisions took the rifle pits and then, with no orders to do so, charged up the steep, boulder-strewn grade of Missionary Ridge in the face of Rebel artillery fire and routed the astonished Confederates. Bragg's headquarters stood on top of the ridge. The Rebel general made a quick exit, mounted his horse, and rode full-tilt down the other side of the ridge and out of his command. Bragg had never been a favorite either among his fellow officers or with the common soldier. He was officious and quarrelsome and did not take criticism well. He alienated everyone except for Jefferson Davis. But even Davis did not possess unlimited patience with the man soldiers claimed had "the iron hand, the iron heart and the wooden head." Davis replaced him with Joseph E. Johnston.[39]

Sherman's opposition retreated. The federal armies could now enjoy Chattanooga. Burnside held off Longstreet at Knoxville long enough for Sherman to arrive and lift that siege. More important, the Federals broke a key east-west rail connection. The road to Georgia now lay open for the Union armies. Yet Bragg's army was mostly intact. Grant's men were too exhausted to pursue the retreating Rebels.

Hooker's crucial assault on Lookout Mountain might never have occurred, or the results could have been very different, were it not for the growing efficiency and centralization of power in Washington. Under normal conditions, it would have taken a month to move Hooker's forces from the East to Chattanooga. The federal government, however, commandeered the railroads and transported Hooker's twenty thousand men and three thousand horses and mules from Virginia to Tennessee in a mere seven days. Contrast that with Longstreet's circuitous journey westward to join Bragg, which required nineteen railroads and six weeks of travel. Timing and the speed of troop movements were crucial variables in determining the outcome of battles. By late 1863, the Union had the logistical support to effect the rapid redeployment of its armies.

The Tennessee campaign was over. The men of the Union armies threw

worn clothing they had not washed for over a month into huge kettles of
boiling brine. Some of the more hardy soldiers dipped in the icy waters of
the Tennessee and scrubbed dirt, lice, and everything else off their bodies
by a roaring fire. They looked forward to a winter of rest, lodged in their
cozy log cabins with a fireplace, where they could play cards or read dime
novels to their heart's content. Once a week a band came through to spon-
sor a "gander dance," at which soldiers taught each other the latest steps,
tying handkerchiefs on the arms of the men who were to be girls. Sherman
had requisitioned all of the railroads in the region, ensuring a steady supply
of rations. One hundred and twenty ten-ton carloads of supplies arrived
each day, and the mail came and went on a regular basis. When the snow
fell and the creeks froze in Tennessee, the soldiers huddled under comfortable blankets and overcoats. They drank real coffee in the morning. The
Union war machine, at least in this theater, operated with great efficiency.
Photographers and topographers went out in advance of the army to map
the terrain. If a stream or river needed crossing, pontoniers would throw
a makeshift pontoon bridge across the water. Engineers repaired damaged
railroads with lightning speed. When news arrived that Confederates had
wrecked a tunnel behind the federal lines, a Rebel prisoner told his comrades, "It's no use, boys, Sherman's sure to carry a duplicate. The thing's
all fixed by now."[40]

Constructing Telegraph Lines, April 1864.
(National Archives and Records Administration)

Confederate quarters in the brutal winter of 1863–64, when temperatures dropped below zero even in the Lower South, were not as comfortable. Patchwork tents housed the common soldier, and neither horses nor cows had much meat on them. For those fortunate to possess an overcoat, it was likely threadbare by this time. The prized possessions consisted of canteens, haversacks, writing paper, and clothing from dead Yankees or prisoners. Rags and newspapers were stuffed into boots to provide warmth against the cold. Hard meal bread and bacon washed down by something called coffee made from parched corn kernels comprised the common meal. The Confederates had maps, but they were mostly outdated. Reading material, unless filched from a Union soldier, consisted of letters and newspapers, at least until newsprint and paper ran out.[41]

The Rebels knew the contrast between their situation and that of the enemy. They took prisoners and they rifled haversacks of the dead. When Jefferson Davis reviewed the troops on Missionary Ridge, some soldiers called out, "Send us something to eat, Massa Jeff." Sam Watkins of Bragg's Army of Tennessee reported that he and his comrades were "starved and almost naked, and covered all over with lice and camp itch and filth and dirt. The men looked sick, hollow-eyed, and heart-broken, living principally upon parched corn, which had been picked out of the mud and dirt under the feet of officers' horses." These were the men sent into battle against Grant's armies. When Joseph Johnston took over command of the Army of Tennessee, he found a force depleted by desertion, perhaps in the thousands. Watkins admitted, "The morale of the army was gone. The spirit of the soldiers was crushed, their hope gone. The future was dark and gloomy." The federal soldiers lived and looked like they were winning the war.[42]

Recognition from the European powers, promising in the spring, now seemed further away than ever for the Rebels. Confederate battlefield reverses damaged the Davis government's credibility abroad, but European realpolitik hindered the Rebels' diplomatic objectives as well. The elite of both Great Britain and France could barely conceal their delight at the possible breakup of a rival nation. Throughout the war, however, they were constrained by the realities of European politics. The staunchest supporter of the Union cause was Russia. That the most despotic regime on the continent supported the most democratic nation on earth was strictly a matter of self-interest. The Russians viewed a united America as an effective rival to their perennial enemies, France and England. When the Russian Atlantic and Pacific fleets called on New York and San Francisco, respectively, in 1863, many observers interpreted the maneuver as a signal of support for the federal navy and a warning against

British or French intervention. In truth, the tsar wished to remove his fleet from Russia's ice-bound harbors for the winter in case tensions with Great Britain escalated into war.[43]

The British and French positions were of vital interest to the Confederacy. Early in the conflict, both countries recognized the Confederate States of America as a belligerent, which enabled the Davis administration to obtain loans and munitions. When a U.S. naval ship intercepted a British vessel carrying two Confederate envoys and detained them, British authorities threatened retaliation and sent two troop vessels to Canada to support their claim. The Lincoln administration wisely apologized and released the captives. The crisis passed.

The Confederacy was never able to gain recognition from Britain and France as an independent nation. The European powers feared American reprisal, and the military situation of the Confederacy deteriorated after the losses at Gettysburg and Vicksburg in July 1863. Also, Europe experienced a number of short grain crops and now relied increasingly on shipments from the North.

The French would not intrude into the American conflict without the British, though they managed to make trouble elsewhere, invading Mexico in 1862 over the alleged nonpayment of a debt and installing Maximilian of Austria as emperor. They were confident that the Americans, engaged in a civil war, would not interfere. When the Civil War ended in April 1865, the Lincoln administration massed troops at the Mexican border as a warning, and the French withdrew. Mexican nationalists overthrew Maximilian and established a republic in 1867.

Though the British aristocracy favored the Confederacy, the middle and working classes championed the Union cause, especially once emancipation became a war aim. Even the textile workers who suffered from the cessation of the cotton trade supported the Union cause. A statue of Abraham Lincoln graces a square in the center of Manchester, England. The inscription on the pedestal reads in part, "This statue commemorates the support that the working people of Manchester gave in their fight for the abolition of slavery during the American Civil War."

Despite the Confederacy's diplomatic reverses, the result of the war was not foregone in that bitter winter of 1863–64. The Davis government had substantial armies in the field and the will to continue the fight. The Rebels, though, no longer confronted the same enemy they had battled earlier in the war. Behind and in support of the Union forces loomed a new nation. A nation energized and inspired by the war's ideals, fueled by the prosperity of factories, railroads, technology, and entrepreneurial endeavors, and coordinated by a government stretching its influence across the vast continent. The South had changed as well from the war's outset. States bound together by slavery had forged a national government, a national currency, a national army, and national legislation to prosecute the war. They had not yet, however, forged a nation. The conflict between North and South had transformed from a conflict of regions to a war between insurgents and a nation, between yesterday and tomorrow. Now, the South battled America.

CHAPTER 14

WAR IS CRUELTY

WAR REVERSED THE SEASONS. Soldiers looked forward to winter as a time of regeneration. Spring brought death. The men settled in winter quarters could not know that the spring of 1864 would also mark a change in the rhythm of the conflict. Relentless, unforgiving war lay ahead. Had they known, perhaps the soldiers would have cherished their time in camp. Maybe they would have tolerated better the bitter cold, incessant lice, constant diarrhea, ranting preachers, and crashing boredom. As it was, the soldiers appreciated their sabbatical from death well enough. They appreciated the regular mail from home, and the food and clothing that often accompanied the letters. And every winter everyone hoped for the end of the war. That hope spurred rumors, and those rumors produced more hope. Marion Fitzpatrick, in winter quarters with Lee's Army of Northern Virginia, wrote to his wife optimistically, "It is prophesied by a good many that this cruel war will end before a great while and then we will all get furloughs." He added, "I long for the time to come when I can return to you and my darling boy."[1]

Confederate and Union troops sometimes established winter quarters near each other, adhering to a gentleman's agreement not to fight during this season of renewal. On one cold, clear night, Union troops camped in Tennessee lifted their spirits and voices in patriotic song, accompanied by regimental bands. Bands on the Confederate side of the river struck up competing songs. Before long "Yankee Doodle" battled with "Dixie," and "The Bonnie Blue Flag" answered "Hail, Columbia." As the evening wound down and the campfires glowed to embers, the Union bands played "Home, Sweet Home." The Rebels joined in, and the bitter enemies raised their voices into the star-splashed sky till they were one.[2]

Some fortunate soldiers obtained furloughs during the winter hiatus. Henry Abbott of the 20th Massachusetts enjoyed a two-week leave over Christmas. Images of a cozy holiday season abounded in the North, reflecting the good news from the front. Thomas Nast, the Union's most popular cartoonist, debuted the jolly figure of Santa Claus in the pages of *Harper's Weekly*. His drawing "Merry Christmas" depicted a wife welcoming home her soldier-husband for a brief visit. The children are excited to see their father, especially as he is bearing gifts. The hearth burns brightly, and the home exudes a happy middle-class prosperity. The poignancy of the drawing lay in the realization to all who viewed it that the joy would be temporary. And so was Abbott's visit. Upon leaving, he "broke down and wept like a child." It was the last time Abbott would ever see his family. He was killed four months later.[3]

The longing for peace mixed with a resolve to fight until the war's objectives were achieved. The protection of home and family continued to motivate the Confederate soldier. Federal soldiers persisted for the cause of the Union, and many embraced the idea of freedom as well. Home and family also motivated the Federals, though usually framed by the notion that saving the Union would secure both. All agreed that the war was transformative. New York private John Foote wrote, "By war, God is regenerating this Nation."[4]

God hovered over winter quarters as He had over the battlefield. By early 1864, however, the religious meaning of the war was more complex for soldiers on both sides. Skepticism about God's role, if indeed He had a role, had grown since First Bull Run. Nearly three years of battle and blood led to deeper soul-searching. A wave of religious revivals swept over Confederate camps that winter. Military reverses and mounting casualties drove the Rebels to interpret events within the context of their faith. If the Confederacy was waging a holy war, why were they losing? The preachers reminded the men that God gave victory to the Chosen People often at the darkest hours and against overwhelming forces. Ministers cited Judges 6:13: "If the Lord be with us, why then is all this befallen us?" The text concerned the story of Gideon, one of the judges of Israel, weak in faith and convinced he is both unworthy and unready to lead his people to certain destruction against a force of overwhelming odds. "Surely I will be with thee," God assures, "and thou shalt smite the Midianites as one man." With a force of only three hundred men, Gideon defeats the Midianites, who, in a reassuring coincidence, attacked the Israelites from the north.[5]

To ensure victory, ministers stressed, southern soldiers and civilians must live more righteous lives. Their faith must not flag in the face of adversity. Confederate defeats and hard circumstances resulted from both a weakness in faith and a failure to expiate sin. This was a difficult demand for soldiers and families who had already made great sacrifices. Jefferson Davis proclaimed days of fast and humiliation so southerners could atone for their sins and re-dedicate themselves to their holy war. In his October 1864 fast day proclamation, Davis wrote, "And let us not forget that, while graciously vouchsafing to us His protection, our sins have merited and received grievous chastisement."

Some southerners greeted Davis's exhortations with cynicism. They wondered how the president's fast days differed from any other day in the Confederacy late in the war.[6]

The mounting carnage turned soldiers and civilians away from theological explanations, if not from their faith. Kate Cumming reported in 1864 that religious revivals in her hometown of Mobile, Alabama, had fallen flat. Sam Watkins mocked the self-righteous preachers who visited the Army of Tennessee in the winter of 1863–64. Clergy commented on the falling away of piety among Confederate soldiers by 1864. The "deep, intense, religious fervor soon changed to indifference; and I certainly saw nothing and heard nothing of an out-door prayer-meeting or a conversion among the cavalry during the last year of the war," one said. A southern minister lamented, "At the beginning of the war, every soldier had a Testament in his pocket; three years later there was not a half dozen in each regiment." Did the loss of piety invite God's wrath, or vice versa?[7]

Given the rise in northern fortunes, Union soldiers should have thanked God for their success. Bloodshed, however, raised the level of skepticism in federal ranks as it had among Confederates. Ministers, like their counterparts in the South, regretted lapses in piety. Soldiers tossed away Bibles ("bibles and blisters didn't go well together," one soldier explained) and showed open disdain for preachers. Theodore Lyman of the Army of the Potomac dismissed a minister he encountered in Petersburg, Virginia, in 1864. "He was like all of that class, patriotic and one-sided, attributing to the Southerners every fiendish passion; in support of which he had accumulated all the horrible accounts of treatment of prisoners, slaves, etc., etc., and had worked himself into a great state." Righteous retribution would have a short season in the remaining year of the war. Soldiers wanted to get the job done and go home.[8]

These comments represented less a loss of faith—America was a religious nation—than a belief that God did not have His hand in this bloody war. Rather than the personal, interventionist God of evangelical Christianity, this Supreme Being was more detached and more inscrutable. Soldiers maintained their personal piety even as they grew increasingly skeptical of God's role in the war. Any soldier who participated in battle and looked out over the field afterward found it difficult to fathom what God had in mind. "War is cruelty, and you cannot refine it," General William T. Sherman declared. He advised his men not to look for God on the battlefield. "When preachers clamor . . . don't join in, but know that war, like the thunderbolt, follows its own laws, and turns not aside even if the beautiful, the virtuous and charitable stand in its path."[9]

If God was out of it, then what was the purpose of all this misery? Soldiers and their families could not believe they were fighting for nothing. Not after the sacrifices, the deaths, and the pain. Secular meanings—the Union, independence, family, freedom—were lofty enough, even stripped of holy anointment. Yet a weariness had tarnished even these exalted objectives by the winter of 1863–64. A Union general's wife asked, "What is all this struggling and fighting for? This ruin and death to thousands of families? . . . What advancement of mankind is to compensate for the present horrible calamities?"[10]

If the answers were elusive in the camps, they were even less clear in places where soldiers languished in more horrid conditions. The battle for life over death continued in the hospitals. The contest was more desperate in the military prisons. If it was difficult to imagine a divine presence on the battlefield, it required an immense leap of faith to think of a God who would countenance a Civil War prison.

A large army lived in prisons. More than 410,000 soldiers (200,000 Union and 210,000 Confederate) spent time as forced guests of the enemy. Of these, 56,000 died, mostly from disease. These deaths accounted for nearly 10 percent of all fatalities during the war. This tragedy, like the war that spawned it, was avoidable. In July 1862, Union General John A. Dix and Confederate General D. H. Hill concluded an agreement to exchange prisoners on a systematic basis. The pact worked well for more than a year until black troops entered the Union ranks. The Davis administration announced that it would not exchange black prisoners of war or their white officers. The Lincoln administration, in turn, declared that it would halt all prisoner exchanges.[11]

Union authorities stood on the high moral ground, but the cessation of exchanges benefited their military operations more than their mortal souls. The Confederacy, strapped for manpower, could ill afford the loss of tens of thousands of soldiers from their ranks. Federal forces, on the other hand, easily replaced those taken prisoner with new recruits. General Grant rationalized the issue, admitting that "it is hard on our men held in Southern prisons not to exchange them, but it is humanity to those left in our ranks to fight our battles. We have got to fight until the military power of the South is exhausted, and if we release or exchange prisoners captured it simply becomes a war of extermination."[12]

The result of the end of exchange was severe overcrowding, rampant disease, inadequate food and clothing, and sadistic treatment by overworked guards. Given the Union's greater resources, its prisons should have provided better conditions for their Confederate captives. Neither side, however, was willing to invest beyond the bare minimum in its prison system. The death rates were roughly comparable, with 15.5 percent of Union prisoners in Confederate custody dying and a 12 percent mortality rate among Confederate inmates. No other prison had as high a mortality rate as the notorious Andersonville, where 29 percent of the Union inmates perished. At Elmira, the worst Union facility, the death rate stood at 24 percent.

Letters from POWs on both sides told similar stories. Louis Leon, a Confederate soldier confined at Elmira, wrote of a bustling trade in dead rats to supplement meager rations, and of a "frightful" smallpox epidemic that took away twenty men a day. A Rebel prisoner at Point Lookout, Maryland, documented his food ration consisting of "crackers as hard as flint stone, and full of worms." He fixed the blame on the respective governments: "Dam Old Abe and old Jeff Davis," he wrote, "dam the day I 'listed."[13]

George Comstock, a Union soldier held at Belle Isle near Richmond, worried, "It is a stiff battle now against insanity. We are so hungry." Another resident of Belle Isle, J. Osborn Coburn, wrote in his diary a common question among his comrades: "Why does a just God permit them to continue evil doing? We are literally freezing and starving. . . . We must have something done or all shall perish in a little while."[14]

Fifty-eight miles below Macon lay the south Georgia town of Anderson. It consisted of five buildings: a church without a steeple, a tiny railroad depot, a shed that served as the county post office, and two dwellings. Nearby a new town took shape, mainly to serve a Confederate prison. Forty buildings rose from the dirt in early 1864, including homes for officers, hospitals, and storehouses. A stockade twelve feet high went up, enclosing a pleasant area of thirty acres covered with trees. The trees soon disappeared; all that remained when the Union prisoners arrived was a large open space with no shelter other than what the inmates could provide for themselves, though abundant pine forests surrounded the camp. Digging holes, erecting shelters from bits of cloth, sticks, and mud, or merely suffering the elements, from the blazing hot Georgia summer sun to the bone-chilling, damp winters, the prisoners, forty thousand in a facility built to hold about ten thousand, did the best they could. The Rebels named this place Andersonville.[15]

Inside the stockade, guards set off an area twenty feet from the inner wall. This marked the "dead line," a common feature in prisons on both sides. If an unfortunate prisoner staggered beyond the boundary, Rebel sentries opened fire. On more than one occasion, the body remained where it fell, devoured by rats, as a warning to any who might contemplate escaping. Any guard who killed a Union prisoner trespassing over or even near the dead line received a two-week furlough.

A stream ran through the prison, quickly becoming a fetid sewer. The prisoners drew their drinking water from it; they also emptied their bowels into the sluggish channel, having no other choice in the crowded conditions. By the summer of 1864, the stream was a black slash through the sandy dirt of the prison, reeking of excrement and swarming with flies. They would go without water. Those too weak to make it to the dried streambed relieved themselves where they slept. They died covered with grime and filth, emitting an unimaginable stench that was multiplied by the number of fatalities. Private Charles Mosher recalled one unfortunate prisoner "with not only the lice and fleas feeding on him, but out of every aperture of his body the maggots were crawling."[16]

The death rate was so high that summer—one man every eleven minutes on some days—sixteen thousand overall—that Rebel guards relaxed discipline as long as the prisoners avoided the dead line. Frank Bailey of the 6th Pennsylvania Reserves saw comrades dying "like dogs." Another confided to his diary, "It is plain to me that all will die." Some soldiers deliberately stepped over the dead line as a quick dispatch from their misery. Rumors circulated that Captain Henry Wirz, the Swiss immigrant who commanded the facility, shot inmates near death to expedite the process and make room for newcomers. Occasionally, the men would catch a glimpse of a wagon parked outside the prison's main entrance, weighed down with stripped Yankee corpses stacked on top of each other, rigid as logs, and covered with black flies. The wagons carried the bodies to a ditch some distance from the camp, where they were tumbled out and covered with a thin layer of dirt.[17]

The prison shocked visitors, but they rationalized what they saw as the fault of federal authorities. Kate Cumming visited Andersonville during that fatal summer of 1864. She admitted, "My heart sank within me at seeing so many human beings crowded so closely together." As for culpability, she had no doubts: "O how I thought of him who is the cause of all this woe on his fellow-countrymen—Abraham Lincoln. What kind of a heart can he have, to leave these poor wretches here? . . . To think of how often we have begged for exchange; but this unfeeling man knows what a terrible punishment it is for our men to be in northern prisons, and how valuable every one of them is to us. . . . May Heaven help us all! But war is terrible."[18]

The absence of an exchange agreement provided a good cover for both sides to disavow deliberate mistreatment. The situation of prisoners, even prior to the breakdown of exchanges, however, was scarcely better. Neither side was equipped to absorb and maintain the volume of prisoners that the war generated. Franklin Dick, in charge of a Union prison in St. Louis, wrote to his commander in Illinois in November 1862, pleading for relief. "The military prisons here are overcrowded and sickness prevailing amongst the prisoners and is rapidly increasing." Dick reported that large numbers of sick and dying men lay on the prison floor. He appealed unsuccessfully to the commander to remove a group of prisoners across the river to Illinois.[19]

Everyone in the Andersonville stockade knew of Dr. White, the chief surgeon. The smallest wound, a splinter or even a scratched mosquito bite, could lead to gangrene, at which point Dr. White would perform an amputation, sawing off limbs without anesthesia or a shot of whiskey. The lack of fruit and vegetables meant that few prisoners avoided scurvy, a disease that, among other symptoms, resulted in the loss of feeling in the extremities, therefore leaving the sufferer exposed to the threat of gangrene and a visit to Dr. White.

Captain Wirz either relished torturing the prisoners by withholding food and water or was a victim of ungenerous officers up the line who would not or could not provision the facility properly. The Confederacy could barely feed its own soldiers, let alone a burgeoning prison population. Union authorities believed the worst version of events, and after the war Captain Wirz became the only Rebel officer or official hanged for war crimes. The local chapter of the United Daughters of the Confederacy erected a statue to Captain Wirz in the town of Anderson. The inscription quotes Jefferson Davis: "When time shall have softened passion and prejudice, when Reason shall have stripped the mask from misrepresentation, then Justice, holding evenly her scales, will require much of past censure and praise to change places."[20]

The prisoners blamed Wirz and the guards for their plight, though often as part of a longer list of guilty parties. Union prisoner Amos Stearns wondered, "Day after day passes, and nothing is done about taking us out of this bull pen. Can it be that our government does not care for men who have served it faithfully for most three years?" Private William Tritt blamed "Old Abe and the niggers" for his plight, as did many other inmates in Confederate prisons who understood that were it not for the impasse over black prisoner exchanges, they would be free. Another captive, Sergeant William Stevens from Vermont, claimed he harbored "*abolition principles*" prior to his imprisonment, but he knew "that the only reason our Government has for leaving us in such a condition was a miserable quibble, about the '*exchange*' Negroes." In truth, there were not many blacks to exchange. Confederates sent relatively few African Americans to prison. Rebel forces typically executed captured black troops or remanded them into slavery. The comments of the Union captives, though, indicated that the emancipationist sentiment even among sympathetic federal troops was fragile.[21]

The press on both sides used the prison atrocities as rallying points to continue the war. The southern press, low on newsprint by 1864, and dwindling in circulation as Union forces advanced, could not win this propaganda contest. Northern papers and magazines published shocking pictures of emaciated former inmates with accompanying stories of the horrors of their captivity. *Harper's* chronicled the story of Private Jackson Broshers, a twenty-year-old soldier from Indiana incarcerated at Belle Isle until he escaped in March 1864. Broshers stood six feet and one inch tall and weighed 185 pounds upon his capture. After a little over three months at Belle Isle, his weight had dropped to 108 pounds. The writer instructed, "It is not the effect of disease that we see in these pictures; it is the consequence of starvation. . . . There is no civilized nation in the world with which we could be at war which would suffer the prisoners in its hands to receive such treatment . . . and the reason is, that none of them are slaveholding nations, for nowhere are human life and human nature so cheap as among those who treat human beings like cattle."[22]

As Sherman's army prepared to march through Georgia in the fall of 1864, the Confederates disbanded most of Andersonville. They exchanged the remaining prisoners when Sherman took Savannah in December. The following month, the Davis administration agreed to parole black prisoners, and the exchanges accelerated. As the prisoners trickled out from liberated camps or were exchanged, their condition provoked horror and demands for retribution. "Now sir," an Indiana Republican railed, "if this is to be a war of extermination, let not the extermination be all upon one side." Walt Whitman, who had seen almost every form of human deformity imaginable, was shaken to his core by the sight of emaciated Union prisoners. "The sight is worse than any sight of battlefields, or any collection of wounded, even the bloodiest. . . . Can these be *men*—these little, livid brown, ash-streaked, monkey-looking dwarfs? Are they really not mummied, dwindled corpses? . . . Probably no more appalling sight was ever seen on this earth."[23]

The prisoners' fate shocked civilian sensibilities on both sides in a war that had already produced shocking casualties and cruelty. The prisons were an atrocity because war was an atrocity. And the war was not yet finished. The grim rhythm of death continued in the hospitals and prisons. On the battlefield, the slaughter quickened, and this time with no respite. With the approaching spring, the Civil War would become a war for all seasons.

Ulysses S. Grant became an advocate of relentless war. The conflict had gone on too long with too many casualties and too many of the enemy's soldiers still in the field. Grant understood that the Union successes in the second half of 1863 would not sustain northern support if the Federals continued to prosecute the war at the leisurely pace that had characterized the first three years of the struggle. War-weariness and peace movements sprouted like wildflowers on both sides as winter turned to spring. Grant believed that a massive, sustained, and coordinated campaign could end the war, save the Union, and preserve freedom for the slaves. Peace through victory.

President Lincoln promoted Grant to commander of all Union armies in March 1864. Grant deduced that Confederate strength by this time was "far

180.32

inferior" to the federal forces. Seasonal campaigning and the lack of coordination between the eastern and western theaters enabled the Confederacy to shift troops between the regions and maintain the integrity of its two armies, the Army of Northern Virginia in the East under Lee, and the Army of Tennessee in the West, now under the command of Joseph Johnston. As long as these two armies lived, the Confederacy would not die.

To change this equation required a comprehensive plan. As Grant explained, "I therefore determined, first, to use the greatest number of troops practicable against the armed force of the enemy, preventing him from using the same force at different seasons [and] . . . second, to hammer continuously against the armed force of the enemy and his resources, until by mere attrition . . . there should be nothing left to him but submission." Lincoln had advocated this strategy almost since the outset of the war but lacked the right general to implement it. Grant was the right general.[24]

Northerners enthusiastically supported Grant's appointment. Walt Whitman learned of the general's presence in Washington and wrote excitedly that Grant "is determined to bend everything to take Richmond and break up the banditti of scoundrels that have stuck themselves up there as a 'government.' He is in earnest about it; his whole soul and all his thoughts night and day are upon it." Yet both sides had heard the "On to Richmond" cry before. Grant had built a credible reputation in the West, but he had never faced an army commanded by Robert E. Lee.[25]

On May 4, 1864, the Army of the Potomac, 118,000 strong, following the dubious footsteps of Fighting Joe Hooker a year earlier, crossed the Rapidan River to confront the 62,000-man Army of Northern Virginia in the Wilderness, near the site of the Confederates' last great victory at Chancellorsville. Grant's immediate objective was Lee's army, not Richmond. If he could destroy the Army of Northern Virginia, Richmond would fall. Setting the western phase of his grand plan in motion, Grant directed General William T. Sherman, the new commander of the Army of the Cumberland, to attack Joseph Johnston's Army of Tennessee, "break it up and get into the interior of the enemy's country as far as you can, inflicting all the damage you can against their war resources." These coordinated offensives, pursued without surcease, would strain Rebel resources to the breaking point, prohibit the shifting of troops, and bring an end to the war, Grant believed.[26]

A private in Lee's army awoke on May 5 and pronounced it "a beautiful spring day." Parts of the two armies joined battle that day in fierce fighting that ended inconclusively. The area's tangled undergrowth negated Grant's troop advantage and rendered artillery ineffective. Soldiers aimed by ear more than sight. The armies spent the night entrenching and waiting for the onslaught at sunrise. The Federals attacked part of the Rebel line, and the Confederates launched an assault of their own, both to little advantage but much carnage. Dry weather had turned the Wilderness into tinder for gunfire. Forest fires killed many of the wounded, sometimes horribly by exploding the cartridge belts around their waists. Wounded soldiers committed suicide to avoid being consumed by the flames. A North Carolina soldier reduced the battle to its basic element: "a butchery pure and simple." Colonel Horace Porter, Grant's aide-de-camp, agreed. "It seemed as though Christian men had turned to fiends, and hell itself had usurped the place of earth." The battle ended in a tactical draw, though at a frightful toll to both armies. The Federals suffered nearly 18,000 casualties and the Confederates 7,800.[27]

Despite the casualties, Grant had raised Lincoln's hopes. "The great thing about Grant," the president offered, "is his perfect coolness and persistency of purpose. . . . [H]e is not easily excited . . . and he has the *grit* of a bull-dog! Once let him get his 'teeth' *in*, and nothing can shake him off." Indeed, after a particularly bloody day on the battlefield, Grant could be found in his tent, puffing on a cigar and calmly planning the next day's assault.[28]

Rather than withdrawing across the Rapidan in the face of his losses as Hooker had done the previous year, Grant pressed on, to the cheers of his men. He attacked Lee's right flank at nearby Spotsylvania Court House on May 8. The Confederates met the challenge and halted the Union advance. Lee entrenched now whenever he fought, making Union assaults particularly costly. Grant's charge on the trenches produced no significant gains and considerable casualties. In nearly two weeks of fighting at Spotsylvania, the Union casualties stood at nearly eighteen thousand, and the Confederates lost twelve thousand men. Grant wired Secretary of War Edwin Stanton, "I propose to fight it out on this line if it takes all summer." Grant believed ultimate victory was in his grasp. In a dispatch to General Meade at the conclusion of the Spotsylvania battles, he asserted, "Lee's army is really whipped. The prisoners we now take show it. . . . Our men feel that they have gained the *morale* over the enemy, and attack him with confidence. I may be mistaken, but I feel that our success over Lee's army is already assured."[29]

This was a new kind of war, and while it initially exhilarated some, it soon exhausted all. A week into the offensive, a Union officer wrote home, "Dust is sweeping over me like smoke; my face is black with dirt and perspiration, clothes soiled and torn almost to pieces. I am too tired to sleep, too tired to stand." Confederate private Marion Fitzpatrick expressed what most soldiers on both sides already knew, that they were experiencing a dramatic change in the war: "Never has such fighting been known before. . . . It is useless to talk about how tired and sore I am. I have not changed clothes or shaved since the fighting commenced. Now it is nothing but fight, fight, and we are in danger more or less all the time and God alone knows when it will end." Two weeks into the fighting, and a growing disgust at the cost joined the feeling of exhaustion. Oliver Wendell Holmes Jr. wrote home to his parents, "Before you get this you will know how immense the butchers bill has been— . . . [N]early every Regimental off[icer] I knew or cared for is dead or wounded—I have made up my mind to stay on the staff if possible till the end of the campaign & then if I am alive, I shall resign—I have felt for sometime that I didn't any longer believe in this being a duty." Holmes left the army later that summer, admitting, "I am not the same man" as when he enlisted.[30]

Grant marched forward toward Richmond. Lee dashed along with him to keep his army between the Federals and the capital. He entrenched his forces at Cold Harbor, so named because the local tavern offered cold drinks but no hot meals. The crossroads lay near the site of the Seven Days' Battles two years earlier. By now, the soldiers of the Army of the Potomac knew that entrenchments would not deter their general. Many pinned their names and addresses to the back of their tunics so burial parties could identify them and notify their families. If Grant's army smashed through Lee's fortifications, Richmond loomed just eight miles away. On June 3, at four thirty in the morning, Grant threw his troops at Lee. The result was catastrophic. The Federals lost seven thousand men in less than thirty minutes. If ever a Civil War battle proved the futility of charging over open ground before entrenched soldiers firing rifled weapons, this was the place. The Confederates suffered fifteen hundred casualties.[31]

From the Wilderness to Cold Harbor, Grant had lost fifty-two thousand men, 41 percent of his army, or almost the size of Lee's army. Lee did not escape the slaughter. His total losses for the month amounted to twenty thousand men, or 32 percent of his force. Grant knew he would receive replacements; Lee could not cover his casualties. The Army of the Potomac continued to move forward. An astonished Rebel soldier remarked of Grant, "We have met a man this time, who either does not know when he is whipped, or who cares not if he loses his whole Army."[32]

Grant simply refused to accept defeat. Blocked from Richmond from the north, he swung south to attack Petersburg, twenty-five miles below the Confederate capital, and where three of the four rail lines serving the capital converged. Lincoln endorsed the move in a dispatch to Grant, though the mounting casualties disturbed him. He hoped Grant "may find a way that the effort shall not be desparate [sic] in the sense of great loss of life."[33]

General P. G. T. Beauregard protected Petersburg with only four thousand men but held off an assault by forty-eight thousand federal troops on June 16, proving again the value of trenches in overcoming superior numbers of an attacking enemy. Lee's force quickly joined Beauregard, increasing the Rebel army to forty-one thousand men. Grant's army, though, was exhausted, and some troops mutinied against the order to launch yet another assault against entrenched Confederates. The Federals attacked Petersburg four times, the last on June 18, with a listless and uncoordinated performance that one might expect from a tired and demoralized army. Private Frank Wilkeson described the mood of the troops sent forward on these futile charges. "The soldiers were thoroughly discouraged. They had no heart for the assault. It was evident that they had determined not to fight staunchly, not to attempt to accomplish the impossible. . . . The infantry was sent to the slaughter, and the Confederates promptly killed a sufficient number of them to satisfy our generals that the works could not be taken by assaults delivered by exhausted and discouraged troops."[34]

Grant dug trenches and settled into a siege that would last almost until the end of the war the following year. After six weeks of fighting, Grant had lost sixty-five thousand men. The Confederates suffered thirty-five thousand casualties. Grant had hoped to destroy Lee's army in open field combat but had not counted on the Confederates' strategy of fighting a defensive war from entrenchments. A war of attrition prolonged the conflict, which was Lee's only realistic hope: that northern public opinion would rebel against the war as too costly and force a peace.

The unrelieved fighting left both sides precious little time to bury their dead. Grant rejected Lee's request for a forty-eight-hour truce to attend to the corpses after Cold Harbor, offering a twenty-four-hour pause instead. The Union general explained, "Lee was on his knees begging for time to bury his dead. But in this cruel war the business of generals is with the living." A long line of ambulances from the battlefields of Virginia wended its way through the streets of Washington. Walt Whitman was at his post at the Armory Hospital in the city, where soldiers were dying at the rate of one every hour. President Lincoln, spotting the procession of ambulances, exclaimed, "Look yonder at those poor fellows. I cannot bear it. This suffering this loss of life is dreadful."[35]

The northern press, with an assist from War Department censors, had translated Grant's persistent forward movements into triumphs, exclaiming that the general had "won a great victory," that the Army of the Potomac "again is victorious," and that Grant had forced Lee "to retreat step by step to the very confines of Richmond." The usually staid *New York Times* blared, "GLORIOUS NEWS . . . IMMENSE REBEL LOSSES." Horace Greeley's *New York Tribune* was even more declarative. "Lee's Army as an effective force has practically ceased to exist," he wrote, and "LIBERTY—UNION—PEACE" were moments away. Then the casualty lists appeared, hospital beds filled up, and letters from exhausted and troubled soldiers arrived at homes throughout the North, and the mood shifted. Murmurs about Grant's profligate use of troops turned into demands for his removal. "The fumbling butcher," they called him. The Democratic press called Grant's campaign "a national humiliation." The massive casualties and meager results repulsed even staunch Republicans. "The immense slaughter of our brave men chills and sickens us all," wrote Secretary of the Navy Gideon Welles. Perhaps this was the beginning of the shift in northern public opinion that Confederates had hoped for.[36]

The two months of uninterrupted battle had a significant impact on the soldiers of both sides. They were unaccustomed to the new tempo of the war. Though casualty figures listed only the dead and wounded, an unknown number of men had succumbed to the stress in other ways. A report from the front in July 1864 suggested that the problem was fairly widespread, at least among Union soldiers. "The unexampled campaign of sixty continuous days, the excitement, exhaustion, hard work and loss of sleep broke down great numbers of men who had received no wounds in battle. Some who began the campaign with zealous and eager bravery, ended it with nervous and feverish apprehension of danger in the ascendancy."[37]

Though Grant had failed to destroy Lee's army, he prevented the Confederates from sending reinforcements south to support Joseph E. Johnston's troops in their battle for Georgia. William T. Sherman's hundred-thousand-man army moved against Johnston on May 7, three days after Grant's army crossed the Rapidan in Virginia. Sherman would not hurl his army directly at Johnston. He would, rather, outmaneuver it and take Atlanta, the prized rail junction, without huge casualties. The city had become a manufacturing center, the main connecting point between the Confederate forces in the East and West, and a nexus for the distribution of food and supplies to the armies. Neither would Johnston confront Sherman; rather he would snipe, stall, and frustrate the Union's advance to the city. Johnston traded territory to conserve his army and protract the war. He would not be lured into a war of attrition.

Sherman and Johnston danced through northwest Georgia, the latter attempting to lure the former into a deadly frontal assault while the former sashayed around the Confederate army. Johnston fell back and established a line, invariably on a hill or some other defensible position, and the process repeated itself, with Sherman covering much more territory sideways than forward and Johnston keeping his smaller army of sixty-two thousand men intact and harassing the Federals at every opportunity. President Davis wondered why his general would not stand and fight, and Confederate officials called Johnston "the Great Retreater," but the dance continued. Frustration also mounted in Washington. At this pace, Sherman would be in Atlanta in another year or so.[38]

Sherman broke first. Whether it was the frustration over Johnston's maneuvers, mounting criticism in the North, or his confidence in his men, Sherman violated his own rule of avoiding direct assaults. Johnston's Confederates were entrenched on Kennesaw Mountain near Marietta in an almost impregnable position. Sherman's attack, launched in 110-degree heat, was futile and costly, losing 2,000 men to 440 for the Rebels. For the first time, however, the residents of Atlanta could hear the sound of battle. Kennesaw was only twenty-two miles away.[39]

The dance resumed, both armies marching in a fog of dust. By mid-July Sherman's army could see the spires of Atlanta quivering through the haze of heat. Johnston set up defensive positions on the outskirts of the city. It had taken Sherman seventy-four days to advance one hundred miles. Johnston had almost the same number of men as he had at the outset of the campaign. Jefferson Davis, however, had seen enough. One more retreat by Johnston and Atlanta would be flying the Stars and Stripes. Johnston's maneuvers had harassed the enemy and preserved his army, but at some point he had to fight. On July 17, Davis relieved Johnston of his command and appointed General John Bell Hood of Texas to lead the Army of Tennessee. Lee's assessment of the change: "We may lose Atlanta and the army too."[40]

By mid-July, Grant's grand plan was stalled. The Army of the Potomac squatted in damp trenches before Petersburg, much reduced in size since the early spring and unlikely to destroy the Army of Northern Virginia anytime soon. Sherman camped on the Chattahoochee seven miles outside Atlanta with both the city and his opposing army very much intact. In the midst of a growing malaise in the North, Confederate General Jubal Early launched a series of cavalry raids that, while strategically inconsequential, served as a metaphor for Union ineffectiveness.

The origin of Early's quixotic campaign lay in Union attempts to seize the valuable farmlands of the Valley of Virginia in the spring of 1864. The campaign was part of Grant's grand plan. Union control of the valley would eliminate a vital source of food for the Confederacy and would end guerrilla operations in the region, freeing up troops for Grant's operations against Lee. The Federals failed but caused considerable property damage, motivating Early to cross the Potomac River and boldly advance on Washington with ten thousand men on July 9. Along the way, he marched into Frederick, Maryland, and imposed a $200,000 levy on city officials, an expeditious if unorthodox means of replenishing the depleted Confederate treasury. As Early advanced on Washington's suburbs, General Halleck called up every soldier in the city, including invalids, to defend against the expected attack. Early swept through Silver Spring as the president left his White House sanctuary for nearby Fort Stevens to get a better view of the action. He stood on a parapet, his trademark stovepipe hat making an inviting target for Rebel snipers. Naturally, he drew enemy fire. When a bullet wounded the man standing next to the president, Lincoln's alarmed military escort, Oliver Wendell Holmes Jr., cried out, "Get down, you damn fool, before you get shot!"[41]

The Federals fortified Washington sufficiently to deter Early from an assault, but the Confederate general was not through. Early returned to the valley and then headed north into Maryland and Pennsylvania. He rode into Chambersburg on July 30 and threatened to burn the town to ashes unless its residents paid a ransom of $500,000 in currency or $100,000 in gold. The citizens could not raise such a sum, and Early set fire to the town, justifying it as retaliation for federal depredations in the valley. "It was a most disagreeable duty to inflict such damage upon those citizens," he wrote later, "but I deemed it an imperative necessity to show the people of the Federal States that war has two sides." Confederate soldiers looted and robbed citizens and left three hundred families homeless. Miraculously, no citizen was killed in the conflagration. The only casualty was a Confederate officer who lingered too long in the town enjoying the contraband he had looted from a liquor store. Incensed townspeople shot him dead and buried him outside of town only up to his shoulders, so that birds and varmints could feast on his head. That Early could operate with relative impunity so close to the federal capital and destroy a northern town dealt another blow to the administration, already reeling from the bloody stalemates in Virginia and Georgia.[42]

Sherman would cite Chambersburg as a justification for his army's harsh treatment of Georgians during his march through that state later in the year, explaining, "The Rebels were notoriously more cruel than our men." While both armies pledged to minimize the impact of war on civilians, much of that restraint had dissipated by the third year of the war. Since most of the battles occurred in the South, southern civilians suffered considerably more than their counterparts in the North.[43]

The month of July ended appropriately for the Union in a spectacular fiasco at Petersburg. The 48th Pennsylvania regiment, composed mainly of coal miners familiar with explosives, concocted a plan to build a tunnel under Confederate entrenchments, plant eight thousand pounds of black powder, and blow the Army of Northern Virginia sky high. Just before dawn on July 30, a thunderous explosion occurred underneath one of the Rebel lines, sending men and cannon hurtling high in the air like leaves on a windy fall day. The blast created a large crater, 170 feet long, 30 feet deep, and about

70 feet wide. Poorly led Union soldiers stood gaping at the hole in amazement for four hours before entering and advancing toward the enemy rather than skirting the crater's rim. Confederate units, stunned at first, surrounded and charged the hole and picked off the Federals before Union officers sounded the retreat. The Federals lost four thousand men that morning, while the Rebels counted fifteen hundred casualties.

The peace movement intensified in the North, just as Lee had hoped. The huge losses sustained by Union armies since the early spring necessitated another draft. The cries of "Stop the War!" came from an expected quarter, the so-called Copperheads or Peace Democrats residing mainly in the southern-leaning areas of the Lower Midwest. But they also emanated from Republicans who, party leader Thurlow Weed of New York asserted, were "wild for peace." In early July, Republican editor Horace Greeley informed Lincoln that Confederate agents in Canada had contacted him, with the approval of President Davis, to serve as Lincoln's intermediary to negotiate a peace settlement. Greeley pleaded with the president, "Our bleeding, bankrupt, almost dying country longs for peace—shudders at the prospect of fresh conscriptions of further wholesale devastations, and of new rivers of human blood." Here was an opportunity to end the carnage, Greeley insisted.[44]

Lincoln believed little if anything would emerge from these negotiations, but, given the public uproar in the North over the recent course of the war, he sent John Hay, his private secretary, to Canada to meet with Greeley and the Confederate agents. Hay carried a letter from Lincoln detailing the Union's conditions for peace: "Any proposition which embraces the restoration of peace, the integrity of the whole Union, and the abandonment of slavery . . . will be received and considered by . . . the United States." The Rebel agents, who, in fact, had no authority to negotiate anything, broke off the meeting, condemning Lincoln for his bad faith in submitting preconditions for peace that he knew the Confederate government could not accept. The agents postured, "If there be any citizen of the Confederate States who has clung to the hope that peace is possible," the terms of Lincoln's letter "will strip from their eyes the last film of such delusion." Turning to northerners, the agents urged the "patriots and Christians who shrink appalled from the illimitable vistas of private misery and public calamity" guaranteed by further pursuit of the war to throw Lincoln and the Republicans out of office in the November elections.[45]

The Confederates had scored a public relations victory in a North hungry for peace. Greeley was apoplectic in the *Tribune*. "No truce! No armistice! No negotiation! No mediation! Nothing but [Confederate] surrender at discretion! I never heard of such fatuity before." Lincoln could not ignore the anguish of his friends, not to mention the millions of northerners who would

COLUMBIA DEMANDS HER CHILDREN !

*"Columbia Demands Her Children!" 1864. The summer of 1864 was a
horrible time for President Lincoln and the Union war effort. Huge casualties
overwhelmed the promise of Grant's spring offensive, a movement was under way
to dump the President as the Republican Party candidate in the fall, and a
new draft calling for five hundred thousand conscripts outraged many
in the North. Here Columbia is saying, in effect, enough is enough. Lincoln
responds not with gravity, but by telling a joke. (Courtesy of the Library of Congress)*

vote in November. On July 17, two emissaries from the North, one a journalist
and the other a soldier and Methodist minister, met with Jefferson Davis and
the Confederate secretary of war, Judah P. Benjamin, in Richmond. The northerners repeated Lincoln's terms: reunion and emancipation. Now it was
Davis's turn for apoplexy: "We are not fighting for slavery. We are fighting for
Independence—and that, or extermination we *will* have. . . . You may emancipate every negro in the Confederacy, but *we will be free*. We will govern
ourselves . . . if we have to see every Southern plantation sacked, and every
Southern city in flames."[46]

Davis implied that independence was now more important than the maintenance of slavery. Whether he really believed that and whether his constituents
would agree with him were beside the point. Davis was well aware of the propaganda value of his declaration. And, even if Lincoln were to abandon emanci-

pation as a condition for peace, Davis would never accept reunion. The *New York Times* placed the matter in its proper context. The meeting in Richmond "established that Jeff. Davis will listen to no proposals of peace that do not embrace disunion. . . . In view of the efforts now being made by the Peace Party of the North to delude our people into a belief that peace is now practicable without disunion," Davis's conditions were "peculiarly timely and valuable."[47]

The "Peace Party" referred to the Peace Democrats, or Copperheads. They elided the issue of reunion and focused instead on Lincoln's condition of abolition. The Democratic *New York World* asserted that Lincoln "prefers to tear a half million more white men from their homes . . . to continue a war for the abolition of slavery rather than entertain a proposition for the return of the seceded states with their old rights." Davis would never have accepted such a compromise, but Democrats hoped to convince northerners that slavery was the only stumbling block to peace.[48]

Some Republicans either ignored or misunderstood Jefferson Davis's adherence to southern independence as a nonnegotiable issue and also focused on slavery. The failure to resolve the slavery issue resulted in a civil war. Now slavery appeared as the major obstacle to ending that war. Greeley, who two years earlier had attacked Lincoln for dragging his feet on emancipation, wrote in the *Tribune*, "We do not contend that reunion is possible or endurable only on the basis of Universal Freedom. . . . War has its exigencies which cannot be foreseen . . . and Peace is often desirable on other terms than those of our own choice." Lincoln remained steadfast, however. Nearly a hundred thousand blacks had joined the Union army, and their contributions had been significant. The president believed he would "be damned in time and eternity" if he abandoned his commitment to the former slaves.[49]

The July peace initiatives revealed three things. First, given the positions of each president, the war would not end until one side surrendered unconditionally to the other. Second, northern support for emancipation was soft. Most northerners acknowledged the military benefits of freeing the slaves, but fewer recognized its moral dimension, or they believed that an end to the killing represented a higher morality. Finally, the issues of war and peace and of race and rebellion were likely to dominate the unfolding presidential election of 1864.

The Republicans renominated Lincoln for the presidency at a subdued convention in Baltimore in June. A movement by Radicals concerned about Lincoln's commitment to emancipation to nominate John C. Frémont came to naught. As the military situation deteriorated in late June and July, and the peace negotiations went nowhere, Lincoln's prospects looked dim. In August, Thurlow Weed pronounced that the president's reelection was "an impossibility." Lincoln agreed. "I am going to be beaten, and unless some great change takes place *badly* beaten." In a desperate move, *New York Times* editor Henry Raymond urged Lincoln to appoint a commissioner to "*make distinct proffers of peace to Davis . . . on the sole condition of acknowledging the supremacy of the Constitution.*" Lincoln hesitated, but eventually dismissed the proposal as a betrayal of trust.[50]

On August 31, the Democrats nominated George B. McClellan for president and approved a platform that demanded "immediate efforts . . . for a cessation of hostilities," without any preconditions. McClellan's acceptance letter contradicted the platform. He supported peace negotiations, but only on the precondition of reunion. The Peace Democrats had their platform, and the War Democrats had their candidate. Whether this "compromise" would divide or unite the party depended in great part on the course of the war over the next several months. In the meantime, the Democrats launched the most racist presidential campaign in American history, a strategy they believed would resonate in a war-weary North.[51]

The Democratic press and party leaders hammered on two themes: that the Republican Party was the party of blacks and, therefore, against the best interests of white Americans, and second, that the Republican fixation with the African was the major obstacle to ending the bloodshed. Typical among the campaign literature published by the Democrats was *The Lincoln Catechism*, which, among other slanders, called the president "Abraham Africanus the First" and posted Lincoln's personal Ten Commandments, the first of which declared, "Thou shalt have no other God but the negro." A new word entered the American lexicon, courtesy of the Democrats: miscegenation. Victorian sensibilities prohibited the discussion of interracial sexual relations on the stump, but everyone understood the meaning of the new word by its context. Democrats falsely charged that the Republicans promoted racial intermarriage, and routinely referred to the Emancipation Proclamation as the Miscegenation Proclamation.[52]

The Democrats carefully wove together the themes of peace and white supremacy, less to take the hard edge off their racial obsession than to sharpen it. McClellan did not descend to such tactics, though everyone knew the meaning behind his oft-repeated declaration, "The Union is the one condition of peace—we ask no more." The Democratic press informed readers more directly, "Tens of thousands of white men must yet bite the dust to allay the negro mania of the President." Editors reprinted "scientific" articles asserting the racial inferiority of African Americans. A London publication wrote, "We do not hesitate to recognize [the negro] as a member of the human family. All we maintain is, that he is an inferior member. . . . What mockery,

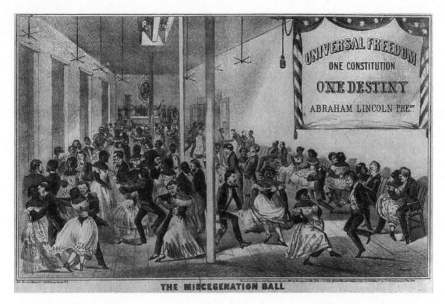

UNIVERSAL FREEDOM
ONE CONSTITUTION
ONE DESTINY
ABRAHAM LINCOLN PRE"

THE MISCEGENATION BALL

"Miscegenation Ball," 1864. During the presidential campaign of 1864, the Democrats portrayed the Republicans, and Lincoln in particular, as favoring the intermingling of the races and as being so obsessed with racial equality that they would continue a bloody war to achieve that end. In this caricature white men and black women consort, dance, and flirt with each other in a suggestive manner.
(Courtesy of the Library of Congress)

then, if not madness, to think of placing them on an equality in the powers of Government!" These arguments would persist through the Reconstruction era, and northern whites would become well versed in their implications. The Democratic press also reprinted articles of dubious veracity from southern newspapers alleging orgies of rape and looting by freed slaves, including the rape of a "Mrs. G" no less than eleven times while she suckled a six-month infant at her breast. At least twenty similar cases occurred, the article noted.[53]

The reelection of Lincoln, these articles warned, guaranteed that these fiends would come north to take white jobs and white daughters. Such articles energized the Democrats' urban working-class constituencies. Workingmen received the least benefit from the war's economic boom, and the Republican administration dealt harshly with protesting laborers. In New York City, a Democratic stronghold, workers feared competition from emancipated blacks. "We do not want the freed negroes overrunning the North as paupers for us to support, or as low priced laborers, crowding white men out of work. . . . If the negro is everywhere freed, the laboring man of the North is reduced to the vassalage of the middle ages." This was precisely the point made by pro-slavery apologists like George Fitzhugh before the war: that slavery guaranteed the freedom of the white man by ensuring the permanent subordination of the African. At an August rally, the city's workers charged the Lincoln administration with refusing to "make peace or restore the Union until white men and negroes are reduced to a common level—until our heretofore proud white republic shall become a disgusting mass of mongrels and hybrids; until, indeed, we adopt and practice amalgamation!" At Democratic rallies in Ohio, young girls paraded with banners imploring, "Father, save us from Negro Equality." Democratic cartoonists depicted Lincoln as a simian creature, craven before his black masters.[54]

The Republicans rarely responded directly to these arguments, except to dismiss them as fantasy. Many white northerners believed in black inferiority and were jittery about the prospect of four million freed slaves descending on their towns and cities. Conditions in the prisons, the mounting casualties of war, and the dashed prospects for peace convinced Republican strategists to steer away from racial issues. Their strategy instead tarred the Democrats with disloyalty, a difficult argument when the war was going badly. Thomas Nast summarized the Republican argument in a memorable cartoon, "Compromise with the South," which appeared in *Harper's* on September 3, 1864. A crippled and defeated Union veteran shakes hands with a vigorous and victorious Rebel soldier while Columbia, kneeling by a tombstone for Union soldiers who died in a "Useless War," weeps. In the background, Nast depicts life in the North as totally prostrate as a result of the "compromise." The article accompanying the drawing summarized the sentiment: "Compromise with armed rebellion is abject submission."[55]

Then, news from the front suddenly and dramatically altered the dynamics of the campaign. On September 3, Horace Greeley and several Republican governors were polling the party's rank and file to gauge interest in a new nominating convention to dump Lincoln. That same day, the Democratic Party, with much fanfare, issued a proclamation pronouncing the war a "failure." In the midst of these events, Lincoln received a telegram from General Sherman: "Atlanta is ours, and fairly won."[56]

Jefferson Davis had his wish for a fighting general fulfilled. John Bell Hood abandoned his predecessor's defensive posture and went after Sherman, sustaining over fourteen thousand casualties to less than half that for the Federals in a series of disorganized and ill-planned attacks. In the eleven days since he had taken command, Hood lost almost as many men as Johnston had in seventy-four days. The citizens of Atlanta stood on their rooftops to watch the fighting and pray for a Rebel victory. When Sherman launched artillery shells, they fled to the cellars or dug holes in the ground. The remaining Atlantans were mostly women, children, and the elderly, as the able-bodied men had been conscripted. The morale of Hood's army plunged. Private Sam Watkins reported that he and his comrades "were broken down with their long days' hard marching—were almost dead with hunger and fatigue. Every one was taking his own course, and wishing and praying to be captured. . . . Each one prayed that all this foolishness might end one way or the other."[57]

Sherman took control of the railroads, cutting off Atlanta from its supplies. Hood had given his left arm and right leg to the Rebel cause, but he would not give up his army. Rather than suffer the fate of Pemberton in Vicksburg, Hood abandoned the city on September 1, setting off explosions to prevent the Federals from seizing munitions and other supplies. Six days later, Sherman ordered the city's remaining citizens to leave. He aimed to "make old and young, rich and poor, feel the hard hand of war as well as the organizing armies." Atlanta's strategic rail connections had enabled the Confederacy to prolong the war against the Union, and Sherman expressed little concern for the city or its residents. "Now that war comes home," he explained, "you feel very different—you deprecate its horrors, but did not feel them when you sent carloads of soldiers and ammunition and molded shells and shot, to carry war into Kentucky and Tennessee." Wagons loaded with possessions and the elderly filled the roads from Atlanta. Hood protested to Sherman that the evacuation "transcended in studied and ingenious cruelty,

"Refugeeing." The war disrupted southern civilian life as most of the conflict was fought in the Confederate states. Here a family leaves home to escape Sherman's oncoming troops. (National Archives and Records Administration)

all acts ever before brought to my attention in the dark history of war," but he did nothing to stop the exodus, and, in fact, could do nothing. Sherman responded, "If the people raise a howl against my barbarity and cruelty, I will answer that war is war and not popularity-seeking."[58]

The news of Sherman's victory electrified North and South. George Templeton Strong, a persistent critic of the president, wrote joyously in his diary, "Glorious news this morning. Atlanta is taken at last!!!! . . . It is (coming at this political crisis) the greatest event of the war." The victory infused northerners with a sense that the war was winnable, that the battlefield and not the negotiating table offered the best opportunity for achieving the war's objectives. *Harper's* advised that "no other effort for an immediate cessation of hostilities should be made by the loyal American people except renewed and overwhelming vigor in the war to confirm the absolute supremacy of the Government." While northerners rejoiced, southerners plunged into despair at the broader meaning of Atlanta's capitulation. "The disaster at Atlanta," the *Richmond Examiner* editorialized, came "in the very nick of time" to "save the party of Lincoln from irretrievable ruin. . . . It will diffuse gloom over the South."[59]

Two other important military victories occurred that late summer and early fall to seal Lincoln's reelection. Mobile was the last remaining Gulf Coast port open to the Confederacy's blockade-runners. On the morning of August 5, Admiral David Farragut and his fleet of eighteen ships, including four ironclads, sailed into Mobile Bay, guarded by two heavily armed forts and by the CSS *Tennessee*, reputedly the most powerful ironclad vessel afloat. When a torpedo sank his lead ironclad, Farragut allegedly shouted to his men, "Damn the torpedoes, full speed ahead." Despite the rocky start, Farragut took the forts and closed Mobile Bay to Confederate shipping. Now only Wilmington, North Carolina, remained as a viable Rebel base for blockade-running.

The Valley Campaign, another unfulfilled piece of Grant's grand plan, reversed in the Federals' favor. The turning point came on August 1, when Grant placed General Philip H. Sheridan in command of the operation. Grant's instructions to Sheridan and the Army of the Shenandoah reflected his thinking that only relentless war against soldier and civilian alike would bring the conflict to its speediest conclusion: "Take all provisions, forage, and stock wanted for the use of your command; such as cannot be consumed destroy. . . . [T]he people should be informed that so long as an army can subsist among them recurrences of these raids must be expected, and we are determined to stop them at all hazards. . . . Give the enemy no rest. . . . If the war is to last another year, we want the Shenandoah Valley to remain a barren waste." The valley became a sea of fire, and the flames took provisions and dwellings alike. Sheridan made no apologies: "Death is popularly considered the maximum of punishment in war, but it is not; reduction to poverty brings prayers for peace more surely and more quickly than does the destruction of human life." Sheridan's actions in the valley so incensed southerners that the *Richmond Whig* set out a detailed plan on how to "burn one of the chief cities of the enemy, say Boston, Philadelphia or Cincinnati."[60]

Sheridan did not operate unchallenged. John Singleton Mosby commanded a group of eight hundred irregulars in the area. They destroyed supplies and sniped at Sheridan's men, fighting mainly at night or from ambush. Mosby had developed such a menacing reputation in the North that many believed the normal rules of engagement, such as they were, should not apply to guerrillas like him. Walt Whitman averred that Mosby's guerrillas were "men who would run a knife through the wounded, the aged, the children, without compunction." After Mosby's men killed one of Sheridan's aides, the general ordered George Armstrong Custer to burn every house within a five-mile radius of the incident. Custer not only carried out Sheridan's orders but also rounded up and executed seven of Mosby's men, vowing, "I mean to return evil for evil until these scoundrels cease their depredations." The war had been cruel from the beginning, but it was clearly entering an even more retributive phase. Both sides were desperate—the Union to finish off the Rebels, and the Confederates to sustain their fading dream of independence.[61]

Jubal Early was the greater threat to Sheridan's mission. He gave the squat, bow-legged Union general a spirited fight. A crucial and climactic confrontation at Cedar Creek in October saw Sheridan riding back and forth waving his odd-shaped little hat, rallying his troops forward. His superior numbers, thirty thousand to eighteen thousand for the Confederates, helped Sheridan prevail, nearly destroying Early's army and giving Union forces virtually free reign in the Valley. Several thousand of Sheridan's troops left for Petersburg to assist in Grant's siege of the city. Grant ordered a hundred-gun salute in Sheridan's honor. He aimed the guns at Petersburg.

The work of Sherman and Sheridan secured the reelection of Abraham Lincoln. It was a remarkable achievement to hold a presidential election in the midst of a bloody civil war. The election demonstrated the commitment to government by the consent of the governed among civilians, government officials, and the military. The Union proved itself not only to Americans but also to the rest of the world. Franklin Dick wrote of the election, "It proves to the world & all times the ability of the People for self government—Oh, it is today an honor to be an American. Our strength is re-established—our permanency assured; for the ability of the nation now to suppress the rebellion cannot be doubted." The experiment that many Americans considered fragile now seemed stronger. *Harper's* summarized the ultimate import of the election. "Yet the grandest lesson of the result is its vindication of the American system of free popular government." Many northerners came to believe that the election was as great a victory over the Rebels as Gettysburg or Atlanta, and more lasting.[62]

The Republicans called themselves the Union party in this election to broaden their appeal. Just as the North was becoming synonymous with America, the Republicans hoped to forge an identity in the minds of voters between the party and the nation. The Democrats, by implication, represented the old-fashioned factional politics, loyal to local constituencies, not to a national entity. Their calls for peace, or as Republicans phrased it "peace at any price," and their racist rants sounded parochial and hollow after the Atlanta and Valley campaigns. The Republicans won 55 percent of the vote, regaining almost all of the seats lost in the off-term elections of 1862.

Nearly four out of five soldiers voted for Lincoln, a testimony to their belief in the war and the president's leadership. It was an impressive figure considering many soldiers came from Democratic families. Some soldiers had worried as much about the declining support at home as about the enemy confronting them on the battlefield. After troops voted, many for the first time, they sat around their campfires and sang a song they first learned when they marched off to war.

> Way down in old Virginni, I suppose you all do know,
> They have tried to bust the Union but they find it is
>   no go,
> The Yankee boys are starting out de Union for to sabe,
> And we're going down to Washington,
> To fight for Uncle Abe.

In their new version, however, they substituted "vote" for "fight."[63]

The soldiers sensed that a Lincoln victory would further demoralize Rebel forces. The Confederacy's only hope for peace and for at least some concessions lay with a Democratic victory. George Hannaford, a Union soldier, wrote home to his wife, "If [Lincoln] is elected, it will do more to discourage the rebels than to lose a dozen battles." As another cold winter settled in, the assertion seemed to be accurate. A Rebel soldier wrote, "The Armey is very much demoralized. I don't believe that the men will fight much." Another admitted, "Every thing looks quite gloomy at the present & prospects don't seem to get no brighter." Indeed, when southerners looked around at the end of 1864, there was precious little, if anything, to encourage a spark of hope. Quite the opposite. The *Weekly Register*, a southern paper, confessed, "We cannot contemplate this verdict of the Northern masses with any other than painful emotions. . . . We must take it as an avowal of the people of the North that this war is to continue until *we are subjugated*—until the last vestige of liberty is gone—until our homes are abandoned, and our lands become the property of the hireling soldiery who are sent to destroy us." If, as many southerners still believed, "this war is waged not for a reconstruction of the Union . . . [but] for our property— our lands and houses—our broad rivers—our beautiful valleys, for the posses- sion of a country which they have long envied us," then the cruel war would go on, and the beautiful land would continue to be stained with blood.[64]

On November 10, a group of supporters serenaded Lincoln at the White House. In his brief remarks to the revelers, he typically placed the election in a global context. His affirmation by voters "demonstrated that a people's govern- ment can sustain a national election in the midst of a great civil war. Until now it has not been known to the world that this was a possibility. It shows also how *sound*, and how *strong* we still are." It was important, however, not to lose sight of the task at hand. The election may have been a great step forward in constituting a new Union, but, Lincoln warned, "the rebellion continues; and now that the election is over, may not all, having a common interest, reunite in a common effort, to save our common country?" To achieve that result would yet require uncommon sacrifice, including the president himself.[65]

CHAPTER 15

ONE NATION, INDIVISIBLE

MARCH 4, 1865. America had come to town. Washington, D.C., over-
flowed with visitors. Hotels were jammed, sidewalks impassable, and pedestrians and horse-drawn vehicles battled for space in the streets. Late arrivals
bedded down in firehouses if they were lucky, outdoors if they were not. The
blustery March weather did not dampen the revelry. Citizens began to gather
in front of the Capitol's East Portico several hours before Abraham Lincoln
would deliver his inaugural address. The Capitol dome, unfinished at Lincoln's first inauguration, was now portentously complete.

Some in the crowd recalled the event four years earlier when the new president delivered a careful speech balancing his constitutional duty as he saw it
with the unfolding reality of a nation falling apart. That had been a somber
day. Today was different. The flags flew higher and brighter, even in the rain.
The bands played "Hail, Columbia!" "Yankee Doodle," and one of the president's favorites, "Dixie." Soldiers in fresh blue uniforms with shiny brass buttons milled about, smiling and chatting with comrades. Ten inches of mud
clogged the city's unpaved streets. The soldiers felt at home. Women wore their
finest dresses anyway, getting their "crinolines smashed, skirts bedaubed, and
velvet, laces and such dry goods streaked with mud from end to end." Who
cared? The war was as good as over, and America had come to its capital city to
hear the president deliver a victory speech, thank God for His support, and
look forward to the new nation's bright future.[1]

Looking back on the four months since Lincoln's reelection, they saw the
Union's ascendancy on the battlefield, and the Confederacy's marked disintegration. On November 16, Sherman burned what remained of Atlanta and
began his march to the sea. The undulating blue ranks stretched for miles,
thousands of gun barrels glinting in the autumn sun, followed by a train of
white-topped wagons five miles long and a huge drove of cattle. The men sang
as they marched, "Mine eyes have seen the glory of the coming of the Lord /
He is trampling out the vintage where the grapes of wrath are stored." Corydon

Foote, a Michigan soldier in Sherman's legion, recalled, "Anything seemed possible with an army like that."[2]

With Confederate General John Bell Hood's tattered troops marching in the opposite direction toward Tennessee, Sherman expected few challenges. He had failed to destroy Hood's army as Grant had hoped. Georgia would be a good consolation. Noting the parallel between removing the Indians and removing the slaveholders to make way for a new nation, Sherman explained, "We must reconquer the country . . . as we did from the Indians. We are not only fighting hostile armies, but a hostile people. We cannot change the hearts of those people of the South, but we can make war so terrible . . . that generations would pass away before they would again appeal to it." Sherman vowed to "make Georgia howl!" Cut off from his supply base, he determined that his army would "forage liberally on the country during the march." Sherman relished his growing reputation as the cool angel of vengeance. Sentiment was for civilians.[3]

Moving his sixty-thousand-man army along four separate routes, Sherman had his way with Georgia. Residents fled in advance, carrying what they could, while the Federals took or burned the rest, though Sherman had issued orders to destroy property only if the residents resisted the troops. A chaplain accompanying the Federals reported, "The question . . . is never asked how much the farmer needs for his subsistence, but all is taken—literally everything." Only the slaves remained behind, despite masters' warnings that the Yankees would drown their babies, sell them to Cuba, or work them to death building fortifications. They followed Sherman's army to the sea, often bearing "gifts" of the masters' livestock. Other men came into camp as well. They were haggard figures, emaciated, weeping at the sight of food and the flag—fugitives from Andersonville. If the soldiers required additional motivation, these men provided it.[4]

The march became a romp. No Union army ate better than Sherman's. Daily fare included turkey, pork, chicken, beef, and sweet potatoes. Soldiers woke up every morning to the pleasant aroma of coffee and bacon. Corydon Foote recalled, "There were times when the Georgia campaign seemed like a gorgeous holiday, a skylarking reward for past hardships." Soldiers broke into the abandoned state legislature in Milledgeville and amused themselves by holding a mock session to repeal the ordinance of secession. Sherman slept in the governor's mansion. The Federals' rampage through Georgia was hardly worse than Sheridan's depredations in the Valley of Virginia, though it garnered considerably more publicity, then and now. Sherman was the better promoter, and several New York journalists had come along for the ride.[5]

On December 20, the ten thousand Confederate troops protecting Savannah abandoned the city, and Sherman walked in the following day. He telegraphed the president: "I beg to present you, as a Christmas gift, the city of Savannah, with 150 heavy guns and plenty of ammunition, and also about 25,000 bales of cotton." Along the way Sherman's army had destroyed or confiscated property and resources worth $100 million. For six hundred miles along a swath twenty-five to fifty miles wide scarcely any resources remained. A wave of fire had swept over the land, leaving only a dark scar. "This may seem a hard species of warfare," he acknowledged, "but it brings the sad realities of war home to those who have been directly or indirectly instrumental in involving us in its attendant calamities."[6]

When the news of Sherman's feat spread across the North, the elation brightened an already festive holiday season. Northerners compared Sherman favorably to Napoleon. He had marched six hundred miles in forty days without losing a wagon or a gun to the enemy. The ease with which Sherman carried out his campaign depressed southerners. A soldier in Lee's army expressed a common sentiment: "In my opinion every man killed or wounded after this it will be cold blooded murder. All know that it is useless for the war to be further persisted."[7]

The absence of most military-age men, who were off with either Hood or Lee, leaving only boys and old men to defend the state, played a significant role in Sherman's rout. The lack of resistance left the impression that southerners had given up the fight. Though some southerners appeared to lack the will to fight on, they did not embrace their conquerors. A woman who lost all of her food, crops, and livestock to Sherman's army understood the war was coming to an end, but she pronounced herself "a much stronger Rebel!" The weakening resolve to fight did not imply an accommodation with the victor or his principles.[8]

As Sherman marched through Georgia, Hood moved into Tennessee. Hood hoped to disrupt the Federals' supply lines (which Sherman no longer needed in any case) and to draw their army away from Georgia by threatening Union-held Nashville. Sherman sent George Thomas with thirty thousand troops to reinforce the Tennessee capital and destroy Hood's force of thirty-three thousand.

While Thomas secured Nashville, he dispatched General John M. Schofield with most of the troops to confront Hood. Schofield entrenched outside of Franklin, fifteen miles south of Nashville. On November 30, while Sherman roared through Georgia, Hood's army charged over a mile of open field to attack the Union's defensive positions, with predictably disastrous results. The Rebels encountered a sheet of fire directly in their faces until the men could take no more and ran away at full tilt from the Union barrage. Some Confederate soldiers stopped in their tracks and allowed themselves to be taken prisoner. Hood retreated to his headquarters, where he broke down and wept.[9]

Hood's army, now at 27,000 men, suffered 6,200 casualties, while Schofield's force of 25,000 lost 2,300 men in one of the few major Civil War battles where Confederates outnumbered the Federals. A mark of Confederate desperation was the sight of freezing Rebel soldiers stripping the bodies of their own generals, six of whom fell during the battle. One general, Patrick Cleburne, received forty-nine bullet wounds, attesting to the ferocity of the Union bombardment. Sam Watkins woke up the next morning and exclaimed, "O, my God! what did we see! It was a giant holocaust of death." During the night, Schofield retreated to the defenses of Nashville, and Hood followed. Schofield later observed, "Was it not, in fact, such attacks as that of Franklin, Atlanta and Gettysburg, rather than any failures of defense, that finally exhausted and defeated the Confederate Armies?" For a regime with limited resources in men and materiel, the question was merely rhetorical. A senseless war was getting more senseless by the day. It would end only when one army lay down its arms.[10]

On December 3, Grant ordered Thomas to come out from his defensive positions and attack Hood, as the Federals enjoyed a better than two-to-one troop advantage. Thomas waited. On December 6, Grant, fearing Hood would bypass Nashville, reach the Ohio River, and menace the Midwest, issued a new order: "Attack at once and wait no longer." Thomas waited. On December 11, Grant issued the attack order again, threatening to remove Thomas from command. Thomas replied he would move when the icy weather improved. The ice melted on December 14, and the following morning, Thomas's Army of the Cumberland emerged as an apparition from thick fog and smashed Hood's Army of Tennessee. The Confederates, numbering now little more than twenty thousand men, lost six thousand soldiers; the Union army, which had grown to fifty thousand men, lost three thousand. Though a hard core of fighters remained in Hood's army, the defeat at Nashville ended both the Rebels' potential threat to the Midwest and an attempt to link up with Lee at Petersburg. Lincoln's Christmas became even merrier. The remnants of Hood's army retreated across the Tennessee River into Alabama, singing a derisive verse to the tune of "The Yellow Rose of Texas":

> *You may talk about your Beauregard,*
> *And sing of General Lee,*
> *But the Gallant Hood of Texas*
> *Played hell in Tennessee!*

Hood sent a telegram to Richmond asking to be relieved of command, which President Davis granted immediately.[11]

Sherman, like Grant, did not believe in winter vacations. On February 1, 1865, Sherman marched out of Savannah into South Carolina. His objectives were to establish a base at Goldsboro, North Carolina, and join up with Grant's army to lift the siege of Petersburg, destroy Lee's army, and end the war. The Federals viewed the Carolina campaign with great anticipation. An Ohio soldier wrote home, "No man ever looked forward to any event with more joy than did our boys to have a chance to meet the sons of the mother of traitors, 'South Carolina.'" As the men crossed into South Carolina, a division commander rode through the ranks asking, "Boys, are you well supplied with matches, as we are now in South Carolina?" The soldiers felt a special responsibility to create havoc there. A Michigan soldier noted, "Grim as the business of destruction was, there was not a man of those who marched with Uncle Billy who did not feel but that he was right." Jefferson Davis understood the stakes of Sherman's renewed march: "Sherman's campaign has produced a bad effect on our people, success against his future operations is needed to reanimate public confidence." The Confederate command tried desperately to raise an army to oppose Sherman in South Carolina, but where would the men come from? Deserters flowed from the Rebel armies in torrents. Those who remained in the ranks were either pinned down at Petersburg or demoralized remnants of the Army of Tennessee now camped in Tupelo, Mississippi.[12]

The rivers and swamps of South Carolina were more of a hindrance to Sherman than the token Confederate resistance. On February 17, the mayor of Columbia, South Carolina, the state capital, rode out to surrender the city to Sherman. The Union army entered the city, and some soldiers repeated their charade from Milledgeville by "convening" the state legislature. A retreating force of Confederate cavalry set fire to cotton bales to prevent them from falling to the Federals. The blaze, fanned by high winds, touched off a more general conflagration, helped along by inebriated Union soldiers who had discovered and consumed a large cache of liquor. Though Sherman issued orders against vandalism, he was even less inclined to enforce them in South Carolina. He explained, with more than a touch of sarcasm, "Somehow, our men had got the idea that South Carolina was the cause of all our troubles . . . and therefore on them should fall the scourge of war in its worst form."[13]

The Federals entered homes and absconded with everything they could carry, leaving the residents, mainly women and children, unmolested. A Columbia woman noted that though the soldiers were "plundering and raging," they seemed "curiously civil and abstaining from personal insult." Other women barely concealed their rage at the invasion. "If I were but a man how firm would be my arm to strike," one victim declared. That the soldiers destroyed what they could not carry struck some women as more despicable than the theft itself. "One expects . . . [Yankees] to lie and steal," a resident noted, "but it does seem an outrage that those who practice such wanton and useless cruelty should call themselves men." Despite the hostile reception, the troops generally found Carolina women more refined than their sisters in other parts of the Confederacy. An Iowa sergeant observed the women of the Carolinas were "much better educated and more enlightened than they were in Ala. & Georgia, they do not use quite so much tobacco &tc."[14]

The verdict among Union troops was clear: "Never in modern times did soldiers have such fun." In Columbia, some Federals emptied a barrel of molasses, and then tracked it all over a house. They attired their horses in women's dresses and impaled chickens on their bayonets and marched through the halls of a fine home dripping blood on imported carpets. South Carolinians taunted Sherman that he would encounter a more hostile reception in the Palmetto State than he had in Georgia. As with most Confederate boasts at this stage of the war, the threat was empty air. General Wade Hampton wished Sherman a quick passage through his state. He wrote to his fellow South Carolinian Matthew C. Butler, "Do not attempt to delay Sherman's march by destroying bridges, or any other means. For God's sake let him get out of the country as quickly as possible."[15]

Confederate troops in Charleston, the birthplace of the rebellion, hearing of Columbia's fate, abandoned the city, as did many of its white residents. The Federals entered Charleston on February 18 to the cheers of the city's black population. Leading the procession was a black Union soldier on a mule, carrying a banner emblazoned "Liberty." Black soldiers from the famed 54th Massachusetts marched behind him singing "John Brown's Body."[16]

Sherman did not linger over these triumphs but continued northward, taking Wilmington, North Carolina, on February 22, closing the South's last major port. Jefferson Davis appointed Joseph Johnston to command what remained of the Army of Tennessee, with orders to confront Sherman in North Carolina. Combined with militia and cavalry scattered in the Carolinas and Georgia, Johnston could field an army of about twenty thousand men. Johnston obeyed his orders, but he confided to Lee, "In my opinion, these troops form an army far too weak to cope with Sherman."[17]

By the beginning of March 1865, it was apparent that the Confederate States of America could not perform a basic responsibility of any government: to protect its citizens and their property. It is true that Union armies

had not yet vanquished Lee, but even that superb military strategist understood that if he sent his troops to stop Sherman, Grant would walk into Richmond. Joseph Johnston also knew that, at best, he would delay Sherman but
could not alter the inevitable final result. Josiah Gorgas, the Confederacy's
chief of ordnance, asked, "Where is this to end? No money in the Treasury,
no food to feed Gen. Lee's Army, no troops to oppose Gen. Sherman. . . .
Wife & I sit talking of going to Mexico to live out the remnant of our days."[18]

If the Confederates could no longer win the war on the battlefield, they
would try to negotiate a peace. It was an unlikely prospect, given the ironclad
preconditions of both sides and the recent lopsided military results. In January 1865, Francis Preston Blair, with the tacit approval of President Lincoln,
traveled to Richmond to meet with Jefferson Davis. Blair was an old friend of
Davis's. Like Gorgas, he had Mexico on his mind. In 1864, Louis Napoleon
had installed Archduke Ferdinand Maximilian of Austria as emperor of
Mexico, backed by thirty-five thousand French troops. Blair believed that a
joint campaign by Union and Confederate armies would drive the French
from Mexico, after which North and South would reunite and live happily
ever after. The unlikely scheme had some support in the northern and southern press, but neither Davis nor Lincoln endorsed it. Instead, Davis proposed
the appointment of commissioners to "enter into conference with a view to
secure peace to the two countries." Lincoln agreed to accept any commissioner Davis "may *informally* send to me with the view of securing peace to
the people of our *one common country.*" The distinction between "country"
and "countries" escaped neither president, but the initiative went forward.[19]

Lincoln held little optimism concerning the talks, but he could not be perceived as rejecting a peace initiative. Davis also expected failure, but he hoped
to use it to rally flagging southern morale and continue the fight. Davis appointed three commissioners, including Vice President Stephens. Secretary of
State Seward represented Lincoln, though at the last minute the president decided to join his colleague for the meeting on a Union steamer anchored in
Hampton Roads, Virginia. If nothing else, it would be good to see his old friend
Stephens.

The night before the meeting, Stephens had dinner with General Grant. It
was a convivial social evening. Stephens had spent more time at his Georgia
home than in Richmond during the war. He had clashed with President
Davis concerning the centralizing tendencies of the Confederate government
and restrictions on civil liberties. Davis had marginalized his vice president
but allowed him to take part in the February peace mission as Rebel fortunes
were desperate and Stephens had a cordial relationship with Lincoln.

The following morning, February 3, Stephens boarded the president's steamer and greeted Lincoln warmly. Stephens seemed frailer than the last time the two former Whigs met, nearly seven years earlier. The Confederate vice president wore a thick gray overcoat that descended to his ankles and threatened to swallow him. He had always looked cadaverous, but the coat made his appearance even more ghostly. A Union soldier guarding the gathering exclaimed, "My God! He's dead now, but he don't know it." Stephens doffed his overcoat, and Lincoln chuckled, "Never have I seen so small a nubbin come out of so much husk." The atmosphere immediately relaxed, and the two men chatted amiably about the old days before settling down to business.[20]

Lincoln held fast to his conditions for peace: the establishment of national authority throughout all the states and the abolition of slavery. Stephens mentioned the Mexican scheme and raised the idea of an armistice. Lincoln dismissed both suggestions, and the conference disbanded. Before the two former friends parted, Stephens asked Lincoln to secure the release of his nephew, who was a prisoner on Johnson's Island. Lincoln agreed. After the release of Stephens's nephew, Lincoln invited him to the White House and presented him with an autographed portrait of himself with the inscription, "Don't have these where you're from."[21]

Davis used the failure of the conference to renew enthusiasm for the war in a speech to a large throng in Richmond on February 9. Stephens admitted the speech was "brilliant . . . but little short of dementation." The southern press, though, picked up Davis's rallying cry. The *Richmond Examiner* paraphrased Lincoln's terms: "Down upon your knees, Confederates! . . . your mouths in the dust; kiss the rod, confess your sins." Davis was defiant. There would be a fight to the finish, and the Confederacy would prevail. Southern armies, he predicted, would "compel the Yankees, in less than twelve months, to petition us for peace on our own terms." Richmond settled down to a bunker mentality. We must "conquer or die," one newspaper declared. "There is no alternative. We must make good our independence, defend our institutions . . . or give up the . . . lands we have tilled, the slaves we have owned . . . all indeed that makes existence valuable." Many Rebel soldiers, though war-weary, looked upon the failure of peace negotiations as a declaration of continuous warfare on the South. "We have been awakened to the solemn reality," soldier Robert Bunting declared, and the southern man would refuse "to stretch out his hand for Northern fetters, and bow his dishonored head for the yoke which abolitionism stands ready to place upon him."[22]

The passage of the Thirteenth Amendment to the Constitution by the U.S. Congress added to the Confederacy's sense of urgency. Seward had informed the Confederate commissioners of the landmark vote. Once three quarters of the states ratified the amendment, it would become the law of the land. Slavery was dead. Lincoln saw that the news rattled the commissioners perhaps more than any other disclosure that day. The president advocated a constitutional amendment because he perceived the Emancipation Proclamation as a wartime measure that would not withstand the scrutiny of federal courts once the war ended. The proclamation applied only to those states in rebellion. Kentucky, Missouri, Maryland, and Delaware remained in the Union. Slavery continued in those states through the end of the war. A constitutional amendment, however, would apply to all states.

The close association between slavery and rebellion in the minds of many northerners generated widespread support for the amendment. "If [Southern slaveowners] made war once, they may make it again. Therefore the restoration of slavery is restoration of political strife," noted one lawmaker. The *Philadelphia Inquirer* stated the matter simply: "The two terms, slavery and rebellion, are now synonymous, the one will live as long as the other, and both will expire together." Most Democrats denounced the amendment. "The law of [God's] providence is inequality," one Democratic legislator declared, amazed that the Republicans were "vain enough to imagine that . . . we can improve upon the workmanship of the Almighty." The Democrats, however, had gotten ahead of themselves, no doubt for political reasons. The amendment guaranteed freedom for the African, not equality.[23]

The Thirteenth Amendment was one manifestation of the remarkable transformation that had occurred in Americans' thinking about their nation. Many northerners saw the amendment as a logical extension of federal power, an outcome of a soon-to-be victorious conflict. The experience of war, its sacrifices, and the demands placed on the administration during the crisis clearly justified the transfer of powers from the individual states to the federal government. An Ohio Republican supporting the amendment stated unequivocally, "The supreme power of the national Government is rigorously maintained throughout the constitution. We must keep steadily in view the fact that the [and here he did not employ the common usage of "these"] United States are not a confederation, but a nation."[24]

The House passed the measure on January 31, 1865, by the required two-thirds majority with two votes to spare, as sixteen of the eighty Democrats joined the Republicans. Immediately, the chamber erupted into pandemonium with cheers, embraces, men's hats and ladies' handkerchiefs flying through the air, and not a few tears. African Americans joined in the celebration, a change in itself, as blacks were not allowed in the galleries prior to this time. Lincoln added his signature the following day and sent it on to the states for ratification. The United States became the only nation to abolish slavery without compensation. The *New York Times* captured the epic nature of the amendment. "With its passage, the Republic enters upon a new stage of its great career . . . aiming at the greatest good and the highest happiness of all its people." Indeed, the sense that a nation and a people had been reborn filled the hall. A congressman observed, "It seemed to me I had been born into a new life, and that the world was overflowing with beauty and joy."[25]

Lincoln, observing the reaction to Seward's announcement at the peace conference, especially from his former friend, offered some advice to Stephens: "If I were in Georgia, I would go home and get the governor of the state to call the legislature together . . . and ratify this constitutional amendment *prospectively*, so as to take effect, say, in five years. Such a ratification would be valid in my opinion." That way, Lincoln explained, southerners "will avoid, as far as possible, the evils of immediate emancipation." Lincoln, according to Stephens, pledged "to remunerate the southern people for their slaves," on the grounds that both North and South were responsible for slavery.[26]

To support his pledge, Lincoln prepared legislation that would offer all the slaveholding states $400 million in government bonds, half payable by April 1, if "all resistance to national authority shall be abandoned and cease," and the other half payable on the southern states' ratification of the Thirteenth Amendment. Lincoln presented this proposal to his cabinet, pleading for approval as he surmised the war would continue for "at least a hundred days" or more and cost "three millions a day, besides all the blood which will be shed." The resolution received no support in the cabinet. Lincoln adjourned the meeting, sighing, "You are all against me." Lincoln wanted to abolish slavery, but he understood the difficulties both black and white southerners would face during the transition from slavery to freedom. Most of all, he wanted to stop the war and its carnage.[27]

The loss of slaves aside, the Confederacy was descending into chaos. As many whites as blacks were now flooding Union lines to avoid impressment in Rebel service or to escape reprisal for deserting, advocating the Union cause, or simply expressing a desire for peace. Many of these whites were poor. "I have left the Rebell army," a Louisiana soldier wrote to his mother in late 1864, "and I intend in a few days to Seek protection in the federal lines. . . . I will not be governed by a people where there is no justice. . . . [T]hey press Cattle and hogs and take the last feed of corn from a mans Wife and Children. . . . I am determined in my mind not to Serve them any longer they have allways made laws to oppress the poor Since this war commenced." Other whites joined Union foragers and former slaves in pillaging farms. A Georgia woman in the path of Sherman's army reported a wave of thievery in her town, "some by the Yankees and a great deal by the poor people and negroes."[28]

Chaos and destitution reinforced each other. The raids of Union and

Confederate soldiers and various bands of outlaws, deserters, and people desperate for food left many parts of the South without livestock or draft animals.
Without horses and mules, there would be no spring planting. And with the
continuing raids, it was impossible to keep what little people could plant.

A new "underground railroad" appeared in the South, spiriting deserters
and draft dodgers to a series of safe houses, especially in the mountains of
North Carolina and Tennessee. In North Carolina, a shadowy pro-Union
group, the "Heroes of America" or "Red Strings," claimed ten thousand members distinguished by a secret handshake and the display of red string hanging from their windows. Still, Unionist southerners often found themselves
targets of vandalism and violence from their neighbors. There was little recourse to a rapidly disintegrating law enforcement apparatus.[29]

The Rebel army was "melting like a Scotch mist." One in eight Confederate
soldiers deserted (compared to one in ten Union soldiers), but the rate accelerated dramatically in late 1864 and early 1865. As the siege of Petersburg
dragged on, soldiers walked away from the Army of Northern Virginia, many
figuring the war was lost and it was time for spring planting. Lee complained
that "hundreds of men are deserting nightly and I cannot keep the army together unless examples are made of such cases." There would need to be mass
executions, however, to implement Lee's wish, a prospect even he would not
countenance. Conscription laws expanded the draft age to include boys and
men from the ages of fourteen to sixty, robbing both cradle and grave, and
even those measures were insufficient to replenish the thinning ranks.[30]

Few events reflected the Confederacy's desperation more than the attempt
to arm and free slaves. The scheme was ill advised for two reasons. First, tens
of thousands of slaves had already left their masters, and 150,000 of them
were fighting for the Union. There was little incentive for slaves to take up
arms against the same men who liberated them. Second, if the slaves were
capable of bailing out a failing regime, then the entire theory supporting their
enslavement was wrong. Pro-slavery ideology rested on the premise of black
inferiority. Confederate general and politician Howell Cobb struck at the
heart of the contradiction: "If slaves will make good soldiers our whole theory of slavery is wrong. . . . The day you make soldiers of them is the beginning of the end of the revolution." The northern press saw the proposal as
both an act of desperation and the height of all contradictions. "The structure
can not be raised," *Harper's* pointed out, "without knocking away the cornerstone!" Besides, if slaves were content with their condition, why would they
risk death for a freedom they supposedly neither wanted nor needed?[31]

Sentiment for arming slaves began to build in the South in early 1864 when
enlistments dried up. Patrick Cleburne, a division commander in the Army

of Tennessee and a native of Ireland, presented a document proposing the
idea at a general officers' meeting in January 1864. Davis quashed the proposal and forbade further discussion of the issue as too divisive.

As the military situation worsened during the latter part of the year, discussion resumed. By November, the topic of conscripting slaves was the talk of
the army. "I had much rather gain our independence without it but if necessary I say put them in and make them fight," was Marion Fitzpatrick's view.
More typical, though, was the reaction of Charles Baughman, a Rebel soldier,
who stated, "I think it is the worse measure that could be proposed. The army
would not submit to it and half if not more than half would lay down their
guns if forced to fight with negroes." Robert E. Lee offered a crucial endorsement for both freedom and fighting. He believed that emancipated slaves
would prefer to fight with the Confederacy rather than with the Yankees. "I
think we could at least do as well with them as the enemy," he predicted. On
March 13, the Confederate Congress narrowly passed a bill to enlist black
soldiers, but not to free them. Davis, however, issued an executive order eman-
cipating slaves upon enlistment thus assuring that they would fight as free
men. The Confederacy enrolled and drilled its first black recruits, and a Richmond newspaper informed readers that they were drilling with "as much apt-
ness and proficiency . . . as is usually shown by any white troops we have ever
seen." The paper predicted that freedmen fighting in Union armies would
desert to the Rebel side. The war ended before any black troops appeared on
a battlefield.[32]

A walk through a southern town on a Sunday morning in March revealed
in human terms the desperation of the Confederate cause. Silence. No church
bells tolled, as congregations had melted down their bells for military ordnance. Women, some with young children, begged openly in the streets. Runaway inflation had rendered even simple items beyond the reach of many.
Potatoes, for example, cost twenty-five dollars per bushel at a time when soldiers' pay was eleven dollars a month. Few men were about. Basic maintenance on buildings and streets ceased, offering a portrait of dilapidation that
reflected the sagging spirit of the citizens. Inside one home, parched corn is
the only thing edible for the women and children. In another house, a young
woman tends to her boy, wounded by the bursting of a federal shell. In another
dwelling, a woman rocks her child beside a cold hearth as there is no wood to
kindle a fire. Schools were closed and churches were empty not only of people,
but also of furniture and whatever else of value they possessed. There was no
paper to publish a newspaper or write a letter. Money was scarcer, even though
it was close to worthless.[33]

Little wonder that the damp weather did not darken the mood of the growing crowd in front of the East Portico. The Confederacy tottered at the precipice of extinction. Only a push from General Grant was necessary to end the rebellion. At that very moment, Sherman's war machine was churning into North Carolina. It was only a matter of time. A little after twelve noon, the president appeared on the platform. The rain ceased, the fog lifted, and rays of sunshine pierced the clouds. God blessed the man and the nation.

In the crowd before him, Lincoln recognized Frederick Douglass, to whom he nodded. Near a column of the portico, but out of Lincoln's sight, stood the actor John Wilkes Booth. As the president was introduced, "a roar of applause shook the air."[34]

Lincoln's Second Inaugural Address puzzled many in the audience, inspired others, and left some cold. Most newspaper accounts of the speech were critical or politely praised its brevity; it was the second-shortest inaugural address in American history, at 701 words. It began in a low key and did not raise its tone conspicuously from then on. The opening sentence was almost apologetic for

The scene at President Lincoln's Second Inauguration, March 4, 1865. The president may be seen in the center of this photo by Alexander Gardner, hatless and looking down at a sheet of paper in front of a small podium. (Courtesy of the Library of Congress)

the short speech that would follow: "At this second appearing to take the oath of the presidential office, there is less occasion for an extended address than there was at the first." His only comment on the status of war appeared a few sentences later in the same low-key tone: "The progress of our arms ... is as well known to the public as to myself, and it is, I trust, reasonably satisfactory and encouraging to all. With high hope for the future, no prediction in regard to it is ventured." In other words, everyone knows what is happening at the front, so there is no point in discussing it. In the remainder of the speech, the tone was even more detached—Lincoln rarely used personal pronouns in this address.[35]

Lincoln did not blame the South for the war. Rather, the war happened despite good intentions on both sides: "All dreaded it [the war]—all sought to avert it. . . . Both parties deprecated war. . . . And the war came." Nor was the cause of the war unequivocally self-evident: "All knew that this interest [slavery] was, somehow, the cause of the war." The word "somehow" qualified the cause. He took no side in the conflict: "Neither party expected for the war the magnitude, or the duration, which it has already attained. Neither anticipated that the cause of the conflict might cease with, or even before, the conflict itself should cease. Each side looked for an easier triumph, and a result less fundamental and astounding."

The speech took a religious turn in the third paragraph. At a place where listeners could have expected the president to invoke God's grace on the Union, he instead invoked God's inscrutability. "Both [sides] read the same Bible, and pray to the same God; and each invokes His aid against the other." Yet God might not favor either side. "In great contests each party claims to act in accordance with the will of God. Both may be, and one must be wrong. God can not be for, and against the same thing at the same time."

Even on the question of slavery, first as a cause and then as an institution, there was no certitude of sin, a significant departure from the "higher law" doctrine advocated by many Republicans. Paraphrasing Genesis 3:19, Lincoln admitted, "It may seem strange that any men should dare to ask a just God's assistance in wringing their bread from the sweat of other men's faces," then, switching to Jesus's Sermon on the Mount, "but let us judge not that we be not judged." As the leader of a party that transformed the slavery issue from a political question to a moral imperative, Lincoln refused to judge the slaveholder or the South.

If slavery caused the war—and that was not certain to Lincoln—the mark was not on the South alone, but on the nation: "He gives to both North and South this terrible war, as the woe due to those by whom the offence came."

Both sides, therefore, were complicit in slavery, and both sides must suffer God's judgment, if that was indeed His purpose. For this reason, only God, not men, could end the war. This was the Puritan theology of his father, not the evangelical tenets of free will and man's transcendence. Man figured little in the outcome; here was God's preordained plan. With both sides responsible for the war and slavery, and with the outcome in God's hands, postwar America should focus on reconciliation, not retribution. The latter judgment rested with God in any case. Lincoln concluded the address calling on all Americans to dig deep in the reservoir of mercy for the sake of a lasting peace:

> With malice toward none; with charity for all; with firmness in the right, as God gives us to see the right, let us strive on to finish the work we are in; to bind up the nation's wounds; to care for him who shall have borne the battle, and for his widow, and his orphan—to do all which may achieve and cherish a just, and a lasting peace, among ourselves, and with all nations.

More a sermon about the limits of man, the inscrutability of God, and the nature of forgiveness—views that challenged prevailing evangelical Protestant beliefs—than a political speech, the Second Inaugural did not receive good notices from the leading Republican newspapers. With the end of a bloody war in sight, the press wanted less contemplation and more information. The *New York Times* expressed its disappointment in a petulant editorial: "He makes no boasts of what he has done, or promises of what he will do. He does not re-expound the principles of the war; does not re-declare the worth of the Union; does not re-proclaim that absolute submission to the Constitution is the only peace." Horace Greeley's *New York Tribune* regretted the absence of an "appeal to the rebels for a cessation of hostilities."[36]

Lincoln managed to touch a chord with some Republicans. Charles Francis Adams Jr. was in the crowd that day. Adams, who was from a prominent New England family that had given the nation two presidents, wrote to his father, who had served as Lincoln's ambassador to Great Britain, "That rail-splitting lawyer is one of the wonders of the day. Once at Gettysburg and now again on a greater occasion he has shown a capacity for rising to the demands of the hour. This inaugural strikes me in its grand simplicity and directness as being for all time the historical keynote of the war." Frederick Douglass acknowledged that many around him in the crowd did not approve the conciliatory tone of the address. He was invited to a reception at the White House that evening (his third such visit), but two policemen barred him from the door until Lincoln spotted him and shouted out, "Here comes my friend Douglass. . . . I am glad to see you. I saw you in the crowd today, listening to my inaugural address; how did you like it?" Douglass replied, "Mr. Lincoln, that was a sacred effort." Later, Douglass observed, "The address sounded more like a sermon than a state paper." Lincoln was pleased with the speech, but he wrote to a friend, "I believe it is not immediately popular. Men are not flattered by being shown that there has been a difference of purpose between the Almighty and them."[37]

Five weeks earlier, Henry Ward Beecher, the self-righteous conscience of antebellum America, gave a sermon at Fort Sumter to commemorate the recapture of that landmark by federal troops. He charged, "The whole guilt of this war rests upon the ambitious, educated, plotting, political leaders of the South. They have shed this ocean of blood. . . . A day will come when God will reveal judgment, and arraign at his bar these mighty miscreants. . . . And then, [they] shall be whirled aloft and plunged downward forever and forever in an endless retribution." This imagined a very different future from the one Lincoln had suggested.[38]

The Second Inaugural reflected the evolution of Lincoln's thinking on both religion and the war. Perhaps his most impressive quality was the ability to apply new facts to alter old opinions. It was evident in his beliefs on racial equality, on the issue of slavery and the arming of freedmen, on the soundness of paper money, and on reconstructing the southern states; it was also evident in his pursuit of military strategy. Today, Lincoln would be open to the charge of inconsistency—"flip-flopping"—but it was his informed flexibility and his remarkable intuition of what the public was thinking and what it needed to hear from a leader at a given point in time that marked his success as a man and as a president.

For a nation that believed weighty political issues could be parsed into good or evil, Lincoln's words offered a complexity that many found difficult to accept. The war had thrashed the certitude of evangelical Protestantism, its belief that mankind could perfect itself, its confidence in the approaching millennium and America's special role in that event, and its hubristic affirmation that it was possible to know God and His intentions. If any specific event of the war buried the Second Great Awakening, it was Abraham Lincoln's Second Inaugural Address.

Evangelicals attempted one last major intrusion into America's civil religion during the war. Eleven Protestant denominations from seven northern states banded together to promote a constitutional amendment proclaiming the United States as a Protestant Christian nation. The "Bible Amendment" would modify the opening paragraph of the U.S. Constitution to read, "We, the people of the United States, *humbly acknowledging Almighty God as the source of all authority and power in civil government, the Lord Jesus Christ as the Ruler among the nations, His revealed will as the supreme law of the land,* [italics mine] in order to form a more perfect union." Two lobbying efforts earlier in the war had proved successful. First, "In God We Trust" was engraved on coins, and second, Lincoln had proclaimed Thanksgiving, which had been a Protestant religious feast, as a national holiday in 1863. These were ecumenical measures, he believed.[39]

By 1864, the persistent flow of blood was giving soldiers and civilians alike second thoughts about God's role, if any, in the conflict and about the wisdom of injecting theology into public policy. The use of force to advance "Christian civilization" had left an American region in ruins and mourning crepe draped on dwellings across the land. Lincoln received the petition politely. "The general aspect of your movement I cordially approve, [but] in regard to particulars I must ask time to deliberate, as the work of amending the Constitution should not be done hastily." That time never came.[40]

Evangelical religion had not prevented America from going to war; to the contrary, it fueled the passions for a dramatic solution to transcendent moral questions. Evangelical religion did not prepare either side for the carnage, and its explanations seemed less relevant as the war continued. The Civil War destroyed the Old South civilization resting on slavery; it also discredited evangelical Protestantism as the ultimate arbiter of public policy. Ideas, soldier Oliver Wendell Holmes Jr. believed, must be adaptable to survive. Ideas should never become ideologies. Flexibility, adaptability, and humility, the strengths of Abraham Lincoln and the message of his Second Inaugural, did not suit the absolutes of evangelical Protestantism. Living a life of uncertainty with respect to one's mortal soul is considerably more uncomfortable than the evangelicals' certitude of eternal salvation, but it is likely to be more compatible with a democratic society and a political process that depends on accommodation.[41]

The war continued. Philip Sheridan and two divisions of his Army of the Shenandoah had joined Grant at Petersburg in late March, swelling the federal force to 125,000 men. Lee's army, whittled away by desertions and battle, had shrunk to 30,000 troops. Perhaps if Grant waited another month or two, Lee's army would just melt away and the war would end in a whimper. Then again, it might not. It was time to end the siege of Petersburg and take Richmond. Lee understood this, having written to his daughter on March 28, "Genl Grant is evidently preparing for something." Lee's only hope was to dash to the West and join forces with the remnants of the Army of Tennessee, now in North Carolina attempting to slow Sherman's advance. Spring was in full bloom in Virginia.[42]

On April 1, Sheridan, with fifty thousand men, attacked ten thousand Rebels under the command of General George E. Pickett at Five Forks, west of Petersburg, and near a key railroad junction. While Pickett attended a fish fry (or shad bake, as Virginians called it), the Federals smashed through the thin Confederate lines, taking five thousand prisoners. News of Sheridan's victory encouraged Grant to challenge the Rebel entrenchments in front of Petersburg. By this time, there were simply not enough Confederate soldiers remaining to man the trenches. The Federals overran the defenses, sending Lee westward toward Lynchburg in a desperate attempt to meet up with Joseph Johnston's army. The siege of Petersburg was over.

It was Sunday, and Jefferson Davis sat worshiping at St. Paul's Church in Richmond. The congregation consisted mainly of women, many in mourning clothes. The few men present had hobbled in on crutches or were cabinet officers. A messenger found the president, who then quietly excused himself. When other officials began to peel out of their pews, the congregation knew something major was happening. The note told of Lee's evacuation of Petersburg and of Richmond's imminent danger.

By midnight, the Confederate government and their families abandoned the capital. Flickering gaslights cast a yellow pall over crowds in the streets, drunken mobs looting shops, and throngs at the railroad depot. Confederate General Richard Ewell ordered evacuating troops to burn cotton, tobacco, and military stores, and the glow grew brighter, punctuated by explosions from ordnance, turning the city into an inferno. Dogs, cats, and rats ran alongside citizens fleeing the conflagration. The fire destroyed nearly 90 percent of the city center. All that remained of Richmond's industrial might was isolated brick chimneys and the piers of the city's three burned bridges. Lincoln telegraphed Grant, "Allow me to tender to you, and all with you, the nation's grateful thanks for this additional, and magnificent success." Richmond had finally fallen.[43]

Sheridan's cavalry galloped into the charred Rebel capital on Monday, April 3. Major Atherton H. Stevens Jr. of Massachusetts raised the American flag atop the Capitol. A Richmond woman watching the ceremony wrote, "I saw them unfurl a tiny flag, and I sank on my knees, and the bitter, bitter tears came in a torrent." As more federal troops entered the city, blacks clustered on the streets and cheered each column as it passed, reserving the loudest acclaim for a black regiment whose band struck up a lively rendition of "Dixie." The city's black residents "danced and shouted, men hugged each other, and women kissed." The following day, President Lincoln, escorted by only ten sailors, toured the still-smoldering city, nodding to thousands of cheering former slaves. "Thank God I have lived to see this," he exclaimed. "It seems to me that I have been dreaming a horrid dream for four years, and now the nightmare is gone." A freed slave exulted, "I know I am free, for I have seen Father Abraham and felt him." Lincoln toured the Confederate White House, sat at Jefferson Davis's desk, ate lunch, and resumed his tour. When officers asked him what policy they should pursue in occupying the city, Lincoln replied, "If you were in my place, you would not press them."[44]

Lee, with his fast dissolving army now numbering fewer than thirty thousand men, found Grant blocking his way to Lynchburg and Sheridan harassing him from the rear, a combined force of more than eighty thousand troops. On Friday, April 7, Grant wrote to Lee: "The result of the last week must convince you of the hopelessness of further resistance . . . and [I] regard it as my duty to shift from myself the responsibility of any further effusion of blood, by asking of you the surrender of the . . . Army of Northern Virginia." Lee's depleted men would have to fight through a force three times as large to reach Lynchburg. At dawn on April 9, he tried, but abandoned the assault when he saw the numbers arrayed against him. He had reached a decision. Borrowing Grant's turn of phrase, he announced, "It would be useless and therefore cruel to provoke the further effusion of blood, and I have arranged to meet with General Grant with a view to surrender."[45]

In the early afternoon, Lee and Grant met in the home of Wilmer McLean at Appomattox Court House. The apple and peach trees surrounding the house were in full color, a beautiful backdrop for a momentous occasion. McLean, ironically, had owned a house near Manassas that the Confederates used as their headquarters during the First Battle of Bull Run. He had moved to a more remote portion of the state to this sturdy brick house with a small green lawn in front to escape the war, and now found himself in the midst of the war's final act. Lee, resplendent in his finest dress uniform, and Grant, in a crumpled, soiled private's jacket, reminisced about their Mexican War service, avoiding for some moments the awkward conversation that must follow. Grant allowed the Confederate soldiers to go home with their horses for spring planting, a gesture that Lee remarked "will have the best possible effect upon the men. It will be very gratifying and will do much toward conciliating our people." Grant ordered twenty-five thousand rations for Lee's famished army, a welcome sight to soldiers who had been living on parched corn for the past week. It also reflected a well-oiled war machine that could come up with enough food to feed an enemy army so quickly.[46]

Grant, initially jubilant at the prospect of meeting Lee, found himself saddened as he stood before the stoic Confederate general. "I felt like anything rather than rejoicing at the downfall of a foe who had fought so long and valiantly, and had suffered so much for a cause, though that cause was, I believe, one of the worst for which a people ever fought." When news spread among

Union ranks about the purpose of the meeting, the men began firing a hundred-gun salute, which Grant immediately stopped, as "we did not want to exult over their downfall." Some of Grant's officers requested permission of Lee to go inside the Confederate lines to visit old friends. Lee acquiesced, and soon Union and Confederate were mingling in the gentle spring afternoon at Appomattox. Grant marveled that the former enemies seemed as "friends separated for a long time while fighting battles under the same flag."[47]

Lee walked out of the house and faced his men. Speaking softly, he confided, "I have done for you all that it was in my power to do. You have done all your duty. Leave the result to God. Go to your homes and resume your occupations. Obey the laws and become as good citizens as you were soldiers." Recently wounded Rebel soldiers lay on wooden pallets as Lee spoke. They asked their comrades to prop them up so they could see the general. Tears streaked down the begrimed faces of the Rebel soldiers. When he finished, there was silence, except for a few muffled groans. Lee mounted his horse, Traveler, and cheers erupted as he rode toward the men, his head uncovered, his countenance reflecting a deep sorrow. All the men took off their hats, including the Union soldiers. Some noticed water welling in the general's eyes. As his horse waded slowly through the ranks, the men brushed their hats against the animal's withers. The soldiers stacked their arms, some smashing their weapons on rocks so that a serviceable gun would not fall into the hands of the enemy, and set down their cartridge boxes. They tenderly folded their battle-worn, torn, and bloodstained flags, and laid them down as well. Some men rushed forward to press the flags to their lips. The war was over.[48]

In Chicago early Monday morning, citizens awakened by the roar of cannon thought for a moment their city was under attack. Washington set off a five-hundred-gun salute that shattered all the windows in Lafayette Square. Lincoln appeared before a large crowd around the White House and asked the band to play "Dixie," "one of the best tunes I have ever heard." He joked with his attorney general that the song was now a "lawful prize" of war. Similar celebrations erupted in cities throughout the North. It would be another two weeks before Joseph Johnston surrendered his army to Sherman in North Carolina, and more than a month before the last Confederate force, the Army of Trans-Mississippi under the command of General E. Kirby Smith, surrendered, but the war ended, for all intents and purposes, on that bright day in Virginia, April 9, 1865. An array of factors converged to doom the Confederacy: a disintegrating economy, a war-weary civilian population, the inability to manufacture and distribute provisions for the armed forces, social class and geographic divisions, and a limited reservoir of manpower. The most important failure, though, occurred on the battlefield. The Union victory was not inevitable. General George Pickett had it right when asked about the reasons for the demise of the Confederate States of America: "The Yankees had something to do with it."[49]

Some Rebels wanted to continue the conflict and undertake a guerrilla war against the Yankee invaders. Jefferson Davis toyed with the idea for a time. Lee would have none of it. Guerrillas, he said, "would become mere bands of marauders, and the enemy's cavalry would pursue them and overrun many sections they may [otherwise] never have occasion to visit." A private in the Army of Northern Virginia summarized the feelings of some of his comrades: he "would be very much tempted to become a desperado and prey upon our enemy in every possible way that a strong feeling of hate and vengeance could devise." But he thought better of it. "With my little ones still living and looking so anxiously for my safe return, I must take care of myself and try to live to protect them, and care for them." Most white southerners, whatever their personal animus toward Yankees, thought continuation of the war by any means was, as a former Confederate senator from Texas noted, "madness." Going home was what the Rebel soldier thought about after April 9.[50]

As news of Appomattox spread throughout the South, despair and depression were much more common emotions than defiance. A soldier noted that he and his comrades, as well as the civilians they encountered on their way home, were "steeped in a fatal lethargy, unwilling or unable to resist or forward anything." A Georgia girl confided to her diary, "The demoralization is complete. We are whipped, there is no doubt about it." A woman in North Carolina confessed that she slept "endlessly." The paralysis would eventually dissipate, but not the memory.[51]

According to friends who saw President Lincoln on Good Friday, April 14, he seemed "in perfect health and in exuberant spirits," as if a great burden had lifted. During a cabinet meeting that day Lincoln related a recurring dream of a ship "moving with great rapidity toward a dark and indefinite shore." If anyone in attendance offered an interpretation, it has been lost to posterity, though the president had similar dreams when he anticipated good news. He hoped to hear soon from General Sherman that Joseph Johnston had surrendered the Army of Tennessee. Lincoln had also experienced darker dreams recently about an assassination and funeral services in the East Room of the White House. He had received enough death threats that he created a special compartment marked "Assassinations" on his stand-up desk. He made light of these menacing messages, but lately, they had begun to trouble him.[52]

An especially heavy schedule of appointments kept the president busy until 8:30 P.M., when he and Mrs. Lincoln departed for Ford's Theatre to take in the comedy *Our American Cousin*. He had invited Grant and his wife to accompany them, but the general declined, saying he wanted to spend time with his family in New Jersey. The Washington rumor mill buzzed that Mrs. Lincoln and Mrs. Grant did not get along.

The Lincoln party arrived while the play was in progress. Abraham and Mary Todd Lincoln had a pleasant carriage ride to the theater with another couple, who reported that the Lincolns had acted like "newlyweds," talking about taking trips together to Paris and California. At Ford's, the audience and the members of the cast cheered as Lincoln entered his box over the stage and settled into his specially provided rocking chair. Shortly after 10:00 P.M. a shot rang out from the direction of the box. Some in the audience thought it was part of the play, until a man, recognized as John Wilkes Booth, the actor, jumped from the box to the stage, brandishing a knife, staggering on an injured left leg, and shouting, "Sic semper tyrannis"—"Thus always to Tyrants"—before exiting stage right. At that moment, a cry rang out, "Our President! our President is shot! catch him—hang him!" Twelve days later, a federal agent shot Booth inside a flaming barn in the northern Virginia countryside. The popular actor had played his final role as Brutus. The assassin's last entry in his diary: "I am abandoned, with the curse of Cain upon me."[53]

A small group of men carried the unconscious president to a house across the street and placed him in a rear bedroom. It was clear that the president's condition was grave. A bullet had gone from the back of his head to lodge near his right eye. Government officials, doctors, and military personnel assembled inside the house, and a larger throng collected on the street outside. News circulated that another assassin had attacked Secretary of State William H. Seward and only the quick actions of his son and nurse (Seward was recovering from a carriage accident) saved his life.

Abraham Lincoln died at 7:22 on the morning of April 15. Vice President Andrew Johnson assumed the presidency. Johnson, a former Democrat from Tennessee, was the only U.S. senator from the seceded states to remain loyal to the Union. Republicans placed him on the ticket to legitimize their designation as the Union party in the 1864 presidential election. Belligerent toward the Rebels, he had a considerable following among Radical Republicans, especially those wary of Lincoln's prayer, "with malice for none; with charity for all."[54]

Northerners, still in the midst of celebrations, now plunged into mourning. On April 19, Lincoln reposed in the East Room of the White House. Mary Todd Lincoln and her son Tad remained sequestered, too overcome with grief to attend the ceremony. Her eldest son, Robert, represented the family. General Grant stood alone at the head of the catafalque. Government officials, military officers, and the diplomatic corps filled the rest of the room.

A funeral carriage, led by a detachment of black troops, followed by a rider-less horse and ranks of wounded soldiers on crutches, transported the president's body to the Capitol Rotunda as bells tolled throughout Washington, bands played dirges, and people along the route up Pennsylvania Avenue wept. It was spring in the nation's capital and the lilacs were in bloom. On Friday, April 21, Lincoln's body began the sixteen-hundred-mile journey back home to Springfield, Illinois.

Walt Whitman was at his mother's home in Brooklyn when he heard of Lincoln's assassination. "Mother prepared breakfast—and other meals after-wards—as usual; but not a mouthful was eaten all day by any of us." He hurried back to Washington to view the funeral procession. And he wrote,

> When lilacs last in the door-yard bloom'd
> And the great star early droop'd in the western sky in
>   the night,
> I mourn'd—and yet shall mourn with ever-returning
>   spring.[55]

Lincoln had forged a personal bond with Americans, white and black, and they with him. During the long, cruel war, he articulated their frustrations, softened their grief, elevated their hopes, and allowed them to laugh, even at him occasionally. He led his nation through the fire of a bloody civil war and convinced his constituents that the Union and their freedom would be stronger for it. "He has been appointed . . . to be laid as the costliest sacrifice of all upon the altar of the Republic and to cement with his blood the free institutions of this land," a group of ministers memorialized. A grieving soldier wrote that he and his comrades "had all come to look upon [Lincoln] as the chosen leader under whose guidance, peace, and prosperity, the gift of the dear God would come to the nation and to them all." The annealing process would facilitate a national healing. He had become Walt Whitman's prophesied "Redeemer President," securing salvation for a nation and its people.[56]

More than seven million mourners lined the railways from Washington to Springfield to salute, stare, wave, or weep as the "Lincoln Special," its nine cars draped in black, passed, with an outsized portrait of the president wreathed in garlands on the cowcatcher. At the larger cities, mourners were able to pay their respects as Lincoln's body lay in state in a government building. In Phila-delphia, three hundred thousand people forming a column three miles long filed by the coffin. In New York City, where citizens had often voiced criticism of Lincoln and the war, a half-million citizens jammed sidewalks and rooftops to view the cortege. When Lincoln's body reached Chicago, nearly two weeks after it left Washington, D.C., his skin had darkened appreciably, requiring a quick cosmetic touch-up to restore a "natural" color to his face. A procession up Michigan Avenue drew thirty-seven thousand people. Two days later, on May 4, the train arrived in Springfield, where more mourners viewed Lincoln's body lying in state. As the president was finally laid to rest, the minister read the Second Inaugural Address. And Whitman wrote:

> *Coffin that passes through lanes and streets,*
> *Through day and night with the great cloud darkening*
>   *the land,*
> *With the pomp of the inloop'd flags with the cities*
>   *draped in black,*
> *With the show of the States themselves as of crapeveil'd*
>   *women standing. . . .*
>
> *With the tolling bells' perpetual clang,*
> *Here, coffin that slowly passes,*
> *I give you my sprig of lilac.*[57]

Southerners had mixed responses to Lincoln's death. Many exulted in his demise: "Lincoln's death seemed . . . like a gleam of sunshine on a winter's day." The black crepe hanging from businesses and homes in southern cities owed less to deep affection for the departed president than to fears of retaliation from occupying federal troops. A minority, however, believed that Lincoln's Second Inaugural hinted at a relatively mild program of reconstruction. General Joseph E. Johnston declared the assassination "the greatest possible calamity to the South." A planter wrote in his diary that Lincoln's death "is . . . in my judgment one of the greatest misfortunes that could have befallen the country. . . . [It is] in my opinion, a great loss to the whole country & especially to the South—as from him, we had a right to expect better terms of peace than from any one else. . . . Oh! my poor country—What have you yet to Suffer."[58]

Lincoln was shot on Good Friday, a fact not lost on a religious people. It was almost as if the president died for the nation's sins, the final expiation. The parallels with Christ seemed obvious, not sacrilegious, though Lincoln himself rarely mentioned Jesus in his speeches or private conversations. James A. Garfield, who had served in the Union army, was now an Ohio congressman, and would become the nation's second assassinated president, made that connection. "It may be almost impious to say it, but it does seem that Lincoln's death parallels that of the Son of God."[59]

Ministers were less hesitant in drawing the parallel, especially in their Sunday sermons that "Black Easter." Referring to Lincoln's visit to Richmond ten days earlier, a Methodist minister drew this comparison: "As Christ entered into Jerusalem, the city that above all others hated, rejected, and would soon slay Him, so did this, His servant, enter the city that above all others hated and rejected him, and would soon be the real if not intentional cause of his death." The Rev. C. B. Crane of Hartford, Connecticut, intoned, "Jesus Christ died for the world, Abraham Lincoln died for his country." Lincoln's death provoked an ecumenical outpouring of grief that transcended Protestantism. The nation's Jewish and Roman Catholic citizens emphasized Lincoln's biblical qualities of mercy, forgiveness, and humility. "Father Abraham" belonged to all people of faith. "With malice toward none; with charity for all" became a recurring phrase in the banners, memorials, and obituaries.[60]

"Young America Crushing Rebellion and Sedition." By 1864 many northerners believed that a new nation was emerging from the war. This engraving by William Sartain (1843–1924) captures that spirit, as a baby, "Young America," vanquishes the serpents "Rebellion" and "Sedition." (Courtesy of the Library of Congress)

   Some Radical Republicans came to view the president's death as fortuitous. "His death," a prominent Radical declared, "is a godsend to our cause." Not only politicians but also evangelical ministers discerned God's message in Lincoln's death. A New York Baptist minister echoed the politicians: the president might have been removed because he was "too lenient," and in his place was now "an avenger" to "execute wrath."[61]

   These were the dogmas Lincoln had preached against in his Second Inaugural Address. The greatest tragedy of a tragic war was that it ended with Abraham Lincoln's death. We will never know if the troubled decade that followed would have turned out differently if Lincoln had lived. America, though, would not wait to cast backward glances. The country would soon place its mourning clothes in storage and barrel forward. Almost ninety years after the noble experiment began, it was now secure. A new and stronger nation emerged from the fire of war. Walt Whitman placed the events of April 1865 in their proper perspective. "He [Lincoln] was assassinated—but the Union is not assassinated. . . . [T]he Nation is immortal." One nation, indivisible.[62]

CHAPTER 16

THE AGE OF REASON

HARRIET BEECHER STOWE became an Episcopalian. No need to be born again in Christ. One biological birth was enough. Surround yourself with liturgy, doctrine, and ritual and experience God through safe filters. Tired of wrestling with God and losing, she opted for a more sedate spiritual life. She moved to Florida. Stowe came to teach former slaves to read and write and stayed to promote Florida real estate. She coauthored a book with her sister Catharine, *The American Woman's Home* (1869), which served as the middle-class bible for home design through World War I. Stowe's kitchen resembled a medical operating theater with its bright lighting, extensive ventilation, and immaculate surfaces. Metal countertops and cement or tiled floors enabled housewives or servants to maintain a sanitary domain. If the Civil War had taught Stowe anything, it was that dirt was bad. Cleanliness was godliness. As much interested in domestic technology as in sanitation, Stowe promoted central heating for both its health-fulness and how it opened floor plans to encourage family interaction. While southern women decorated graves, northern women renovated their homes.[1]

Stowe began the book during the last year of the war. She sensed correctly that the public was war-weary and would rather read about efficient homes and imaginative decorating ideas than the monotony of death. Her first essay on the subject, "Ravages of a Carpet," appeared in the *Atlantic Monthly* in January 1864. The piece urged families to undertake a home makeover to create a modern dwelling. The nation was new, the home must follow suit. Gone were the clutter, the darkness, and the old furniture and carpets. In came the sun, lighter floor coverings, and more functional furniture. The home literally blossomed, opening up to air, light, and sleek furnishings.[2]

Gone also was Stowe's passion for the plight of the slave. She applauded William Lloyd Garrison's decision to dissolve the Anti-Slavery Society. Now that the slave was free, God would take care of the rest. God would finish the "great work [of Liberty] he has begun among us," she wrote to Garrison, for the task was clearly beyond her abilities. Attempting to educate the freedmen, Stowe concluded they were suitable only for manual labor. The bright side of

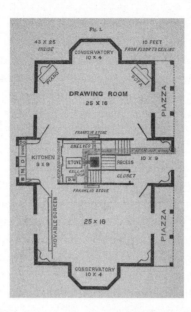

Main floor plan from Catharine Beecher and Harriet Beecher Stowe,
The American Woman's Home, *1869. (Courtesy of the*
Museum of Fine Arts, Houston; Hirsch Library)

the matter was that they would find considerable work in Florida, as whites found the tropical climate debilitating. Whites were fortunate to have "a docile race who both can and will bear [the climate] for them."[3]

Florida's exotic environment captivated Stowe. When she arrived on the banks of the St. Johns River in north Florida in February 1867, the orange blossoms were in bloom. She immediately "stripped off the woolen garments of my winter captivity, put on a thin dress white skirt . . . & sat down to enjoy the view of the river & the soft summer air." She pulled her writing desk out-doors to face "the glorious blue river." At this desk, Stowe wrote a breezy ac-count of her early experiences in Florida, *Palmetto Leaves* (1873), describing her work with the freedmen, but mostly promoting Florida tourism and of-fering advice on growing citrus trees.[4]

Henry Ward Beecher, Harriet's famous preacher brother, did not move to Florida. He remained in Brooklyn. After praying that the "mighty miscreants" of the Confederacy be "whirled down to perdition" in February 1865, he soft-ened his outlook once the war ended. Perhaps the spirit of Lincoln's Second Inaugural Address had entered his heart, or maybe he realized that condemn-ing one third of American citizens to hell was inconsistent with evangelical Christianity's message of God's everlasting love. And speaking of advertising, as the national spokesman for Waltham watches, Beecher did not wish to alienate millions of potential customers. More likely, his congregation tired of hearing about the war and preferred more current and uplifting fare. Beecher's most notable contribution to the public realm in the decade after the Civil War was a sizzling adultery trial where he stood accused of seducing a young and married member of his congregation. Though a jury acquitted him, the trial's testimony revealed serious lapses in the preacher's memory and copious titillating details that the tabloids and the American public eagerly devoured.[5]

Beecher had little faith in the press, except when it promoted his ministry or his watches. In the months following Appomattox, he advised fellow northerners to ignore newspaper reports of southern whites attacking former slaves. "You must not be disappointed or startled because you see in the newspapers accounts of shocking barbarities committed upon these people [freedmen]." Forbearance was a Christian virtue, and northerners should understand that southern whites required a period of adjustment to the sudden reality of freedom. "Above all," northerners must have "patience with Southern men as they are, and patience with Southern opinion as they have been, until the great normal, industrial, and moral laws shall work such gradual changes as shall enable them to pass from the old to the new." Like his sister, Beecher believed that southern problems were beyond mortal solution. Things would work out, whether through God or immutable "laws."[6]

Still, Beecher advocated some human intervention to facilitate God's work. He knew, of course, the precise policies God required. In 1866, Beecher lobbied for the restoration of all rights to former Rebels and the immediate return of the late Confederate states to the Union without preconditions. Only then, he argued, would relations between the races achieve stability. "The negro is part and parcel of Southern society," he reasoned. "He cannot be prosperous while it is unprospered. Its evils will rebound upon him. . . . The restoration of the south . . . [will] rebound to the freedmen's benefit." Yet it was clear by this time that the restoration southern whites sought most was their dominance over the former slaves.[7]

As he had made abolition the focus of his antebellum ministry, Beecher promoted reconciliation as the theme of his postwar sermonizing. Reconciliation was not a mutual exercise, however. White southerners did not reciprocate, and when they seemed to, it was often superficial. Northern reconciliation involved accepting the perspective of southern whites. Beecher carried this theme from the pulpit to a novel, *Norwood* (1868), where he portrayed the white protagonist, Tom Heywood, as a "brilliant young Southerner." The black character in the book, Pete Sawmill, was a "great, black, clumsy-moving fellow." Worse, Pete lacked the Yankee virtue of hard work. "He had no purpose in life, had no trade or calling. He was an idle fellow," little more than "an overgrown child."[8]

William Dean Howells, one of the leading literary figures of the postwar era, reviewed *Norwood* in the *Atlantic Monthly* and commended Beecher for his realistic portrayal of Sawmill. "Unlike most negroes, as we find them in New-England novels, he is a genuine 'nigger,' not a saint in charcoal, nor a paragon of virtue. A faithful, warmly attached servant, he has his little human failings, and has a great weakness for whiskey. It is really pleasant to meet with a darkey in a New-England novel, who isn't a living reproach to all white men." It was a not-so-veiled swipe at Beecher's sister and *Uncle Tom's Cabin*. The postwar era would not be a time for saints, white or black. The crusading spirit of the antebellum years rested with the bones of the dead young men.[9]

Beecher backed off from crusades after the war, excepting his watches. He had always interspersed his sermons with secular humor, and some critics complained that he was Barnum in the pulpit. After the war, his sermons at Plymouth Church dwelt on topics such as civic duty, child rearing, and voting rights. It was nondenominational entertainment, punctuated by such aphorisms as "The mother's heart is the child's schoolroom" and "The difference between perseverance and obstinacy is that one often comes from a strong will, and the other from a strong won't." Fellow Brooklynite Walt Whitman stated flatly, "It was only fair to say to Beecher that he was not a minister." Showmanship and fortune-cookie advice overtook theology, and most northerners welcomed the transition.[10]

Sentiment was out; reality was in. Charles Francis Adams Jr., a Union veteran, angrily attributed the war and its bloody train to Harriet Beecher Stowe and "that female and sentimentalist portrayal . . . that the only difference between the Ethiopian and the Caucasian is epidermal." White Americans would not make the same mistake again. They would not allow a cloying, feminine Christianity, tugging at the heartstrings, to lure young men to their graves for a cause not grounded in reason. Oliver Wendell Holmes Jr. remarked that the war caused him to cross "the threshold of reality." The businessman, not the philosopher, now received Holmes's admiration. "Business," he declared, "often seems mean, and always challenges your power to idealize the brute fact—but it hardens the fibre and I think is more likely to make more of a man of one who turns it to success." Philosophy will only get you killed.[11]

Acceding to the views of southern whites did not signal a belief among northerners in the moral equivalency of the combatants' causes as much as a desire to put the war to rest. Victory, of course, nurtured magnanimity. Bitterness was backward looking; it inhibited citizens from acting in the present and planning for the future. It was better to live at peace with former enemies than at war with yourself.

John T. Trowbridge, a Boston writer, set out for Gettysburg in the summer of 1865. He had published several anti-slavery novels and had vigorously supported the Union cause. His guide at the famous battlefield pointed out the field upon which Pickett made his fateful charge. The guide seemed unconcerned that so many young southern men perished on this ground and were buried in mass graves beneath their feet. Trowbridge, moved by the scene, beseeched the guide to "consider . . . though they were altogether in the wrong, and their cause was infernal, these, too, were brave men; and under different circumstances, . . . they might have been lying in honored graves . . . instead of being buried in heaps, like dead cattle, down here." Trowbridge looked forward to the time "when we shall at least cease to hate them."[12]

The seeds of reconciliation lay in the war itself. Both sides fraternized during the long intermissions between battles. None of these fleeting encounters prevented either side from bashing out the other's brains later, but there were numerous examples of restraint on the battlefield—the reluctance to shoot at pickets and the forbearance of generals to destroy the enemy's army when pursuit or a timely artillery barrage would have done the work. Lee at Fredericksburg and Grant at Chattanooga pulled punches. Not all failures to pursue a beaten enemy could be attributed to exhaustion. Theodore Lyman, a Union soldier at Petersburg, wrote, "The great thing that troubles me is, that it is not a gain to kill off these people—now under a delusion that amounts to a national insanity. They are a valuable people, capable of heroism that is too rare to be lost."[13]

Both sides were American, after all, and despite what divided them, they had much in common. The real surprise after the war would have been an absence of reconciliation. Some have argued that reconciliation occurred at the expense of the freedmen; that whites, north and south, recognized the common racial bond and built a new nation on that ground. There is some truth in this interpretation, but the simple fact that both were Americans, that both, as Lincoln stated, prayed to the same God and read the same Bible, provided the initial impetus for a national rapprochement. After that, a desire to move on motivated northerners to forgive and forget.[14]

The case of Jefferson Davis is an example of reconciliation over retribution. Lincoln hoped the Confederate president would abscond to some distant country so he would not need to deal with a man many in the North considered a traitor. A group of Union soldiers captured Davis in north Florida two months after the surrender, forcing the issue. Incarcerated for two years, Davis received his parole thanks to the efforts of Horace Greeley, the editor of the leading Republican newspaper, the *New York Tribune*, and the sermons of Henry Ward Beecher.

Mark Twain, on one of his nocturnal perambulations about Manhattan that summer, spotted a hatless man with wispy gray hair standing on the sidewalk in front of the New York Hotel. It was midnight, and the gentleman seemed to be enjoying the air of a summer evening before retreating to his stuffy hotel room. On closer inspection, Twain realized that the man was Jefferson Davis. He had come to the city to have dinner and visit with Greeley and some friends. Here was a man who led a bloody civil war against his country but now "went about his business as unheralded as any country merchant visiting town." What, Greeley and others asked, would be accomplished by Davis's continued incarceration, or his execution? The war was over, slavery was dead, and the Union was secure. What else mattered?[15]

General John Logan helped to organize the Grand Army of the Republic in 1866, an organization for Union veterans to lobby for pensions, employment, and financial aid. He understood that, in order to fulfill the group's agenda, he would need to keep the issue of the war before the public, but in such a manner as to inspire support, not opposition. "To keep the scenes of war with all its horrors vivid before the [public] mind, without some still more important motive, would hardly meet with the approval of this intelligent age." A sanitized war became part of the North's collective memory.[16]

Who can blame them? To dwell on a bloody war, the loss of comrades, the carnage of the battlefield, the stench of the hospital, and the hopelessness of the prison was to invite nightmares without end. Military doctors at the time reported soldiers who suffered from extreme "exhaustion" so severe that it was difficult to rouse them from sleep in the morning. They also noted "disordered actions of the heart," a type of arrhythmia traumatized soldiers experienced after combat. When the soldiers returned home after the war, the symptoms persisted. The first professional paper diagnosing what is now termed post-traumatic stress disorder appeared in 1876.[17]

It was much healthier to engage in selective forgetting, to remember courage rather than carnage. Remembering the war in this manner eased the personal pain and facilitated reconciliation. Friedrich Nietzsche wrote that personal happiness and the will to move on required selective forgetfulness: "Forgetting is essential to action of any kind. Thus, it is possible to live almost without memory . . . but it is altogether impossible to live at all without forgetting." Ambrose Bierce, a union veteran from Ohio, flailed against a romantic view of the war yet admitted his own failing in that regard. "Is it not strange," he asked, "that the phantoms of a blood-stained period have so airy a grace and look with so tender eyes?—that I recall with difficulty the danger and death and horrors of the time, and without effort all that was gracious and picturesque?" Not so strange, after all. This was not a question of mutually recognized white privilege. It was a matter of self-preservation.[18]

The war nearly broke Walt Whitman's heart. He had tended both Confederate and Union soldiers with equal care and love. He had wept over their deaths and rejoiced in their recoveries. He expressed the nation's grief over its martyred president in "When Lilacs Last in the Door-yard Bloom'd." It was time now for the nation to heal, time for "Reconciliation" (1865):

> *Word over all, beautiful as the sky!*
> *Beautiful that war, and all its deeds of carnage, must*
> *   in time be utterly lost;*
> *That the hands of the sisters Death and Night*
> *   incessantly softly wash again,*
> *   And ever again, this soil'd world;*
> *. . . For my enemy is dead—a man divine as myself is*
> *   dead;*
> *I look where he lies, white-faced and still, in the*
> *   coffin—I draw near;*
> *I bend down, and touch lightly with my lips the white*
> *   face in the coffin.*[19]

The rush to reconcile restored the sanity of the Union veteran, though it mellowed his memory of bloodshed. Northern civilians moved on to other things, notably making their way amid the economic transformation accelerated by war. Reconciliation came at a price, however. For all his bravado about reconciliation, Whitman sensed that the war's ultimate bloody lesson would evaporate in forgetfulness. "Future years will never know the seething hell and the black infernal background . . . of the Secession War." He lamented the "mushy influences of current times" where "the fervid atmosphere and typical events of those years are in danger of being totally forgotten."[20]

The end of the war ended an era for many northerners. A new chapter in their lives and in the nation's life had opened. As the guns went silent, a finality settled over the North. George Templeton Strong, the acerbic New York diarist, wrote his last entry and closed the book: "PEACE. Peace herself at last. . . . So here I hope and believe ends, by God's great and undeserved mercy, the chapter of this journal I opened with the heading of War on the night of April 13, 1861."[21]

The salvation of the Union restored confidence in America's exceptionalism. It spurred northerners to a giddy nationalism. They had always held great pride in America, but only after the war did they identify closely with the national state. And that state was synonymous with the future, with innovation, technology, and prosperity. Ulysses S. Grant had discerned the "spirit of independence and enterprise" abroad in the land in 1865, a nation of limitless possibility. Even in high culture, Americans would not bow to any nation.[22]

Mark Twain's *Innocents Abroad* (1869) captured this confidence. The war had worked its transformative powers on the young man from Hannibal, Missouri. Twain had entered the war as Samuel L. Clemens, Confederate recruit, and exited as Mark Twain, the American writer. His book was a stream-of-consciousness travelogue that satirized European culture, to the delight of American readers accustomed to reverential treatment of the various cradles of Western civilization and their cultures. Twain poked fun at tourists viewing the Italian masters. "They stand entranced before [a da Vinci] with bated breath and parted lips, and when they speak, it is only in the catchy ejaculations of rapture. . . . I envy them their honest admiration, if it be honest. . . . But at the same time the thought *will* intrude . . . How can they see what is not visible?" He wandered by Lake Como and pronounced Lake Tahoe superior. As for the rest of Italy, "We were in the heart and home of priestcraft—of a happy, cheerful, contented ignorance, superstition, degradation, poverty, indolence, and everlasting uninspiring worthlessness." He did not think much of Italians.[23]

Nor of Italy. Venice? Forget "La Serenissima." Venice "sits among her stagnant lagoons, forlorn and beggared, forgotten of the world." He saved his worst invectives for Rome, imagining himself a Roman traveler writing his impressions of America: "I saw common men and common women who could read. . . . [I]f I dared think you would believe it, I would say they could write, also. . . . Jews, there, are treated like human beings, instead of dogs." As for Twain's own impressions, Rome was a giant torture chamber, a stage set for rotting corpses and public slaughter.[24]

Twain's recounting of his tour of Jerusalem was even more abrasive. Having blasted the cultural pretensions of Europe, he deflated the sacred solemnity of the Holy Land. His delighted audience was in the mood for this religious comeuppance. At the alleged tomb of Adam in Jerusalem, Twain waxed sarcastic. "I leaned upon a pillar and burst into tears. I deem it no shame to have wept over the grave of my poor-dead relative. . . . [H]e died before I was born—six thousand brief summers before I was born. But let us try to bear it with fortitude." Overall, the Holy Land was "not a beautiful place." He concluded, "No Second Advent. Christ been here once—will never come again." The book was the type of smart, witty honesty that postwar Americans devoured. It proved that America was new, real, and cleansed of both the burdens and the pretenses of the past. History would begin anew. Twain was the chronicler of this new nation, and Whitman was its poet.[25]

Northerners understood that this new united nation almost hadn't been. There was little point in maintaining the bitter animosities that nearly led to the destruction of a grand experiment. America would not flourish if citizens persisted in dividing themselves into the righteous and the damned. Armageddon exacted a heavy price, and northerners understood that apocalyptic visions become self-fulfilling prophecies. The new nation—at least the northern part of it—was wiser, chastened by war and eager to move on. It was good to lose the self-righteousness and the overweening pride that accompanied triumph. Work remained, to be sure. Four million former slaves had attained freedom, but little else, and much of the white South was intent on ensuring that the "little else" remained that way. It is ever the dilemma between righteousness and reason. Reinhold Niebuhr put it best: "Justice cannot be approximated if the hope of its perfect realization does not generate a sublime madness in the soul. Nothing but such madness will do battle with malignant power. . . . The illusion is dangerous because it encourages terrible fanaticisms. It must therefore be brought under the control of reason. One can only hope that reason will not destroy it before its work is done."[26]

It was reasonable for northerners to move on. The war generated a booming economy. A beneficent government primed businesses with currency and credit reform, land subsidies, and protective tariffs. The scale and efficiency of Union military operations transferred to the new industries of oil, steel, and railroads, creating new workforces, disorienting for some, but exhilarating and remunerative for many others. Great cities flexed their economic power, and great entrepreneurs demonstrated their creativity. Americans, northerners in particular, had no time for caring about government policies toward the South—a region forgotten, if not gone. Not only was it healthy for the veterans to put the gory war behind them, but dwelling on the past proved distracting. Besides, northern civilians already had a head start in the new economy, and returning veterans were anxious to plunge into the prosperity stream as soon as possible.

The stream became a mighty river. The corporation, a new way to organize business pursuits that limited the financial liability of owners, was the preferred vehicle for integrating into the national economy created by government policies. Before the war, most states required businesses seeking incorporation to demonstrate that their activities promoted the public good. During and after the war, the moral imperative became secondary and the number of corporations receiving charters mushroomed. The number of corporations selling stock to raise money increased accordingly, as did the opportunity for fraud. The establishment of the New York Stock Exchange in 1869 was both a market response to weed out fraudulent businesses and a mechanism to match corporate borrowers with lenders. Within a year, the exchange handled more than $22 billion in stock sales. Wall Street became the nation's financial center. When John D. Rockefeller required substantial infusions of capital to purchase rival companies and build new businesses, Cleveland banks could no longer fulfill his credit needs. He went to New York, both for his money and, eventually, for his corporate headquarters.[27]

The federal government and many state administrations maintained intimate ties with businesses. In an era without standards governing conflicts of interest, it was not unusual to have William E. Chandler, chairman of the Republican National Committee, on the payroll of four railroad companies, including the transcontinental railroad so favored by his party. Federal largesse to corporations seemed boundless. The 1866 National Mineral Act allocated millions of acres of mineral-rich public lands to mining companies for free. Many of the entrepreneurs may have been self-made men, but the government had lent a hand in their creation. Though these relationships seem highly unethical by present-day standards, the government and the nation had a strong interest in settling the West and creating a national market for both economic and military reasons. Subsidies played crucial roles in reaching these objectives.[28]

The entrepreneurs were America's new heroes. The citizen-soldiers of the Union armies were happy to cede center stage. The war had set the entrepreneurs' sights to incomparable heights. As Ohio Republican senator John Sherman of Ohio noted in 1865 in a letter to his brother William, "The truth is, the close of the war with our resources unimpaired gives an elevation, a scope to the ideas of leading capitalists, far higher than anything ever undertaken in this country before. They talk of millions as confidently as formerly of thousands." Not only the "leading capitalists" but also many regular Americans elevated their ambitions as the buoyant economy carried ever-increasing numbers to prosperity.[29]

The press broadcast the biographies of the great industrial moguls as proof of the nation's ability to replicate the rags-to-riches story time and again. Every man could become wealthy. Merit, not inherited wealth or accident of birth, determined success. The Scottish immigrant Andrew Carnegie, who began work as a bobbin boy in a Pennsylvania textile mill for $1.20 a week, built an empire of steel; John D. Rockefeller rose from lower-middle-class mediocrity to lead an oil empire; and Cornelius Vanderbilt escaped from an impoverished childhood to become a railroad tycoon. "In ninety-nine cases out of every hundred," *Harper's* related, "greatness is achieved by hard, earnest labor and thought. . . . And thus it happens that the really great, the really successful men of our country have been self-taught and self-made."[30]

Horatio Alger captured the nation's imagination beginning in the late 1860s with a series of best-selling stories about such rags-to-riches heroes. He was an unlikely hero himself. Born in Massachusetts in 1832 to a comfortable family, he overcame a stutter to climb the academic ladder and enter Harvard's Divinity School, graduating as a Unitarian minister in 1860. In 1866, allegations that he had molested two children forced him to resign from the ministry and move to New York City, where he pursued a different gospel. In New York, Alger saw an opportunity to atone for his sins and save the children of the city. The result was his first rags-to-riches novel, *Ragged Dick; or, Street Life in New York with the Boot-Blacks*, published in 1867. Dick Hunter shines shoes for his meager living and sleeps on the streets until, fortuitously, he saves a boy from drowning. The boy's grateful father, a successful businessman, offers Dick a clerkship in his countinghouse. With his new position, Dick assumes the name Richard Hunter, "a young gentleman on the way to fame and fortune," and leaves behind his street existence. Alger's novels stressed the importance of order—neat clothes, cleanliness, thrift, and hard work. The books also highlighted the importance of chance and the responsibility of those better off to serve as mentors and role models. The city may be a place of fantastic wealth and abysmal poverty, but the two worlds could and should be mutually supportive to smooth out the rough spots of capitalism. Labor and capital needed each other and, like North and South, must be reconciled for the economy and the nation to function well.[31]

Alger's stories resonated because Americans were flush with confidence and enthusiasm after the Civil War. And because there were abundant examples, in the press and in the real world of young men who had risen from modest circumstances to comfortable, if not wealthy, lives. The leading architects of the Republican-inspired economic revolution were themselves products of low beginnings and hard work, not least of whom was Abraham Lincoln. In his December 1861 message to Congress, he outlined the upward mobility available to young American men, "the prudent, penniless beginner in the world labors for wages awhile, saves a surplus with which to buy tools or land for himself; then labors on his own account another while, and at length hires another new beginner to help him." Americans believed these examples abounded in the postwar nation. Banker Thomas Mellon looked back on this extraordinary time when ordinary people could realistically hope for riches:

> It was such a period as seldom occurs, and hardly ever more than
> once in anyone's lifetime. The period between 1863 and 1873 was one

in which it was easy to grow rich. There was a steady increase in the value of property and commodities, and an active market all the time. One had only to buy anything and wait, to sell at a profit; sometimes, as in real estate for instance, at a very large profit in a short time.[32]

The spirit captured Mark Twain, a fellow not likely to be taken in by pie-in-the-sky promises. On January 12, 1867, a boat carrying Twain maneuvered through the ice of New York Harbor and docked at Castle Garden in the Battery. Twain aimed to take the metropolis by storm. "Make your mark in New York and you are a made man," he reported back to California. "With a New York endorsement you may travel the country over, without fear—but without it you are speculating up a dangerous issue."[33]

Depositing himself at a rooming house on East Sixteenth Street, he immediately took to Broadway on foot, accurately discerning it to be the most efficient mode of travel on this crowded thoroughfare. It was nearly impossible to cross the street. The city erected a cast-iron bridge at Fulton Street so pedestrians could get to the other side of Broadway. The ceaseless energy of the city impressed Twain. "It is hard even for an American to understand this. But it is a toiling, thinking, determined nation, this of ours, and little given to dreaming. Our Alexanders do not sit down and cry because there are no more worlds to conquer, but snatch off their coats and fall to shinning around and raising corn and cotton, and improving sewing machines."[34]

Twain set about to attain a cosmopolitan demeanor, though his skepticism and sense of humor often compromised the effort. He took a bride from an abolitionist family, which raised his northern bona fides considerably. He moved to Hartford, a prominent center of publishing and insurance that had grown immensely prosperous from the war as the site of the Colt revolver works and the Sharps rifle factory. Twain, like many other Americans, became a great baseball fan, attending the games of the Hartford Dark Blues of the National Association, the forerunner of the National League. And he counted Harriet Beecher Stowe as his friend and next-door neighbor when she traveled up from Florida. Twain would pad over to Stowe's house several mornings a week to converse and swap off-color jokes. The encounters would drive Twain's wife to tears, not because she was concerned about any improper doings but because Twain went there in his pajamas, something no high-bred New England gentleman would consider when visiting a lady. Stowe did not seem to mind, and Twain made a poor study of Brahmin etiquette anyway. He particularly enjoyed tweaking the local religious establishment, often referring to the Congregational church down the street as "the Church of the Holy Speculators," again much to his wife's dismay.[35]

Yet he was not immune to the siren of speculation. Twain was not only a successful author but a wealthy one as well. The reason was the subscription system of publication, headquartered in Hartford. Under the subscription system, a book would not go to press until the publisher's door-to-door salesmen had secured enough advance orders—subscriptions—for the book. The typical reader resided on a farm or in a small town and had relatively little formal education. The book, therefore, had to read easily and provide enough excitement and melodrama to sustain the interest of such an audience. The formula proved successful for Twain, who boasted to his friend and fellow novelist William Dean Howells, "Anything but subscription publishing is printing for private circulation." Howells retorted, more accurately, "No book of literary quality was made to go by subscription except Mr. Clemens' books, and I think these went because the subscription public never knew what good literature they were." Nevertheless, subscription publishing flourished as, like other postwar businesses, it rationalized the production and marketing of a commodity, in this case, literature.[36]

Twain was also America's first national celebrity. Taking advantage of his homespun humor and the rapidly expanding rail network, Twain traveled across the country on the lecture circuit. The lectures resembled stand-up comedy more than erudite ruminations, and audiences loved it. His popularity soared to the point that he even had his own cigar brand. "DON'T FAIL TO SMOKE MARK TWAIN CIGARS," blared the advertising copy. Like subscription publishing, the lecture circuit became rationalized in the years after the Civil War with the formation of bureaus that booked presentations for an array of worthies, taking 10 percent of the fee. James Redpath, who had fought alongside John Brown in Kansas, headed the most notable of these organizations, the Boston Lyceum Bureau. Popular lecturers could earn five hundred dollars an evening, a significant sum considering that an annual salary of two thousand dollars placed one solidly in the middle class in the late 1860s. Before the Civil War, preachers and intellectuals dominated the lecture circuit, as did the idea that talks should improve listeners' minds and souls. After the war, entertainment and practical information eclipsed spiritual stimulation. Henry Ward Beecher's standard lyceum lecture, "The Ministry of Wealth," and former abolitionist Thomas Wentworth Higginson's presentation on "The Natural Aristocracy of the Dollar" give an idea of what listeners wanted to hear after the war.[37]

Twain embraced modern technology as much as he had modern publishing. He was the first resident of Hartford to install a phone in his house, in 1877. In 1874, he spied a "type-machine" in a Boston store window, bought it, and took it back to Hartford. He pecked out "The boy stood on the burning deck" over and over again until he could type twelve words per minute, at which point he figured it was fast enough to write a novel on the machine. Twain turned out *Life on the Mississippi* (1876), the first book ever typed before being sent to the printer.[38]

Many young men like him were migrating to the great American cities, a fact not lost on Twain. These were the places where imaginations could run free and the possibilities for success seemed boundless. In *The Gilded Age* (1873), a book he wrote with his Hartford neighbor Charles Dudley Warner and which gave its name to the period, Twain described the optimism of these recent urban recruits, himself included: "To the young American . . . the paths to fortune are innumerable and all open; there is invitation in the air and success in all his wide horizon." America's Romantic Age was over, or at least it had subsumed itself in the pursuit of wealth. As a character in William Dean Howells's novel *The Rise of Silas Lapham* (1885) put it: "There is no doubt but money is to the fore now. It is the romance, the poetry of our age." That romance, more than likely, would be requited in the city.[39]

In 1880, the United States Census Bureau, for the first time in its history, published two supplementary volumes on American cities. The volumes surveyed 222 cities, providing historical, economic, infrastructural, and political details for each. The *Report on the Social Statistics of Cities* also delineated an array of urban problems, but expressed confidence that experts, armed with the bureau's statistics, would find the best scientific solutions. The application of social science methodology to cities would help urban America to become more efficient and rational, just as the natural sciences helped to harness the natural world. If reforms were necessary, social science would enable policymakers to render informed decisions. Though critics have claimed these early social scientists were oblivious to economic and social misery, they were not opposed to government or private interventions. They argued, rather, for informed and rational decisions based upon verifiable facts, not on emotions or sentiment. This was America's Age of Reason, when faith in science replaced faith in God as the basis for public policy. These attitudes would coalesce by the end of the century into the Progressive movement.[40]

Chicago and New York were the epicenters of the new urban America. The cities epitomized the energy and confidence of the nation. New York was already America's major city by the time of the Civil War, and it was clear Chicago would become the colossus of the West. The change after the war was primarily in scale, a tremendous horizontal and vertical expansion fueled by unprecedented population and economic growth. More than a hundred thousand people called Chicago home in 1860. The city would grow its population almost fivefold over the next the next two decades. This despite the most destructive fire in American history in 1871, which wiped out more than three square miles of the city and left nearly a hundred thousand people homeless.[41]

New York's urban landscape grew vertically after the Civil War. The nation's first apartment building erected exclusively for residential use appeared on East Eighteenth Street in New York in 1869. A six-room apartment rented for one hundred dollars a month. Apartment living offered the affluent private living quarters and proximity to work without the burdens of home ownership. The success of the five-story Stuyvesant House touched off a wave of apartment construction in the city. The *New York Times* proclaimed the apartment "a domiciliary revolution." Structures and flats became ever more luxurious, capped by the Dakota on West Seventy-second Street, which remains an exclusive address today. Boston quickly followed New York's example, and by the late 1870s "miles of new middle-class apartment houses . . . marched out of Boston in every direction." These apartments possessed amenities previously available only to the wealthiest: electricity, central heating, and plumbing innovations.[42]

New York's structural transformation included the incorporation of new and more expensive materials, such as marble, iron, and granite. Commercial buildings boasted these facades of new materials, replacing and supplementing the traditional five- and six-story brownstones that lined Broadway. The nine-story Tribune Building topped off the city's new skyline in 1875, its iron and granite tower a commercial version of a church steeple. Height became more than a practicality in New York and other booming American cities. It conferred status, a confirmation of lofty ambition realized.[43]

Affluent districts of Chicago and New York were the opulent parlors of America's modern mansion of progress. Pittsburgh was the boiler room, where the initial dirty work of generating wealth and prosperity occurred. This was Andrew Carnegie's domain. The telegraph had fascinated Carnegie during the Civil War. He studied it, left his job at the textile mill, and landed a position as a telegrapher for Tom Scott and the Pennsylvania Railroad. Scott, one of the nation's leading railroad entrepreneurs, mentored the young immigrant, advising him to invest in companies poised to benefit from the nation's growing railroad network. Carnegie followed this advice, using money he borrowed from Scott. He soon received his first dividend check. As he noted in his autobiography, "I shall remember that check as long as I live. It gave me the first penny of revenue from capital—something that I had not worked for with the sweat of my brow. 'Eureka!' I cried. 'Here's the goose that lays the golden eggs.'" That goose continued to deliver for Carnegie as he invested in the infant oil industry during the war. Then he returned to Europe. During his tour, he happened upon Henry Bessemer's steel plant in Sheffield,

England. When the Grant administration raised the duty on imported steel in 1870, Carnegie seized the opportunity and poured his life savings into the construction of a steel mill outside Pittsburgh.[44]

Steel and iron works soon lined both banks of the Monongahela, vomiting lurid flames and smoke so dense that black snowflakes filled the air, the eyes, and the mouth. At dusk, the fires from the chimneys illuminated the particles in kaleidoscopic tints of red, purple, pink, and gray. The ships at sea, the locomotives steaming across the Plains, and the skyscrapers and bridges of the great cities began here. Though located at the city's edge, the mills drenched Pittsburgh with their effluvia. Of the city's buildings, an observer wrote, "Whatever their original material and color, [they] are smoked to a uniform, dirty drab." Of the atmosphere during the day, he noted that "a drab twilight hangs over the town, and the gas-lights which are left burning at mid-day, shine out of the murkiness with a dull-reddish glare." The sun, when it could be seen, looked "coppery through the sooty haze." While Thomas Edison worked in his laboratory to turn night into day, the great iron and steel industry of Pittsburgh managed to turn day into night. In either case, man had conquered nature. The first sight of this perpetual twilight on the river usually inspired awe rather than revulsion. A correspondent for *Scientific American* described it as "a scene of variable and indescribable beauty."[45]

The steel mills created thousands of jobs that did not exist before the war, and not merely on the shop floor. The new industries, due to their size and the extent of their markets, required a white-collar army to manage and grow their business. The expansion of such jobs in cities was crucial to the creation of a national economy. Although such positions accounted for only 7 percent of total employment by 1880, they ranked among the fastest-growing sectors of the labor force. During the 1870s, the number of clerks in offices quadrupled, and the number of bookkeepers and accountants doubled. Similar spurts of growth occurred in insurance firms, banks, and railroad offices. Traveling salesmen fanned out across the country on the new rail network. Department stores, relatively rare prior to the war, provided employment for clerks, managers, and buyers. A new professional and managerial class emerged—salaried administrators, accountants, bankers, brokers, advertisers, and magazine editors and writers. It also included new professions requiring technical expertise, such as engineers, landscape architects, and interior designers.

Salaries from these jobs fueled dramatic economic growth. Industry churned out a dazzling array of goods for eager and able customers. Between 1865 and 1873, the nation's industrial production increased by 75 percent. To speed these products and the information to market and sell them efficiently, the nation's railroad and telegraph networks expanded significantly. By 1880,

128,000 miles of railway and 760,000 miles of telegraph traversed America—
more mileage of each than in all of Europe. Old Europe, as Mark Twain had
satirized, was yesterday; America was the future. The jobs created by economic expansion drew many from Old Europe to the New World. More than
eight million immigrants entered the nation during that same time, many
absorbed into the burgeoning industrial cities of the Northeast and Midwest.
One of those immigrants, Andrew Carnegie, declared, "The old nations of the
earth creep on at a snail's pace; the Republic thunders past with the rush of
the express."[46]

Women's work outside the home changed as well. Working-class and immigrant women had concentrated in domestic service and the needle trades.
Those jobs persisted in the industrial city, but new technologies and changing
aspirations attracted middle-class women into the urban labor market. The
advent of the typewriter in the late 1860s opened up office work for middle-
class women. "Type girls" could earn as much as nine hundred dollars per
year in the early 1870s, or about half the salary of the male clerks whom they
replaced. Teachers earned from four hundred to eight hundred dollars a year,
making clerical jobs more attractive to middle-class women. By 1875, the typical office had become totally "feminized."[47]

Hard work and city living left little time for recreation. Critics worried that
the move from farm to city created a generation of overweight and overwrought
Americans. Amateur athletic clubs, some operating out of YMCA organization, sprang up across urban America, and publications such as *Sporting Times*
and *Sports and Games* appeared in the late 1860s to instruct and encourage
the urban middle class on exercise routines and organized sports activities. The
articles urged all family members, regardless of age or gender, to participate and
cease their sedentary habits.

Affluence allowed for more leisure time for some, especially favoring those
activities that involved the entire family. Spectator sports flourished accordingly, especially baseball. In 1869, the first professional baseball team, the
Cincinnati Red Stockings, whose players received seasonal salaries ranging
from eight hundred to fourteen hundred dollars, barnstormed across the country beating almost every amateur squad in sight. Players and entrepreneurs in
other cities took note, and by the mid-1870s they had organized the National
League of Professional Base Ball Clubs out of the old National Association.

While tens of thousands of Americans moved to the city to work, a smaller
but growing number left the city to live. The booming urban economy crowded
out residential uses from city centers. Industry disgorged its essence into residential areas. The influx of immigrants crowding into dwellings near their
places of work made inner cities even less desirable for those with the means to

move. As land uses segregated, so did people. Steam railroads and horse-drawn railways enabled residents to live five to twenty miles away from their work. In the early 1870s, magazines advertised spacious homes for sale in the towns around New York City. By 1873, Chicago boasted nearly one hundred suburbs with a combined population of more than fifty thousand. These suburbanites, part of the new middle class, sought environments conducive to family life, with people much like themselves. As one suburban resident gushed to his city friends, "If you want to bring up a family, to prolong your days, to cultivate the neighborly feeling . . . leave your city block and become like me. It may be a little more difficult for us to attend the opera, but the robin in my elm tree struck a higher note and a sweeter one yesterday than any prima donna ever reached."[48]

The Russells of Short Hills, New Jersey, endorsed this sentiment. Short Hills was a railroad suburb eighteen miles from New York City, founded in

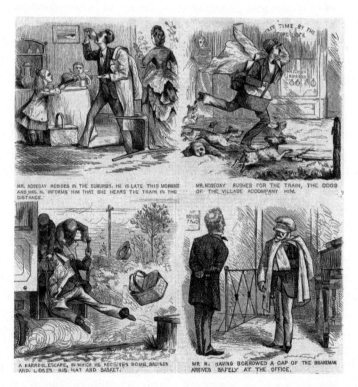

"Hurrying for the Train," September 2, 1871. The American move to the suburbs of northern cities began in earnest after the Civil War. The image of the dashing commuter, familiar to Americans of the mid-twentieth century, has its late-nineteenth-century counterpart here. (Harper's Weekly)

1877. William Russell and his wife, Ella Gibson Russell, were typical of the early residents. They moved from Brooklyn to Short Hills with their six children, seeking a "pleasant cultured people whose society we could enjoy" and a cure for Mr. Russell's rheumatism. Russell, who owned and managed a small metal brokerage in New York, described himself as a "clean liver" who enjoyed gardening, reading, and socializing with his new neighbors. Ella Russell cared for the six children with the help of a servant but also found time to belong to several clubs and charities.[49]

The Russells followed the design principles of Harriet Beecher Stowe and Catharine Beecher. Mrs. Russell, as a "domestic scientist" (in the words of Stowe and Beecher), ensured the cleanliness of her home as well as selecting the appropriate furnishings. Following Stowe and Beecher's recommendations, they located the utility hardware in a central core, freeing wall areas for other functions. Central heating removed the necessity of designing small, compact rooms, each with a fireplace or stove. The new arrangement reduced the number of rooms and encouraged the family to pursue their individual activities in a common space. Gone were parlors and reception rooms. The rigid spatial segregation of the sexes disappeared as well. Such standards as the children's wing, the male "smoking room," and the female parlor were not included in the new allocation of space.

The family enjoyed the Athletic Club, where all members, not just the male head of household, could play tennis, swim, or skate. Because Short Hills bordered on undeveloped woodland traversed by trails, "wheel clubs" sprang up to organize families for bicycle outings. Leisure and sports activities amid bucolic settings, once the preserve of the wealthy, became accessible to middle-class Americans. The new economy, and the employment opportunities it created, enabled many families like the Russells to achieve this latest version of the American dream.

It was now possible to talk about a middle-class "lifestyle," and what that implied in terms of family, living arrangements, work, leisure, education, and consumer preferences. While the pursuit of money may have characterized the postwar age, the pursuit of happiness was equally important, and the two were frequently linked in the American mind. Absorbed in great issues and then a great war for two decades, it was refreshing to focus on home, family, work, and leisure.

The Russells were among many northern families finding a better life after the war. Home ownership was more readily available to Americans in the early 1870s than at any previous time in the nation's history. Middle-class salaries averaged $2,000 per year and a modest suburban home cost $750. Although thirty-year fixed-rate mortgages with little or no down payment would not appear until the mid-twentieth century, building and loan societies emerged during the 1860s to provide financial assistance to prospective homeowners. An income of $2,000 qualified a buyer for a $2,500 loan at 7 percent interest, sufficient to purchase a lot and a two-story home in Brooklyn in 1866, with monthly payments and taxes totaling $400 annually. "House pattern books" flooded the market in the late 1860s, providing consumers with relatively simple and inexpensive plans for home building. "There never was a time," an art critic wrote in 1872, "when so many books written for the purpose of bringing the subject of architecture—its history, its theory, its practice—down to the level of popular understanding were produced as in this time of ours."[50]

New technologies eased middle-class life and made it more affordable. Balloon frame construction (think of a birdcage) reduced the cost of raw materials and facilitated larger and more flexible designs. Power looms lowered the cost of wool carpets to less than one dollar per yard. Advances in paint technology allowed new homeowners to use a variety of colors both inside and outside their dwellings.

Residents could accessorize their homes more cheaply than ever. Currier and Ives produced inexpensive black-and-white lithographs from the 1860s onward ranging in cost from fifteen cents to three dollars. Such bargains allowed homeowners to fill their walls with landscapes and historic scenes just like the rich folks. By the 1860s, gas stoves were replacing cast-iron stoves heated by wood or coal, providing cleaner and more efficient output with considerably less work.

Women especially appreciated the benefits of the gas stove and the access to new foods and ingredients that lent variety and nutrition to mealtimes. The advent of refrigerated rail cars, canned goods, fresh fruits, and factory-made dairy products brought the farm closer to middle-class homes. The old general store gave way to supermarkets. The first chain grocery store—the New York–based Atlantic and Pacific Tea Company, known popularly as the A&P, opened its doors in 1864.

Fashion, once the purview of the wealthy, attracted middle-class devotees already adjusting to new occupations, residences, and leisure activities. Clothes became a mark of class, a means to delineate one's arrival into success. In November 1867, *Harper's* announced the first number of *Harper's Bazaar* magazine, a publication targeting middle-class readers. The objective of the new magazine was to clothe the middle-class with the accouterments of the well-to-do at a fraction of the cost.[51]

America's future lay in these homes in these cities and suburbs. In 1870, for the first time in American history, a majority of citizens no longer lived on farms. Farm life was changing, too, however. In some parts of the North, farming became an industry, taking advantage of new railroad connections and agricultural technology. Well into the 1880s, the majority of patents approved related to farming. "Bonanza" farms appeared on the fertile prairies of the Dakotas and Minnesota, vast tracts of a thousand acres or more, highly mechanized and owned by absentee landlords. These farms hired accountants and purchasing agents, as well as seasonal farmworkers. Managers broke down operations into discrete tasks such as cultivating, harvesting, loading, and shipping, much like an industrial factory. The farms also helped cities grow. Minneapolis became nationally renowned as a flour-milling center primarily through the entrepreneurial skill of Charles A. Pillsbury, who established a state-of-the-art mill there in 1869. By the mid-1870s, a national system of grain exchanges existed as well as standards for grading, storage, and weighing the crop. America was feeding the world, and western farmers fed their profits back into more and better technology, just like the industrialists.[52]

Most farmers in the West, though, were family farmers who felt isolated from the urban industrial boom. Aaron Montgomery Ward, a young man who started working at the age of fourteen in a barrel factory, moved with his family from New York to Niles, Michigan. Though farm families had access to ready-made clothing, country stores charged considerably more for such items than did merchants in the cities. Ward began a mail-order business, sending out printed sheets to farmers across the Midwest with pictures of each item for sale. He purchased and shipped the merchandise from Chicago at a cost considerably below that offered by country merchants by eliminating the middleman. In 1874, Ward published and mailed his first catalog. Within a decade, the catalog included 240 pages listing more than ten thousand items. Ward's Chicago operation employed hundreds of clerks and shippers and an inventory worth over $500,000. Farmers were no longer his only customers. Residents of towns eagerly grasped the opportunity to live at least a little like the folks in the big cities. Ward remained the leading mail-order entrepreneur until Richard Sears and Alvah Roebuck entered the field in the 1890s.

Americans were beginning to live a modern life, a life more recognizable to residents of the twenty-first century than to those who lived in the early nineteenth century. Work, living arrangements, leisure activities, and access to technology separated the eras. As journalist and novelist Henry Adams wrote, "In essentials like religion, ethics, philosophy; in history, literature, art; in the concepts of all science . . . the boy of 1854 stood nearer the year 1 than to the year 1900." The Civil War was the great divide. Though elements of modern life existed before the war, they flourished afterward.[53]

Intellectual historian Louis Menand has argued that, while the Civil War did not make America modern, it marked the birth of a modern nation. "Modern," according to Menand, meant that life was no longer cyclical, that sons and daughters did not automatically follow in their parents' path, that society was not an extension or a repetition of the past. Modern societies, in fact, move in unforeseeable directions. The war, through its vast organizational accomplishments, the technology it unleashed, and the government policies that facilitated mobility and innovation, provided the impetus for modernization. The great entrepreneurs took advantage of the new economic and political landscape, and a growing middle class reaped the benefits of the transition.[54]

The entrepreneurs operated in an environment that allowed them free rein. They had access to capital, markets, and technology. And when they did not, they created it. Above all, they were innovators generating untold wealth that supported not only lavish lifestyles but also a broadening middle class. The integration of the nation's transportation and communication infrastructure, the managerial revolution that rationalized the operation of geographically distant units and large and diverse workforces, and the application of continuous flow production, pioneered in flour mills long before Henry Ford adapted it to car manufacturing, were a few of the innovations entrepreneurs devised to increase efficiency and profitability in the postwar years.

The large corporation changed how Americans lived their daily lives. People moved to cities in unprecedented numbers. They purchased goods that did not exist or that had limited distribution prior to the Civil War. They worked in an environment where management and labor became ever more distinct. And they established new consumption patterns in purchasing and furnishing their dwellings and in their leisure activities. Their lives revolved around family, work, and play. They were modern Americans.

John D. Rockefeller was the entrepreneurial prototype for innovation. He slashed costs by controlling the oil industry from well to market. His empire included companies or subsidiaries that made pipes and barrels, pumped oil, and loaded and hauled oil onto tankers and rail cars. Economists call this vertical integration. Rockefeller was also a master at horizontal integration, gobbling up competing oil refiners and playing railroad companies against each other to receive shipping rebates until his company, Standard Oil of Ohio, stood virtually alone atop the oil industry. By the late 1870s, Standard Oil controlled 90 percent of the nation's petroleum refining capacity. The national banking system established during the Civil War created a stable and lucrative credit environment for Rockefeller. The capital he accumulated served as a war chest to devour smaller companies and reduce competition and, he argued, to increase efficiency and lower the price for consumers.

Recalling the Union army's ability to feed hundreds of thousands of soldiers efficiently by the end of the war, Rockefeller defended his business methods, asking, "Who can buy beef the cheapest—the housewife for her family, the steward for her club or hotel, or the commissary for the army?" And he was right. Prices for almost every major category of goods—farm products, textiles, fuels, metals, building materials, and household furnishings—fell steadily during a thirty-year period beginning in 1865 as manufacturers took advantage of the economies of scale and the technology that accompanied it. The wholesale price index in 1892 stood at less than half of its 1866 level. Falling prices eliminated inefficient enterprises and placed a premium on technological innovation. Wages also fell, but not as much as prices.[55]

Rockefeller and his fellow entrepreneurs were hardly paragons of chivalry when it came to business practices. They used intimidation, stock manipulation, secret rebate deals, outright chicanery, and bribery of public officials to limit competition in their respective industries. When a citizens' group accused railroad magnate Cornelius Vanderbilt of violating the law, he allegedly blustered, "Law! What do I care about the law? Hain't I got the power?" The entrepreneurs operated in an environment largely devoid of regulation. They could be as creative and as destructive as they wanted. At the same time, it is unlikely the economy would have grown so quickly and so enormously in a regulated environment.[56]

Rockefeller, a devout Baptist, placed his business dealings within the context of his religious devotion. He claimed that God endowed him with "the power to make money. . . . I believe it is my duty to make money and still more money, and to use the money I make for the good of my fellow man according to the dictates of my conscience." As for running roughshod over his competitors, Rockefeller had little remorse for his actions, referring to Standard Oil as "the Moses who delivered them [the competing refiners] from their folly which had wrought such havoc in their fortunes." Standard Oil was not a rogue firm. To the contrary, it had "rendered a missionary service to the whole world." Rockefeller was far from the only consolidator in American industry. By the 1880s, several industries had become synonymous with corporate names. Western Union meant telegraphy; Bell signified telephones; Singer, sewing machines; Colt, firearms; and Procter & Gamble, soap.[57]

The entrepreneurial thrust for efficiency, discipline, and rational management blended well with "business Christianity," which first appeared during the religious revival of 1857–58. This was a male-oriented, "muscular," unsentimental, and politically neutral form of Christianity. The war had stripped evangelical Christianity of its romantic and messianic qualities and created a more practical and less emotional religious culture. Harriet Beecher Stowe's conversion (and the conversion of many of her family members) to the Episcopal Church was a small part of this transformation, as were her brother's secular sermons.

Few Americans were more practical and less theoretical than the gaggle of inventors who created the technology that created a modern nation. Invention, like innovation, benefited from the freewheeling postwar environment. *Scientific American* predicted at the beginning of the Civil War that "the inventions resulting from the intellectual activity which generally accompanies a period of war are not confined at all to warlike implements, but are found in every department of science and art." Nothing as far-reaching as the sewing machine, the reaper, or the telegraph came out of the war, but improvements in railroad construction, industrial machinery, agricultural implements, and shipping benefited from the war economy and created a community of inventors that consistently improved on existing technology to make new things. The Brooklyn Bridge, for example, a technological icon of the age, began construction in 1870 after improvements in steel and masonry fabrication rendered John A. Roebling's design feasible. Demand for steel in rails, bridges, and machinery, combined with improved production techniques resulted in the growth of steel manufacturing from two thousand tons in 1867 to over one million tons by 1880. Technological innovations helped to create and expand new postwar industries such as steel, oil refining, food canning, machine tools, electrical equipment, and rubber.[58]

Americans before the war believed they could transcend history and attain perfection as God's Chosen People living in His Chosen Nation. After the war, transcendence came in the form of science and technology, the visual, verifiable proof of man's conquest of Nature. Not angels but engineers, not saints but scientists, lifted the new American nation. Nature was beautiful so long as it could be made useful. "Nature unadorned is not its highest type of beauty," *Scientific American* explained. "A scene of wildness appeals more powerfully to the senses when it is relieved by the sight of a monument of man's ingenuity in a magnificent bridge or an aqueduct.... Man is the improver of visible nature as well as of the latent forces of natural laws. Nature exists for man." The editor acknowledged critics who complained that such a mechanistic view "would destroy all poetry, romance, and sentiment." However, the editor responded, "we do not despair of seeing the poetry of steam, the romance of steamship voyages, and the sentiment of a sewing machine yet embodied in poetry and story."[59]

In that case, the most poetic and sentimental American of the postwar era was Thomas Edison, another young man who rose "from the great mass." Like Mark Twain, Edison headed east in 1868 after being fired from a job in Louisville. He settled in Newark, New Jersey, a rising port and manufacturing city near New York where, nearly penniless, he perfected a printing telegraph, or stock ticker, that printed out up-to-the-minute stock quotations as well as "all general news of the world . . . in advance of all newspapers." Edison next developed a "quadruplex" telegraph that handled four messages over the same wire simultaneously. By 1876, his fortune from telegraphy allowed him to establish the first research and development facility in the United States at Menlo Park, New Jersey, where he worked on such famous inventions as the phonograph and the incandescent lightbulb. Public admiration of Edison was so great that when a New York newspaper ran an April Fool's headline, "Edison Invents a Machine That Will Feed the Human Race," many readers believed it as fact.[60]

Edison's enterprises required a significant infusion of capital and, as in the case of Rockefeller, the ready availability of credit fueled the genius of invention. J. Pierpont Morgan became a prime investor in Edison's work. Edison's inventions would not only conquer Nature but, as *Scientific American* had predicted, improve on it as well. Edison's work obliterated distance, turned night into day, and captured the sound of the human voice. Middle-class households were defined not only by income but also by things. By 1900, electric lighting and the phonograph were so commonplace in middle-class homes they scarcely provoked comment. By 1910, General Electric had debuted an all-electric kitchen.

The North, meaning America, was ablaze with brilliance and innovation after the Civil War. Making money was the least of that brilliance, an entry fee for a new and better life. Creating new things and new ways of creating were the engines building a modern America. Americans moved quickly out of the realm of war and into the land of prosperity. It was no Eden, not with its roiling cities, anxious workers, fresh immigrants, struggling farmers, mourning widows, and traumatized veterans. But it was a land of possibility, a place of realistic aspiration. No illusions, no sentiment; just hard work and a limitless future. That was enough. "Thy great cathedral sacred industry," Whitman called his new nation, replacing the tragedy of war with the triumph of enterprise, as he sang in the "Song of the Exposition" (1871):

> *Away with themes of war! away with war itself!*
> *Hence from my shuddering sight to never more return*
> *that show of blacken'd, mutilated corpses!*

That hell unpent and raid of blood, fit for wild tigers
  or for lop-tongued wolves, not reasoning men,
And in its stead speed industry's campaigns,
With thy undaunted armies, engineering,
Thy pennants labor, loosen'd to the breeze,
Thy bugles sounding loud and clear.

Away with old romance!
Away with novels, plots and plays of foreign courts,
Away with love-verses sugar'd in rhyme, the intrigues,
  amours of idlers,
Fitted for only banquets of the night where dancers to
  late music slide,
The unhealthy pleasures, extravagant dissipations of
  the few,
With perfumes, heat and wine, beneath the dazzling
  chandeliers. . . .

I say I bring thee Muse to-day and here,
All occupations, duties broad and close,
Toil, healthy toil and sweat, endless, without
  cessation, . . .

With latest connections, works, the inter-
  transportation of the world,
Steam-power, the great express lines, gas, petroleum,
These triumphs of our time, the Atlantic's delicate
  cable,
The Pacific railroad, the Suez canal, the Mont Cenis
  and Gothard and Hoosac tunnels, the Brooklyn
  bridge,
This earth all spann'd with iron rails, with lines of
  steamships threading every sea,
Our own rondure, the current globe I bring.[61]

Northerners had docked the war at Lethe's Wharf. They embraced the new nation and all its possibilities. Yet they lived in a time of riddles. The war was over, yet fighting continued. The war had settled the issues of slavery and state sovereignty, yet it had not. The war created a broad prosperity, yet misery persisted. Postwar Americans would address these contradictions, though only within the framework of the Age of Reason and only as secondary to their

personal navigations through the new national economy. Science, not sentiment, would dominate public policy. The trajectory of the South would be
significantly different after the war. White and black southerners would have
other preoccupations that, increasingly, would matter only to each other.

CHAPTER 17

ASPIRATIONS

TWO WEEKS AFTER THE CIVIL WAR ended, N. J. Bell, a railroad conductor, enjoyed a layover in Wilmington, North Carolina. A small boy and a little girl who lived on the edge of the railyard came up to him asking for something to eat. He gave them whatever bread and meat they could carry away. The children were very thankful. Their father had been killed during the war, and both their mother and grandmother were sick. Bell returned to Wilmington two months later. Lounging in the railyard, he inquired about the fate of the boy and girl. He learned that their mother had died and the children had starved to death.[1]

The homecoming of the southern soldier was quite different from that of his counterpart in the North, if either came home at all. Sometimes there was nothing to come home to. A young man on his way home traveled by train through the same Georgia countryside Sherman's army had passed six months earlier. Out his window, he saw "a desolated land. Every village and station we stopped at presented an array of ruined walls and chimneys standing useless and solitary." Beyond the towns, abandoned fields alternated with pine forests. Livestock gone or dead; farm equipment missing or destroyed; heirloom seeds for cotton lost; seedbeds choked with weeds; levees and canals fallen into disrepair; shops shuttered or destroyed. If a family were fortunate enough to salvage a plough, they would have to drag it through the fields themselves. Starvation loomed over a landscape of despair.[2]

Richmond, the once-proud capital of the Confederacy, stood as forlorn and as hollow as the late cause. Blackened chimneys were silhouetted against the sky. Debris clogged streets. Vacant lots here and there punctuated by a granite facade with nothing behind it. Piles of cinders everywhere. Residents lined up to receive rations from federal authorities, a file of "sickly-faced women, jaundiced old men and children in rags, with here and there a seedy gentleman who had seen better days, or a stately female in faded apparel ... whom the war had reduced to want." A resident copied from Lamentations:

> *How doth the city sit solitary, that was full of people!*
> *How is she become as a widow!*
> *She that was great among the nation,*
> *And princess among the provinces,*
> *How is she become tributary!*[3]

For the next forty years, the southerner's per capita income remained stagnant. Two thirds of the South's wealth had disappeared, as had one out of four
white men between the ages of twenty and forty. Confederate currency was
worthless. Total northern wealth increased by a robust 50 percent between 1860
and 1870; southern wealth declined by 60 percent. Even if slaves are removed
from the calculation, the decline was 30 percent. It would take the South sixty
years to reach the level of wealth it possessed in 1860.

Refugeeing women and children making their way back home chronicled
the sorrowful journey. Elizabeth Allston and her mother recalled, "We were
never out of the sight of dead things, and the stench was almost unbearable.
Dead horses along the way and, here and there, a leg or an arm sticking out of
a hastily made too-shallow grave. . . . No living thing was left." It made a difference that the bloody war had been fought on southern ground.[4]

Loss surrounded southerners—a home, a loved one, a favorite heirloom.
Rooms where children had played and grown into adulthood; gardens that
once greeted the spring with lustrous beauty; and soft evenings of tea and
cakes and conversation. It was not only the loss of things, but also the loss of
what those things represented. When Mary Chesnut returned to her Camden,
South Carolina, home from Richmond, she came to a ravaged ruin, furniture
smashed, anything of value plundered. Union soldiers had burned the last reserves of cotton that were her family's livelihood. The land remained, but
burdened by huge debts that she would never be able to repay. The memories
came flooding back to her most vividly at night when the day's chores were
over and everyone had gone to bed. She wrote to a friend, "There are nights
here with the moonlight, cold & ghastly, & the screech owls alone disturbing
the silence when I could tear my hair & cry aloud for all that is past & gone."
All that remained was "lavender and pressed-rose memories."[5]

Wade Hampton III would never forget or forgive. Scion of a prominent
South Carolina family, owner of large tracts of land and slaves before the war,
he never allowed himself to succumb to the fury of some of his comrades in the
years following the surrender. His outward civility did not imply accommodation, however. Appomattox was a way station, not the destination. Together
with his fellow white men of South Carolina, he would help steer the state back
home.

Hampton was a moderate. He had opposed secession, and fire-eaters repulsed him. When Lincoln called for troops, however, the forty-three-year-old planter knew his duty. The Hampton Legion was born. He fought ably and rose to the Confederate high command. He hated the war. As early as October 1862, he wrote home, "My heart has grown sick of the war, & I long for peace." Two years later, Hampton's cavalry confronted three Union infantry corps outside of Petersburg. A Yankee bullet found one of his sons, Preston. Hampton raced over, cradled the dying boy in his arms, and cried, "My son, my son!"[6]

Six months later, the war was over. Hampton returned to his home outside Columbia and discovered there was no home. His property destroyed, many of his slaves gone, and deep in debt from which he would never recover, Hampton faced the future with $1.75 in his pocket. Yet he was not the worst off by far. He had only lost his brother, his son, and his livelihood. He wanted desperately to get back to the past. And he wanted vindication.

As the desperation grew, some took the law into their own hands and looted shops or stole from farmers. "A spirit of lawlessness seems to pervade the town," the *Montgomery Advertiser* complained. The general disorder bred other crimes as well. The *Atlanta New Era* chronicled a crime wave of "rape, murder, suicide, theft, burglary, garroting, pocket picking, embezzlement, elopements, bigamy, [and] adultery." With few police officers and dark streets—most towns and cities lacked gas to light their streetlamps—law enforcement was negligible. A northern journalist visiting Atlanta warned, "Passing about the dark, crooked streets of Atlanta after night, unaccompanied and unarmed, was worse than attempting a similar exploration of the Five Points in New York."[7]

The world had not merely changed for southerners; it had turned upside down, as if, suddenly, they had happened upon a mirror universe of whence they had come. In Charleston, the cradle of rebellion, gaiety ruled the streets in April 1861, like "Paris in the Revolution." On the fourth anniversary of this merriment, Charleston's streets were still crowded, only this time with armed black soldiers. The restaurants were shuttered or destroyed; and their patrons were dead, in prison, or destitute. The taverns were rollicking, but the patrons all wore blue uniforms. Occasionally, a soldier in a Confederate uniform wandered by, not to tweak his former enemy but because he had no other clothes to wear.[8]

The elevation of African Americans grated most on white southerners. Watching a contingent of black soldiers marching through the streets of Mobile, a white resident exclaimed, "There's my Tom. How I'd like to cut the throat of the dirty, impudent good-for-nothing!" The slaves were now masters, and the masters felt like slaves. "Change, change, indelibly stamped upon everything I meet, even upon the faces of the people!" former vice president Alexander Stephens remarked sadly.[9]

The blame for this terrible state of affairs clearly lay with the Yankees. Mary Chesnut expressed the sentiment of many in similarly reduced circumstances: "I . . . wish they were *all* dead—all Yankees." While northerners hurried to forget, southerners wrapped themselves in resentment. What they saw on a daily basis, and the hunger and deprivation they felt, had a great deal to do with it. They had lost the war, to be sure, but to many it was not a fair fight. "You had three things too many for us," a Georgia planter told northern journalist Whitelaw Reid, "the Irish, the niggers, and Jesus Christ." Many southerners accepted as fact that northern armies consisted almost entirely of immigrants conscripted as they landed. It would not be the last myth about the war to prevail in the South.[10]

Resentful southerners were not anxious to take up arms again, at least not against Yankee armies. They would express and act upon their bitterness in safer venues. However cordial they might be to northern visitors and soldiers, and however accepting they seemed of the war's outcome, they were still pursuing the rebellion. Whitelaw Reid reported that he met many professed Unionists in the South, but "to talk of any genuine Union sentiment . . . any intention to go one step further out of the old paths that led to the rebellion . . . is preposterous." Time and again, Reid encountered congenial hosts who informed him that the North forced the South into the war, that the South had no choice but to defend encroachments on its liberty. Reid never heard anyone suggest that, somehow, southerners might have contributed to the conflict. Without accountability, there could be no contrition.[11]

Without contrition, white southerners were likely to respond with hostility to restrictions or conditions imposed by federal authority. Wade Hampton fired off a letter to Andrew Johnson, who favored mild terms for southern re-entry into the Union. Hampton informed the president that the federal government could not demand more of the South than simple loyalty. "You have no right to ask or to expect that she will at once profess unbounded love for the Union." While southerners accepted defeat, Hampton warned Johnson that "the brave men . . . fought to the last in a cause which they believe, *and still believe.*" If Johnson contemplated a form of apprenticeship for southern states, southerners would perceive that as an insult: "She [the South] will never . . . tarnish her name by inscribing on her escutcheon . . . that she has been guilty." Hampton acknowledged the end of both slavery and southern independence, but he did not recognize the rightness of these outcomes. With such attitudes, any conditions imposed on the South would have been perceived as unjust.[12]

White southerners would register their defiance privately for the time being. Careful to maintain an outer demeanor of loyalty for fear of losing their property, their political rights, or worse, they accepted the verdict of the war, but not that it was over. As a Virginian told New England journalist John T. Trowbridge, "The war feeling here is like a burning bush with a wet blanket wrapped around it. Looked at from the outside, the fire seems quenched. But just peep under the blanket and there it is, all alive, and eating, eating in." Georgia humorist Bill Arp put the feelings of fellow white southerners in more earthy terms: "Who's sorry? Who's repentin? Who ain't proud of our people? Who loves our enemies? Nobody but a durned sneak."[13]

Whites in the South sometimes demonstrated their feelings in more public ways, especially in the cities, though subtly. Women refused to walk under the American flag or crossed the street when approaching a northern man. Federal authorities banned the display of Confederate symbols. Veterans covered their buttons with mourning cloth and left them on their coats. The resistance had its song:

> Oh, I'm a good old Rebel,
>   Now that's just what I am;
> For the "fair land of Freedom"
>   I do not care a dam.
> I'm glad I fit against it—
>   I only wish we'd won.
> And I don't want no pardon,
>   For anything I done.
>
> Three hundred thousand Yankees
>   Lie still in Southern dust
> We got three hundred thousand
>   Before they conquered us.
> They died of Southern fever
>   And Southern steel and shot.
> I wish we'd killed three million
>   Instead of what we got.[14]

Many northerners suspected southern professions of loyalty to the Union. Their prewar history of placing state above national interests and their vigorous defense of slavery did not evaporate at Appomattox. Those advocating a strong hand toward the South after the war reminded their colleagues, "Cannon conquer, but they do not necessarily convert." Southerners believed their loss in the war represented a failure of numbers, not of ideas. *Harper's* printed numerous dispatches from the South in the months after the surrender to demonstrate the persistent rebelliousness of the southern white population.

A correspondent from Memphis wrote to *Harper's*, "The rebellious spirit of the people here is as bitter and strong as it has been at any time during the last five years."[15]

Outward acquiescence and inward resistance toward those who have brought down calumny upon your family is a good strategy for survival in the short run. White southerners, however, wanted more than survival. Like Hampton, they wanted vindication. Most of all they wanted to reconstruct their lives, their communities, and their civilization. Loathing the present, fearing the future, they looked to the past.

White southerners groped for meaning in defeat. If, as their ministers and leaders had told them, they were fighting a holy war, then they must have sinned against God. Yet the Old Testament is replete with examples of God's Chosen People receiving severe punishment for serious transgressions against His laws. God held out the possibility of redemption if His people repented. "He loveth whom he chasteneth," from Hebrews 12:6, became the scriptural foundation of a new southern faith. It enabled white southerners to rationalize their loss and move forward in their lives with the belief in their ultimate redemption. As northerners moved away from a civil society informed and directed by evangelical Protestantism, southerners embraced it, and embraced it so fiercely that it became a folk religion indistinguishable from southern culture. Thomas Markham, a Presbyterian minister, took this theme in a sermon he delivered in New Orleans shortly after the end of the war: the "present afflictions which are but for a moment, shall work out for us a far more exceeding and eternal weight of glory." Defeat was not an adverse judgment on the South so much as a motivation to create a perfect society. "Defeat," the Rev. Moses Drury Hoge of Richmond declared, "is the discipline which trains the truly heroic soul to further and better endeavors." For southerners, "it is better to be chastened, than to be let alone."[16]

The religious transformation served two purposes in the South. First, it shored up a shaken faith. Second, the South's status as a Chosen Nation elevated the cause for which it fought. The impurity was in the southerner, not in the cause. Robert Lewis Dabney, the South's leading Presbyterian theologian, wrote in 1867, "Because we believe that God intends to vindicate his Divine Word, and to make all nations honour it . . . we confidently expect that the world will yet do justice to Southern slaveholders." It was not happenstance that white southerners called the men who led the restoration Redeemers.[17]

White southerners had to perceive the North as evil incarnate in order to sustain the belief in their section's ultimate redemption. For God would not allow evil to triumph. At a memorial service in Charleston in 1870, Wade Hampton reminded his listeners that might did not mean right. Just as the sword had "turned over Spain and Portugal to the tender mercies of the Saracens," it was now "directed by unscrupulous power against prostrate States, reeking with fratricidal blood, [enforcing] the laws which it alone has made."[18]

The theme that the South's suffering was temporary and only awaiting redemption became the prevailing arc of southern expression after Appomattox. The lost war was not a heavenly judgment on southern ideals. It was a call for rededication to those ideals. In 1865, the Rev. Dr. A. W. Miller, pastor of the First Presbyterian Church in Charlotte, North Carolina, responded to comments of northern ministers that the South should accept the results of the war as a divine remonstrance against its institutions. Miller replied that "accepting the situation" did not mean that southerners "abandoned their former distinctive views and principles." He cited Old Testament accounts of neighboring nations defeating the Jewish people. "Providence, for wise ends, may permit an ungodly nation to prosper for a time." If southerners had maintained a proper relationship with God, "Southern principles would have been crowned with speedy victory." A purified South would arise from the ashes to serve as God's "last and only hope."[19]

The resurrected South would look a great deal like the Old South, a restored regime of white supremacy, patriarchy, and states' rights. These political and cultural principles became holy tenets, dissent from which threatened redemption. Politics and theology became indistinguishable. A Baptist minister declared, "As a Democrat, I love all Democrats. All Baptists are Democrats. . . . It is THE political faith of the great majority of the members of the church." Politics became a faith, and the vote was an offering to both God and the South.[20]

The Lord would not allow white southerners to suffer long. Benjamin M. Palmer, the Presbyterian minister who had delivered the stirring Thanksgiving Day sermon in November 1860 on the Christian roots of secession, consoled the members of his church that "the next generation would see the South *free* and independent." If the South must wander in the desert, it would eventually reach the Promised Land. Redemption would come. Recall: "It was when Isaac lay upon the altar of sacrifice that Abraham's faith was made perfect by works; it was when the Hebrew children walked in the midst of the fiery furnace that the glory of the Lord was revealed before the eyes of His enemies."[21]

Remain steadfast to the truths of the Old South and southerners would triumph. Robert Lewis Dabney, in a commencement address at Davidson College in 1868, urged the graduates to maintain antebellum ideals: "Resolve to abate nothing, to concede nothing of righteous conviction." Dabney warned the students of the evils of urbanization and technology and the enfranchisement of blacks. He prayed that these future leaders of the South would adopt "scriptural politics." These ideals would not only ensure that the South would prevail, but they would also serve as a "bulwark against the flood of Yankee innovations in religion and morals." The great danger for the South, Dabney concluded, would be to allow the North to *"Yankeeize the South,"* making southerners "become like the conquerors."[22]

Such ideas coalesced into a creed called the Lost Cause. The creed idealized the Old South, elevated the Civil War to a passion play of courage and martyrdom, and depicted the Reconstruction era as a time of unmerited suffering, the time before Redemption. The Confederacy died and the South was reborn, more pure, more chaste, and more obedient to the old values. While northerners looked forward, filed the war away, and relegated religion to a subordinate role, white southerners embraced and sanctified the past. "The present is a very little part of life, sir," a character in an Ellen Glasgow novel informs us. "It's the past in which we store our treasures." Southerners walked backward into the future.[23]

Southern religion merged with southern culture. Churches altered their hymnals to incorporate the Lost Cause creed. Ministers retitled "That Old-Time Religion" to "We Are Old-Time Confederates." The Methodist church adopted a new hymn, "Let Us Pass Over the River, and Rest Under the Shade of the Trees," the final words of Stonewall Jackson.[24]

Southern history imbued the South's religion. Virginia writer James Branch Cabell asserted, "No history is a matter of record; it is a matter of faith." In the chaotic and uncertain months after the end of the war, religion was much more than a solace; it was an explanation and a reason to hope. The home would be rebuilt; the town would prosper; the farm would yield its bounty; and whites would regain their patrimony. It was God's promise. And any means white southerners employed to accomplish the South's redemption were justified. Redemption meant the independence of white southerners to order their lives and their society as ordained by Scripture. God had given white southerners the "great mission of political independence," a writer in *De Bow's Review* asserted in 1868. Now they must fulfill His wish. The war and its aftermath crucified the South; soon would come the resurrection of a great people.[25]

Church became both the cultural and religious center of southern life. The southern white church boomed in the 1860s. Evangelical denominations had 31,000 more church seats and 450 more congregations in 1870 than in 1860. While property values fell throughout the South during this decade, the church property of these denominations rose in value by nearly $1 million.

Southern women played significant roles in the expanded church polity. They had always been more churchgoing than the men. Women kept the family Bible and saw to it that names and traditions were carried down from generation to generation. They were the guardians of memory for their families. As history blended into faith, and as the boundaries between public and private spheres in the South became indistinct, women become the attendants of sacred southern memory. Their work expanded from the family to encompass the community. The cemetery became an extension of the home.

Southerners constructed their lives around their fallen. The women of Richmond painstakingly carried stones to erect a precarious pyramid at Hollywood Cemetery commemorating the late martyrs. Many of these women were never able to bury their loved ones. Their sons and husbands and fathers lay in common graves in Gettysburg or Antietam, or were missing altogether. The graves they tended were surrogates for the loss of a farewell. They followed Jefferson Davis's admonition to "keep the memories of our heroes green." Statues went up and wreaths were placed at the tombs of Jackson, Stuart, then Lee. On May 10, 1866, the women organized the first Confederate Memorial Day, drawing the white community together to commemorate the martyrs. They had not departed; they had merely changed their address. If the boundary between religion and culture had disappeared, so had the distinction between life and death. The women placed a banner at the tomb of J. E. B. Stuart in Hollywood Cemetery: "Stuart: Dead, yet alive. Mortal, yet immortal." By the late 1870s, orators were referring to the Confederacy in the present tense. In the moment of its death, Robert Penn Warren wrote, "the Confederacy entered upon its immortality."[26]

Southerners took pride in their defeat, relished and exaggerated their suffering. They lavished more attention on the dead than on the living. These were the penances before the redemption. Father Abram Ryan, the poet of the Confederacy, wrote, "A land without ruins is a land without memories; a land without memories is a land without liberty. . . . Crowns of roses fade; crowns of thorns endure. Calvaries and crucifixions take deepest hold of humanity; the triumphs of might are transient." As he watched the women lay the wreaths and inscribe the tablets, he wrote, "There's grandeur in graves— There's glory in gloom."[27]

This was history remembered, not learned. It was history as therapy. The reality of life in the South was too harsh, and the contrast between what was and what is too great. Some, like Ashley Wilkes, found the time after the war so much out of joint that they crumbled. He explained to Scarlett O'Hara that life had "suddenly become too real. . . . It isn't that I mind splitting logs here in the mud, but I do mind what it stands for. I do mind, very much, the loss of the beauty of the old life I loved. Scarlett, before the war, life was beautiful. There was a glamour to it, a perfection and a completeness and a symmetry to it like Grecian art." Most southerners, however, were not as incapacitated as Ashley Wilkes. They willed the old life back into existence, even if it never quite existed in those terms. Like their religion, it was a matter of faith. And that faith shaped their view of the world. Father Ryan recalled seeing his young niece standing before a painting of the death of Jesus. He asked her if she knew who crucified her Lord. Without hesitation, she replied, "O yes I know. The Yankees."[28]

There was an air of defiance about all of this. An acceptance of defeat, but a refusal to acknowledge its consequences. A Confederate veteran declared after the surrender, "In the face of the civilized world the honor of the South stands untarnished and her sons will live in the world's memory as a chivalrous, gallant and brave people." Better to think that than to despair about the poverty, the hunger, the devastation, and the world turned upside down. Better to be proud than prostrate. White southerners held the past tightly, as it was all they had left. "Everything," Margaret Mitchell wrote, "in their old world had changed but the forms. The old usages went on, must go on, for the forms were all that were left to them." It was a remarkable piece of alchemy, turning misery into romance. Leave reality to the Yankees.[29]

Edward A. Pollard, editor of the *Richmond Examiner*, wrote one of the first histories of the war in 1866. He called it *The Lost Cause*, borrowing the phrase from the Scottish Jacobites. He wrote, "It would be immeasurably the worst consequence of defeat in this war that the south could lose its moral and intellectual distinctiveness as a people, and cease to assert its well-known superiority in civilization." He accepted the defeat, the restoration of the Union, and the abolition of slavery. "But the war did not decide negro equality; it did not decide negro suffrage; it did not decide State Rights. . . . And these things, which the war did not decide, the southern people will still cling to, still claim, and still assert them in their rights and views." Pollard articulated the sentiment of white southerners: defeated, defiant, unbowed, and unwilling to relinquish the ideals they cherished most, particularly now that they had become not only a matter of conviction but of faith as well.[30]

There were other southerners, black southerners, who held an entirely different perspective on the Old South and the war and its aftermath. These were differences born of distinctive experiences, differences that could not be reconciled. The former slaves failed to advance much beyond their status in 1865 primarily because their white neighbors could not allow it. The subjugation of the black southerner became too much a part of the white southerner's faith. It was essential to redemption.

Frederick Douglass knew that freedom was not enough. While he appreciated the missionary aid societies and the Freedmen's Bureau, the government agency founded in 1865 to ease the transition of the slave to freedom, he wanted equality, not charity. If black people became permanent victims, they would never enjoy full citizenship. The Indian provided a frightening example of a colored race standing outside the pale of white civilization. "The negro needs justice more than pity, liberty more than old clothes," Douglass wrote in May 1865. Grateful for the well-intentioned white educators coming south to tutor the former slaves, he nevertheless asserted that his people needed "rights more than training to enjoy them."[31]

Douglass believed what most whites did not: that the war and its outcome demanded racial equality. "Whether the tremendous war so heroically fought . . . shall pass into history a miserable failure . . . or whether, on the other hand, we shall, as the rightful reward of victory over treason have a solid nation, entirely delivered from all contradictions and social antagonisms, must be determined one way or the other." Full citizenship for the former slaves honored those men who fought and died and the nation they had saved. For northern whites, it was enough that slavery was ended and the great experiment forged in revolution was saved.[32]

Emancipation and the Thirteenth Amendment forced southern whites to acknowledge the black man's freedom, nothing more. Even so, many whites predicted African Americans would wilt in their new status. They would descend to barbarism and penury without the discipline of forced labor. Unable to survive, they would become extinct, as many believed would happen to the Indians. A Mississippi planter predicted to a Union officer, "These niggers will all be slaves again in twelve months."[33]

That was a hope, but it masked many fears. Would the freedmen work without compulsion? Would the former slave become a master supported by federal bayonets? Would there be a race war? Would the Federals confiscate whites' land? Slavery had ended; but what would take its place? Armed black men parading in the streets of southern cities and former slaves coming and going as they pleased and addressing whites in a too-familiar way—were these portents of a greater revolution to come, or merely a passing phase? Southern society was predicated on white supremacy. Without it, redemption would be lost.

Blacks hoped, too. The months after the surrender saw a giddy excitement in black communities across the country as residents contemplated a new equality, an opportunity to reconstruct the nation on egalitarian grounds. A young black man attending a Fourth of July celebration in Washington, D.C., exulted, "We come to the National Capital—our Capital—with new hopes, new prospects, new joys, in view of the future and past of the people." In Little Rock, Arkansas, another young black man proclaimed, "God marked it out with his own finger;... here, where we have been degraded, will we be exalted— AMERICANS IN AMERICA, ONE AND INDIVISIBLE." Such declarations represented different hopes and a different faith from those of white southerners. Both claimed to know God's purpose, but only one would prevail.[34]

Freedmen took to the roads. These were not aimless wanderings to test their freedom but purposeful searches for children, husbands, wives, and relatives, hoping to reconstitute families. They chose their destinations based on rumor or memory or from the master's recollection. So these journeys of hope would not end in frustration, the freedmen placed advertisements in local papers, posted notices in churches, and asked Freedmen's Bureau officials for assistance. A bureau agent in South Carolina recalled, "They had a passion, not so much for wandering, as for getting together, and every mother's son among them seemed to be in search of his mother; every mother in search of her children." In North Carolina, a northern journalist came upon a middle-aged freedman, tired and footsore, who told him he had walked nearly six hundred miles to find his wife and children, who were sold away four years earlier. One freedman sought his mother, whom he had not seen since 1846. He eventually learned that she had died three years earlier. Even as late as the 1880s, advertisements appeared in newspapers requesting the whereabouts of relatives long lost. Here is one:

> Charlotte Brock wishes to hear from her son Alonzo; was taken from her about 1859, to Memphis, Tenn; lived there with a family named Morrison. Think he was in the army during the rebellion. Any information concerning him will be thankfully received by his aged mother.[35]

Many of the attempts at reunion were successful. By 1870, nearly 75 percent of blacks lived in two-parent households. Even when reunions occurred, they were sometimes bittersweet. Laura Spicer's husband had remarried, thinking she had died. After the war, when he discovered Laura was alive, he was both relieved and tormented. He wrote to her, "I would come and see you but I know you could not bear it. I want to see you and I don't want to see you. I love you just as well as I did the last day I saw you, and it will not do for you and I to meet. I am married, and my wife have two children." They continued to correspond. In one letter, he requested, "Send me some of the children's hair in a separate paper with their names on the papers." He concluded the letter crying out to her, "Oh, I can see you so plain, at any-time. The woman is not born that feels as near to me as you do."[36]

Many freedmen went to cities, not only to find loved ones but also to find work. The plantation was the master's domain, the place of whips, chains, and work from sunup to sundown. The city belonged to no man, and a freedman could be his own master. He could find a place to live, negotiate for work, and join a church and a mutual aid society. Although the majority of blacks remained on the farm, many moved to town. Within a year or two, blacks comprised the majority of the population in Charleston, Petersburg, and Memphis. White residents sputtered with rage, "The streets are filled with them. . . . The shops are overflowing with them, squandering on themselves and each other what little money they have acquired in anything that strikes their fancy." If black migrants could not find lodgings in town they erected their own communities on the outskirts, leading to more fears among whites that these instant neighborhoods would become dens of vice and dissipation. What grated on whites was freedom, that former slaves were making their own decisions on where and how to live.[37]

Close contact was a fact of urban life. In rural areas, blacks and whites could maintain their distance. This was more difficult in cities. Sidewalks and streets were crowded. Segregation was not yet the rule in places such as taverns, train stations, and parks. Indiscriminate mingling implied a rough equality. Some cities enacted laws requiring blacks to walk about with passes as in the days of slavery. A black man in Richmond complained, "All that is needed to restore Slavery in full is the auction-block as it used to be." White employers resisted hiring blacks, and cities imposed heavy licensing fees on those who wanted to go into business for themselves. Whites took up many of the city jobs that blacks had held before the war, such as drayman, barman, or barber. Black women had better luck finding jobs as laundresses and domestics. Whites hired armed guards (often former slaves) to patrol their porches and protect them from potential black thieves, murderers, and rapists who were allegedly waiting to pounce.[38]

Some of these black urban migrants moved back to the farm, but not enough to satisfy whites. Within a year of the surrender, white southerners had regained control of many local and state governments. Among the first pieces of business were laws to restrict black movement. Vagrancy laws established lengthy sentences for being about without means of support. Statutes set fines on employers for hiring blacks without checking references or their previous employer. A great fear of the white South was that the loss of black labor would ruin any chance of economic recovery.

These were not the greatest debilities confronting rural blacks. John Trow-bridge, the New England writer, explained why, despite bleak prospects, city blacks were reluctant to move back to the farm. Like most other northerners, he believed that working for wages on the farm was the best path to success for the freedmen. The rural South would prosper, and they along with it. Freed-men would save enough money to purchase a farm of their own someday. It was the story of upward mobility, of free labor's infinite possibilities for suc-cess, that had driven the American dream since the country's birth. Trow-bridge encountered some blacks in straitened circumstances in Petersburg. He tried to persuade them to return to the countryside where there was work. "But they assured me that they could not [go back]; their very lives had been in danger; and they told me of several murders perpetrated upon freedmen by the whites in their neighborhoods, besides other atrocities." Indeed, not much had changed on many plantations. A South Carolina planter admitted to the "uncommon amount of whipping it takes now to keep the plantation niggers in order."[39]

Land ownership would solve many of these problems. What blacks wanted most after the war was independence from the white man. Not separation, but independence to pursue their work and fortune. Whitelaw Reid asked freedmen in rural South Carolina what they desired of freedom, and they said, "Gib us our own land and we take care ourselves; but widout land, de ole massas can hire us or starve us, as dey please." The government donated mil-lions of acres of land to the railroads and begged, cajoled, and forced Indians onto reservations, but drew back when it came to securing land for the newly freed slave. The Republican Congress passed another homestead law in 1866 that enabled a small number of freedmen to purchase marginal land in the South, but a comprehensive grant program never emerged. Northerners con-ceived of freedmen as laborers. If they possessed skills and intelligence, and worked hard, they could aspire to land ownership and become rural Horatio Algers. But they would have to earn it without government subsidy.[40]

Blacks who had accumulated some savings could, of course, purchase land from whites. The official Freedmen's Bureau line was: "The government owns no lands in this State. It therefore can give away none. Freedmen can obtain farms with the money which they have earned by their labor. Every one, there-fore, shall work diligently, and carefully save his wages, till he may be able to buy land and possess his own home." In practice, this was nearly impossible. Traveling in the Mississippi Valley immediately after the war, Whitelaw Reid commented, "The feeling against any ownership of the soil by the negroes is so strong, that the man who should sell small tracts to them would be in actual personal danger." Even renting a parcel to blacks was deemed "unworthy of a good citizen." In a cash-poor South, with very few banks (that would not lend to freedmen anyway), land ownership would be difficult. Land ownership implied independence and the ability to accumulate capital and make decisions, all of which undermined the racial assumptions of whites.[41]

The situation seemed much more promising before the war ended, when General William T. Sherman issued his famous Field Orders No. 15 in January 1865. The orders arose out of a conference between Sherman, Secretary of War Edwin M. Stanton, and a group of black ministers in Savannah. The parties agreed to divide abandoned and confiscated lands on the Sea Islands and a portion of the Low Country coast south of Charleston into forty-acre plots for each black family. Sherman also suggested that the army could loan mules to the freedmen, the likely basis of the phrase "forty acres and a mule" that became a rallying cry for freedmen across the South. Sherman claimed later that the land transfer was a temporary measure to alleviate the tremendous influx of blacks into his lines following his march through Georgia. The freedmen assumed otherwise. By May 1865, forty thousand freedmen had settled on four hundred thousand acres of "Sherman land."[42]

In May 1865, however, President Johnson announced his Proclamation of Amnesty, pardoning most Confederates and remitting any confiscated land. The freedmen were disconsolate. Some armed themselves to prevent the whites from repossessing their farms, but such resistance was short-lived. When Radical Republicans attempted to revive Sherman's orders in February 1866, the House defeated it by a three-to-one margin. Even at the height of the Radical tide in Congress, few lawmakers supported a return of black owners to the Sea Islands. This reversal was heartbreaking for the freedmen. The slaves had remained loyal to the government; their masters had not. They had toiled on these lands without recompense. Many had served in the Union armies, fighting to save the government that now betrayed them.

But hope persisted. A school for black children opened in Marianna, Florida, early in 1866. Each day, the children passed a white school whose students hurled taunts and stones at the black youngsters. The stones would occasionally hit their targets and cause minor but painful injuries. One morning, the black children armed themselves with stones and walked past the white school in formation. Before then, they had walked to school in pairs or small groups. A half-dozen white boys materialized as usual and began to throw their missiles. Instead of running away, the black boys stood their ground. Seeing resistance, more white boys poured out of their school and charged the black children. The black students unleashed their fusillade and waded into the white attackers, who retreated quickly into the safety of their building. "There were many bruises on both sides," one of the black youngsters recalled, "but it taught the white youngsters to leave the colored ones alone."[43]

T. Thomas Fortune was a prominent editor of a black newspaper in New York City at the time he wrote about this incident. In the scheme of Reconstruction events, it did not amount to much. But for ten-year-old Thomas, born a slave in Marianna, it was a revelatory experience. He and his comrades had challenged whites successfully. They could now pursue their goal of getting an education. It also underscored the obstacles the freedmen confronted in their pursuit of the American dream. The eagerness with which black children (and adults) flooded schools was matched by the hostility of the white community that resented any advance toward equality by the former slaves.

Northern missionaries, many of them young middle-class women from New England, came south to teach those whose liberation they had prayed for. Between 1862 and 1870, more than eight thousand northerners traveled to the South to teach former slaves. Their sponsoring organizations, such as the American Missionary Association or evangelical church groups, provided funds to purchase books, pay teachers, and establish schools. The AMA also founded several major black universities during the 1860s, including Hampton Institute in Virginia, Howard University in Washington, D.C., and Fisk University in Tennessee. These institutions would train a cadre of black teachers who eventually replaced white missionaries. The Methodist Church not only sent missionary teachers south; its northern members contributed $2 million to black education in the South between 1865 and 1880. Not all funding came from charity. Black communities in cities across the South donated hard-earned savings to secure better school buildings, books, and higher salaries for teachers. Even the students chipped in. A group of black youngsters in Chattanooga scoured the battlefield for bullets to sell and spent the proceeds on spelling books.

The Freedmen's Bureau coordinated the educational activities of the various church groups. By 1869, the Bureau oversaw three thousand schools serving 150,000 black pupils. In many parts of the South, the black freedom schools were the first public schools of any kind. In a meritocratic society, education is the great leveler. Being born a slave was not a permanent bar on aspiration. In order to achieve independence and financial security, however, education, as much as work, was essential. Even former slaves from the most isolated districts of the South understood the value of an education.

Coming south to educate blacks required not only conviction but also courage. The teachers often received a hostile reception from native whites. A Quaker teacher in Clarksville, Tennessee, believed that local whites "would

*"Teaching the Freedmen" 1866. Visitors to the South immediately after the war
invariably commented on the freedmen's thirst for education. Classrooms
often contained several generations, as this one did. (Schomberg Center
for Research in Black Culture, the New York Public
Library, Astor, Lenox and Tilder Foundations)*

have been glad of the opportunity to have poisoned us. No white person spoke to us, and the town people never moved an inch on the walk for us." From North Carolina, teacher Margaret Thorpe wrote to a friend up north, "You can't imagine how strange it seems never to speak to a white person, and have absolutely no social life, not one visitor."[44]

Silence was preferable to some of the epithets directed at the émigrés. A teacher in Virginia wrote, "From one set of [white] students . . . I habitually received the polite salutation of 'damned Yankee bitch of a nigger teacher.'" Sisters Lucy and Sarah Chase recounted similar experiences in South Carolina, including a neighbor woman who could not imagine why they would come to teach blacks, adding, "I'd poison a Yankee in a moment, if I could get a chance."[45]

Verbal assaults were not the greatest of concerns for Yankee teachers. Alonzo B. Corliss, a partially crippled teacher at a Quaker school for blacks in Louisiana, was dragged out of his house by masked men and given thirty lashes with rawhide and hickory sticks for the crime of "teaching niggers and making them like white men." They shaved one side of his head, painted it black, and suggested that he leave town forthwith. Corliss received no solace from local Southern Baptists, who condemned him for teaching "politics rather than religion" and "equal suffrage rather than repentance." The Baptists had a point. The curriculum of many of these schools included reading lessons in the Bible, the Emancipation Proclamation, the Constitution, the Declaration of Independence, and speeches by Abraham Lincoln and Frederick Douglass. The instructors also taught the importance of self-reliance and obedience to the law. These lessons were undoubtedly not the kind of instruction southern whites would have preferred for blacks.[46]

Some missionaries lived in a constant state of terror. A teacher in Americus, Georgia, noted, "I sometimes feel so utterly helpless and alone and have so many severe and bitter [experiences] to bear that I yell at times. I cannot bear it. My life is in danger every hour." Booker T. Washington and W. E. B. DuBois, who did not agree on much, both praised the courage and value of these teachers. "Whenever it is written—and I hope it will be," Washington stated, "the part that the Yankee teachers played in the education of the Negroes immediately after the war will make one of the most thrilling parts of the history of this country." DuBois in *The Souls of Black Folk* (1903) called the teachers "the gift of New England to the freed Negro, not alms, but a friend; not cash, but character. . . . In actual formal content their curriculum was doubtless old-fashioned, but in educational power it was supreme, for it was the contact of living souls."[47]

Their faith and the eagerness of their pupils drove these teachers. Whitelaw Reid stood amazed at "the feverish anxiety for initiation into the mysteries of print, everywhere strikingly manifest among the negroes." On plantations, it was not unusual for the workers to ask former masters to reserve some of their wages to hire a teacher for their children. The pupils were not only eager, they were also apt. Reid commented, "In reading and writing I do not hesitate to say that the average progress of the children of plantation hands . . . is fully equal to the average progress of white children at the North." Not to mention white children in the South. Reid claimed that about 60 percent of Charleston's blacks could read, while only 12 percent of the city's white population was literate. A black resident explained the discrepancy to Reid: "Dey [whites] haven't learned, because dey don't care; we, because dey wouldn't let us."[48]

John Trowbridge encountered the same indifference among whites and enthusiasm among blacks for education. The public school superintendent of Chattanooga informed Trowbridge, "The colored people are far more zealous in the cause of education than the whites. They will starve themselves and go without clothes in order to send their children to school." The schools they attended were likely to be shabby affairs, converted sheds, old buildings "good for little else," and churches where the students knelt, using pew benches as desks. In Savannah, the most commodious black school was the former slave mart, where teachers taught their students in the large auction room or in the jail over it.[49]

The rapid ascent of black literacy testified to freedmen's enthusiasm. In Richmond, for example, by 1870, almost one third of the adult black population could read and write, compared with less than 10 percent in 1865. Joseph Wilson, a former slave who attended classes, attested to "this longing of ours for freedom of the mind as well as the body." In May 1867, *Harper's* made an announcement that likely caused some initial confusion among readers until they read through. At the end of an article touting the educational successes of African Americans in the South, the editor declared that Jefferson Davis's proposal for arming the slaves had come to fruition, adding, "but in a very different manner from that proposed by him."[50]

In many ways, the former slaves were the South's modernists. They came out of the war with unbounded optimism, eager to accept both the promise and challenge of freedom. They aspired to the same status as the young men and women coming to northern cities or moving out West. They wanted personal and financial independence. They sought land, jobs, and education. They reunited with their families. They established their own churches and associations. Their theology reflected the optimism of their new freedom. They had lived the Book of Exodus. Now they would enter the Promised Land. There was no need to bind themselves up and follow an orthodoxy of thought and action in order to reconcile with the Lord. They had already been saved, and they expressed their faith accordingly in animated and joyous worship. They did everything, in short, to make themselves productive American citizens.

White southerners, on the other hand, nursed their wounds and grievances. They did not, in fact, come out of the war. They remained mired in its mud, gore, and death. They looked backward to the Old South, not forward like northerners or African Americans. There were some prominent merchants and newspapermen in southern cities who promoted economic development just as hard as their northern counterparts. But this so-called New South Creed was a fraud as much as the professions of contrition and reconciliation. The refusal of southern churches to rejoin their northern denominational brethren provided a better indication of southern attitudes. These would-be entrepreneurs wanted to diversify the southern economy and attract northern investment, but they did not invite northern ideas or enterprises that would upset the social and political structure.[51]

All to keep the black man down in his place. For every time a white southerner encountered a black person in the years just after the war, the white was reminded of the defeat, the destruction, the society turned upside down, and his own reduced circumstances. Freedmen reminded the white southerner that there was much work to accomplish before redemption occurred, and the reduction of the black man stood high on the agenda of restoration. They feared God and they feared to think differently. The white southerner stood as the greatest obstacle to the success of the freedman. No Horatio Alger tale provided a recipe for how to get around this barrier.

It was for this reason that African Americans looked hopefully to the federal government in the early days of peace. The Union war had liberated the slaves and a nation. Northerners had paid a heavy price to achieve those objectives. They would not allow them to slip away in the warm glow of peace and prosperity. Or so the former slaves hoped.

CHAPTER 18

A Golden Moment

Andrew Johnson was no Abraham Lincoln. On that there was general agreement. Although some of the biographical details sounded familiar—the birth of low circumstances, the frequent uprooting as a child, and the life in a small town with a modest career that eventually led to politics—the respective individuals were quite different. Johnson was a Democrat, a firm believer in minimum government. A tailor by trade, he rose through the tumultuous ranks of Tennessee politics to become a U.S. senator. Like many other whites of his social class in east Tennessee, he disdained the plantation owners further west, their airs, their slaves, and their influence. Stocky in build, he dressed impeccably and exuded a polish that was acquired rather than inherited. Men appreciated Johnson's direct, sometimes blunt manner, but he could be stubborn and, when pressed, intemperate in his language.[1]

Johnson's sensitivity derived from insecurity over how far he had come in the world. He told his rags-to-riches story often, mostly for his own benefit. Perhaps the greatest distinction from Lincoln was Johnson's total lack of humor. He did not see any purpose in cultivating it in himself and he neither understood nor appreciated its demonstration in others. While he had little use for slavery, he had less regard for the black man, whose inherent and permanent inferiority he did not question. Johnson seemed most invigorated in opposition. While Lincoln's position on several key issues, including emancipation, evolved during the war, and he seemed open to the opinions of others, Johnson remained fixed in his views. He took differing opinions as personal affronts and clung to his position that much more fiercely.

Johnson's tenacity served him well during the war. He refused to join his southern colleagues in their abandonment of the nation's capital when the Civil War began. Johnson became a hero to the Radical Republicans, who hailed his courage and fortitude as they fought Lincoln on his tardy conversion to abolition and his mild views on postwar reconstruction. He assumed the presidency in tragic circumstances. The tailor was handed the task of mending the nation.

Historians have forever asked the question "What would Lincoln have done had he lived?" Would the outcome of Reconstruction been different, better, or worse? It is, of course, impossible to know, but wonderful to speculate. Lincoln never developed a comprehensive reconstruction plan, and, even if he had, given the skill with which he responded to events as they unfolded, he might very well have thrown his initial plan out the window.

During the relatively brief time Lincoln considered reconstruction policy, several general principles emerged. He hoped that the seceding states would return to full-fledged membership in the Union as soon as possible. To do so, the former Confederate states must accept the supremacy of federal authority and the demise of slavery. He had no desire to carry out a campaign of retribution against Confederate leaders. As for the former slaves, he held the same view as most northern whites, that the freedmen's path to success lay as workers for wages. He did not advocate land redistribution, but he did not rule it out. He believed blacks should vote, but perhaps only those who were literate and who served in Union forces. Lincoln would not require black suffrage as a prerequisite for the restoration of a state to full status in the Union. The Union was paramount to Lincoln, both in the war and in the coming peace.

In his December 1863 message to Congress, Lincoln announced a Proclamation of Amnesty and Reconstruction offering the Rebels "full pardon . . . with restoration of all rights of property, except as to slaves." High-ranking Confederate officials would have to take a loyalty oath. He promised to extend recognition to the reorganized states when as few as 10 percent of their voting-age population took an oath of allegiance. This was a wartime measure, meant to encourage Unionism in the occupied states, and not a portent of Lincoln's reconstruction policies. Louisiana was the first state to take up the proposal. About eleven thousand voters who promised to support the Union and agreed to abide by the Emancipation Proclamation elected a governor and a state legislature. The new government, however, did not provide for black suffrage.[2]

Lincoln admitted that he wished Louisiana had conferred voting rights on at least "the very intelligent freedmen." But it was a start. "Concede," he argued, "that the new government of Louisiana is only to what it should be as the egg is to the fowl, we shall sooner have the fowl by hatching the egg than by smashing it." Lincoln wanted to generate as much white support as possible. If he had insisted on black suffrage, it would have derailed the efforts of loyal Union men in Louisiana to gain readmission to the Union. As a constitutionalist, he was deeply concerned about the legitimacy of governments if they rested on a minority of citizens for too long a time. Above all he was a Unionist, and he wanted the nation whole. The Republican Party was still very much a sectional party. If a conciliatory reconstruction policy could help build the party in the South, this would also strengthen the Union.[3]

The Radical Republicans in Congress rejected Louisiana's new representatives and framed their own reconstruction plan, "the main object of which was to counteract the mild and tolerant policy of the Administration." The Wade-Davis bill increased the threshold of eligibility to 50 percent of the voting-age population and barred former Confederate officials from participating. It avoided the issue of black suffrage, as the Radicals understood it would have opened the subject for discussion in the North, where many states barred black residents from voting. Lincoln pocket-vetoed the bill, which, even if implemented, never had a chance of success given the high threshold of loyal citizens it required. The episode highlighted the two dominant themes of reconstruction policy: the tug-of-war between Congress and the president, and the contest over the degree of federal imposition on the rebellious states.[4]

Lincoln was a practical man. He chafed at theoretical debates over whether the seceding states had committed "state suicide," thereby requiring an apprentice period, much like the territories, to gain readmission to the Union. What counted now was whether the Rebel states wanted to be part of the American enterprise. "Finding themselves safely at home," he noted in one of his last ruminations on the subject on April 11, 1865, "it would be utterly immaterial whether they had ever been abroad." He also acknowledged that the process of formulating, let alone implementing, a reconstruction policy could be long and contentious before a consensus emerged. Lincoln understood how much "we, the loyal people, differ among ourselves as to the mode, manner, and means of reconstruction." Compromise, the essence of democratic government, would be necessary.[5]

At his final cabinet meetings during the week of April 10, he was open-minded about a spectrum of policies, including military occupation and black enfranchisement. He wanted an expeditious reconstruction of the Union, but he also wanted it to be fair. Like the good inventor he was, he recognized reconstruction as a work in progress and was prepared to alter the course, if necessary. He returned again to the issue of legitimacy, believing that any federal imposition ran the risk of losing the support of the majority of the white population. "We can't undertake to run State governments," he told his cabinet. "Their people must do that—I reckon that at first some of them may do it badly." He would adjust his program accordingly.[6]

In one of the greater misjudgments in American history, the Radicals believed that Lincoln's removal would aid their cause. At least Johnson would be tougher than his predecessor, "whose tenderness to the Rebels" and views on reconstruction were as "distasteful as possible." Johnson, it turned out, wanted

reconstruction to proceed as quickly as Lincoln. He expressed no commitment to voting rights, land grants, or civil equality for the freedmen. Johnson
wished blacks no ill, nor good. He explained his inattention to black voting
rights by noting that blacks possessed less "capacity for government than any
other race of people. . . . Wherever they have been left to their own devices
they have shown a constant tendency to relapse into barbarism." Black suffrage, therefore, would result in "a tyranny such as this continent has never yet
witnessed." [7]

Johnson had a clear field to formulate a reconstruction, or "restoration,"
policy, as he called it, as Congress was out of session. The president's preferred
term implied a return to what had been. He required an oath of allegiance in
exchange for amnesty and the restoration of property and called for the election of state conventions to formally abolish slavery, nullify state ordinances of
secession, and repudiate Confederate debts. Johnson barred high-ranking
Confederate officers and officials, as well as those individuals worth more
than twenty thousand dollars (reflecting his lifelong animosity against wealthy
planters) from taking the oath. They could, however, petition for pardons.
Soon, Washington, D.C., was crowded with former Confederate civilian and
military leaders petitioning the president. Of the 15,000 southerners who
applied, 13,500 received pardons. [8]

Johnson's plan restored most of the prewar southern leadership to positions of power and effectively removed the federal government from any
role in the South. The occupying soldiers in the rapidly diminishing armed
forces and the Freedmen's Bureau would withdraw once the seceding states
met the relatively simple requirements for readmission. Redemption had
come sooner than expected, and southern whites who had ridiculed Johnson
as "the drunken tailor from the mountains," or "the po' white demagogue,"
now called him a statesman. [9]

Even these mild terms rankled some white southerners. Mississippi refused to ratify the Thirteenth Amendment abolishing slavery, yet Johnson
accepted the state's new government anyway. South Carolina repealed rather
than nullified its ordinance of secession, implying that the ordinance was legal. Many southern whites refused to believe that anything should change as
a result of the war. Whitelaw Reid spent a convivial evening with David Levy
Yulee, the former U.S. senator from Florida, and reported, "It was amusing to
see how ignorant he was that during the last four years anything had happened! . . . That there was any modification of the old order of things . . . had
never occurred to him." [10]

Johnson dispatched Carl Schurz on a fact-finding mission to the South to
determine the impact of his policies. Schurz, a leading Republican politician, a

Civil War general, and a former abolitionist, had the credentials to offer the president an honest appraisal of conditions in the South. Johnson either vastly overestimated southern white contrition or underestimated Schurz's independence, because the report he received concluded that a counterrevolution had occurred in the South. It was as if the Confederate state governments had taken a brief recess and returned to business as usual. Alexander Stephens took up his old seat in Congress. Also elected to Congress in the fall 1865 special elections were numerous Confederate generals, six cabinet members, and fifty-eight men who had served in the Confederate Congress. It seemed only natural, an Alabamian confided to Whitelaw Reid: "We tried to leave the Union. You have defeated us in our effort. What can there be, then, for us to do but to return our Senators and Representatives to the Congress?" More ominously, the state governments armed and reactivated their militias, ostensibly to keep the peace in a still-lawless region. What peacekeeping they would do soon became clear. A Mississippi militiaman predicted, "Our negroes have . . . a tall fall ahead of them. They will learn that freedom and independence are different things."[11]

The restored southern state legislatures enacted Black Codes among their first orders of business. The statutes severely restricted black mobility and imposed heavy fines and prison sentences for relatively minor infractions. Some of the "crimes" included using "insulting" gestures or language and preaching the Gospel without a license. Those blacks who "misspent what they earn" also ran afoul of the law. The laws replaced slavery as the institutional control for black labor. The South Carolina code, for example, prohibited a freedman from entering any employment other than agricultural labor or domestic service unless he obtained a special license from a judge to certify his "skill and fitness" and "good moral character." Freedmen's Bureau officials generally stood back. They lived among southern whites, and the hostility to their presence was great enough without unpopular interventions. The federal officials also believed, along with their southern neighbors, that without some compulsion, the former slave would not work and therefore would retard southern economic recovery.[12]

Schurz's report chronicled southern whites' virulent refusal to allow the freedmen to exercise their rights as citizens. He appended a long list of incidents where whites had murdered, whipped, or persecuted blacks for no apparent crime other than asserting their freedom. Schurz highlighted the fundamental difference between Johnson's view of reconstruction and that of most Republicans. "It is not only the political machinery of the States and their constitutional relations to the general government, but the whole organism of southern society that must be reconstructed, or rather constructed

anew, so as to bring it into harmony with the rest of American society." He asserted that there was "among the southern people an *utter absence of national
feeling.*" As to why, he had no doubt that "the southern people cherished, cultivated, idolized their peculiar interests and institutions in preference to those
which they had in common with the rest of the American people." At the heart
of a fair and lasting reconstruction lay the "negro question." Schurz concluded
that the only solution was a continued and strong federal military presence
in the South.[13]

Johnson believed politics motivated Schurz's findings, but by the late fall of
1865 he needed some affirmation for his policies as public clamor in the North
against the southern restoration grew. In November, he sent General Grant to
the South. Grant's report was, literally, a whitewash. While Schurz had traveled all over the South for three months and interviewed a wide range of
southerners, Grant undertook a whirlwind tour of one week to the Carolinas
and Georgia. He found, accurately, that white southerners wanted "self government, within the Union, as soon as possible." He praised Freedmen's Bureau agents who insisted that the freedmen sign work contracts with planters.
"In some instances," Grant wrote, "I am sorry to say, the freedman's mind
does not seem to be disabused of the idea that a freedman has the right to live
without care or provision for the future." His evidence rested on the continued
agitation of former slaves for land and their propensity to leave farms to look
for work and families in towns and cities. The great objection, in other words,
was that blacks were exercising their freedom. If the freedmen, like the Indians, persisted in testing their freedom, they would suffer a similar and inevitable fate, Grant believed. Unless checked, he predicted, these expressions of
freedom "will tend to the extermination or great reduction of the colored
race."[14]

The Johnson restoration plan enabled white southerners to openly express
their fealty to the Lost Cause and its heroes. Jefferson Davis, whom many Rebels reviled during the war, became a widely sympathetic figure when the Federals incarcerated him. Generals Joseph E. Johnston and P. G. T. Beauregard
received ovations wherever they went in the South. And Robert E. Lee was a
living god. Oath taking, a serious business in nineteenth-century America,
became a meaningless if distasteful hurdle for those petitioning for their
rights. A former Confederate official boasted to Whitelaw Reid, "I've taken the
oath, and I'm just as big a Rebel now as ever I was." The hostility took Reid
aback, but his companion assured him that it would dissipate if the government
did three things: "reestablish slavery; give the old masters in some way power to
compel the negroes to work; or colonize them out of the country, and help us to
bring in white laborers!" Reid was flabbergasted. "Such waste and destruction

all about," he wrote, "and still these insatiable men . . . want more conciliation!" White southerners could not consider themselves redeemed unless they could have their way with the freedmen. That was the essence of the independence they sought.[15]

Northern public opinion objected to the parade of former Confederates returned to power in the South and in the Congress. But how could any other result claim legitimacy? Would governments elected by blacks and a handful of white Unionists receive the respect of the majority any more than the proslavery legislature at Lecompton in Kansas a decade earlier represented the will of the people of that territory? Northern Republicans tended to overestimate the number of southern Unionists. Reid's travels in the South, however, convinced him "there was no such party" as Unionists in the South. Any government that relied on blacks and small numbers of "aggrieved and vindictive whites," as Reid put it, could only be "held up by aid from without, to sway power . . . over a people who, but for the bayonet, would submerge them in a week."[16]

Here was a major dilemma of reconstructing the Union. The process would need to include former Rebels, and it was doubtful if these men would participate in a system that included the freedmen as partners. Any program that extended even modest protections to black men would lack legitimacy in the eyes of many southern whites, even if the Republicans could attract enough whites to form interracial coalitions that resulted in an electoral majority. It was not a question of majority rule. Many white southerners had little use for the concept; they had destroyed the Union because of their opposition to a legitimate democratic election. In South Carolina, African Americans comprised the majority of the voting population. In several states of the Lower South blacks and a small coterie of sympathetic whites could create winning coalitions. The issue of legitimacy had less to do with numbers than with the fact of black participation.

Some have argued that if the federal government had been firm with the white South at the end of the war and established a reconstruction process that proceeded in stages requiring adherence to certain principles including black suffrage, the outcome would have been different. Southern whites from the outset, however, acknowledged only the failure of their independence movement and the demise of slavery (and those only grudgingly). Even prewar moderates such as Wade Hampton made it clear that they would resist any additional requirements. The depth of white southern animosity was reflected in the flurry of legislation and other strictures against the black population during the remainder of 1865. Even Yankee kindness did not soften white southern hearts, or perhaps southerners interpreted small generosities as weakness or expressions of guilt. In late 1865, a destitute elderly white woman in Richmond received a box of rations from federal troops stationed there. As she made her way home, she faltered under her burden. A Union soldier, seeing her distress, ran up and offered his help. The woman seemed relieved and said, "Young man, you Yankees are not as horrid as I've believed. I hope that if there is a cool spot in hell that you will find it."[17]

The most vigorous expression of white sentiment came in the form of violence, despite the presence of Union troops. Sometimes the confrontations occurred for political reasons, other times to maintain social traditions, and most commonly to put the freedman in his proper lowly place. As a white Tennessean commented in late 1865, "Nigger life's cheap now. When a white man feels aggrieved at anything a nigger's done, he just shoots him and puts an end to it."[18]

Thirteen Confederate veterans met in a Pulaski, Tennessee, law office in December 1865 to form the Ku Klux Klan. The Klan was nominally a social club, though its members admitted that intimidating the former slaves and their white allies was their purpose from the outset. By early 1867, the Klan was a full-fledged terrorist organization. Sometimes, their nocturnal visits settled old scores, such as a freedman's service in the Union army. Rhoda Ann Childs, a black woman in Henry County, Virginia, testified that masked men called for her husband one night.

> I said he was not there. . . . They then seized me and took me some distance from the house, where they bucked me down across a log. Stripped my clothes over my head, one of the men standing astride my neck, and beat me across my posterior. Then I was thrown upon the ground on my back, one of the men stood upon my breast, while two others took hold of my feet and stretched my limbs as far as apart as they could, while the man standing upon my breast applied the strap to my private parts until fatigued into stopping, and I was more dead than alive. They swore they ought to shoot me, as my husband had been in the "god damned Yankee Army."[19]

Such individual "lessons" were common throughout the South in the first year after the war. A Freedmen's Bureau official in Kentucky counted, over the course of several months in his district, "twenty-three cases of severe and inhuman beating and whipping of men; four of beating and shooting; two of robbing and shooting; three of robbing; five men shot and killed; two shot and wounded; four beaten to death; one beaten and roasted; three women assaulted and ravished; four women beaten; [and] two women tied up and

"Whipping a Negro Girl in North Carolina," 1867.
(General Research Division, the New York Public Library, Astor,
Lenox and Tilder Foundations)

whipped until insensible." It was almost impossible to bring the perpetrators to trial, as whites refused to testify. A bureau official in Georgia claimed, "The American Indian is not more delighted at the writhings and shrieks of his victim at the stake, than many Georgians are at the agonizing cries of the African negro at the whipping post."[20]

Few venues presented as many challenges to white authority as southern cities. In the spring and summer of 1866, race riots erupted in Memphis and New Orleans. Both episodes involved the assertion by freedmen of their presumed rights. In Memphis, recently discharged black soldiers clashed with white police over the arrest of a black man. The rapid growth of the city's black population and vigorous enforcement of vagrancy laws heightened tensions between the police and freedmen. Retaliating against the assault on the police, white mobs invaded the black section of Memphis, torching homes, businesses, and churches, and attacking residents. The Union army commander refused to intervene, explaining that "he had a large amount of public property to guard; that a considerable part of the troops he had were not reliable; that they hated Negroes too." The dead included forty-six blacks (including three women and two children) and two white men. The local newspaper endorsed the outcome: "The late riots in our city have satisfied all of one thing: that the southern men will not be ruled by the negro. . . . The negroes now know, to their sorrow, that it is best not to arouse the fury of the white man."[21]

In New Orleans, the dispute revolved around a constitutional convention and the demands of the city's black community for a suffrage provision. A white mob confronted a group of black workers who had marched to the convention site, and a melee erupted, resulting in 48 dead (37 of whom were black) and 166 wounded before late-arriving federal troops quelled the disturbance. A New Orleans newspaper had a message for local blacks, similar to the one western journalists transmitted to the Indians: "Every real white man is sick of the negro, and the 'rights' of the negro. Teach the negro that if he goes to work, keeps his place, and behaves himself, he will be protected by *our* white laws; if not, this Southern road will be 'a hard one to trave,' [sic] for the whites must and shall rule to the end of time, even if the fate of Ethiopia be annihilation."[22]

These episodes, and others, demonstrated that the freedmen would not go submissively into their second-class caste status and that southern whites would retaliate forcibly. What unfolded in the decade after the Civil War was another civil war, this one between black and white southerners. A white North Carolinian remarked, "With reference to emancipation, we are at the beginning of the war."[23]

When Congress finally convened on December 4, 1865, having been out of session since March 3, its members were in a fighting mood. Thundered Illinois senator George W. Julian, "Indict, convict and hang Jeff. Davis in the name of God; as for Robert E. Lee, unmolested in Virginia, hang him too. And stop there? Not at all. I would hang liberally while I had my hand in." Ohio senator Benjamin Wade suggested, "If the negroes by insurrection could contrive to slay one-half of the Southern whites, the remaining half would then hold them in respect and treat them with justice." As one Republican noted, "The Confederacy, though beaten, refuses to die."[24]

Northerners looked for contrition on the part of southerners for what many considered treason. The presence of prominent Confederates in elective office, the defiant attitudes of whites, and the persistent verbal and physical assaults against African Americans rankled most northerners. They wanted to put the war behind them as quickly as possible, but they would not cavalierly dismiss the causes for which so many men died. The war supposedly ended slavery and established the supremacy of the federal government. In December 1865, these outcomes were by no means secure.

Attacking the Black Codes was high on the congressional agenda. Of all the legislation and defiance emanating from the defeated South, these measures highlighted white southerners' unwillingness to accept the verdict of the war. The Civil Rights Act of 1866 addressed the Codes by creating the category of national citizenship with rights that superseded state laws. The act reinforced the Republicans' aggressive growth of the government during the war and shifted power even more toward Washington. President Johnson vetoed the act as a usurpation of state prerogative. Congress mustered a two-thirds majority to override the veto, the first time in American history that Congress passed major legislation over a president's veto. The vote set the stage for a bitter contest between the president and Congress over reconstruction policy that nearly resulted in Johnson's impeachment.

To keep freedmen's rights safe from presidential vetoes, state legislatures, and federal courts, Congress moved to incorporate some of the provisions of the Civil Rights Act into the Constitution. The Fourteenth Amendment, which Congress passed and sent on to the states for ratification in June 1866, guaranteed every citizen equality before the law. The two key sections of the amendment prohibited states from violating the civil rights of their citizens, thus rendering the Black Codes unconstitutional, and gave states the choice of enfranchising blacks or losing representation in Congress. Republicans made ratification of the Fourteenth Amendment a prerequisite for any southern state seeking readmission to the Union.

The amendment failed to give African Americans the vote outright. It reflected a compromise between the minority Radical faction and the more moderate Republicans who believed that states should decide voting rights for their residents. The amendment disappointed advocates of woman suffrage, for the first time including the word "male" in the Constitution to define who could vote. Wendell Phillips, a prominent abolitionist, counseled women, "One question at a time. This hour belongs to the Negro." Susan B. Anthony, who had campaigned for the abolition of slavery before the war and helped mount a petition drive that collected four hundred thousand signatures for the Thirteenth Amendment, founded the American Equal Rights Association in 1866 to push for woman suffrage at the state level.[25]

Andrew Johnson opposed the Fourteenth Amendment and carried his case to the people in a swing around key northern states beginning in August 1866. It was an unprecedented campaign for a president. While many of his listeners opposed black suffrage and favored his message of reconciliation, his tone and manner dismayed many more as unbecoming for the chief executive. The off-year elections in November 1866, which generally would favor the party out of power, resulted in embarrassing defeats for the Democrats in the North, giving Republicans a veto-proof two-thirds majority in the House and Senate. Republicans interpreted the results as a mandate to sweep away the president's reconstruction policy and begin anew.

The new Congress passed the Military Reconstruction Acts in March 1867 over another presidential veto. With the exception of Tennessee, the only southern state that had ratified the Fourteenth Amendment and had been readmitted to the Union, Congress divided the former Confederate states into five military districts, enfranchised one million former slaves, and barred ex-Confederate leaders from voting or holding office. The acts charged military commanders to conduct voter-registration campaigns to enroll blacks. The eligible voters would then elect delegates to a state convention to write a new constitution that guaranteed universal male suffrage. Once a majority of eligible voters ratified the document, the state could apply for readmission to the Union.

The Reconstruction Acts fulfilled the Radicals' three major objectives. They secured the freedmen's right to vote. They made it likely that southern states would be run by Republican regimes that would enforce the new constitutions, protect former slaves' rights, and maintain the Republican majority in Congress. Finally, they set standards for readmission that required the South to accept the preeminence of the federal government and the end of slavery. Moderate Republicans agreed with these principles. They did not see them as vindictive but rather as ratifying the results of the war and ending the rebellion once and for all.

It is difficult to overestimate the impact of these measures. Carl Schurz asserted that the program represented "a great political and social revolution." The new legislation placed the power of the federal government behind African Americans' civil and political rights. The government acknowledged that freedom was meaningless without the right and security to exercise that freedom. The Reconstruction Acts, coupled with the Fourteenth Amendment, changed federal-state relations for all time. They ensured all minorities basic rights that individual states could not abrogate or modify. Though court decisions, the actions of white southerners, and the disengagement of white northerners limited the intended impact of these changes for nearly a century after the war, they served as a standard by which America could eventually live up to its promise as a beacon of democracy to the world.[26]

Black suffrage was a key element of the new program. The ballot would not only provide protection for African Americans, but it would also enhance Republican Party fortunes in the South. Given the strong opposition to black suffrage in the South, it would also become a flashpoint for violence. While Congress was considering this issue, it received a petition from white Alabamians: "Do not, we implore you, abdicate your own rule over us, by transferring us to the blighting, brutalizing and unnatural dominion of an alien and inferior race." Other whites viewed suffrage as the beginning of a slippery slope leading, somehow, to interracial sex. A white man in North Carolina reported, "The common white people of the country are at times very much enraged against the negro population. They think that this universal political and civil equality will finally bring about social equality. . . . There are already instances . . . in which poor white girls are having negro children."[27]

Albion W. Tourgée, who left his native Ohio at the age of twenty-three to fight for the Union, moved to North Carolina after the war to open a nursery business. He followed the path of many so-called carpetbaggers—northerners who stayed or ventured south after the war to make their fortune, not necessarily to participate in a social revolution. Seeing injustice in the treatment of the freedmen, Tourgée threw himself into reform politics at considerable personal peril. The new reconstruction policy troubled him, however, and he shared his reservations with Massachusetts Republican senator Charles Sumner, one of the architects of the Reconstruction Acts. His concern focused on the issue of legitimacy. Could any government in the South predicated on black suffrage and the disfranchisement of white leaders earn the support of the larger population? Tourgée warned Sumner, "A party builded upon ignorance, inexperience, and poverty, and mainly composed of a race of pariahs, who are marked and distinguished by their color, can not stand against intelligence, wealth, the pride of a conquered nation, and race prejudice." That party, even if initially successful, would generate such violent opposition that its reign would be short and bloody.[28]

The warning was well taken, though the southern Republican Party was more than a party of freedmen. Northerners like Tourgée who had come to the South to make money and white southerners, the handful of prewar Unionists, small farmers, and town merchants—"scalawags" was the epithet other whites used to identify them—joined the party as its political prospects brightened under the new legislation. The lure of office and its financial rewards undoubtedly motivated some of these whites, but some also had a deep commitment to Americanizing the South. Tourgée's emphasis on black Republicans, however, reflected his experience in North Carolina. To most whites in the state, the upstart Republicans were not an interracial coalition but rather a party of and for blacks. On this basis, the new Reconstruction governments could never be legitimate in the minds of white southerners.

Blacks nevertheless grabbed the opportunity the new suffrage provisions offered. Republican political organizations called Union Leagues popped up all over the South. The league organized black voters, provided voter education, helped to select candidates, conducted registration drives, and collected funds for school buildings and churches. Of greater concern to whites, the league organized self-defense corps that openly drilled with weapons and uniforms. The military commanders generally remained aloof from these activities, with the notable exception of General Philip H. Sheridan, who, as commander of the district that included Texas and Louisiana, vigorously encouraged the formation of Union Leagues and removed ex-Confederates from office. His zealotry on behalf of the Republican Party in general and the black electorate in particular raised the ire of President Johnson, who removed him. Sheridan went west to fight the Indians instead of the Johnson administration.

Legitimacy remained a problem for southern Republican governments. Even some moderate northern Republicans wondered about the contradiction between the advocacy for universal manhood suffrage and the provisions that barred ex-Confederates from exercising their franchise. Republican senator John Sherman of Ohio unsuccessfully urged his colleagues to "reconstruct society in the rebel States upon the broad basis of universal suffrage." He then voiced a sentiment that would become more general in the coming years: "Is it not enough that they are humiliated, conquered, their pride broken, their property lost, hundreds and thousands of their best and bravest buried under their soil, their institutions gone, they themselves deprived of the right to hold office, and placed in political power on the same footing with their former slaves? Is not that enough?"[29]

Thousands of white voters were ineligible because of their roles in the Confederacy, and an untold number of whites refused to register to vote in protest of black suffrage and the disfranchisement of their neighbors. The acts barred as many as ten thousand Confederate officials from elective office. Of the 1,363,000 registered voters in the South by the end of 1867, more than half of them—703,000—were black, and they formed the majority of the electorate in Alabama, Florida, Louisiana, Mississippi, and South Carolina. These figures presented a significant opportunity for the incorporation of the freedmen, only recently property, into both the southern and the national bodies politic.

The mere existence of these governments was a rebuke to the aspirations of white southerners to redeem their region. Even before the states held their first elections under the new constitutions, opponents pronounced the governments-to-be abominations, "the most galling tyranny and most stupendous system of organized robbery that is to be met with in history." The great fear was that these governments would be successful and perpetuate themselves. As W. E. B. DuBois noted correctly, "There was one thing that the white South feared more than negro dishonesty, ignorance, and incompetency, and that was Negro honesty, knowledge, and efficiency."[30]

By late 1867, more northern whites had joined Senator Sherman in their concerns about the new Reconstruction. The Republicans had misread their stunning victories in the 1866 elections. Congress had rightly tossed out the old governments but added a new class of disfranchised whites. It rendered null and void the legal strictures against African Americans but also enfranchised the freedmen. Northerners wanted the Republicans to ensure that the same issues that caused the war would not enjoy a new life. They did not give

Republicans a mandate to engineer an egalitarian society in the South, a society to which most northerners would have objected. While Republicans triumphed across the South in the November 1867 elections, the Democrats gained numerous state and local offices from Republicans in the North. Black suffrage, on the ballot in Minnesota, Ohio, and Kansas, went down to defeat in all three states. Republicans in Congress had applied a different standard to the South from the one they supported in their own jurisdictions. Blacks could vote in only eight of the twenty-two northern states, and between 1865 and 1869 voters rejected equal suffrage referendums in eight of eleven northern states. The reason for these electoral setbacks was clear to the *Nation*, a Republican magazine: "It would be vain to deny, the fidelity of the Republican party to the cause of equal rights . . . has been one of the chief causes of its heavy losses."[31]

Although southern whites would rail about "black rule" for generations, African Americans never held office in proportion to their numbers in the electorate. Except for the lower house in South Carolina, blacks never attained a majority in any southern state legislature. Nor was there a black governor, and there were only two black U.S. senators, both from Mississippi. The African Americans who held these positions were, on the whole, educated, able men, a number of whom had come to the South after the Civil War, and several from the South who were free before the war.

Black suffrage represented the ultimate loss of control for whites in the South. A legislature elected with black votes could pass laws regulating contracts between blacks and whites, authorize public funds to educate blacks, and make judicial appointments to ensure the fair application of justice regardless of race. In the late fall of 1866, the state court of North Carolina met in Raleigh. Every day for nearly a month, a crowd of five hundred people gathered outside the courthouse to witness the public whipping of black men convicted of various crimes. Whites convicted of similar crimes did not receive this sentence. General Daniel E. Sickles, the Union military commander for the Carolinas, put a stop to the practice. The governor immediately petitioned the president for a restoration of the punishment, stating that such laws had "existed with us and our ancestors for many hundred years." Despite the unintended irony of that statement, Johnson granted the request and fired Sickles, though Congress would reinstate him. With the new state constitution and a black electorate in place the following year, the spectacle at the state courthouse in Raleigh ceased.[32]

Despite threats and intimidation, blacks thronged to the polls to ratify new state constitutions providing for universal manhood suffrage in Louisiana, Georgia, North Carolina, South Carolina, and Arkansas. The successful voting drives, the Union Leagues, and the growing confidence of freedmen across the South provoked predictable responses from southern whites. Before the spring of 1868, white attacks on freedmen were, at best, loosely organized. During and after this time, the assaults were organized and included a broad spectrum of social classes. The Ku Klux Klan emerged as the great enforcer of white supremacy in the South, though similar organizations appeared under different names. Its official creed cloaked a violent mission in Old South rhetoric. "This is an institution of chivalry, humanity, mercy, and patriotism to protect the weak, the innocent, and the defenseless from the indignities, wrongs, and outrages of the lawless, the violent, and the brutal." The Klan revealed more of its true purpose in its membership requirements, proscribing membership in "the Radical Republican Party," opposing "Negro equality both social and political," and favoring "a white man's government, the reenfranchisement and emancipation of the white men of the South, and the restitution of the Southern people to all their rights." This was the agenda of Redemption, and it manifested itself most often and most violently during and after election campaigns.[33]

Wyatt Outlaw was the son of a slave mother and a white father. He owned a small carpentry shop in Graham, North Carolina, and organized a Union League chapter in the town. The league built a black school and an AME Zion church. When Republicans took control in North Carolina in 1868, the governor appointed Outlaw to the post of town commissioner. A Klan-like organization called the White Brotherhood threatened Outlaw and his colleagues. In response, Outlaw organized a police force. One night, one hundred members of the Brotherhood dragged Outlaw from his bed and carried him to the central square in Graham. They hanged him from an oak tree across from the county courthouse and pinned a note to his mutilated body, "Beware you guilty both white and black."[34]

Camilla, Georgia, lay in the heart of the Second Congressional District in the southwestern part of the state. Black voters outnumbered whites by a two-to-one margin. The local Union League chapter sponsored a campaign rally on September 19, 1868. Blacks came from the surrounding plantations, some with weapons because of threats from local whites. As they entered the town square, a much larger group of armed whites opened fire, killing nine blacks and wounding dozens more. Despite the Republicans' numerical advantage in voter registration, the district went for the Democrats on election day. White paramilitary groups repeated this scenario in various versions throughout the South as the November 1868 election approached. Ulysses S. Grant, the Republican presidential nominee, campaigned on the slogan "Let Us Have Peace." It was an odd theme considering that the war had ended more than three years earlier. What Grant and the Republicans meant, of course, was that the periodic uprisings in the South must end, and the general was the best man to end them. Just how he would accomplish that remained unclear.[35]

The Democrats nominated former New York governor Horatio Seymour for president and ran their usual race-baiting campaign in the North, focusing on black suffrage, an overreaching federal government, and the disfranchisement of southern whites. Their platform declared the Reconstruction Acts "a flagrant usurpation of power, unconstitutional, revolutionary, and void." For good measure, the Democrats charged that the Republicans' real objective was to impose "negro rule" on the entire country. In a nation of thirty-one million whites and four million blacks, such a coup would have been quite an upset.[36]

The election season opened with the assassination of a Republican congressman from Arkansas and three Republican members of the South Carolina legislature. The Klan would murder more than one thousand black and white Republicans through the November elections. Undeterred, black southerners threw themselves into the campaigning. The 1868 presidential campaign in the South was America's first interracial campaign. Blacks and whites worked together to stage rallies, register voters, and participate in parades. Black women sported Grant buttons as they toted laundry or cooked for their white employers. In those parts of the South where white Democrats attempted to cajole blacks into voting their ticket, or where white paramilitary organizations were weak, black voter participation exceeded 90 percent. Former U.S. congressman and South Carolina governor Francis W. Pickens wrote, "All society stands now like a cone on its Apex," a feeling most southern whites shared.[37]

Grant won the election, but his margin of victory was uncomfortably narrow. Reflecting growing ambivalence in the North over issues of race and federal authority, Seymour probably won a majority of the nation's white vote. In the South, intimidation by the Klan and allied groups cut into the Republican vote, returning Democratic majorities in Louisiana and Georgia. In Georgia, eleven counties with a black voting majority recorded not a single vote for Grant. The new president would immediately confront a dilemma. In order to stabilize the South's Republican regimes and protect the party's members, he would need to mobilize federal resources, particularly the army. As the war against the Plains Indians erupted again, and as army strength dropped sharply from wartime levels, this option became less viable.

Republican party leaders in Washington viewed reconstruction policy in the South through the lens of their fortunes in the North. They recognized the changing political climate in the North, and they contemplated shifting their policy emphasis from the "struggle over the negro" to economic issues. The first piece of legislation enacted in the new Grant administration was the Public Credit Act that pledged the payment of the national debt in gold. The act promised to redeem the flood of greenbacks and bonds issued during the war with gold or silver coin over a ten-year period. The legislation boosted the confidence of creditors concerned about too much unsecured paper money triggering inflation. Some economists argue that the act was responsible for initiating a decade of strong growth, despite the economic downturn in 1873. More important for the long run, it established the Republicans as the party of sound money and was much more indicative of the party's direction than the Reconstruction legislation. A Republican leader declared, "I look forward to Grant's administration as the beginning of a real and true conservative era."[38]

The Republicans were the heirs of the Whigs. Even their anti-slavery positions related to their desire to develop the West and create a national economy. This is not to say that Republicans did not genuinely abhor slavery on moral grounds. Once the war abolished slavery, however, party members were anxious to use their legislative power to enhance the nation's prosperity. A new era was at hand.

Many northerners agreed. Grant won; the South had voted; Reconstruction was over. Albion Tourgée recalled the feeling. "It was all over—the war, reconstruction, the consideration of the old questions. Now all was peace and harmony. The South must take care of itself now. The nation had done its part: it had freed the slaves, given them the ballot, opened the courts to them, and put them in the way of self-protection and self-assertion." The old, obstructive South was finally gone. "For three-quarters of a century," Tourgée explained, "the South had been the 'old Man of the Sea' to the young Republic; by a simple trick of political legerdemain he was now got rid of for ever." The result? "Yankee-land could now bend its undivided energies to its industries and commerce."[39]

Indeed, it seemed as if the South had found its political equilibrium. The Republican governments turned out to be moderate, not radical. There were no schemes to redistribute land, no legislation that particularly favored African Americans as a class, and no laws passed mandating interracial marriage. As the New York Times wrote approvingly, the black lawmakers had been "extremely moderate and modest in their demands," had "been scrupulous in their respect for all the rights of property," and had "in all respects given proof of a capacity to take part in the carrying on of a Republican Government, that can but astonish those who know the condition in which they have till lately been kept." Seven of the former eleven Confederate states had adopted new constitutions and elected Republican legislatures. Congress readmitted those seven states into the Union. By January 1869, the Times could note that "a healthy prosperity" was abroad in the South. Now that the election had put to rest the old issues of the war, southerners "are fast emerging from poverty and depression, and are prepared to profit by the lessons of a painful experience." In May 1869, the first national celebration of Decoration, or Memorial, Day occurred as Union and Confederate veterans exchanged ceremonies and tended the graves of their former enemies. In August, the Gettysburg Memorial Association invited former Union and Confederate soldiers to the battlefield to mark out the lines of battle.[40]

But former Confederates did not reconcile themselves to the black men in their midst, indicating that a winter truce rather than a genuine peace had taken hold. The Georgia legislature expelled its duly elected black representatives. The *Meridian* (Miss.) *Mercury* issued a warning common across the South: "We must make the negro understand we are the men we were when we held him in abject bondage, and make him feel that when forbearance ceases to be a virtue he has aroused a power that will control him or destroy him." The *Nashville Republican Banner* was even more explicit in its threat of violence, evoking a chilling memory. "So far as the white native citizens of this State may be compelled to take part in it they will be very careful throughout the sanguinary carnival which would naturally ensue to remember Fort Pillow in act as well as word, and 'Throughout the bloody conflict / Seek the white man, not the black.'"[41]

The persistent violence in the South sent congressional Republicans back to reconstruction policy. Congress passed the Fifteenth Amendment to the Constitution, barring race as a test for voting. The amendment said nothing about a state's right to determine requirements for voting other than race, a loophole that southern states would exploit over the next century to limit black voter participation. The amendment was also silent, once again, about woman suffrage. Elizabeth Cady Stanton charged that the amendment created an "aristocracy of sex." In an appeal brimming with ethnic and racial animosity, Stanton warned that "if you do not wish the lower orders of Chinese, African, Germans and Irish, with their low ideas of womanhood to make laws for you and your daughters . . . awake to the danger . . . and demand that woman, too, shall be represented in the government!"[42]

The reaction of the northern Republican press to ratification of the Fifteenth Amendment in March 1870 was positive, though accompanied by the conviction that this was the last salvo in the fight for freedmen's rights. Pronouncing the end of Reconstruction was becoming a latter-day version of "On to Richmond." The *Chicago Tribune* expressed relief that at last, blacks had "merged politically with the rest of the people." Now, however, the black man "has to run the race of life, dependent, like all others, upon his own energy, ability, and worth." The *New York World*, a Democratic newspaper, agreed.

The freedman had been "raised as high as he can be put by any action other than his own."[43]

Despite such caveats, this was an epochal moment. There are judges who insist the Constitution is color-blind. It is not. Congress placed the three Reconstruction amendments into the Constitution to free and then establish the full rights of citizenship for African Americans. After the ratification of the Fifteenth Amendment, Frederick Douglass exulted, "The black man is free, the black man is a citizen, the black man is enfranchised, and this by the organic law of the land. . . . Never was revolution more complete."[44]

The Ku Klux Klan remained unimpressed and unbowed. Reconstruction would not be over until they redeemed the South from Republican and black rule. Violence escalated as the 1870 elections approached. Democrats registered gains in the North, not unusual in an off-year election cycle, but also made significant inroads in the South, redeeming several southern states after the Klan and similar groups suppressed the black vote. Republican administrations in Texas and Arkansas successfully fought back against the Klan. Governor Edmund J. Davis of Texas, for example, organized a special force of two hundred state policemen to round up Klansmen. Between 1870 and 1872, Davis's force arrested six thousand men and broke the Klan in Texas. But other governors hesitated to enforce laws directed at the Klan, fearing that this would further alienate whites. Democrats regained power in North Carolina after the state's Republican governor enraged white voters by calling out the state militia to counter white violence during the election of 1870.[45]

Congress, in response to the violence, ventured once again to pass protective legislation, in this case the Enforcement Act of 1870, which authorized the federal government to appoint supervisors in states that failed to protect voting rights. When the attacks continued, Congress followed with a second, more sweeping measure, the Ku Klux Klan Act of 1871 permitting federal authorities, with military assistance if necessary, to arrest and prosecute members of groups that denied a citizen's civil rights if state authorities failed to do so. The act outlawed the Klan, but Klansmen merely reappeared in organizations under different names.

Political violence was not the only obstacle confronting southern blacks. The daily strain of living among neighbors who wished to thwart your ambition, limit your education, and isolate you was enormous. If a black person carved out a modicum of success in this harsh environment, the ill treatment would likely escalate. White southerners turned the American dream on its head as applied to African Americans. Work hard and get hurt. A Republican sheriff in Mississippi explained, "Education amounts to nothing, good behavior counts for nothing, even money cannot buy for a colored man or woman decent treatment and the comforts that white people claim and can obtain." Charles Sumner attempted to address this problem by introducing a civil rights bill in 1871 to ensure blacks' equal access to juries and public accommodations. Congressmen from both parties and sections, however, believed that there were sufficient protections already in place and the rest was up to blacks themselves. The bill veered too close to mandating a social equality few whites, north or south, were willing to accept.[46]

Northerners had wanted to put the Civil War to rest as soon as Grant and Lee signed the surrender documents, but white southerners insisted on continuing the conflict by other means. Satisfied that they had honored those who had fallen and the cause for which they fought by surrounding the freedmen with constitutional amendments and protective legislation, northerners left the land of war for the garden of peace. The array of economic opportunities in a rapidly industrializing and urbanizing nation set northern minds to shaping the future rather than sorting out the past. They hoped the South would now follow a similar course. The *New York Times* wrote the prologue to the new era in the New South. "The bulk of the people in the reconstructed States are realizing the reward of labor; they are fast emerging from poverty and depression, and are prepared to profit by the lessons of a painful experience." The South would eventually become a version of the North, much as Indians should become versions of western white farmers, and blacks versions of white laborers. All lesser incarnations, but given the racial limitations of the red and the black they were consonant with northern visions of stable and prosperous societies.[47]

The Republican governments elected under the new southern state constitutions seemed to herald the fulfillment of such prophecy. The new regimes promoted an activist government that raised taxes, built infrastructure, established charitable institutions, funded public school systems for both races, and reduced the power of local elites by transferring appointment responsibilities to the state. This last policy tilted the local law enforcement system to a more evenhanded dispensation of justice. Republican governments in the South also embarked on extensive programs of economic development. Between 1868 and 1872, Republicans rebuilt the South's railroads and constructed an additional thirty-three hundred miles of track.

There were many smaller, symbolic moments that did not escape the attention of blacks or whites. There was the scene in the statehouse in Columbia, South Carolina, where black lawmakers sat at the very desks of those who had passed the secession ordinance in November 1860. There was Robert Smalls, who had commandeered a Confederate vessel and delivered it to Union troops, and who now took his oath of office as a United States congressman from

South Carolina. And there was Hiram Revels, born a free black in Fayetteville, North Carolina, who became a minister, then a Union army chaplain, and, after the war, a pastor at a church in Natchez, Mississippi. In 1870, he became the first black person to become a U.S. senator, taking the seat once occupied by Jefferson Davis. Indeed, the South had turned upside down.

For many blacks, the new regimes were almost a second emancipation. A Freedmen's Bureau official in the Virginia Piedmont noted in late 1868 that three years earlier, the freedmen were "abject and fearful in the presence of the master class." Now they were "much less abject and more settled, ambitious and industrious." They will "generally resist if attacked." It was, as W. E. B. DuBois would note at a later time, "a Golden Moment," for African Americans, and for America generally.[48]

It would only be a moment. The South could not long remain a region teetering on its "Apex." White and black southerners would not follow the northern script. The transforming national economy held increasing public attention, not only for its promise but also soon for its excesses. Immigrants and urban workers in the North did not share either the profits or the buoyant optimism of the middle and entrepreneurial classes. New scientific theories reinforced racial prejudices and questioned the role of an activist government. Northerners did not become indifferent about the South or about the freedmen. They came to feel that disengagement was best for both and for the nation. It was more important to follow one's own dreams than to protect those of others. A new era was at hand. The war was over, and so was Reconstruction. Stephen Douglas finally got his railroad built, a sure sign that the old issues no longer mattered. Only the Indians now remained in the way, the last obstacle to fulfilling the destiny of the indivisible nation.

CHAPTER 19

THE GOLDEN SPIKE

THE TRANSCONTINENTAL RAILROAD seemed to live a charmed, if precarious, life. After surviving blizzards, subzero temperatures, deadly Indian raids, financing fiascos, and attacks by grizzlies and cougars, workers readied the last rails. Dignitaries were converging on Promontory Point, Utah, for a grand celebration uniting East and West. As the appointed day grew closer, however, luck seemed to have run dry. The Central Pacific Railroad steamed out of Sacramento on May 5, 1869, with California governor Leland Stanford aboard. He planned to link up with a Union Pacific train heading west from Omaha. The trip from Sacramento to Promontory Point would take two days and allow Governor Stanford to preside over the celebration scheduled for Saturday, May 8.[1]

The locomotive carrying Stanford's party from Sacramento carefully climbed to the crest of the Sierra Nevada, providing magnificent vistas over canyons and pine forests. The notables enjoyed a lavish lunch at Donner Lake, near where more than two decades earlier, less appealing fare had been on the menu. Their appetites sated, the group resumed their travel. In the Truckee Valley ahead, Chinese lumbermen felled trees along the tracks. They had not been informed about the unscheduled train about to disrupt their work. A gigantic felled pine lay across the tracks, and though the engineer was able to slow the locomotive sufficiently to avoid injuring his passengers, the log disabled the engine.

Stanford and his party waited for another locomotive, which arrived in due course, and the journey continued. As they crossed the forty-mile desert between the Truckee River and the Sink of the Humboldt, the old forty-niners among the group pointed out the places where their livestock had died and the numerous poisonous streams that killed man and beast. Thus enlightened, the dignitaries retired to their comfortable beds as the train lumbered across Nevada.

Things were not so peaceful at Promontory Point. While the inbound VIPs slept, the Chinese laborers rioted, not against management but against each other. The workers belonged to one of two companies that had brought them from China to work on America's railroads. A dispute erupted over the purported default of a fifteen-dollar payment from one company to another. The partisans of each group, "armed with every conceivable weapon," went at each other, threatening to turn the impending celebration into a civil war.

The warring Chinese laborers belonged to different companies representing distinctive dialects and districts. These groups first appeared in San Francisco in 1851. Like European immigrant mutual benefit societies, the companies provided an array of services for their members such as job placement, housing, welfare and burial services, and facilitated connections with homeland families. Relations were often frosty between the companies. The immigrants exhibited fierce loyalties to their associations. The Central Pacific Railroad hired more than ten thousand Chinese laborers, who brought their affiliations to the construction site. The laborers generally worked out differences peacefully, even banding together in a successful strike for higher wages. But the stress of finishing the road in time for the celebration frayed tempers and now jeopardized the party.

Things were also not peaceful for the Union Pacific heading west. Thomas C. Durant, vice president of the road, had an uneventful journey from Omaha until he reached Piedmont, Wyoming. Hundreds of workers surrounded his railroad car demanding their wages. They had not received their pay in months and, accordingly, were holding Durant and other executives hostage. The disgruntled laborers detached the locomotive, which went on to Utah, leaving Durant stationary in southwestern Wyoming. The strikers told the telegrapher they would hang him if he wired for assistance. They ordered Durant to telegraph for their wages.

As the delayed Central Pacific party rolled into Promontory Point early on May 8 ready to stage the ceremony, their counterparts remained under siege in Wyoming. San Francisco and Sacramento had planned mammoth celebrations on May 8, complete with brass bands, steam whistles, fire bells, and a grand parade. In San Francisco, soldiers would fire cannon from Alcatraz, presumably not in the direction of the city. Not wishing to spoil the party, the two cities carried off the celebrations on May 8 for an event that had not yet occurred, if it would occur at all.

It was a frustrating lead-in to an event that would, Americans believed, reverberate around the world. The project was a tribute to the engineering skills and creativity of the railroad builders who organized the construction of the road, coordinating supplies and labor over a thousand miles of continent, often under hostile conditions. And it came in ahead of schedule, at least until now.

Building a transcontinental railroad had become an obsession in the North during the Civil War. With the future of the Union in doubt, the Pacific railroad symbolized hope for a reunited nation. As much as the war's outcome, the railroad would render the nation indivisible, binding Americans together. The transcontinental railroad would hasten the settlement of the West by northerners. Their hard work, skills, and ingenuity would transform the western wilderness into a region dotted with productive towns and farms to make America "the greatest nation of the earth." The future of the nation depended on sealing the relationship between East and West. "Unless the relations between the East and the West shall be the most perfect and most intimate which can be established," the nation would "break on the crest of the Rocky Mountains." [2]

More accurately, the railroad would connect the West to the North. This was a pact for the future, for economic development and settlement. The South's rebellion, and the insistence of its majority white population to reestablish a past the rest of the nation had discredited, would fix the region as the American outlier for nearly a century: poor in a nation of plenty; ignorant in an enlightened country; and mired in a one-party political system and a biracial society in a diverse, competitive America. The South became the nation's place to leave. After the turn of the twentieth century, the greatest internal migration in American history occurred as more than twenty-eight million southerners donated their ambitions and their children to the rest of the nation. [3]

The construction of the railroad was a wonder in itself. In the public mind, the Rocky Mountains represented a nearly impenetrable barrier to transcontinental travel. The road's engineers and surveyors crossed the summit of the mountains at 8,262 feet above sea level without any grade greater than ninety feet to a mile, and that only for a short distance. The construction also put to rest any lingering assumptions that the territory between the Mississippi and the Rockies was a "Great American Desert." The Plains would soon sprout abundant fields of wheat and corn to be shipped to the great cities of the East and to markets all over the world. The road also employed a workforce that far exceeded the numbers of workers on any other enterprise in American history. More than twenty thousand workers built the railroad, a small army that managers had to house, feed, and (hopefully) pay, accomplishing much of this during a civil war. The "medley of Irishmen and Chinamen" who built the road brought "Europe and Asia face to face, grasping hands across the American Continent." [4]

The managers of the Union Pacific finally won their release, and the strikers received their wages. On Monday, May 10, 1869, two days late, workers laid the two last rails simultaneously, one opposite the other. Nevada provided a silver spike for the next-to-last rail, and California donated a golden spike to secure the union of East and West. Even then, the ceremony went awry as the first strikes hit the rail and not the silver spike. Governor Stanford was more accurate with his hammer. A telegraph wire connected to the golden spike told the world that the deed of spanning a continent was done. Bells pealed all over the North, and, in New York a celebratory service was held in Trinity Church near Wall Street. The minister there called the ceremony at Promontory Point "a great event of the world . . . one of the victories of peace. . . . It is a triumph of commerce. . . . It will preserve the union of these States." The *New York Times* echoed the theme of Union. The railroad "binds the States of the Atlantic and Pacific into one nation."[5]

A few days after the ceremony, a telegram arrived at the Post Office Department in Washington, D.C., informing the postmaster general that the new railroad had delivered mail from New York to San Francisco. Transmitting mail across the country by stagecoach or Pony Express cost $1,100 per mile annually. By the railroad, it was only $200 per mile. The same savings would accrue to private passengers, military personnel, and crops, livestock, and precious metals. *Harper's* expressed the prevailing opinion in the North: "No work of this century can compare in the grandeur both of the undertaking and of its probable results with the Pacific Railroad." Soon, middle-class

Joining the tracks at Promontory Point, Utah Territory, for the first transcontinental railroad. May 1869. (National Archives and Records Administration)

Americans on the East Coast could glide across the continent, sleep in spring beds in a Pullman Palace Car, eat meals with fine cutlery and china, enjoy the stunning landscapes, and arrive refreshed in San Francisco a mere ten days after leaving. Before the railroad, the fastest journey to the West took four weeks.[6]

Naysayers predicted the railroad would burden the national treasury and never live up to its expectations. They were wrong. Within a year of its completion, the railroad had $100 million in capital from the sale of stock and government bonds and turned a profit of $4 million that doubled the following year. The savings to the nation in terms of cheaper freight rates and military and private passenger fares were incalculable. The road was both a consumer and a shipper of lumber, steel, coal, and oil, thereby stimulating those industries as well.

By the 1880s, the United States contained nearly one third of the world's railroad mileage, blotting out distance and even altering the concept of time. On November 18, 1883, the American Railway Association reduced the number of time zones in America from fifty to four. The change helped the trains run on time, or at least according to a schedule that shippers and passengers anywhere in the country could understand. A standard gauge for all railroads followed three years later. Cities constructed "Union" terminals, often their most imposing structures, to consolidate the various rail lines heading into and out of town. The railroad became the symbol for an age enamored of science, technology, and innovation. The golden spike cemented the Union materially as the war had done politically. Like God, the iron rails would bring peace and harmony to all mankind, as Walt Whitman wrote in his tribute to the ceremony at Promontory Point, "Passage to India" (1870):

> SINGING my days,
> Singing the great achievements of the present,
> Singing the strong, light works of engineers, . . .
> The New by its mighty railroad spann'd,
> The seas inlaid with eloquent, gentle wires; . . .
>
> The earth to be spann'd, connected by net-work,
> The races, neighbors, to marry and be given in
>   marriage,
> The oceans to be cross'd, the distant brought near,
> The lands to be welded together. . . .
>
> I see over my own continent the Pacific Railroad,
>   surmounting every barrier; . . .

> Bridging the three or four thousand miles of land
>   travel,
> Tying the Eastern to the Western sea,
> The road between Europe and Asia.[7]

Not everyone sang along with Whitman. The transcontinental railroad traveled through Indian territory, bringing more settlers who established homesteads, prospected for gold or silver, and threatened the buffalo as well as the Indians themselves. Most white Americans viewed the Indian in the same manner as they saw the Mexican or the slaveholder: an obstacle to progress. Indians were yesterday's people; primitive, savage, and content to live with rather than over nature.

The transcontinental railroad was viewed as the "final solution" to ending the Native American threat to white settlement in the West. The road would facilitate transforming the region's environment and rendering it immensely prosperous. Four months before the golden spike joined East and West, the Committee on the Pacific Railroad in the U.S. Senate cited the military application of the new road. "As the thorough and final solution of the Indian question," the committee's report stated, "by taking the buffalo range out from under the savage, and putting a vast stock and grain farm in its place, the railroads to the Pacific surely are a military necessity."[8]

The construction of the transcontinental railroad heated up the long-standing conflict during the Civil War. Alliances of some Plains tribes with the Confederacy angered the federal government. Other tribes took advantage of the dissension among whites to press for reforms or regain their lands.

The Santee Sioux in Minnesota launched an attack on farmsteads during the late summer of 1862, killing more than 350 white men, women, and children, the largest massacre of whites by Indians in U.S. history. The federal government had forced the tribe onto a reservation in 1858, hoping they would become Christian farmers and provide food for themselves. In the meantime, the government would feed the Indians. Corrupt agents and inadequate training to help the Santee transition from hunting to farming worsened conditions on the reservation. The removal of federal troops from the Upper Midwest to the South led to more civilian abuses and severe food shortages among the Santee. An increase in white settlement reduced game and diminished the Santee's treaty domain. Their supplier, trader Andrew Jackson Myrick, pocketed government money and shrugged, "So far as I am concerned, if they are hungry let them eat grass or their own dung."[9]

Two hundred starving Santee carried out the Great Sioux Uprising, throwing the state's white population into a state of panic for six weeks. State militiamen found Myrick's mutilated body, his mouth stuffed with grass. Jane Grey Swisshelm, a leading abolitionist in Minnesota and editor of the *Saint Cloud Democrat*, demanded, "Every Sioux found on our soil deserves a permanent homestead six feet by two. Shoot the hyenas. Exterminate the wild beasts." The federal government dispatched General John Pope, recently humiliated by Robert E. Lee at Second Bull Run, and a detachment of Union troops to quell the uprising. Pope vowed to fulfill Swisshelm's wish: "It is my purpose utterly to exterminate the Sioux. . . . They are to be treated as maniacs or wild beasts." Fortunately for Pope, the Sioux were much fewer in number and arms than the Army of Northern Virginia. Thirty-eight Santee were executed the day after Christmas—the largest mass hanging in U.S. history—and several hundred were placed in an internment camp in Davenport, Iowa, where about half died from exposure, disease, or starvation. The camp commander, responding to pressure from the town, allowed curious residents to view the prisoners two hours every day except Sunday. The Federals buried the executed Indians on a sandbar in the Minnesota River. Physicians dug up the bodies and carried them off for use in medical experiments. Government officials used the uprising as an excuse to remove all Indians from Minnesota and place them on a reservation in South Dakota territory.[10]

The list of condemned Sioux would have been considerably longer had Lincoln not commuted the death sentences of 260 Indians, a decision that infuriated many whites in Minnesota. Lincoln, despite his perfunctory "service" in the Black Hawk War in 1836, had little knowledge of Indian affairs. Caught up in the midst of a horrible civil war, he could not devote much time to the issue. He welcomed Indian delegations to the White House, addressing them with condescension, noting the "great difference between this pale-faced people and their red brethren," and lecturing that whites were prosperous because they were farmers rather than hunters. Another reason for white success, Lincoln offered with unintended irony, was that "we are not, as a race, so much disposed to fight and kill one another as our red brethren."[11]

Chauncey Cooke was a white boy of sixteen in 1862. Lying about his age, he joined the 25th Wisconsin Infantry. As a member of an abolitionist family, Cooke was eager to fight the Rebels and liberate the slaves. Instead, his first assignment was to track down fugitive Santee Sioux in Minnesota. In late November, he guarded a contingent of seventeen hundred forlorn Santee at Fort Snelling in Minneapolis waiting to be taken to a reservation in South Dakota. Few if any of these Santee had been involved in the raids of the previous summer. "They are going to be shipped West into the Black Hills Country," Cooke wrote to his parents. "They were weary and broken hearted and desperate at the broken promises of the government. And when they took up arms in desperation for their homes and the graves of their sires, they are called savages and red devils. When we white people do the same things we are written down in history as heroes and patriots. Why this difference?" Cooke did not receive an answer to his question, and few whites in Minnesota shared his sympathies. Most whites in America, including Lincoln, found it difficult to place themselves in the position of the Indians. Unlike Cooke, most did not recognize a common humanity between white and red, any more than between white and black.[12]

White settlement often occurred in surges, exacerbating conflicts with the Indians over land and water rights. In the Colorado Territory, for example, the discovery of gold in the Pike's Peak region in 1858 and again in the following year at Clear Creek sent a hundred thousand whites to the region. In an effort to protect both whites and Indians, a treaty in 1861 confined the Southern Cheyennes and Arapahoes to the Sand Creek reservation in southeastern Colorado. The government's failure to provide sufficient resources, particularly food, caused the tribes to forage on their old lands, now under white control, creating the same tensions that provoked the uprising in Minnesota.

In April 1864, a white rancher reported that Cheyennes had stolen livestock from his ranch. The state militia, about to be deployed to the South, seized on the incident as an opportunity to stay home and also to teach the Indians a lesson. Colonel John Chivington, a Methodist minister and militia commander, launched an attack on the Sand Creek reservation, training artillery on the village at point-blank range. Chivington's soldiers castrated Indian men, some saving the organs for use as tobacco pouches. They sliced open the stomachs of pregnant women, leaving both mother and baby to die. They dragged children from their hiding places and murdered them. The *Rocky Mountain News*, based in Denver, proclaimed, "All acquitted themselves well. Colorado soldiers have again covered themselves with glory." Chivington defended the killing of children with the simple comment, "Nits make lice."[13]

Back east, news of the Sand Creek massacre outraged citizens and officials alike. The congressional Joint Committee on the Conduct of the [Civil] War recessed from deliberations on Union military strategy to investigate the incident. The committee's report concluded that Chivington "deliberately planned and executed a foul and dastardly massacre which would have disgraced the veriest savage among those who were the victims of his cruelty." Colonel Amos Miksch broke ranks with his commander, testifying that on the morning after the battle, he saw a boy still alive in a ditch filled with dead Indians. A major drew his pistol and shot off the top of the boy's head. Soldiers cut off fingers and ears to get jewelry and collected scalps as trophies. "Next morning

Black Kettle (center) and other Cheyenne chiefs meeting with Major
Edward W. Wynkoop (kneeling with hat) at Fort Weld, Colorado, September 1864.
As a result of an agreement reached at this meeting, Black Kettle led his
people back to the Sand Creek reservation where, in late November,
they were massacred. (National Archives and Record Service Administration)

after they were dead and stiff," Miksch related, "these men pulled out the bodies of the squaws and pulled them open in an indecent manner." Robert Bent, a half-Indian, half-white guide and interpreter, was at Sand Creek along with his brother, George, and offered this testimony to the investigators:

> Some thirty or forty squaws and children were hiding in a hole for protection. [They] sent out a little girl about six years old with a white flag on a stick. She was shot and killed, all the [others] in the hole were killed. . . . I saw quite a number of infants in arms killed along with their mothers.[14]

Coloradoans saw it differently. The transfer of militia to the South would have left whites in the territory without protection. Sand Creek was a preemptive strike. Clearing the Indians from the territory had the added benefit of encouraging further white settlement, enhancing Colorado's application for statehood.

The government responded to Sand Creek by writing a new treaty offering the Cheyenne and Arapaho other reservations. As with previous treaties, federal officials did not enforce its provisions. None of the tribes ever received the land the government promised. When the Civil War ended, it was clear a new federal Indian policy was in order if the benefits of peace—a stable Union, a transcontinental railroad, and a verdant and productive West—were to be realized. Western settlers were single-minded on the best course. The *Topeka Weekly Leader* articulated western sentiment, describing the Indians as "a set of miserable, dirty, lousy, blanketed, thieving, lying, sneaking, murdering, graceless, faithless, gut-eating skunks as the Lord ever permitted to inflict the earth, ... whose immediate and final extermination all men ... should pray for." Easterners, on the other hand, believed in redemption. Indians must cease their nomadic life for their own survival. The government should provide land and education to transform them into productive Christian farmers.[15]

The West and the East would engage in this dialogue for another two decades before the nation settled on a coherent policy, and even then the implementation wavered between diligence and criminal neglect. The issue confounded even General William T. Sherman, a man rarely at a loss for a decisive strategy. Sherman, fresh from his Civil War exploits, commanded the Division of the Missouri and was responsible for implementing Indian policy in the trans-Mississippi West. He expressed his perplexity to General John M. Schofield, one of his field commanders who requested advice on the proper course of action. "The whole Indian question is in such a snarl, that I am utterly powerless to help you by order or advice."[16]

Western settlers wanted Indians out of the way, permanently. They felt that easterners, far removed from the frontier, had no conception of how daily raids on livestock, attacks on emigrant wagon trains, and the persistent fear for safety of women and children shaped the settlers' lives. Easterners sought a more humane accommodation of both parties, which many whites in the East believed the reservation system offered. *Harper's* expressed the prevailing sentiment in the East in a March 1867 editorial reminding readers that "whites are equally guilty with the Indians.... Any policy which encourages the whites to regard the Indians as mere vermin to be shot at sight, which is substantially the present policy, will only teach the Indians to retaliate." The magazine called for "the strictest supervision of the whites with the utmost possible protection of the Indians." The army, as the referee, was too thin to keep the parties separated. Most of the million-man Union army had been mustered out of the service. By 1867, the army had dwindled to fifty-five thousand men, not enough to carry out congressional policies in both the South and the West.[17]

Easterners viewed the reservation as a compromise between extinction and continued warfare, even if it meant the end of Indian culture, or perhaps *because* it meant the end of Indian culture. Adopting the white man's values would make a productive citizen out of the red man, just as freed blacks would discover the benefits of paid farm labor over political and social equality. These were the best futures for inferior races. More bloodshed in the West and the South would occur before all sections of the country reconciled to a mutually acceptable policy toward Indians and blacks. In both cases, the racial assumptions of white Americans played a significant role in the course of events.

The West continued to yield riches that attracted hordes of prospectors and settlers. Five million dollars in gold out of Colorado in 1860; thirty million in silver in 1864 from the Comstock Lode in Nevada; and prospectors in Montana and Idaho struck gold in 1864. The Nevada *Territorial Enterprise* joined the familiar western chorus in 1865, blaring, "THE INDIANS MUST BE EXTERMINATED." Identifying the Indians as a major obstacle to progress, the editor declared, "They have thrown themselves in front of the advancing giant, and must be hurled from his path or crushed."[18]

In March 1865, Congress, alarmed by the escalating violence in the West, established the Joint Committee on the Condition of the Indian Tribes. The committee's report bluntly blamed white settlers for the "irrepressible conflict between a superior and an inferior race when brought in presence of each other." The committee adopted the eastern approach to Indian policy. A Peace Commission was appointed to reach agreements with the various Indian tribes and establish reservations. Sherman endorsed the basic premise of the report, as he wrote to General Ulysses S. Grant, "I have no doubt our people have committed grievous wrong to the Indians and I wish we could punish them."[19]

Touring the West in the months after his appointment, Sherman complained of "premature settlement" by whites. The Indian could no longer pursue his way of life, so "the poor devil naturally wriggles against his doom." Sherman ordered his officers to "act against all people," including whites who provoked Indians, and to make every possible effort to discern peaceful Indians from the more belligerent tribes, a task the army neither seemed willing nor able to undertake. His colleague General Philip H. Sheridan took a harder line, sounding very much like the soldier who left a trail of destruction in the Valley of Virginia two years earlier. He recommended to the committee that Indians who refused to enter reservations should have "such destruction of their property made, as will render them very poor." Sheridan believed that the tactics that worked successfully against the Confederacy would produce similar results against the Indians.[20]

Conflict on the Plains continued while the government debated. The transcontinental railroad construction entered Indian territory in 1866. General Grant, while acknowledging the construction of the road as a provocation, viewed the railroad as "one of its [the government's] most efficient aids in the control of the Indians," as it would facilitate troop movements.

When Thomas C. Durant of the Union Pacific Railroad vowed that he would suspend construction unless his workers secured military protection, Sherman responded, "We are not going to let a few thieving, ragged Indians check and stop the progress of a work of national and world-wide importance." But the overextended army could not protect a thousand miles of railroad and separate the white settlers from the Indians at the same time. The railroad received priority, and the army generally maintained the safety of the workers and the company's property. The task of serving as a referee between white settlers and Indians proved impossible. Drawn into the conflict, the army heightened the bloodshed without materially alleviating the instability of the region.[21]

The construction of the Bozeman Trail to the Montana goldfields through Indian territory and the establishment of three forts along the trail sent the Sioux on a series of deadly raids in 1866. Captain William J. Fetterman and his cavalrymen rode out to confront the Sioux, and the result cost eighty-four soldiers their lives, including Fetterman. It was the worst massacre for the army in the West up to that time. Fetterman had expressed disdain for the fighting abilities of the Sioux, and he had ignored warnings not to mount a frontal assault on the warriors. The Sioux did not fight like the Confederates. Chief Red Cloud and his Oglala Sioux warriors mutilated Fetterman's troops in much the same manner as Chivington's men had defiled the Cheyenne at Sand Creek. Post physician C. M. Hines described the bodies of Fetterman's cavalry as looking "like . . . hogs brought to market." The official report of the battle noted "eyes, ears, mouth, and arms penetrated with spearheads, sticks and arrows; ribs slashed to separation with knives; [and] muscles of calves, thighs, stomach, breast, back, arms, and cheeks taken out."[22]

Sherman resolved, "We must act with vindictive earnestness against the Sioux, even to their extermination, men, women, and children. Nothing else will reach the root of this case." The army, however, demonstrated little enthusiasm for a campaign in the dead of winter. Instead, in the Fort Laramie Treaty of April 1868 the government agreed to dismantle the forts on the Bozeman Trail in exchange for the cessation of hostilities. Federal negotiators also guaranteed fixed boundaries for the Sioux lands comprising what is now the western half of South Dakota, for "as long as the grasses grow." The government gave up nothing, as the transcontinental railroad obviated the need for a trail to the Montana goldfields. And, as it turned out, the growing season for grass was very short.[23]

The Indians of the southern Plains, seeing the success of their northern brethren in getting the government to back down, and angered by the Federals' failure to comply with treaty guarantees, attacked army posts and settlers in Kansas in the late summer of 1868. Sherman ordered Sheridan to "go ahead in your own way, and I will back you with my authority. If it results in the utter annihilation of these Indians, it is but the result of what they have been warned again and again." Sheridan reminded his commander that an all-out campaign would inevitably result in the deaths of women and children, a price he was willing to pay. Recalling their work in the Civil War, Sheridan noted, "During the war did any one hesitate to attack a village or town occupied by the enemy because women and children were within its limits? Did we cease to throw shells into Vicksburg or Atlanta because women and children were there?"[24]

With Sherman and Sheridan directing the campaign, many whites believed that the Indian wars would end soon. *Harper's* regretted that the current campaign would probably result in "the extermination of the Indian tribes," as "neither General Sherman nor General Sheridan are men to be turned back from their purposes by false sentiments of humanity." In this unsentimental age they would pursue their objectives aggressively. Sheridan defended his policy of total war against the Plains Indians, asking, "Who shall be killed—the whites or the Indians? . . . Since 1862 at least 800 men, women, and children have been murdered within the limits of my present command in the most fiendish manner. . . . I have myself conversed with one woman who, while some months gone in pregnancy, was ravished over 30 times successively by different Indians. . . . Also another woman, ravished with more fearful brutality over 50 times, and the last Indian sticking the point of his sabre into the person of the woman." Sheridan decried the government policy of "making presents to these savages. . . . If a man commits murder . . . we hang him. . . . If an Indian does the same we have been in the habit of giving him more blankets."[25]

Sheridan launched an unprecedented winter campaign in 1868–69. When a Comanche chief asked Sheridan, "Why am I and my people being tormented by you? I am a good Indian," the general replied infamously, "The only good Indians I ever saw were dead," often misquoted as "The only good Indian is a dead Indian." The sentiment, however, was the same. Sheridan's winter campaign was a bloody success even as the members of the Peace Commission condemned it. The southern tribes conceded defeat and most returned to reservations.[26]

When Ulysses S. Grant took office as president in March 1869, he tried to steer a middle course on Indian-white relations, an approach he would also apply to the southern front. He had spent time in the West as a young soldier, and he sympathized with the plight of the Indians. In a rare mention of Indian policy in an inaugural address, Grant declared, "The proper treatment of the original occupants of this land—the Indians—is one deserving of careful study." He endorsed "any course toward them which tends to their civilization and ultimate citizenship." Rather than exterminating or permanently isolating the Indians from whites, Grant hoped to transform them into American citizens much like the immigrants from Europe. In his first year in office, he replaced the troublesome Indian agents with Quaker missionaries noted for their pacifism and "strict integrity and fair dealings."[27]

Grant appointed Brigadier General Ely S. Parker as commissioner of Indian affairs, charging him to root out corrupt agents. Parker, a Seneca Indian from New York State, was the first Native American to occupy that position and also the first of his race to hold a cabinet-level office. He had a lengthy association with Grant, having served as his adjutant during the Civil War. Parker was present at Appomattox when Lee surrendered to Grant. He drew up the documents with the terms of surrender. According to eyewitness accounts, Lee went around the room shaking hands with the Union officers but hesitated before the dark-skinned Parker. Grant introduced Parker as his adjutant, adding that he was a Native American. Lee took Parker's hand and reportedly replied, "I'm glad to see that there is at least one real American here," to which Parker responded, "We are all Americans."[28]

Parker believed, with Grant, that the surge of migration to the West could ultimately lead to the Indians' extinction. He told the president, "Unless they [the Indian nations] fall in with the current of destiny as it rolls and surges around them . . . they must succumb and be annihilated by its overwhelming force." Parker would eventually run afoul of powerful congressmen who challenged his authority to eliminate waste and corruption in the Bureau of Indian Affairs. He left Washington and made a distinguished career as a member of the Board of Commissioners in New York City, where he died in 1895.[29]

Parker's appointment indicated Grant's seriousness to formulate an Indian policy that would be as fair as possible to Native tribes. Grant refused to consider the systematic "extinction of a race," instead advocating "placing all the Indians on large reservations, as rapidly as it can be done, and giving them absolute protection there." Once acclimated to the new environment, they would receive individual plots of land and establish self-government, a policy not implemented until 1887. The former general advanced an enlightened view for the time, though he shared the racial condescension of most white Americans toward nonwhites. Grant avowed he was on the "side of the Civilization & Christianization of the Indian. I do not believe our Creator ever placed different races of men on this earth with the view of having the stronger exert all his energies in exterminating the weaker." Grant's proposals did not represent a significant break with earlier policies favoring concentration of the tribes. He tried, however, to introduce fairness and honesty into the system. Destroying the Native American culture was the price, steep though it was, for the preservation of the Indian race.[30]

In practical terms, and this was a practical age, it would have been extremely difficult for the Indians to survive as they had in the past. The settlement of the trans-Mississippi West in the three decades after the Civil War was the largest migration of people in American history to that time. These new arrivals were well aware of the threats the Indians presented, both to their property and to their lives. As the western population grew, so did the political pressure on the army and on the Grant administration. With Republican fortunes more uncertain by the day in the South, the West required nurturing. While the reservation system moved the Indians out of the way of white harm, it did not remove the Indians. Nor did it guarantee that the Indians would remain there. The Grant administration could hardly ignore the clamor from white westerners demanding a tougher Indian policy.

In 1870, Red Cloud and several other Sioux chiefs visited Washington, D.C. Red Cloud had moved onto the reservation, and his journey to Washington was a reward for that decision. The Grant administration hoped that Red Cloud would return to the Plains and persuade the other bands of Sioux to do the same. Red Cloud ate strawberries and cream with the president and Mrs. Grant and gave a speech at Cooper Union in New York to a packed house and a standing ovation. The *New York Times* gave Red Cloud's presentation a rave review: "His earnest manner, his impassioned gestures, the eloquence of his hands, and the magnetism which he evidently exercises over an audience, produced a vast effect on the dense throng. . . . 'You have children, and so have we. We want to rear our children well, and ask you to help us in doing so.' It seems to us that this is not an unreasonable request even though it does come from a 'savage.'"[31]

Red Cloud also delivered an address to the Department of the Interior and its secretary, Jacob Cox. This speech encapsulated the failure of U.S. Indian policy to that point and the growing misery of the Native American population that the next seven years of warfare would only exacerbate. It was both a summary and an elegy. "What has been done in my country," Red Cloud spoke, "I did not want, did not ask for it; white people going through my country. . . . The white children have surrounded me and have left me nothing but an island. When we first had this land we were strong, now are melting like snow on the hillside, while you are grown like spring grass." Red Cloud knew, of course, that he could not stem the tide of migration, but he hoped for a more enlightened government policy.[32]

Although Red Cloud had agreed to bring his people onto the reservation, he regretted his decision. "I do not want my reservation on the Missouri; this is the fourth time I have said so. . . . Our children are dying off like sheep; the country does not suit them. I was born at the forks of the Platte, and I was told that the land belonged to me." Moreover, the promised annuities and goods fell far short of the agreement. "When you send goods to me, they are stolen all along the road, so when they reached me they were only a handful. They held a paper for me to sign, and that is all I got for my lands. The railroad is passing through my country now; I have received no pay for the land." The officials listened politely. Nothing changed.[33]

In 1872, P. T. Barnum was already famous for his circus shows. In that year, he introduced a new attraction, a "Wild West" show that featured an Indian camp with real squaws and warriors sitting in wigwams, performing war dances, hunting real buffalo, and racing their ponies. This idyllic scene was suddenly crashed by a horde of swarthy Mexicans who attacked the camp, igniting "such a scene of savage strife and warfare as is never seen except upon our wild western borders." Wild West shows soon became a staple form of entertainment rivaling minstrel shows in popularity. Buffalo Bill Cody eclipsed Barnum as the leading impresario of these staged dramas, trading on his experience and fame as a man of the West. White men replaced Mexicans, and the Indians became the aggressors. The Indians, and the West, had passed into the realm of caricature, much as African Americans and the South became the stereotype of minstrel shows. White Americans came to "know" both races and regions from what they saw on the stage. What they saw was two races of limited intelligence and ability to compete in the modern world without the assistance and direction of whites. The policies governments devised over the next century for these two races reflected more the act than the reality. For an age that exalted reason and realism, this was the ultimate abstraction.[34]

Reservation boundaries continued to shrink or shift as white settlement expanded. The administrative overhaul notwithstanding, problems persisted in feeding, clothing, and sheltering reservation Indians. When reservation Indians did not receive goods and annuities as promised and when their territories disappeared, they conducted raids. Then policy shifted toward extermination. While easterners acknowledged corruption and inefficiency, they also placed some of the blame upon the Indian. Harper's, normally a sympathetic voice for the Indian, conceded, "These Indians have farms and do a little at farming; but it is evident that they are idle and shiftless, and unable to take care of themselves." Just as North and South would eventually concur on Reconstruction policy based upon the racial limitations of blacks, so East and West would accommodate on Indian policy.[35]

By the early 1870s such concurrence was relatively easy to come by. Douglas's railroad drew East and West together not only in economic terms but intellectually as well. The Age of Reason had elevated science to an exalted role once reserved for religion as a major arbiter of public policy. The new science reinforced old racial views. The competitive, Darwinian view of society also privileged individual initiative and innovation, attributes lacking in "lesser" races. While white southerners banded together to work for redemption, white northerners raced off to make money.

CHAPTER 20

POLITICAL SCIENCE

MONEY RAN EVERYTHING and people ran after money. Sometimes too hard. Russell Conwell was a believer. A Union veteran and an attorney, he became a Baptist preacher building a struggling congregation in Philadelphia into what became Temple University. In 1878, he delivered a sermon, "Acres of Diamonds," that he would give over six thousand times. Not quite as famous as the "Sermon on the Mount," to which some followers compared it, the speech went through numerous print editions. The advertising blurb on the back of the 1978 centennial edition claimed, "This is the beloved, all-time bestseller that has helped more Americans find more happiness than any other book besides the Bible!"[1]

Some sermons do not age well. They are too reflective of their time and place. "Acres of Diamonds" struck a responsive chord in Americans of the 1870s and kept on striking it because it articulated the theme of modern America. God wanted all Americans to be wealthy, the sooner the better. Forget about "Money is the root of all evil." That is not in the Bible. The biblical passage reads, "*Love* of money that is the root of all evil." As long as you do not fall in love, money is wonderful. "Money is power, money is force. . . . I say that you ought to get rich, and it is your duty to get rich." People asked Conwell, "Why don't you preach the gospel instead of preaching about man's making money?" He replied, "Because to make money honestly is to preach the gospel. . . . The men who get rich may be the most honest men you find in the community."

Money can do good things. It can make a man more masculine, for one thing. "A man is not really a true man until he owns his own home." Ultimately, Conwell asserted, "Money is power, and you ought to be reasonably ambitious to have it!" He proclaimed to his congregation, "I say, then, you ought to have money. If you can honestly attain unto riches in Philadelphia, it is your Christian and godly duty to do so. It is an awful mistake of these pious people to think you must be awfully poor in order to be pious." Poverty, in fact, revealed impiety. "There is not a poor person in the United States who was not made poor by his own shortcomings. . . . It is all wrong to be poor, anyhow."

Mark Twain pilloried the Gospel of Money in "The Revised Catechism," published in the *New York Tribune*. Twain wanted to get rich as much as the next man. He was a friend to Andrew Carnegie, who would send him barrels of whiskey from his cellars; and he hobnobbed with Henry H. Rogers, an official of Standard Oil. Twain despised hypocrisy, however, especially in religion. For him, the Gospel of Money was no Gospel at all, just a self-serving patina for greed. Twain wrote:

> What is the chief end of man?—to get rich. In what way?—dishonestly if we can; honestly if we must. Who is God, the one only and true? Money is God. Gold and Greenbacks and Stock—father, son, and the ghost of same—three persons in one; these are the true and only God, mighty and supreme.[2]

Where Twain saw hypocrisy, Conwell's comfortable congregants in Philadelphia heard validation. They never tired of hearing the sermon, nor, apparently, did millions of other Americans. Religions emerge initially as challenges to the prevailing culture. It was true of the Mormons and of the evangelical Protestant denominations in early nineteenth-century America. Success in the form of converts and in the wider acceptance of its theology poses a dilemma for all religions. Inevitably that religion becomes part of or subservient to the host culture. This happened in post–Civil War America in both the North and the South, though for different reasons. In the South, evangelical Protestantism sanctified the war and its causes, the Old South civilization it defended, and the crusade for redemption. Northerners, on the other hand, recoiled from the self-righteous certitude and idealism that nearly destroyed a nation even as they abolished its greatest sin. Russell Conwell, a man who came to the pulpit from a business background, represented the new voice of northern evangelical Protestantism. Conwell believed faith could only be relevant if it reinforced rather than challenged the prevailing culture.

The Gospel of Money was totally apolitical; it represented no party or candidate, reflecting the turn away from great moral issues to the pursuit of happiness. The new gospel left little room for sentiment. If the poor are always with us, then that is their problem; if the former slaves, guarded by constitutional amendments and a ring of statutes, cannot make their way in society, then the shortcoming is theirs. If the Indians cannot compete for land and sustenance with whites, then that is due to their inferiority. These were not only matters of faith but also matters of science. For governments to intervene on behalf of such unfortunates would contravene the natural order and produce chaos. And chaos would destroy democracy.

The Gospel of Money assumed that everyone pursued success on a level playing field. Conwell's assertion that the wealthiest men were perhaps the most honest was debatable, but honesty was essential for the integrity of the pursuit. No government to put its thumb on the scale of prosperity, no entrepreneur to deceive those less well informed or endowed, and no group unduly favored or burdened to skew the competition. The war had created a unified nation and abundant opportunities for a much broader range of people than at any other previous time in American history.

The lure of lucre was irresistible. Never was there so much, and never were there as many ways to use it and to grow it. Among the most popular nonfiction titles of the era were future president James A. Garfield's *Elements of Success* (1869) and P. T. Barnum's *The Art of Money-Getting* (1882). States and cities plunged into railroad construction. Between 1866 and 1873, twenty-nine state legislatures approved over eight hundred proposals to grant local aid to railroads. New York, Illinois, and Missouri were the most generous, each authorizing over $70 million in aid. Most of the funds to purchase rail stock, sometimes at inflated value, came from municipal tax-secured bonds. Mark Twain would look back on the 1870s and conclude, "I think that the reason Americans seem to be so addicted to trying to get rich suddenly is merely because the *opportunity* to make promising efforts in that direction has offered itself with a frequency out of all proportion to the European experience." The postwar nation provided a dazzling array of opportunities, and many took advantage of them, some more than others.[3]

William Marcy Tweed never heard Russell Conwell's sermon, but he would have been an enthusiastic disciple. Tweed believed fervently in individual initiative; yet he was generous to a fault, helping friends and relatives, as well as his city, New York. Conwell would have delighted in Tweed's background, another Horatio Alger tale. His father was a brush maker, and the younger Tweed was a carpenter and then a fireman. He joined a Democratic Party that, in New York, included a large contingent of Irish immigrants. The great entrepreneurs were ordering disparate activities into large corporations, so Tweed, always a quick study, decided to organize New York politics.

Tweed befriended two influential men, Peter B. "Brains" Sweeny, an Irish saloon keeper who maintained the Democratic organization, Tammany Hall, and Richard "Slippery Dick" Connolly, an Irish ward boss who organized the city's districts and bestowed patronage liberally to secure their loyalty. In those days, politicians, not gangsters, had the colorful nicknames. Sweeny and Connolly developed a well-oiled system, or "machine," much in the spirit of the great entrepreneurs. They hung around the docks of lower Manhattan, greeting new arrivals from the Old World with clothes, food, and cash to tide them over during the cold winters. The grateful newcomers, in turn, provided Tammany with substantial majorities in local elections, often well beyond the number of registered voters. As Tweed explained, "The ballots made no result, the counters made the result." Tweed rose through the ranks to become chairman of the New York City Board of Supervisors, the body responsible for the day-to-day operation of America's largest city. The city became a series of construction projects that never seemed to end: road paving, public buildings, sewer and water systems, and that iron bridge over Broadway that Mark Twain navigated on his first day in New York. Doing business with the city of New York was a privilege, and Tweed aimed to make contractors pay for it.[4]

By the late 1860s, Tweed was making about a million dollars a month. Like all good businessmen of the era, Tweed was a student of vertical integration. He established his own business, the New York Printing Company, which billed the city for all its printing needs. One bill, submitted in 1870, charged the city $10,000 for three inkbottles, six reams of paper, and a few boxes of rubber bands. In an era when welfare was rarely public, Tweed spent some of his profits on the poor, distributing $50,000, in food, fuel, and clothing to impoverished New Yorkers in the winter of 1870. The city's bonded indebtedness increased from zero in 1867 to $90 million by 1871, with Tweed and his coterie siphoning off about $50 million for kickbacks, payoffs, and their own pockets. He was especially proud of the new county courthouse, whose initial cost was pegged at $250,000. It wound up costing taxpayers $13 million. Andrew Garvey, known for good reason as "the Prince of Plasterers," charged $3 million for $20,000 worth of plastering. "Lucky George" Miller, another contractor true to his name, earned over $360,000 a month for carpentry, though the building's structural materials were primarily iron and marble. What galled New Yorkers was less Tweed's $750 million profit on the project than the fact that it sat unfinished.[5]

Investigative journalism might have uncovered these details, except that most of the region's eighty-nine newspapers received considerable advertising revenue from Tammany Hall, and those editors who were especially friendly to Tweed earned handsome Christmas bonuses. After Tweed was exposed, twenty-seven of these newspapers folded, having existed primarily on the income from Tammany. Not only did journalists ignore Tweed's defalcations, but they also praised him as a reformer and a builder. The Republican press might have brought him down, but Tweed had worked out an arrangement with Thurlow Weed, the Republican Party boss in New York State, by which the Democrats would leave Albany to Weed, if Weed left the city to Tweed. Weed and Tweed worked together well.

The arrangement lasted until the *New York Times*, one of the Republican newspapers that had praised Tweed's acumen, "broke" the story in September 1870. The graft had become too obvious for the newspaper to ignore, and it identified Tweed and his cronies as "a gang of burglars." The broader theme was "the Irish Catholic despotism that rules the City of New York, the Metropolis of Free America." Thomas Nast, the Bavarian-born cartoonist for *Harper's* who had given America Santa Claus and whose drawings articulated what many northerners were feeling in their hearts during the Civil War, helped bring down Boss Tweed, perhaps more than the *Times*.[6]

By 1870, Nast had become an oracle for middle-class New Yorkers, many of them Republicans predisposed to despising the Irish Catholics and their sway over the city's politics. Nast depicted Tweed as a bloated bureaucrat sucking the lifeblood out of democracy, aided by his simian-like Irish allies. In one drawing, Tweed and his Tammany cohorts are vultures picking over the bones of city taxpayers, with the caption "Let Us Prey." In another, the Tammany Tiger is in the Roman Colosseum devouring Christians with Tweed taunting, "What are you going to do about it?" Downright nasty. Tweed, recognizing the threat to his empire, offered Nast $5 million to lay down his pencil. "I don't care a straw for your newspaper articles," Tweed told Nast. "My constituents don't know how to read, but they can't help seeing them damned pictures." The attempted bribe became part of the evidence that finally convicted Tweed, sending him to prison for twelve years. The sheriff reportedly blushed and apologized when he arrived to arrest Tweed. Less than five years into his sentence, he bribed his way out, was rearrested, and died the following year in prison.[7]

Tweed's rule in New York was wasteful. Could anyone, though, corral the spirit of New York or other burgeoning American cities? The *New York Times* pronounced the city's government "worse than a failure. . . . It is corrupt, inefficient, wasteful and scandalous." These comments appeared in 1867, four years before Tweed's deeds came to light. But when have Americans not complained about their cities? Thomas Jefferson's statement about cities as "sores on the human body" was hardly the last bad word against urban America. In the 1890s, writer Josiah Strong described the American city as "a menace to state and nation" because it was incapable of governance. The classic handwringing study of urban horror, Lincoln Steffens's *Shame of the Cities*, appeared soon after. In a nation that consistently elevated the farm and small town as the apotheosis of the democratic ideal, such attitudes were not unusual. What is indisputable, though, is that people with education and ambition left farms and small towns for large cities posthaste. Any place that held

"Let Us Prey," 1871. One of a series of merciless cartoons
Thomas Nast drew satirizing William
M. Tweed and his Tammany gang in New York City.
In this drawing, Tweed and his crew of "vultures"—Peter B. "Brains" Sweeny,
Richard B. "Slippery Dick" Connolly, and A. "Elegant"
Oakey Hall are waiting for the storm of protest to "Blow Over."
It didn't, and Tweed was convicted and imprisoned due in no small part
to Nast's caricatures. (Courtesy of the Library of Congress)

so many dreams was bound to be chaotic and volatile. Great energy, however, produced great things. For all the attention to Tweed and other urban bosses, the engineer, the landscape architect, and other professionals and technicians shaped American cities in the decades after the Civil War. The infrastructure and architectural styles they pioneered created the modern urban landscape.[8]

In the wake of the Tweed scandal, a group of citizens appointed a blue-ribbon panel, the Committee of Seventy, to study reform measures including imposing literacy and property qualifications for voting. The clamor to limit democracy was considerable. Historian Francis Parkman complained it was foolish if not criminal to leave the city's destiny to "the dangerous classes." Liberty, he argued, "means license and politics means plunder." The committee managed to end public welfare (in the midst of a depression) but accomplished little else. By the late 1870s, Tammany was back in business. The city instituted civil service reform to limit the politicians' power of appointment. In 1882, Congress would pass a federal Civil Service Act, placing the reins of government in the hands of professionals who would carry out their responsibilities in an objective, apolitical, and honest manner. Or so the theory went.[9]

Southern whites opposed to the Republican governments and black suffrage learned from the media frenzy surrounding Tweed and his cohorts. They understood that corruption as a practice was not as important as corruption *as an issue*, especially if they could tie it to suffrage. Corruption played well to northern audiences, who need only reference their own backyards to sympathize with white southerners. The issue of corruption lent more credence to the charges that these southern governments were illegitimate.

This is not to say that southern Republican governments were chaste. The Republican administrations in South Carolina were especially profligate. The state government expanded services and infrastructure but grew the state debt from $5.4 million to $15.8 million between 1868 and 1872. Evidence indicated that some lawmakers benefited financially from these expenditures. The South Carolina General Assembly spent $125,000 on wine and whiskey for lawmakers during one session alone. A printing firm, the Republican Printing Company, bribed legislators to award it state contracts at inflated rates. South Carolina's printing bill soared from $21,000 in 1868 to $450,000 in 1873.

Some of the lawmakers enjoyed well-furnished quarters. Between 1868 and 1872, South Carolina spent $200,000 on furniture for the statehouse. An inventory taken in 1877 indicated that only $17,775 worth of furnishings remained. There were also bond frauds involving state securities and discounted railroad stock sold to legislators in exchange for favorable votes. Key officials in the state government led the carnival, including Republican governor Robert K. Scott (a white northerner) and his successor, Franklin J. Moses Jr. (a white southerner). Perhaps the most notorious of the crew was John J. "Honest John" Patterson, who bought a U.S. Senate seat in 1872 for forty thousand dollars, bribing state legislators who elected him. These lapses were not unique for the Gilded Age, but they indelibly tainted regimes whose legitimacy was already suspect. The *New York Times* spoke for many disgusted northerners when it noted in 1874 that "ignorant negroes [in South Carolina] transplanted from the cotton fields to the halls of the Capitol, where they have been drilled by unscrupulous white adventurers, have naturally made a mockery of government and bankrupted the State." Little wonder that support for southern regimes was eroding quickly, even among staunch northern Republicans.[10]

Not all Republican governments in the South were tainted, but the few examples afforded the Democrats opportunities to attack all these regimes as the logical outcome of universal suffrage. The improvements in infrastructure, education, and the economy accomplished by southern Republicans provided, ironically, visible evidence of alleged profligate spending, higher taxes, and the opportunity, if not the reality, for graft.

Democratic chicanery in the South did not raise a similar concern in the North. Southern Democrats stuffed ballot boxes, levied poll taxes, prevented Republicans from voting, and changed polling places without general notification. One rarely heard of corruption once the low-tax, low-service, lily-white Redeemer governments took office. In Georgia, for example, corruption charges in 1875 led to the impeachment and resignation of the Democratic state treasurer, the impeachment and conviction of the comptroller general, and the resignation of the commissioner of agriculture. James "Honest Dick" Tate, the Redeemer state treasurer of Kentucky, was so popular voters re-elected him to ten consecutive terms. One day he was gone, and, officials discovered, so was $229,000. None of this condoned Republican failings, but a double standard operated in the nation.[11]

Investigations into government corruption typically revealed cozy relationships between public officials and corporate leaders. Entrepreneurs, the heroes of the postwar era, began to receive closer scrutiny after the Tweed investigation uncovered ties between Tammany and railroad executives. Mark Twain enjoyed taking the moguls to task. He taunted railroad magnates "Commodore" Cornelius Vanderbilt and Jay Gould, two of the most unlovable of the era's entrepreneurs. "Go and surprise the whole country by doing something right," he baited Vanderbilt. "I didn't remember ever reading anything about you which you oughtn't be ashamed of." Of Gould Twain wrote, "The people had *desired* money before this day, but *he* taught them to fall down and worship it." Gould attempted to corner the gold market; he manipulated railroad stock, and he ruthlessly bought out competitors. Small in stature, dark in complexion, he was rumored to be Jewish.[12]

The scandals swept over public opinion in rapid succession. Gould, Vanderbilt, Tweed, and then the Credit Mobilier revelations splashed into the press and nearly drowned the Grant administration. Transcontinental railroad promoters had set up Credit Mobilier (named after a French bank that failed in 1867) as the independent construction company through which all funds to build the railroad were funneled. The construction company raised funds from the sale of stocks and bonds and repaid investors with government subsidies as each section of the road was completed. The men who ran the railroad and the construction company were one and the same, and they spread stocks and bonds liberally throughout the Congress to obtain friendly legislation. Credit Mobilier was the only company bidding on construction contracts. Congress set the upper limit for bids, and, miraculously, Credit Mobilier's bids matched the ceilings, enabling the directors to sell bonds to that amount, though construction costs for each section were well below the bids. The directors of both companies pocketed the difference and provided gifts to friendly congressmen and Vice President Schuyler Colfax. The Pacific road was a moneymaking enterprise long before a single train crossed the continent.[13]

Credit Mobilier erupted into a scandal in September 1872 when someone discovered a railroad company notebook with congressmen's names alongside the amount of stock each would receive. Credit Mobilier, however, was the product of decades of intimate relationships between government and railroads. The arrangements uncovered by the investigation broke no laws. It was doubtful whether the Pacific railroad would have been completed without close ties between legislators and directors. Still, the lawmakers' supplemental income shocked many Americans. Mark Twain, in the preface to the London edition of *The Gilded Age*, hoped the book would illuminate America's "all-pervading speculativeness" and "the shameful corruption which lately crept into our politics, and in a handful of years has spread until the pollution has affected some portion of every State and Territory in the Union."[14]

When the smoke cleared from these financial shenanigans in 1873, Jay Gould stood atop the Pacific railroad's organizational chart. Within a decade he ran much of the country's rail system. Gould also controlled New York City's rapid transportation system, several newspapers, and Western Union, the nation's leading telegraph operator. Conspiracy theories about Gould abounded to such a degree that even the *New York Times* saw humor in the situation. "But straightaway we are assured that 'JAY GOULD' is at the bottom of the whole affair, as he is said to be at the bottom of everything that goes on nowadays. We strongly suspect that he will yet be found to . . . have had something to do with the hard Winter, frozen water-pipes, and plumbers' extravagant bills."[15]

The reformers were not amused. Gould represented the Gospel of Money run amok, the rogue individual who could buy a Congress and seize the nation's key transportation and communication networks. In 1869, Gould and his partner "Diamond" Jim Fisk sought to wrest control of the Erie Railroad from Cornelius Vanderbilt by printing bogus stock. Gould showed up at the New York State legislature in Albany, hoping to convince the lawmakers to legalize the stock and thereby gain control of the road. Vanderbilt and Gould conducted a bidding war, paying off legislators to vote their way. Both entrepreneurs had suites in the same hotel, trunks full of cash, and a parade of lawmakers coming and going. Gould gave away $600,000, sufficient to gain a 101-to-5 vote in the legislature to legitimize his stock.[16]

Gould set up a five-man executive committee to run the Erie Railroad. Two of the five spots went to Boss Tweed and Brains Sweeny, ensuring there would be no future challenges to the Erie empire. The Empire State, indeed. Nor was New York an isolated case. One journalist described the government of New Jersey as "a lobby containing a State Legislature." Nor was New York City the only metropolis where such financial hi-jinks occurred. Washington, D.C., went bankrupt in 1870 after a spending spree grading streets and paying off black voters to elect the Republican ticket. That ended democracy in the nation's capital; Congress took control of the city. Cleveland city councilmen concocted a system in which each city contract let out would let in a given amount to each member.[17]

The collective apoplexy over Gould and his ilk was out of proportion to their alleged crimes. The Pacific railroad finished ahead of schedule and under budget. Conflict of interest, shocking in our day, was business as usual in theirs. And corruption was hardly an invention of the Grant administration. The scale of it, the intense competition among the press for a juicy story, and the general insecurity at a time of great economic and urban transformation fueled fears that the country had taken the Gospel of Money too far. Under ordinary circumstances, such reformist tantrums would eventually dissipate. In the context of continued unrest in the South, disorder in northern cities, and an impending presidential election, the advocates of pure government and pure electorates persisted. They did not end corruption, but they succeeded in ending the hopes of black Americans to become equal citizens.

The most serious charge against official corruption was that it corroded democracy by cheating the public of wealth and elevating unfit individuals to power. Walt Whitman lamented in 1871, "The depravity of the business classes of our country is not less than has been supposed, but infinitely greater." Governments, put into power by an incompetent electorate, condoned and participated in the "depravity." The productive middle classes were the main victims of these activities. Whitman worried about the "appalling dangers of universal suffrage" that enabled the brigands to function unrestrained. The stories of greed and graft crowding the columns of the major dailies proved too much for Whitman, who vowed to close his ears and eyes to such news. He could no longer hear America singing:

> Nay, tell me not to-day the publish'd shame,
> Read not to-day the journal's crowded page,

> *The merciless reports still branding forehead after*
>   *forehead,*
> *The guilty column following guilty column,*
> *To-day to me the tale refusing,*
> *Turning from it—from the white capitol turning.*[18]

For Whitman and many other Americans, the fire of war should have cleansed the body politic. That evidence abounded to the contrary was a matter of great heartbreak. America may have been reborn, but its new incarnation was hardly a state of grace. Preparing a new edition of *Leaves of Grass* in 1871, Whitman tellingly inserted this addition to his poem "Respondez!" originally written in 1856:

> *Stifled, O days! O lands! in every public and private*
>   *corruption!*
> *Smother'd in thievery, impotence, shamelessness,*
>   *mountain-high;*
> *Brazen effrontery, scheming, rolling like ocean's waves*
>   *around and upon you, Oh my days! my lands!*
> *For not even those thunderstorms, nor fiercest lightnings*
>   *of the war have purified the atmosphere.*[19]

Mark Twain shared Whitman's concerns about untrammeled democracy. In *The Gilded Age*, there is no mawkish sentimentality about the common man. The people on the western frontier are "animals" and "cattle." They spend their time gossiping, spitting, and whittling. New York is hardly better. Surveying a jury, Twain and Warner wrote, "Low foreheads and heavy faces they all had; some had a look of animal cunning, while the most were only stupid." Washington lawmakers reflected their constituents, both in morals and physiognomy. Twain quipped in a banquet speech, "There is a Congressman—I mean a son of a bitch—But why do I repeat myself?" A dinner companion noted Twain's agitation on the subject, inveighing against "this wicked ungodly suffrage, where the vote of a man who knew nothing was as good as the vote of a man of education and industry; this endeavor to equalize what God has made unequal was a wrong and a shame." In an *Atlantic* article in 1875, Twain wrote, only half in jest, that instead of contracting the suffrage, the country should expand it so that "men of education, property, and achievement would receive five or even ten votes each."[20]

The ethically challenged governments elected by immigrants and poor laborers in the North and black men in the South gave many Americans pause
in the 1870s, hardening their views toward blacks, whose aspirations now
seemed more like pretensions, while white southerners' violence looked more
like self-defense. Soon there would be widespread approbation concerning
the use of police and federal troops against immigrant workers. What concerned Twain, Whitman, and many others was that unrestricted suffrage
could, ironically, threaten democracy itself. It might be prudent to restrict democracy in order to save it. Of the immigrants to the cities, one observer
wrote that they "follow blindly leaders of their own race, are not moved by
discussion, exercise no judgment of their own." They "are not fit for the suffrage." These were the arguments white southerners put forward concerning
the freedmen. Eventually, an immoral equivalency emerged: two regions of
the country with similar problems with similar inferior peoples.[21]

A consensus formed in the early 1870s that democracy was a privilege, not
a right. Americans did not need to draw on the experience of the failed European revolutions of 1848 to see the dangers of too much democracy. The Paris
Commune of 1871 provided a more immediate example, and many who questioned the expansion of the franchise cited the Commune as the logical outcome of "bottom-side up" government.[22]

The Paris Commune, the name of the city's governing body between late
March and late May 1871, arose after France's humiliating defeat in the Franco-
Prussian War. Consisting of mostly workers and some professionals, many of
whom were socialists or anarchists, the Commune challenged the authority of
the central government. During its brief tenure, the Commune enacted a series of measures separating church and state, extending debt relief, granting
pensions to unmarried companions, abolishing night work, and remitting
rents. The French army marched into Paris and attacked the Commune's bar-
ricades. In what became known as *la semaine sanglante* (the blood-soaked
week), the military put an end to the Commune, killing 30,000 communards while losing 7,500 troops. By comparison, during a year and a half of
the French Revolution from 1789–90, the death toll stood at 19,000. Both the
Commune's revolutionary programs and the bloody battles that followed
repelled many Americans, who attributed the violence to the radicalism of
the communards.

The Commune debacle resulted from unqualified citizens—workers, anarchists, and socialists—participating in government. Americans in 1871 saw
a similar danger in the daily reports of violence in the South, labor unrest in
the cities of the North, and corrupt governments put in place by a largely

uneducated electorate. The *Chicago Tribune* made this connection explicitly: "New York is abandoned by her property-owners to the rule of one set of adventurous carpet-baggers and vagabonds. . . . South Carolina is ruled by carpet-baggers and irresponsible non-property-holders for other reasons." When the New York branch of the International Workingmen's Association, which included socialists, anarchists, and various women's rights groups, marched through the city to promote the eight-hour workday in September 1871, just as the Tweed scandal broke, the connection seemed obvious. Reports of the march noted the ominous presence of "a group of negro workers," and members carrying "the red flag and a banner with the French slogan, 'Liberty, Equality and Fraternity.'" Suffragist Victoria Woodhull, a member of the IWA, passed out flyers advocating "free-love, anarchy, and every extreme doctrine that appealed to their speculative fancy."[23]

Northerners questioned the legitimacy of their governments, much as white southerners denied the legitimacy of the Republican regimes in their states. The "bogus state governments" of the South and the degraded "Celtocracy" of New York City were two examples of the same problem. The *Nation* identified South Carolina as the breeding ground of "a swarm of little Tweeds." Up until the early 1870s, the national trend moved toward expanding the suffrage, first of non-property-holders, then of naturalized immigrants, and finally of African Americans. Then it stopped, and courts and states began to circumscribe the franchise and remove some offices from the electorate and others from politicians' appointive powers. The corruption and violence, north and south, provided the context for this democratic contraction.[24]

Susan B. Anthony also questioned the legitimacy of her government. The culprits in her interpretation were not unqualified workers, blacks, or immigrants but white men in power. Police arrested Anthony and several other suffragists as they attempted to vote in the 1872 presidential election. After her conviction, Anthony proclaimed, "This government is not a democracy. . . . It is an odious aristocracy; a hateful oligarchy of sex" that placed "father, brothers, husbands, sons . . . over the mother and sisters, the wife and daughters, of every household." At a time when the concept of universal suffrage came under attack, Anthony reminded Americans that suffrage was hardly universal. Her cause, however, was lost in an era when many sought means to narrow rather than to expand the franchise.[25]

The northern evangelical churches that had been in the forefront of antebellum reform upheld the status quo. Evangelicals were less scolds than cheerleaders, as Conwell's sermon indicated. Walt Whitman was concerned that everyone pursued everything except the collective good, and the churches encouraged such behavior. "Genuine belief seems to have left us. . . . The spec-

*"The Ignorant Vote—Honors are Easy," 1876. Many white northerners
drew parallels between the corruption and inefficiency
of their local and state governments, supported by
immigrant and working-class votes, with similar problems in
southern states where African Americans voted. Thomas Nast, who,
in earlier years, had championed civil rights for the freedmen, confirms
that connection with an unflattering portrayal of a black
voter and an Irish voter. (Courtesy of the Library of Congress)*

tacle is appalling. We live in an atmosphere of hypocrisy throughout. . . . A lot
of churches, sects, etc., the most dismal phantasm I know, usurp the name
of religion."[26]

Evangelicals built sturdy churches in the great cities, and their ministers
mingled with leading entrepreneurs and politicians. They withdrew their blessings from the Republican governments in the South, curtailing or ending their
funding of missionaries and schools, and they would support the use of force
against unruly strikers during the economic downturn following the Panic of
1873. Northern Presbyterians pulled out of missionary efforts to the freedmen
in 1871 to avoid "all unpleasant collisions with the Southern churches." The
American Missionary Association, which had supplied hundreds of teachers to

the former slaves, disavowed that it had ever endorsed the idea that the races were equal and cut funding to the missions. Northern evangelicals harbored futile hopes that their orthodoxy on race and politics could win the favor of their southern brethren. Northern Methodists, hoping for a reunion, joined southern Methodists in prohibiting "mixed Conferences, mixed congregations, and mixed schools." They explained candidly, "The [Church] south must be appeased." To what end? A Presbyterian minister in North Carolina summarized the feeling among many southern churchmen: "You may put me down as one of the number that will never, no never, consent to a union with the Yankees. I hope that this is the sentiment of every Presbyterian."[27]

The crusades of northern churches in the postwar era focused on outlawing behavioral sins and on symbolic acts that filled their coffers but not their faith. Efforts to enact another "Christian amendment" to the Constitution failed, as did campaigns to prohibit the consumption of alcohol. Evangelicals managed to convince Congress to outlaw obscenity and Mormon polygamy. Those pale victories testified to their waning influence.[28]

One old crusade survived the transition to postwar America, and it reinforced the decline of northern evangelicals. Like a favorite threadbare blanket, the Roman Catholic Church comforted evangelicals in its traditional role as a menace to American civilization. The fact that Tweed's minions were mostly Irish, and many of the new immigrants were Catholic, enabled evangelicals to join with secular bigots to appear relevant. Thomas Nast's monkey-like caricatures of the Irish were a well-known signature for the artist. His cartoons attacking Catholics for threatening the separation of church and state and depicting foreign prelates slithering ashore to lure young children to God-knows-what were widely circulated in the early 1870s. Abolitionist stalwarts among the evangelicals, many of whom had harbored almost as much disdain for Catholics as for slaveholders, now honed their religious bigotry. Harriet Beecher Stowe's daughter, Hatty, writing from Chicago, informed her mother, "Mary Neugent who used to live with us . . . brought her oldest boy with her to see us—And you have no idea what a nice pretty refined looking little fellow he is—you would never in the world take him to be the child of Irish parents." Mom understood. In her novel celebrating the small-town, homogeneous New England of her youth, *Poganuc People: Their Loves and Lives* (1878), Stowe wrote, "Such were our New England villages in the days when its people were of our own blood and race, and the pauper population of Europe had not as yet been landed upon our shores."[29]

While evangelicals both north and south harked back to a halcyon and irrelevant past, the nation turned to a new faith, science. Activist governments upset the natural evolution of the economy and society. Cities were inefficient because experts and professionals were either closed out or turned off by a corrupt political process. States in the South and cities in the North were ill governed because unqualified electorates ruled. Science had predicted these problems.

Charles Darwin's *On the Origin of Species* (1859) had an enormous impact on American thought and practice in the post–Civil War era. Darwin's theory of natural selection transferred power from God to nature. Scientific laws governed the universe, and as natural and social scientists discovered those laws, people could act in harmony with nature. People once sought faith to uncover truth; now they pursued the scientific method. Andrew Dickson White, president of Cornell University, announced his institution would "afford an asylum for Science [often capitalized]—where truth shall be sought for truth's sake, where it shall not be the main purpose of the Faculty to stretch or cut sciences exactly to fit 'Revealed Religion.'"[30]

Empirical research in America's Age of Reason would save America from itself. As the evangelicals believed man could attain perfectibility by following God, the acolytes of science asserted that man would attain perfectibility through research. Science was a marvelous recipe for doing nothing, at least until all the data were in. As economist Lyman Atwater put it, "Legislation cannot alter the laws of nature, of man, of political economics." Mankind's dominion over nature and society would occur once scientists unlocked the secrets of the universe. Here was America's new millennial vision. It was a philosophy of innocence as much as the evangelical promise of a heaven on earth. Ralph Waldo Emerson described the process: "Infancy is the perpetual Messiah, which comes into the arms of fallen men, and pleads with them to return to Paradise."[31]

Darwin's theory came as a revelation even to those steeped in evangelical theology. In November 1865, Charles Francis Adams Jr. was convalescing from what we would today describe as post-traumatic stress disorder. He came across an essay by the positivist August Comte, and it "revolutionized" his "whole mental attitude. I emerged from the theological stage, in which I had been nurtured, and passed into the scientific. I had up to that time never heard of Darwin. . . . From reading [Comte] I date a changed intellectual and moral being."[32]

For the realists of the postwar age, Darwin shattered faith. Andrew Carnegie described the revelatory process he went through after his first introduction to Darwin's work in 1867. "Not only had I got rid of theology and the supernatural, but I had found the truth of evolution. 'All is well since all grows better' became my motto, my true source of comfort." This was the message of Russell Conwell in a secular context, that accumulating money and doing good are mankind's highest callings. By the tenth anniversary of the book's publication, *Scientific American* asserted that Darwin's theory of natural selection was making converts so "rapidly" that many considered it no longer a theory, but a "truth."[33]

The concept of evolution suited the prejudices of the age. Evolution implied a slow inexorable process that established a hierarchy of living organisms. Though Darwin made clear that natural selection occurred by chance and that not all adaptations were useful, popularizers of his theory focused on the progressive nature of evolution. These ideas comported with general notions of racial differences. The full title of Darwin's book, *On the Origin of Species by Means of Natural Selection, or The Preservation of Favoured Races in the Struggle for Life*, made the racial connection explicit. Human societies evolved much like organisms. At the apex stood western Europeans and Anglo-Americans. The African persisted on the lower end of the evolutionary continuum. As proof, scholars pointed out that "the Negro has had centuries of independence within which to show the metal [*sic*] that is in him—what has he done in Africa but evolve monsters that put our monkey ancestors to shame?" Therefore, black suffrage was not only foolish but also dangerous, both to the African and to the higher civilization.[34]

Politics must adhere to scientific truths, and the distinction among races was self-evident. This was not racism but incontrovertible political science. The frequent appearance of such words as "extinction" and "extermination" in writings and discussions of other races was not a crude reference to genocide but an acknowledgment of the inevitability of science. In *The Descent of Man* (1871), Darwin predicted, "At some future period, not very distant as measured by centuries, the civilized races of man will almost certainly exterminate and replace the savage races throughout the world." Those species that could not adapt to new environments ultimately become extinct. Evolution was impersonal and inexorable.[35]

These ideas did not posit a laissez-faire policy toward inferior races. Interventions grounded in scientific research were appropriate to protect the lesser races for their own survival and for the order of the greater society. Both racial segregation and disfranchisement were examples of suitable policies toward the African. Legislation promoting black suffrage and officeholding and land ownership was not appropriate given the inherent limitations of the race. The new discipline of social science, employing empirical research to discover the natural laws through which society operated, could calibrate what policies would benefit the races' different capabilities.

Legislation based on sentiment or religious ideals was doomed to fail. Thomas Huxley, an English biologist and Darwin disciple, argued, "It is simply incredible that, when all [the black's] disabilities are removed . . . he will be able to compete successfully with his bigger-brained and smaller-jawed rival, in a context which is to be carried out by thoughts and not by bites." Huxley had been an abolitionist. He believed that whites did not need slavery to maintain their superiority over the African. Nature had already accomplished that. And while "the highest places in the hierarchy of civilization will assuredly not be within the reach of our dusky cousins, . . . it is by no means necessary that they should be restricted to the lowest." Once the African attained a "stable equilibrium into which the laws of social gravitation may bring [him], all responsibility for the result will henceforward lie between Nature and him. The white man may wash his hands of it, and the Caucasian conscience be void of reproach for evermore." When northerners turned away from Radical Reconstruction, they could justify it on scientific principles and take comfort in the assurances of southern whites that they knew the blacks in their midst best and would protect them with policies in concert with nature.[36]

John William DeForest was a Freedmen's Bureau agent sympathetic to the former slave. Like many other educated Americans in the late 1860s, he had read Darwin and had seen the world in a new way as a result. In an article in the *Atlantic* in May 1868, DeForest wrote, "I am convinced that the Negro as he is, no matter how educated, is not the mental equal of the European," but it would be a cruel mistake not to educate blacks "mentally and morally," to enable some of the more conscientious and talented of the race to survive. For those blacks, their survival depended on isolation from whites, perhaps in "those lowlands where the white race cannot or will not labor." In direct competition, DeForest feared, the freedman was doomed. Similar logic guided the reservation policy for Native Americans.[37]

Herbert Spencer applied Darwin's theory to society, coining the phrase "survival of the fittest" in *Principles of Biology* (1864). Peoples who are best adapted to society will flourish; those who are not will fail. Any attempt to short-circuit the process by intervening with natural selection was futile and counterproductive to society at large. Darwin, in *The Descent of Man*, agreed with Spencer, up to a point. It was injurious, he argued, for "the weak members of civilized societies [to] propagate their kind." Yet man cannot help himself because, through the process of evolution, he has developed the instinct of sympathy. It was correct, in this view, to make Indians wards of the state and teach them the basics of a sedentary civilization. It was correct to offer the African freedom, but he would thrive only if placed under the close supervision of whites, preferably in agricultural labor. The problem with Reconstruction policy was that it installed Africans in positions of power beyond their natural capacities and allowed them to be manipulated by members of the superior race. As for workers' antagonistic attitude toward capital, the market, like the organism, would set the wages and working conditions.[38]

Spencer insisted that society must grow and develop without artificial interference, which he equated with government policy. Otherwise, he believed, there would be a severe erosion of liberty. He already saw that happening in "the late catastrophes on the continent," referring to the Paris Commune, and in the political corruption in postwar America. Spencer was a champion of abolition for the same reason as Huxley: slavery was an unnecessary imposition.[39]

America's embrace of Darwin reflected and accelerated the decline of religious faith as a force in public policy. Charles Hodge, a leading northern evangelical theologian, complained that "in using the expression Natural Selection, Mr. Darwin intends to exclude design, or final causes." Other divines attempted to reconcile religion and science, but most were clearly troubled about the implications of Darwin's theory for their faith. The universities, close allies of the religious establishment and often founded as seminaries, followed Harvard's lead and reinvented themselves as research institutions predicated on the scientific method. They did not abandon their divinity schools, if they had them, but by the 1870s theology was subordinate to higher education's new mission.[40]

There were dissenters from this new pedagogy, such as Frederic Henry Hedge, a New England Unitarian minister who warned, "An education which looks only at the practical, may help to fill the purse, but it can never enrich the mind. It can never impart that dignity of character, that respect for our intellectual nature, that veneration for the beautiful and the good, that zeal for improvement, that longing after the infinite, to impart which, is the true object of all education." This was precisely what America's Age of Reason wanted to leave behind: the sentimental longing for grace that characterized the antebellum evangelical crusade and that led to a bloody civil war. The attractiveness of Darwin was that, in a nation of laws, he offered the ultimate law, the law of nature from which there could be no escape or modification.[41]

At the newly formed Social Science Association in 1879, William Graham Sumner, a disciple of Spencer, noted, "The law of the survival of the fittest was not made by man. We can only, by interfering with it, produce the survival of the unfittest." To Sumner, harsh as it was, this was realism deduced from science. For a nation that prized the rugged individual and had grown increasingly wary of government institutions, Darwin and Spencer resonated well with postwar culture. The answer to Tweed and the southern Republican governments was not to limit the ambition of those who sought public service, but rather to limit the access of those whom nature had designated as unfit to participate in a democratic political process.[42]

Trust in science was such that it eclipsed faith as a missionary force. *Scientific American* argued that new technology "in obscure quarters of the globe where the mind of the heathen is as dark as his skin" performed the "great mission of lifting up and restoring to the world regions and men lost to it." As examples, the editor noted the impact of technology on manufacturing enterprises in China and India that were modernizing both societies. Soon they would be harvesting "Acres of Diamonds." "As the ax of the woodman lets sunlight into the forest, so the advent of machinery breaks down the prejudices of the uncultivated; where sloth was, industry is, and where only force had sway, reason enters."[43]

The faith in science arrived just in time to save America. A group calling themselves Liberal Republicans gathered in late 1871 to introduce scientific principles into American government. Corruption, in their view, was the new slavery, just as unnatural, and just as threatening to the body politic. Carl Schurz, a founder of the movement, pronounced civil service reform the great crusade of the postwar era, just as abolition stirred a nation before the war. Reform would turn government over to experts who could apply the scientific method to the political process. Henry Ward Beecher insisted, "The government must be conducted by men who study government—men who are not amateurs, but who make it the business of life." *Harper's*, referring to the Tweed scandals, advised, "The peace and prosperity of the country are now to be perpetuated, as they were a few years ago to be secured, only by prostrating the Tammany tyranny and corruption as effectually and finally as those of slavery were prostrated."[44]

Corruption gave government a bad name. Less government meant less corruption. More safeguards such as suffrage restrictions, civil service reform, and shifting power away from legislatures provided the cure, or so the reformers assumed. Limit the access of those less fit to govern, and increase the numbers of experts and professionals to run government scientifically. As the scandals mounted, so did agitation for major reforms. The 1872 presidential election provided a forum for those issues.

The Liberal Republicans distanced themselves from the party organization tied to the now-tainted Grant administration. They advocated civil service reform to reduce reliance on patronage and the abuses that accompanied office seeking. To constrain government and remove temptation, they supported an end to federal grants to railroads and a reduction in the tariff to reduce government revenues. For the South, addressing the issue of legitimacy, they recommended restoring the voting rights of high-ranking Confederates and a return to "local self-government" by men of "property and enterprise." The Liberals depicted themselves as modernists. They also hoped for a restructuring of the American party system, to create a new party from a coalition of bright young men, both northern and southern, who would pursue power for the good of the nation, not of themselves.[45]

Schurz believed that a conciliatory policy toward the South would enable these intelligent men to emerge and join forces with like-minded northern colleagues. "A very large number of Southerners, especially young men who have become disgusted with their old leaders . . . are sincerely willing to uphold the new order of things *in every direction*, if they are generously treated. . . . This will be a power fit to absorb the best elements of both parties." This was a delusion other Republicans held as well.[46]

The Liberals sought to capture the Republican Party, toss out Grant, and select a reformist presidential candidate. They failed. Other Republicans were unwilling to cashier a war hero whose personal integrity was unquestioned. Democrats, sensing an opportunity to split the Republicans and win the White House, forged an alliance with the Liberals. Together they nominated Horace Greeley to challenge Grant.

Having made the *New York Tribune* one of the nation's most widely read Republican organs before the Civil War, Greeley reduced his involvement with the paper after 1860. He pursued an erratic course during the war, pressing Lincoln on one hand to abolish slavery, and on the other meeting with Peace Democrats to arrange a compromise with the Confederacy to end the war. After the war, he sided with the Radicals against Andrew Johnson, but he also joined a group that posted bond for the release of former Confederate president Jefferson Davis. Greeley first entered electoral politics in 1869 as the losing Republican candidate for New York State comptroller. When he became the presidential nominee for both the Liberal Republicans and the Democrats in 1872, opponents had a treasure trove of contradictory editorials, speeches, and actions to hurl against him and his supporters.[47]

The irony was inescapable. Greeley's *New York Tribune* had spent most of its career attacking the Democratic Party. Now he was its standard-bearer. Voters may have been angry about the political scandals and the purported elevation of unqualified and unethical officeholders, but the conversion of convenience perpetrated by Greeley and the Democrats seemed to be the greater fraud.

Northerners were amenable to appeals for national reconciliation. They were not receptive, however, to Horace Greeley, whose contortions to make himself fit into the Democratic Party mold were both comic and sad. As *Harper's* noted, "Greeley's career for nearly forty years has been one of uncompromising hostility to every cardinal principle and measure of the Democratic party." This former abolitionist confessed, "I was, in the days of slavery, an enemy of slavery. . . . That might have been a mistake." Greeley mimicked the white southerners' indictment of the freedmen, declaring, "Had [blacks] saved the money they have since 1865 spent in drink, tobacco, balls, gambling, and other dissipations, they might have bought therewith at least Ten Million acres of soil in their respective states." Greeley made no mention of statutes that prohibited land sales to blacks or of the opprobrium faced by whites who rented land to black families.[48]

Voters also wondered whether the Liberals' commitment to clean government was a genuine conviction or a campaign ploy. The Democrat-controlled legislature of Georgia changed the election date from November to October, passed a poll tax, reduced the number of polling places, and patrolled the roads leading to the polls with armed "sabre clubs." Democratic "poll watchers" disposed of ballot boxes in Republican precincts and returned large Democratic majorities in districts that were overwhelmingly Republican. Yet the Greeley campaign hailed the results from Georgia as an early indication of an electoral tide favoring their candidate.[49]

Grant won a resounding victory, aided by a strong turnout among black voters in the South despite the perils they faced. He also benefited from quick-footed friends in Congress who lowered the tariff and passed an amnesty law restoring voting rights to almost all former Confederate officials, thus depriving the Liberals of two key issues in their platform. Grant carried all southern states except Georgia, Tennessee, and Texas. In the North, Republicans used Greeley's own words against the Democrats, and they "waved the bloody shirt," reminding voters who had saved the Union. Grant won every state in the North. Many Democrats simply stayed home.

Thomas Nast, who played a significant role in bringing down Tweed, worked his blistering artistry against Greeley. The talk at the office, at the dinner table, and on the streets in towns and cities across the North was of the latest Nast illustration. In a series of "clasping hands" cartoons showing Greeley in various settings shaking or offering a hand, Nast exposed the hypocrisy of the Democratic campaign. The first appeared in *Harper's* on July 20, 1872, and, using Greeley's own denunciation of the Democratic Party's constituents, showed him shaking hands with criminals, Irish immigrants, and assorted subhuman characters clearly on the lower side of the evolutionary continuum.

Greeley only made matters worse, retorting, "I never said all Democrats were saloonkeepers. What I said was that all saloonkeepers were Democrats."[50]

Perhaps the most famous of the clasping hands cartoons appeared on August 3 and showed Greeley shaking hands with an Irishman hiding a revolver with which he has just killed a Massachusetts soldier, a reference to the attack on Union troops in Baltimore at the start of the Civil War. On August 24, Nast's drawing, "It Is Only a Truce to Regain Power," portrayed Greeley and Charles Sumner urging a black man to grasp the bloody hand of a Klansman who hides a knife behind his back that he has used to kill the man's wife. Also extending a hand is an Irishman concealing a revolver. Greeley implores the black man to "Clasp hands over the bloody chasm," in an effort to reconcile North and South. On September 21, "Let Us Clasp Hands Across the Bloody Chasm" summarized the Republicans' strategy. The drawing placed Greeley at the notorious Andersonville stockade, now a Union cemetery, leaning against the fence with hand outstretched over the rows of tombstones below. Nast's offering on October 19 depicted Greeley shaking hands with a Confederate veteran trampling an American flag and standing on the corpses of black men who had attempted to vote in Georgia. A quote on the facade of the polling place, "What Are You Going to Do About It?" recalled Tweed's response to initial allegations of corruption in New York City.

Nast concluded the series on November 13 following Grant's victory. "Clasping Hands Over the Bloodless (Sar)c(h)asm" showed Grant and "Uncle Sam" clasping hands, the latter much relieved by the outcome. The Republic is tranquil once more now that the Liberals and the Democrats have been relegated to the nether regions. Greeley is hanging upside down; below him is Whitelaw Reid, the interim editor of the *Tribune*, who predicted Greeley's victory six weeks earlier. Greeley, discouraged and broken from the campaign, and disconsolate over the death of his wife just before election day, died two weeks later. Shortly after the election, Mark Twain congratulated his friend: "Nast you, more than any other man, have won a prodigious victory for Grant—I mean, rather, for Civilization & progress."[51]

The Republican Party began its existence as an ideology. It carried the antislavery banner from the 1850s through the Civil War. By the 1870s, the party had benefited from the expansion of government and become a machine for the dispensation of patronage and a partner with large corporations. The ideological bent of the party diminished. During elections, the party would recycle its bloody shirt and then stuff it in a drawer until the next campaign. Carl Schurz, ever the idealist, complained bitterly, "The organization of the Republican party is almost entirely in the hands of the office-holders and ruled by selfish interest." The Liberals and the Democrats lost the 1872 elec-

"Baltimore, 1861–1872," *Thomas Nast, August 3, 1872. Perhaps the most
famous of the "Clasp of Hands" series Nast drew opposing the candidacy of
Democrat/Liberal Republican Horace Greeley during the presidential campaign
of 1872, the cartoon reminds voters of the ambush
of Massachusetts soldiers passing through the city at the
outset of the Civil War.* (Harper's Weekly)

tion, primarily because of Greeley's inept candidacy and Grant's popularity. The Republicans were wise enough afterward to absorb some of the
Liberals' ideas such as civil service reform and ending Reconstruction in
the South.[52]

The strategy worked, as the Republicans became the majority party in the
North. They would lose a national election only twice (to the Democrat Gro-
ver Cleveland) between 1865 and 1912, and during that time, the South would
secure only seven of thirty-one Supreme Court appointments, two of twelve
House speakerships, and only fourteen of 133 cabinet positions. Considering
the dominance of the South in the federal government before the Civil War, a
historian's comment, "Never in the history of the country, and rarely in the
history of any country, had there been a comparable shift in the geography of

political power," is hardly an overstatement. The Republicans no longer needed the South and, therefore, no longer needed the African American.[53]

Redemption was well under way by the end of 1872. Despite the strong Republican showing in the South, only Arkansas, Louisiana, Mississippi, and South Carolina remained in undisputed Republican control. Democrats and their paramilitary organizations would redouble their efforts during the next four years to redeem the remaining states. A financial downturn in 1873 and continued revelations of corruption in high places led Republicans to focus on shoring up their majority in the North. Northern public opinion had already turned against the southern Republican governments. The specter of the Paris Commune, growing labor unrest in the cities, corrupt urban political machines, and persistent violence in the South blended in the public mind as assaults on order. Disruptive elements must be contained (as with the Indians), restrained (as with labor), or eliminated and the "natural" order restored.

Early in the 1872 election campaign, Horace Greeley dispatched Republican James S. Pike of Maine to the South. The purpose of Pike's trip was to send back reports to Greeley's *Tribune* substantiating the Liberals' charge that southern Republican governments were corrupt and inefficient. Pike's first stop was South Carolina, where his main source was Wade Hampton. The result of these interviews appeared in the *Tribune* under the title "A State in Ruins."[54]

South Carolina, Pike began, was a state turned "bottom-side up." "Men of weight and standing in the communities they represent" were displaced in government by "the most ignorant democracy that mankind ever saw invested with the functions of government." Pike was unsparing in his depiction of black lawmakers. He called them "snug-built, thick-lipped, woolly-headed, small-brained," an example of "barbarism overwhelming civilization by physical force." The freedmen were only instruments, however, in Pike's telling. The carpetbaggers used black votes to loot the state treasury. That, ultimately, instigated the violence. Leave the blacks "to the kind feeling of the white race at the South," and they would benefit as the state was restored to its "natural" order.[55]

Pike's report did not have the impact on the election Greeley had hoped. Voters in the North believed that Grant would protect their patrimony and the nation best. The report confirmed for some and convinced many, however, that any further federal intervention in the South or protective legislation for blacks was both futile and dangerous. The lesson Henry Ward Beecher took away from "A State in Ruins," later published as a best-selling book, *The Prostrate State: South Carolina Under Negro Government* (1873), was the necessity for "the speedy achievement of rule by the classes who ought always to rule." A few months after the book appeared, Thomas Nast, who had usually drawn positive portraits of the freedmen, published a hostile caricature of a chaotic South Carolina legislature dominated by blacks while Columbia, against a backdrop reading "Let Us Have Peace," unsuccessfully attempts to call the body to order. As one scholar noted, Pike's report was "the *Uncle Tom's Cabin* of the redemption of the South."[56]

A consensus was forming that transcended party lines. The consensus was that Reconstruction was over, at last, regardless of what African Americans and their white allies in the South believed. The consensus was stronger for the fact that northerners connected the unrest and discord fomented by immigrants, crooked politicians, and laborers in their midst to the persistent disorder in the South. Poet and diplomat James Russell Lowell expressed the sentiment of many northern intellectuals, noting, "What is bad among ignorant foreigners in New York will not be good among ignorant natives in South Carolina." Charles Francis Adams Jr., a staunch Republican, expressed concern about the rising "Celtic proletariat on the Atlantic coast, an African proletariat on the shores of the Gulf, and a Chinese proletariat on the Pacific."

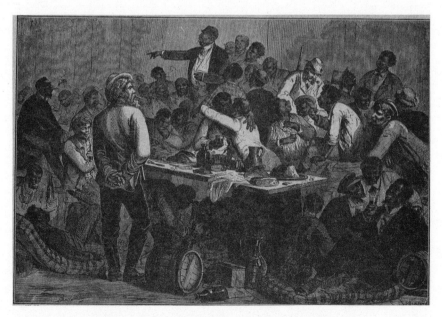

*A black legislature during Reconstruction. The memory of
Reconstruction in the South as an era of Yankee oppression
and black misrule persisted for nearly a century after the war.
This particular caricature was produced in 1901 and comes from a high school
textbook. (New York Public Library, Astor, Lenox and Tilden foundations)*

Expanding the suffrage to include these groups while restricting the franchise of the white southern "intelligent class" was unwise. Adams's brother Henry, talking about northern cities, though he could have been discussing the situation in the South, observed, "The great problem of every system of Government has been to place administration and legislation in the hands of the best men"—those with "the loftiest developments of moral and intellectual education." This hope would attain partial fruition during the Progressive Era of the late nineteenth and early twentieth centuries. In the meantime, the dissonant elements of American society must be dealt with in a way that comported with natural laws and economic well-being.[57]

CHAPTER 21

LET IT BE

THE WINTER OF 1873-74 was a bitter time. Jobs were scarce, and the weather was cold. The worst economic depression in American history to that time had settled in. Casualty lists of the unemployed came in from cities around the country as if from bloody battlefields. In New York City, a hundred thousand workers went jobless, one quarter of the city's workforce. It was worse elsewhere. Economists estimated that nearly half of the nation's working population was either wholly or partially unemployed that winter.

In January 1874, fifteen thousand workers gathered in New York's Tompkins Square to protest wage cuts, job losses, and the lack of public relief programs. They carried placards demanding "Work or Bread." The crowd included a sizable number of German and Bohemian socialists. The press likened the demonstrators to the communards of Paris. By midmorning the workers had packed the square. At 10:30 A.M., a squad of mounted police officers galloped into the square wielding clubs. Samuel Gompers, future labor leader and one of the organizers of the protest, recalled, "The mounted police charged the crowd . . . riding them down and attacking men, women, and children without discrimination. It was an orgy of brutality." Gompers barely escaped injury by jumping into a cellar. The police continued their attacks, chasing down workers through the streets of the Lower East Side. The police claimed they were protecting the city from "communists."[1]

The depression overwhelmed local charities. The Society for Improving the Condition of the Poor, the city's largest relief organization, ceased operations. A spokesman for St. John's Guild in New York warned that the charity had run out of food and money and must "bar the door against the prayers and tears of thousands of women and children who are in utter destitution and terrible suffering." The press and public opinion, however, were unmoved. An "army of tramps" menacing "the peace of the community" had taken advantage of the economic downturn to rob charities. "The bread of charity would be wasted" on such reprobates.[2]

*"The Red Flag in New York," 1874. This rendering of the Tompkins Square workers'
riot in New York City in January 1874 shows little sympathy for the
unemployed workers, the artist noting "riotous Communist workingmen driven from
Tompkins Square by the mounted police." "Communist" referred to the communards
of the Paris Commune of 1871, a reference which repulsed many middle-class northerners
as proof of the dangers of an excess of democracy. (Courtesy of the Library of Congress)*

The depression, later called the Panic of 1873, originated in the nation's
overheated railroad finance market. An investment-banking firm, Jay Cooke &
Co., had financed construction for a second transcontinental railroad, the
Northern Pacific. The road broke ground in 1870. The contraction of the money
supply with the return to the gold standard and the retirement of greenbacks
issued during the Civil War tightened money markets. When the Northern
Pacific required a new infusion of capital in 1873, Cooke tried and failed to float
a $300 million bond issue. His firm collapsed, as did other banks and railroads
across the country as financial institutions called in loans and companies could
not respond.

Despite the genuine misery it caused, the economic downturn was neither
as long-lasting nor as severe as many have claimed. The Panic of 1873 was an
adjustment during a time of major economic transition. The 1870s were a
healthy decade from an economic perspective. Although the economy stumbled
downward from late 1873 to late 1874, annual growth rates for every year until
the end of the decade fluctuated between 4.5 percent and 6 percent, making

the 1870s a period of some of the fastest economic growth on record. Wages went up by between 10 and 20 percent during the 1870s, while the cost of living declined. Consumption, an important indicator of economic well-being, grew even faster than total output. Despite high immigration and population growth, real consumption per capita grew by almost 50 percent during the decade, the highest total in the industrialized world. While railroad construction slowed—the system was built far ahead of demand—freight loadings went up every year of the decade.[3]

Steel and oil led the nation's industrial output. The United States scarcely had a steel industry in 1870. By 1880, the nation rivaled Great Britain as the world's top steel producer. Oil production increased by 500 percent in the 1870s, unrivaled in the world. The number of workers employed in manufacturing grew by nearly a third between 1873 and 1880. Mechanized agriculture spurred farm productivity to feed a rapidly growing urban and international market. Americans ate 20 percent more beef in the 1870s and 50 percent more grains. The new industries required vast networks of support services including financial institutions, marketing firms, accountants, and managers. Housing construction increased steadily during the 1870s, and families such as the Russells who moved from Brooklyn to Short Hills, New Jersey, purchased suburban homes at an accelerating rate. The gap between the wealthy and the poor increased, as usually happens during a time of economic transformation. The failure of eighty-nine railroads and dozens of banks contributed to high unemployment during the winter of 1873–74. Railroads, the largest employer in the nation, were responsible for nearly two million jobs. Outside of the railroad sector, business was booming, especially in the new industries.

Technology reduced the need for skilled workers, one reason why Boss Tweed transitioned from making chairs to making friends. American entrepreneurs, confronted with chronic labor shortages, particularly during the war, thought of technological solutions first. Technology depressed wages in some sectors of the economy. This was especially the case in the sewing trades dominated by young women. The sewing machine opened up the garment industry for female workers. Unscrupulous contractors often cheated women out of wages and exposed them to abysmal working conditions. Women sat crowded together in long rows in poorly ventilated rooms sewing piecework, earning between twenty and twenty-five cents a day. The cheapest room for rent in New York cost one dollar a week, so wages barely covered shelter, not to mention food. To survive, many young women often shared a room. Even then, it was difficult to cover basic living costs.[4]

Factory work offered higher wages—about two dollars a week by 1880—but harsh working conditions. For a single woman attempting to fend for herself in the city, such wages allowed her to eat, in writer O. Henry's words, little that was more nourishing "than marshmallows and tea." Lodging rarely meant more than one room, and recreation was affordable only once or twice a year, a trip to Coney Island or a ticket to a vaudeville show.[5]

Not surprisingly, some working-class women turned to prostitution. Maggie Johnson's brother in Stephen Crane's novel *Maggie: A Girl of the Streets* (1893) described the choice facing young women, many of them immigrants new to the city: "Mag, I'll tell yeh dis! See? Yeh've eeder got t' go on d' toif er go t' work." The rise in prostitution would energize urban churches during the 1880s as ministers came out foursquare against vice. Cities appointed vice commissioners to regulate or eliminate the trade, ignoring its causes. "So is it any wonder," asked the Chicago vice commissioner, "that a tempted girl who receives only a few dollars per week working with her hands sells her body for twenty-five dollars per week, when she learns there is a demand for it and men are willing to pay the price?"[6]

Women organized trade unions and protective associations by the end of the 1870s. At that point, women comprised about 10 percent of the membership of the Knights of Labor, the nation's largest labor union, founded in 1869. After the mid-1880s, however, union activity among women declined. The issues of working-class women rarely engaged the middle class. Many middle-class women frowned upon their gender working at all. They believed married women who worked neglected their families, and single working women skirted the limits of propriety. Besides, many believed working-class women, unlike men, labored for frills, not necessities, as the U.S. commissioner of labor asserted: "A large proportion of [working girls] will work for small pay, needing money only for dress or pleasure," hence the low wages. Yet his office released a report in 1882 acknowledging, "A family of workers can always live well, but the man with a family of small children to support, unless his wife works also, has a small chance of living properly." The *Boston Daily Evening Voice* proposed a solution to the problems of working women: "get husbands." The newspaper solicited funds to ship women to the West, where a gender imbalance existed.[7]

Most middle-class urban residents scarcely knew, in the words of Danish-born reformer Jacob Riis, "how the other half lives." The city was becoming residentially, ethnically, and racially segregated. Separation occurred on the job as well. The array of mid-level managers of large corporations insulated directors from workers. If they interacted at all, it was often as parts of larger organizations. As entrepreneurs organized the components of their industry, workers organized each other. Union membership reached an all-time high by the mid-1870s.

These trends pointed to a distinction between labor and capital that Americans had long denied. Labor, they believed, was a way station to management. Abraham Lincoln had outlined that path of upward mobility in his annual message to Congress in December 1861. The American economy no longer worked that way in 1873 and probably had not in 1861. Technology and industrial workforces of lower skill levels replaced artisans and their shops. Americans were slow to admit that labor was a permanent status and that workers did not see themselves as entrepreneurs-in-waiting. When workers acted contrary to this image, there was a sense of betrayal. Like Indians protecting their lands and blacks demanding their rights, workers became part of the "dangerous classes," a phrase that made its first appearance in the decade after the Civil War. That many of these militant workers were also immigrants merely confirmed their place outside "normal" American society. They threatened both democracy and prosperity. The fact that the urban middle classes fared relatively well during the downturn reinforced the view that workers' demands were unmerited. The problem lay not with the economy but with people who lacked the ambition, fortitude, or character to compete.

Science, especially Darwinian applications, and the Paris Commune also informed middle-class perspectives on the "dangerous classes." Northern Republicans firmly rejected any government aid for the unemployed, fearing that such measures recalled "the revolutionary and Socialistic doctrines of the French." It was not "the proper sphere of Congress to enter on a general system of providing for pauperism." Northern clergymen generally agreed with this assessment, especially those who led urban, middle-class congregations. Strikes and protests, Henry Ward Beecher asserted in Darwinian rhetoric, demonstrated that workers were "unfit for the race of life."[8]

Events in Paris served as a prevalent analogy for Americans as they interpreted unrest in northern cities and the South. Charles Loring Brace, a founder of the Children's Aid Society, wrote in 1873, "In the judgment of one who has been familiar with 'dangerous classes' for twenty years, there are just the same explosive social elements beneath the surface of New York as of Paris." *Scribner's Monthly*, in language that recalled reformers' denunciations of black suffrage in the South, warned that *"the interference of ignorant labor with politics is dangerous to society."* The *New York Times* was hopeful that the experience of the Paris Commune would dampen rather than excite labor militancy in the United States. "Possibly the very extravagances and horrible crimes of the Parisian Communists will, for some years, weaken the influence of the working classes in all countries." Regardless of the merits of workers' grievances, public opinion typically favored the employers or the authorities whenever conflict occurred.[9]

Governors who called out state militias against strikers received widespread public approbation. When Governor John Hartranft of Pennsylvania, a former Union general, ordered the militia to disperse striking miners in 1875, both political parties applauded his action. Employers typically used strikebreakers from outside the community, often Eastern Europeans or blacks, calculated to provoke violence from striking workers. Once violence erupted, employers counted on government officials to intervene on their behalf. Northern states and localities passed a flurry of vagrancy statutes in the mid-1870s to use against the unemployed, much as southern states had applied such laws to freedmen. The South, accustomed to a suppressed labor force, issued a warning to any of its textile, tobacco, or iron and steel workers who might consider organizing. "Labor organizations are to-day the greatest menace to this Government," N. F. Thompson, secretary of the Southern Industrial Convention, asserted. "A law should be enacted that would make it justifiable homicide for any killing that occurred in defense of any lawful occupation."[10]

Management would argue that capital costs, especially in new industries that required expensive technology, demanded a cheap labor force to maintain profit margins. John D. Rockefeller's Standard Oil Company was among the best employers in the 1870s, providing reading rooms and recreational facilities for its workers and, extremely rare for the time period, industrial accident insurance policies for each worker. Yet when barrelmakers in his employ struck in 1877 in response to a wage cut, Rockefeller was collecting dividends at a rate of $720 an hour, more than most of his workers earned in a year. During the first half of 1877, Standard Oil paid out eighty dollars in dividends on each hundred-dollar share of its stock.[11]

Workers found themselves estranged not only from management but also from the middle class. America may have yet been a nation of shopkeepers and farmers, but that was changing. Postwar society provided great opportunities for the urban middle class, and its members opposed any group or idea that threatened their advance. "The great 'middle-class,'" the New York Times observed, "which now governs the world, will everywhere be terrified at these terrible outburst[s] and absurd[ities], they will hold a strong rein on the lower classes."[12]

Walt Whitman, the poet of the middle class, was singing again, a sure sign that things were getting better. He saw through the joblessness, the hunger, and the violence to a brighter future. Whitman believed science would right the wrongs of labor unrest, of corruption and compromised electorates, and set America back on its course to greatness. Manifest destiny had become a theorem, not a theology. He wrote in "Song of the Universal" (1874):

Lo! keen-eyed, towering Science!
As from tall peaks the Modern overlooking,
Successive, absolute fiats issuing. . . .

For it, the mystic evolution;
Not the right only justified—what we call evil also
justified. . . .

Out of the bulk, the morbid and the shallow
Out of the bad majority—the varied, countless frauds
of men and States,

Electric, antiseptic yet—cleaving, suffusing all,
Only the good is universal.[13]

Whitman's salute to science reflected the transformation of American thinking on labor. Perhaps workers were no longer proto-capitalists after all. In "A Song for Occupations," composed in 1855, Whitman described an array of workers and jobs, concluding with an affirmation of the individual worker as an exalted figure: "You workwomen and workmen of these States having your own divine and strong life, / And all else giving place to men and women like you." By the 1870s, his perspective on "workwomen" and "workmen" had changed. In "Song of the Exposition" (1871), Whitman wrote of "sacred industry." The individual worker had blended into industrial "armies," fuel to feed American enterprise.[14]

Scientists urged lawmakers not to interfere with natural law to aid laborers. Simon Newcomb, a pioneer in the application of mathematical models to economics, warned that if the government intervened in "the peculiar and limited field of political economy, nothing but harm will result." Sociologist William Graham Sumner told his students at Yale that adhering to natural law comported with God's will, or at least the will of God the Scientist. "You need not think it necessary to have Washington exercise a political providence over the country," he lectured. "God has done that a great deal better by the laws of political economy." America, the nation of laws, had just accrued a large number of new statutes.[15]

Sumner was quick to add that it was appropriate for the government to enhance the ability of the worker to accumulate capital. The state could do this by offering the laborer "the greatest possible measure of liberty in the directing of his own energies for his own development," and, second, "giv[ing] him the greatest possible security in the possession and use of the products of his own industry." The state, however, should not become the employer of last resort. "The moment that government provided work for one," Sumner warned, "it would have to provide work for all, and there would be no end whatever possible. Society does not owe any man a living." Sumner's advice to the worker: "He has got to fight the battle with nature as every other man has."[16]

The entrepreneurs were not particularly Darwinian with respect to their own enterprises. They had no intention of sending their companies into "the battle of nature." Competition, they felt, was wasteful; it encouraged inefficiency, unethical behavior, and instability. Consolidation quieted volatile markets and enabled companies to take advantage of economies of scale that benefited shareholders and consumers alike. Samuel Dodd, the chief counsel for Rockefeller's Standard Oil empire, remarked that competition "carried to the furthest extreme without cooperation or compromise . . . would be a fit mode for savages, not for civilized men." Yet when it came to workers or blacks, the competitive, not the cooperationist, model prevailed. The scientific conclusion should have been that social ethics and policy do not derive from the laws of nature. Darwin intended no such analogy. Yet the application of Darwin to society went forward.[17]

Workers, apparently following Sumner's advice to "fight the battle with nature," organized into labor unions at a record pace during the 1870s. The largest, the Knights of Labor, embraced a variety of occupations and skills. Other unions divided along craft lines, such as miners and carpenters. There were also unions based on ethnic background. From 1870 onward, roughly one third of factory workers were foreign-born. The various and often competing labor communities inhibited the formation of a major proletarian political movement as in Europe. The presence of immigrants in the workplace, for example, created tensions that common grievances rarely transcended. California laborers led the fight for legislation barring Chinese workers from the United States. The campaign resulted in the Chinese Exclusion Act of 1882, the first law to close the United States to all citizens from a foreign country. Said one native-born ironworker: "Immigrants work for almost nothing and seem to be able to live on wind—something which I can not do."[18]

Workers should not have been so anxious. Science, as Whitman sang, would cure the world's problems. Edward Livingston Youmans, a social scientist from New York, wrote to Spencer at the height of the corruption scandals in the early 1870s, "There is no salvation for this continent except in the acquirement of some proximately scientific conception of the nature of governments." Youmans and other intellectuals believed that only a thorough application of science would generate the stability necessary for national progress. Policies based on laws derived from scientific research into government and society would eliminate corruption, solve conflicts between capital and labor, and restore harmony to the democratic process.[19]

The consensus against government intervention not grounded in the scientific method called into question even private ameliorations. Charities came under increasing scrutiny. Many faltered under the great burdens of the depression. Charities were likely to be underfunded in the best of times, with varying criteria for aid. They were generally aware of demographic, geographic, and ethnic changes in their cities, though they rarely studied the nature and extent of their clientele. This ad hoc approach to charity began to change in the 1870s with the arrival of English clergyman Samuel Humphreys Gurteen. In 1877, Gurteen founded the Charity Organization Society in Buffalo, New York. The idea was to establish a "scientific philanthropy." Within five years, the COS spread to twenty-five cities. COS organizers contended that poverty resulted from individual moral defects. Charity, traditionally dispensed, worsened the problem by indulging the poor. The COS proposed to change the culture by organizing all local charities under one roof, a Union Station of giving. The new organization proposed thorough investigations of applicants to determine their worthiness for relief and advocated tying charity to work. The COS depended on an army of middle-class women who volunteered as "friendly visitors" to mentor the poor out of poverty and wean them off assistance. The orderly transformation of charity did not end poverty or even make a serious impact. The COS did, however, provide a scientific basis for later reforms such as the settlement house movement and public welfare departments.[20]

The debate over intervention in the economy and in the South infiltrated the off-year elections in 1874. The economy had not recovered by then, and unrest in the South persisted. In one of the greatest swings in American history, the Democrats turned a 110-seat Republican majority in the House into a 60-vote advantage for their party. Federal Reconstruction was already moribund by late 1874, but the Democratic resurgence sounded the death knell for the remaining southern Republican governments. Northern Republicans retreated as quickly as they could from their party's remaining regimes in the South. The Republican press, once the staunchest defender of black suffrage, turned against the involvement of freedmen in southern governments. E. L. Godkin, editor of the *Nation*, who suddenly fancied himself an expert on evolution, informed his readers that the "blackest" legislators were always the worst, especially in South Carolina, where the black population possessed an overall "average of intelligence but slightly above the level of animals."[21]

The Republicans' infighting also reflected their concern that instability in the South inhibited economic recovery. Republicans urged Grant to allow nature to run its course in the South. Hard on the heels of James Pike's report serialized in the *Tribune* came the articles of Charles Nordhoff for the rival *New York Herald*. Nordhoff collected his essays in a book, *The Cotton States in the Spring and Summer of 1875* (1876), concluding that a return to power of responsible whites would guarantee blacks' rights and restore law and order to the South.[22]

The economy and the intellectual consensus against government intervention shredded what remained of federal Reconstruction policy. The recession hit the South hard. Many of the railroads forced into receivership were located there. Northern roads purchased the companies at bargain prices and would set freight rates that placed southern shippers at a competitive disadvantage for the next century. Republican governments in the South had invested heavily in the railroads, leaving thin treasuries in the wake of the Panic. This forced tax increases that broadened discontent. To compound matters, the price of cotton, the South's major money crop, dropped 50 percent during the depression, barely covering the costs of production. Part of the problem was a serious oversupply. Cotton growing even penetrated the southern upcountry, a stranger to cultivation before the war. Cleveland County, North Carolina, grew only 520 bales of cotton in 1870 and more than ten times that amount a decade later. In a cash-poor region, cotton was readily convertible into money, so everyone grew it. By 1880, southern per capita income had fallen to one third that of the North. None of this boded well for the remaining Republican regimes in the South.[23]

Northerners had hoped to remake the South into the North's own image—a region of productive and efficient family farms following the tenets of scientific agriculture and mechanized cultivation and harvesting. White southerners were uninterested in northern visions. Their focus was always on controlling the freedmen, especially their labor. The former slave was not helpless in negotiating work contracts, though the power in the relationship rested with the landowner. Blacks' refusal to work in teams ended the gang labor system. After experimentation with various land tenure and employment arrangements, sharecropping emerged as the prevailing agricultural labor system in the South in the 1870s. It suited the cash-poor region, and it enabled black sharecroppers to cultivate in families, make decisions about their crop, and gain some autonomy. Promising from one quarter to one half of the crop's proceeds to the landowner, sharecropping allowed the black farmer to generate an income and savings. Some croppers graduated to tenancy, which allowed more autonomy and the prospects of higher profits. A few sharecroppers eventually became landowners.

The system often broke down, however, as a result of the declining price of cotton, swindling by landlords, and inflated prices at the company store. Some croppers never escaped debt, and debt peonage appeared in the South by the mid-1870s. It resembled slavery, except the landowner was under no compulsion to provide food and medical care for his croppers. The system created a permanent and marginally literate black underclass and blocked land improvements, maintenance, and mechanization that reinforced the South's colonial economic status through the first half of the twentieth century. The major difference between labor in the North and the South was the greater degree of control exercised by southern employers. Strikes and demonstrations in the cotton fields were few.[24]

The white South used the cover of the 1873 depression and the attendant problems of labor unrest and corruption to speed the redemption process. The popularity of Darwin and the smoldering example of the Paris Commune also worked in favor of the Redeemers. After the 1874 elections, three states in the Lower South remained under Republican control: Louisiana, Mississippi, and South Carolina, all with large black electorates that maintained the party in power. White leaders in the three unredeemed states embarked on campaigns of publicity and violence to overthrow the alien regimes. They could count on the absence of a coherent response from Washington and a growing consensus among northerners that the experiment with black suffrage was a failure. It was best to allow natural laws to take their course. If white southerners helped nature along, so much the better.

On Easter Sunday 1873, the bloodiest peacetime massacre in nineteenth-century America occurred in Colfax, Louisiana. Colfax, a small town in the state's fertile Red River Valley, was named after Schuyler Colfax, Grant's vice president. It was the seat of a new parish, created by the Republican state government and called Grant Parish. The choice of names did not generate great support among the area's white inhabitants. The state's Republican governor, Henry Clay Warmoth, recognizing the shifting political winds, attempted to attract more whites to the party by joining with conservatives to form a fusion party. Many black Republicans objected to these overtures. One of them, William Ward, an ex-slave from Virginia, commanded the state militia unit in Grant Parish. The November 1872 election had seen widespread fraud and intimidation. Both the Warmoth fusionists and the regular Republicans claimed victory. The Grant administration recognized the regular Republican ticket, and Ward took possession of the Grant Parish courthouse on behalf of that group.[25]

White leaders in Grant Parish retaliated by unleashing a reign of terror in rural districts, forcing blacks to flee into Colfax for protection. Four hundred black refugees, only about eighty of whom were armed, erected defenses around the courthouse. Klansmen from surrounding parishes rushed to Colfax to dislodge Ward and the black refugees. Ward slipped away to New Orleans to recruit reinforcements. Before he returned, the white "army" attacked the courthouse, taking forty prisoners, who were shot that night in a cotton field outside of town. An additional one hundred blacks lay dead from the assault.

Federal authorities arrested nine of the white attackers, and a jury convicted three of violating the Enforcement Act of 1871. The Democratic Party hired top attorneys for the defendants and appealed the convictions. The case reached the U.S. Supreme Court as *U.S. v. Cruikshank* (1876). The Court found for the defendants, holding that the Fourteenth and Fifteenth Amendments created no national rights except the right not to be discriminated against on the basis of race. The Court ruled that the government had not offered proof of a racially discriminatory purpose. It was an election dispute, not a racial confrontation. For the protection of all other rights, including voting rights, citizens had standing only with their states, not with the federal government. The postwar amendments empowered the federal government to prohibit violations of blacks' rights by *states*, not by *individuals*. For the latter violations, plaintiffs must seek redress from the state. The *Cruikshank* decision, coming in the midst of escalating political violence in the South, amounted to a judicial endorsement of that violence. The decision made it virtually impossible for the federal government to prosecute crimes against blacks unless they were perpetrated by a state and unless it could prove a racial motive unequivocally.[26]

It was the second time in three years that the High Court had eviscerated a key measure of Congressional Reconstruction. The aversion to further accrual of federal authority appeared most tellingly in a case having nothing to do with Reconstruction or African American rights. The *Slaughter-House Cases* (1873) involved the issue of whether the state of Louisiana could require New Orleans butchers to ply their trade in a central, state-franchised facility. The state cited health and safety issues for its monopoly (though revenue probably played a more important role). The butchers claimed that the state, by forcing them to operate in a state facility rather than independently, had violated the Fourteenth Amendment, depriving them of "liberty and property without due process of law."[27]

In a five-to-four decision, the Court upheld the right of Louisiana to create a monopoly for health and safety reasons. Justice Samuel F. Miller in his majority opinion went beyond the specific case to remark more generally that the

Fourteenth Amendment applied only to those "privileges and immunities" already protected by the federal government. These included access to ports and navigable waterways, the right to run for federal office, the ability to travel to Washington, D.C., and the right to protection on the high seas and in foreign countries. None of these federal rights interested most blacks. In other words, the amendments did not protect individuals from *states* abridging a broader list of rights enumerated in the Bill of Rights. The butchers, as citizens of Louisiana, could not invoke federal citizenship in this case to seek their remedy.

Miller used the specific case to ruminate more generally on the nature of federal relations emerging from the war and on the intent of the amendments' framers. Miller argued that the Reconstruction amendments applied only to African Americans, not to white Louisiana butchers. These were not the views of the amendments' proponents, however. House Judiciary Chairman James F. Wilson, an Iowa Republican, and Ohio Republican John A. Bingham, who authored portions of the Fourteenth Amendment, clearly stated their intent to provide federal protection to *all* citizens when states violated their civil rights. The amendments, its framers contended, did not augment federal power as much as they provided enforcement for Article IV, Section 2 of the U.S. Constitution that required states to uphold the Bill of Rights.

Justice Miller, an anti-slavery Republican, worried that the power tilt toward the federal government during and after the war threatened the balance of power between state and federal authority and the balance between the legislative, executive, and judiciary branches. His decision to go well beyond the facts of the case before him reflected this concern. In early 1868, as Congressional Reconstruction was in full swing in the South, Miller wrote, "In the threatened collision between the Legislative branch of the government and the Executive and Judicial branches I see consequences from which the cause of free government may never recover in my day. The worst feature I now see is the passion which governs the hours in all parties and all persons who have controlling influence." In his opinion, Justice Miller hoped to restore "the balance between State and Federal power."

The passions Miller cited, a perpetual concern of Americans since the burning of the Ursuline convent in 1834 and the subsequent violent outbursts eventually leading to civil war, had the potential of veering toward despotism. Lincoln had articulated these fears in the late 1830s, and the failed revolutions in Europe in 1848 and the Paris Commune of 1871 provided warning memories of popular excess. Justice David Davis, Lincoln's campaign manager during the 1860 presidential election race, in joining Miller's majority opinion, worried in 1868 that "both parties have run into extremes," leaving him with "great alarm at the tendency to consolidated Government. . . . This alarms me more than all other things."

Justice Stephen J. Field, another Lincoln appointee, dissented, expressing the view that the amendments rendered national citizenship paramount to state citizenship: "A citizen of a State is now only a citizen of the United States residing in the State." Therefore, the federal government could hold states accountable for enforcing the Reconstruction amendments and the Bill of Rights. Justice Noah H. Swayne, a Virginian, went further, hailing the Reconstruction amendments as "a new departure" and "an important epoch" in constitutional history. These amendments "trench directly upon the power of the States." Swayne noted that before the war, there was "ample" protection against national "oppression" and "little . . . against wrong and oppression by the states." The Reconstruction amendments resolved this imbalance.

Swayne's opinion reflected a minority view among northern Republicans by 1873. The disillusionment with Reconstruction and the concern over corruption and disorder made federal power suspect. The Civil War created a unified nation, but the debate over the balance between state and federal authority would continue to rage. The result, as Justice Joseph P. Bradley noted in his dissent, was that the Court had relegated the "rights, privileges, and immunities of the greatest importance to the state's protection alone." The decision left African Americans in particular at the mercies of redeemed southern states with little or no recourse to federal redress.

The cumulative impact of these decisions and the prevailing social and economic contexts of the era encouraged bolder attacks against the remaining Republican governments. White paramilitary groups closely tied to the Democratic Party now operated openly in Louisiana, Mississippi, and South Carolina. Leaders announced a "white line" policy, inviting all white men, regardless of party affiliation, to "unite" and redeem the states. Black Republicans feared not only for their political future but also for their lives.[28]

The boldest assault occurred in New Orleans in September 1874 when leading citizens and Confederate veterans, organized as the White League, led eighty-five hundred men in an attempted coup to oust Republican governor William P. Kellogg and members of his administration. The league's manifesto, promulgated in July 1874, offered a clear indication of its intentions: "Having solely in view the maintenance of our hereditary civilization and Christianity menaced by a stupid Africanization, we appeal to the men of our race . . . to unite with us against that supreme danger . . . in an earnest effort to re-establish a white man's government in this city and the State." These were no mincing words or veiled threats.[29]

The New Orleans Leaguers overwhelmed the city's racially mixed Metropolitan Police Force under the command of former Confederate general James B. Longstreet. Only the timely arrival of federal troops, ordered to the scene by President Grant, prevented the takeover attempt. The aftermath of the "Battle of Liberty Place" was not good for either Longstreet or President Grant. When Confederate-leaning historians wrote about the Civil War in future decades, the turncoat Longstreet appeared as the cause of every major defeat. In the more immediate future, northerners denounced the use of military force to prop up a government many felt was illegitimate. The league was more successful in the Louisiana countryside in the weeks preceding the Democratic victory in November 1874. League troops overthrew or murdered Republican officials in eight parishes.[30]

The Democratic victory in Louisiana encouraged white paramilitarists in Mississippi. Blacks dominated the Warren County government headquartered in Vicksburg. The White Liners, as they called themselves, demanded the resignations of all black officials including the sheriff, Peter Crosby, a black Union veteran. Republican governor Adelbert Ames, a native of Maine, ordered the Liners to disperse and granted Crosby's request to raise a protective militia to respond to future threats. Ames, a hero at Gettysburg, settled in Mississippi because of a deep commitment to the freedman. As part of that desire, he hoped to remake Mississippi as a modern state, much in the image of his native Maine. Almost from the beginning of his administration, however, internal disputes among the state's Republicans and political pressure and violence from Democrats undermined his progressive agenda. Ames ran one of the most honest administrations in the South, yet Democrats constantly charged him and his colleagues with corruption. No charges were ever filed, but the Democrats understood that mere accusations played sympathetically in the North.[31]

Peter Crosby's efforts to gather a militia force were too successful. An army of several hundred armed African Americans marched in three columns from the surrounding countryside to Vicksburg. Whites responded to the challenge, firing on the militia and terrorizing blacks in the city and county over the next ten days. Among the victims were a black Presbyterian minister and several of his congregants kneeling in prayer. Liners killed at least twenty-nine blacks and wounded countless more. Democrats gained control of the county government.

The Vicksburg incident was a rehearsal for Democratic victories in statewide elections in 1875. The *Birmingham News* cheered on the Mississippi White Liners in the popular Darwinian rhetoric of the time: "We intend to beat the negro in the battle of life, and defeat means one thing—EXTERMINATION."

Liners focused on the state's majority black counties and vowed to "overawe the negroes and exhibit to them the ocular proof of our power." In September, Governor Ames wrote to his wife, whom he had sent out of state, recounting a Republican barbecue attended by fifteen hundred African Americans in Clinton, Mississippi. White Liners opened fire on the gathering, killing two women and two children, then marauded through the countryside and killed three more blacks, including a man nearly one hundred years old, "defenseless and helpless." Blacks fought back and killed four of the Liners, but they were no match for the superior numbers and firepower of the whites. "It is cold-blooded murder on the part of the 'white liners,'" Ames wrote. "You ask what are we to do. That is a question I find it difficult to answer." Ames requested troops from Grant, but, as he informed his wife, "it will be a difficult thing [for Grant] to do."[32]

Such intimidation worked, and the Democrats swept to victory in Mississippi. They would not allow Governor Ames to finish his term, threatening him with impeachment. Fearing for his safety, Ames resigned and fled the state. A federal grand jury convened several months later and concluded that the "fraud, intimidation, and violence perpetuated" in the 1875 state elections were "without a parallel in the annals of history." The South's second war of independence was reaching its climax.[33]

The southern white evangelical churches, which had roundly condemned the political activities of northern missionaries and the Republican governments, praised the restoration of Democratic rule. The means justified the ends. The editor of the *Christian Index* of Georgia hailed the outcomes of the 1874 elections throughout the South, proclaiming that "every Christian in the southern States should devoutly thank God for His mercies bestowed in the political victories of last week." The "trials" and "oppressions" of the past decade had been so great that "many of our people—otherwise good citizens—have been led to doubt the overruling Providence of God." Admitting that churchmen ought to devote themselves to "*Religion* and not to *Politics*," the editor excused himself, noting that the "political revolution" was "a Christian triumph," wrought "by the hands of an All-wise and merciful Providence."[34]

Frederick Douglass despaired. What began as a promising experiment in racial equality was quickly deteriorating into anarchy and murder. The Grant administration and Republican leaders resisted further interventions in the South. After the Democrats battered them in 1874, Republicans listened more carefully to their northern constituents. Reconstruction, as much as the economic downturn, caused the broad rejection of Republican candidates throughout the North. Douglass saw only one alternative for southern blacks: "My own impression is that when the Government will not or can not protect the black man, he ought to and will finally try to protect himself." That he did; up to the point of reason. Whites commanded the firepower, and many of the attackers had military experience in the Confederate armies. Rarely did black defenders succeed in overwhelming white assaults in these last years of Reconstruction. Nor could blacks turn to federal troops stationed in the South. By 1874, there were fewer than three thousand federal troops in the region, barely enough to contain even a minor insurgency. The rest of the troops were in the West fighting the Indians.[35]

The *Methodist Advocate*, a northern missionary publication located in Atlanta, shared Douglass's concern about the safety of the freedmen in an era of laissez-faire government. It stated in April 1875, "To leave the States to manage their own affairs without restriction or interference from the central power is simply to put them mostly into the hands of those who were and now are bitter and persistent enemies of the government, of national union, and of universal freedom and education." While not refuting the *Advocate*'s characterization of southern white attitudes, *Harper's* challenged its solution. The editor claimed that "incessant and direct national control of the States has so alarmed the republican instinct of the most intelligent part of the country that the chances of Democratic success have been visibly increased." Republican leaders in the North supported the freedman as long as that support did not interfere with the party's standing among the northern electorate. Now it did. *Harper's* concluded in a condescending tone, "It is certainly not the least pressing duty of all sincere friends of the colored race to teach them self-dependence and the essential character of the government under which they are citizens and voters." It was incumbent on southern whites themselves to dispose of the bullies in their midst as "New York disposed of Tweed and his Ring." Self-determination for southern whites was now the vogue; the same for blacks was not.[36]

Grant's inaction was political, not personal. In the early days of Congressional Reconstruction, he intervened in several southern states to protect African Americans and the electoral process. He sent troops to North Carolina in 1870 to assist Republican governor William Holden's fight against the Klan. In 1872, he dispatched soldiers to Alabama to prevent violence after a disputed election in that state. Grant's most extensive military operation occurred during the fall of 1871 when he rounded up South Carolina Klansmen. Declaring nine upcountry counties to be "in a state of rebellion," he suspended the writ of habeas corpus and ordered federal military authorities to arrest suspected Klansmen. The effort netted nearly six hundred Klansmen, though the leaders escaped to northern states or to Canada. The intervention broke the Klan in South Carolina. By July 1872, however, reports from the state indicated "the K.K.'s are becoming very much emboldened and their organizations are coming together again." Out of 1,300 Klan cases, 1,200 never went to trial. Juries convicted twenty Klansmen, and seventy others pleaded guilty. Grant's actions yielded sparse results and managed to serve as an excellent recruiting tool for white paramilitarists.[37]

Louisiana was an especially difficult case for the Grant administration, given the level of violence and the precarious position of Governor William P. Kellogg, who held office from 1872 to 1876. The president's periodic intrusions into Louisiana saved the Republican government, but Kellogg failed to mend political fences in his own party or hold off opponents sufficiently to strengthen his position within the state. The more Grant intervened, the less legitimacy the Kellogg administration could claim to govern the state.

From 1874 until the end of his administration, Grant resolved to draw back from federal intervention in the South. Members of his party, especially the Liberal branch, opposed further involvement both on philosophical and practical grounds. In the midst of a recession, government involvement could only worsen the situation everywhere. E. L. Godkin stated the case for northern public opinion: "The government must get out of the 'protective' business and the 'subsidy' business and the 'improvement' and 'development' business." When Mississippi Republicans requested federal intervention to protect their state government in January 1874, Grant had had enough. "This nursing of monstrosities has nearly exhausted the life of the party. I am done with them, and they will have to take care of themselves." Everyone was on his own now.[38]

The Democrats' victories in 1874 were the final arguments against intervention. Northerners had never really endorsed the extent of the Radical program to begin with. Except for a brief period of collective anger in 1866–67 when white southerners threatened to reverse the verdict of the war, northerners were keen to let the South go on its way as long as it did not interfere with the nation's progress. Unlike in the era before the Civil War, southerners no longer wielded power nationally. White southerners simply wanted to rule at home.

Events in Louisiana provided a good gauge of northern public opinion on the issue of federal intervention in the South. For months after the November 1874 elections in the state, Democratic and Republican legislators battled, each contending that the other's election resulted from fraud. Two rival governments set themselves up. The standoff ended in January 1875 when a contingent of federal troops under the command of Colonel Philippe R. de Trobriand entered the legislative chamber and expelled five Democrats. General Philip Sheridan, overall commander of federal troops in Louisiana and recently returned from the Plains, recycled his old rhetoric for the new venue.

He commended the action, adding that some southerners deserved to be "exterminated." Sheridan's comment and de Trobriand's intrusion outraged northerners already disgusted with the continued chaos in the South. New York politicians and merchants "without distinction of party," held an "Indignation Meeting" in the city to oppose the maneuver and any further involvement of the government in Reconstruction generally. Even citizens of Boston, the erstwhile hotbed of abolitionism, called for a federal withdrawal from the South. The Republican Party could no longer associate itself with southern Republican governments. It no longer needed to. As the *New York Times* explained, the abolitionists "Wendell Phillips and William Lloyd Garrison . . . represent ideas in regard to the South which the majority of the Republican party have outgrown."[39]

The Republican Party had descended mainly from the Whigs, who were economic nationalists and well connected to merchants, prosperous farmers, shopkeepers, and nascent manufacturing interests. The abolitionist wing of the party was always small, even during the war. The Republican Party was not changing in the 1870s as much as it was reverting to its roots as an organization committed to promoting commerce, manufacturing, and sound money policies. Northerners were unwilling to continue fighting the Civil War. If white southerners wished to do so, they could carry on the battle with their black neighbors, not with the Yankees. Jane Addams, the founder of Hull House in Chicago and a pioneer in social work, recalled growing up in Freeport, Illinois, during the Reconstruction era. Her father, John, was a banker and a founding member of the local Republican Party. She told of his desire to put the war behind him and of his growing discomfort with the party's southern policies. Addams remembered her father's thinking, "We freed the slaves by war & had now to free them all over again individually, & pay the costs of the war & reckon with the added bitterness of the Southerner beside." One crusade a century was enough.[40]

White southerners knew their northern Republican adversaries well. Rather than emphasize white supremacy in their appeals for greater home rule, they railed against excessive taxes, waste, and corruption. A white South Carolinian declared, "Taxation is robbery, when imposed for private gain, or to build up monopolies for the benefit of the few at the expense of the many." These words resonated among northerners who experienced similar problems in their cities. The source of these difficulties lay with the undue power of an unfit electorate. Northerners were ignorant of conditions in the South, and particularly of the black men and women struggling for full citizenship and the right to earn a living. They were more than willing to concede the argument that white southerners knew best how to deal with African Americans.[41]

White northerners scarcely knew the relatively few blacks in their midst, let alone the millions of freedmen in the South. The Rev. Alexander Crummell, a prominent black minister, lamented in 1875, "We are living in this country, a part of its population, and yet, in diverse respects, we are as foreign to its inhabitants as though we were living in the Sandwich Islands." Northerners' knowledge of the lives of blacks came from a northern press that grew increasingly critical of their political efforts and attempts to attain social equality. The press consistently understated the degree of violence against blacks in the South, the extent of white control over black labor, and the daily indignities freedmen suffered, especially in southern towns and cities. When whites murdered thirty blacks in Jackson, Mississippi, in September 1875, the northern press scarcely noted the episode. A despairing southern Republican editor wrote, "There was little use in even calling attention to these outrages, for almost no one seemed to care." Future president James A. Garfield agreed. "I have for some time had the impression that there is a general apathy among the people concerning the War and the Negro. The public seems to have tired of the subject."[42]

On the other hand, the reports of James Pike and Charles Nordhoff attained wide circulation and credence in the North. Northerners came to see southern white violence as heavy-handed but understandable amid the frustrating circumstances. Readers of the *New York Tribune*, the largest circulating daily in the country, received a persistent education on conditions in the South. Sources were almost exclusively white leaders. In one article, "Political Problems in South Carolina," the correspondent wrote of "the great mass of the negroes . . . the plantation 'field-hands,'" who were not only indolent but also "given to petty thieving to great extent." Holding "absolute political supremacy," they elevated their own leaders and reduced white people to "thralldom" as they enacted their own legislative program. Regardless of party, the northern press was equally eager to print conciliatory remarks and speeches by white southerners as proof of goodwill both toward the North and the freedmen.[43]

The northern reaction to the 1875 Civil Rights Act provided another benchmark from which to measure public opinion. Among other provisions, the act guaranteed blacks equal access to public accommodations. The act was a parting gift to the recently deceased Charles Sumner, who had introduced a much stronger version four years earlier. The Republican *New York Times*, a strong supporter of Sumner since the 1850s, lectured, "Respect for the dead is incumbent on us all—but legislation should be based on a careful and wise regard for the welfare of the living, not upon 'mandates,' real or fictitious, of the dead." The U.S. Supreme Court would rule it unconstitutional in 1883, but in its few years of existence, the act created more problems for Republicans in the North than for whites in the South.[44]

The white consensus was that the legislation singled out blacks for preferential treatment that other minorities, particularly Jewish and Irish American citizens, did not possess. Government should be blind to distinctions of race, religion, and ethnicity. The *Chicago Tribune* asked the question: "Is it not time for the colored race to stop playing baby?" In a nation that prized individual initiative and self-reliance, and that now possessed the scientific affirmation of such traits, the entire array of Reconstruction legislation smacked of unnatural privilege. The belief was so widespread that when Justice Joseph P. Bradley spoke for the Court in the 1883 case, few whites contested the logic: "When a man has emerged from slavery, and by the aid of beneficent legislation has shaken off the inseparable concomitants of that state, there must be some stage in the progress of his elevation when he takes the rank of a mere citizen, and ceases to be the special favorite of the laws, and when his rights as a citizen are protected in the ordinary modes by which other men's rights are protected." There is no quarreling with such egalitarian logic, except it did not take into account the context in which black Americans lived their lives, especially in the South. In an age that prided itself on realism, the reality of black life in late nineteenth-century America eluded white consciousness.[45]

By mid-1875, Americans looked forward to the centennial celebration of their independence. After commemorations at Lexington and Concord, thoughts turned to plans for the festivities in Philadelphia the following year. Such a momentous birthday also generated considerable reflection on the American experiment. The lingering effects of economic depression, the discontent of a seemingly permanent labor population, the ongoing Indian war on the Plains, and the persistent unrest in the South did not dampen the mood of optimism. The strength of the economy shone through the gloom of depression, new inventions appeared almost monthly, it seemed, and middle-class Americans enjoyed an incomparable lifestyle of new things, new houses, and new opportunities.

There were signs also that the country was coming together, finally. In June 1875, *Harper's* predicted that the "Centennial year" would be a year "of increased national harmony." As evidence, the editor offered "the disuse of the habit of speaking of certain States of the Union as 'the South,' as if there were a section of the country separate and peculiar." Though the death of the South has had significantly more pronouncements than the imminent capture of Richmond, *Harper's* was certain the event was at hand. The editor chirped that southerners had abandoned the theory of secession and it was nearly impossible to find anyone "who would resort to war as a remedy for governmental grievances, or who would restore slavery." And while southerners continued to oppose Reconstruction, they "no longer oppose established results." Probably not, since the results in most states by the middle of 1875 were the restorations of white leadership and black subjugation.[46]

The Confederates finally took Boston. At the Bunker Hill centennial celebration in April 1875, from which visitors could still see the charred remains of the Ursuline convent, two thousand ex-Confederates marched through Boston on some of the same streets where the 54th Massachusetts had stepped proudly. John Quincy Adams II, son of the former president and congressman who railed against southern slaveholders, offered a golden olive branch to the guests. "You are come so that once more we may pledge ourselves to a new union, not to a union merely of the law, or simply of the lips; not to a union . . . of the sword, but gentlemen, the only true union, a union of hearts." Edward Atkinson, a Boston industrialist and a former supporter of John Brown, accepted an honorary membership in the Society of Ex-Confederate Soldiers for his investment in New South industries. The former abolitionist and officer of a black regiment Thomas Wentworth Higginson spoke of his high regard for his new southern friends. And Ralph Waldo Emerson, the poet conscience of New England, visited the University of Virginia, where he delivered an address praising the southern people, at least the whites among them.[47]

Such testimonials to national fealty in 1875 came mainly from the North. Northerners did not mind the imbalance. They were going off to the future, and the South could come along, or not. The North was America, and that was what counted.

Northerners would celebrate the centennial year counting the blessings of victory. The war unleashed an economic revolution, unparalleled innovation, and a degree of affluence across a broader segment of society than any Western nation had known to that time. It was a nation primarily of northern European Protestants with an abiding faith in science, imbued with self-reliance and optimism. Historians have agreed that Americans missed a golden opportunity to broaden its definition of "all men are created equal" in the decade after the Civil War. Americans at the time would beg to differ. They had come through a war that threatened to destroy their experiment, and during the succeeding decade they had nurtured a shaky peace into unbounded progress. When the world convened at Philadelphia in 1876 for the centennial exhibition, that was the accomplishment they would see and celebrate.

The new American nation was obviously not all-inclusive. Workers, African Americans, Native Americans, women, Roman Catholics, and many immigrant groups remained outside the story Americans wove for themselves as they approached the centennial. There were few dissenting voices, for example, when the Grand Army of the Republic, the organization of Union veterans, barred Irish Americans from membership. It seemed odd that a group that gave lives and blood for their new nation could not find acceptance among their fellow soldiers. Neither, of course, could blacks. Or Native Americans. It was not a matter of racial, gender, class, religious, or ethnic exclusion. It was all of the above. America's second century would become more inclusive, and it would do so primarily because the Union victory had saved the ideals of the first century.

CHAPTER 22

CENTENNIAL

JULY FOURTH, 1876. America's one-hundredth birthday. A modest celebration unfolded in Hamburg, South Carolina, a small town in the Edgefield district across the Savannah River from Augusta, Georgia. Blacks comprised more than 75 percent of the town's population. They held most of the political offices, including the head of the state militia, the town marshal, and the judge of the town court. Doc Adams, captain of the militia, read the Declaration of Independence. His men paraded down Market Street in full regalia before a festive crowd to honor America on this blistering hot day.[1]

A buggy approached from the opposite direction. The two young white men driving the wagon demanded passage through the procession. After a heated argument, Adams ordered his men to stand aside and allow the wagon to pass. The following day, the father of one of the drivers appeared before the judge, Prince Rivers, demanding the arrest of Doc Adams and other officers for obstructing a public road. Rivers, hearing conflicting versions of the incident, decided to hold a hearing.

On the day of the hearing, July 8, the town filled up with armed whites. Rivers pressed both parties to reach a settlement. Matthew C. Butler, a prominent attorney and former Confederate general, demanded that Adams disarm the militia. Adams refused. By this time, more than a thousand armed whites were milling in front of the wooden "armory" where one hundred black militiamen had taken refuge. A shot rang out and shattered a second-floor window. Soon a pitched battled was raging. The white attackers fired a cannon that turned most of the building into splinters. As blacks fled, whites tracked them down. Several blacks escaped across the river to Georgia; others hid underneath a railroad trestle and witnessed the massacre. The white men also burned homes and shops and robbed residents of the town. One of the white hunters exclaimed, "God damn it, boys, what better fun do we want than this?"[2]

On July 15, Robert Smalls, a black Union war hero and now a congressman from South Carolina, rose in the House to read a letter from a constituent. "The United States Government is not powerless. . . . In this Centennial year, will she stand idly by and see her soil stained with the blood of defenseless citizens? . . . God forbid that such an attitude will be assumed toward the colored people of the South by the 'best Government the world ever saw.'"[3]

The northern Republican press called it "the Hamburg Butchery." Thomas Nast contributed "The 'Bloody Shirt' Reformed" in August. The cartoon depicted Justice holding a balance scale, with one scale containing the seven black men who died and the other, one white man. She demands that the scale be balanced with more dead whites. The nation's two sacred documents, the Constitution and the Declaration of Independence, frame her. In the background, posters appear with the names of white terrorist groups: the Ku Klux Klan, the White League, and the White Liners.[4]

*"The 'Bloody Shirt' Reformed," August 12, 1876. This Thomas Nast cartoon expresses the outrage of northern public opinion to the Hamburg, South Carolina, massacre of July 1876. The figure of Justice demands the prosecution of the white men responsible for the execution-style murder of six blacks after the riot. The wall posters represent a roll call of the South's Democratic paramilitary organizations. Despite the outrage, a weary Grant administration did nothing to stem the violence in South Carolina and the white perpetrators not only escaped prosecution, but their exploits were celebrated in subsequent decades. (*Harper's Weekly)

In an election year, such cold-blooded mayhem was difficult to ignore. Thomas Wentworth Higginson confessed to self-deception in his assessment of white southern public opinion. "I have been trying hard to convince myself," he wrote, "that the Southern whites had accepted the results of the war, and that other questions might now come uppermost." Still, there was no groundswell for federal intervention. The prevailing view was to abandon the South and its disorderly population to focus on the "other questions."[5]

South Carolina governor Daniel H. Chamberlain, a Massachusetts native who was instrumental in allowing black students to enroll at the state university at Columbia, informed President Grant, "This affair at Hamburg is only the beginning of a series of similar race and party collisions in our State, the deliberate aim of which is ... the political subjugation and control of this State." Grant responded with sympathy but little else. In a resigned tone, he stated, "How long these things are to continue, or what is to be the final remedy, the Great Ruler of the universe only knows." The inscrutable God invoked by Lincoln had clearly triumphed in Washington at least. It was clear, however, that the Great Ruler of the United States was not going to assist his celestial counterpart to achieve a "final remedy." Grant expressed his confidence in Chamberlain to handle the situation "without aid from the federal government." In the meantime, confirming Chamberlain's fears, Matthew C. Butler vowed, "This won't stop until after November." He characterized the murders in Hamburg as a worthy effort toward putting the black man in his appropriate place. "This collision was the culmination of the system of insulting and outraging of white people which the negroes had adopted there for several years." As proof, he offered Doc Adams's refusal to accept his conditions for a settlement, showing that Adams was "wholly unfit for so important a station."[6]

Butler correctly pinpointed the grievances of whites in the Edgefield district. As a result of their superior numbers, blacks held key positions in the town and county. When southern whites talked of their world turned "bottomside up," the situation in Edgefield was a prime example. South Carolina whites were well aware of how their friends in Mississippi and Louisiana had redeemed their states from Republican rule, and they sought to follow suit.

In May 1876, South Carolina Democrats drafted *The Plan of the Campaign of 1876*, a manual on how to redeem the state. Some of the recommended strategies included: "Every Democrat must feel honor bound to control the vote of at least one negro, by intimidation, purchase, keeping him away or as each individual may determine how he may best accomplish it." The instructions concluded with this chilling reminder: "Never threaten a man individually. If he deserves to be threatened, the necessities of the times require that he should die."[7]

Wade Hampton received the Democratic nomination for governor. He would try to steer a moderate course during the campaign as much because of his patrician sensibilities as because of his fear of federal intervention if more violence erupted in South Carolina. His platform was mild enough. He campaigned on "home rule" and promises to end corruption and cut spending and taxes. Hampton held out an olive branch to blacks, promising to support the Reconstruction amendments. Yet he presided over what one historian has called "one of the bloodiest electoral campaigns in American history."[8]

Hampton's supporters knew what was at stake in the election, and he articulated it at every turn even while eschewing violence. In his acceptance speech, he energized his supporters, now conspicuous by their red shirts modeled after Giuseppe Garibaldi's Italian "Redshirts." "You are struggling for the highest stake for which a people ever contended, for you are striving to bring back to your prostrate State the inestimable blessings which can only follow orderly and regulated liberty under free and good government." Hampton benefited from more than three hundred gun clubs throughout the state with a membership of over fifteen thousand.[9]

Hampton was a master at transforming political rallies into cultural spectacles. He entered on a flower-bedecked chariot to the cheers of his supporters. On the stage a young white woman sat, head bowed, draped in black, and chained. Hampton descended from the chariot and mounted the platform to martial music. The young woman arose, cast off her mourning clothes, and appeared white, radiant, and free, with a tiara emblazoned "South Carolina." Reporters confirmed that men wept openly when the young woman transformed herself. Hampton presented himself as a selfless medieval knight rescuing his state from evil forces. The correspondent painted Hampton for his audience: "simple, unaffected gentleman, dauntless warrior of South Carolina, loving and reverencing his God, his cause and his commonwealth to the last recess of his clean soul." Governor Chamberlain witnessed a Hampton event and exclaimed, "Never since the passage of the Ordinance of Secession has [sic] there been such scenes in this state." He became the Redeemer incarnate to his followers. As one supporter recalled, "Wade Hampton was the Moses of his people, the God-given instrument to help them free themselves from their enemies."[10]

It was not unusual to see black Red Shirts at Hampton's rallies. He often reserved the front rows for these supporters. A few of the blacks may have been coerced, but most had good economic or political reasons to support Hampton. Their presence enabled Hampton to rebut northern critics and claim that the election was about home rule, not about reestablishing white supremacy. Hampton often displayed a large poster at his rallies showing a prostrate palmetto tree being raised by white and black men over the caption "While There's Life, There's Hope." Democrats urged white Republicans to "cross Jordan" and join the effort to save South Carolina, reserving places of honor on the reviewing stand for those who had "come over to the Lord's side." Religious imagery figured large at Hampton rallies. Ministers offered prayers both before and after the events and urged voters to consider themselves "Confederate Christians." They prayed for God to deliver South Carolina from her "more than Egyptian bondage." The election, they informed the crowd, was a contest between "Hampton" and "Hell." A choir closed the rally singing both southern patriotic and sacred songs.[11]

The rifle clubs delivered a more forceful message. They disrupted Republican rallies, often firing guns in the air. Armed members made personal visits to white and black Republicans to deliver threats. That these warnings were serious was evidenced by a wave of political murders across the state during the campaign.

The November election went off in relative calm. The Red Shirts had prepared well. In Edgefield District, out of 7,000 potential voters, 9,200 ballots were cast. Similar fraud occurred throughout the state. Had fraudulent ballots been tossed out, Chamberlain would have won the governor's race outright. Still, the result was a dead heat. Both Democrats and Republicans claimed victory and set up rival governments. The following April, after a deal brokered in Washington between the parties, federal troops were withdrawn from South Carolina and the Hampton government installed in Columbia. The victorious Democrats expelled twenty-four Republicans from the state legislature and elected Matthew C. Butler to the U.S. Senate. South Carolina was redeemed.[12]

Redemption of another sort occurred elsewhere. Dwight L. Moody had replaced the tarnished Henry Ward Beecher as America's favorite evangelist. He was an unlikely crowd favorite. A former shoe salesman who found God in Chicago, Moody worked for the Young Men's Christian Association and became a Union chaplain during the Civil War. Before Lincoln went off to the White House, he visited Moody's "Y" Bible class and gave his first and last Sunday school lecture. Short in stature and progressively chubbier through the years, he murdered syntax in his sermons and was not half the spellbinding orator that Beecher was. Yet a ticket to one of his revivals became more prized than Standard Oil stock. Even President Grant sat on Moody's platform, though, truth be told, he looked confused most of the evening.[13]

Moody's stature grew after the war as a YMCA fund-raiser. Following Chicago's disastrous 1871 fire, he persuaded Philip Armour, the meatpacking king, and Cyrus McCormick to invest in building the largest lending library in the city. A Chicago newspaper called Moody "an up and comer." The business analogy was appropriate. Moody prepared the groundwork for his traveling revivals by launching massive advertising campaigns, wooing the local press, and ensuring area dignitaries attended and were accorded due recognition. He placed the leaders on his stage, and at the climactic moment in his sermon he turned and asked if they were ready to meet their Maker. "Are you ready?" he shouted at each man, lingering until he received an affirmative response. His friend John Wanamaker reportedly replied, "Yes, ready-made," repeating his department store's advertising slogan.[14]

Critics charged Moody with purveying "salvation of the slop-shop character." Others noted the overwhelmingly middle- and upper-class nature of the audience. Few workers and fewer blacks attended the revivals. To those who complained that his ministry resembled more a commercial than a religious enterprise, he replied, "This is the age of advertisement and you have to take your chance." Though his revivals seemed spontaneous, he planned them carefully, the placement of leading citizens, the musical selections, the design and copy for the programs, the spacing of the seating, and the decoration of the venue. The revivals ran like clockwork and permitted no deviation from the script. At his Philadelphia revival on New Year's Eve 1875, he notified the press that the door would close promptly at 7:30 P.M. "and if the President of the United States comes after that he can't get in." If an audience member was moved by the spirit and shouted "Hallelujah!" ushers would escort the offender out of the auditorium. A rival preacher marveled, "His expertise and management of men was worthy of a field general."[15]

Moody dispensed with aphorisms and politics and kept his message simple. Salvation and only salvation was his inventory. The stories he told, allegedly from real-life experiences, concluded with a punch line for salvation. Moody's revivals were slick commercial operations, with sales of his version of the Bible and various tracts and sermons guaranteed to snatch the reader from the everlasting jaws of hell. Moody mugs, kitchen utensils, prayer cloths, and gloves were also hawked before and after his appearances. John Wanamaker offered him a large railroad depot for one of his revivals, after which he turned it into one of the nation's largest department stores. Patrons scarcely noticed the change.

Moody returned to the United States in mid-1875 after a two-year mission to Great Britain. He set northern cities on fire, inspiring the *Cleveland Leader* to proclaim that "the United States is now in the midst of the throes of the third of [its] great Religious Awakening[s]." Judging by the sartorial splendor of the crowds, Moody's revivals were beneficial for Wanamaker and other retail entrepreneurs. Moody's message resonated with his urban audiences. It comported with the deepening belief that natural laws governed society, so there was no point worrying about how to fix its problems. "I have noticed," he preached, "that when a Christian man goes into the world to get an influence over the world, he suffers more than the world does." Here was Darwin's preacher.[16]

Moody also preached love, which is one reason why women flocked to his revivals. In addition to love, he also preached reconciliation. In Chicago in 1875 he proclaimed, "Let me tell everyone in this hall tonight that I bring good news . . . the Gospel of Reconciliation." As whites were murdering blacks in Vicksburg, Mississippi, Moody told ten thousand rapt New Yorkers, "I love the South as well as I do the North." It was a message Moody took south during the centennial year. As southern audiences embraced him, the *New York Tribune* rejoiced, "Denominational differences are forgotten, the Christian people, long separated by church barriers are coming together, and are thinking less of Creed and more of Christ."[17]

There was, in fact, very little "creed" in Moody's sermons. He was not a biblical scholar. E. L. Godkin, a fan, conceded that very "little dogmatic theology or biblical exegesis" appeared in Moody's preaching. Moody's great talent was that he told stories. While Mark Twain traveled the lecture circuit, Moody traveled the revival trail. Instead of humor for a punch line, Moody delivered salvation. Walt Whitman, a religious skeptic, called Moody a "boss story-teller." During his southern tour, his stories emphasized sectional reconciliation: "*We* had to give up *our young* men, both North and South, to death." The war, not the respective causes, was the killer. Although Moody impressed Whitman, the poet confessed, "I do not believe in him. Nor his God . . . nor his stories which sound like lies."[18]

On New Year's Eve 1875, with the centennial year just hours away and his southern crusade looming, Moody held a massive rally in Philadelphia. The guest of honor was the noted South Carolina Presbyterian minister William Plumer Jacobs. That night, Moody stressed the theme of reconciliation, of coming together as one people under God. He persisted in this theme throughout his southern crusade. On Confederate Memorial Day, he prayed for "brokenhearted ones, both North and South . . . who were mourning for friends lost in the late war." He "had no sympathy at all with men in any section of the country who were continually seeking to stir up strife and embitter the people against each other."[19]

As Moody traveled around the country in 1875 and 1876, he divined the great problem confronting America. It was not the unrest in the South, in the city streets, or out on the Plains. It was alcohol. "I fear," he intoned, "unless a great temperance reform sweeps over our whole land, the Republic itself may be imperiled." He was all for a sober Centennial. It was also a good business model. John D. Rockefeller was so smitten with Moody's temperance message that he donated liberally to his ministry. Moody articulated from the pulpit what middle-class Americans felt in their hearts, and just as importantly he never articulated what they did not want to hear. It is too much to say that Americans were nurturing a celebrity culture and individuals such as Mark Twain and Dwight L. Moody were the earliest examples, but since Darwin had nudged God from His pedestal, someone had to take His place.[20]

As the accolades poured down on Moody during his centennial tour of the South, Frederick Douglass took a different perspective: "Of all the forms of negro hate in this world, save me from that one which clothes itself with the name of loving Jesus." Referring to Moody's crusade, a segregated affair, Douglass reported, "The Negro can go into the circus, the theatre . . . but he cannot go into an evangelical Christian meeting." It is only fair to note that, toward the end of his life in 1895, Moody finally defied Jim Crow laws and physically removed the barriers separating the races at a revival in Houston.[21]

As Moody preached, Americans celebrated. On May 10, 1876, the International Exhibition of Arts, Manufactures and Products of the Soil and Mine opened in Philadelphia. The nation marked its centennial by showing off its technological and artistic creativity, industrial prowess, and natural abundance. Americans invited the world. The fair's organizers did not believe that an exhibition heavy on economic development slighted the accomplishments of the Founders. Rather, it was the Founders' work, in the Declaration of Independence and the Constitution, that made the displayed wealth and genius possible. A decade after the Civil War, the exhibition provided an opportunity to demonstrate the progress of a united nation.[22]

The exposition rose in Fairmount Park on the western bank of the Schuylkill River. Exhibits occupied 450 acres with an additional 42 acres given over to displays of livestock and agricultural machinery. All together 167 buildings housing 30,000 exhibits covered the grounds. Thirty-seven foreign nations erected pavilions, with the British, German, Austrian, and French structures among the most impressive. Beer gardens, cigar shops, popcorn stands, and ethnic restaurants were scattered throughout the park. In Machinery Hall more than 1,500 exhibitors showed off their latest technologies. Here was the heart of the exposition. The organizers also erected a cultural building to show the works of contemporary American and foreign artists. The fair had its own lodging, the Continental Hotel, the largest in the country with over 1,300 rooms.

On opening day, nearly a hundred thousand people crowded the front gate. A smaller contingent of invited guests, including President Grant and

Dom Pedro II, the emperor of Brazil, filed into the Main Exhibition Hall, the largest building in the world, covering twenty acres and built with Andrew Carnegie's iron and steel. Once seated, they heard the symphony orchestra break into an enthusiastic rendition of Richard Wagner's "Centennial March." The Rev. Matthew Simpson, a Methodist bishop, blessed the fair. A choir sang a hymn written by John Greenleaf Whittier for the occasion and a cantata composed from the words of southern poet Sidney Lanier, who had become a northern favorite in the years after the war. President Grant then stepped to the podium and delivered a brief speech. Noting that the first hundred years of America's existence were devoted to building the infrastructure of a civilization, Grant declared it was time for America to rival "older and more advanced nations in law, medicine, and theology, in science, literature, philosophy, and fine arts." America had built; now it would soar. The president pronounced the exhibition open, and the choir and orchestra struck up the "Hallelujah Chorus," accompanied by a peal of chimes, the blasts of cannon, and the unfurling of the largest American flag in existence. These latter additions were not in Handel's original score, but everyone agreed they added great emphasis to the music.[23]

The procession of dignitaries made its way into Machinery Hall, at the center of which, mounted on a platform that resembled an altar, stood the giant Corliss steam engine, forty-five feet tall. The president and "my brother the Emperor" mounted the platform. Why Grant invited Dom Pedro II, absolute monarch of the only nation in the Western world where slavery still prevailed, is unclear. Commercial interests, more than exhibitions, were probably on Grant's mind as he escorted the emperor around the grounds. George Corliss, the proud inventor of the iron colossus, greeted the two leaders and stationed the president at the left throttle-valve and the emperor at the right, where they awaited their orders from this former grocery store clerk. Only in America. "Are you both ready? Then your Majesty will turn that handle." Suddenly, the sound of rushing steam filled the hall. "Now, Mr. President, yours." The sound multiplied and parts of the metal monster began to move, brought to life by a mere handle turn. The engine reached 2,500 horsepower and powered fourteen acres of machinery in the hall engaged in various activities such as sawing logs, shaving metal, and printing newspapers. Yet, other than the initial rush of steam, the engine emitted barely a sound. One young lady who watched the engine reach its climactic power wrote home, "Dear Mother, Oh! Oh! O-o-o-o-o-o-o-o-o!!!!!!"[24]

The Corliss engine was the ultimate masculine symbol of the fair. William Dean Howells called it "an athlete of steel and iron with not a superfluous ounce of metal on it." He marveled at the pistons thrusting downward and

*The mighty Corliss engine at the Centennial Exposition, 1876, with President Grant
on the left and Emperor Dom Pedro II of Brazil next to him, both waiting
to turn their handles to set the giant machine into motion. The engine symbolized
American ingenuity and might. (Courtesy of Jeffery Howe, Boston College)*

the "vast and almost silent grandeur" of its silhouette. A mechanic sat at the
base of the giant, quietly reading a newspaper. Every so often, he would as-
cend a narrow stairway and lubricate "some irritated spot on the giant's body
with a drop of oil."[25]

Small houses representing the states dotted the grounds, though only seventeen of the thirty-nine states participated. State exhibitors received strict

a

instructions not to make any political statements or "offensive" references to the Civil War. The federal government occupied the largest of these American buildings. Officials designed the exhibits to "illustrate the functions and administrative facilities of the Government in time of peace, and its resources as a war power, and thereby serve to demonstrate the nature of our institutions and their adaptations to the wants of the people." The displays were as dull as the introduction. Exhibits demonstrated the operation of various federal agencies, including a functioning post office, a wonder in itself. The building also contained an array of military hardware.[26]

The building also housed an exhibit on the American Indian. It included tepees, which fairgoers could enter, tools, pottery, weapons, and life-size wax figures of the indigenous people. It was as if the Indians were a vanished race, ancient primitive precursors to the European. Custer's encounter with Sitting Bull in late June doubtless colored visitors' experiences, reading into the exhibit their contemporary impressions of Native Americans. "The red man, as he appears in effigy and in photograph in this collection, is a hideous demon, whose malign traits can hardly inspire any emotion softer than abhorrence," wrote one visitor. Another reported, "Novelists with subdued fancies may sit in their cozy back parlors, and write pretty little stories of the noble red man, but let them once see the wax figures of those red gentlemen with . . . small, cruel, black eyes, . . . coarse, unkempt locks, . . . and large animal mouth," and they would surely write something different.[27]

There was also a Women's Pavilion on the grounds, where the ladies exhibited their needlework and the latest household appliances. In keeping with the apolitical theme of the fair, there was no mention of woman's suffrage, and the pavilion's exhibitors ignored the July 4 protest by Susan B. Anthony and her followers.

The exposition displayed several firsts, chief among them Alexander Graham Bell's telephone. Heinz ketchup and Hires root beer also made their debuts. The Japanese pavilion offered a momentous gift to the American South. The emperor had sent over some samples of a plant reputed to prevent soil erosion. The Japanese called it kudzu. Eventually, it would conquer the South in a more lasting and comprehensive way than Sherman's army.

Scientific explanations for virtually any phenomenon being in vogue, the Declaration of Independence came in for its share of empirical analysis. Mostly these interpretations adopted a racial tone. Experts viewed the Declaration as the natural evolutionary offspring of the Magna Carta, and the Magna Carta, in turn, of "old Teutonic traditions from which English political civilization emerged." America owed its unique existence, then, not to God but to those prescient knights in a long-ago dark forest in Germany. The Declaration "was but an extension of that assertion of individual independence which is instinctive in the English race. . . . And this anniversary shows what the political genius of a race has accomplished in a century."[28]

A major celebration occurred at the exposition on July 4. General Philip Sheridan was among a host of dignitaries that day. When a messenger rushed up to him on the platform to pass him a note, the general blanched and departed hastily. The message informed Sheridan of the destruction of the 7th Cavalry and the death of its commander, General George Armstrong Custer.

Sheridan's winter campaign of 1868–69 ended the Plains war, but only temporarily. The familiar cycle of inadequate provisions, the need to roam far and wide to find alternative food supplies in the face of the decimation of the buffalo, and incursions by white settlers touched off another round of hostilities in 1874. Sheridan was philosophical about the situation: "We took away their country and their means of support, broke up their mode of living, their habits of life, introduced disease and decay among them, and it was for this and against this they made war. Could any one expect less?" Sheridan's empathy did not deter him from his mission to force Indians onto reservations or annihilate them. Scouring the southern Plains for Indian camps, Sheridan's men destroyed food, livestock, and weapons, leaving the tribes with neither sustenance nor shelter and a hard winter at hand.[29]

Rumors circulated that the Black Hills, sacred land for the Sioux, hid an untold treasure store of gold. Sheridan ordered Custer into the Black Hills, ostensibly to survey the region for the location of a fort to protect the construction of a second transcontinental railroad. Gold was on Custer's unofficial agenda. Custer found only modest amounts of gold, but the press inflated it as a second Sutter's Mill, and thousands of eager miners flooded the region. Though the Fort Laramie Treaty of 1868 gave the Sioux rights to the land, whites in the region wanted them evicted. The *Yankton* (S.D.) *Press and Dakotan* called the treaty an "abominable compact" and a barrier to "improvement and development." The editor asked, "What should be done with these Indian dogs in our manger? They will not dig the gold or let others do it. . . . They are too lazy and too much like mere animals to cultivate the fertile soil, mine the coal, develop the salt mines, bore the petroleum wells, or wash the gold." The free labor ideology of hard work, improving oneself and one's surroundings, and achieving upward mobility was foreign to the Indians, westerners argued. They did not deserve stewardship over this vast and rich domain.[30]

President Grant, seeking to avoid a bloody confrontation, directed Sherman to keep miners out of the Black Hills "by force if necessary." Sheridan torched the wagons and possessions of the intruding miners and hauled the prospectors off to the stockade. These policies created an uproar in the mining camps, and for a while it appeared as if the army would be fighting prospectors instead of Indians. Large numbers of soldiers, dismayed at Sheridan's actions, deserted and set off to find gold themselves. With more than one thousand miners entering the Black Hills per month, Sherman could not effectively carry out Grant's order. The president, still seeking a fair resolution, offered to purchase the Black Hills from the Lakota Sioux chief Sitting Bull, who angrily rejected the offer. Seeing no alternative, Grant ordered all Indians in the Black Hills region onto reservations by January 31, 1876. If they declined, the army would force compliance. The Plains Indian war now entered its final phase.[31]

By the early summer of 1876 a sizable proportion of the Lakota Sioux led by Chiefs Sitting Bull and Crazy Horse refused to enter the reservation. The army moved to end their rebellion. On June 17, 1876, Crazy Horse fought General George Crook to a standstill at the Battle of Rosebud Creek. A week later, Custer, or "Long Hair," as the Sioux called him, led five hundred men to a large Sioux village containing twenty-five hundred warriors commanded by Sitting Bull. The settlement lay in the valley of the Little Big Horn in southeastern Montana. The Sioux referred to the area as the Greasy Grass. It was a hot, dry, and windy day. The cottonwood trees on the banks of the Greasy Grass released their white fluffy seedpods simulating a snowfall along the river.[32]

Custer dangerously divided his troops. Crazy Horse attacked and overran the contingent led by Major Marcus Reno, sending them into full flight. The Sioux warrior and his men galloped to aid Sitting Bull, who engaged Custer's 260 cavalrymen. Crazy Horse arrived on the battle scene late; Sitting Bull wiped out Custer and his men in about forty-five minutes, or "about as long as a hungry man to eat his dinner," recalled one Cheyenne chief. In an interview given in his Canadian refuge the following year, Sitting Bull commented, "Where the last stand was made, the Long Hair stood like a sheaf of corn with all the ears fallen around him." He had assumed, incorrectly, that Custer and his men were drunk; no sober person would have attempted an assault of so few against so many.[33]

The western press renewed its call for a war of extinction against the Sioux. The *Black Hills Pioneer* thundered, "There is but one sentiment on the Indian question here—the hostile Sioux should be exterminated." The southern Democratic press used Custer's defeat as a metaphor for the failure of Reconstruction policies and the allegedly inept and corrupt Republican regimes both in the South and in Washington. The "tragic events," the *Charleston Journal of Commerce* noted, were "hardly more than the logical results of the scandalous mismanagement of the army by our military President and the infamous frauds, peculation and inefficiency which flourished in the Indian Bureau."[34]

Custer's defeat shocked Sheridan and northerners generally, though not everyone clamored for revenge. By now, most white Americans east of the Mississippi understood the reduced options confronting the Native Americans. A writer in the *Nation* praised "the gallantry of General Custer and his men" and added, "but who shall blame the Sioux for defending themselves?" *Harper's* used the occasion of Custer's death to depict him as a victim of a misguided Indian policy. The contradictions were obvious, if the means to correct them were not. "We make solemn treaties with them [the Indians] as if they were civilized and powerful nations, and then practically regard them as vermin to be exterminated. . . . We make treaties . . . and then leave swindlers and knaves of all kinds to execute them. . . . [We] respect their rights to reservations, and then permit the reservations to be overrun. . . . [We] treat them as men, and then hunt them like skunks." Custer's fate illuminated the failure of the administration's Indian policy as much as the persistent racial violence in the South demonstrated the futility of its Reconstruction policy.[35]

The summer victories of Crazy Horse and Sitting Bull were sensational though hollow triumphs. The army under Sheridan's direction was relentless after Custer's fall. Black Elk, who fought with Crazy Horse, recalled, "Wherever we went, soldiers came to kill us." Crazy Horse and his Sioux band went deep into their country, and they encountered what many southerners experienced when they returned to their homes in the Valley of Virginia or along Sherman's route in Georgia and the Carolinas. The Sioux came upon a land "black from the fire, and the bison had gone away." A hard winter came early. "It snowed much," Black Elk related. "Game was hard to find, and it was a hungry time for us. Ponies died, and we ate them. . . . There had been thousands of us together that summer, but there were not two thousand now." The buffalo were gone; the Black Hills were lost; and soon, so was a way of life.[36]

Sheridan pursued the Sioux and their Cheyenne allies through the winter, the most serious blow being inflicted on a Cheyenne village where American soldiers burned two hundred tepees, destroyed all food stores, buffalo robes, and ponies, and made a bonfire of blankets and sacred objects. That night, the temperature fell to thirty below zero. A dozen babies froze to death, and the Cheyenne killed the few horses they had saved so the elderly could place their hands and feet into the warm entrails of the dead horses. Sitting Bull fled to Canada, and most of the Sioux tribes entered the reservation.

Crazy Horse escaped defeat, but it was only a matter of time before hunger and the overwhelming odds forced him and his dwindling band into Fort Robinson. Placed under arrest, which he had not expected, Crazy Horse resisted, and an army private thrust a bayonet into his back while members of his own tribe held him down. He died that evening, September 5, 1877. The soldiers released his body to his parents the following day, and they carried him away on a horse-drawn travois. Young women uncovered Crazy Horse's body, as is the Sioux custom, washed him, and anointed his arms with red paint and painted his face as if for war. They tied a reddish brown stone behind his ear. His mother wrapped him in new deer hides as his father chanted a song. Both parents lifted him onto a scaffold, and at sunset the following day, they took him down, loaded him back on the travois, and rode off into the night to bury their son. The final resting place of Crazy Horse is unknown, but some have said that his grave lies on the banks of a creek in South Dakota called Wounded Knee.[37]

The incident rated only brief comments in the eastern press. Americans had placed the Indian wars behind them, just as they were relegating the issues of Reconstruction to oblivion. Economic recovery and the centennial celebration held public attention, not the fate of men and women of color. Crazy Horse was a man out of time, a man of yesterday. The *New York Times* observed, "In the tribe over which he ruled he was almost worshiped on account of his personal bravery; and yet he was greatly dreaded by his people, for his way was that of a despot. He had been a bad Indian ever since he had obtained manhood." The *New York Tribune* condemned Crazy Horse as a "religious enthusiast." The writer noted darkly and with unintended irony that "during his campaign . . . he used to boast that he held communion with a spirit from above that aided, sustained and directed him." The Plains Indian war was over. Chief Red Cloud, who had led the attack on Fetterman,

Crazy Horse and his Oglala Sioux people on the way to
Fort Sheridan to surrender to General George Crook, May 1877.
(National Archives and Records Administration)

offered a fitting epitaph: "They made us many promises, more than I can remember, but they never kept but one. They promised to take our land, and
they took it."[38]

The army could no more stem the tide of white migration than a farmer
could plough the sea. By 1880, an agricultural empire had arisen on former
Indian lands in Minnesota, the Dakotas, Nebraska, and Kansas. Between 1860
and 1880, the population in these states grew from three hundred thousand to
over two million, an amazing advance considering the predominantly rural
nature of these states. Their bountiful crops, transported on railroads, fed the
nation and the world. For the great middle classes of the North and their entrepreneurial partners, the rise of the West more than compensated for the fall
of the South.

Whites agreed that the confinement of Indians to reservations and the demise of the buffalo were good things. In an era when Americans expected
their generation to both transcend and improve upon nature, the Indians were
hopelessly retrograde. General Nelson Miles, a veteran of the Indian wars of
the 1860s and 1870s, looked out over the prairie and saw the amber waves of
grain and the fat livestock and noted with satisfaction, "The buffalo, like the
Indian, stood in the way of civilization and in the path of progress. . . . The
same territory which a quarter of a century ago was supporting those vast
herds of wild game, is now covered with domestic animals which afford the
food supply for hundreds of millions of people in civilized countries."[39]

The Quaker missionaries dispatched by President Grant proved more com-
passionate than the old Indian agents, but just as convinced that the Indians
must adopt the white man's culture. The Quakers proposed in the late 1870s to
begin the conversion to white civilization with the Indian children. Merrill
Gates, president of the Friends of the Indian, vowed, "We are going to conquer
barbarism, but we are going to do it by getting at the barbarism one by one. . . .
We are going to conquer the Indians by a standing army of school teachers,
armed with ideas, winning victories by industrial training, and by the gospel
of love and the gospel of work." The belief among whites grew that adult Indians were too set in savagery to successfully convert to the white man's ways.
Reformers instead proposed bringing "the savage-born infant to the surroundings of civilization," so "he will grow to possess a civilized language and
habit."[40]

Army Captain Richard Henry Pratt became a leading advocate of this philosophy. He had led black soldiers during the Civil War and believed that it
was possible to "train up" an inferior race. He coined a phrase for his policy:
"Kill the Indian, Save the Man." Pratt opened the Carlisle Indian Industrial
School in Pennsylvania in 1879. Its first class consisted of 129 Plains Indians

*Buffalo lying dead in the snow, 1872. The booming market for buffalo hides
and the sporting attraction of buffalo hunts diminished herds to the point where
Native Americans, who relied on the animal for food, shelter,
and clothing, had few options but to settle on reservations or near
American forts for sustenance. (National Archives and Records Service)*

youngsters. Carl Schurz, appointed interior secretary in 1877, believed that
the Indians should follow the example of southern blacks and get an education in the agricultural and mechanical arts. He advocated for their admission to Hampton Institute in Virginia, a school established for freedmen after
the Civil War. As educated Christian workers, both Indians and blacks could
make their way as farmers and mechanics in industrial America. That was
the best possible scenario for these races. Without the discipline of work, the
black man and the red man would literally fade away.[41]

The Centennial Exhibition reinforced the lesson of American ingenuity.
The evidence of hard work and the innovation it spawned among white
Americans enthralled the visitors. By the time the exhibition closed on November 10, over eight million people had paid fifty cents apiece to see it. They
came not merely to view but to learn. Manufacturing demonstrations were
a major part of the exhibition. Visitors learned how to make carpets, bricks, and

typewriters, should they care to enter the ranks of manufacturers. One could chat with Thomas Edison as he explained his latest version of the telegraph. The Age of Reason was a practical era. It was in things that America excelled.

Some things visitors did not see. While Indians had a display, African Americans had none, which, considering the nature of the Native American exhibit, may have been a good thing. Two black artists, Edmonia Lewis and Edward Bannister, had their paintings displayed. There was a concession called the "Southern Restaurant," where, the guidebook breezily informed visitors, "a band of old-time plantation 'darkies' . . . sing their quaint melodies and strum the banjo before visitors in every clime." Philadelphia had one of the largest black populations in the North, yet not one African American worked on the construction of the fair. Once the exhibition opened, blacks found work as entertainers, waiters, and janitors.[42]

Fairgoers were overwhelmingly middle class. The admission price equaled half a day's work for some, and unemployment was still a problem. Still, the poor and working classes could get a flavor of the exposition at "Centennial City," a countercultural exhibition outside Fairmount Park. The "City" was a ramshackle collection of wooden structures on a mile-long strip populated with cheap restaurants, cheaper hotels, and seedy bars. Vendors sold peanuts, pies, sausages, and lemonade from stands along the strip, and sideshows promised sights not available inside the fair to gullible passersby, such as "the wild man of Borneo, and the wild children of Australia, the fat woman . . . heavy enough to entitle her to a place in Machinery Hall, and a collection of 'Feejees,'" who were "pure and unadulterated man-eaters." Within a few months of opening, "Centennial City," was a muddy firetrap that, sure enough, went up in flames. By then fall had arrived, and the city authorities discouraged rebuilding efforts.[43]

The Philadelphia Centennial Exhibition was a snapshot of America in 1876. It was not a summary of the events, ideals, and peoples of the previous century. Yet it offered the visitor a summation of sorts. The fair was a paean to progress. It exalted technology and the making and the inventing of things. It appealed overwhelmingly to the white urban middle class who, though still a minority in the nation, was coming to be synonymous with the national culture. President Grant's simple opening speech implied that the exposition represented both an end and a beginning. The first one hundred years of American life were over, the really hard work of building a nation accomplished. America had gone through a gruesome civil war and then a difficult adjustment to peace. And now, the country could focus on consolidating its continental empire, broadening the opportunities for its ambitious citizens, improving their lives with science and industry, all watched over by the benevolent government of a united republic. A new nation had emerged from the crucible of war, and Americans were trying to make sense of the urban, industrial behemoth arising in their midst, for which the Corliss engine was a fit metaphor.

From the vantage of the twenty-first century, the flaws in this vision are obvious, and one need look no further than the lily-white exposition or the portrayal (or nonportrayal) of minorities, workers, and women. Yet for white visitors to Philadelphia, the only conclusion they could rightfully draw was that America was a wonderful country. Its abundance was not the province of a small minority of wealthy moguls but spread far and wide, there for the taking. The problem with those other groups, if indeed the visitors thought about it, was that they would not or could not avail themselves of those incomparable opportunities. Once they did, they would enjoy the blessings of the first century of American life. The American Revolution was over, its promise and unique ideals secure. As Andrew Carnegie expressed it, America was on the fast track: "The old nations of the earth creep on at a snail's pace; the Republic thunders past with the rush of the express."[44]

America would travel lighter and faster once it jettisoned Reconstruction from its policy agenda. The South would become for the rest of the nation increasingly distant and more exotic, shrouded in perpetual moonlight, covered with magnolia groves, and unmoved by the winds of time and progress. The ritual of disengagement began with the end of the war, but markedly different perspectives on what the war accomplished kept the South in the public consciousness for more than a decade after the conflict ended. The election of 1876 provided the means for ending the nation's involvement in its tar baby region for another century.

President Grant toyed with the idea of an unprecedented third term, but very few of his Republican colleagues encouraged him. Scandal had touched close to his administration and its efforts in the South. Certain sectors of the economy continued to limp along, and the Republicans believed a clean slate, both literally and figuratively, would be a more prudent choice. Rutherford B. Hayes, governor of Ohio, an important state to hold in the fall elections, became the party's nominee for president. Hayes was a thrice-wounded Civil War general who had been active in anti-slavery politics before the war. His main attribute was that he was offensive to no one. Henry Adams called him, not unfairly, a "third-rate nonentity." The most interesting qualification of his running mate, lawyer William A. Wheeler of New York, was that public speaking "in the presence of crowds" made him ill. The party platform was notable for the absence of anything substantive concerning the South, though Hayes pledged himself to the principle of "local self government," which everyone took to mean an end to Republican Reconstruction.[45]

The Democratic nominee, Samuel J. Tilden, governor of New York, had battled corruption within his own party in New York City. Like many other New York politicians, he had a nickname: "the Great Forecloser," because of his legal work for bankrupt railroads. Republicans had other names for him, such as "Slippery Sam" and "Tammany Sammy." An early opponent of Tweed, he became governor on a reform platform vowing to clean up politics throughout the state. His running mate was Governor Thomas A. Hendricks of Indiana, the first Democratic governor of a northern state after the Civil War.[46]

The Democrats hammered on the themes of corruption and persistent economic problems, while the Republicans continued to wave the bloody shirt, though they avoided discussion about the rights of African Americans. Grant's refusal to help the embattled Chamberlain in South Carolina reflected Republican campaign strategy. On election night, it appeared that Tilden had won the presidency. General Daniel Sickles, who had given his leg and nearly his life for the Union cause, limped into Republican headquarters in New York City on his way home on election night. Nearly a decade earlier, Andrew Johnson had fired him from his commander's post in the Carolinas for insisting on voting rights for African Americans. For Sickles, the Democratic Party was the party of treason. As he dolefully watched the returns come in on the telegraph ticker, he suddenly realized that Hayes had a chance despite Tilden's lead in the popular vote. If Hayes did not lose any more states, and if he picked up the electoral votes in Florida, Louisiana, and South Carolina—all three potentially Republican states because of the large black vote—he would become the next president.

Sickles was back at Gettysburg, ordering his men to the charge, only this time it was the telegraph that he commanded, firing off messages to party leaders in the contested southern states over the signature of Republican National Chairman Zachariah Chandler, who was too drunk to function. Republican election boards in each of the three states dutifully followed their commander's directive and invalidated enough Democratic ballots—typically in those counties prone to Democratic paramilitary violence—to declare Hayes the winner. No doubt the Louisiana election board took a close look at East Feliciana Parish, where, despite a black voting majority, not one Republican vote was cast. The Red Shirts discouraged Republicans from voting in South Carolina, and in Florida, among the ruses engineered by Democrats was to pass out Tilden ballots under the Republican emblem to trick illiterate blacks into voting for the Democrat. Tilden partisans in Florida also stopped a train going through a town and voted all the white passengers as local residents. In New Orleans, Republicans uncovered ten thousand Democratic votes by nonexistent voters. Outraged Democrats, beaten at their own game, challenged the results. Thus the election was taken out of the hands of the voters and into the arms of the dealmakers.

The outcome, known as the Compromise of 1877, was that Hayes would receive the contested electoral votes and become the nineteenth president of the United States, the last of the federal troops would be withdrawn from the South (they did not actually leave, but were confined to their barracks), and the federal government and northern investors would rebuild the southern economy. Democrats and Republicans reached the compromise at the home of James Wormley, one of Washington's wealthiest black residents. The last element of the bargain, concerning the South's economic development, was never fulfilled, and the military withdrawal was symbolic. The South's real victory was a permanent end to any threat of federal meddling in southern affairs. Hayes had assured Louisiana Democrats, "I believe, and I have always believed that the intelligence of any country ought to govern it." It was a sentiment many northerners shared.[47]

Grant sighed a great relief as well. His administration would end on a quiet rather than on a contentious note. Looking back on the Reconstruction debacle at the end of his term, he confided to his cabinet that black suffrage was probably a mistake. "It had done the Negro no good, and had been a hindrance to the South, and by no means a political advantage to the North." Northerners agreed. They were pleased to see the South and, especially, blacks disappear as an issue. E. L. Godkin announced, "The negro will disappear from the field of national politics. Henceforth, the nation, as a nation, will have nothing more to do with him." Blacks in the South recognized the end of a noble but doomed experiment. Henry Adams, a black leader in Louisiana, despaired, "The whole South—every state in the South had got into the hands of the very men that held us as slaves." Redemption at last. Reconstruction did not formally end with the triumph or failure of a particular policy but with a deal. The Republicans got the White House, the North got rid of the South and its fractious population, and the South went its own peculiar way.[48]

Alexander Stephens, now a congressman from Georgia, summarized the southern point of view. Though a Democrat, Stephens assured Hayes he supported the compromise. "What," Stephens asked, "do the [southern] people care who governs? All they care for is a good government." As for blacks, Stephens dismissed them entirely. "[The Negro] is nothing but a machine, an instrument in the hands of the politicians to vote as they want. . . . He is not to be taken into account in making up the estimate."[49]

Most writers have agreed that Reconstruction failed the freedmen. If so, it was a preordained failure. Given the nation's racial attitudes before, during, and after the Civil War, permanent concessions to black equality were unrealistic. Only the baldest defiance of white southerners brought the Radical program to fruition, and then for only a short while. Northerners wanted to put the war behind them, and the incessant reminders drifting up from the South at first alarmed, then annoyed, and finally bored them. Mary Livermore, who worked during the war for the U.S. Sanitary Commission, found her northern neighbors during the postwar "turn[ing] with relief to the employments of peaceful life, eager to forget the fearful years of battle and carnage." As long as white southerners could see and feel, however, they could not forget. W. E. B. DuBois summarized the Reconstruction experience for southern blacks. "The slave went free; stood a brief moment in the sun; then moved back again toward slavery." DuBois was only partially correct, however. Reconstruction failed the freedman, but it also failed the South and the nation.[50]

For some blacks, that "moment" lasted longer. By 1870, blacks in the South owned $68,528,200 worth of property, an average estate of only $408 per owner, but an increase of 240 percent over 1860. By 1880, one in five black farmers in the South owned his farm; in the Upper South, it was one out of three. In Virginia, 43 percent of black farmers owned their farms—more than twice as many African American farm owners than there were in the entire South in 1860. It is true that many of these farms were small, less than half the average acreage of white farms; and it was also true that black farms were worth less per acre than white-owned acreage. It was an impressive showing, however, for a people recently out of bondage.[51]

More significant gains occurred in education. In 1865, less than 10 percent of southern blacks were literate. Five years later, that figure had climbed to 18.6 percent, but by 1890, 55 percent of southern blacks were literate. American blacks ranked far ahead of former slaves in other post-emancipation societies such as Trinidad, Haiti, and British Guiana. Black literacy rates compared favorably with some European countries as well. In 1900, Spain had a literacy rate of 37 percent, and Italy, 52 percent. When northern missionaries left due to fear or lack of funds, black teachers took over and schools persisted. By the early 1890s, there were 150 black newspapers in the South.[52]

These figures indicated that freedom itself was enough to hope; that adversity discouraged but did not paralyze the freedmen. Some considered emigration—to Liberia, Central America, or the Caribbean. Roughly twenty-five thousand blacks, "Exodusters," they were called, emigrated to Kansas. These were small movements, however, born of great frustration. Most blacks stayed in the South, at least until race relations worsened in the 1890s and more opportunities opened in the North after the turn of the twentieth century.[53]

For all the advances, however, the sense of betrayal prevailed, not only for the lost promise of equal citizenship but also for the memory of Reconstruction. It was not enough that whites succeeded in subjugating blacks in politics and on the job; the prevailing memory of Reconstruction justified those positions. "Yankee oppression and black misrule" summarized the white memory of the era. The constitutional amendments, the presence of federal troops, and the disfranchisement of some whites provided the evidence for oppression. The courts, however, severely restricted the application of the amendments to black civil and voting rights; most federal troops were on the Plains, not in the South—at the time of the Hamburg massacre, Governor Chamberlain could call upon ten federal soldiers in the vicinity; and only a small proportion of the white electorate was affected by suffrage restrictions, which, in any case, were lifted in 1872. Black misrule is even a weaker argument, as African Americans formed a majority in only one state legislature. What whites objected to was black freedom, the right to vote, the right to hold office, to serve on juries, in short, to exercise their rights as citizens. Remembering Reconstruction as a "Tragic Era" had significant policy and social consequences. It froze white thinking on the subject and justified continued restrictions on black suffrage and civil rights. Dissent from the prevailing view was an attack on redemption, and an attack on redemption was an attack against faith and heritage.[54]

On February 16, 1916, a group of white leaders gathered for a ceremony in North Augusta, South Carolina, formerly known as Hamburg, the site of a deadly confrontation forty years earlier. They had come to dedicate a monument to Thomas McKie Merriweather, the only white man killed during that event. Daniel S. Henderson, a state legislator from the district, addressed the crowd: "We are to Unveil today a Monument, erected by the General Assembly of the State and admiring friends to the memory of one who shed the first blood that started that revolution of 1876, which redeemed the Palmetto State from the yoke of the African and the stranger, and which established beyond a question that this is a white man's country, to be ruled by white men forever." By 1916, stone and bronze tributes to the Confederacy and the Redemption covered the southern landscape. Blacks were as absent in these representations as they were in the meaningful participation in southern life.[55]

There were opposing views. Blacks, Frederick Douglass understood, fought a losing battle of memory, but he urged them to fight with words for what they could not win with arms. "Well the nation may forget," he noted in 1888, "it may shut its eyes to the past, and frown upon any who may do otherwise, but the colored people of this country are bound to keep the past in lively memory till justice shall be done them." The compulsion for national reconciliation created a moral equivalency that buried the injustices of Reconstruction and the causes of the war. On Memorial Day 1893, a black newspaper in Kansas asked its readers:

> *Why should we praise the gray, and blue,*
> *And honor them alike?*
> *The one was false, the other true—*
> *One wrong, the other right.*[56]

John R. Lynch, a black former Mississippi congressman, wrote *The Facts of Reconstruction* (1913) to counter the prevailing white interpretations. He was, after all, an eyewitness to the era's events. Congressional Reconstruction, he wrote, was not a crime but a plan that "could have saved to the country the fruits of the victory that had been won on the battlefield." That it did not succeed was less the fault of the freedmen than of the violent resistance of the South's white population. Two decades later, W. E. B. DuBois published his extensive study of the period, *Black Reconstruction* (1935), taking issue especially with the characterization of southern Republican governments as corrupt and incompetent. These works of careful scholarship did not change national public opinion, or the views of white professional historians. Two years after Lynch's book appeared, D. W. Griffith's film *The Birth of a Nation* thrilled audiences across the country with its story of redemption and reconciliation. One year after the publication of DuBois's study, Margaret Mitchell's *Gone with the Wind* became an instant bestseller, and three years later, one of the most popular motion pictures of all time. In Mitchell's defense, she had read thoroughly the works of leading historians of the era, and the book reflected the latest white scholarship on the Civil War and Reconstruction. *Harper's* recognized, as early as 1873, what would become a chronic frustration for blacks and the interpretation of Reconstruction: "The colored race has never yet been permitted to tell its wrongs." That was true well into the next century.[57]

Though most northerners willingly adopted and even enhanced the southern memory of the war and the Reconstruction era, some refused to acquiesce in this alchemy. Henry Cabot Lodge of Massachusetts, who had grown to adulthood during the Reconstruction era, recalled the great optimism in the North in the decade after the war. He decried, however, the tendency of northerners to accept uncritically the southern perspective on the war and Reconstruction. "We should think ill of the Southern people if they did not" cherish their own institutions and patriots, but "that which is most praiseworthy in Southerners is discreditable in a Northerner."[58]

Most northerners cherished the manufactured South precisely because it was not the North: a genteel, rural, homogeneous, and harmonious region of languid days and starry nights where people moved as softly as the breeze on a summer evening and where paternalism counted more than profit. It was a docile South, uncompetitive economically and unthreatening politically. If the North represented Reason, the South was Romance. Northerners shared, however, the racial beliefs of southern whites. The immigrants, outspoken women, and discontented workers in their midst provided the flash of recognition of how it was to live among an inferior population.

Travel guides prepared by northerners depicted the South as a stage set, a foreign land with hospitable people and quaint customs. Take a train journey south and see "the negro huts along the way, with a grinning turbaned colored woman standing in each doorway." Such a scene "apprises the Northerner that he is certainly 'right smart down South.'" Southern women were more beautiful and comely than their northern counterparts. *Cosmopolitan* writer Marion Baker criticized "the masculinity and independence of too many Northern women," finding them "less charming, less womanly" than their southern sisters. Another editor rhapsodized, "The young ladies of the South are, with very few exceptions, beautiful, and we see no sickly, ugly or consumptive-looking females, such as are to be found in all similar gatherings in the North." Only when tens of thousands of northerners came south during World War II and when African Americans began to protest for their rights as Americans did America scrape away the fairy-tale veneer to expose an ugly, festering secret of racial bigotry, economic stagnation, political repression, and religious self-righteousness.[59]

Robert Penn Warren called the memory of the South's victimization in the war and Reconstruction "the Great Alibi," an excuse white southerners offered for their poverty, ignorance, and peculiar race relations. The war and the Reconstruction provided the white South with the cover to restore a facsimile of the Old South, and the North obliged. Even New South promoters such as D. A. Tompkins and Richard H. Edmonds acknowledged the seamlessness between Old and New Souths. Edmonds chided those who wondered if "the New South is a new creation altogether different from the Old South." Such views, Edmonds argued, were completely false. Using the Darwinian rhetoric familiar to his time, he asserted, "The South of today is no novel creation. It is an evolution." Edmonds's preferred phrase for the South after the war was the "revived South."[60]

Not all white southerners adhered to the redemption myth, though they dissented at their peril. Ellen Glasgow, the noted novelist from Richmond, came of age in the late nineteenth century when the myth attained full bloom. She knew it was a lie. "I hated—I had always hated—the inherent falseness in much Southern tradition." The South was a society of appearances. If the North represented itself as the paragon of reality, the South was a dream province. No less a southern heroine than Varina Howell Davis, the wife of the former Confederate president, recognized the skewed memories of the war and its aftermath. "Between us," she confided to Mary Chesnut, "no one is so tired of Confederate history as the Confederates—they do not want to tell the truth or to hear it."[61]

By the time of Hayes's inauguration in March 1877, the nation was moving out of the economic depression. A bitter and violent railroad strike throughout the Northeast and Midwest later that year highlighted the persistent discontent as well as the solid anti-labor stance of the urban middle classes, the press, and the pulpit. America, to borrow a Carnegie metaphor, was thundering forward to the future, and those who would not or could not come aboard could only blame themselves.

Walt Whitman composed "Song of the Exposition" in 1871. The managers of the Centennial Exhibition in Philadelphia appropriated parts of it for the printed program, as it exemplified the fair's buoyant optimism, its nationalistic tenor, and its emphasis on the great abundance of the land and the inventiveness of its people.

> *And thou America,*
> *Thy offspring towering e'er so high, yet higher Thee*
> *   above all towering,*
> *With Victory on thy left, and at thy right hand Law;*
> *Thou Union holding all, fusing, absorbing, tolerating*
> *   all,*
> *Thee, ever thee, I sing. . . .*
>
> *Mark, thy interminable farms, North, South,*
> *Thy wealthy daughter-states, Eastern and Western,*
> *The varied products of Ohio, Pennsylvania, Missouri,*
> *   Georgia, Texas, and the rest,*
> *Thy limitless crops, grass, wheat, sugar, oil, corn, rice,*
> *   hemp, hops,*
> *Thy barns all fill'd, the endless freight-train and the*
> *   bulging store-house,*
> *The grapes that ripen on thy vines, the apples in thy*
> *   orchards,*
> *Thy incalculable lumber, beef, pork, potatoes, thy coal,*
> *   thy gold and silver,*
> *The inexhaustible iron in thy mines.*

All thine O sacred Union!

Ships, farms, shops, barns, factories, mines,

City and State, North, South, item and aggregate . . . [62]

The managers invited Whitman to the fair, and he came. He visited all of
the major buildings and enjoyed himself immensely. Machinery Hall fascinated him the most, and, after he had toured the grounds, Whitman returned
to gaze once again on the massive Corliss steam engine. It was a revelation. A
visitor, just like Whitman, had stood before it and expressed his faith that
here were embodied America's ideals, a fitting centennial symbol. "Yes, it is
still in these things of iron and steel that the national genius most freely
speaks." And again: "Surely here . . . is true evidence of man's creative power;
here is Prometheus unbound."[63]

Whitman walked up to the engine and climbed onto the platform. Borrowing a chair from the mechanic, he sat in front of the meshing gears and

*"The Stride of a Century," 1876. The figure of Brother Jonathan (precursor to Uncle Sam)
straddles the main building of the Centennial Exhibition in Philadelphia and the
entire American continent. (Courtesy of the Library of Congress)*

thrusting pistons and worshiped. For thirty minutes, he did not move but sat agape in front of this metal god atop its altar. Whitman marveled at the repetitive, efficient movements dispensing power as a god would do. The poet saw America's future. The new nation as a mighty machine powering prosperity and generating opportunity for anyone who could harness its energy. America, realizing the promise of its creation, heralding a century of untrammeled progress.[64]

ACKNOWLEDGMENTS

Research for this book began when I was ten years old. At that time, and for at least a decade thereafter, my aunt and uncle Mary and Charles Gainor showered me with books on the Civil War era. The fascination continued through graduate school. My doctoral dissertation and first book concerned the origins of the war in Virginia. I have been moving forward in time professionally ever since. If, as some say, the aging process eventually initiates a second childhood, that might account for the resurgence of my Civil War passion, the one that produced this book.

That only tells part of the story, however. Along the way, family, friends, historians, and an array of librarians, archivists, and students have helped me immeasurably. These do not include the much larger number of scholars whose fine works I have relied upon and whom I acknowledge in my notes. I honed my interest in the origins of the war at the University of Maryland, where I was fortunate to have George H. Callcott as a mentor and a friend. He taught me many things, foremost of which was that history is a story and we should write it that way. At Maryland I encountered a group of fellow graduate students who encouraged my work and helped me maintain a healthy balance between work and recreation. Pete Daniel, Jim Lane, and Ray Smock have become lifelong friends.

My ideas as a historian and my values as a person derive from such relationships and also from close friendships formed after graduate school with fellow historians Peter Kolchin, Betsy Jacoway, Ray Mohl, Howard Rabinowitz, and especially Blaine A. Brownell. Blaine and I have written books together and have shared countless meals as well as each other's joys and sorrows. He is a part of this book as well.

Though research and writing are solitary activities, they are also products of collaborations. What would we do without the professional help of librarians and archivists? Not much, and it would take much longer to do it. My gratitude goes out to Ed Bray of the Smithsonian Institution, Jennifer Ericson of the Abraham Lincoln Presidential Library, Kristi Finefield of the Library of Congress, Kevin Grogan of the Morris Museum of Art in Augusta, Georgia, Yuhua Li of the Widener Library at Harvard, and Matthew Turi at the Southern Historical Collection in the Wilson Library of the University of North Carolina, Chapel Hill. Sherry Jordon and Marilyn Elysse of the interlibrary loan department at the University of North Carolina at Charlotte have provided invaluable service to me.

I am especially grateful to Robert Barrett of Brigham Young University for making his artwork available to me. The same goes for Harmony Haskins of the Johnson Collection in Spartanburg, South Carolina. Jeffery Howe of the fine arts department at Boston College was kind enough to share his high-resolution image of that impressive Corliss steam engine.

I have been fortunate to receive the assistance of several stellar graduate students. Boyd Harris, La Shonda Mims, Donna Ward, and Kathryn B. Wells were all that I could ask for and more. Kathy Wells not only engaged in research and lightened my editorial responsibilities but also read parts of the manuscript and shared her vast theological expertise with me.

Dr. Martina Kohl of the American Embassy in Berlin was brave enough to allow me to try out my ideas on the Civil War era in front of diverse audiences across Germany. I have benefited from this European perspective as well as from the ideas and friendship of Jörg Nagler of the University of Jena.

Working in a nurturing department at the University of North Carolina at Charlotte has facilitated my research and writing. No one has been more supportive than Jürgen Buchenau, department chair. I also appreciate the support of the late Schley Lyons, dean of the College of Liberal Arts and Sciences, and his successor, Nancy Gutierrez. I hope that my Civil War–era historian-colleagues Mark R. Wilson and Jim Hogue will forgive me for pestering them with questions. I also hope I have transcribed their knowledge correctly. I very much appreciate the continued financial support of my research by the Davenport family.

I have also benefited from my association with Bloomsbury Press, first and foremost with Peter Ginna, who believed in this book from the outset, and his fine staff, including Pete Beatty, Nathaniel Knaebel, and Peter Miller. India Cooper was a copy editor nonpareil. To say Geri Thoma is my agent is to say only the half of it. I have enjoyed her sense of humor, benefited from her suggestions, and appreciated her dedication.

And speaking of dedication, it is a very easy thing to dedicate this book to my wife, Marie-Louise Hedin. George Callcott told me that history was a jealous mistress. It is my great vocational passion. Without the presence of family, however, it is a hollow pursuit. Marie-Louise and my wonderful family—my son, Erik; daughter, Eleanor; my late mother, Sarah; and my father, Alex, who at ninety-three is still teaching—have supported that passion. I can never match their support, but I return their love at least as equally. Marie-Louise is always my first reader and first friend. This book is especially for her.

NOTES

ABBREVIATIONS

CG   *Congressional Globe*

CW   *Collected Works of Abraham Lincoln,* ed. Roy P. Basler (New Brunswick: Rutgers University Press, 1953)

FD:SSW   *Frederick Douglass: Selected Speeches and Writings,* ed. Philip S. Foner (Chicago: Lawrence Hill Books, 1999)

CHAPTER I: CRUSADES

1. The following account of the Ursuline convent derives from these sources: Nancy Lusignan Schultz, *Fire and Roses: The Burning of the Charlestown Convent, 1834* (New York: Free Press, 2000); Ray Allen Billington, "The Burning of the Charlestown Convent," *New England Quarterly* 10 (March 1937): 4–24; Jeanne Hamilton, OSU, "The Nunnery as Menace: The Burning of the Charlestown Convent, 1834," *Catholic Historian*, Winter 1996, http://www.ewtn.com/library/HUMANITY/BURNING.TXT; Carmine A. Prioli, "The Ursuline Outrage," *American Heritage* 33 (February/March 1982): 101–5.

2. Quoted in Billington, "Burning," 5.

3. Quoted in Schultz, *Fire and Roses,* 115.

4. Quoted in Hamilton, "Nunnery as Menace," 16.

5. Quoted in Schultz, *Fire and Roses,* 159.

6. Quoted in Billington, "Burning," 15.

7. Quoted in ibid., 12.

8. Quoted in ibid., 15.

9. Quoted in ibid.

10. Quoted in Hamilton, "Nunnery as Menace," 17.

11. Quoted in ibid, 8.

12. Rebecca Reed, *Six Months in a Convent, or the Narrative of Rebecca Theresa Reed, Who Was Under the Influence of the Roman Catholics About Two Years, and an Inmate of the Ursuline Convent on Mount Benedict, Charlestown, Mass., Nearly Six Months in the Years 1831–32* (Boston: Russell, Odiorne & Metcalf, 1835), available on Google Books. The Mother Superior's reply is available at the American Catholic History Research Center and University Archives of the Catholic University of America.

13. Rebecca Theresa Reed, *Supplement to "Six Months in a Convent"* (Boston: Russell, Odiorne, 1835): 69, available on Google Books.

14. Maria Monk, *Awful Disclosures* (New York: Maria Monk, 1836): 104, available on Google Books.

15. William L. Stone, *Maria Monk and the Nunnery of the Hotel Dieu* (New York: Howe and Bates, 1836), 26, available on Google Books.

16. Quoted in A. James Reichley, *Faith in Politics* (Washington: Brookings Institution, 2002), 175–76.

17. Mark A. Noll, *America's God: From Jonathan Edwards to Abraham Lincoln* (New York: Oxford University Press, 2002), 236–37. In additional to Noll's excellent work, I am especially indebted to the insights of the following authors concerning the connection between politics, the economy, and religion in antebellum America: Robert H. Abzug, *Cosmos Crumbling: American Reform and the Religious Imagination* (New York: Oxford University Press, 1994); Richard Carwardine, *Evangelicals and Politics in Antebellum America* (New Haven: Yale University Press, 1993); Daniel Walker Howe, *What Hath God Wrought: The Transformation of America, 1815–1848* (New York: Oxford University Press, 2007); Mark A. Noll, ed., *Religion and American Politics: From the Colonial Period to the 1980s* (New York: Oxford University Press, 1990); Ernest Lee Tuveson, *Redeemer Nation: The Idea of America's Millennial Role* (Chicago: University of Chicago Press, 1968).

18. Joan D. Hedrick, *Harriet Beecher Stowe: A Life* (New York: Oxford University Press, 1994), 102–19.

19. "William Jay Mocks and Dismisses the Proslavery Argument," in *Major Problems in the Early Republic, 1747–1848*, ed. Sean Wilentz and Jonathan Earle, 2nd ed. (Boston: Cengage Learning, 2007), 394–95.

20. Quoted in Leon F. Litwack, *North of Slavery: The Negro in the Free States, 1790–1860* (Chicago: University of Chicago Press, 1961), 96.

21. Ibid.

22. Quoted in William W. Freehling, *The Road to Disunion*, vol. 1, *Secessionists at Bay, 1776–1854* (New York: Oxford University Press, 1990), 294.

23. Lyman Beecher, *A Plea for the West* (Cincinnati: Truman & Smith, 1835), 22, 26.

24. Henry David Thoreau, "Walking" (1862), http://www.bartleby.com, paragraph 22; John Patrick Diggins, ed., *The Portable John Adams* (New York: Penguin, 2004), 214.

25. Quoted in Reinhold Niebuhr, *The Irony of American History* (New York: Charles Scribner's Sons, 1962), 70.

26. Quoted in Terry A. Barnhart, "'A Common Feeling': Regional Identity and Historical Consciousness in the Old Northwest, 1820–1860," *Michigan Historical Review* 29 (Spring 2003): 67–68.

27. John O'Sullivan, "Annexation," *United States Magazine and Democratic Review* 17 (July/August 1845): 6.

28. The following works informed my discussion of the Latter-day Saints: Richard Lyman Bushman, *Joseph Smith: Rough Stone Rolling* (New York: Knopf, 2005); Reid L. Nielson and Terryl L. Givens, eds., *Joseph Smith, Jr.: Reappraisals After Two Centuries* (New York: Oxford University Press, 2009), especially the essay by Richard H. Brodhead, "Prophets in America Circa 1830: Ralph Waldo Emerson, Nat Turner, Joseph Smith," 13–30; Ray Allen Billington, *The Far Western Frontier, 1830–1860* (New York: Harper Torchbooks, 1956), chapter 9; Nathan O. Hatch, "The Democratization of Christianity and the Character of American Politics," in Noll, *Religion and American Politics*, 102; Donald C. Swift, *Religion and the American Experience* (Armonk, N.Y.: M. E. Sharpe, 1998), 95–101; Tuveson, *Redeemer Nation*, 176.

29. This assessment appeared in an unflattering article on the Mormons, "Memoir of the Mormons," *Southern Literary Messenger* 14 (November 1848): 653–54.

30. Quoted in Brodhead, "Prophets in America," 24 (Smith), 25 (Emerson).

31. Quoted in Tuveson, *Redeemer Nation*, 176.

32. Quoted in Billington, *Far Western Frontier*, 196.

33. Quoted in ibid., 199.

34. Thomas Jefferson to John Dickinson, March 6, 1801, in Paul Leicester Ford, ed., *The Writings of Thomas Jefferson* (New York: G. P. Putnam's Sons, 1892–99), 9: 343, http://oll.libertyfunding.org/title/757.

35. Quoted in Richard Carwardine, "Trauma in Methodism: Property, Church Schism, and Sectional Polarization in Antebellum America," in *God and Mammon: Protestants, Money, and the Market, 1790–1860,* ed. Mark A. Noll (New York: Oxford University Press, 2002), 206, 208. Mitchell Snay offers an excellent account of the evangelical sectional schism in *Gospel of Disunion: Religion and Separatism in the Antebellum South* (New York: Cambridge University Press, 1993).

36. Quoted in Snay, *Gospel of Disunion*, 135.

37. Both quoted in Noll, *America's God*, 199.

38. The best analysis of the Whig Party is Michael F. Holt, *The Rise and Fall of the American Whig Party: Jacksonian Politics and the Onset of the Civil War* (New York: Oxford University Press, 1999). See 118.

39. Quoted in Carwardine, *Evangelicals and Politics*, 75.

40. Quoted in ibid., 53.

41. Quoted in ibid., 137.

42. The following works have informed my discussion of the annexation controversy, in addition to the others noted: Robert F. Durden, *The Self-Inflicted Wound: Southern Politics in the Nineteenth Century* (Lexington: University Press of Kentucky, 1985), 49–51; John D. Eisenhower, *So Far from God: The U.S. War with Mexico, 1846–1848* (New York: Random House, 1989), 13–26; Freehling, *Secessionists at Bay*, part 6; Joel H. Silbey, *Storm over Texas: The Annexation Controversy and the Road to Civil War* (New York: Oxford University Press, 2005).

43. Irving H. Bartlett, *John C. Calhoun: A Biography* (New York: Norton, 1994) and John Niven, *John C. Calhoun and the Price of Union: A Biography* (Baton Rouge: Louisiana State University Press, 1988) are among the best of several Calhoun biographies. See also Lacy K. Ford Jr., "Republican Ideology in a Slave Society: The Political Economy of John C. Calhoun," *Journal of Southern History* 54 (August 1988): 405–24. Calhoun's works are collected in a well-edited series of volumes, Clyde N. Wilson, ed., *The Papers of John C. Calhoun,* 28 vols. (Columbia: University of South Carolina Press, 1959–2003).

CHAPTER 2: EMPIRE

1. James K. Polk, "First Annual Message," December 2, 1845, American Presidency Project, http://www.presidency.ucsb.edu.

2. Quoted in John D. Eisenhower, *So Far from God: The U.S. War with Mexico, 1846–1848* (New York: Random House, 1989), 45, 23.

3. Quoted in Ray Allen Billington, *The Far Western Frontier, 1830–1860* (New York: Harper Torchbooks, 1956), 171.

4. U. S. Grant, *Personal Memoirs of U. S. Grant* (New York: Charles L. Webster, 1972; first published in 1886), 63.

5. Quoted in Eisenhower, *So Far from God*, 47.

6. John C. Pinheiro, "'Religion Without Restriction': Anti-Catholicism, All Mexico, and the Treaty of Guadalupe Hidalgo," *Journal of the Early Republic* 23 (Spring 2003): 69–96.

7. Soldier quoted in Billington, *Far Western Frontier*, 173; Taylor quoted in Eisenhower, *So Far from God*, 65.

8. James K. Polk, "Message on War with Mexico," May 11, 1846, Archives of *The West*, http://www.pbs.org/weta/thewest/resources/archives/two/mexdec.htm.

9. "War with Mexico," May 11, 1846, in *The Gathering of the Forces by Walt Whitman: Editorials, Essays, Literary and Dramatic Reviews and Other Material Written by Walt Whitman as Editor of the Brooklyn Daily Eagle in 1846 and 1847*, ed. Cleveland Rodgers and John Black (New York: G. P. Putnam's Sons, 1920), 240.

10. "Our Territory on the Pacific," July 7, 1846, in ibid., 246.

11. Philip Callow, *From Noon to Starry Night: A Life of Walt Whitman* (Chicago: Ivan R. Dee, 1992), 24–25.

12. George Bancroft, *History of the United States, from the Discovery of the American Continent*, 10 vols. (1834–74). The books appeared in numerous editions, some abridged over the years (the latest in 2010). Little, Brown published several editions beginning in 1846.

13. Quoted in Richard Carwardine, *Evangelicals and Politics in Antebellum America* (New Haven: Yale University Press, 1993), 145.

14. Editor quoted in Thomas E. Schott, *Alexander H. Stephens of Georgia: A Biography* (Baton Rouge: Louisiana State University Press, 1988), 71; Hitchcock quoted in Bernard DeVoto, *The Year of Decision, 1846* (Boston: Houghton Mifflin, 1960), 15.

15. *CG*, 29th Congress, 1st Session (May 11, 1846): 96; Emerson quoted in DeVoto, *Year of Decision*, 492.

16. "Sermon of War," in Theodore Parker and Frances Power Cobbe, eds., *Collected Works of Theodore Parker, Part Four* (Whitefish, Mont.: Kessinger Publishing, 2004; first published in 1876), 4.

17. James K. Polk, "Special Message," August 4, 1846, American Presidency Project, http://www.presidency.ucsb.edu.

18. *CG*, 29th Congress, 1st Session (August 12, 1846): 1217.

19. Milo Milton Quaife, ed., *The Diary of James K. Polk during his Presidency, 1845 to 1849* (Chicago: A. C. McClurg, 1910), August 10, 1846, 2:75, available on Google Books; *Boston Whig* quoted in Robert F. Durden, *The Self-Inflicted Wound: Southern Politics in the Nineteenth Century* (Lexington: University Press of Kentucky, 1985), 53.

20. Delano Quoted in David M. Potter, *The Impending Crisis, 1848–1861* (New York: Harper & Row, 1976), 67–68; Toombs quoted in Schott, *Stephens*, 116.

21. Quoted in Potter, *Impending Crisis*, 49.

22. Quoted in Eisenhower, *So Far from God*, 160.

23. William Gilmore Simms to James Henry Hammond, April 2, 1847, in *Voices from the Gathering Storm: The Coming of the American Civil War*, ed. Glenn M. Linden (Wilmington, Del.: Scholarly Resources, 2001), 24.

24. Quoted in Carwardine, *Evangelicals and Politics*, 94.

25. All quotes in the preceding three paragraphs are from ibid., 150–51.

26. Frederick Douglass, "The Blood of the Slave on the Skirts of the Northern People," *North Star*, November 17, 1848, in *FD:SSW*, 122–23.

27. The discussion of the gold rush draws on the following sources: Gunther Barth, *Instant*

Cities: Urbanization and the Rise of San Francisco and Denver (New York: Oxford University Press, 1975); Billington, *Far Western Frontier*, 218–41; H. W. Brands, *The Age of Gold: The California Gold Rush and the New American Dream* (New York: Doubleday, 2002); DeVoto, *Year of Decision*, 499–500; Susan Lee Johnson, *Roaring Camp: The Social World of the California Gold Rush* (New York: Norton, 2000); Malcolm J. Rohrbough, *Days of Gold: The California Gold Rush and the American Nation* (Berkeley: University of California Press, 1997); John D. Unruh Jr., *The Plains Across: The Overland Emigrants and the Trans-Mississippi West, 1840–1860* (Urbana: University of Illinois Press, 1979), 68–244.

28. James K. Polk, "Fourth Annual Message," December 5, 1848, American Presidency Project, http://www.presidency.ucsb.edu.

29. Unless otherwise noted, the discussion of Harriet Beecher Stowe and Charley relies on Joan D. Hedrick, *Harriet Beecher Stowe: A Life* (New York: Oxford University Press, 1994), 190–92.

30. Harriet Beecher Stowe to Calvin Stowe, July 26, 1849, in *Life and Letters of Harriet Beecher Stowe*, ed. Annie Fields (Boston: Houghton Mifflin, 1897), 119, available on Google Books.

CHAPTER 3: REVOLUTIONS

1. The discussion of the European revolutions of 1848 relies on Jonathan Sperber, *The European Revolutions, 1848–1851*, 2nd ed. (Cambridge: Cambridge University Press, 2005).

2. Quoted in Philip Callow, *From Noon to Starry Night: A Life of Walt Whitman* (Chicago: Ivan R. Dee, 1992), 171; quoted in Timothy M. Roberts, " 'Revolutions Have Become the Bloody Toy of the Multitude': European Revolutions, the South, and the Crisis of 1850," *Journal of the Early Republic* 25 (Summer 2005): 263; see also Timothy M. Roberts, *Distant Revolutions: 1848 and the Challenge to American Exceptionalism* (Charlottesville: University of Virginia Press, 2009); Michael A. Morrison, "American Reaction to European Revolutions, 1848–1852: Sectionalism, Memory, and the Revolutionary Heritage," *Civil War History* 49 (June 2003): 111–32.

3. James K. Polk, "Fourth Annual Message," December 5, 1848, James K. Polk Papers: American Presidency Project, http://www.presidency.ucsb.edu.

4. Quoted in Jack P. Greene, ed., *The Ambiguity of the American Revolution* (New York: Harper & Row, 1968), 49–50.

5. For a full treatment of the Compromise of 1850, see Holman Hamilton, *Prologue to Conflict: The Crisis and Compromise of 1850* (Lexington: University Press of Kentucky, 2005); Merrill D. Peterson, *The Great Triumvirate: Webster, Clay, and Calhoun* (New York: Oxford University Press, 1988); Robert V. Remini, *At the Edge of the Precipice: Henry Clay and the Compromise That Saved the Union* (New York: Basic Books, 2010).

6. Calhoun confided this to James M. Mason, senator from Virginia and a close friend. Virginia Mason, *The Public Life and Diplomatic Correspondence of James Murray Mason* (New York: Neale Publishing, 1906), 72–73.

7. *CG*, 31st Congress, 1st Session (March 4, 1850): 451–55.

8. Both quotes from Thomas E. Schott, *Alexander H. Stephens of Georgia: A Biography* (Baton Rouge: Louisiana State University Press, 1988), 99.

9. *Register of Debates*, 21st Congress, 1st Session (January 27, 1830): 80.

10. *CG*, 31st Congress, 1st Session (March 7, 1850): 477.

11. John Greenleaf Whittier, "Ichabod" (1850), http://www.bartleby.com.

12. *CG*, 31st Congress, 1st Session, Appendix (March 11, 1850): 265.

13. Wooster Parker quoted in Richard Carwardine, *Evangelicals and Politics in Antebellum America* (New Haven: Yale University Press, 1993), 178.

14. *CG*, 31st Congress, 1st Session, Appendix (July 22, 1850): 482.

15. Quoted in David M. Potter, *The Impending Crisis, 1848–1861* (New York: Harper & Row, 1976), 121.

16. George Templeton Strong, *The Diary of George Templeton Strong*, ed. Allan Nevins and Milton Halsey Thomas, (New York: Macmillan, 1952), September 9, 1850, 2: 19–20.

17. Quoted in Carwardine, *Evangelicals and Politics*, 183.

18. Both quotes from Schott, *Stephens*, 129.

19. S.L.C., "Isaac and Ishmael," *Southern Literary Messenger* 17 (January 1851): 23.

20. Quoted in Vincent Harding, *There Is a River: The Black Struggle for Freedom in America* (New York: Vintage, 1983), 160.

21. These and subsequent quotes from the speech of Frederick Douglass, "The Meaning of July Fourth for the Negro," in *FD:SSW*, 188–205.

22. Walt Whitman, "Blood-Money," initially appeared in the *New York Daily Tribune*, March 22, 1850, http://www.bartleby.com.

23. Unless otherwise noted, the discussion of Stowe relies on Joan D. Hedrick, *Harriet Beecher Stowe: A Life* (New York: Oxford University Press, 1994).

24. Quoted in Elizabeth Fox-Genovese, "Days of Judgment, Days of Wrath: The Civil War and the Religious Imagination of Women Writers," in *Religion and the American Civil War*, ed. Randall M. Miller, Harry S. Stout, and Charles Reagan Wilson (New York: Oxford University Press, 1998), 234.

25. Quoted in Andrew Delbanco, "Sentimental Education," *New Republic*, April 18, 1994, 42.

26. Quoted in Fox-Genovese, "Days of Judgment," 235.

27. Hedrick, *Stowe*, 104.

28. Quoted in ibid., 25.

29. Harriet Beecher Stowe, *Uncle Tom's Cabin, or Life Among the Lowly* (New York: Norton, 1994; first published in 1852), 385.

30. Ibid., first quote, 247; second quote, 77.

31. Ibid., 385.

32. Ibid., first quote, 115; second quote, 357.

33. Ibid., first quote, 277; second quote, 340; third quote, 344.

34. Ibid., first quote, 249; second quotes, 246.

35. Ibid., 257.

36. Ibid., 383.

37. Ibid., 384.

38. Ibid., 385.

39. Ibid., 388.

40. Ibid.

41. First quote, Hedrick, *Stowe*, vii; second quote, Felix Gregory de Fontaine, *History of American Abolitionism: Its Four Great Epochs* (New York: D. Appleton, 1861), 53.

42. Quotes in Annie Fields, ed., *Life and Letters of Harriet Beecher Stowe* (Boston: Houghton Mifflin, 1898), 135, 136, available on Google Books.

43. Frederick Douglass to Harriet Beecher Stowe, March 8, 1853, in *FD:SSW*, 216–17; Stowe quoted in Thomas Graham, "Harriet Beecher Stowe and the Question of Race," *New England Quarterly* 46 (December 1973): 621.

44. *Frederick Douglass' Paper*, March 4, 1853, in *Voices from the Gathering Storm: The Coming of the American Civil War*, ed. Glenn M. Linden (Wilmington, Del.: Scholarly Resources, 2001), 65.

45. "A Methodist," *Liberator*, October 22, 1858; see also Catherine Clinton, *Harriet Tubman: The Road to Freedom* (New York: Little, Brown, 2004), 114.

46. George Frederick Holmes, "Notices of New Work," *Southern Literary Messenger* 18 (October 1852): 630.

47. George Frederick Holmes, "A Key to Uncle Tom's Cabin," *Southern Literary Messenger* 19 (June 1853): 325.

48. Ibid., 329.

49. "Editor's Table," *Southern Literary Messenger* 19 (January 1853): 58.

50. Harriet Beecher Stowe to Eliza Cabot Follen, December 16, 1852, in *The Limits of Sisterhood*, ed. Jeanne Boydston, Mary Kelley, and Anne Margolis (Chapel Hill: University of North Carolina Press, 1988), 178–80.

51. Abraham Lincoln, "The Perpetuation of our Political Institutions," January 27, 1838, *CW* 1:112.

CHAPTER 4: RAILROADED

1. Greeley quoted in Adam-Max Tuchinsky, "'The Bourgeoisie Will Fall and Fall Forever': The *New-York Tribune*, the 1848 French Revolution, and American Social Democratic Discourse," *Journal of American History* 92 (September 2005): 494.

2. Quoted in Hans L. Trefousse, *Carl Schurz: A Biography* (Knoxville: University of Tennessee Press, 1982), 41.

3. William Edward Forster quoted in John Francis Maguire, *Father Mathew: A Biography* (New York: D. & J. Sadlier, 1864), 383.

4. Quoted in Oscar Handlin, *Boston's Immigrants, 1790–1880: A Study in Acculturation* (Cambridge: Harvard University Press, 1991; first published in 1941 as *Boston's Immigrants, 1790–1865*), 84.

5. For this biographical material on Carl Schurz, I rely on Hans Trefousse's biography.

6. For a discussion of this connection, see Gilbert Sykes Blakely, "Introduction," Sir Walter Scott, *Ivanhoe* (New York: Charles E. Merrill, 1911).

7. Frederick Douglass, *Narrative of the Life of Frederick Douglass, an American Slave* (New York: Modern Library, 2000), 103.

8. See John Bodnar, *The Transplanted: A History of Immigrants in Urban America* Bloomington: Indiana University Press, 1985).

9. The following discussion relies on Tyler Anbinder, *Nativism and Slavery: The Northern Know Nothings and the Politics of the 1850s* (New York: Oxford University Press, 1992); Ray Allen Billington, *The Protestant Crusade, 1800–1860: A Study of the Origins of American Nativism* (New York: Macmillan, 1938); Michael F. Holt, *The Political Crisis of the 1850s* (New York: Norton, 1978); and Bruce C. Levine, "Conservatism, Nativism, and Slavery: Thomas R. Whitney and the Origins of the Know-Nothing Party," *Journal of American History* 88 (September 2001): 455–88.

10. Quoted in Richard Carwardine, *Evangelicals and Politics in Antebellum America* (New Haven: Yale University Press, 1993), 86.

11. Quoted in ibid., 220.

12. Henry A. Wise, "Governor Wise's Letter on Know-nothingism and His Speech at Alexandria" (1854), YA Pamphlet Collection, Library of Congress.

13. Quoted in Thomas E. Schott, *Alexander Stephens of Georgia: A Biography* (Baton Rouge: Louisiana State University Press, 1988), 185.

14. Biographical details come from Schott, *Stephens.*

15. Quoted in ibid., 27.

16. Quoted in ibid., 185, 186.

17. Quoted in Carwardine, *Evangelicals and Politics,* 231.

18. Quoted in Isaac Kramnick and R. Laurence Moore, *The Godless Constitution: The Case Against Religious Correctness* (New York: Norton, 1997), 122.

19. First quote in Anbinder, *Nativism and Slavery,* 96; second quote in Levine, "Conservatism, Nativism, and Slavery," 477.

20. Quoted in Trefousse, *Schurz,* 50.

21. Quoted in Robert W. Johannsen, *Stephen A. Douglas* (Urbana: University of Illinois Press, 1997), 399.

22. Quoted in Robert R. Russel, *Improvement of Communication with the Pacific Coast as an Issue in American Politics, 1783–1864* (Cedar Rapids, IA: Torch Press, 1948), 25.

23. First quote in Johannsen, *Douglas,* 405; second quote in James L. Huston, *Stephen A. Douglas and the Dilemmas of Democratic Equality* (Lanham, Md.: Rowman & Littlefield, 2007), 105; third quote in David M. Potter, *The Impending Crisis, 1848–1861* (New York: Harper & Row, 1976), 160.

24. *CG,* 33rd Congress, 1st Session (January 24, 1854): 281–82.

25. "Slavery Militant," *New York Tribune,* January 11, 1854.

26. Quoted in William W. Freehling, *Road to Disunion,* vol. 1, *Secessionists at Bay* (New York: Oxford University Press, 1990), 557.

27. *CW* 2:130.

28. *CW* 2:255.

29. First quote in *CW* 2:282; second quote in *CW* 2:248.

30. Quoted in Johannsen, *Douglas,* 422.

31. *CW* 2:281, 266.

32. *CW* 2:546.

33. *CW* 2:255, 266.

34. *CW* 2:242.

35. Speech at Chicago, October 30, 1854, in *FD:SSW,* 310.

36. *New York Tribune,* January 11, 1854; Atchison quoted in Louis A. De Caro Jr., *"Fire from the Midst of You": A Religious Life of John Brown* (New York: NYU Press, 2002), 217.

CHAPTER 5: BLOOD ON THE PLAINS

1. The discussion on the Plains Indians in this chapter benefited particularly from the following works: Colin G. Calloway, ed., *Our Hearts Fell to the Ground: Plains Indian Views of How the West Was Lost* (Boston: Bedford/St. Martin's, 1996); Arrell Morgan Gibson, *The American Indian: Prehistory to the Present* (Lexington, Mass.: D. C. Heath, 1980); Patricia Nelson Limerick, *The Legacy of Conquest: The Unbroken Past of the American West* (New

York: Norton, 1987); Joseph M. Marshall III, *The Journey of Crazy Horse: A Lakota History* (New York: Penguin, 2004); Mike Sajna, *Crazy Horse: The Life Behind the Legend* (New York: John Wiley & Sons, 2000); Philip Weeks, *Farewell, My Nation: The American Indian and the United States, 1820–1890* (Arlington Heights, Ill.: Harlan Davidson, 1990); Richard White, *"It's your misfortune and none of my own": A History of the American West* (Norman: University of Oklahoma Press, 1991).

2. Quoted in Weeks, *Farewell*, 63.

3. Both quotes in Marshall, *Journey of Crazy Horse*, 34.

4. Quoted in Sajna, *Crazy Horse*, 91.

5. Quoted in George M. Fredrickson, *The Black Image in the White Mind: The Debate on Afro-American Character and Destiny, 1817–1914* (New York: Harper & Row, 1971), 98; see also Thomas F. Gossett, *Race: The History of an Idea in America* (Dallas: Southern Methodist University Press, 1963), 89–96.

6. Frederick Law Olmsted, *A Journey in the Seaboard Slave States, with Remarks on their Economy* (New York: Mason Brothers, 1861), 18, available on Google Books; William C. Daniell, "Southern Agricultural Congress," *Southern Literary Messenger* 18 (October 1852): 616.

7. Horace Greeley, *An Overland Journey from New York to San Francisco in the Summer of 1859* (New York: C. M. Saxton, Barker, 1860). Letter 13: "Lo! the Poor Indian!" http://etext .virginia.edu/railton/roughingit/map/indgreeley.html.

8. See Marshall, *Journey of Crazy Horse*, 39–46, for additional details on this episode.

9. Quotes are from Sajna, *Crazy Horse*, 109, 110.

10. Quoted in ibid., 111.

11. Quoted in ibid., 118.

12. Quoted in ibid., 119.

13. Seward and Rhett quoted in Robert F. Durden, *The Self-Inflicted Wound: Southern Politics in the Nineteenth Century* (Lexington: University Press of Kentucky, 1985), 69; Atchison quoted in Robert Kagan, *Dangerous Nation: America's Foreign Policy from Its Earliest Days to the Dawn of the Twentieth Century* (New York: Knopf, 2006), 236.

14. *New York Tribune*, May 28, 1856.

15. *CG*, 34th Congress, 1st Session, Appendix (June 21, 1856): 641.

16. "The Political Aspect," *Putnam's Monthly Magazine* 8 (July 1856): 89.

17. Quoted in Timothy M. Roberts, "The European Revolutions of 1848 and Antebellum Violence in Kansas," *Journal of the West* 44 (Fall 2005): 66.

18. Quoted in ibid., 67.

19. *CG*, 34th Congress, 1st Session, Appendix (May 19, 1856): 530.

20. Ibid. (May 20, 1856): 543.

21. *New York Tribune*, May 23, 1856.

22. *Edgefield* (S.C.) *Advertiser*, May 28, 1856, http://history.furman.edu/editorials/see.py ?ecode=sceasu560528a.

23. Quoted in Thomas E. Schott, *Alexander H. Stephens of Georgia: A Biography* (Baton Rouge: Louisiana State University Press, 1988), 205.

24. Frederick Douglass, *Life and Times of Frederick Douglass* (Mineola, N.Y.: Dover, 2003; first published in 1892), 195.

25. Ibid., 194.

26. Quoted in David M. Potter, *The Impending Crisis, 1848–1861* (New York: Harper & Row, 1976), 222.

27. De Bow, "The War Against the South—Opinions of Freesoilers and Abolitionists, Their Denunciations, etc.," *De Bow's Review* 21 (September 1856): 271–72, 276.

28. Ibid., 274.

29. Ibid., 276.

30. *CW*, 2:322, 341.

31. Quoted in Allen C. Guelzo, *Abraham Lincoln: Redeemer President* (Grand Rapids, Mich.: Eerdmans, 1999), 205.

32. Quoted in Joan D. Hedrick, *Harriet Beecher Stowe: A Life* (New York: Oxford University Press, 1994), 258.

33. Quoted in Schott, *Stephens*, 208.

34. Quoted in David Herbert Donald, *Lincoln* (New York: Simon & Schuster, 1995), 315.

35. Alexander K. McClure, *Recollections of Half a Century* (Salem, Mass.: Salem Press, 1902), 357.

36. Quoted in Richard Carwardine, *Evangelicals and Politics in Antebellum America* (New Haven: Yale University Press, 1993), 260, 262.

37. Quoted in ibid., 260.

38. Quotes in Durden, *Self-Inflicted Wound*, 171, 172.

39. Quotes in Carwardine, *Evangelicals and Politics*, 263, 264.

40. Quoted in ibid., 268.

41. Quoted in ibid., 269.

42. Quoted in Guelzo, *Redeemer President*, 206.

43. Quoted in William E. Gienapp, *The Origins of the Republican Party, 1852–1856* (New York: Oxford University Press, 1987), 442.

CHAPTER 6: REVIVAL

1. The definitive work on the Revival is Kathryn Teresa Long, *The Revival of 1857–58: Interpreting an American Religious Awakening* (New York: Oxford University Press, 1998).

2. "The Commercial Crisis of 1857," *Hunt's Merchants' Magazine and Commercial Review* 10 (November 1857): 533.

3. Quoted in Long, *Revival*, 52.

4. Walt Whitman, "Song of Myself," in *Leaves of Grass*, ed. Harold W. Blodgett and Sculley Bradley (New York: New York University Press, 1965), 36.

5. *Harper's New Monthly Magazine* 13 (July 1856): 272; George Templeton Strong, *The Diary of George Templeton Strong*, ed. Allan Nevins and Milton Halsey Thomas, (New York: Macmillan, 1952), October 27, 1850, 2:24.

6. Quoted in Sean Wilentz, *Chants Democratic: New York City and the Rise of the American Working Class* (New York: Oxford University Press, 1984), 108.

7. Quoted in Stuart M. Blumin, *The Emergence of the Middle Class: Social Experience in the American City, 1760–1900* (Cambridge: Cambridge University Press, 1989), 14.

8. Quotes in David Goldfield and Blaine A. Brownell, *Urban America: A History* (Boston: Houghton Mifflin, 1990), 145.

9. *Harper's Weekly* 11 (July 1855): 272.

10. Quoted in Goldfield and Brownell, *Urban America*, 173.

11. Quoted in ibid.

12. Quoted in Heather D. Curtis, "Views of Self, Success, and Society Among Young Men in Antebellum Boston," *Church History* 73 (September 2004): 629–30.

13. Quoted in Gunther Barth, *City People: The Rise of Modern City Culture in Nineteenth-Century America* (New York: Oxford University Press, 1980), 123.

14. On department stores and suburban development, see Goldfield and Brownell, *Urban America*, 117–28.

15. On urban reform and innovation in the 1850s, see ibid., chapter 6.

16. Walt Whitman, "Pioneers! O Pioneers!" *Leaves of Grass*, 229–230.

17. "Self Reliance," in *Ralph Waldo Emerson: Essays and Lectures*, ed. Joel Porte (New York: Literary Classics of the U.S., 1983), 270.

18. For biographical material on Whitman, I have relied on Philip Callow, *From Noon to Starry Night: A Life of Walt Whitman* (Chicago: Ivan R. Dee, 1992); Roy Morris Jr., *The Better Angel: Walt Whitman in the Civil War* (New York: Oxford University Press, 2000); and David S. Reynolds, *Walt Whitman's America: A Cultural Biography* (New York: Knopf, 1995).

19. See Tyler Anbinder, *Five Points: The 19th-Century New York City Neighborhood That Invented Tap Dance, Stole Elections, and Became the World's Most Notorious Slum* (New York: Free Press, 2001).

20. "Self-government in Large Cities," *Harper's*, November 20, 1858, 738; Nevins and Thomas, *Diary of Strong*, October 22, 1857, 2:357.

21. Quoted in Reynolds, *Whitman's America*, 109.

22. "Questionable Progress of the Age," *De Bow's Review* 16 (April 1854): 369; George Fitzhugh, *Sociology for the South: or, The Failure of Free Society* (Richmond: A. Morris, 1854), 201.

23. J. D. B. De Bow, "Cannibals All, or Slaves without Masters," *De Bow's Review* 22 (May 1857): 546.

24. Quoted in Reynolds, *Whitman's America*, 140.

25. Malcolm Cowley, ed., *Walt Whitman's* Leaves of Grass (New York: Viking, 1959), 16; Tocqueville quoted in Aurelian Craiutu and Jeremy Jennings, "The Third *Democracy*: Tocqueville's Views of America After 1840," *American Political Science Review* 98 (August 2004): 399.

26. Quoted in R. Kent Newmyer, *The Supreme Court Under Marshall and Taney*, 2nd ed. (Wheeling, Ill.: Harlan Davidson, 2006), 93.

27. On the Dred Scott case, see Don E. Fehrenbacher, *The Dred Scott Case: Its Significance in American Law and Politics* (New York: Oxford University Press, 1978).

28. *Dred Scott v. Sandford*, 60 U.S. 404–5 (1857).

29. *Richmond Enquirer*, March 10, 1857.

30. *CG*, 35th Congress, 1st Session (March 3, 1858): 941.

31. *New York Tribune*, March 11, 1857.

32. Ibid.

33. Quoted in Carwardine, *Evangelicals and Politics*, 280.

34. Quoted in David M. Potter, *The Impending Crisis, 1848–1861* (New York: Harper & Row, 1976), 281.

35. Quoted in Vincent Harding, *There Is a River: The Black Struggle for Freedom in America* (New York: Harcourt Brace, 1981), 203.

36. Quoted in ibid.

37. Quoted in John Sherman, *John Sherman's Recollections of Forty Years in the House, Senate and Cabinet* (Chicago: Warner, 1895), 1:149.

38. Quoted in Thomas E. Schott, *Alexander H. Stephens of Georgia: A Biography* (Baton Rouge: Louisiana State University Press, 1988), 245.

39. Both quotes in Robert W. Johannsen, *Stephen A. Douglas* (New York: Oxford University Press, 1973), 590–91, 586.

40. Quoted in Schott, *Stephens*, 251.

41. Quoted in Ernest Lee Tuveson, *Redeemer Nation: The Idea of America's Millennial Role* (Chicago: University of Chicago Press, 1968), 71.

42. Quoted in Jan C. Dawson, "The Puritan and the Cavalier: The South's Perception of Contrasting Traditions," *Journal of Southern History* 44 (November 1978): 600.

43. Bangs quoted in Mark A. Noll, *America's God: From Jonathan Edwards to Abraham Lincoln* (New York: Oxford University Press, 2002), 344; Hildreth quoted in Allen C. Guelzo, "'The Science of Duty': Moral Philosophy and the Epistemology of Science in Nineteenth-Century America," in *Evangelicals and Science in Historical Perspective*, ed. David N. Livingstone, D. G. Hart, and Mark A. Noll (New York: Oxford University Press, 1999), 281.

44. Quotes from Long, *Revival of 1857–58*, 36.

45. Quotes from ibid., 33.

46. Quoted in ibid., 44.

47. Quoted in ibid., 105–6.

48. Quoted in ibid., 48.

49. Quoted in Richard Carwardine, *Evangelicals and Politics in Antebellum America* (New Haven: Yale University Press, 1993), 293.

50. Quoted in Schott, *Stephens*, 255.

51. Douglas quoted in David Herbert Donald, *Lincoln* (New York: Simon & Schuster, 1995), 209; platform quoted in William E. Gienapp, "Nativism and the Creation of a Republican Majority in the North Before the Civil War," *Journal of American History* 72 (December 1985): 548.

52. *CW* 2:461–62.

53. See Allen C. Guelzo, *Lincoln and Douglas: The Debates That Defined America* (New York: Simon & Schuster, 2009).

54. Quoted in Hans L. Trefousse, *Carl Schurz: A Biography* (Knoxville: University of Tennessee Press, 1982), 71.

55. Quoted in Donald, *Lincoln*, 214. Donald has an excellent discussion of the debates, 211–27.

56. Quotes in William S. McFeely, *Frederick Douglass* (New York: Touchstone, 1992), 188.

57. *CW* 1:369.

58. Harold Holzer, ed., *The Lincoln-Douglas Debates* (New York: Fordham University Press, 2004), 258.

59. *CW* 3:220.

60. Holzer, *Lincoln-Douglas*, 35.

61. Quoted in Craiutu and Jennings, "The Third *Democracy*," 401, 402.

62. Quoted in Eugene D. Genovese, "Religion in the Collapse of the American Union," in *Religion and the American Civil War*, ed. Randall M. Miller, Harry S. Stout, and Charles Reagan Wilson (New York: Oxford University Press, 1998), 74.

CHAPTER 7: THE BOATMAN

1. Quoted in William S. McFeely, *Frederick Douglass* (New York: Touchstone, 1992), 197; see also Frederick Douglass, *Admiration and Ambivalence: Frederick Douglass and John Brown* (New York: Gilder Lehrman Institute of American History, 2005).

2. See Catherine Clinton, *Harriet Tubman: The Road to Freedom* (Boston: Little, Brown, 2004).

3. Brown quote in Jean M. Humez, *Harriet Tubman: The Life and the Life Stories* (Madison: University of Wisconsin Press, 2003), 32; Mary Thacker Higginson, ed. *Letters and Journal of Thomas Wentworth Higginson, 1846–1906* (Boston: Houghton Mifflin, 1921), 81.

4. See Stephen B. Oates, *Our Fiery Trial: Abraham Lincoln, John Brown, and the Civil War Era* (Amherst: University of Massachusetts Press, 1979); David S. Reynolds, *John Brown, Abolitionist: The Man Who Killed Slavery, Sparked the Civil War, and Seeded Civil Rights* (New York: Knopf, 2005).

5. Quoted in Reynolds, *John Brown*, 354.

6. Quoted in Steven Mintz, *Moralists and Modernizers: America's Pre–Civil War Reformers* (Baltimore: Johns Hopkins University Press, 1995), 139.

7. George Templeton Strong, *The Diary of George Templeton Strong*, ed. Allan Nevins and Milton Halsey Thomas, (New York: Macmillan, 1952), December 2, 1859, 2:473; Edward Arlington Robinson, "John Brown," *Collected Poems* (1921), http://www.bartleby.com.

8. "Insurrection at Harper's Ferry," *Harper's*, October 29, 1859, 690.

9. *CW* 3:503, 541.

10. Quoted in Clinton, *Harriet Tubman*, 134.

11. *Raleigh Register*, December 3, 1859, Secession Era Editorial Project, Furman University, http://history.furman.edu/editorials.

12. *Frankfort Yeoman* quoted in Oswald Garrison Villard, *John Brown: A Biography, 1800–1859* (Garden City, N.Y.: Doubleday, 1929), 502.

13. Both quotes in David M. Potter, *The Impending Crisis, 1848–1861* (New York: Harper & Row, 1976), 383, 384.

14. *Charleston Mercury*, November 1, 1859, Secession Era Editorials Project, Furman University, http://history.furman.edu/editorials.

15. Quoted in Potter, *Impending Crisis*, 390.

16. Whitman, "Rulers Strictly out of the Masses," http://www.bartleby.com.

17. Quoted in David Herbert Donald, *Lincoln* (New York: Simon & Schuster, 1995), 235.

18. Much of the foregoing biographical material on Lincoln derives from Donald, *Lincoln*. Other helpful Lincoln biographies include Richard Carwardine, *Lincoln: A Life of Purpose and Power* (New York: Knopf, 2006) and Allen C. Guelzo, *Abraham Lincoln: Redeemer President* (Grand Rapids, Mich.: Eerdmans, 1999).

19. Quoted in Donald, *Lincoln*, 239.

20. "The Great Union Meeting at New York," *Harper's*, January 7, 1860, 2.

21. *CW* 3:550.

22. *CW* 4:25.

23. Quoted in Donald, *Lincoln*, 247.

24. Quoted in Thomas E. Schott, *Alexander H. Stephens of Georgia: A Biography* (Baton Rouge: Louisiana State University Press, 1988), 289.

25. "The Wide-Awake Parade," *Harper's*, October 13, 1860.

26. Quotes in Richard Carwardine, *Evangelicals and Politics in Antebellum America* (New Haven: Yale University Press, 1993), 301, 302.

27. Quotes in Robert P. Swierenga, "Ethnoreligious Political Behavior in the Mid-Nineteenth Century: Voting, Values, Cultures," in *Religion and American Politics: From the Colonial Period to the 1980s*, ed. Mark A. Noll (New York: Oxford University Press, 1990), 159.

28. Quoted in Guelzo, *Redeemer President*, 247.

29. Quoted in Charles B. Dew, *Apostles of Disunion: Southern Secession Commissioners and the Causes of the Civil War* (Charlottesville: University Press of Virginia, 2001), 53.

30. First quote in Guelzo, *Redeemer President*, 250; *Charleston Mercury*, January 21, 1861.

31. Quotes in Guelzo, *Redeemer President*, 247.

32. Quotes in Schott, *Stephens*, 299, 301.

33. Lincoln used this phrase in his inaugural address on March 4, 1861.

34. Quoted in C. C. Goen, "Broken Churches, Broken Nation: Regional Religion and North-South Alienation in Antebellum America," *Church History* 52 (March 1983): 33

35. Lucretia Mott, "Righteousness Exalteth a Nation," June 6, 1860, http://www.qhpress .org/quakerpages/qhoa/mott.htm. The quote is from Proverbs 14:34.

36. "The Relative Political Status of the North and South," *De Bow's Review* 22 (February 1857): 119.

37. "Editor's Table," *Southern Literary Messenger* 31 (July 1860): 70; L. W. Spratt of South Carolina, quoted in *New York Times*, March 14, 1861.

38. First quote in Dew, *Apostles of Disunion*, 43; second quote in William W. Freehling, *The Road to Disunion*, vol. 2, *Secessionists Triumphant, 1854–1861* (New York: Oxford University Press, 2007), 267.

39. First quote in John B. Adger and John L. Girardeau, eds., *The Collected Writings of James Henley Thornwell*, vol. 4 (Richmond: Presbyterian Committee of Publication, 1873), 550, available on Google Books; second quote in James O. Farmer Jr., *The Metaphysical Confederacy: James Henley Thornwell and the Synthesis of Southern Values* (Macon, Ga.: Mercer University Press, 1999; first published in 1986), 182.

40. Washington, "The Races of Men," *Southern Literary Messenger* 30 (April 1860): 254.

41. See, for example, "The Relative Political Status of the North and South," *De Bow's Review* 22 (February 1857): 114–29; "The South and Progress," ibid. 26 (February 1859): 214–16.

42. "The Great Issue: Our Relations to It," *Southern Literary Messenger* 32 (March 1861): 173.

43. "Progress of the Republic," *De Bow's Review* 17 (August 1854): 129.

44. First quote in "Disfederation of the States," *Southern Literary Messenger* 32 (February 1861): 119; second quote in "The Difference of Race Between the Northern and Southern People," ibid. (June 1861): 401, 404.

45. Quoted in Schott, *Stephens*, 296.

46. Quoted in Eric Foner, *Free Soil, Free Labor, Free Men: The Ideology of the Republican Party Before the Civil War* (New York: Oxford University Press, 1970), 41.

47. Quoted in Doris Kearns Goodwin, *Team of Rivals: The Political Genius of Abraham Lincoln* (New York: Simon & Schuster, 2005), 274.

48. Quoted in Thomas B. Alexander, "The Civil War as Institutional Fulfillment," *Journal of Southern History* 47 (February 1981): 16.

49. "The Late Election," *Douglass' Monthly*, December 1860, in *FD:SSW*, 415.

CHAPTER 8: THE TUG COMES

1. Quoted in David S. Reynolds, *Walt Whitman's America: A Cultural Biography* (New York: Knopf, 1995), 406.

2. James Buchanan, "Fourth Annual Message to Congress on the State of the Union," December 3, 1860, American Presidency Project, http://www.presidency.ucsb.edu; Stephens

quoted in Thomas E. Schott, *Alexander H. Stephens of Georgia: A Biography* (Baton Rouge: Louisiana State University Press, 1988), 316.

3. "Editor's Table," *Southern Literary Messenger* 31 (December 1860): 468.

4. Holcombe, "The Alternative: A Separate Nationality, or the Africanization of the South," ibid. 32 (February 1861): 81.

5. Both quotes in Charles B. Dew, *Apostles of Disunion: Southern Secession Commissioners and the Causes of the Civil War* (Charlottesville: University Press of Virginia, 2001), 12.

6. Quoted in ibid., 29.

7. Quoted in David M. Potter, *The Impending Crisis, 1848–1861* (New York: Harper & Row, 1976), 549–50.

8. *CW* 4:149–50.

9. First quote in *CG*, 36th Congress, 2nd Session (January 21, 1861): 487; second quote in *A Belle of the Fifties: Memoirs of Mrs.* [Virginia] *Clay* [-Clopton], *of Alabama, Covering Social and Political Life in Washington and the South, 1853–66* (New York: Doubleday, Page, 1905), 147–48, http://docsouth.unc.edu/fpn/clay/clay.html#clay138.

10. Quoted in Schott, *Stephens*, 308, 309.

11. Quoted in ibid., 321.

12. Quoted in ibid., 326.

13. Quoted in Carol K. Bleser, "The Marriage of Varina Howell and Jefferson Davis: 'I gave the best and all my life to a girdled tree,'" *Journal of Southern History* 65 (February 1999): 18.

14. Quoted in Gary W. Gallagher, ed., *Lee the Soldier* (Lincoln: University of Nebraska Press, 1996), 302.

15. Quoted in Marc Egnal, "Rethinking the Secession of the Lower South: The Clash of Two Groups," *Civil War History* 50 (September 2004): 288.

16. The full text of the "Cornerstone" speech may be found in Henry Cleveland, *Alexander H. Stephens, in Public and Private: With Letters and Speeches, Before, During, and Since the War* (Philadelphia: National Publishing, 1866), 717–29.

17. Quoted in Schott, *Stephens*, 334.

18. James D. Richardson, ed., *A Compilation of the Messages and Papers of the Confederacy* (Nashville: U.S. Publishing, 1905), 1:67.

19. See Schott, *Stephens*, 317.

20. Both quotes in Potter, *Impending Crisis*, 506.

21. Quoted in ibid., 511.

22. Both quotes in Bertram Wyatt-Brown, "Church, Honor, and Secession," in *Religion and the American Civil War*, ed. Randall M. Miller, Harry S. Stout, and Charles Reagan Wilson (New York: Oxford University Press, 1998), 100.

23. Both quotes in Potter, *Impending Crisis*, 508.

24. Quoted in Schott, *Stephens*, 310.

25. "The Non-Slaveholders of the South: Their Interest in the Present Sectional Controversy Identical with That of the Slaveholders," *De Bow's Review* 30 (January 1861): 73. Italics in original.

26. Ibid., 76.

27. Quoted in Leon F. Litwack, *Been in the Storm So Long: The Aftermath of Slavery* (New York: Random House, 1979), 3.

28. Quoted in David B. Chesebrough, *Clergy Dissent in the Old South, 1830–1865* (Carbondale: Southern Illinois University Press, 1996), 16.

29. Quoted in Mitchell Snay, *Gospel of Disunion: Religion and Separatism in the Antebellum South* (New York: Cambridge University Press, 1993), 173.

30. For the full text of Palmer's sermon, see http://www.civilwarcauses,org/palmer.htm. For a discussion of the impact of the sermon, see Snay, *Gospel of Disunion*, 177–79, and Richard T. Hughes, "A Civic Theology for the South: The Case of Benjamin M. Palmer," *Journal of Church and State* 25, no. 3 (1983): 447–67.

31. Quoted in Snay, *Gospel of Disunion*, 179.

32. "Reconstruction," *Harper's*, March 9, 1861, 146.

33. Ibid.

34. Wendell Phillips, *Speeches, Lectures, and Letters* (Boston: Lee and Shepard, 1894), 1:374.

35. Quoted in Richard Carwardine, *Evangelicals and Politics in Antebellum America* (New Haven: Yale University Press, 1993), 311.

36. *CG*, 37th Congress, 1st Session, Appendix (July 4, 1861): 2–3.

37. Ibid.

38. Quoted in David Herbert Donald, *Lincoln* (New York: Simon & Schuster, 1995), 269.

39. First quote in ibid.; second quote, *CW* 4:149–50.

40. Quoted in Donald, *Lincoln*, 272.

41. *CW* 4:192.

42. *CW* 4:192, 195–96, 237.

43. *CW* 4:240.

44. "The City of Washington and the Capitol," *Harper's*, December 15, 1860, 786.

45. Quoted in Doris Kearns Goodwin, *Team of Rivals: The Political Genius of Abraham Lincoln* (New York: Simon & Schuster, 2005), 319.

46. *CW* 4:271.

47. Quotes in Donald, *Lincoln*, 284.

48. "The Prayer at Sumter," *Harper's*, January 26, 1861, 49.

49. "Wanted—A Policy!" *New York Times*, April 3, 1861.

50. Quoted in Allen C. Guelzo, *Abraham Lincoln: Redeemer President* (Grand Rapids, Mich.: Eerdmans, 1999), 266.

51. *CW* 4:323.

52. C. Vann Woodward and Elisabeth Muhlenfeld, eds., *The Private Mary Chesnut: The Unpublished War Diaries* (New York: Oxford University Press, 1984), 57.

53. Quoted in Gamaliel Bradford Jr., "Robert Toombs," *Atlantic Monthly* 112 (August 1913): 215.

54. Quoted in Donald, *Lincoln*, 293.

55. Revelation 20:9, 21:1.

56. Quoted in Philip Callow, *From Noon to Starry Night: A Life of Walt Whitman* (Chicago: Ivan R. Dee, 1992), 282.

CHAPTER 9: JUST CAUSES

1. Whitman, "First O Songs for a Prelude," *Leaves of Grass*, ed. Harold W. Blodgett and Sculley Bradley (New York: New York University Press, 1965), 281.

2. First quote in James M. McPherson, *Ordeal by Fire*, vol. 2, *The Civil War* (New York: Knopf, 1982), 149; second and third quotes in Louis Menand, *The Metaphysical Club: A Story of Ideas in America* (New York: Farrar, Straus and Giroux, 2001), 31, 32.

3. Quoted in Garry Wills, *Head and Heart: American Christianities* (New York: Penguin, 2007), 323.

4. "War as a Schoolmaster," *Harper's*, October 19, 1861, 658; "Our History of the War," *Scientific American*, May 11, 1861, 297.

5. Quoted in McPherson, *Ordeal*, 149.

6. First quote in Charles P. Roland, *An American Iliad: The Story of the Civil War*, 2nd ed. (Lexington: University Press of Kentucky, 2004; first published in 1991), 39; second quote in Frank Moore, ed., *The Rebellion Record: A Diary of American Events* (New York: G. P. Putnam, 1861), 1:324.

7. First quote in James M. McPherson, *For Cause and Comrades: Why Men Fought in the Civil War* (New York: Oxford University Press, 1997), 20; second quote in Chandra Manning, *What This Cruel War Was Over: Soldiers, Slavery, and the Civil War* (New York: Knopf, 2007), 28.

8. See Roy Morris Jr., *Lighting Out for the Territory: How Samuel Clemens Headed West and Became Mark Twain* (New York: Simon & Schuster, 2010), 24–34.

9. First quote in McPherson, *Cause and Comrades*, 112; second quote in McPherson, "'For a Vast Future Also': Lincoln and the Millennium," Jefferson Lecture, March 27, 2000, http://www.neh.gov/whoweare/mcpherson/speech.html.

10. Quotes in Bertram Wyatt-Brown, "Church, Honor, and Secession," in *Religion and the American Civil War*, ed. Randall M. Miller, Harry S. Stout, and Charles Reagan Wilson (New York: Oxford University Press, 1998), 103; Reid Mitchell, "Christian Soldiers? Perfecting the Confederacy," in ibid., 302.

11. First quote in McPherson, *Cause and Comrades*, 19; second quote in Gerald F. Linderman, *Embattled Courage: The Experience of Combat in the American Civil War* (New York: Free Press, 1987), 82.

12. First quote in Douglass, "Sudden Revolution in Northern Sentiment," *Douglass' Monthly*, May 1861, in FD:SSW, 445; second quote in Douglass, "The Decision of the Hour," *Douglass' Monthly*, July 1861, in ibid., 463.

13. All quotes from Joan D. Hedrick, *Harriet Beecher Stowe: A Life* (New York: Oxford University Press, 1994), 300.

14. Mark Grimsley and Todd D. Miller, ed. *The Union Must Stand: The Civil War Diary of John Quincy Adams Campbell, Fifth Iowa Volunteer Infantry* (Knoxville: University of Tennessee Press, 2000), xvii.

15. Quoted in Kurt O. Berends, "'Wholesome Reading Purifies and Elevates the Man': The Religious Military Press in the Confederacy," in Miller, Stout, and Reagan, *Religion and the American Civil War*, 144.

16. Ellen Glasgow, *The Battle-Ground* (Tuscaloosa: University of Alabama Press, 2002; originally published in 1902), 284; Margaret Mitchell, *Gone with the Wind* (New York: Macmillan, 1936), 231.

17. For the discussion of Confederate politics, I relied on George C. Rable, *The Confederate Republic: A Revolution Against Politics* (Chapel Hill: University of North Carolina Press, 1994) and Emory M. Thomas, *The Confederate Nation, 1861–1865* (New York: Harper & Row, 1979).

18. First quote in McPherson, *Ordeal by Fire*; second quote in Thomas E. Schott, *Alexander H. Stephens of Georgia: A Biography* (Baton Rouge: Louisiana State University Press, 1988), 356; third quote in Woodward and Muhlenfeld, eds., *Private Mary Chesnut*, 166.

19. Quoted in Georgia Lee Tatum, *Disloyalty in the Confederacy* (Lincoln: University of Nebraska Press, 2000), 111.

20. See McPherson, *Ordeal by Fire*, 181–82, for discussion of conscription issue; C. Vann Woodward, ed., *Mary Chesnut's Civil War* (New Haven: Yale University Press, 1993; first published in 1981), 773.

21. Quoted in McPherson, *Ordeal by Fire*, 182.

22. A good discussion of tactics and weaponry is Earl J. Hess, *The Union Soldier in Battle: Enduring the Ordeal* (Lawrence: University Press of Kansas, 1997), especially chapter 1.

23. Quoted in Heather Cox Richardson, *The Greatest Nation of the Earth: Republican Economic Policies During the Civil War* (Cambridge: Harvard University Press, 1997), 8.

24. For a good summary of northern economic advantages, see Orville Vernon Burton, *The Age of Lincoln* (New York: Hill and Wang, 2007), 142–45.

25. Bates in Martin E. Marty, *The War-Time Lincoln and the Ironic Tradition*, Annual Robert Fortenbaugh Memorial Lecture (Gettysburg, Pa.: Gettysburg College, 2000), 21; second quote in David Herbert Donald, *Lincoln* (New York: Simon & Schuster, 1995), 425; third quote in Allen C. Guelzo, *Abraham Lincoln: Redeemer President* (Grand Rapids, Mich.: Eerdmans, 1999), 274.

26. *CW* 6:260–269.

27. *CW* 7:512.

28. *CW* 4:438.

29. Sherman to Thomas Ewing Jr., May 23, 1861, in *Home Letters of General Sherman*, ed. M. A. DeWolfe Howe (New York: Charles Scribner's Sons, 1909), 198, available on Google Books.

30. On the construction of the Union army, see Dora L. Costa and Matthew E. Kahn, "Cowards and Heroes: Group Loyalty in the American Civil War," *Quarterly Journal of Economics* (May 2003): 519–48.

31. See Guelzo, *Redeemer President*, 292–93.

32. See Donald, *Lincoln*, 297–98; Guelzo, *Redeemer President*, 272, 280.

33. *CW* 7:281–82.

34. "Our Institutions on Their Trial," *Harper's*, August 3, 1861, 482.

35. *CW* 4:507; on the border states generally, see McPherson, *Ordeal by Fire*, 150–62.

36. Ballou's letter may be found at http://www.pbs.org/civilwar/war/ballou_letter.html.

37. Lincoln quoted in James M. McPherson, *Tried by War: Abraham Lincoln as Commander in Chief* (New York: Penguin, 2008), 39; *New York Tribune*, June 26, 1861.

38. For battle details, unless otherwise noted, I relied on E. B. Long, *The Civil War Day by Day: An Almanac, 1861–1865* (Garden City, N.Y.: Doubleday, 1971) and Russell F. Weigley, *A Great Civil War: A Military and Political History, 1861–1865* (Bloomington: Indiana University Press, 2000). I also used the works cited above by Orville Vernon Burton, David Herbert Donald, Allen C. Guelzo, Earl J. Hess, Gerald F. Linderman, James M. McPherson, and Emory M. Thomas.

39. Quoted in James I. Robertson Jr., *Stonewall Jackson: The Man, the Soldier, the Legend* (New York: Macmillan, 1997), 264. Although there are many biographies of Jackson, Robertson's is the definitive work.

40. Both quotes in Thomas, *Confederate Nation*, 117, 118.

41. Quoted in Mitchell Snay, *Gospel of Disunion: Religion and Separatism in the Antebellum South* (Cambridge: Cambridge University Press, 1993), 195.

42. First quote in Thomas, *Confederate Nation*, 118; second quote in George Templeton Strong, *The Diary of George Templeton Strong*, ed. Allen Nevins and Milton Halsey Thomas,

(New York: Macmillan, 1952), July 22, 1861, 3:169; third quote in Guelzo, *Redeemer President*, 295; last quote in "The Lesson of Defeat," *Harper's*, August 10, 1861, 499.

43. "The Necessity of War," *Harper's*, August 17, 1861, 514.

CHAPTER 10: SHILOH AWAKENING

1. I drew biographical details from the following works, unless otherwise noted: William S. McFeely, *Grant: A Biography* (New York: Norton, 2002; first published in 1981); Brooks D. Simpson, *Ulysses S. Grant: Triumph over Adversity* (Boston: Houghton Mifflin, 2000); Jean Edward Smith, *Grant* (New York: Simon & Schuster, 2001). Grant's memoirs also provided valuable insights: U. S. Grant, *Personal Memoirs of U.S. Grant* (New York: Charles L. Webster, 1972; first published in 1886).

2. Quoted in Earl J. Hess, *The Union Soldier in Battle: Enduring the Ordeal of Combat* (Lawrence: University Press of Kansas, 1997), 16.

3. Quoted in Frank Moore, ed., *The Rebellion Record: A Diary of American Events* (New York: G. P. Putnam, 1864), 3:431, available on Google Books.

4. Quoted in David A. Nichols, *Lincoln and the Indians: Civil War Policy and Politics* (Columbia: University of Missouri Press, 1978), 48.

5. *CG*, 37th Congress, 2nd Session, Appendix, 3.

6. Gari Carter, ed., *Troubled State: Civil War Journals of Franklin Archibald Dick* (Kirksville, Mo.: Truman State University Press, 2008), January 26, 1862, 50; February 17, 1862, 60.

7. "The Beginning of the End," *Harper's*, March 1, 1862, 130; quoted in Allen C. Guelzo, *Abraham Lincoln: Redeemer President* (Grand Rapids, Mich.: Eerdmans, 1999), 302.

8. Grant, *Memoirs*, 188.

9. First quote in Emory M. Thomas, *The Confederate Nation, 1861–1865* (New York: Harper & Row, 1979), 147; second quote in Morgan Ebenezer Wescott, *Civil War Letters, 1861 to 1865: Written by a Boy in Blue to His Mother* (Mora, Minn.: privately published, 1909), 5.

10. Quoted in Bruce Catton, "The Generalship of Ulysses S. Grant Defended," in *Grant, Lee, Lincoln, and the Radicals: Essays on Civil War Leadership*, ed. Grady McWhiney (Evanston, Ill.: Northwestern University Press, 1973), 10.

11. First quote in Winston Groom, *Vicksburg, 1863* (New York: Knopf, 2009), 265; second quote in E. B. Long, *The Civil War Day by Day: An Almanac, 1861–1865* (New York: Doubleday, 1971), 196.

12. First quote, Sherman to his wife (Ellen Ewing Sherman), April 11, 1862, in *Home Letters of General Sherman*, ed. M. A. DeWolfe Howe (New York: Charles Scribner's Sons, 1909), 222; second quote in Chandra Manning, *What This Cruel War Was Over: Soldiers, Slavery, and the Civil War* (New York: Knopf, 2007), 55.

13. Derived from a compilation of soldiers' accounts: Ambrose Bierce, "What I Saw of Shiloh," in Bierce, *Civil War Stories* (Mineola, N.Y.: Dover, 1994), 4–17; Corydon Edward Foote, *With Sherman to the Sea: A Drummer's Story of the Civil War* (New York: John Day, 1960), 35; Grant, *Memoirs*, 211; Sam R. Watkins, *"Co. Aytch": A Confederate Memoir of the Civil War* (New York: Touchstone, 2003; first published in 1990), 25–28; William T. Sherman quoted in Hess, *Union Soldier*, 1.

14. First quote in Richard Barksdale Harwell, ed., *Kate: The Journal of a Confederate Nurse* (Baton Rouge: Louisiana State University Press, 1987), 14; second quote in Charles P.

Roland, *An American Iliad: The Story of the Civil War*, 2nd ed. (Lexington: University Press of Kentucky, 2004, first published in 1991), 65.

15. Olynthus B. Clark, ed., *Downing's Civil War Diary* (Des Moines: Iowa State Department of History and Archives, 1916), 41.

16. Watkins, *"Co. Aytch,"* 27.

17. Quotes in Ellen Glasgow, *The Battle-Ground* (Tuscaloosa: University of Alabama Press, 2002; originally published in 1902), 175, 307, 315; Drew Gilpin Faust, *This Republic of Suffering: Death and the American Civil War* (New York: Knopf, 2008), 58.

18. Quoted in Gerald Linderman, *Embattled Courage: The Experience of Combat in the American Civil War* (New York: Free Press, 1987), 117.

19. Quoted in Hess, *Union Soldier*, 10.

20. Quoted in ibid., 16.

21. First quote in ibid., 137; second quote in Faust, *Suffering*, 37.

22. Quoted in Linderman, *Embattled Courage*, 101.

23. Quoted in ibid., 217.

24. Quoted in Manning, *Cruel War*, 58; Elisha Franklin Paxton, *Memoir and Memorials* (privately published, 1905), 74, available on Google Books.

25. First quote in Faust, *Suffering*, 37; second quote in Hess, *Union Soldier*, 1.

26. First quote in Grant, *Memoirs*, 218; second quote in John T. Trowbridge, *The Desolate South, 1865–1866: A Picture of the Battlefields and of the Devastated Confederacy*, ed. Gordon Carroll (Boston: Little, Brown, 1956), 134.

27. Theresa M. Collins and Lisa Gitelman, eds., *Thomas Edison and Modern America: A Brief History with Documents* (Boston: Bedford/St. Martin's, 2002), 5–6.

28. Quoted in Faust, *Suffering*, 188.

29. *CW* 5:403–4.

30. Herman Melville's poem, "Shiloh: A Requiem" (1862), may be accessed at: http://www.poetryfoundation.org.

31. Quoted in Linderman, *Embattled Courage,* 159.

32. Margaret Mitchell, *Gone with the Wind* (New York: Macmillan, 1936), 212.

33. First quote in Glasgow, *Battle-Ground*, 291; second quote in Hess, *Union Soldier*, 124.

34. Henry Timrod, "Two Armies," in Timrod, *Poems of Henry Timrod: Memoir and Portrait* (Boston: Houghton Mifflin, 1899), 158–60, available on Google Books; last quote in Drew Gilpin Faust, "Altars of Sacrifice: Confederate Women and the Narrative of War," *Journal of American History* 76 (March 1990): 1207.

35. First quote, T. Buchanan Read, "The Brave at Home," in *The Rebellion Record: A Diary of American Events*, ed. Frank Moore (New York: G. P. Putnam, 1861), 1:51; second quote in Drew Gilpin Faust, "Altars of Sacrifice" 1211; third quote in Jeffrey C. Lowe and Sam Hodges, eds., *Letters to Amanda: The Civil War Letters of Marion Hill Fitzpatrick, Army of Northern Virginia* (Macon, Ga.: Mercer University Press, 1998), May 8, 1862, 3.

36. Quoted in Faust, "Altars of Sacrifice," 1217–18, 1219.

37. C. Vann Woodward and Elisabeth Muhlenfeld, eds., *The Private Mary Chesnut: The Unpublished Civil War Diaries* (New York: Oxford University Press, 1984), August 29, 1861, 145.

38. Quoted in Giselle Roberts, "The Confederate Belle: The Belle Ideal, Patriotic Womanhood, and Wartime Reality in Louisiana and Mississippi, 1861–1865," *Louisiana History* 43 (Spring 2003): 207.

39. Quoted in James Marten, *Children for the Union: The War Spirit on the Northern Home Front* (Chicago: Ivan R. Dee, 2004), 65.

40. Quoted in ibid., 59.

41. Quoted in Linderman, *Embattled Courage*, 108.

42. Both quotes in ibid., 83, 87.

43. Lowe and Hodges, *Fitzpatrick*, June 8, 1865, 210.

44. "The Second Division at Shiloh," *Harper's New Monthly Magazine*, May 1864, 830.

45. Robert Garth Scott, ed., *Fallen Leaves: The Civil War Letters of Major Henry Livermore Abbott* (Kent, Ohio: Kent State University Press, 1991), December 20, 1862, 160.

46. Watkins, *"Co. Aytch,"* 188.

47. Hess, *Union Soldier*, 7.

48. Ambrose Bierce, "Chickamauga," in Bierce, *Civil War Stories* (Mineola, N.Y.: Dover, 1994), 45.

49. Watkins, *"Co. Aytch,"* 64.

CHAPTER 11: BORN IN A DAY

1. Fanny Burdock, interviewed by the Federal Writers Project and quoted in Allan Gurganus, *Oldest Living Confederate Widow Tells All* (New York: Knopf, 1989), xiii–xiv.

2. Nat Love, *The Life and Adventures of Nat Love* (electronic ed., 1999; first published in 1907), 14, http://docsouth.unc.edu/neh/natlove/natlove,html#nlove14.

3. "The Steamer *Planter* and Her Captor," *Harper's*, June 14, 1862, 372–73.

4. Quoted in Chandra Manning, *What This Cruel War Was Over: Soldiers, Slavery, and the Civil War* (New York: Knopf, 2007), 45.

5. Quoted in ibid., 50.

6. Lincoln quote in Allen C. Guelzo, *Abraham Lincoln: Redeemer President* (Grand Rapids, Mich.: Eerdmans, 1999), 330; Wade quote in David Herbert Donald, *Lincoln* (New York: Simon & Schuster, 1995), 317.

7. "Slavery and the War," *Harper's*, August 24, 1861, 530.

8. *CG*, 37th Congress, 2nd Session (March 6, 1862), 1102.

9. Quoted in Allen C. Guelzo, *Lincoln's Emancipation Proclamation: The End of Slavery in America* (New York: Simon & Schuster, 2004), 19.

10. Quoted in Emory Upton, *Military Policy of the United States* (Washington: GPO, 1916), April 9, 1862, 297.

11. Walker Freeman's notes on the Peninsula Campaign appear in Keith D. Dickson's forthcoming book, *Keeping Southern Memories Alive: Douglas Southall Freeman and Identity in the Modern South* (Baton Rouge: Louisiana State University Press, 2011).

12. Quoted in Donald, *Lincoln*, 357.

13. For details on the life of Robert E. Lee, unless otherwise noted, I relied on Michael Fellman, *The Making of Robert E. Lee* (Baltimore: Johns Hopkins University Press, 2003); Douglas Southall Freeman, *R. E. Lee: A Biography*, 4 vols. (New York: Scribner's, 1934–35); Elizabeth Brown Pryor, *Reading the Man: A Portrait of Robert E. Lee Through His Private Letters* (New York: Penguin, 2008); Emory M. Thomas, *Robert E. Lee: A Biography* (New York: Norton, 1997).

14. Stephen Vincent Benét, "Army of Northern Virginia," http://oldpoetry.com/opoem/38925-Stephen-Vincent-Benet-Army-Of-Northern-Virginia.

15. Quotes in Pryor, *Lee*, 285.

16. Quoted in ibid., 288.

17. Quoted in Elizabeth Brown Pryor, "Robert E. Lee's 'Severest Struggle,'" *American Heritage* 58 (Winter 2008): 23.

18. Sam R. Watkins, *"Co. Aytch": A Confederate Memoir of the Civil War* (New York: Touchstone, 2003), 11.

19. Quoted in Fellman, *Lee*, 115.

20. Quoted in James I. Robertson Jr., "Stonewall Jackson: A 'Pious Blue-Eyed Killer'?" in *New Perspectives on the Civil War: Myths and Realities of the National Conflict*, ed. John Y. Simon and Michael E. Stevens (Lanham, Md.: Rowman & Littlefield, 2002), 86.

21. Quoted in ibid.

22. First quote in John S. Salmon, "Land Operations in Virginia in 1862," in *Virginia At War, 1862*, ed. William C. Davis and James I. Robertson Jr. (Lexington: University Press of Kentucky, 2007), 10; second quote in Doris Kearns Goodwin, *Team of Rivals: The Political Genius of Abraham Lincoln* (New York: Simon & Schuster, 2005), 443.

23. Olmsted compiled his observations from the Peninsula Campaign in a memoir. It is most recently available in Laura L. Behling, ed., *Hospital Transports: A Memoir of the Sick and Wounded from the Peninsula of Virginia in the Summer of 1862* (Albany: State University of New York Press, 2005; first published in 1863), 115.

24. Quoted in Stephen W. Sears, *Landscape Turned Red: The Battle of Antietam* (Boston: Houghton Mifflin, 1983), 42.

25. Quoted in Guelzo, *Emancipation Proclamation*, 120.

26. Stephen W. Sears, ed., *The Civil War Papers of George B. McClellan: Selected Correspondence, 1860–1865* (Cambridge, Mass.: Da Capo Press, 1992), 239.

27. Quoted in Stephen W. Sears, "Getting Right with Robert E. Lee," *American Heritage* 42 (May/June 1991): 63.

28. Jeffrey C. Lowe and Sam Hodges, eds., *Letters to Amanda: The Civil War Letters of Marion Hill Fitzpatrick, Army of Northern Virginia* (Macon, Ga.: Mercer University Press, 1998), September 2, 1862, 26.

29. Quoted in Joseph L. Harsh, *Taken at the Flood: Robert E. Lee and Confederate Strategy in the Maryland Campaign of 1862* (Kent, Ohio: Kent State University Press, 1999), 60.

30. First quote in Guelzo, *Redeemer President*, 310; second quote in James M. McPherson, *Tried by War: Abraham Lincoln as Commander in Chief* (New York: Penguin, 2008), 125.

31. John T. Trowbridge, *The Desolate South, 1865–1866: A Picture of the Battlefields and of the Devastated Confederacy*, ed. Gordon Carroll (Boston: Little, Brown, 1956), 22.

32. Quoted in Douglas Southall Freeman, *Lee's Lieutenants: A Study in Command* (New York: Scribner, 1998; abridged by Stephen W. Sears from original published in 1934), 362.

33. Quoted in Fellman, *Lee*, 301.

34. First quote in Alfred Lewis Castleman, *The Army of the Potomac, Behind the Scenes: A Diary of Unwritten History; From the Organization of the Army to the Close of the Campaign in Virginia, About the First Day of January, 1863* (Milwaukee: Strickland, 1863), September 18, 1862, 230; second quote in E. B. Long. *The Civil War Day by Day: An Almanac, 1861–1865* (New York: Doubleday, 1971), 268.

35. Castleman, *Diary*, September 17, 1862, 227.

36. Quoted in Donald, *Lincoln*, 387.

37. Quoted in John F. Ross, "Treasures of Robert E. Lee Discovered," *American Heritage* 58 (Winter 2008): 28.

38. *New York Times*, October 20, 1862.

39. "Diary of Gideon Welles" in *Atlantic Monthly* 103 (February 1909): 155.

40. Both quotes in Guelzo, *Emancipation Proclamation*, 26, 160.

41. *New York Tribune*, August 19, 1862; *CW* 5:388–89.

42. Quoted in McPherson, *Tried by War*, 132.

43. Quoted in Guelzo, *Redeemer President*, 341.

44. First quote in James M. McPherson, *For Cause and Comrades: Why Men Fought in the Civil War* (New York: Oxford University Press, 1997), 124; second quote in Robert Garth Scott, ed., *Fallen Leaves: The Civil War Letters of Major Henry Livermore Abbott* (Kent, Ohio: Kent State University Press, 1991), January 10, 1862, 161.

45. Both quotes in Manning, *This Cruel War*, 94, 93.

46. First quote, "Fair Play," *Harper's*, January 24, 1863, 50; second quote in Leon F. Litwack, *Been in the Storm So Long: The Aftermath of Slavery* (New York: Random House, 1979), 223.

47. Quoted in Edward J. Cashin, "Paternalism in Augusta: The Impact of the Plantation Ethic upon Urban Society," in *Paternalism in a Southern City: Race, Religion, and Gender in Augusta, Georgia*, ed. Edward J. Cashin and Glenn T. Eskew (Athens: University of Georgia Press, 2001), 29.

48. *CW* 5:537.

49. The song is widely available on the Web. Hear two versions at http://www.youtube .com.

50. First quote in E. B. Long, *The Civil War Day by Day: An Almanac, 1861–1865* (Garden City, N.Y.: Doubleday, 1971), 296; second quote in Douglas Southall Freeman, *R. E. Lee: A Biography*, 4 vols. (New York: Scribner's, 1934–35), 2:462.

51. First quote, Robert E. Lee, *Recollections and Letters of General Robert E. Lee*, ed. Robert E. Lee [his son] (New York: Doubleday, Page, 1905), 87, available on Google Books; second quote in John Beauchamp Jones, *A Rebel War Clerk's Diary at the Confederate States Capital* (Philadelphia: J. B. Lippincott, 1866), 1:214.

52. Both quotes in Roy Morris Jr., *The Better Angel: Walt Whitman in the Civil War* (New York: Oxford University Press, 2000), 58–59.

53. First two quotes in Linderman, *Embattled Courage*, 63; third quote in La Salle Corbell Pickett, ed., *The Heart of a Soldier: As Revealed in the Intimate Letters of General George Pickett* (New York: Seth Moyle, 1913), December 14, 1862, 66.

54. Scott, *Abbott*, December 17 and 21, 1862, 155.

55. First quote in "The Reverse at Fredericksburg," *Harper's*, December 27, 1862, 818; cartoon appeared in ibid., January 3, 1863, 16; final quote in George C. Rable, *Fredericksburg! Fredericksburg!* (Chapel Hill: University of North Carolina Press, 2002), 325. Rable's work is an excellent source on the battle.

56. Quoted in Long, *Civil War Day by Day*, 308, 309.

57. Both quotes in Louis Menand, *The Metaphysical Club: A Story of Ideas in America* (New York: Farrar, Straus and Giroux, 2001), 43, 45.

58. Quoted in William S. McFeely, *Frederick Douglass* (New York: Touchstone, 1992), 215.

CHAPTER 12: BLOOD AND TRANSCENDENCE

1. "A Sight in Camp in the Day-Break Gray and Dim," *Leaves of Grass*, ed. Harold W. Blodgett and Sculley Bradley (New York: New York University Press), 307.

2. "The Wound-Dresser," ibid., 310–311.

3. Roy Morris Jr., discusses hospital and sanitary conditions contributing to high death

rates, as well as the John Holmes story, in *The Better Angel: Walt Whitman in the Civil War* (New York: Oxford University Press, 2000), 86–119.

4. All quotes in ibid., 86.

5. Both quotes in ibid., 109.

6. Quoted in Drew Gilpin Faust, *This Republic of Suffering: Death and the American Civil War* (New York: Knopf, 2008), 59.

7. For details of Barton's life, I relied on Elizabeth Brown Pryor, *Clara Barton: Professional Angel* (Philadelphia: University of Pennsylvania Press, 1987).

8. Quoted in Morris, *Better Angel*, 53.

9. Quotes in Pryor, *Barton*, 88, 89.

10. Quoted in ibid., 99.

11. Quoted in ibid., 106.

12. Both quotes in Richard Barksdale Harwell, ed., *Kate: The Journal of a Confederate Nurse* (Baton Rouge: Louisiana State University Press, 1987), 11, 14.

13. Ibid., 65, 124.

14. "Have We a General Among Us?" *Harper's*, January 17, 1863, 34.

15. Quoted in David Herbert Donald, *Lincoln* (New York: Simon & Schuster, 1995), 409.

16. "No Surrender!" *Harper's*, January 31, 1863, 66.

17. "The Irrepressible Conflict Again," *Harper's*, February 21, 1863, 114.

18. See Walter H. Hebert, *Fighting Joe Hooker* (Lincoln: University of Nebraska Press, 1999; first published in 1944); see also "Brigadier-General Hooker," *Harper's*, July 5, 1862, 421–22.

19. Quoted in Aaron Charles Sheehan-Dean, *Why Confederates Fought: Family and Nation in Civil War Virginia* (Chapel Hill: University of North Carolina Press, 2007), 113.

20. Quoted in E. B. Long, *The Civil War Day by Day: An Almanac, 1861–1865* (Garden City, N.Y.: Doubleday, 1971), 307.

21. Quoted in Stephen Chicoine, "'. . . Willing Never to Go in Another Fight': The Civil War Correspondence of Rufus King Felder of Chappell Hill," *Southwestern Historical Quarterly* 106 (April 2003): 584.

22. Jeffrey C. Lowe and Sam Hodges, eds., *Letters to Amanda: The Civil War Letters of Marion Hill Fitzpatrick, Army of Northern Virginia* (Macon, Ga.: Mercer University Press, 1998), April 27, 1863, 65.

23. Quoted in Gamaliel Bradford, "Joseph Hooker," *Atlantic Monthly* 114 (July 1914): 23.

24. The best analysis of the battle is Stephen W. Sears, *Chancellorsville* (New York: Mariner Books, 1996).

25. Quotes in Donald, *Lincoln*, 436.

26. Quoted in Michael Fellman, *The Making of Robert E. Lee* (New York: Random House, 2000), 132.

27. All quotes in James I. Robertson Jr., *Stonewall Jackson: The Man, the Soldier, the Legend* (New York: Macmillan, 1997), 746, 753, 754.

28. All quotes in Daniel W. Stowell, "Stonewall Jackson and the Providence of God," in *Religion and the American Civil War*, ed. Randall M. Miller, Harry S. Stout, and Charles Reagan Wilson (New York: Oxford University Press, 1998), 189, 194.

29. Ibid., 194.

30. Ibid., 193.

31. Quoted in John C. Abbott, "Siege and Capture of Port Hudson," *Harper's New Monthly Magazine* 30 (March 1865): 435.

32. Quoted in Charles P. Roland, *An American Iliad: The Story of the Civil War*, 2nd ed. (Lexington: University Press of Kentucky, 2004; first published in 1991), 99.

33. Both quotes in Chandra Manning, *What This Cruel War Was Over: Soldiers, Slavery, and the Civil War* (New York: Knopf, 2007), 178, 141.

34. "Slaves in Louisiana," *Harper's*, February 21, 1863, 114.

35. Quoted in Manning, *Cruel War*, 121.

36. Quoted in ibid., 122.

37. "Missouri Slave Woman to Her Soldier Husband," in *Freedom Series II: The Black Military Experience: A Documentary History of Emancipation, 1861–1867*, ed. Ira Berlin, Joseph Patrick Reidy, and Leslie S. Rowland (Cambridge: Cambridge University Press, 1985), December 30, 1863, 244.

38. Quoted in Jordan Ross, "Uncommon Union: Diversity and Motivation Among Civil War Soldiers," *American Nineteenth Century History* 3 (Spring 2002): 17.

39. Robert Garth Scott, ed., *Fallen Leaves: The Civil War Letters of Major Henry Livermore Abbott* (Kent, Ohio: Kent State University Press, 1991), August 7, 1863, 205.

40. First quote in Ethan S. Rafuse, *Robert E. Lee and the Fall of the Confederacy, 1863–1865* (Lanham, Md.: Rowman & Littlefield, 2008), 44; second quote in Thomas E. Schott, *Alexander H. Stephens of Georgia: A Biography* (Baton Rouge: Louisiana State University Press, 1988), 376.

41. First quote in Scott, *Abbott*, 191; second quote in Edwin B. Coddington, *The Gettysburg Campaign: A Study in Command* (New York: Touchstone, 1997; first published in 1963), 196. Coddington's is the most comprehensive single-volume work on Gettysburg.

42. Quoted in Manning, *Cruel War*, 131.

43. Quoted in Altina Laura Waller and William Graebner, eds., *True Stories from the American Past: To 1865* (New York: McGraw-Hill, 1996), 244.

44. See Jeffry D. Wert, *General James Longstreet: The Confederacy's Most Controversial Soldier: A Biography* (New York: Simon & Schuster, 1993).

45. Quoted in Freeman Cleaves, *Meade of Gettysburg* (Norman: University of Oklahoma Press, 1960), 157.

46. Earl J. Hess, *Pickett's Charge—The Last Attack at Gettysburg* (Chapel Hill: University of North Carolina Press, 2000). This is the most definitive account of this tragic episode. See also Carol Reardon, *Pickett's Charge in History and Memory* (Chapel Hill: University of North Carolina Press, 1997).

47. Scott, *Abbott*, July 28, 1863, 194.

48. Quoted in Earl J. Hess, *The Union Soldier in Battle: Enduring the Ordeal of Combat* (Lawrence: University Press of Kansas, 1997), 39.

49. Quoted in Elizabeth D. Leonard, *Yankee Women: Gender Battles in the Civil War* (New York: Norton, 1994), 37.

50. Quotes in Jim Weeks, *Gettysburg: Memory, Market, and an American Shrine* (Princeton: Princeton University Press, 2003), 39, 45.

51. Quoted in Joseph T. Glatthaar, *General Lee's Army: From Victory to Collapse* (New York: Free Press, 2008), 286.

52. First quote in Fellman, *Lee*, 152; second quote in Roland, *An American Iliad*, 146.

53. Quoted in Fellman, *Lee*, 154.

54. Quoted in James Howell Moorhead, "Religion in the Civil War: The Northern Side," http://nationalhumanitiescenter.org/tserve/nineteen/nkeyinfo/cwnorth.htm.

55. *CW* 6:329, 327–28.

56. Quoted in Donald, *Lincoln*, 447.

57. U. S. Grant, *Personal Memoirs of U. S. Grant* (New York: Charles L. Webster, 1972; first published in 1886), 332.

58. First quote in Manning, *Cruel War*, 132; Grant, *Memoirs*, 336; Lincoln quote in *CW* 6:406; final Lincoln quote in Brooks D. Simpson, *Ulysses S. Grant: Triumph over Adversity, 1822–1865* (Boston: Houghton Mifflin, 2000), 215.

59. Mark Grimsley and Todd D. Miller, eds., *The Union Must Stand: The Civil War Diary of John Quincy Adams Campbell, Fifth Iowa Volunteer Infantry* (Knoxville: University of Tennessee Press, 2000), 110.

60. First quote in Winston Groom, *Vicksburg, 1863* (New York: Knopf, 2009), 423; second quote in James M. McPherson, *Ordeal By Fire*, vol. 2, *The Civil War* (New York: Knopf, 1982), 333; third quote in Orville Vernon Burton, *The Age of Lincoln* (New York: Hill and Wang, 2007), 208; final quote in Groom, *Vicksburg*, 422.

61. Lowe and Hodges, *Fitzpatrick*, July 20, 1863, 79.

62. Quoted in Randall M. Miller, "Catholic Religion, Irish Ethnicity, and the Civil War," in Miller, Stout, and Wilson, *Religion and the American Civil War*, 283. An excellent analysis of the draft riots is Iver Bernstein, *The New York City Draft Riots: Their Significance for American Society and Politics in the Age of the Civil War* (New York: Oxford University Press, 1990).

63. Quoted in Morris, *Better Angel*, 139.

64. Lowe and Hodges, *Fitzpatrick*, July 20, 1863, 79.

65. "'The People,'" *Harper's*, August 1, 1863, 482–83.

66. Quoted in Reid Mitchell, "Christian Soldiers? Perfecting the Confederacy," in Miller, Stout, and Wilson, *Religion and the American Civil War*, 303.

67. For an excellent discussion on the background of the address and the speech itself, see Donald, *Lincoln*, 460–66.

68. See Allen C. Guelzo, *Abraham Lincoln: Redeemer President* (Grand Rapids, Mich.: Eerdmans, 1999), 369–73; "Gettysburg," *Harper's*, December 5, 1863, 770–71.

69. Quoted in Weeks, *Gettysburg*, 13.

70. Both quotes in Morris, *Better Angel*, 118, 119.

CHAPTER 13: A NEW NATION

1. First quote in James M. McPherson, *Ordeal By Fire*, vol. 2, *The Civil War* (New York: Knopf, 1982), 378; second quote in John Beauchamp Jones, *A Rebel War Clerk's Diary at the Confederate States Capital* (Philadelphia: J. B. Lippincott, 1866), 2:78.

2. Quoted in Emory M. Thomas, *The Confederate Nation, 1861–1865* (New York: Harper & Row, 1979), 203.

3. Quoted in ibid., 204.

4. Quoted in ibid.

5. First quote in W. Buck Yearns and John G. Barrett, eds., *North Carolina Civil War Documentary* (Chapel Hill: University of North Carolina Press, 1980), 221; second quote, Anne Morehead to Mrs. Rufus Patterson, April 1, 1863, Folder 40, Jones and Patterson Family Papers, 578. Southern Historical Collection, University of North Carolina, Chapel Hill.

6. First quote in Drew Gilpin Faust, "Altars of Sacrifice: Confederate Women and the Narratives of War," *Journal of American History* 76 (March 1990): 1224; second quote in James I. Robertson Jr., *Soldiers Blue and Gray* (Columbia: University of South Carolina Press, 1998), 136.

7. Jeffrey C. Lowe and Sam Hodges, eds., *Letters to Amanda: The Civil War Letters of Marion Hill Fitzpatrick, Army of Northern Virginia* (Macon, Ga.: Mercer University Press, 1998), October 29, 1863, 96; October 8, 1863, 93.

8. C. Vann Woodward, ed., *Mary Chesnut's Civil War* (New Haven: Yale University Press, 1981), 461; last quote in George C. Rable, *Civil Wars: Women and the Crisis of Southern Nationalism* (Urbana: University of Illinois Press, 1989), 117.

9. Richard Barksdale Harwell, ed., *Kate: The Journal of a Confederate Nurse* (Baton Rouge: Louisiana State University Press, 1987), May 29, 1865, 296.

10. Yearns and Barrett, *North Carolina Documentary*, 104.

11. First quote in Faust, "Altars of Sacrifice," 1227; second quote in Drew Gilpin Faust, *This Republic of Suffering: Death and the American Civil War* (New York: Knopf, 2008), 139.

12. Phoebe Yates Pember, *A Southern Woman's Story* (Columbia: University of South Carolina Press, 2002), quote in Introduction by George C. Rable, xv.

13. Both quotes in Faust, "Altars of Sacrifice," 1225, 1222.

14. Quoted in Roy Morris Jr., *The Better Angel: Walt Whitman in the Civil War* (New York: Oxford University Press, 2000), 154.

15. Quoted in Emerson David Fite, *Social and Industrial Conditions in the North During the Civil War* (New York: Macmillan, 1910), 151.

16. Quoted in ibid., 213.

17. *CW* 4:394. The definitive account of the expansion of the federal government and its partnering with private enterprise during the Civil War is Mark R. Wilson, *The Business of Civil War: Military Mobilization and the State, 1861–1865* (Baltimore: Johns Hopkins University Press, 2006).

18. For an excellent discussion of Civil War legislation and its impact, see Heather Cox Richardson, *The Greatest Nation of the Earth: Republican Economic Policies During the Civil War* (Cambridge: Harvard University Press, 1997). See also Peter A. Coclanis, "The American Civil War in Economic Perspective: Basic Questions and Some Answers," *Southern Cultures* 2 (Winter 1996): 165–68.

19. Quoted in Richardson, *Greatest Nation*, 146.

20. For a fuller discussion of Lincoln's invention, see "President Lincoln as an Inventor," *Scientific American*, May 27, 1865, 340.

21. Quoted in John Fiske, *Edward Livingston Youmans: Interpreter of Science for the People* (New York: D. Appleton, 1894), 179, available on Google Books.

22. Quoted in Richardson, *Greatest Nation*, 157.

23. Quoted in ibid., 151.

24. Both quotes in ibid., 179, 180.

25. "A Few Figures," *Harper's*, May 11, 1861, 290.

26. See Richardson, *Greatest Nation*, chapter 3.

27. Quoted in Allen C. Guelzo, *Abraham Lincoln: Redeemer President* (Grand Rapids, Mich.: Eerdmans, 1999), 382.

28. See Claudia Dale Goldin, "The Economics of Emancipation," *Journal of Economic History* 33 (March 1973): 66–85.

29. Both quotes in Ron Chernow, *Titan: The Life of John D. Rockefeller, Sr.* (New York: Random House, 1998), 78, 99.

30. *Executive Documents*, 39th Congress, 1st Session, "Diplomatic Correspondence," 64.

31. Quoted in Wilson, *Business of Civil War*, 179–80. "Song of the Shoddy" made its first appearance in *Vanity Fair*, September 21, 1861.

32. Mary Pratt quoted in Mark R. Wilson, "The Business of Civil War: Military Enterprise, the State, and Political Economy in the United States, 1850–1880" (Ph.D. diss., University of Chicago, 2002), 707; "The Fortunes of War. How They Are Made and Spent," *Harper's New Monthly Magazine* 29 (July 1864): 227.

33. Quoted in Wilson, *Business of Civil War*, 182.

34. Mark Wahlgren Summers, *The Era of Good Stealings* (New York: Oxford University Press, 1993), 20.

35. See John Bowers, *Chickamauga and Chattanooga: The Battles That Doomed the Confederacy* (New York: Harper Perennial, 2001); Steven E. Woodworth, ed., *The Chickamauga Campaign* (Carbondale: Southern Illinois University Press, 2010).

36. Corydon Edward Foote, *With Sherman to the Sea: A Drummer's Story of the Civil War* (New York: John Day, 1960), 121; see also U. S. Grant, *Personal Memoirs of U. S. Grant* (New York: Charles L. Webster, 1972; first published in 1886), 350–94.

37. Grant, *Memoirs*, 362.

38. Foote, *Sherman to the Sea*, 145.

39. Quoted in Sarah E. Gardner, *Blood and Irony: Southern White Women's Narratives of the Civil War, 1861–1937* (Chapel Hill: University of North Carolina Press, 2004), 261.

40. Foote, *Sherman to the Sea*, 179. Foote also comments on the relatively comfortable winter quarters for Sherman's army, 161–78.

41. Sam R. Watkins, *"Co. Aytch": A Confederate Memoir of the Civil War* (New York: Touchstone, 2003), 115.

42. Ibid., 98, 99, 112.

43. See Donald, *Lincoln*, 468.

CHAPTER 14: WAR IS CRUELTY

1. Jeffrey C. Lowe and Sam Hodges, eds., *Letters to Amanda: The Civil War Letters of Marion Hill Fitzpatrick, Army of Northern Virginia* (Macon, Ga.: Mercer University Press, 1998), February 24, 1864, 120.

2. Earl J. Hess, *The Union Soldier in Battle: Enduring the Ordeal of Combat* (Lawrence: University Press of Kansas, 1997), 113.

3. "Merry Christmas," *Harper's*, December 1863, 818, drawing on 824; Abbott's sad departure from home is related by the editor of his letters, Robert Garth Scott, in *Fallen Leaves: The Civil War Letters of Major Henry Livermore Abbott* (Kent, Ohio: Kent State University Press, 1991), 26.

4. Quoted in Chandra Manning, *What This Cruel War Was Over: Soldiers, Slavery, and the Civil War* (New York: Knopf, 2007), 188.

5. Quoted in Daniel W. Stowell, *Rebuilding Zion: The Religious Reconstruction of the South, 1863–1877* (New York: Oxford University Press, 1998), 37.

6. James Daniel Richardson, ed., *A Compilation of the Messages and Papers of the Confederacy* (Nashville: U.S. Publishing, 1905), 1:564.

7. Richard Barksdale Harwell, ed., *Kate: The Journal of a Confederate Nurse* (Baton Rouge: Louisiana State University Press, 1987), April 10, 1864, 198; Sam R. Watkins, *"Co. Aytch": A Confederate Memoir of the Civil War* (New York: Touchstone, 2003), 88; both quotes in Gerald F. Linderman, *Embattled Courage: The Experience of Combat in the American Civil War* (New York: Free Press, 1987), 255.

8. Both quotes in Linderman, *Embattled Courage*, 254.

9. First quote in William Tecumseh Sherman, *Memoirs of General William T. Sherman* (New York: Penguin, 1990), 601; second quote in Linderman, *Embattled Courage*, 209.

10. Quoted in James M. McPherson, *Battle Cry of Freedom: The Civil War Era* (New York: Oxford University Press, 1988), 742.

11. For a comprehensive view and statistics of Civil War prisons, especially the notorious Andersonville, see Benjamin G. Cloyd, *Haunted by Atrocity: Civil War Prisons in American Memory* (Baton Rouge: Louisiana State University Press, 2010).

12. Quoted in McPherson, *Battle Cry of Freedom*, 799–800.

13. Both quotes in Cloyd, *Haunted by Atrocity*, 24, 22 (page numbers refer to manuscript in author's possession).

14. Both quotes in ibid., 26.

15. Jay Parini has a forthcoming novel, *Anderson Depot*, based on extensive research on the facility; see also "Letter from a Soldier," *Harper's*, February 11, 1865, 93–94.

16. Quote in Cloyd, *Haunted by Atrocity*, 27.

17. Both quotes in Linderman, *Embattled Courage*, 258.

18. Harwell, *Kate*, August 19, 1864, 228.

19. Gari Carter, ed., *Troubled State: Civil War Journals of Franklin Archibald Dick* (Kirksville, Mo.: Truman State University Press, 2008), November 20, 1862, 91–92.

20. Quoted in Charles P. Roland, *An American Iliad: The Story of the Civil War* (Lexington: University Press of Kentucky, 2004; first published in 1991), 108.

21. First quote in Cloyd, *Haunted by Atrocity*, 29; second quote in Manning, *Cruel War*, 156.

22. "Further Proofs of Rebel Inhumanity," *Harper's*, June 18, 1864, 386.

23. First quote in Steven Hahn, "The Politics of the Dead," *New Republic*, April 23, 2008, 50; second quote in Linderman, *Embattled Courage*, 260.

24. U. S. Grant, *Personal Memoirs of U. S. Grant* (New York: Charles L. Webster, 1972; first published in 1886), 781.

25. Quoted in Roy Morris Jr., *The Better Angel: Walt Whitman in the Civil War* (New York: Oxford University Press, 2000), 173.

26. Quoted in David Coffey, *Sheridan's Lieutenants: Phil Sheridan, His Generals, and the Final Year of the Civil War* (Lanham, Md.: Rowman & Littlefield, 2005), 18.

27. First quote in E. B. Long, *The Civil War Day by Day: An Almanac, 1861–1865* (Garden City, N.Y.: Doubleday, 1971), 492; second quote in Morris Schaff, "The Battle of the Wilderness," *Atlantic Monthly* 104 (November 1909): 638; third quote in Morris, *Better Angel*, 176.

28. Quoted in Jean Edward Smith, *Grant* (New York: Simon & Schuster, 2001), 284.

29. First quote in "The Intellectual Character of President Grant," *Atlantic Monthly* 23 (May 1869): 631; second quote in Grant, *Memoirs*, 569.

30. First quote in John Gardner Perry, *Letters from a Surgeon of the Civil War*, ed. Martha Derby Perry (Boston: Little, Brown, 1906), 174, available on Google Books; second quote in Louis Menand, *The Metaphysical Club: A Story of Ideas in America* (New York: Farrar, Straus and Giroux, 2001), 55.

31. See Noah Andre Trudeau, *Bloody Roads South: The Wilderness to Cold Harbor, May–June 1864* (Baton Rouge: Louisiana State University Press, 2000).

32. Quoted in Herman Hattaway, "The Evolution of Tactics in the Civil War," in Hattaway, *Reflections of a Civil War Historian: Essays on Leadership, Society, and the Art of War* (Columbia: University of Missouri Press, 2003), 219.

33. *CW* 7:444.

34. Frank Wilkeson, *Reflections of a Private Soldier in the Army of the Potomac* (New York: G. P. Putnam's Sons, 1887), 173.

35. First quote in Drew Gilpin Faust, *This Republic of Suffering: Death and the American Civil War* (New York: Knopf, 2008), 66; second quote in David Herbert Donald, *Lincoln* (New York: Simon & Schuster, 1995), 513.

36. First three quotes in Donald, *Lincoln*, 513; remainder in James M. McPherson, "No Peace Without Victory, 1861–1865," *American Historical Review* 109 (February 2004): 5, 6.

37. Quoted in Linderman, *Embattled Courage*, 167.

38. C. Vann Woodward, ed., *Mary Chesnut's Civil War* (New Haven: Yale University Press, 1981), 733.

39. See Noah Andrew Trudeau, *Southern Storm: Sherman's March to the Sea* (New York: Harper, 2008).

40. Quoted in Emory M. Thomas, *Robert E. Lee: A Biography* (New York: Norton, 1995), 343.

41. Quoted in McPherson, *Battle Cry of Freedom*, 757.

42. *Valley Spirit*, August 31, 1864, http://valley.lib.virginia.edu/news/vs1864/pa.fr.vs.1864.08.31.xml.

43. Quoted in *Southern Historical Society Papers* 9 (July/August 1881): 380, available on Google Books.

44. Quotes in Donald, *Lincoln*, 528, 513.

45. First quote in ibid., 522; second quote in James M. McPherson, *Tried by War: Abraham Lincoln as Commander in Chief* (New York: Penguin, 2008), 236.

46. First quote in McPherson, *Tried by War*, 236; second quote in Robert F. Durden, *The Self-Inflicted Wound: Southern Politics in the Nineteenth Century* (Lexington: University Press of Kentucky, 1985), 99–100.

47. "The Testimony of Jeff. Davis," *New York Times*, August 20, 1864.

48. Quoted in McPherson, "No Peace Without Victory," 11.

49. Both quotes in ibid., 11, 12.

50. All quotes in Donald, *Lincoln*, 528, 529, 532.

51. Quoted in "Lincoln's Triumph in 1864," *Atlantic Monthly* 41 (April 1878): 457.

52. Quoted in Donald, *Lincoln*, 537.

53. First quote in McPherson, *Battle Cry of Freedom*, 776; second quote in "The Negro in His Native [text is unclear]," *Campaign Age*, September 1, 1864; third quote in McPherson, *Battle Cry of Freedom*, 768; final quote in "Horrible Crimes of the Negro Soldiers," *Campaign Age*, August 18, 1864. *Campaign Age* and other Civil War newspapers and magazines are available online from Alexander Street Press, http://alexanderstreet.com/products/cwdb.htm.

54. First quote in "Sensible," *Campaign Age*, August 25, 1864; second quote in "The Working Men," ibid., August 18, 1864.

55. "Compromise with the South," *Harper's*, September 3, 1864, 563.

56. Both quotes in McPherson, "No Peace Without Victory," 13, 14.

57. Watkins, *"Co. Aytch,"* 198–99.

58. First two quotes in Sherman, *Memoirs*, 705, 602; third quote in David W. Blight, *Race and Reunion: The Civil War in American Memory* (Cambridge: Harvard University Press, 2001), 163; final quote in Sherman, *Memoirs*, 585.

59. George Templeton Strong, *The Diary of George Templeton Strong*, ed. Allan Nevins and Milton Halsey Thomas, (New York: Macmillan, 1952), September 3, 1864, 3:480; "General Sherman," *Harper's*, September 17, 1864, 594; last quote in McPherson, *Battle Cry of Freedom*, 775.

60. First quote in John Y. Simon, ed., *The Papers of Ulysses S. Grant*, vol. 11, *June 1–August 15, 1864* (Carbondale: Southern Illinois University Press, 1984), 378; second quote in William J. Miller, "'Never Has There Been a More Complete Victory': The Cavalry Engagement at Tom's Brook, October 9, 1864," in *The Shenandoah Valley Campaign of 1864*, ed. Gary W. Gallagher (Chapel Hill: University of North Carolina Press, 2006), 136; third quote in Linderman, *Embattled Courage*, 213; final quote in *Richmond Whig*, October 15, 1864, quoted in *New York Times*, October 19, 1864.

61. Both quotes in Linderman, *Embattled Courage*, 200.

62. Carter, *Troubled State*, November 9, 1864, 160–61; "The Election," *Harper's*, November 19, 1864, 738.

63. Corydon Edward Foote, *With Sherman to the Sea: A Drummer's Story of the Civil War* (New York: John Day, 1960), 207.

64. First three quotes in Manning, *Cruel War*, 184, 202; last two quotes, "The Re-Election of Abraham Lincoln," *Weekly Register*, December 3, 1864.

65. *CW* 8:101.

CHAPTER 15: ONE NATION, INDIVISIBLE

1. Quoted in David Herbert Donald, *Lincoln* (New York: Simon & Schuster, 1995), 565.

2. Corydon Edward Foote, *With Sherman to the Sea: A Drummer's Story of the Civil War* (New York: John Day, 1960), 209.

3. Quotes in James M. McPherson, *Battle Cry of Freedom: The Civil War Era* (New York: Oxford University Press, 1988), 809, 810; last quote in William Tecumseh Sherman, *Memoirs of General William T. Sherman* (New York: Penguin, 1990), 652.

4. George S. Bradley, *The Star Corps: or, Notes of an Army Chaplain During Sherman's Famous "March to the Sea"* (Milwaukee: Jermain & Brightman, 1865), 184, available on Google Books.

5. Foote, *With Sherman to the Sea*, 212.

6. First quote in James M. McPherson, *Tried by War: Abraham Lincoln as Commander in Chief* (New York: Penguin, 2008), 254; second quote in "Sherman's Report of the Georgia Campaign," in *The Story of the Great March: From the Diary of a Staff Officer*, ed. George Ward Nichols (Bedford, Mass.: Applewood Books, 2008; first published in 1865), 335.

7. Quoted in Joseph T. Glatthaar, *General Lee's Army: From Victory to Collapse* (New York: Free Press, 2008), 451.

8. Dolly Sumner Lunt, *A Woman's Wartime Journal* (New York: Century, 1918), 84.

9. Sam R. Watkins, *"Co. Aytch": A Confederate Memoir of the Civil War* (New York: Touchstone, 2003), 219–27.

10. Ibid., 21; second quote in Russell F. Weigley, *A Great Civil War: A Military and Political History, 1861–1865* (Bloomington: Indiana University Press, 2000), 415.

11. U. S. Grant, *Personal Memoirs of U. S. Grant* (New York: Charles L. Webster, 1972; first published in 1886), 567; second quote in Archer Jones, *Civil War Command and Strategy: The Process of Victory and Defeat* (New York: Free Press, 1992), 214.

12. First quote in James M. McPherson, *What They Fought For, 1861–1865* (Baton Rouge: Louisiana State University Press, 1994), 36; second quote in Charles P. Roland, *An American Iliad: The Story of the Civil War* (Lexington: University Press of Kentucky, 2004; first published in 1991), 242; final quote in Jones, *Civil War Command and Strategy*, 214.

13. Sherman, *Memoirs*, 254.

14. First quote in Marion Brunson Lucas, *Sherman and the Burning of Columbia* (Columbia: University of South Carolina Press, 2000; first published in 1976), 111; second quote in George C. Rable, *Civil Wars: Women and the Crisis of Southern Nationalism* (Urbana: University of Illinois Press, 1989), 178; remaining quotes in Emma LeConte, *Diary*, 35, electronic ed., http://docsouth.unc.edu/fpn/leconteemma/leconte.html.

15. Quoted in Judith N. McArthur and Orville Vernon Burton, eds., *A Gentleman and an Officer: A Military and Social History of James B. Griffin's Civil War* (New York: Oxford University Press, 1996), 78.

16. Description in James M. McPherson, *Ordeal by Fire*, vol. 2, *The Civil War* (New York: Knopf, 1982), 471–73.

17. Quoted in E. B. Long, *The Civil War Day by Day: An Almanac, 1861–1865* (Garden City, N.Y.: Doubleday, 1971), 644.

18. Quoted in James M. McPherson, "No Peace Without Victory, 1861–1865," *American Historical Review* 109 (February 2004): 15.

19. *CW* 8:220–21.

20. First quote in Thomas E. Schott, *Alexander H. Stephens of Georgia: A Biography* (Baton Rouge: Louisiana State University Press, 1988), 445; second quote in Donald, *Lincoln*, 557.

21. Quoted in Schott, *Stephens*, 447.

22. First quote in ibid., 448; second and third quotes in McPherson, "No Peace Without Victory," 17; final quote in Manning, *Cruel War*, 204.

23. All quotes in Heather Cox Richardson, *The Greatest Nation of the Earth: Republican Economic Policies During the Civil War* (Cambridge: Harvard University Press, 1997), 241, 243.

24. Quoted in ibid., 247.

25. Both quotes in ibid., 249.

26. Quotes in William C. Harris, "The Hampton Roads Peace Conference: A Final Test of Lincoln's Presidential Leadership," *Journal of the Abraham Lincoln Association*, Winter 2000, http://www.historycooperative.org/journals/jala/21.1/harris.html.

27. Quoted in Allen C. Guelzo, *Abraham Lincoln: Redeemer President* (Grand Rapids, Mich.: Eerdmans, 1999), 409.

28. Both quotes in Stephen V. Ash, "Poor Whites in the Occupied South, 1861–1865," *Journal of Southern History* 47 (February 1991): 53, 51.

29. See Paul D. Escott, *Many Excellent People: Power and Privilege in North Carolina, 1850–1900* (Chapel Hill: University of North Carolina Press, 1985); see also Albion W. Tourgée, *A Fool's Errand: A Novel of the South During Reconstruction* (New York: Harper, 1961; first published in 1879), 124; Victoria Bynum, "'War Within a War': Women's Participation in the Revolt of the North Carolina Piedmont, 1863–1865," *Frontiers* 9, no. 3 (1987): 43–49.

30. First quote in C. Vann Woodward, ed., *Mary Chesnut's Civil War* (New Haven: Yale University Press, 1981), 777; second quote in McPherson, *Battle Cry of Freedom*, 820.

31. First quote in Winston Groom, *Shrouds of Glory: From Atlanta to Nashville—the Last Great Campaign of the Civil War* (New York: Pocket Books, 1995), 274; second quote in "The End of Rebel Logic," *Harper's*, December 3, 1864, 770.

32. Jeffrey C. Lowe and Sam Hodges, eds., *Letters to Amanda: The Civil War Letters of Marion Hill Fitzpatrick, Army of Northern Virginia* (Macon, Ga.: Mercer University Press, 1998), November 3, 1864, 182; Baughman quoted in Bruce C. Levine, *Confederate Emancipation: Southern Plans to Free and Arm Slaves During the Civil War* (New York: Oxford Uni-

versity Press, 2006), 44; third quote in McPherson, *Battle Cry of Freedom*, 836; last quote in Emory M. Thomas, *The Confederate Nation, 1861–1865* (New York: Harper & Row, 1979), 297.

33. See Roland, *American Iliad*, 216–219.

34. Quoted in Ronald C. White Jr., "Lincoln's Sermon on the Mount: The Second Inaugural," in *Religion and the American Civil War*, ed. Randall M. Miller, Harry S. Stout, and Charles Reagan Wilson (New York: Oxford University Press, 1998), 211.

35. Lincoln's Second Inaugural Address is widely available. The Library of Congress Web site for the address contains related useful links: http://www.loc.gov/rr/program/bib/ourdocs/Lincoln2nd.html.

36. "The Inaugural," *New York Times*, March 6, 1865; *Tribune* quoted in "The Inaugural Address," *Harper's*, March 18, 1865, 162.

37. Quotes in White, "Lincoln's Sermon on the Mount," 222.

38. Quoted in Mark A. Noll, "'Both . . . Pray to the Same God': The Singularity of Lincoln's Faith in the Era of the Civil War," *Journal of the Abraham Lincoln Association*, Winter 1997, http://www.historycooperative.org/journals/jala/18.1/noll.html.

39. "Amending the Constitution," *New York Times*, February 2, 1864. The editorial opposed the amendment.

40. Quoted in Jon Meacham, *American Gospel: God, the Founding Fathers, and the Making of a Nation* (New York: Random House, 2007), 130.

41. See Louis Menand, *The Metaphysical Club: A Story of Ideas in America* (New York: Farrar, Straus and Giroux, 2001), preface.

42. Quoted in E. B. Long, *The Civil War Day by Day: An Almanac, 1861–1865* (Garden City, N.Y.: Doubleday, 1971), 659.

43. Lincoln to Lt. Gen. Grant, April 2, 1865, in *The War of the Rebellion: A Compilation of the Official Records of the Union and Confederate Armies, Series I—Volume XLVI—Part III*, 449. The OR is a valuable resource for the Civil War. It may be accessed online: http://digital.library.cornell.edu/m/moawar/waro.html.

44. First quote in Douglas Southall Freeman, ed., *A Calendar of Confederate Papers* (Richmond: Confederate Museum, 1908), 251; second and third quotes in Jay Winik, *April 1865: The Month That Saved America* (New York: HarperCollins, 2001), 116, 119; fourth quote in K. M. Kostyal, *Abraham Lincoln's Extraordinary Era: The Man and His Times* (New York: National Geographic, 2009), 188; final quote, *CW* 8:406.

45. Both quotes in Grant, *Memoirs*, 624.

46. Quoted in Brooks D. Simpson, *Let Us Have Peace: Ulysses S. Grant and the Politics of War and Reconstruction, 1861–1868* (Chapel Hill: University of North Carolina Press, 1991), 85.

47. Grant, *Memoirs*, 631, 633, 634.

48. Quoted in Long, *Civil War Day by Day*, 671.

49. *CW* 8:393.

50. Quotes in Gaines M. Foster, *Ghosts of the Confederacy: Defeat, the Lost Cause, and the Emergence of the New South, 1865 to 1913* (New York: Oxford University Press, 1987), 12.

51. Quoted in ibid., 13.

52. First quote in Guelzo, *Redeemer President*, 432; second quote in Donald, *Lincoln*, 592.

53. First quotes in Timothy S. Good, *We Saw Lincoln Shot: One Hundred Eyewitness Accounts* (Oxford: University Press of Mississippi, 1995), 53; last quote in Jay Winik, "'American Brutus': The Lone Gunman," *New York Times*, December 19, 2004.

54. See David Donald's account of the assassination in *Lincoln*, 596–99.

55. Quoted in Philip Callow, *From Noon to Starry Night: A Life of Walt Whitman* (Chicago: Ivan R. Dee, 1992), 317; "When Lilacs Last in the Door-yard Bloom'd," *Leaves of Grass*, ed. Harold W. Blodgett and Sculley Bradley (New York: New York University Press, 1965), 328.

56. Quotes in James Howell Moorhead, "Religion in the Civil War: The Northern Perspective," http://nationalhumanitiescenter.org/tserve/nineteen/nkeyinfo/cwnorth.htm.

57. "When Lilacs Last in the Door-yard Bloom'd," *Leaves of Grass*, 330–31. See "President Lincoln's Burial," *Harper's*, May 27, 1865, 321–22.

58. All quotes in Charles P. Roland, *An American Iliad: The Story of the Civil War* (Lexington: University Press of Kentucky, 2003; first published in 1991), 253–254.

59. Quoted in Richard Wightman Fox, "The President Who Died for Us," *New York Times*, April 14, 2006.

60. Quotes in Guelzo, *Redeemer President*, 440, 441.

61. Quoted in David Herbert Donald, *Lincoln Reconsidered: Essays on the Civil War Era* (New York: Vintage, 2001; first published in 1947), 4.

62. Quoted in Roy Morris Jr., *The Better Angel: Walt Whitman in the Civil War* (New York: Oxford University Press, 2000), 221.

CHAPTER 16: THE AGE OF REASON

1. Catharine E. Beecher and Harriet Beecher Stowe, *The American Woman's Home* (New Brunswick: Rutgers University Press, 2002; first published in 1869).

2. "Ravages of a Carpet," in Harriet Beecher Stowe, *House and Home Papers* (Bedford, Mass.: Applewood Books, 2008; first published in 1865), 1–22.

3. First quote in Joan D. Hedrick, *Harriet Beecher Stowe: A Life* (New York: Oxford University Press, 1994), 325; second quote in Laura Wallis Wakefield, "'Set a Light in a Dark Place': Teachers of Freedmen in Florida, 1864–1874," *Florida Historical Quarterly* 81 (Spring 2003): 413.

4. Quoted in Hedrick, *Stowe*, 329.

5. See Debby Applegate, *The Most Famous Man in America: The Biography of Henry Ward Beecher* (New York: Doubleday, 2006).

6. Quoted in Edward J. Blum, *Reforging the White Republic: Race, Religion, and American Nationalism, 1865–1898* (Baton Rouge: Louisiana State University Press, 2005), 88.

7. Quoted in ibid., 93.

8. Quoted in ibid., 96.

9. Quoted in ibid., 97.

10. First quote in Ron Powers, *Mark Twain: A Life* (New York: Free Press, 2005), 183; second quote in David S. Reynolds, *Walt Whitman's America: A Cultural Biography* (New York: Knopf, 1995), 256.

11. First quote in Michael DeGruccio, "Manhood, Race, Failure, and Reconciliation: Charles Francis Adams, Jr., and the American Civil War," *New England Quarterly* 81 (December 2008): 673; second quote in G. Edward White, *Justice Oliver Wendell Holmes: Law and the Inner Self* (New York: Oxford University Press, 1993), 206.

12. John T. Trowbridge, *The Desolate South, 1865–1866: A Picture of the Battlefields and of the Devastated Confederacy*, ed. Gordon Carroll (Boston: Little, Brown, 1956), 8.

13. Quoted in Gerald F. Linderman, *Embattled Courage: The Experience of Combat in the American Civil War* (New York: Free Press, 1987), 219.

14. The most insightful of these memory studies is David W. Blight, *Race and Reunion: The Civil War in American Memory* (Cambridge: Harvard University Press, 2001).

15. Justin Kaplan, *Mr. Clemens and Mark Twain: A Biography* (New York: Simon & Schuster, 1966), 36.

16. Quoted in Stuart McConnell, *Glorious Contentment: The Grand Army of the Republic, 1865–1900* (Chapel Hill: University of North Carolina Press, 1992), 181.

17. Quoted in David Goldfield et al., *The American Journey: A History of the United States*, 5th ed. (Upper Saddle River, N.J.: Pearson, 2009), 405.

18. First quote in David W. Blight, "'For Something Beyond the Battlefield': Frederick Douglass and the Struggle for the Memory of the Civil War," *Journal of American History* 75 (March 1989), 1173; second quote in Ambrose Bierce, "What I Saw of Shiloh," in Bierce, *Civil War Stories* (Mineola, N.Y.: Dover, 1994), 17.

19. Walt Whitman, "Reconciliation," *Leaves of Grass*, ed. Harold W. Blodgett and Sculley Bradley (New York: New York University Press, 1965), 321.

20. Quoted in Roy Morris Jr., *The Better Angel: Walt Whitman in the Civil War* (New York: Oxford University Press, 2000), 240.

21. George Templeton Strong, *The Diary of George Templeton Strong*, ed. Allan Nevins and Milton Halsey Thomas, (New York: Macmillan, 1952), May 29, 1865, 3:601.

22. U. S. Grant, *Personal Memoirs of U. S. Grant* (New York: Charles L. Webster, 1972; first published in 1886), 665.

23. Quoted in Powers, *Twain*, 207.

24. Quoted in ibid., 207, 208.

25. Quoted in ibid., 216.

26. Reinhold Niebuhr, *Moral Man and Immoral Society: A Study in Ethics and Politics* (Louisville: Westminster John Knox Press, 2001; first published in 1932), 277.

27. See Charles R. Morris, *The Tycoons: How Andrew Carnegie, John D. Rockefeller, Jay Gould, and J. P. Morgan Invented the American Supereconomy* (New York: Holt, 2005) and Heather Cox Richardson, *West from Appomattox: The Reconstruction of America After the Civil War* (New Haven: Yale University Press, 2007).

28. For a thorough discussion of the connections between lawmakers and corporations during this era, see Mark Wahlgren Summers, *The Era of Good Stealings* (New York: Oxford University Press, 1993).

29. John Sherman to William T. Sherman, November 10, 1865, in *The Sherman Letters*, ed. Rachel Sherman Thorndike (New York: C. Scribner's Sons, 1894), 258–59, available on Google Books.

30. Quoted in Heather Cox Richardson, *The Death of Reconstruction: Race, Labor, and Politics in the Post–Civil War North, 1865–1901* (Cambridge: Harvard University Press, 2001), 36.

31. Horatio Alger, *Ragged Dick* (Philadelphia: John C. Winston, 1910; first published in 1868), in *Religion in America*, vol. 2, ed. James T. Baker (Belmont, Calif.: Thomson Wadsworth, 2006), 255.

32. First quote in *CG*, 37th Congress, 2nd Session, Appendix (December 3, 1861): 4; second quote in Thomas Mellon, *Thomas Mellon and His Times* (Pittsburgh: Pittsburgh University Press, 1994), 238.

33. Quoted in Kaplan, *Mr. Clemens and Mark Twain*, 21.

34. Quoted in ibid.

35. Quoted in ibid., 141.

36. Quotes in ibid., 62.

37. First quote in Powers, *Twain*, 280; remaining quotes in Kaplan, *Mr. Clemens and Mark Twain*, 85.

38. Quoted in Powers, *Twain*, 363.

39. Mark Twain and Charles Dudley Warner, *The Gilded Age: A Tale of Today* (New York: Penguin, 2001; first published in 1873), 86; William Dean Howells, *The Rise of Silas Lapham* (Boston: Houghton Mifflin, 1884), 87.

40. See Zane L. Miller, "The Rise of the City," *Hayes Historical Journal* 3 (Spring and Fall 1980): 73–83.

41. On urbanization during this period, see Raymond A. Mohl, *The New City: Urban America in the Industrial Age, 1860–1920* (Arlington Heights, Ill.: Harlan Davidson, 1985).

42. Both quotes in ibid., 48.

43. Mona Domosh, "The Symbolism of the Skyscraper: Case Studies of New York's First Tall Buildings," *Journal of Urban History* 14 (May 1988): 321–45.

44. Quoted in David Nasaw, *Andrew Carnegie* (New York: Penguin, 2006), 60.

45. Willard W. Glazier, *Peculiarities of American Cities* (Philadelphia: Hubbard Brothers, 1884), 333–334; "American Iron and Steel—Pittsburgh, the Iron City," *Scientific American* 20 (January 23, 1869): 49–50.

46. Andrew Carnegie, *Triumphant Democracy; or, Fifty Years' March of the Republic* (Boston: Elibron, 2006; first published in 1888), 1.

47. See David Goldfield and Blaine A. Brownell, *Urban America: A History* (Boston: Houghton Mifflin, 1990), 198–200; see also Alice Kessler-Harris, *Out to Work: A History of Wage-Earning Women in the United States* (New York: Oxford, 1982).

48. Quoted in Howard Allen Bridgman, "The Suburbanite," *Independent*, April 10, 1902, 863.

49. The Russells' story is presented in Mary Corbin Sies, "The City Transformed: Nature, Technology, and the Suburban Ideal, 1877–1917," *Journal of Urban History* 14 (November 1987), 81–111.

50. Quoted in Daniel E. Sutherland, *The Expansion of Everyday Life, 1860–1876* (New York: Harper & Row, 1989), 29.

51. "Harper's Bazaar," *Harper's*, November 2, 1867, 691; see also Sutherland, *Everyday Life*, 70.

52. See Morris, *Tycoons*, 108–11.

53. Henry Adams, *The Education of Henry Adams* (Forgotten Books, 2008; first published in 1919), 44, http://www.forgottenbooks.org.

54. Louis Menand, *The Metaphysical Club: A Story of Ideas in America* (New York: Farrar, Straus and Giroux, 2001), x.

55. Quoted in Ron Chernow, *Titan: The Life of John D. Rockefeller, Sr.* (New York: Random House, 1998), 116.

56. Quoted in T. J. Stiles, *The First Tycoon: The Epic Life of Cornelius Vanderbilt* (New York: Knopf, 2009), 435.

57. Both quotes in Chernow, *Rockefeller*, 153.

58. "War and Inventions," *Scientific American*, May 25, 1861, 329.

59. "Useful Improvements Not Opposed to the Harmony of Nature," ibid., September 29, 1866, 221.

60. Quotes in Theresa M. Collins and Lisa Gitelman, eds., *Thomas Edison and Modern America: A Brief History with Documents* (Boston: Bedford/St. Martin's, 2002), 7, 8, 12.

61. "Song of the Exposition," *Leaves of Grass*, 201–03.

CHAPTER 17: ASPIRATIONS

1. James A. Ward, ed., *Southern Railroad Man: Conductor N. J. Bell's Recollections of the Civil War Era* (DeKalb: Northern Illinois University Press, 1994; first published in 1896), 26.

2. Quoted in Eric Foner, *Reconstruction: America's Unfinished Revolution, 1863–1877* (New York: Harper & Row, 1988), 124.

3. John T. Trowbridge, *The Desolate South, 1865–1866: A Picture of the Battlefields and of the Devastated Confederacy*, ed. Gordon Carroll (Boston: Little, Brown, 1956), 92; quoted in Michael B. Chesson, *Richmond After the War, 1865–1890* (Richmond: Virginia State Library, 1981), 90.

4. Quoted in Heather Cox Richardson, *West from Appomattox: The Reconstruction of America After the Civil War* (New Haven: Yale University Press, 2007), 17.

5. Quoted in C. Vann Woodward, ed., *Mary Chesnut's Civil War* (New Haven: Yale University Press, 1993; first published in 1981), xii.

6. Both quotes in Rod Andrew Jr., *Wade Hampton: Confederate Warrior to Southern Redeemer* (Chapel Hill: University of North Carolina Press, 2008), 120, 243.

7. First two quotes in Richardson, *West from Appomattox*, 17, 18; last quote in Whitelaw Reid, *After the War: A Tour of the Southern States, 1865–1866* (New York: Harper & Row, 1965; first published in 1866), 356.

8. Reid, *After the War*, 66.

9. First quote in ibid., 213; second quote in Thomas E. Schott, *Alexander H. Stephens of Georgia: A Biography* (Baton Rouge: Louisiana State University Press, 1988), 458.

10. C. Vann Woodward and Elisabeth Muhlenfeld, eds., *The Private Mary Chesnut: The Unpublished Civil War Diaries* (New York: Oxford University Press, 1984), May 13, 1865, 243; Reid, *After the War*, 345.

11. Quoted in Anne Sarah Rubin, *A Shattered Nation: The Rise and Fall of the Confederacy, 1861–1868* (Chapel Hill: University of North Carolina Press, 2005), 156.

12. Quoted in Andrew, *Hampton*, 322–23. Italics in original.

13. Trowbridge, *Desolate South*, 41; Bill Arp [Charles Henry Smith], *Bill Arp's Peace Papers: Columns on War and Reconstruction, 1861–1873* (Columbia: University of South Carolina Press, 2009; first published in 1873), 120.

14. Hear Ry Cooder's interpretation of the song: http://www.lyricstime.com/ry-cooder-i-m-a-good-old-rebel-lyrics.html.

15. First quote in "What Next?" *Harper's*, April 22, 1865, 242; second quote in "From Memphis," ibid., October 7, 1865, 627.

16. First quote in Gaines M. Foster, *Ghosts of the Confederacy: Defeat, the Lost Cause, and the Emergence of the New South, 1865 to 1913* (New York: Oxford University Press, 1987), 14; second quote in David Goldfield, *Still Fighting the Civil War: The American South and Southern History* (Baton Rouge: Louisiana State University Press, 2002), 54.

17. Quoted in Daniel W. Stowell, *Rebuilding Zion: The Religious Reconstruction of the South, 1863–1877* (New York: Oxford University Press, 1998), 43.

18. Quoted in Andrew, *Hampton*, 326.

19. Quoted in Stowell, *Rebuilding Zion*, 113.

20. Quoted in Paul Harvey, "'Yankee Faith' and Southern Redemption: White Southern Baptist Ministers, 1850–1890," in *Religion and the American Civil War*, ed. Randall M. Miller, Harry S. Stout, and Charles Reagan Wilson (New York: Oxford University Press, 1998), 178.

21. First quote in Edward J. Blum, *Reforging the White Republic: Race, Religion, and American Nationalism, 1865–1898* (Baton Rouge: Louisiana State University Press, 2005), 33; second quote in Charles Reagan Wilson, *Baptized in Blood: The Religion of the Lost Cause, 1865–1920* (Athens: University of Georgia Press, 1980), 72.

22. First quote in Robert Lewis Dabney, "The Duty of the Hour," *The Land We Love* 6 (December 1868): 117; remaining quotes in Charles Reagan Wilson, "Robert Lewis Dabney: Religion and the Southern Holocaust," *Virginia Magazine of History and Biography* 89 (January 1981): 82.

23. Ellen Glasgow, *The Deliverance: A Romance of the Tobacco Fields* (BiblioBazaar, 2007; first published in 1904), 57, http://www.bibliobazaar.com.

24. Wilson, *Baptized in Blood*, 26.

25. "Exodus," *De Bow's Review* 6 (July 1868): 579.

26. First quote in Goldfield, *Still Fighting*, 25; second quote in David Goldfield, *Southern Histories: Public, Personal, and Sacred* (Athens, Ga.: University of Georgia Press, 2003), 8; third quote in Robert Penn Warren, *The Legacy of the Civil War* (Lincoln: University of Nebraska Press, 1998; first published in 1961), 15.

27. Quoted in Wilson, *Baptized in Blood*, 59.

28. Margaret Mitchell, *Gone with the Wind* (New York: Macmillan, 1936), 529; last quote in Wilson, *Baptized in Blood*, 25.

29. First quote in Catherine Clinton, *Harriet Tubman: The Road to Freedom* (New York: Little, Brown, 2004), 189; second quote in Mitchell, *Gone with the Wind*, 608.

30. First quote in James C. Cobb, *Away Down South: A History of Southern Identity* (New York: Oxford University Press, 2005), 66; second quote in "The Lost Cause," *Hours at Home* 3 (September 1866): 477. The journal may be accessed through the American Periodicals Series, an electronic resource.

31. Quoted in William S. McFeely, *Frederick Douglass* (New York: Touchstone, 1992), 242.

32. Frederick Douglass, "Reconstruction," *Atlantic Monthly* 18 (December 1866): 761.

33. Carl Schurz, "Report on the Condition of the South," *CG*, 39th Congress, 1st Session, Appendix (December 19, 1865): 76.

34. Both quotes in Blum, *Reforging the White Republic*, 49.

35. Both quotes in Dorothy Sterling, ed., *We Are Your Sisters: Black Women in the Nineteenth Century* (New York: Norton, 1997; first published in 1984), 311, 313.

36. Quotes in Wilbert L. Jenkins, *Climbing Up to Glory: A Short History of African Americans During the Civil War and Reconstruction* (Wilmington, Del.: Scholarly Resources, 2002), 144.

37. Quoted in Hannah Rosen, *Terror in the Heart of Freedom: Citizenship, Sexual Violence, and the Meaning of Race in the Postemancipation South* (Chapel Hill: University of North Carolina Press, 2009), 271n.

38. Quoted in Foner, *Reconstruction*, 155.

39. First quote in Trowbridge, *Desolate South*, 114; second quote in Reid, *After the War*, 150.

40. Reid, *After the War*, 59.

41. First quote in Patricia Click, *Time Full of Trial: The Roanoke Island Freedmen's Colony, 1862–1867* (Chapel Hill: University of North Carolina Press, 2001), 164; second quote in Reid, *After the War*, 565.

42. See Irvin Kitrell III, "40 Acres and a Mule," *Civil War Times Illustrated* 41 (May 2002): 54.

43. Fortune tells his story in Dorothy Sterling, ed., *The Trouble They Seen: Black People Tell the Story of Reconstruction* (Garden City, N.Y.: Doubleday, 1976), 22–24.

44. Both quotes in Blum, *Reforging the White Republic*, 77. Blum has a good discussion of black education during Reconstruction.

45. Both quotes in ibid., 78, 79.

46. Quotes in ibid., 79.

47. First quote in ibid., 80; second quote in Booker T. Washington, *Up from Slavery: An Autobiography* (New York: Doubleday, Page, 1902), 62; third quote, W. E. B. DuBois, *The Souls of Black Folk* (Forgotten Books, 2008; first published in 1903), 64, http://www.forgottenbooks .org.

48. Both quotes in Reid, *After the War*, 255, 59.

49. Trowbridge, *Desolate South*, 131.

50. First quote in Peter J. Rachleff, *Black Labor in the South: Richmond, Virginia, 1865–1890* (Philadelphia: Temple University Press, 1984), 38; second quote in "Educating the Freedmen," *Harper's*, May 25, 1867, 321–22.

51. See Paul M. Gaston, *The New South Creed: A Study in Southern Mythmaking* (New York: Knopf, 1970).

CHAPTER 18: A GOLDEN MOMENT

1. Biographical details are from Hans L. Trefousse, *Andrew Johnson: A Biography* (New York: Norton, 1989).

2. *CG*, 38th Congress, 1st Session, Appendix (December 8, 1863): 3.

3. *CW* 8:403.

4. Quoted in Allen C. Guelzo, *Abraham Lincoln: Redeemer President* (Grand Rapids, Mich.: Eerdmans, 1999), 392.

5. Abraham Lincoln, *Speeches and Writings, 1859–1865* (New York: Penguin, 1989), 699, 697. This useful compilation of Lincoln's major speeches and writings derives from the primary source of Lincoln's work, Roy P. Basler's *Collected Works of Abraham Lincoln*, published in 1953.

6. Quoted in David Herbert Donald, *Lincoln* (New York: Simon & Schuster, 1995), 591.

7. First two quotes in William C. Harris, *With Charity for All: Lincoln and the Restoration of the Union* (Lexington: University Press of Kentucky, 1997), 262; Johnson's quotes in *CG*, 40th Congress, 2nd Session, Appendix (December 3, 1867): 2–3.

8. On Johnson's reconstruction plan, see Eric Foner, *Reconstruction: America's Unfinished Revolution, 1863–1877* (New York: Harper & Row, 1988), chapter 5.

9. Quotes in Whitelaw Reid, *After the War: A Tour of the Southern States, 1865–1866* (New York: Harper & Row, 1965), 291.

10. Ibid., 163–64.

11. First quote in ibid., 264; second quote in Foner, *Reconstruction*, 134.

12. Quoted in Foner, *Reconstruction*, 199–200.

13. Carl Schurz, "Report on the Condition of the South," *CG*, 39th Congress, 1st Session, Appendix, (December 19, 1865): 38, 13, 23.

14. U. S. Grant, "Letter of General Grant Concerning Affairs at the South," *CG*, 39th Congress, 1st Session, Appendix (December 19, 1865): 107.

15. Both quotes in Reid, *After the War*, 360, 361.

16. Quotes in ibid., 404.

17. Quoted in W. Scott Poole, "Uncertain Legacy," H-Civil War, August 8, 2003, http://h-net.msu.edu/cgi-bin/logbrowse.pl?trx=vx&list=H-CivWar&month=0308&week=b&msg=UgqV3iN9Z7bL/jDXaCWsng&user=&pw=.

18. Quoted in Christopher Waldrep, *Roots of Disorder: Race and Criminal Justice in the American South, 1817–80* (Urbana: University of Illinois Press, 1998), 106.

19. Ira Berlin, Joseph P. Reidy, and Leslie S. Rowland, eds., *Freedom's Soldiers: The Black Military Experience in the Civil War* (Cambridge: Cambridge University Press, 1998), 173.

20. *Executive Documents of the House of Representatives* (Washington: GPO, 1866), 39th Congress, 1st Session, "Inspector's Report of Affairs in Kentucky," March 5, 1866, 8:201. A comprehensive account of such violence is Stephen Budiansky, *The Bloody Shirt: Terror After the Civil War* (New York: Plume, 2009).

21. *The Reports of the Committees of the House of Representatives* (Washington: GPO, 1866), 39th Congress, 1st Session, "Memphis Riots and Massacres," July 25, 1866, 3:51, 324.

22. Reid, *After the War*, 411.

23. Eric Foner, *A Short History of Reconstruction* (New York: Harper & Row, 1990), 54.

24. Quotes in Avery Craven, *Reconstruction: The Ending of the Civil War* (New York: Holt, Rinehart and Winston, 1969), 93.

25. Quoted in Melanie S. Gustafson, *Women and the Republican Party, 1854–1924* (Urbana: University of Illinois Press, 2001), 35.

26. Carl Schurz, "The True Problem," *Atlantic Monthly* 19 (March 1867): 371.

27. Quoted in Martha Hodes, *White Women, Black Men: Illicit Sex in the 19th-Century South* (New Haven: Yale University Press, 1997), 169.

28. Albion W. Tourgée, *A Fool's Errand: A Novel of the South During Reconstruction* (New York: Harper Torchbooks, 1961; first published in 1897), 167.

29. *CG*, 39th Congress, 2nd Session (February 19, 1867): 1564.

30. W. E. B. DuBois, "Reconstruction and its Benefits," in *W. E. B. DuBois: A Reader*, ed. David Levering Lewis (New York: Holt, 1995), 187.

31. Quoted in Foner, *Short History of Reconstruction*, 136.

32. Jonathan Worth, "Inaugural Address," March 1868, http://www.atgpress.com/inform/govo65.htm.

33. Quoted in Heather Cox Richardson, *West from Appomattox: The Reconstruction of America After the Civil War* (New Haven: Yale University Press, 2007), 91.

34. Quoted in Steven Hahn, *A Nation Under Our Feet: Black Political Struggles in the Rural South from Slavery to the Great Migration* (Cambridge: Harvard University Press, 2003), 275.

35. See Lee W. Formwalt, "The Camilla Massacre of 1868: Racial Violence as Political Propaganda," *Georgia Historical Quarterly* 71 (Fall 1987): 399–426. For a discussion of Grant's presidential campaign, see Brooks D. Simpson, *Let Us Have Peace: Ulysses S. Grant and the Politics of War and Reconstruction, 1861–1868* (Chapel Hill: University of North Carolina Press, 1991).

36. J. M. H. Frederick, comp., *National Party Platforms of the United States* (Akron, Ohio: J. M. H. Frederick, 1896), 36.

37. Quoted in Foner, *Reconstruction*, 291.

38. Quoted in ibid., 344.

39. Tourgée, *Fool's Errand*, 169.

40. Quotes in Heather Cox Richardson, *The Death of Reconstruction: Race, Labor, and Politics in the Post–Civil War North, 1865–1901* (Cambridge: Harvard University Press, 2001), 74, 76.

41. Quoted in "The Stars and Bars at the Democratic Peak," *Harper's*, September 5, 1868, 562.

42. Quoted in Louise Michele Newman, *White Women's Rights: The Racial Origins of Feminism in the United States* (New York: Oxford University Press, 1999), 64.

43. Both quotes in Richardson, *West from Appomattox*, 101.

44. Quoted in Richardson, *Death of Reconstruction*, 80.

45. See Randolph B. Campbell, *Grass-Roots Reconstruction in Texas, 1865–1880* (Baton Rouge: Louisiana State University Press, 1998).

46. Quoted in Foner, *Reconstruction*, 369.

47. Quoted in Richardson, *Death of Reconstruction*, 76.

48. Quoted in Hahn, *Nation Under Our Feet*, 248.

CHAPTER 19: THE GOLDEN SPIKE

1. For a full discussion of these events, see Michael Johnson, "Rendezvous at Promontory: A New Look at the Golden Spike Ceremony," *Utah Historical Quarterly* 72 (Winter 2004): 47–68.

2. Quoted in Heather Cox Richardson, *The Greatest Nation of the Earth: Republican Economic Policies During the Civil War* (Cambridge: Harvard University Press, 1997), 179.

3. See James N. Gregory, *The Southern Diaspora: How the Great Migrations of Black and White Southerners Transformed America* (Chapel Hill: University of North Carolina Press, 2007).

4. "The Pacific Railroad," *Harper's*, May 29, 1869, 342.

5. First quote in ibid., 341; second quote in "East and West," *New York Times*, May 11, 1869.

6. "Pacific Railroad," May 29, 1869, 342.

7. "Passage to India," *Leaves of Grass*, ed. Harold W. Blodgett and Sculley Bradley (New York: New York University Press, 1965), 411, 412, 413, 414.

8. *Miscellaneous Documents*, 43rd Congress, 2nd Session (Washington: GPO, 1875), December 8, 1874, 3.

9. Quoted in Dee Brown, *Bury My Heart at Wounded Knee: An Indian History of the American West* (New York: Holt, 1970), 41.

10. Quotes in Philip Weeks, *Farewell, My Nation: The American Indian and the United States, 1820–1890* (Arlington Heights, Ill.: Harlan Davidson, 1990), 94, 93.

11. *CW* 6:151–52.

12. Chauncey H. Cooke, *A Badger Boy in Blue: The Civil War Letters of Chauncey H. Cooke* (Detroit: Wayne State University Press, 2007; first published in 1920–22), 24–25.

13. First quote in "The Battle of Sand Creek," *Rocky Mountain News*, December 17, 1864, http://www.kclonewolf.com/History/SandCreek/sc-reports/rocky-editorials.html; last quote in Weeks, *Farewell, My Nation*, 104.

14. "The Chivington Massacre," Report of the Joint Special Committee, in *The Reports of the Committees of the Senate of the United States for the Second Session Thirty-ninth Congress, 1866–67* (Washington: GPO, 1867), Appendix, 75, 95–96.

15. Quoted in Evan S. Connell, *Son of the Morning Star: Custer and the Little Bighorn* (New York: North Point Press, 1984), 148–49.

16. Quoted in Robert Wooster, *The Military and United States Indian Policy, 1865–1903* (New Haven: Yale University Press, 1988), 144.

17. "Our Indian Policy," *Harper's*, March 9, 1867, 147.

18. Quoted in Heather Cox Richardson, *West from Appomattox: The Reconstruction of America after the Civil War* (New Haven: Yale University Press, 2007), 36.

19. Grant to Lt. Gen. W. T. Sherman, May 29, 1867, in John Y. Simon, ed., *The Papers of Ulysses S. Grant*, vol. 17, *January 1–September 30, 1867* (Carbondale: Southern Illinois University Press, 1991), 174.

20. First Sherman quote in Robert G. Athearn, *William Tecumseh Sherman and the Settlement of the West* (Norman: University of Oklahoma Press, 1956), 67; second Sherman quote in Letter of the Secretary of War in *Executive Documents of the Senate of the United States for the First Session, Fortieth Congress, and for the Special Session, 1867* (Washington: GPO, 1868), 1–2; Sheridan quote in George W. Manypenny, *Our Indian Wards* (Cincinnati: Robert Clarke, 1880), 206, available on Google Books.

21. Grant to Secretary of War Edwin M. Stanton, January 15, 1867, in Simon, *Papers of Grant* 17:22; Sherman to Thomas Durant, May 28, 1867, ibid., 162.

22. Testimony of Col. Henry B. Carrington, January 3, 1867, Records Relating to the Investigation of the Ft. Philip Kearney (or Fetterman) Massacre, National Archives and Record Service, 5, http://freepages.history.rootsweb.ancestry.com/~familyinformation/fpk/car_5.html.

23. Quoted in Athearn, *Sherman and the West*, 99.

24. Sherman to Maj. Gen. Philip H. Sheridan, October 15, 1868, Letter of the Secretary of War in *Executive Documents of the Senate for the Third Session of the Fortieth Congress, 1868–69* (Washington: GPO, 1869), 4; Sheridan to Sherman, March 18, 1870, Letter of the Secretary of War in *Executive Documents of the House of Representatives for the Second Session of the Forty-first Congress, 1869–70* (Washington: GPO, 1870), 12:70–71.

25. "A Policy of Peace," *Harper's*, April 2, 1870, 210.

26. Quoted in Brown, *Wounded Knee*, 194.

27. "First Inaugural Address of Ulysses S. Grant," March 4, 1869, http://avalon.law.yale.edu/19th_century/grant1.asp.

28. Quote in "Grant and Lee in War and Peace," New-York Historical Society exhibit, October 17, 2008–March 29, 2009. See also http://historyperspectives.blogspot.com/2008/03/bureau-of-indian-affairs.html.

29. Quoted in William H. Armstrong, *Warrior in Two Camps: Ely S. Parker, Union General and Seneca Chief* (Syracuse: Syracuse University Press, 1978), 120.

30. First quote in Richardson, *West from Appomattox*, 115; second quote in John Y. Simon, ed., *Papers of Ulysses S. Grant*, vol. 23, *February 1–December 31, 1872* (Carbondale: Southern Illinois University Press, 2000), 270.

31. "The Last Appeal of Red Cloud," *New York Times*, June 17, 1870.

32. Quoted in Dee Brown, *The American West* (New York: Touchstone, 1994), 133.

33. Quoted in Brown, *Wounded Knee*, 184.

34. See Louis S. Warren, *Buffalo Bill's America: William Cody and the Wild West Show* (New York: Knopf, 2005).

35. "The Modocs," *Harper's*, May 3, 1873, 364.

CHAPTER 20: POLITICAL SCIENCE

1. Russell H. Conwell, *Acres of Diamonds* (New York: Jove Press, 1978; first published in 1878). The following paragraphs quote from the sermon, which may be accessed at http://www.americanrhetoric.com/speeches/rconwellacresofdiamonds.htm.

2. Quoted in Justin Kaplan, *Mr. Clemens and Mark Twain: A Biography* (New York: Simon & Schuster, 1966), 96.

3. Quoted in ibid., 165.

4. Quoted in Mark Wahlgren Summers, *Party Games: Getting, Keeping, and Using Power in Gilded Age Politics* (Chapel Hill: University of North Carolina Press, 2004), 110.

5. Kenneth D. Ackerman, *Boss Tweed: The Rise and Fall of the Corrupt Pol Who Conceived the Soul of Modern New York* (New York: Carroll & Graf, 2005), 169.

6. Quoted in Bruce J. Evensen, *God's Man for the Gilded Age: D. L. Moody and the Rise of Modern Mass Evangelism* (New York: Oxford University Press, 2003), 102; see also "The Lessons of the Frauds Continued," *Harper's*, August 19, 1871, 762–63.

7. "Let Us Prey," *Harper's*, September 23, 1871, 889; "The Tammany Tiger Loose—'What Are You Going to Do About It?'" ibid., November 11, 1871, 1056–57; Tweed quote in Charles F. Wingate, "An Episode in Municipal Government," *North American Review* 121 (July 1875): 150.

8. "City Government," *New York Times*, March 9, 1867; Josiah Strong, *The Twentieth Century City* (New York: Baker & Taylor, 1898), 81; see also Lincoln Steffens, *The Shame of the Cities* (Mineola, N.Y.: Dover, 2007; first published in 1904).

9. Francis Parkman, "The Failure of Universal Suffrage," *North American Review* 127 (July/August 1878): 1–20.

10. *New York Times*, February 17, 1874. On the corruption of southern Republican governments, see Eric Foner, *Reconstruction: America's Unfinished Revolution, 1863–1877* (New York: Harper & Row, 1988), 383–92.

11. For a more detailed discussion of "Honest Dick" Tate, see Mark Grossman, *Political Corruption in America: An Encyclopedia of Scandals, Power, and Greed* (Santa Barbara, Calif.: ABC-CLIO, 2003), 322.

12. Quoted in Kaplan, *Mr. Clemens and Mark Twain*, 95, 157.

13. "Human Sacrifices in the Republican Party," *Nation* 16 (February 20, 1873): 128–29. See also Mark Wahlgren Summers, *The Era of Good Stealings* (New York: Oxford University Press, 1993), 226–37.

14. Mark Twain and Charles Dudley Warner, "Author's Preface to the London Edition," *The Gilded Age: A Tale of Today* (New York: Penguin, 2001; first published in 1873), 451.

15. Quoted in Maury Klein, *The Life and Legend of Jay Gould* (Baltimore: Johns Hopkins University Press, 1986), 196.

16. See Ackerman, *Boss Tweed*, 52.

17. Quoted in Summers, *Era of Good Stealings*, 115.

18. First Whitman quote in "Democratic Vistas" (1871), in *Specimen Days and Collect* (Philadelphia: David McKay, 1882), 210; Whitman, "Nay, Tell Me Not To-Day the Publish'd Shame," *Leaves of Grass*, ed. Harold W. Blodgett and Sculley Bradley (New York: New York University Press, 1965), 578. The poem appeared originally in the *New York Daily Graphic*, March 5, 1873, http://www.whitmanarchive.org/published/periodical/poems/per.00127.

19. Whitman, "Respondez!" (lines added in 1871) *Leaves of Grass*, 591–92.

20. First quote in Kaplan, *Mr. Clemens and Mark Twain*, 166; second quote in Ron Chernow, *The Life of John D. Rockefeller, Sr.* (New York: Random House, 1998), 206; final quote in Mark Twain, "The Curious Republic of Gondour," *Atlantic Monthly* 36 (October 1875): 461–62.

21. John T. Wheelwright, "Public Opinion as a Force," *Harvard Review* 8 (April 1889): 46–47.

22. See Philip M. Katz, *From Appomattox to Montmartre: Americans and the Paris Commune* (Cambridge: Harvard University Press, 1998).

23. All quotes in Heather Cox Richardson, *West from Appomattox: The Reconstruction of America after the Civil War* (New Haven: Yale University Press, 2007), 105.

24. First quote in Nina Silber, *The Romance of Reunion: Northerners and the South, 1865–1900* (Chapel Hill: University of North Carolina Press, 1993), 45; second quote in *Nation* 18 (April 16, 1874): 247.

25. For Anthony's entire speech, see "On Woman's Right to Suffrage" (1873) in *The World's Famous Orations*, vol. 10, *America–III, 1861–1905* (New York: Funk and Wagnalls, 1906), 59.

26. Whitman, "Democratic Vistas," 210.

27. First quote in Edward J. Blum, *Reforging the White Republic: Race, Religion, and American Nationalism, 1865–1898* (Baton Rouge: Louisiana State University Press, 2005), 107; remaining quotes in Daniel W. Stowell, *Rebuilding Zion: The Religious Reconstruction of the South, 1863–1877* (New York: Oxford University Press, 1998), 174, 163.

28. "Christianity and the Constitution," *Harper's*, March 2, 1872.

29. Quoted in Joan D. Hedrick, *Harriet Beecher Stowe: A Life* (New York: Oxford University Press, 1994), 387, 393.

30. Quoted in Mark A. Noll, "Science, Theology, and Society: From Cotton Mather to William Jennings Bryan," in *Evangelicals and Science in Historical Perspective*, ed. David N. Livingstone, D. G. Hart, and Mark A. Noll (New York: Oxford University Press, 1999), 105.

31. First quote in Michael Les Benedict, "Reform Republicans and the Retreat from Reconstruction," in *The Facts of Reconstruction: Essays in Honor of John Hope Franklin*, ed. Eric Anderson and Alfred A. Moss Jr. (Baton Rouge: Louisiana State University Press, 1991), 56; second quote in Ralph Waldo Emerson, "Prospects," in Emerson, *Emerson: Essays and Lectures* (New York: Penguin, 1983), 46.

32. Quoted in Michael DeGruccio, "Manhood, Race, Failure, and Reconciliation: Charles Francis Adams Jr. and the American Civil War," *New England Quarterly* 81 (December 2008): 670.

33. First quote in Andrew Carnegie, *The Autobiography of Andrew Carnegie and His Essay "The Gospel of Wealth*," ed. Gordon Hunter (New York: Signet, 2006; first published in 1920), 291; second quote in "The Darwinian Theory," *Scientific American* 20 (June 19, 1869): 393.

34. Quoted in W. Fitzhugh Brundage, *The Southern Past: A Clash of Race and Memory* (Cambridge: Harvard University Press, 2005), 90.

35. Charles Darwin, *The Descent of Man, and Selection in Relation to Sex*, 2 vols. (New York: D. Appleton, 1872), 1:193.

36. Quoted in Robert C. Bannister, *Social Darwinism: Science and Myth in Anglo-American Social Thought* (Philadelphia: Temple University Press, 1979), 180.

37. J. W. DeForest, "The Man and Brother," *Atlantic Monthly* 22 (October 1868): 416.

38. Darwin, *Descent of Man* 1:181.

39. Herbert Spencer, "The Study of Sociology," *Popular Science Monthly* 1 (June 1872): 160.

40. Quoted in David N. Livingstone, "Situating Evangelical Responses to Evolution," in Livingstone, Hart, and Noll, *Evangelicals and Science*, 196.

41. Quoted in Allen C. Guelzo, "'The Science of Duty': Moral Philosophy and the Epistemology of Science in Nineteenth-Century America," in ibid., 284.

42. Quoted in Bannister, *Social Darwinism*, 105.

43. "Machinery the Great Missionary," *Scientific American* 12 (April 8, 1865): 231.

44. First quote in "Politicians," *Harper's*, January 11, 1873; second quote in "The Lessons of the Frauds Continued," ibid., August 19, 1871.

45. Quoted in Foner, *Reconstruction*, 500.

46. Quoted in Richardson, *West from Appomattox*, 122.

47. See Robert C. Williams, *Horace Greeley: Champion of American Freedom* (New York: New York University Press, 2006).

48. First quote in "Mr. Greeley and the Colored Citizens," *Harper's*, June 15, 1872, 467; Greeley quotes in Blum, *Reforging the White Republic*, 116.

49. "The Georgia Election," *Harper's*, October 19, 1872, 803.

50. Nast titled the first cartoon "Old Honesty," *Harper's*, July 20, 1872, 573; Greeley quoted in Foner, *Reconstruction*, 508.

51. Quoted in Ron Powers, *Mark Twain: A Life* (New York: Free Press, 2005), 327.

52. Frederic Bancroft, ed., *Speeches, Correspondence and Political Papers of Carl Schurz*, 6 vols. (New York: G. P. Putnam's Sons, 1913), 2:311.

53. C. Vann Woodward, *Origins of the New South, 1877–1913*, 2 vols. (Baton Rouge: Louisiana State University Press, 1971; first published in 1951), 2:457.

54. Bruce E. Baker, *What Reconstruction Meant: Historical Memory in the American South* (Charlottesville: University of Virginia Press, 2007), 15.

55. Quoted in Heather Cox Richardson, *The Death of Reconstruction: Race, Labor, and Politics in the Post–Civil War North, 1865–1901* (Cambridge: Harvard University Press, 2001), 106.

56. Quoted in ibid., 111; Claude Bowers, *The Tragic Era: The Revolution After Lincoln* (New York: Retail Press, 2008; first published in 1929), 418. Bowers meant it as a compliment.

57. All quotes in Benedict, "Reform Republicans," 69, 60.

CHAPTER 21: LET IT BE

1. Quoted in Heather Cox Richardson, *West from Appomattox: The Reconstruction of America After the Civil War* (New Haven: Yale University Press, 2007), 151.

2. Quoted in Bruce J. Evensen, *God's Man for the Gilded Age: D. L. Moody and the Rise of Modern Mass Evangelism* (New York: Oxford University Press, 2003), 104.

3. See Charles R. Morris, *The Tycoons: How Andrew Carnegie, John D. Rockefeller, Jay Gould, and J. P. Morgan Invented the American Supereconomy* (New York: Holt, 2005), 99–117.

4. See David Goldfield and Blaine A. Brownell, *Urban America: A History* (Boston: Houghton Mifflin, 1990), 196–200.

5. O. Henry, "An Unfinished Story," in *The American Disinherited: A Profile in Fiction*, ed. Abe C. Ravitz (Belmont, Calif.: Dickenson, 1970), 34.

6. First quote in Stephen Crane, *Maggie: A Girl of the Streets and Other New York Writings* (New York: Random House, 2001; first published in 1893), 18; second quote in Allen F. Davis, *Spearheads for Reform: The Social Settlements and the Progressive Movement, 1890–1914* (New York: Oxford University Press, 1967), 137.

7. First quote in Alice Kessler-Harris, *Out to Work: A History of Wage-Earning Women in the United States* (New York: Oxford University Press, 1982), 100; second quote in Massa-

chusetts Department of Labor, *Thirteenth Annual Report on the Statistics of Labor* (Boston: Rand, Avery, 1882), 300; last quote in Kessler-Harris, *Out to Work*, 98.

8. First two quotes in Heather Cox Richardson, *The Death of Reconstruction: Race, Labor, and Politics in the Post–Civil War North, 1865–1901* (Cambridge: Harvard University Press, 2001), 137; final quote in Donald C. Swift, *Religion and the American Experience* (Armonk, N.Y.: M. E. Sharpe, 1998), 212.

9. All quotes in Richardson, *Death of Reconstruction*, 87, 86, 89.

10. Quoted in John A. Garraty, *The New Commonwealth, 1877–1890* (New York: Harper & Row, 1968), 145.

11. Ibid., 152–53.

12. Quoted in Richardson, *Death of Reconstruction*, 89.

13. "Song of the Universal," *Leaves of Grass*, ed. Harold W. Blodgett and Sculley Bradley (New York: New York University Press, 1965), 226, 227.

14. "A Song for Occupations," ibid., 218; "Song of the Exposition," ibid., 199.

15. First quote in Simon Newcomb, "The Method and Province of Political Economy," *North American Review* 121 (October 1875): 269; second quote in Morton Keller, *Affairs of State: Public Life in Late Nineteenth-Century America* (Cambridge: Harvard University Press, 1977), 183.

16. All quotes in Barry Werth, *Banquet at Delmonico's: Great Minds, the Gilded Age, and the Triumph of Evolution in America* (New York: Random House, 2009), 186, 187.

17. Quoted in Michael Zuckerman, "Holy Wars, Civil Wars: Religion and Economics in Nineteenth-Century America," *Prospects* 16 (1991): 222.

18. Quoted in Garraty, *New Commonwealth*, 142.

19. Quoted in Robert C. Bannister, *Social Darwinism: Science and Myth in Anglo-American Social Thought* (Philadelphia: Temple University Press, 1979), 71.

20. Raymond A. Mohl, *The New City: Urban America in the Industrial Age, 1860–1920* (Arlington Heights, Ill.: Harlan Davidson, 1985), 157.

21. Quoted in Richardson, *Death of Reconstruction*, 117.

22. Charles Nordhoff, *The Cotton States in the Spring and Summer of 1875* (New Castle, Del.: Burt Franklin, 1988; first published in 1876).

23. Eric Foner, *Reconstruction: America's Unfinished Revolution, 1863–1877* (New York: Harper & Row, 1988), 536.

24. See Douglas A. Blackmon, *Slavery by Another Name: The Re-Enslavement of Black Americans from the Civil War to World War II* (New York: Doubleday, 2008); Pete Daniel, *The Shadow of Slavery: Peonage in the South, 1901–1969* (Urbana: University of Illinois Press, 1972).

25. For a comprehensive treatment of the massacre, see LeeAnna Keith, *The Colfax Massacre: The Untold Story of Black Power, White Terror, and the Death of Reconstruction* (New York: Oxford University Press, 2008).

26. See Charles Lane, *The Day Freedom Died: The Colfax Massacre, the Supreme Court, and the Betrayal of Reconstruction* (New York: Henry Holt, 2008).

27. The following discussion of the *Slaughter-House Cases* and the quotes from the justices involved in the decision draw from Richard L. Aynes, "Justice Miller, the Fourteenth Amendment, and the *Slaughter-House* Cases," *Chicago-Kent Law Review* 70 (1994): 627.

28. For a detailed discussion of the formulation and implementation of the white-line policy in Mississippi, see *Mississippi in 1875: Report of the Select Committee to Inquire into the Mississippi Election of 1875*, 2 vols. (Washington: GPO, 1876).

29. "Condition of the South," *Index to Reports of Committees of the House of Representatives for the Second Session of the Forty-third Congress* (Washington: GPO, 1875), 2:1005.

30. See Lawrence N. Powell, "Reinventing Tradition: Liberty Place, Historical Memory, and Silk-Stocking Vigilantism in New Orleans," *Slavery & Abolition* 20 (April 1999): 127–49.

31. On Ames and the Vicksburg episode, see Nicholas Lemann, *Redemption: The Last Battle of the Civil War* (New York: Farrar, Straus and Giroux, 2006).

32. First quote in Thomas Nast, "Shall We Call Our Troops Home?" *Harper's*, January 9, 1875, 37; second quote in Adelbert Ames to Blanche Ames, September 5, 1875, in Stephen Budiansky, *The Bloody Shirt: Terror After the Civil War* (New York: Plume, 2009), 197.

33. "Report of the Grand Jury," *Report of the Select Committee* 2:150.

34. Quoted in Daniel W. Stowell, *Rebuilding Zion: The Religious Reconstruction of the South, 1863–1877* (New York: Oxford University Press, 1998), 148.

35. "Frederick Douglass's View," *Harper's*, October 2, 1875, 795.

36. "The Union and the States," ibid., April 24, 1875, 334.

37. Quoted in Lou Falkner Williams, *The Great South Carolina Ku Klux Klan Trials, 1871–1872* (Athens: University of Georgia Press, 1996), 110.

38. First quote in Michael Perman, *Emancipation and Reconstruction, 1862–1879* (Arlington Heights, Ill.: Harlan Davidson, 1987), 121; second quote in Perman, *The Road to Redemption: Southern Politics, 1869–1879* (Chapel Hill: University of North Carolina Press, 1984), 161.

39. All quotes in Edward J. Blum, *Reforging the White Republic: Race, Religion, and American Nationalism, 1865–1898* (Baton Rouge: Louisiana State University Press, 2005), 125–26.

40. Quoted in Louis Menand, *The Metaphysical Club: A Story of Ideas in America* (New York: Farrar, Straus and Giroux, 2001), 313.

41. Quoted in Michael Les Benedict, "Reform Republicans and the Retreat from Reconstruction," in *The Facts of Reconstruction: Essays in Honor of John Hope Franklin*, ed. Eric Anderson and Alfred A. Moss Jr. (Baton Rouge: Louisiana State University Press, 1991), 76.

42. All quotes in Blum, *Reforging the White Republic*, 110, 127.

43. Quoted in Richardson, *Death of Reconstruction*, 99.

44. Quoted in ibid., 142; *Civil Rights Cases*, 109 U.S. 3 (1883), http://supreme.justia.com/us/109/3/case.html.

45. First quote in Richardson, *Death*, 137; *Civil Rights Cases*, 109 U.S. 3, 31.

46. "Decoration-Day," *Harper's*, June 12, 1875, 474.

47. Quoted in Nina Silber, *The Romance of Reunion: Northerners and the South, 1865–1900* (Chapel Hill: University of North Carolina Press, 1993), 55; other examples of reconciliation in ibid., 96.

CHAPTER 22: CENTENNIAL

1. For a detailed account of the Hamburg massacre and its aftermath, see Stephen Budiansky, *The Bloody Shirt: Terror After the Civil War* (New York: Plume, 2009), 225–53. See also Stephen Kantrowitz, *Ben Tillman and the Reconstruction of White Supremacy* (Chapel Hill: University of North Carolina Press, 2000).

2. Testimony of John Fryer, *South Carolina in 1876. Testimony as to the Denial of the Elective Franchise in South Carolina at the Elections of 1875 and 1876 Taken Under the Resolution of the Senate of December 5, 1876, Forty-fourth Congress, 2nd Session* (Washington: GPO, 1877), 28.

3. *A Centennial Fourth of July Democratic Celebration. The Massacre of Six Colored Citizens of the United States at Hamburgh, S.C., on July 4, 1876. Debate in the U.S. House of Representatives, July 15 and 18, 1876*, 2, http://www.archive.org/details/centennialfourtho1unit.

4. "The Hamburg Butchery," *Harper's*, August 19, 1876, 671; "The 'Bloody Shirt' Reformed," ibid., August 12, 1876, 657.

5. Quoted in *New York Times*, October 15, 1876.

6. Governor Chamberlain to President Grant, July 22, 1876, "South Carolina in 1876—Hamburgh Massacre," *The Miscellaneous Documents of the Senate of the United States for the Second Session of the Forty-fourth Congress* [1876–77] (Washington: GPO, 1877), 6:481; President Grant to Governor Chamberlain, July 26, 1876, "Recent Election in South Carolina," *Index to Reports of Committees of the House of Representatives for the Second Session of the Forty-fourth Congress, 1876–77* (Washington: GPO, 1877): 2:17; first Butler quote in "South Carolina in 1876" 6:493; final Butler quote in Budiansky, *Bloody Shirt*, 241.

7. Paul D. Escott et al., eds., *Major Problems in the History of the American South*, vol. 2, *The New South*, 2nd ed. (Boston: Houghton Mifflin, 1999), 37–38.

8. Rod Andrew Jr., *Wade Hampton: Confederate Warrior to Southern Redeemer* (Chapel Hill: University of North Carolina Press, 2008), 386.

9. "Speech of General Hampton," *Index to the Miscellaneous Documents of the House of Representatives for the First Session of the Forty-fifth Congress* (Washington: GPO, 1877), 2:527.

10. First quote in Andrew, *Wade Hampton*; second quote in W. Scott Poole, *Never Surrender: Confederate Memory and Conservatism in the South Carolina Upcountry* (Athens: University of Georgia Press, 2004), 123; third quote in Andrew, *Wade Hampton*, 383.

11. All quotes in W. Scott Poole, "Religion, Gender, and the Lost Cause in South Carolina's 1876 Governor's Race: 'Hampton or Hell!'" *Journal of Southern History* 68 (August 2002): 585, 586, 594, 596.

12. The election of 1876 is covered in Andrew, *Wade Hampton*, 394–408.

13. These and subsequent biographical details, unless otherwise noted, are from Bruce J. Evensen, *God's Man for the Gilded Age: D. L Moody and the Rise of Modern Mass Evangelism* (New York: Oxford University Press, 2003).

14. First quote in ibid., 17; remaining quotes in Charles Rosenbury Erdman, *D. L. Moody, His Message for Today* (New York: Fleming H. Revell, 1928), 156.

15. First two quotes in Evensen, *God's Man*, 88, 25; New Year's Eve quote in Kathryn Teresa Long, *The Revival of 1857–58: Interpreting a Religious Awakening* (New York: Oxford University Press, 1998), 128; final quote in Evensen, *God's Man*, 27.

16. Both quotes in Edward J. Blum, *Reforging the White Republic: Race, Religion, and American Nationalism, 1865–1898* (Baton Rouge: Louisiana State University Press, 2005), 128.

17. All quotes in ibid., 129, 130.

18. All quotes in ibid., 132, 135, 136.

19. Both quotes in ibid., 141.

20. Quoted in Ron Chernow, *Titan: The Life of John D. Rockefeller, Sr.* (New York: Random House, 1998), 231.

21. Quoted in Blum, *Reforging the White Republic*, 143.

22. The following details on the Centennial, unless otherwise noted, come from "The Centennial," *Harper's*, January 1, 1876, 10, and "Our Centennial," ibid., May 27, 1876, 422.

23. Quoted in Joseph Horowitz, *Wagner Nights: An American History* (Berkeley: University of California Press, 1994), 61.

24. First quote in Dee Brown, *The Year of the Century: 1876* (New York: Scribner, 1966), 129; second quote in Charles R. Morris, *The Tycoons: How Andrew Carnegie, John D. Rockefeller, Jay Gould, and J. P. Morgan Invented the American Supereconomy* (New York: Holt, 2005), 119.

25. William Dean Howells, "A Sennight of the Centennial," *Atlantic Monthly* 38 (July 1876): 96.

26. Quoted in Heather Cox Richardson, *West from Appomattox: The Reconstruction of America After the Civil War* (New Haven: Yale University Press, 2007), 173.

27. First quote in Howells, "Centennial," 103; second quote in Daniel E. Sutherland, *The Expansion of Everyday Life, 1860–1876* (New York: HarperCollins, 1989), 268.

28. "1776–1876," *Harper's*, July 15, 1876, 570.

29. "Report of Lieutenant-General Sheridan," *Index to the Executive Documents of the House of Representatives for the Third Session of the Forty-fifth Congress, 1878–79*, vol. 2, *Report of the Secretary of War* (Washington: GPO, 1879), 36.

30. First part of quote in Jon E. Lewis, ed., *The Mammoth Book of Native Americans: The Story of America's Original Inhabitants in All its Beauty, Magic, Truth, and Tragedy* (New York: Carroll & Graf, 2004), 253; second part in Dorothy M. Johnson, *Warrior for a Lost Nation: A Biography of Sitting Bull* (Philadelphia: Westminster Press, 1969), 67.

31. Quoted in Richard G. Athearn, *William Tecumseh Sherman and the Settlement of the West* (New York: Hewlett Press, 2007), 223.

32. The sources I used, unless otherwise noted, for the Greasy Grass/Little Big Horn battles include Wooden Leg, "A Cheyenne Account of the Battle," in Thomas B. Marquis, *Wooden Leg: A Warrior Who Fought Custer* (Minneapolis: Midwest, 1931), 217–21; Iron Hawk, "Killing Custer's Men," in John G. Neihardt, *Black Elk Speaks* (Albany, N.Y.: SUNY Press, 2008; first published in 1932), 119–25; Joseph M. Marshall III, *The Day the World Ended at Little Bighorn* (New York: Penguin, 2007).

33. First quote in Colin G. Calloway, ed., *Our Hearts Fell to the Ground: Plains Indian Views of How the West Was Lost* (Boston: Bedford/St. Martin's, 1996), 134; second quote in Stephen E. Ambrose, *Crazy Horse and Custer: The Parallel Lives of Two American Warriors* (New York: Anchor, 1996), 443.

34. Both quotes in Mike Sajna, *Crazy Horse: The Life Behind the Legend* (New York: John Wiley & Sons, 2000), 282, 292.

35. First quote in Philip Weeks, *Farewell, My Nation: The American Indian and the United States, 1820–1890* (Arlington Heights, Ill.: Harlan Davidson, 1990), 186; remaining quotes in "A National Disgrace," *Harper's*, August 5, 1876, 631.

36. Quoted in Neihardt, *Black Elk Speaks*, 105.

37. See Sajna, *Crazy Horse*, 316–27.

38. Newspapers quoted in ibid., 325; Red Cloud quoted in Robert W. Larson, *Red Cloud: Warrior-Statesman of the Lakota Sioux* (Norman: University of Oklahoma Press, 1997), 263.

39. Nelson A. Miles, "Hunting Large Game," *North American Review* 161 (October 1895): 492.

40. Gates quote in James Wilson, *The Earth Shall Weep: A History of Native America* (New York: Grove Press, 2000), 311; last quote in Francis Paul Prucha, *Americanizing the American Indian: Writings by the "Friends of the Indian," 1880–1900* (Cambridge: Harvard University Press, 1973), 268.

41. Richard Henry Pratt, *Battlefield and Classroom: An Autobiography*, ed. Robert M. Utley (Norman: University of Oklahoma Press, 2003; first published in 1964), xi.

42. Quoted in W. Fitzhugh Brundage, "Meta Warrick's 1907 'Negro Tableaux' and (Re) Presenting African American Historical Memory," *Journal of American History* 89 (March 2003): 1373.

43. Quoted in Robert W. Rydell, *All the World's a Fair: Visions of Empire at American International Expositions, 1876–1916* (Chicago: University of Chicago Press, 1984), 34.

44. Andrew Carnegie, *Triumphant Democracy; or, Fifty Years' March of the Republic* (Boston: Elibron, 2006; first published in 1888), 1.

45. Quoted in Mark Wahlgren Summers, *The Era of Good Stealings* (New York: Oxford University Press, 1993), 281. For a full discussion of the contested election of 1876, see Summers, chapters 19 and 20, and Roy Morris Jr., *Fraud of the Century: Rutherford B. Hayes, Samuel Tilden and the Stolen Election of 1876* (New York: Simon & Schuster, 2003).

46. Quoted in Summers, *Era of Good Stealings*, 283.

47. Quoted in Eric Foner, *Reconstruction: America's Unfinished Revolution, 1863–1877* (New York: Harper & Row, 1988), 577.

48. Grant quoted in John Y. Simon, ed., *The Papers of Ulysses S. Grant*, vol. 28, *November 1, 1876–September 30, 1978* (Carbondale: Southern Illinois University Press, 2005), 116; Godkin quoted in Douglas A. Blackmon, *Slavery by Another Name: The Re-Enslavement of Black America from the Civil War to World War II* (New York: Doubleday, 2008), 87; Adams quoted in Morris, *Fraud of the Century*, 116.

49. Quoted in Thomas E. Schott, *Alexander H. Stephens of Georgia: A Biography* (Baton Rouge: Louisiana State University Press, 1988), 504.

50. Livermore quoted in Mary Ashton Rice Livermore, *My Story of the War: A Woman's Narrative of Four Years Personal Experience* (Hartford, Conn.: A. D. Worthington, 1890), 7; DuBois quoted in Foner, *Reconstruction*, 602.

51. See Loren Schweninger, "Black Economic Reconstruction in the South," in *The Facts of Reconstruction: Essays in Honor of John Hope Franklin*, ed. Eric Anderson and Alfred A. Moss Jr. (Baton Rouge: Louisiana State University Press, 1991), 180–87.

52. Blum, *Reforging the White Republic*, 83.

53. See Steven Hahn, *A Nation Under Our Feet: Black Political Struggles in the Rural South from Slavery to the Great Migration* (Cambridge: Harvard University Press, 2003), 321–60.

54. See Bruce E. Baker, *What Reconstruction Meant: Historical Memory in the American South* (Charlottesville: University of Virginia Press, 2007).

55. Daniel S. Henderson, *The White Man's Revolution in South Carolina: Address of Hon. D. S. Henderson. Delivered at the Unveiling of the McKie Merriweather Monument, North Augusta, South Carolina, 16th February, 1916*, South Caroliniana Library, University of South Carolina, Columbia, SC.

56. Frederick Douglass, "I Denounce the So-Called Emancipation as a Stupendous Fraud," April 16, 1888, in *FD:SSW*, 714–15; poem in Nina Silber, *The Romance of Reunion: Northerners and the South, 1865–1900* (Chapel Hill: University of North Carolina Press, 1993), 157.

57. John R. Lynch, *The Facts of Reconstruction* (New York: Neale Publishing, 1913), 110; W. E. B. DuBois, *Black Reconstruction in America, 1860–1880*, Introduction by David Levering Lewis (New York: Free Press, 1998; first published in 1935); "A Colored Orator," *Harper's*, September 13, 1873, 795.

58. Henry Cabot Lodge, *Early Memories* (New York: Charles Scribner's Sons, 1913), 128.

59. All quotes in Silber, *Romance of Reunion*, 78, 87.

60. Robert Penn Warren, *The Legacy of the Civil War* (Lincoln: University of Nebraska

Press, 1998; first published in 1961), 55; remaining quotes in Paul M. Gaston, *The New South Creed: A Study in Southern Mythmaking* (New York: Knopf, 1970), 173.

61. Ellen Glasgow, *The Woman Within* (Charlottesville: University of Virginia Press, 2004; first published in 1954), 97; C. Vann Woodward and Elisabeth Muhlenfeld, eds., *The Private Mary Chesnut: The Unpublished Civil War Diaries* (New York: Oxford University Press, 1984), xxv.

62. Walt Whitman, "Song of the Exposition," *Leaves of Grass*, ed. Harold W. Blodgett and Sculley Bradley (New York: New York University Press, 1965), 203, 204.

63. Howells, "Centennial," 96; William Dean Howells, "Characteristics of the International Fair," *Atlantic Monthly* 38 (September 1876): 359.

64. See Charles R. Morris, *The Tycoons: How Andrew Carnegie, John D. Rockefeller, Jay Gould, and J. P. Morgan Invented the American Supereconomy* (New York: Holt), 120.

BIBLIOGRAPHY

PRIMARY SOURCES

LETTERS, MEMOIRS, DIARIES, PAMPHLETS, BOOKS, ARTICLES, AND SPEECHES

Adger, John B. and John L. Girardeau, eds. *The Collected Writings of James Henley Thornwell. Volume IV: Ecclesiastical.* Richmond: Presbyterian Committee of Publication, 1873. http://books.google.com/books?id=DqlZAAAAMAAJ&pg=PR1&lpg=PR1&dq =John+B.+Adger,+James+Henley+Thornwell&source=bl&ots=z5XHyp-z42&sig= hpYOiAvgmL3EWv14Z_Tmx1tV10M&hl=en&ei=cnBgTO-2BIH88AbKh9y0DQ &sa=X&oi=book_result&ct=result&resnum=8&ved=0CDcQ6AEwBw#v=onepage& q=John%20B.%20Adger%2C%20James%20Henley%20Thornwell&f=false.

Alger, Horatio. *Ragged Dick.* Philadelphia: John C. Winston, 1910; first published in 1868.

Anthony, Susan B. "On Woman's Right to the Suffrage." 1873. In *The World's Famous Orations*, vol. 10, *America–III, 1861–1905.* New York: Funk and Wagnalls, 1906.

Arp, Bill [Charles Henry Smith]. *Bill Arp's Peace Papers: Columns on War and Reconstruction, 1861–1873.* Columbia: University of South Carolina Press, 2009; first published in 1873.

"The Battle of Sand Creek." *Rocky Mountain News*, December 17, 1864. http://www.kclone wolf.com/History/SandCreek/sc-reports/rocky-editorials.html.

Bancroft, Frederic, ed. *Speeches, Correspondence and Political Papers of Carl Schurz.* 6 vols. New York: G. P. Putnam's Sons, 1913.

Bancroft, George. *History of the United States from the Discovery of the American Continent.* 10 vols. Boston: Little, Brown, 1854–1878.

Ballou, Sullivan, to Sarah Ballou, July 14, 1861. http://www.pbs.org/civilwar/war/ballou_letter .html.

Basler, Roy P. *The Collected Works of Abraham Lincoln.* 8 vols. New Brunswick: Rutgers University Press, 1953.

Beecher, Catharine E., and Harriet Beecher Stowe. *The American Woman's Home.* New Brunswick: Rutgers University Press, 2002; first published in 1869.

Behling, Laura L., ed. *Hospital Transports: A Memoir of the Sick and Wounded from the Peninsula of Virginia in the Summer of 1862.* Albany, N.Y.: SUNY Press, 2005; first published in 1863.

Berlin, Ira, Joseph Patrick Reidy, and Leslie S. Rowland, eds. *Freedom Series II: The Black Military Experience: A Documentary History of Emancipation, 1861–1867.* Cambridge: Cambridge University Press, 1982.

Bierce, Ambrose. *Civil War Stories*. Mineola, N.Y.: Dover, 1994.

Bradley, George S. *The Star Corps; or, Notes of an Army Chaplain During Sherman's Famous "March to the Sea."* Milwaukee: Jermain & Brightman, 1865. http://books. google.com/books?id=vK6jXo-zKQUC&printsec=frontcover&dq=George+S. +Bradley,+The+Star+Corps&hl=en&ei=juIUTNj5AsH68AbWvYWKCg&sa=X&oi =book_result&ct=result&resnum=1&ved=0CC8Q6AEwAA#v=onepage&q&f= false

Buchanan, James. "Fourth Annual Message to Congress on the State of the Union." December 3, 1860. http://www.presidency.ucsb.edu/ws/index.php?pid=29501&st=Buchanan &st1=fourth.

Carnegie, Andrew. *The Autobiography of Andrew Carnegie and His Essay "The Gospel of Wealth."* Edited by Gordon Hunter. New York: Signet, 2006; first published in 1920.

———. *Triumphant Democracy; or, Fifty Years' March of the Republic*. Boston: Elibron, 2006; first published in 1888.

Carter, Gari, ed. *Troubled State: Civil War Journals of Franklin Archibald Dick*. Kirksville, Mo.: Truman State University Press, 2008.

Castleman, Alfred Lewis. *The Army of the Potomac, Behind the Scenes: A Diary of Unwritten History; from the Organization of the Army, by General George B. McClellan, to the Close of the Campaign in Virginia, About the First Day of January, 1863*. Milwaukee: Strickland, 1863. http://books.google.com/books?id=AMB6WyapTGQC&printsec= frontcover&dq=Alfred+Lewis+Castleman,+The+Army+of+the+Potomac&cd=1#v= onepage&q&f=false.

Clark, Olynthus B., ed. *Downing's Civil War Diary*. Des Moines: Iowa State Department of History and Archives, 1916.

Clay-Clopton, Virginia. *A Belle of the Fifties: Memoirs of Mrs. [Virginia] Clay [-Clopton] of Alabama, Covering Social and Political Life in Washington and the South, 1853–66*. New York: Doubleday, Page, 1905. http://docsouth.unc.edu/fpn/clay/clay.html #clay138.

Cleveland, Henry, ed. *Alexander H. Stephens, in Public and Private: With Letters and Speeches, Before, During, and Since the War*. Philadelphia: National Publishing, 1866. http://books.google.com/books?id=EE-pryuHiVoC&printsec=frontcover&dq= Henry+Cleveland,+Alexander+H.+Stephens&source=bl&ots=Z-Hy4-Veoh&sig= FDvzuiEyvYyr2R7KiA4kc_peHZo&hl=en&ei=NO8TTP.

Conwell, Russell H. *Acres of Diamonds*. New York: Jove Books, 1978; first published in 1878. http://www.americanrhetoric.com/speeches/rconwellacresofdiamonds.htm.

Cooke, Chauncey H. *A Badger Boy in Blue: The Civil War Letters of Chauncey H. Cooke*. Detroit: Wayne State University Press, 2007; first published in 1920–22.

Crane, Stephen. *Maggie: A Girl of the Streets and Other New York Writings*. New York: Random House, 2001; first published in 1893.

Dabney, Robert Lewis. "The Duty of the Hour." *The Land We Love* 6 (December 1868): 108–19.

Darwin, Charles. *The Descent of Man, and Selection in Relation to Sex*. 2 vols. New York: D. Appleton, 1872. Most recent edition: BiblioLife, 2009.

———. *On The Origin of Species by Means of Natural Selection, or The Preservation of Favoured Races in the Struggle for Life*. London: John Murray, 1859. http://books.google .com/books?id=tojb8-O6efoC&printsec=frontcover&dq=Darwin

,+Origin+of+Species & source = bl & ots = DpdotLHDPt & sig = ztFY l6OTbn5NkVKn5PR4Wveo2T4&hl=en&ei=AMVgTKi_AYT48AbM-aStCg&sa=X& oi=book_result&ct=result&resnum=4&ved=0CCsQ6AEwAw#v=onepage&q&f= false

de Fontaine, Felix Gregory. *History of American Abolitionism: Its Four Great Epochs*. New York: D. Appleton, 1861.

Diggins, John Patrick, ed. *The Portable John Adams*. New York: Penguin, 2004.

Douglass, Frederick. *Admiration and Ambivalence: Frederick Douglass and John Brown*. New York: Gilder Lehrman Institute of American History, 2005.

———. *Frederick Douglass: Selected Speeches and Writings*. Edited by Philip S. Foner. Chicago: Lawrence Hill Books, 1999.

———. *Life and Times of Frederick Douglass*. Mineola, N.Y.: Dover, 2003; first published in 1892.

———. *Narrative of the Life of Frederick Douglass, an American Slave*. New York: Modern Library, 2000; first published in 1845.

Emerson, Ralph Waldo. "Self-Reliance." In *Ralph Waldo Emerson: Essays and Lectures*. Edited by Joel Porte. New York: Literary Classics of the U.S., 1983.

Fitzhugh, George. *Sociology for the South, or The Failure of Free Society*. Richmond: A. Morris, 1854. http://books.google.com/books?id=OvwDAQAAIAAJ&printsec=front cover&dq=George+Fitzhugh,+Sociology+for+the+South&lr=&cd=1#v=onepage &q&f=false.

Foote, Corydon Edward. *With Sherman to the Sea: A Drummer's Story of the Civil War*. New York: John Day, 1960.

Ford, Paul Leicester, ed. *The Writings of Thomas Jefferson*. 10 vols. New York: G. P. Putnam's Sons, 1892–99.

Frederick, J. M. H., compiler. *National Party Platforms of the United States*. Akron, Ohio: J. M. H. Frederick, 1896.

Freeman, Douglas Southall, ed. *A Calendar of Confederate Papers*. Richmond: Confederate Museum, 1908.

Grant, Ulysses S. "First Inaugural Address." March 4, 1869. http://avalon.law.yale.edu/19th_ century/grant1.asp.

———. *Personal Memoirs of U. S. Grant*. New York: Charles L. Webster, 1972; first published in 1886.

Greeley, Horace. *An Overland Journey from New York to San Francisco in the Summer of 1859*. New York: C. M. Saxton, Barker, 1860. http://etext.virginia.edu/railton/roughin git/map/indgreeley.html.

Grimsley, Mark and Todd D. Miller, eds. *The Union Must Stand: The Civil War Diary of John Quincy Adams Campbell, Fifth Iowa Volunteer Infantry*. Knoxville: University of Tennessee Press, 2000.

Harwell, Richard Barksdale, ed. *Kate: The Journal of a Confederate Nurse*. Baton Rouge: Louisiana State University Press, 1987.

Henderson, Daniel S. *The White Man's Revolution in South Carolina: Address of Hon. D. S. Henderson. Delivered at the Unveiling of the McKie Merriweather Monument, North Augusta, South Carolina, 16th February, 1916*. South Caroliniana Library, University of South Carolina, Columbia.

Higginson, Mary Thacker, ed. *Letters and Journal of Thomas Wentworth Higginson, 1846– 1906*. Boston: Houghton Mifflin, 1921.

Holzer, Harold, ed. *The Lincoln-Douglas Debates*. New York: Fordham University Press, 2004.

Howe, M. A. DeWolfe, ed. *Home Letters of General Sherman*. New York: Charles Scribner's Sons, 1909. http://books.google.com/books?id=c4ES-yGLTtoC&pg=PA1&lpg=PA1& dq=Howe,+Home+Letters+of+General+Sherman&source=bl&ots=cvEpMJQPwP& sig=xKN5NQ1kato32Ek2af3HJ61uEow&hl=en&ei=9wkUTIGdJsL38Aadyam6Cg&sa= X&oi=book_result&ct=result&resnum=1&ved=0CBIQ6AEwAA#v=onepage&q&f= false.

Howells, William Dean. *The Rise of Silas Lapham*. New York: Penguin, 2002; first published in 1884.

Iron Hawk. "Killing Custer's Men." In *Black Elk Speaks*. Edited by John G. Neihardt. Albany, N.Y.: SUNY Press, 2008; first published in 1932.

Jones, John Beauchamp. *A Rebel War Clerk's Diary at the Confederate States Capital*. 2 vols. Philadelphia: J. B. Lippincott, 1866.

LeConte, Emma. *Diary, 1864-1865*. http://docsouth.unc.edu/fpn/leconteemma/leconte.html.

Lee, Robert E. [the son], ed. *Recollections and Letters of General Robert E. Lee*. New York: Doubleday, Page, 1909. http://books.google.com/books?id=y4QZAAAAYAAJ &printsec=frontcover&dq=Robert+E.+Lee,+Recollections+and+Letters&cd=1#v= onepage&q&f=false.

Lincoln, Abraham. "Second Inaugural Address." March 4, 1865. http://www.loc.gov/rr/pro gram/bib/ourdocs/Lincoln2nd.html.

———. *Speeches and Writings, 1859-1865*. New York: Penguin, 1989.

Livermore, Mary Ashton Rice. *My Story of the War: A Woman's Narrative of Four Years of Personal Experience*. New York: Da Capo Press, 1995; first published in 1888.

Lodge, Henry Cabot. *Early Memories*. Vol. 1. New York: Charles Scribner's Sons, 1913.

Love, Nat. *The Life and Adventures of Nat Love*. 1907. http://docsouth.unc.edu/neh/natlove/ natlove.

Lowe, Jeffrey C., and Sam Hodges, eds. *Letters to Amanda: The Civil War Letters of Marion Hill Fitzpatrick, Army of Northern Virginia*. Macon, Ga.: Mercer University Press, 1998.

Lunt, Dolly Sumner. *A Woman's Wartime Journal*. New York: Century, 1918. http://docsouth .unc.edu/fpn/burge/lunt.html

Maguire, John Francis. *Father Mathew: A Biography*. New York: D&J Sadlier, 1864. http:// books.google.com/books?id=uN4XAAAAYAAJ&printsec=frontcover&dq= John+Francis+Maguire,+Father+Mathew&source=bl&ots=txpXgPqnCm&sig= 5LwTf-fE321HzuNcO2rjgHAWcFQ&hl=en&ei=_1thTMDqKoL78AbinaC5Cg&sa=X &oi=book_result&ct=result&resnum=1&ved=0CBIQ6AEwAA#v=onepage&q&f= false

Manypenny, George W. *Our Indian Wards*. Cincinnati: Robert Clarke, 1880. http://books. google.com/books?id=aGSzSDtvA8MC&printsec=frontcover&dq=Manypenny ,+Our+Indian+Wards&cd=1#v=onepage&q&f=false.

Mason, Virginia, ed. *The Public Life and Diplomatic Correspondence of James Murray Mason*. New York: Neale Publishing, 1906. http://books.google.com/books?id=at3sbO4U1ZoC &printsec=frontcover&dq=Virginia+Mason,+The+Public+Life&source=bl&ots=g- iwmZPKyd&sig=SpJa1zXFFgmuZWo6Mj_2-7mk_Tk&hl=en&ei=UVxhTNo hwvjwBtXY3bMK&sa=X&oi=book_result&ct=result&resnum=1&ved=0CBIQ6AE wAA#v=onepage&q&f=false

McArthur, Judith N., and Orville Vernon Burton, eds. *A Gentleman and an Officer: A Military and Social History of James B. Griffin's Civil War*. New York: Oxford University Press, 1996.

McClure, Alexander K. *Recollections of Half a Century*. Salem, Mass.: Salem Press, 1902. http://books.google.com/books?id=ACNCAAAAIAAJ&printsec=frontcover&dq=Alexander+K.+McClure,+Recollections&source=bl&ots=oXGiEZGyQR&sig=GG51Rp3PCyey7yOVLNWKFz22Z6E&hl=en&ei=hVxhTOiDK8T58Aahk7S0Cg&sa=X&oi=book_result&ct=result&resnum=6&ved=0CCgQ6AEwBQ#v=onepage&q&f=false

Mellon, Thomas. *Thomas Mellon and His Times*. Pittsburgh: Pittsburgh University Press, 1994.

Melville, Herman. "Shiloh: A Requiem." 1862. http://www.poetryfoundation.org.

Monk, Maria. *Awful Disclosures of the Hotel Dieu Nunnery of Montreal*. London: James S. Hodson, 1837; first published in 1836. http://books.google.com/books?id=RkoEAAAAQAAJ&printsec=frontcover&dq=Maria+Monk.+Awful+Disclosures&lr=&cd=3#v=onepage&q&f=false.

Moore, Frank, ed. *The Rebellion Record: A Diary of American Events*. 11 vols. New York: G. P. Putnam, 1861.

Morehead, Anne to Mrs. Rufus Patterson, April 1, 1863. Jones and Patterson Family Papers, Southern Historical Collection, Wilson Library, University of North Carolina, Chapel Hill.

Mott, Lucretia. "Righteousness Exalteth a Nation." June 6, 1860. http://www.qhpress.org/quakerpages/qhoa/mott.htm.

Nichols, George Ward. *The Story of the Great March: From the Diary of a Staff Officer*. Bedford, Mass.: Applewood Books, 2008; first published in 1865.

Nordhoff, Charles. *The Cotton States in the Spring and Summer of 1875*. New Castle, Del.: Burt Franklin, 1988; first published in 1876.

O. Henry. "An Unfinished Story." In *The American Disinherited: A Profile in Fiction*. Edited by Abe C. Ravitz. Belmont, Calif.: Dickenson, 1970.

Olmsted, Frederick Law. *A Journey in the Seaboard Slave States, with Remarks on their Economy*. New York: Mason Brothers, 1861. http://books.google.com/books?id=koMIAAAAQAAJ&printsec=frontcover&dq=Olmsted,+Journey+through+Seaboard&lr=&cd=2#v=onepage&q&f=false.

O'Sullivan, John. "Annexation." *United States Magazine and Democratic Review* 17 (July/August 1845): 6.

Palmer, Benjamin M. "Thanksgiving Sermon." November 29, 1860. http://civilwarcauses.org/palmer.htm.

Parker, Theodore. "Sermon of War." In *Collected Works of Theodore Parker, Part Four*. Edited by Theodore Parker and Frances Power Cobbe. Whitefish, Mont.: Kessinger Publishing, 2004; first published in 1876.

Paxton, Elisha Franklin, *Memoir and Memorials*. Privately published, 1905. http://books.google.com/books?id=b9ItAAAAYAAJ&printsec=frontcover&dq=Elisha+Franklin+Paxton,+Memoir+and+Memorials&cd=1#v=onepage&q&f=false.

Pember, Phoebe Yates. *A Southern Woman's Story*. Introduction by George C. Rable. Columbia: University of South Carolina Press, 2002.

Perry, John Gardner. *Letters from a Surgeon of the Civil War*. Edited by Martha Derby Perry. Boston: Little, Brown, 1906. http://books.google.com/books?id=C0571D9xgIsC

&printsec=frontcover&dq=John+Gardner+Perry,+Letters+from+a+Surgeon&cd=1 #v=onepage&q&f=false.

Phillips, Wendell. *Speeches, Lectures, and Letters*. Vol. 1. Boston: Lee and Shepard, 1872. http://quod.lib.umich.edu/cgi/t/text/text-idx?c=moa;idno=ABT7101.0001.001.

Pickett, La Salle Corbell, ed. *The Heart of a Soldier: As Revealed in the Intimate Letters of General George Pickett*. New York: Seth Moyle, 1913. http://docsouth.unc.edu/fpn/ pickett/pickett.html.

Polk, James K. *The Diary of James K. Polk During His Presidency, 1845 to 1849*. Vol. 2. Edited by Milo Milton Quaife. Chicago: A. C. McClurg, 1910. http://books.google.com/ books?id=vRcOAAAAIAAJ&pg=PR7&dq=The+Diary+of+James+K .+Polk+during+his+Presidency,+Volume+II&lr=&cd=1#v=onepage&q&f=false.

———. "First Annual Message." December 2, 1845. http://www.presidency.ucsb.edu/ws/ index.php?pid=29486&st=Polk&st1=annual.

———. "Fourth Annual Message." December 5, 1848. http://www.presidency.ucsb.edu/ws/ index.php?pid=29489.

———. "Message on War with Mexico." May 11, 1846. http://www.pbs.org/weta/thewest/ resources/archives/two/mexdec.htm.

———. "Special Message." August 4, 1846. http://www.presidency.ucsb.edu/ws/?pld=67937.

Pollard, Edward A. "The Lost Cause." *Hours at Home* 3 (September 1866): 475–82. http:// books.google.com/books?id=DuARAAAAYAAJ&pg=PA5&dq= Hours+at+Home+Volume+III&cd=1#v=onepage&q=Hours%20at%20Home %20Volume%20III&f=false.

Pratt, Richard Henry. *Battlefield and Classroom: An Autobiography*. Edited by Robert M. Utley. Norman: University of Oklahoma Press, 2003; first published in 1964.

Reed, Rebecca Theresa. *Six Months in a Convent, or, the Narrative of Rebecca Theresa Reed, Who Was Under the Influence of the Roman Catholics About Two Years, and an Inmate of the Ursuline Convent on Mount Benedict, Charlestown, Mass., Nearly Six Months in the Years 1831–32*. Boston: Russell, Odiorne & Metcalf, 1835. http://books .google.com/books?id=4LoOAQAAIAAJ&pg=PA40&dq=Rebecca+Reed ,+Six+Months+in+a+Convent&cd=1#v=onepage&q&f=false.

———. *Supplement to "Six Months in a Convent."* Boston: Russell, Odiorne, 1835. http:// books.google.com/books?id=9PsaAAAAYAAJ&pg=PA196&dq=An+Answer+to+Six+ Months+in+a+Convent&cd=6#v=onepage&q=An%20Answer%20to%20Six %20Months%20in%20a%20Convent&f=false.

Reid, Whitelaw. *After the War: A Tour of the Southern States, 1865–1866*. New York: Harper & Row, 1965; first published in 1866.

Richardson, James D., ed. *A Compilation of the Messages and Papers of the Confederacy*. Vol. 1. Nashville: U.S. Publishing, 1905. http://books.google.com/books?id=HUea DyPa39YC&printsec=frontcover&dq=James+D.+Richardson,+A+Compilation+of+t he+Messages+and+Papers+of+the+Confederacy&source=bl&ots=5Yz1Q33oWR &sig=vNmbFm9BGZwIMLtAhGWeWUaMTMY&hl=en&ei= ZvATTPeQG8L48Aa86M2dDA&sa=X&oi=book_result&ct=result&resnum=6&ved= 0CCgQ6AEwBQ#v=onepage&q&f=false.

Robinson, Edward Arlington. "John Brown." In *Collected Poems*. 1921. http://www.bartleby.com.

Scott, Robert Garth, ed. *Fallen Leaves: The Civil War Letters of Major Henry Livermore Abbott*. Kent, Ohio: Kent State University Press, 1991.

Sears, Stephen W., ed. *The Civil War Papers of George B. McClellan: Selected Correspondence, 1860–1865*. Cambridge, Mass.: Da Capo Press, 1992.

Secession Era Editorial Project. Furman University. http://history.furman.edu/editorials.

Sherman, John. *John Sherman's Recollections of Forty Years in the House, Senate and Cabinet*. Vol. 1. Chicago: Warner, 1895. http://books.google.com/books?id=bR9HNwZEC TAC&printsec=frontcover&dq=John+Sherman,+John+Sherman%27s+Recollections &lr=&cd=1#v=onepage&q&f=false.

Sherman, William Tecumseh. *Memoirs of General William T. Sherman*. New York: Penguin, 1990.

Simon, John Y., ed. *The Papers of Ulysses S. Grant*. 30 volumes to date. Carbondale, Ill.: Southern Illinois University Press, 1967–.

Southern Historical Society Papers. Vol. 9. July/August 1881. http://books.google.com/books ?id=3iwUAAAAYAAJ&pg=PP5&dq=Southern+Historical+Society+Papers+Volume +IX&hl=en&ei=QUUSTPuWIIP6lwfq5OizAQ&sa=X&oi=book_result&ct=result& resnum=2&ved=0CDAQ6AEwAQ#v=onepage&q=Southern%20Historical%20Soci ety%20Papers%20Volume%20IX&f=false.

Spencer, Herbert. "The Study of Sociology." *Popular Science Monthly* 1 (June 1872): 159–74.

Stone, William L. *Maria Monk and the Nunnery of the Hotel Dieu*. New York: Howe and Bates, 1836. http://books.google.com/books?id=JY2gCW1ea8UC&pg=PA1&dq= William+Stone,+Maria+Monk&cd=2#v=onepage&q&f=false.

Stowe, Harriet Beecher. *House and Home Papers*. Bedford, Mass.: Applewood Books, 2008; first published in 1865.

———. *Uncle Tom's Cabin, or Life Among the Lowly*. New York: Norton, 1994; first published in 1852.

Stowe, Harriet Beecher, to Calvin Stowe, July 26, 1849. In *Life and Letters of Harriet Beecher Stowe*. Edited by Annie Fields. Boston: Riverside Press, 1898. http://books.google. com/books?id=vNo7AAAAYAAJ&printsec=frontcover&dq=Annie+Fields, +Life+and+Letters&lr=&cd=1#v=onepage&q&f=false.

Strong, George Templeton. *The Diary of George Templeton Strong*. 4 vols. Edited by Allan Nevins and Milton Halsey Thomas. New York: Macmillan, 1952.

Thoreau, Henry David. "Walking." 1862. http://www.bartleby.com.

Thorndike, Rachel Sherman, ed. *The Sherman Letters*. New York: Scribner's, 1894. http:// books.google.com/books?id=bUUYJ9oYN7wC&printsec=frontcover&dq= Rachel+Sherman+Thorndike,+The+Sherman+Letters&source=bl&ots=FZ1o7ruAeT& sig=BeL6fTDN4KDLzDKdYH9_KjwZQfU&hl=en&ei=FiYVTLeTI4T68A beprGdDA&sa=X&oi=book_result&ct=result&resnum=1&ved=0CBIQ6AEwAA#v= onepage&q&f=false.

Timrod, Henry. *Poems of Henry Timrod: Memoir and Portrait*. Boston: Houghton Mifflin, 1899. Richmond: B. F. Johnson Publishing, 1901. http://books.google.com/books? id=4BOxAAAAIAAJ&printsec=frontcover&dq=Henry+Timrod, +Poems+of+Henry+Timrod&cd=1#v=onepage&q&f=false.

Tourgée, Albion W. *A Fool's Errand: A Novel of the South During Reconstruction*. New York: Harper, 1961; first published in 1879.

Trowbridge, John T. *The Desolate South, 1865–1866: A Picture of the Battlefields and of the Devastated Confederacy*. Edited by Gordon Carroll. Boston: Little, Brown, 1956; first published in 1866.

Twain, Mark, and Charles Dudley Warner. *The Gilded Age: A Tale of Today*. New York: Penguin, 2001; first published in 1873.

Ward, James A., ed. *Southern Railroad Man: Conductor N. J. Bell's Recollections of the Civil War Era*. DeKalb: Northern Illinois University Press, 1994; first published in 1896.

Washington, Booker T. *Up from Slavery: An Autobiography*. New York: Doubleday, Page, 1902.

Watkins, Sam. *"Co. Aytch": A Confederate Memoir of the Civil War*. New York: Touchstone, 2003; first published in 1990.

Wescott, Morgan Ebenezer. *Civil War Letters, 1861 to 1865: Written by a Boy in Blue to His Mother*. Mora, Minn.: Privately published, 1909.

Wheelwright, John T. "Public Opinion as a Force." *Harvard Review* 8 (April 1889): 47–48.

Whitman, Walt. *Leaves of Grass*. Edited by Harold W. Blodgett and Sculley Bradley. New York: New York University Press, 1965.

———. "Blood-Money." 1850. http://www.bartleby.com.

———. "Democratic Vistas." 1871. In *Specimen Days and Collect*. Philadelphia: David McKay, 1882.

———. "Rulers Strictly out of the Masses." 1856. http://www.bartleby.com.

———. "War with Mexico," May 11, 1846, and "Our Territory on the Pacific," July 7, 1846. In *The Gathering of the Forces by Walt Whitman: Editorials, Essays, Literary and Dramatic Reviews and Other Material Written by Walt Whitman as Editor of the Brooklyn Daily Eagle in 1846 and 1847*. Edited by Cleveland Rodgers and John Black. New York: G. P. Putnam's Sons, 1920.

Whittier, John Greenleaf. "Ichabod." 1850. http://www.bartleby.com.

Wilkeson, Frank. *Reflections of a Private Soldier in the Army of the Potomac*. New York: G. P. Putnam's Sons, 1887.

Wilson, Clyde, ed. *The Papers of John C. Calhoun*. 28 vols. Columbia: University of South Carolina Press, 1959–2003.

Wise, Henry A. "Governor Wise's Letter on Know-nothingism and his Speech at Alexandria." 1854. YA Pamphlet Collection, Library of Congress.

Wooden Leg. "A Cheyenne Account of the Battle." In *Wooden Leg: A Warrior Who Fought Custer*. Edited by Thomas B. Marquis. Minneapolis: Midwest, 1931.

Woodward, C. Vann, ed. *Mary Chesnut's Civil War*. New Haven: Yale University Press, 1993; first published in 1981.

Woodward, C. Vann, and Elisabeth Muhlenfeld, eds. *The Private Mary Chesnut: The Unpublished War Diaries*. New York: Oxford University Press, 1984.

Worth, Jonathan. "Inaugural Address." March 1868. http://www.atgpress.com/inform/gov065.htm.

Yearns, W. Buck, and John G. Barrett, eds. *North Carolina Civil War Documentary*. Chapel Hill: University of North Carolina Press, 1980.

NEWSPAPERS AND MAGAZINES

Atlantic Monthly
Campaign Age, http://alexanderstreet.com/products/cwdb.htm
De Bow's Review
Harper's New Monthly Magazine

Harper's Weekly
Liberator
Nation
New York Times
New York Tribune
North American Review
Putnam's Monthly Magazine
Scientific American
Southern Literary Messenger
Valley Spirit, http://valley.lib.virginia.edu/news/vs1864/pa.fr.vs.1864.08.31.xml
Weekly Register, http://alexanderstreet.com/products/cwdb.htm

GOVERNMENT DOCUMENTS

A Centennial Fourth of July Democratic Celebration. The Massacre of Six Colored Citizens of the United States at Hamburgh, S.C., on July 4, 1876. Debate in the U.S. House of Representatives, July 15 and 18, 1876. http://www.archive.org/details/centennialfourth o1unit.

"The Chivington Massacre." Report of the Joint Special Committee. Appendix to *Reports of the Committees of the Senate.* 39th Congress, 2nd Session. Washington: GPO, 1867.

Civil Rights Cases. 109 U.S. 3.

"Condition of the South." *Index to Reports of Committees of the House of Representatives.* 43rd Congress, 2nd Session. Washington: GPO, 1875.

Congressional Globe.

"Diplomatic Correspondence." *Executive Documents.* 39th Congress, 1st Session. Washington: GPO, 1866.

Inspector's Report of Affairs in Kentucky. *Executive Documents of the House of Representatives.* 39th Congress, 1st Session. Washington: GPO, 1866.

Executive Documents of the Senate. 40th Congress, 1st Session, and Special Session, 1867. Washington: GPO, 1868.

——. *Executive Documents of the Senate.* 40th Congress, 3rd Session. Washington: GPO, 1869.

——. *Executive Documents of the House of Representatives.* 41st Congress, 2nd Session. Washington: GPO, 1870

Massachusetts Department of Labor. *Thirteenth Annual Report on the Statistics of Labor.* Boston: Rand, Avery, 1882.

"Memphis Riots and Massacres." July 25, 1866. *Reports of the Committees of the House of Representatives.* 39th Congress, 1st Session. Washington: GPO, 1866.

Miscellaneous Documents. 43rd Congress, 2nd Session. December 8, 1874. Washington: GPO, 1875:

Mississippi in 1875. Report of the Select Committee to Inquire into the Mississippi Election of 1875. 2 vols. Washington: GPO, 1876.

"Recent Election in South Carolina." *Index to Reports of Committees of the House of Representatives.* 44th Congress, 2nd Session. Washington: GPO, 1877.

Register of Debates. 21st Congress, 1st Session. January 27, 1830.

"Report of Lieutenant-General Sheridan." *Index to the Executive Documents of the House of Representatives*, vol. 2, *Report of the Secretary of War*. 45th Congress, 3rd Session. Washington: GPO, 1879.

"South Carolina in 1876—Hamburgh Massacre." *Miscellaneous Documents of the Senate*. 44th Congress, 2nd Session. Washington: GPO, 1877.

"Speech of General Hampton." *Index to the Miscellaneous Documents of the House of Representatives*. 48th Congress, 1st Session. Washington: GPO, 1877.

Testimony of Col. Henry B. Carrington, January 3, 1867. *Records Relating to the Investigation of the Ft. Philip Kearney (or Fetterman) Massacre*. National Archives and Record Service, 5. http://freepages.history.rootsweb.ancestry.com/~familyinformation/fpk/car_5.html.

Testimony of John Fryer. *South Carolina in 1876. Testimony as to the Denial of the Elective Franchise in South Carolina at the Elections of 1875 and 1876 Taken Under the Resolution of the Senate of December 5, 1876, Forty-fourth Congress, 2nd Session*. Washington: GPO, 1877.

Upton, Emory. *Military Policy of the United States*. Washington: GPO, 1916.

The War of the Rebellion: A Compilation of the Official Records of the Union and Confederate Armies. Ser. 1, vol. 44. http://digital.library.cornell.edu/m/moawar/waro.html.

SECONDARY SOURCES

BOOKS

Abzug, Robert H. *Cosmos Crumbling: American Reform and the Religious Imagination*. New York: Oxford University Press, 1994.

Ackerman, Kenneth D. *Boss Tweed: The Rise and Fall of the Corrupt Pol Who Conceived the Soul of Modern New York*. New York: Carroll & Graf, 2005.

Adams, Henry. *The Education of Henry Adams*. Forgotten Books, 2008; first published in 1919. http://www.forgottenbooks.org

Ambrose, Stephen E. *Crazy Horse and Custer: The Parallel Lives of Two American Warriors*. New York: Anchor, 1996.

Anbinder, Tyler. *Five Points: The 19th-Century New York City Neighborhood that Invented Tap Dance, Stole Elections, and Became the World's Most Notorious Slum*. New York: Free Press, 2001.

———. *Nativism and Slavery: The Northern Know Nothings and the Politics of the 1850s*. New York: Oxford University Press, 1992.

Anderson, Eric, and Alfred A. Moss Jr., eds. *The Facts of Reconstruction: Essays in Honor of John Hope Franklin*. Baton Rouge: Louisiana State University Press, 1991.

Andrew, Rod, Jr. *Wade Hampton: Confederate Warrior to Southern Redeemer*. Chapel Hill: University of North Carolina Press, 2008.

Applegate, Debby. *The Most Famous Man in America: The Biography of Henry Ward Beecher*. New York: Doubleday, 2006.

Armstrong, William H. *Warrior in Two Camps: Ely S. Parker, Union General and Seneca Chief*. Syracuse: Syracuse University Press, 1978.

Athearn, Robert B. *William Tecumseh Sherman and the Settlement of the West*. Norman: University of Oklahoma Press, 1956.

Baker, Bruce E. *What Reconstruction Meant: Historical Memory in the American South.* Charlottesville: University of Virginia Press, 2007.

Bannister, Robert C. *Social Darwinism: Science and Myth in Anglo-American Social Thought.* Philadelphia: Temple University Press, 1979.

Barth, Gunther. *City People: The Rise of Modern City Culture in Nineteenth-Century America.* New York: Oxford University Press, 1980.

———. *Instant Cities: Urbanization and the Rise of San Francisco and Denver.* New York: Oxford University Press, 1975.

Bartlett, Irving H. *John C. Calhoun: A Biography.* New York: Norton, 1994.

Benét, Stephen Vincent. "Army of Northern Virginia." 1930. http://oldpoetry.com/opoem/38925-Stephen-Vincent-Benet-Army-Of-Northern-Virginia.

Bernstein, Iver. *The New York City Draft Riots: Their Significance for American Society and Politics in the Age of the Civil War.* New York: Oxford University, 1990.

Billington, Ray Allen. *The Far Western Frontier, 1830–1860.* New York: Harper Torchbooks, 1956.

———. *The Protestant Crusade, 1800–1860: A Study of the Origins of American Nativism.* New York: Macmillan, 1938.

Blackmon, Douglas A. *Slavery by Another Name: The Re-Enslavement of Black Americans from the Civil War to World War II.* New York: Doubleday, 2008.

Blight, David W. *Race and Reunion: The Civil War in American Memory.* Cambridge: Harvard University Press, 2001.

Blum, Edward J. *Reforging the White Republic: Race, Religion, and American Nationalism, 1865–1898.* Baton Rouge: Louisiana State University Press, 2005.

Blumin, Stuart M. *The Emergence of the Middle Class: Social Experience in the American City.* Cambridge: Cambridge University Press, 1989.

Bodnar, John. *The Transplanted: A History of Immigrants in Urban America.* Bloomington: Indiana University Press, 1985.

Bowers, Claude. *The Tragic Era: The Revolution After Lincoln.* New York: Retail Press, 2008; first published in 1929.

Bowers, John. *Chickamauga and Chattanooga: The Battles That Doomed the Confederacy.* New York: Harper Perennial, 2001.

Boydston, Jeanne, Mary Kelley, and Anne Margolis, eds. *The Limits of Sisterhood.* Chapel Hill: University of North Carolina Press, 1988.

Brands, H. W. *The Age of Gold: The California Gold Rush and the New American Dream.* New York: Doubleday, 2002.

Brown, Dee. *The American West.* New York: Touchstone, 1994.

———. *Bury My Heart at Wounded Knee: An Indian History of the American West.* New York: Holt, 1970.

———. *The Year of the Century: 1876.* New York: Scribner, 1966.

Brundage, W. Fitzhugh. *The Southern Past: A Clash of Race and Memory.* Cambridge: Harvard University Press, 2005.

Budiansky, Stephen. *The Bloody Shirt: Terror After the Civil War.* New York: Plume, 2009.

Burton, Orville Vernon. *The Age of Lincoln.* New York: Hill and Wang, 2007.

Bushman, Richard Lyman. *Joseph Smith: Rough Stone Rolling.* New York: Knopf, 2005.

Callow, Philip. *From Noon to Starry Night: A Life of Walt Whitman.* Chicago: Ivan R. Dee, 1992.

Calloway, Colin G., ed. *Our Hearts Fell to the Ground: Plains Indian Views of How the West Was Lost*. Boston: Bedford/St. Martin's, 1996.

Campbell, Randolph. *Grass-Roots Reconstruction in Texas, 1865–1880*. Baton Rouge: Louisiana State University Press, 1998.

Carwardine, Richard. *Evangelicals and Politics in Antebellum America*. New Haven: Yale University Press, 1993.

———. *Lincoln: A Life of Purpose and Power*. New York: Knopf, 2006.

Chernow, Ron. *Titan: The Life of John D. Rockefeller, Sr*. New York: Random House, 1998.

Chesebrough, David B. *Clergy Dissent in the Old South, 1830–1865*. Carbondale: Southern Illinois University Press, 1996.

Chesson, Michael B. *Richmond After the War, 1865–1890*. Richmond: Virginia State Library, 1981.

Cleaves, Freeman. *Meade of Gettysburg*. Norman: University of Oklahoma Press, 1960.

Click, Patricia. *Time Full of Trial: The Roanoke Island Freedmen's Colony, 1862–1867*. Chapel Hill: University of North Carolina Press, 2001.

Clinton, Catherine. *Harriet Tubman: The Road to Freedom*. New York: Little, Brown, 2004.

Cloyd, Benjamin G. *Haunted by Atrocity: Civil War Prisons in American Memory*. Baton Rouge: Louisiana State University Press, 2010.

Cobb, James C. *Away Down South: A History of Southern Identity*. New York: Oxford University Press, 2005.

Coddington, Edwin B. *The Gettysburg Campaign: A Study in Command*. New York: Touchstone, 1997; first published in 1963.

Coffey, David. *Sheridan's Lieutenants: Phil Sheridan, His Generals, and the Final Year of the Civil War*. Lanham, Md.: Rowman & Littlefield, 2005.

Collins, Theresa M., and Lisa Gitelman, eds. *Thomas Edison and Modern America: A Brief History with Documents*. Boston: Bedford/St. Martin's, 2002.

Connell, Evan S. *Son of the Morning Star: Custer and the Little Bighorn*. New York: North Point Press, 1984.

Craven, Avery. *Reconstruction: The Ending of the Civil War*. New York: Holt, Rinehart, and Winston, 1969.

Daniel, Pete. *The Shadow of Slavery: Peonage in the South, 1901–1969*. Urbana: University of Illinois Press, 1972.

Davis, Allen F. *Spearheads for Reform: The Social Settlements and the Progressive Movement, 1890–1914*. New York: Oxford University Press, 1967.

DeCaro, Louis A., Jr. *"Fire from the Midst of You": A Religious Life of John Brown*. New York: New York University Press, 2002.

DeVoto, Bernard. *The Year of Decision, 1846*. Boston: Houghton Mifflin, 1960; first published in 1942.

Dew, Charles B. *Apostles of Disunion: Southern Secession Commissioners and the Causes of the Civil War*. Charlottesville: University Press of Virginia, 2001.

Dickson, Keith D. *Keeping Southern Memories Alive: Douglas Southall Freeman and Identity in the Modern South*. Baton Rouge: Louisiana State University Press, 2011.

Donald, David Herbert. *Lincoln*. New York: Simon & Schuster, 1995.

———. *Lincoln Reconsidered: Essays on the Civil War Era*. New York: Vintage, 2001; first published in 1947.

DuBois, W. E. B. *Black Reconstruction in America, 1860–1880*. Introduction by David Levering Lewis. New York: Free Press, 1998; first published in 1935.

———. *The Souls of Black Folk.* http://www.forgottenbooks.org, 2008; first published in 1903.

Durden, Robert F. *The Self-Inflicted Wound: Southern Politics in the Nineteenth Century.* Lexington: University Press of Kentucky, 1985.

Eisenhower, John D. *So Far from God: The U.S. War with Mexico, 1846–1848.* New York: Random House, 1989.

Erdman, Charles Rosenbury. *D. L. Moody, His Message for Today.* New York: Fleming H. Revell, 1928.

Escott, Paul D. *Many Excellent People: Power and Privilege in North Carolina, 1850–1900.* Chapel Hill: University of North Carolina Press, 1985.

———, et al. *Major Problems in the History of the American South*, vol. 2, *The New South.* 2nd ed. Boston: Houghton Mifflin, 1999.

Evensen, Bruce J. *God's Man for the Gilded Age: D. L. Moody and the Rise of Modern Mass Evangelism.* New York: Oxford University Press, 2003.

Farmer, James O., Jr. *The Metaphysical Confederacy: James Henley Thornwell and the Synthesis of Southern Values.* Macon, Ga.: Mercer University Press, 1999; first published in 1986.

Faust, Drew Gilpin. *This Republic of Suffering: Death and the American Civil War.* New York: Knopf, 2008.

Fite, Emerson David. *Social and Industrial Conditions in the North During the Civil War.* New York: Macmillan, 1910. http://books.google.com/books?id=wIo-AAAAYAAJ& printsec=frontcover&dq=Emerson+David+Fite,+Social+and+Industrial+Conditions +in+the+North&source=bl&ots=A5A1VsFYpM&sig=4lbNF5QcQ6LC6eI FvYe3kokKo_8&hl=en&ei=X2BhTP6NBMGB8gbXtu2ICg&sa=X&oi=book_result &ct=result&resnum=1&ved=0CBUQ6AEwAA#v=onepage&q&f=false

Fehrenbacher, Don E. *The Dred Scott Case: Its Significance in American Law and Politics.* New York: Oxford University Press, 1978.

Fellman, Michael. *The Making of Robert E. Lee.* Baltimore: Johns Hopkins University Press, 2003.

Fiske, John. *Edward Livingston Youmans: Interpreter of Science for the People.* New York: D. Appleton, 1894. http://books.google.com/books?id=f_s4AAAAMAAJ&printsec= frontcover&dq=John+Fiske,+Edward+Livingstone+Youmans&lr=&cd=1#v=onepage &q&f=false.

Foner, Eric. *Free Soil, Free Labor, Free Men: The Ideology of the Republican Party Before the Civil War.* New York: Oxford University Press, 1970.

———. *Reconstruction: America's Unfinished Revolution, 1863–1877.* New York: Harper & Row, 1988.

Foster, Gaines M. *Ghosts of the Confederacy: Defeat, the Lost Cause, and the Emergence of the New South, 1865 to 1913.* New York: Oxford University Press, 1987.

Frederickson, George M. *The Black Image in the White Mind: The Debate on Afro-American Character and Destiny, 1817–1914.* New York: Harper & Row, 1971.

Freehling, William W. *The Road to Disunion*, vol. 1, *Secessionists at Bay, 1776–1854.* New York: Oxford University Press, 1990.

———. *The Road to Disunion*, vol. 2, *Secessionists Triumphant, 1854–1861.* New York: Oxford University Press, 2007.

Freeman, Douglas Southall. *Lee's Lieutenants: A Study in Command.* New York: Scribner, 1998. Abridged by Stephen W. Sears from original published in 1934.

———. *R. E. Lee: A Biography.* 4 vols. New York: Scribner's, 1934–35.

Gallagher, Gary W., ed. *Lee the Soldier*. Lincoln: University of Nebraska Press, 1996.

Gardner, Sarah E. *Blood and Irony: White Women's Narratives of the Civil War, 1861–1937*. Chapel Hill: University of North Carolina Press, 2004.

Garraty, John A. *The New Commonwealth, 1877–1890*. New York: Harper & Row, 1968.

Gaston, Paul M. *The New South Creed: A Study in Southern Mythmaking*. New York: Knopf, 1970.

Gibson, Arrell Morgan. *The American Indian: Prehistory to the Present*. Lexington, Mass.: D. C. Heath, 1980.

Gienapp, William E. *The Origins of the Republican Party, 1852–1856*. New York: Oxford University Press, 1987.

Glasgow, Ellen. *The Battle-Ground*. Tuscaloosa: University of Alabama Press, 2002; first published in 1902.

———. *The Woman Within*. Charlottesville: University of Virginia Press, 2004; first published in 1954.

Glatthaar, Joseph T. *General Lee's Army: From Victory to Collapse*. New York: Free Press, 2008.

Goldfield, David. *Southern Histories: Public, Personal, and Sacred*. Athens: University of Georgia Press, 2003.

———. *Still Fighting the Civil War: The American South and Southern History*. Baton Rouge: Louisiana State University Press, 2002.

Goldfield, David, and Blaine A. Brownell. *Urban America: A History*. Boston: Houghton Mifflin, 1990.

Goldfield, David, et al. *The American Journey: A History of the United States*. Upper Saddle River, NJ: Pearson, 2009.

Good, Timothy S. *We Saw Lincoln Shot: One Hundred Eyewitness Accounts*. Oxford: University Press of Mississippi, 1995.

Goodwin, Doris Kearns. *Team of Rivals: The Political Genius of Abraham Lincoln*. New York: Simon & Schuster, 2005.

Gossett, Thomas F. *Race: The History of an Idea in America*. Dallas: Southern Methodist University Press, 1963.

Gregory, James N. *The Southern Diaspora: How the Great Migrations of Black and White Southerners Transformed America*. Chapel Hill: University of North Carolina Press, 2007.

Greene, Jack P., ed. *The Ambiguity of the American Revolution*. New York: Harper & Row, 1968.

Groom, Winston. *Shrouds of Glory: From Atlanta to Nashville: The Last Great Campaign of the Civil War*. New York: Pocket Books, 1995.

———. *Vicksburg, 1863*. New York: Knopf, 2009.

Grossman, Mark. *Political Corruption in America: An Encyclopedia of Scandals, Power, and Greed*. Santa Barbara, Calif.: ABC-CLIO, 2003.

Guelzo, Allen C. *Abraham Lincoln: Redeemer President*. Grand Rapids, Mich.: Eerdmans, 1999.

———. *Lincoln and Douglas: The Debates That Defined America*. New York: Simon & Schuster, 2009.

———. *Lincoln's Emancipation Proclamation: The End of Slavery in America*. New York: Simon & Schuster, 2004.

Gurganus, Allan. *Oldest Living Confederate Widow Tells All*. New York: Knopf, 1989.

Gustafson, Melanie S. *Women and the Republican Party, 1854–1924*. Urbana: University of Illinois Press, 2001.

Hahn, Steven. *A Nation Under Our Feet: Black Political Struggles in the Rural South from Slavery to the Great Migration*. Cambridge: Harvard University Press, 2003.

Hamilton, Holman. *Prologue to Conflict: The Crisis and Compromise of 1850*. Lexington: University Press of Kentucky, 2005.

Handlin, Oscar. *Boston's Immigrants, 1790–1880: A Study in Acculturation*. Cambridge: Harvard University Press, 1991; first published in 1941.

Harding, Vincent. *There Is a River: The Black Struggle for Freedom in America*. New York: Vintage, 1983.

Harris, William C. *With Charity for All: Lincoln and the Restoration of the Union*. Lexington: University Press of Kentucky, 1997.

Harsh, Joseph L. *Taken at the Flood: Robert E. Lee and Confederate Strategy in the Maryland Campaign of 1862*. Kent, Ohio: Kent State University Press, 1999.

Hebert, Walter H. *Fighting Joe Hooker*. Lincoln: University of Nebraska Press, 1999; first published in 1944.

Hedrick, Joan D. *Harriet Beecher Stowe: A Life*. New York: Oxford University Press, 1994.

Hess, Earl J. *Pickett's Charge—The Last Attack at Gettysburg*. Chapel Hill: University of North Carolina Press, 2000.

———. *The Union Soldier in Battle: Enduring the Ordeal*. Lawrence: University Press of Kansas, 1997.

Hodes, Martha. *White Women, Black Men: Illicit Sex in the 19th-Century South*. New Haven: Yale University Press, 1997.

Holt, Michael. *The Political Crisis of the 1850s*. New York: Norton, 1978.

———. *The Rise and Fall of the American Whig Party: Jacksonian Politics and the Onset of the Civil War*. New York: Oxford University Press, 1999.

Horowitz, Joseph. *Wagner Nights: An American History*. Berkeley: University of California Press, 1994.

Howe, Daniel Walker. *What Hath God Wrought: The Transformation of America, 1815–1848*. New York: Oxford University Press, 2007.

Humez, Jean M. *Harriet Tubman: The Life and the Life Stories*. Madison: University of Wisconsin Press, 2003.

Huston, James L. *Stephen A. Douglas and the Dilemmas of Democratic Equality*. Lanham, Md.: Rowman & Littlefield, 2007.

Jenkins, Wilbert L. *Climbing Up to Glory: A Short History of African Americans during the Civil War and Reconstruction*. Wilmington, Del.: Scholarly Resources, 2002.

Johannsen, Robert W. *Stephen A. Douglas*. Urbana: University of Illinois Press, 1997.

Johnson, Dorothy M. *Warrior for a Lost Nation: A Biography of Sitting Bull*. Philadelphia: Westminster Press, 1969.

Johnson, Susan Lee. *Roaring Camp: The Social World of the California Gold Rush*. New York: Norton, 2000.

Jones, Archer. *Civil War Command and Strategy: The Process of Victory and Defeat*. New York: Free Press, 1992.

Kagan, Robert. *Dangerous Nation: America's Foreign Policy from its Earliest Days to the Dawn of the Twentieth Century*. New York: Knopf, 2006.

Kantrowitz, Stephen. *Ben Tillman and the Reconstruction of White Supremacy*. Chapel Hill: University of North Carolina Press, 2000.

Kaplan, Justin. *Mr. Clemens and Mark Twain: A Biography*. New York: Simon & Schuster, 1966.

Katz, Philip M. *From Appomattox to Montmartre: Americans and the Paris Commune*. Cambridge: Harvard University Press, 1998.

Keith, LeeAnna. *The Colfax Massacre: The Untold Story of Black Power, White Terror, and the Death of Reconstruction*. New York: Oxford University Press, 2008.

Keller, Morton. *Affairs of State: Public Life in Late Nineteenth-Century America*. Cambridge: Harvard University Press, 1977.

Kessler-Harris, Alice. *Out to Work: A History of Wage-Earning Women in the United States*. New York: Oxford University Press, 1982.

Klein, Maury. *The Life and Legend of Jay Gould*. Baltimore: Johns Hopkins University Press, 1986.

Kostyal, K. M. *Abraham Lincoln's Extraordinary Era: The Man and His Times*. New York: National Geographic, 2009.

Kramnick, Isaac, and R. Laurence Moore. *The Godless Constitution: The Case Against Religious Correctness*. New York: Norton, 1997.

Lane, Charles. *The Day Freedom Died: The Colfax Massacre, the Supreme Court, and the Betrayal of Reconstruction*. New York: Holt, 2008.

Larson, Robert W. *Red Cloud: Warrior-Statesman of the Lakota Sioux*. Norman: University of Oklahoma Press, 1997.

Lemann, Nicholas. *Redemption: The Last Battle of the Civil War*. New York: Farrar, Straus and Giroux, 2006.

Leonard, Elizabeth D. *Yankee Women: Gender Battles in the Civil War*. New York: Norton, 1994.

Levine, Bruce C. *Confederate Emancipation: Southern Plans to Free and Arm Slaves During the Civil War*. New York: Oxford University Press, 2006.

Lewis, Jon E., ed. *The Mammoth Book of Native Americans: The Story of America's Original Inhabitants in All its Beauty, Magic, Truth, and Tragedy*. New York: Carroll & Graf, 2004.

Limerick, Patricia Nelson. *The Legacy of Conquest: The Unbroken Past of the American West*. New York: Norton, 1987.

Linden, Glenn M. ed. *Voices from the Gathering Storm: The Coming of the American Civil War*. Wilmington, Del.: Scholarly Resources, 2001.

Linderman, Gerald F. *Embattled Courage: The Experience of Combat in the American Civil War*. New York: Free Press, 1987.

Litwack, Leon F. *Been in the Storm So Long: The Aftermath of Slavery*. New York: Random House, 1979.

———. *North of Slavery: The Negro in the Free States, 1790–1860*. Chicago: University of Chicago Press, 1961.

Livingstone, David N., D. G. Hart, and Mark A. Noll, eds. *Evangelicals and Science in Historical Perspective*. New York: Oxford University Press, 1999.

Long, E. B. *The Civil War Day by Day: An Almanac, 1861–1865*. Garden City, N.Y.: Doubleday, 1971.

Long, Kathryn Teresa. *The Revival of 1857–58: Interpreting an American Religious Awakening*. New York: Oxford University Press, 1998.

Lucas, Marion Brunson. *Sherman and the Burning of Columbia*. Columbia: University of South Carolina Press, 2000; first published in 1976.

Lynch, John R. *The Facts of Reconstruction*. New York: Neale Publishing, 1913.

Manning, Chandra. *What This Cruel War Was Over: Soldiers, Slavery, and the Civil War.* New York: Knopf, 2007.

Marshall, Joseph M., III. *The Day the World Ended at Little Bighorn.* New York: Penguin, 2007.

———. *The Journey of Crazy Horse: A Lakota History.* New York: Penguin, 2004.

Marten, James. *Children for the Union: The War Spirit on the Northern Home Front.* Chicago: Ivan R. Dee, 2004.

Marty, Martin. *The War-Time Lincoln and the Ironic Tradition.* Annual Robert Fortenbaugh Memorial Lecture. Gettysburg, Pa.: Gettysburg College, 2000.

McConnell, Stuart. *Glorious Contentment: The Grand Army of the Republic, 1865–1900.* Chapel Hill: University of North Carolina Press, 1992.

McFeely, William S. *Frederick Douglass.* New York: Touchstone, 1992.

———. *Grant: A Biography.* New York: Norton, 2002; first published in 1981.

McPherson, James M. *Battle Cry of Freedom: The Civil War Era.* New York: Oxford University Press, 1988.

———. *For Cause and Comrades: Why Men Fought in the Civil War.* New York: Oxford University Press, 1997.

———. *Ordeal by Fire,* vol. 2, *The Civil War.* New York: Knopf, 1982.

———. *Tried by War: Abraham Lincoln as Commander in Chief.* New York: Penguin, 2008.

Meacham, Jon. *American Gospel: God, the Founding Fathers, and the Making of a Nation.* New York: Random House, 2007.

Menand, Louis. *The Metaphysical Club: A Story of Ideas in America.* New York: Farrar, Straus and Giroux, 2001.

Miller, Randall M., Harry S. Stout, and Charles Reagan Wilson, eds. *Religion and the American Civil War.* New York: Oxford University Press, 1998.

Mintz, Steven. *Moralists and Modernizers: America's Pre–Civil War Reformers.* Baltimore: Johns Hopkins University Press, 1995.

Mitchell, Margaret. *Gone with the Wind.* New York: Macmillan, 1936.

Mohl, Raymond A. *The New City: Urban America in the Industrial Age, 1860–1920.* Arlington Heights, Ill.: Harlan Davidson, 1985.

Morris, Charles R. *The Tycoons: How Andrew Carnegie, John D. Rockefeller, Jay Gould, and J. P. Morgan Invented the American Supereconomy.* New York: Holt, 2005.

Morris, Roy, Jr. *The Better Angel: Walt Whitman in the Civil War.* New York: Oxford University Press, 2000.

———. *Fraud of the Century: Rutherford B. Hayes, Samuel Tilden and the Stolen Election of 1876.* New York: Simon & Schuster, 2003.

———. *Lighting Out for the Territory: How Samuel Clemens Headed West and Became Mark Twain.* New York: Simon & Schuster, 2010.

Nasaw, David. *Andrew Carnegie.* New York: Penguin, 2006.

Neilson, Reid L., and Terry L. Givens, eds. *Joseph Smith, Jr.: Reappraisals After Two Centuries.* New York: Oxford University Press, 2009.

Newman, Louise Michele. *White Women's Rights: The Racial Origins of Feminism in the United States.* New York: Oxford University Press, 1999.

Newmyer, R. Kent. *The Supreme Court Under Marshall and Taney.* 2nd ed. Wheeling, Ill.: Harlan Davidson, 2006.

Nichols, David A. *Lincoln and the Indians: Civil War Policy and Politics.* Columbia: University of Missouri Press, 1978.

Niebuhr, Reinhold. *The Irony of American History*. New York: Charles Scribner's Sons, 1962.

———. *Moral Man and Immoral Society: A Study in Ethics and Politics*. Louisville: Westminster John Knox Press, 2001; first published in 1932.

Niven, John. *John C. Calhoun and the Price of Union: A Biography*. Baton Rouge: Louisiana State University Press, 1988.

Noll, Mark A. *America's God: From Jonathan Edwards to Abraham Lincoln*. New York: Oxford University Press, 2002.

———, ed. *Religion and Politics: From the Colonial Period to the 1980s*. New York: Oxford University Press, 1990.

Oates, Stephen B. *Our Fiery Trial: Abraham Lincoln and John Brown, and the Civil War Era*. Amherst: University of Massachusetts Press, 1979.

Perman, Michael. *Emancipation and Reconstruction, 1862–1879*. Arlington Heights, Ill.: Harlan Davidson, 1987.

———. *The Road to Redemption: Southern Politics, 1869–1879*. Chapel Hill: University of North Carolina Press, 1984.

Peterson, Merrill D. *The Great Triumvirate: Webster, Clay, and Calhoun*. New York: Oxford University Press, 1988.

Poole, W. Scott. *Never Surrender: Confederate Memory and Conservatism in the South Carolina Upcountry*. Athens: University of Georgia Press, 2004.

Potter, David M. *The Impending Crisis, 1848–1861*. New York: Harper & Row, 1976.

Powers, Ron. *Mark Twain: A Life*. New York: Free Press, 2005.

Prucha, Francis Paul. *Americanizing the American Indian: Writings by the "Friends of the Indian," 1880–1900*. Cambridge: Harvard University Press, 1973.

Pryor, Elizabeth Brown. *Clara Barton: Professional Angel*. Philadelphia: University of Pennsylvania Press, 1987.

———. *Reading the Man: A Portrait of Robert E. Lee Through His Private Letters*. New York: Penguin, 2008.

Rable, George C. *Civil Wars: Women and the Crisis of Southern Nationalism*. Urbana: University of Illinois Press, 1989.

———. *The Confederate Republic: A Revolution Against Politics*. Chapel Hill: University of North Carolina, 1994.

———. *Fredericksburg! Fredericksburg!* Chapel Hill: University of North Carolina Press, 2002.

Rafuse, Ethan S. *Robert E. Lee and the Fall of the Confederacy, 1863–1865*. Lanham, Md.: Rowman & Littlefield, 2008.

Rachleff, Peter J. *Black Labor in the South: Richmond, Virginia, 1865–1890*. Philadelphia: Temple University Press, 1984.

Reardon, Carol. *Pickett's Charge in History and Memory*. Chapel Hill: University of North Carolina Press, 1997.

Reichley, A. James. *Faith in Politics*. Washington: Brookings Institution, 2002.

Remini, Robert V. *At the Edge of the Precipice: Henry Clay and the Compromise That Saved the Union*. New York: Basic Books, 2010.

Reynolds, David S. *John Brown, Abolitionist: The Man Who Killed Slavery, Sparked the Civil War, and Seeded Civil Rights*. New York: Knopf, 2005.

———. *Walt Whitman's America: A Cultural Biography*. New York: Knopf, 1995.

Richardson, Heather Cox. *The Death of Reconstruction: Race, Labor, and Politics in the Post-Civil War North, 1865–1901*. Cambridge: Harvard University Press, 2001.

——. *The Greatest Nation of the Earth: Republican Economic Policies During the Civil War.* Cambridge: Harvard University Press, 1997.

——. *West from Appomattox: The Reconstruction of America After the Civil War.* New Haven: Yale University Press, 2007.

Roberts, Timothy M. *Distant Revolutions: 1848 and the Challenge to American Exceptionalism.* Charlottesville: University of Virginia Press, 2009.

Robertson, James I., Jr. *Soldiers in Blue and Gray.* Columbia: University of South Carolina Press, 1998.

——. *Stonewall Jackson: The Man, the Soldier, the Legend.* New York: Macmillan, 1997.

Roland, Charles P. *An American Iliad: The Story of the Civil War.* Lexington: University Press of Kentucky, 2004; first published in 1991.

Rosen, Hannah. *Terror in the Heart of Freedom: Citizenship, Sexual Violence, and the Meaning of Race in the Postemancipation South.* Chapel Hill: University of North Carolina Press, 2009.

Rubin, Anne Sarah. *A Shattered Nation: The Rise and Fall of the Confederacy, 1861–1868.* Chapel Hill: University of North Carolina Press, 2005.

Russel, Robert R. *Improvement of Communication with the Pacific Coast as an Issue in American Politics, 1783–1864.* Cedar Rapids, Iowa: Torch Press, 1948.

Rydell, Robert W. *All the World's a Fair: Visions of Empire at American International Expositions, 1876–1916.* Chicago: University of Chicago Press, 1984.

Sajna, Mike. *Crazy Horse: The Life Behind the Legend.* New York: John Wiley & Sons, 2000.

Schott, Thomas E. *Alexander H. Stephens of Georgia: A Biography.* Baton Rouge: Louisiana State University Press, 1988.

Schultz, Nancy Lusignan. *The Burning of the Charlestown Convent, 1834.* New York: Free Press, 2000.

Sears, Stephen W. *Landscape Turned Red: The Battle of Antietam.* Boston: Houghton Mifflin, 1983.

Sheehan-Dean, Aaron Charles. *Why Confederates Fought: Family and Nation in Civil War Virginia.* Chapel Hill: University of North Carolina Press, 2007.

Silber, Nina. *The Romance of Reunion: Northerners and the South, 1865–1900.* Chapel Hill: University of North Carolina Press, 1993.

Silbey, Joel H. *Storm over Texas: The Annexation Controversy and the Road to Civil War.* New York: Oxford University Press, 2005.

Simpson, Brooks D. *Let Us Have Peace: Ulysses S. Grant and the Politics of War and Reconstruction, 1861–1868.* Chapel Hill: University of North Carolina Press, 1991.

——. *Ulysses S. Grant: Triumph over Adversity.* Boston: Houghton Mifflin, 2000.

Smith, Jean Edward. *Grant.* New York: Simon & Schuster, 2001.

Snay, Mitchell. *Gospel of Disunion: Religion and Separatism in the Antebellum South.* New York: Cambridge University Press, 1993.

Sperber, Jonathan. *The European Revolutions, 1848–1851.* Cambridge: Cambridge University Press, 2005.

Steffens, Lincoln. *The Shame of the Cities.* Mineola, N.Y.: Dover, 2007; first published in 1904.

Sterling, Dorothy, ed. *The Trouble They Seen: Black People Tell the Story of Reconstruction.* Garden City, N.Y.: Doubleday, 1976.

——, ed. *We Are Your Sisters: Black Women in the Nineteenth Century.* New York: Norton, 1997; first published in 1984.

Stiles, T. J. *The First Tycoon: The Epic Life of Cornelius Vanderbilt*. New York: Knopf, 2009.

Stowell, Daniel W. *Rebuilding Zion: The Religious Reconstruction of the South, 1863–1877*. New York: Oxford University Press, 1998.

Strong, Josiah. *The Twentieth Century City*. New York: Baker & Taylor, 1898. http://books.google.com/books?id=y2cAAAAAYAAJ&printsec=frontcover&dq= Josiah+Strong,+The+Twentieth+Century+City&source=bl&ots=Y1IHyEz7j_&sig= Gn5oDo1ERlQQgBuxUr3KBMtPPtE&hl=en&ei=P<->lhTN6EMoy48wSMh7G_Cw &sa=X&oi=book_result&ct=result&resnum=1&ved=0CBIQ6AEwAA#v=onepage &q&f=false

Summers, Mark Wahlgren. *The Era of Good Stealings*. New York: Oxford University Press, 1993.

———. *Party Games: Getting, Keeping, and Using Power in Gilded Age Politics*. Chapel Hill: University of North Carolina Press, 2004.

Sutherland, Daniel E. *The Expansion of Everyday Life, 1860–1876*. New York: Harper & Row, 1989.

Swift, Donald C. *Religion and the American Experience*. Armonk, N.Y.: M. E. Sharpe, 1998.

Tatum, Georgia Lee. *Disloyalty in the Confederacy*. Lincoln: University of Nebraska Press, 2000.

Thomas, Emory M. *The Confederate Nation, 1861–1865*. New York: Harper & Row, 1979.

———. *Robert E. Lee: A Biography*. New York: Norton, 1997.

Trefousse, Hans. *Andrew Johnson: A Biography*. New York: Norton, 1989.

———. *Carl Schurz: A Biography*. Knoxville: University of Tennessee Press, 1982.

Trudeau, Noah Andre. *Bloody Roads South: The Wilderness to Cold Harbor, May–June 1864*. Baton Rouge: Louisiana State University Press, 2000.

———. *Southern Storm: Sherman's March to the Sea*. New York: Harper, 2008.

Tuveson, Ernest Lee. *Redeemer Nation: The Idea of America's Millennial Role*. Chicago: University of Chicago Press, 1968.

Unruh, John D., Jr. *The Plains Across: The Overland Emigrants and the Trans-Mississippi West, 1840–1860*. Urbana: University of Illinois Press, 1979.

Villard, Oswald Garrison. *John Brown: A Biography, 1800–1859*. Garden City, N.Y.: Doubleday, 1929.

Waldrep, Christopher. *Roots of Disorder: Race and Criminal Justice in the American South, 1817–80*. Urbana: University of Illinois Press, 1998.

Waller, Altina Laura, and William Graebner, eds. *True Stories from the American Past: To 1865*. New York: McGraw-Hill, 1996.

Warren, Louis S. *Buffalo Bill's America: William Cody and the Wild West Show*. New York: Knopf, 2005.

Warren, Robert Penn. *The Legacy of the Civil War*. Lincoln: University of Nebraska Press, 1998; first published in 1961.

Weeks, Jim. *Gettysburg: Memory, Market, and an American Shrine*. Princeton: Princeton University Press, 2003.

Weeks, Philip. *Farewell, My Nation: The American Indian and the United States, 1820–1890*. Arlington Heights, Ill.: Harlan Davidson, 1990.

Weigley, Russell F. *A Great Civil War: A Military and Political History, 1861–1865*. Bloomington: Indiana University Press, 2000.

Wert, Jeffry D. *General James Longstreet: The Confederacy's Most Controversial Soldier: A Biography.* New York: Simon & Schuster, 1993.

Werth, Barry. *Banquet at Delmonico's: Great Minds, the Gilded Age, and the Triumph of Evolution in America.* New York: Random House, 2009.

White, G. Edward. *Justice Oliver Wendell Holmes: Law and the Inner Self.* New York: Oxford University Press, 1993.

White, Richard. *"It's Your Misfortune and None of My Own": A History of the American West.* Norman: University of Oklahoma Press, 1991.

Wilentz, Sean. *Chants Democratic: New York City and the Rise of the American Working Class.* New York: Oxford University Press, 1984.

Williams, Lou Falkner. *The Great South Carolina Ku Klux Klan Trials, 1871–1872.* Athens: University of Georgia Press, 1996.

Williams, Robert C. *Horace Greeley: Champion of American Freedom.* New York: New York University Press, 2006.

Wills, Garry. *Head and Heart: American Christianities.* New York: Penguin, 2007.

Wilson, Charles Reagan. *Baptized in Blood: The Religion of the Lost Cause, 1865–1920.* Athens: University of Georgia Press, 1980.

Wilson, James. *The Earth Shall Weep: A History of Native America.* New York: Grove Press, 2000.

Wilson, Mark R. *The Business of Civil War: Military Mobilization and the State, 1861–1865.* Baltimore: Johns Hopkins University Press, 2006.

Winik, Jay. *April 1865: The Month That Saved America.* New York: HarperCollins, 2001.

Woodward, C. Vann. *Origins of the New South, 1877–1913.* Baton Rouge: Louisiana State University Press, 1951.

Woodworth, Steven E., ed. *The Chickamauga Campaign.* Carbondale: Southern Illinois University Press, 2010.

Wooster, Robert. *The Military and United States Indian Policy, 1865–1903.* New Haven: Yale University Press, 1988.

ARTICLES AND BOOK CHAPTERS

Alexander, Thomas B. "The Civil War as Institutional Fulfillment." *Journal of Southern History* 47 (February 1981): 3–32.

Ash, Stephen V. "Poor Whites in the Occupied South, 1861–1865." *Journal of Southern History* 57 (February 1991): 39–62.

Aynes, Richard L. "Constricting the Law of Freedom: Justice Miller, the Fourteenth Amendment, and the *Slaughter-House* Cases." *Chicago-Kent Law Review* 70 (1994): 627.

Barnhart, Terry A. "'A Common Feeling': Regional Identity and Historical Consciousness in the Old Northwest, 1820–1860." *Michigan Historical Review* 29 (Spring 2003): 39–70.

Billington, Ray Allen. "The Burning of the Charlestown Convent." *New England Quarterly* 10 (March 1937): 4–24.

Blakely, Gilbert Sykes. Introduction to *Ivanhoe*, by Sir Walter Scott. New York: Charles E. Merrill, 1911.

Bleser, Carol K. "The Marriage of Varina Howell and Jefferson Davis: 'I gave the best and all my life to a girdled tree.'" *Journal of Southern History* 65 (February 1999): 3–40.

Blight, David W. "'For Something Beyond the Battlefield': Frederick Douglass and the Struggle for the Memory of the Civil War." *Journal of American History* 75 (March 1989): 1156–78.

Bridgman, Howard Allen. "The Suburbanite." *Independent,* April 10, 1902, 862–63.

Brodhead, Richard H. "Prophets in America Circa 1830: Ralph Waldo Emerson, Nat Turner, Joseph Smith." In *Joseph Smith, Jr.: Reappraisals After Two Centuries,* edited by Reid L. Neilson and Terry L. Givens. New York: Oxford University Press, 2009.

Brundage, W. Fitzhugh. "Meta Warrick's 1907 'Negro Tableaux' and (Re)Presenting African American Historical Memory." *Journal of American History* 89 (March 2003): 1368–400.

Bynum, Victoria. "'War Within a War': Women's Participation in the Revolt of the North Carolina Piedmont, 1863–1865." *Frontiers: A Journal of Women Studies* 9, no. 3 (1987): 43–49.

Catton, Bruce. "The Generalship of Ulysses S. Grant Defended." In *Grant, Lee, Lincoln, and the Radicals: Essays on Civil War Leadership,* edited by Grady McWhiney, 3–29. Evanston, Ill.: Northwestern University Press, 1973.

Carwardine, Richard. "Trauma in Methodism: Property, Church Schism, and Sectional Polarization in Antebellum America." In *God and Mammon: Protestants, Money, and the Market, 1790–1860,* edited by Mark A. Noll, 195–216. New York: Oxford University Press, 1990.

Cashin, Edward J. "Paternalism in Augusta: The Impact of the Plantation Ethic upon an Urban Society." In *Paternalism in a Southern City: Race, Religion, and Gender in Augusta, Georgia,* edited by Edward J. Cashin and Glenn T. Eskew, 1–43. Athens: University of Georgia Press, 2001.

Chicoine, Stephen. "'. . . Willing Never to Go in Another Fight': The Civil War Correspondence of Rufus King Felder of Chappell Hill." *Southwestern Historical Quarterly* 106 (April 2003): 574–97.

Coclanis, Peter A. "The American Civil War in Economic Perspective: Basic Questions and Some Answers." *Southern Cultures* 2 (Winter 1996): 163–75.

Costa, Dora L., and Matthew E. Kahn. "Cowards and Heroes: Group Loyalty in the American Civil War." *Quarterly Journal of Economics* 118 (May 2003): 519–48.

Craiutu, Aurelian, and Jeremy Jennings, "The Third *Democracy*: Tocqueville's Views of America After 1840." *American Political Science Review* 98 (August 2004): 391–404.

Curtis, Heather D. "Views of Self, Success, and Society Among Young Men in Antebellum Boston." *Church History* 73 (September 2004): 613–34.

Dawson, Jan C. "The Puritan and the Cavalier: The South's Perception of Contrasting Traditions." *Journal of Southern History* 44 (November 1978): 597–614.

DeGruccio, Michael. "Manhood, Race, Failure, and Reconciliation: Charles Francis Adams, Jr., and the American Civil War." *New England Quarterly* 81 (December 2008): 636–75.

Domosh, Mona. "The Symbolism of the Skyscraper: Case Studies of New York's First Tall Buildings." *Journal of Urban History* 14 (May 1988): 321–45.

DuBois, W. E. B. "Reconstruction and Its Benefits." In *W. E. B. DuBois: A Reader,* edited by David Levering Lewis, 174–92. New York: Holt, 1995.

Egnal, Marc. "Rethinking the Secession of the Lower South: The Clash of Two Groups." *Civil War History* 50 (September 2004): 261–90.

Faust, Drew Gilpin. "Altars of Sacrifice: Confederate Women and the Narratives of War." *Journal of American History* 76 (March 1990): 1200–1228.

Formwalt, Lee W. "The Camilla Massacre of 1868: Racial Violence as Political Propaganda." *Georgia Historical Quarterly* 71 (Fall 1987): 399–426.

Ford, Lacy K., Jr. "Republican Ideology in a Slave Society: The Political Economy of John C. Calhoun." *Journal of Southern History* 54 (August 1988): 405–24.

Fox, Richard Wightman. "The President Who Died for Us." *New York Times*, April 14, 2006.

Gienapp, William E. "Nativism and the Creation of a Republican Majority in the North Before the Civil War." *Journal of American History* 72 (December 1985): 529–99.

Goen, C. C. "Broken Churches, Broken Nation: Regional Religion and North-South Alienation in Antebellum America." *Church History* 52 (March 1983): 21–35.

Goldin, Claudia Dale. "The Economics of Emancipation." *Journal of Economic History* 33 (March 1973): 66–85.

Graham, Thomas. "Harriet Beecher Stowe and the Question of Race." *New England Quarterly* 46 (December 1973): 614–22.

Hahn, Steven. "The Politics of the Dead." *New Republic*, April 23, 2008, 48–52.

Hamilton, Jeanne, O.S.U. "The Nunnery as Menace: The Burning of the Charlestown Convent, 1834." *Catholic Historian*, Winter 1996. http://www.ewtn.com/library/HUMANITY/BURNING.TXT.

Harris, William C. "The Hampton Roads Peace Conference: A Final Test of Lincoln's Presidential Leadership." *Journal of the Abraham Lincoln Association*, Winter 2000. http://www.historycooperative.org/journals/jala/21.1/harris.html.

Hatch, Nathan O. "The Democratization of Christianity and the Character of American Politics." In *Religion and American Politics: From the Colonial Period to the 1980s*, edited by Mark A. Noll, 92–120. New York: Oxford University Press, 1990.

Hattaway, Herman. "The Evolution of Tactics in the Civil War." In Hattaway, *Reflections of a Civil War Historian: Essays on Leadership, Society, and the Art of War*, 200–20. Columbia: University of Missouri Press, 2003.

Hughes, Richard T. "A Civic Theology for the South: The Case of Benjamin M. Palmer." *Journal of Church and State* 25, no. 3 (1983): 447–67.

Johnson, Michael. "Rendezvous at Promontory: A New Look at the Golden Spike Ceremony." *Utah Historical Quarterly* 72 (Winter 2004): 47–68.

Kitrell, Irvin, III. "40 Acres and a Mule." *Civil War Times Illustrated* 41 (May 2002): 54–61.

Levine, Bruce C. "Conservatism, Nativism, and Slavery: Thomas R. Whitney and the Origins of the Know Nothing Party." *Journal of American History* 88 (September 2001): 455–88.

McPherson, James M. "'For a Vast Future Also': Lincoln and the Millennium." Jefferson Lecture. March 27, 2000. http://www.neh.gov/whoweare/mcpherson/speech.html.

———. "No Peace Without Victory, 1861–1865." *American Historical Review* 109 (February 2004): 1–18.

Miller, William J. "'Never Has There Been a More Complete Victory': The Cavalry Engagement at Tom's Brook, October 9, 1864." In *The Shenandoah Valley Campaign of 1864*, edited by Gary W. Gallagher, 134–60. Chapel Hill: University of North Carolina Press, 2006.

Miller, Zane L. "The Rise of the City." *Hayes Historical Journal* 3 (Spring and Fall 1980): 73–83.

Moorhead, James Howell. "Religion in the Civil War: The Northern Side." http://national humanitiescenter.org/tserve/nineteen/nkeyinfo/cwnorth.htm.

Morrison, Michael A. "American Reaction to European Revolutions, 1848–1852: Sectionalism, Memory, and the Revolutionary Heritage." *Civil War History* 49 (June 2003): 111–32.

Noll, Mark A. "'Both . . . Pray to the Same God': The Singularity of Lincoln's Faith in the Era of the Civil War." *Journal of the Abraham Lincoln Association*, Winter 1997. http://www.historycooperative.org/journals/jala/18.1/noll.html.

Pinheiro, John C. "'Religion Without Restriction': Anti-Catholicism, All Mexico, and the Treaty of Guadalupe Hidalgo." *Journal of the Early Republic* 23 (Spring 2003): 69–96.

Poole, W. Scott. "Religion, Gender, and the Lost Cause in South Carolina's 1876 Governor's Race: 'Hampton or Hell!'" *Journal of Southern History* 68 (August 2002): 573–98.

Powell, Lawrence N. "Reinventing Tradition: Liberty Place, Historical Memory, and Silk-Stocking Vigilantism in New Orleans." *Slavery & Abolition* 20 (April 1999): 127–49.

Prioli, Carmine A. "The Ursuline Outrage." *American Heritage* 33 (February/March 1982): 101–5.

Pryor, Elizabeth Brown. "Robert E. Lee's 'Severest Struggle.'" *American Heritage* 58 (Winter 2008): 18–25.

Roberts, Giselle. "The Confederate Belle: The Belle Ideal, Patriotic Womanhood, and Wartime Reality in Louisiana and Mississippi, 1861–1865." *Louisiana History* 43 (Spring 2002): 189–214.

Roberts, Timothy M. "The European Revolutions of 1848 and Antebellum Violence in Kansas." *Journal of the West* 44 (Fall 2005): 58–68.

———. "'Revolutions Have Become the Bloody Toy of the Multitude': European Revolutions, the South, and the Crisis of 1850." *Journal of the Early Republic* 25 (Summer 2005): 255–83.

Robertson, James I., Jr. "Stonewall Jackson: A 'Pious Blue-Eyed Killer'?" In *New Perspectives on the Civil War: Myths and Realities of the National Conflict*, edited by John Y. Simon and Michael E. Stevens, 69–92. Lanham, Md.: Rowman & Littlefield, 2002.

Ross, John F. "Treasures of Robert E. Lee Discovered." *American Heritage* 58 (Winter 2008): 26–29.

Ross, Jordan. "Uncommon Union: Diversity and Motivation Among Civil War Soldiers." *American Nineteenth-Century History* 3 (Spring 2002): 17–44.

Salmon, John S. "Land Operations in Virginia in 1862." In *Virginia at War*, edited by William C. Davis and James I. Robertson Jr., 1–15. Lexington: University Press of Kentucky, 2007.

Schaff, Morris. "The Battle of the Wilderness." *Atlantic Monthly* 104 (November 1909): 721–31.

Sears, Stephen W. "Getting Right with Robert E. Lee." *American Heritage* 42 (May/June 1991): 58–72.

Sies, Mary Corbin. "The City Transformed: Nature, Technology, and the Suburban Ideal, 1877–1917." *Journal of Urban History* 14 (November 1987): 81–111.

Tuchinsky, Adam Max. "'The Bourgeoisie Will Fall and Fall Forever': The *New-York Tribune*, the 1848 French Revolution, and American Social Democratic Discourse." *Journal of American History* 92 (September 2005): 470–97.

Wakefield, Laura Wallis. "'Set a Light in a Dark Place': Teachers of Freedmen in Florida, 1864–1874." *Florida Historical Quarterly* 81 (Spring 2003): 401–17.

Wilson, Charles Reagan. "Robert Lewis Dabney: Religion and the Southern Holocaust." *Virginia Magazine of History and Biography* 89 (January 1981): 79–89.

Winik, Jay. "'American Brutus': The Lone Gunmen." *New York Times*, December 19, 2004.

Zuckerman, Michael. "Holy Wars, Civil Wars: Religion and Economics in Nineteenth-Century America." *Prospects* 16 (1991): 205–40.

EXHIBIT

"Grant and Lee in War and Peace." New York Historical Society, October 17, 2008–March 29, 2009.

DOCTORAL DISSERTATION

Wilson, Mark R. "The Business of Civil War: Military Enterprise, the State, and Political Economy in the United States, 1850–1880." Ph.D. dissertation, University of Chicago, 2002.

INDEX

Abbott, Henry Livermore, 262, 265, 283, 286, 318–19
abolitionists, 25, 115, 246, 474
  anti-slavery literature of, 26–27, 28, 93
  John Brown, 158–61, 162–63
  opponents of, 27, 35, 69, 75, 145, 194
  as out of date, 501
  and peace proposals, 335
  and secession, 194
"Acres of Diamonds" (Conwell), 13, 456–58, 468, 472
Adams, Charles Francis Jr., 358, 373, 471, 481
Adams, Doc, 506, 508
Adams, Henry, 390, 482
Adams, Henry (black leader), 526
Adams, John, 29
Adams, John Quincy II, 504
Addams, Jane, 501
African Americans:
  Colfax massacre, 493–94
  and draft riots, 291–92
  and education, 411–15, 527
  Exodusters, 527
  and Fifteenth Amendment, 435, 436, 494
  and Fourteenth Amendment, 427, 436, 494–95
  freedmen, *see* blacks, free
  independence sought by, 410–11, 412, 422
  labor of, 27, 49, 142
  land sought by, 410–11, 422
  as lesser race, 13, 14, 175, 186
  in postwar years, 406–16, 421–26
  in prisons, 27
  restrictions against, 5, 27–28, 142
  violence against, 410, 424–26, 428, 432, 433, 435–36, 480, 494, 502, 506–10
  voting rights of, 419, 423, 427–28, 429–32, 469, 472, 493, 508, 526, 528
  migration to Canada, 70, 81, 142
  and miscegenation, 336
  property ownership by, 527
  in public office, 431, 481, 508
  rights of, *see* civil rights
  sharecropping, 492–93

  soldiers, 267, 280–83, 295, 321, 354–55, 399
  war for freedom, 208
Age of Reason, 13, 383, 384, 395–96, 455
Agriculture Department, U.S., 304
Alcorn, James, 185
Alger, Horatio, 9, 380
Allston, Elizabeth, 398
American Anti-Slavery Society, 27, 370
American Colonization Society, 101
American Missionary Association, 248, 412, 469–70
American Party, 90
American Railway Association, 443
American Revolution:
  Civil War as completion of, 1, 207
  legacy of, 4, 6, 18, 24, 26, 28, 46, 47, 58, 59, 61, 70, 84, 86, 115, 206, 207, 212, 219, 524
Ames, Adelbert, 497, 498
Anderson, Robert, 200–203, 205
Andersonville prison, 322–25, 345
Andrew, Bishop James O., 34
Anthony, Susan B., 427, 468, 516
anti-Catholicism, 1, 3, 7, 13, 18, 25–26, 291, 293, 470
  and conversion, 24, 25
  and Lyman Beecher, 19, 20, 21–22, 24, 26
  and Mexican War, 49
  and nativism, 90–91, 170
  Ursuline convent, 4, 17–23, 24, 495
Arapaho Indians, 446, 447
Armour, Philip, 301, 510
Army of Northern Virginia, 250, 256, 283–84, 286, 318, 326, 331
Army of Tennessee, 313, 315, 326, 331, 347, 348
Army of the Cumberland, 312, 313, 326, 347
Army of the Potomac, *see* Union army
Army of the Shenandoah, 340, 360
Army of Virginia, 254, 255
Arnold, Benedict, 215
Arp, Bill, 401
Atchison, David, 103–4, 113
Atkinson, Edward, 504
Atwater, Lyman, 471

624   INDEX

Kossuth, Lajos, 59, 61, 86
Ku Klux Klan, 424, 432, 433, 436, 494, 499–500

labor:
  artisanal, 24
  of freed slaves, 27, 49
  of immigrants, 27, 88, 92, 93–94, 487, 490
  vs. capital, 190, 487–90
  wages of, 485–86
labor unions:
  Irish strikebreakers, 18, 20
  membership in, 486, 490
  public cynicism toward, 468, 484, 489, 531
  public demonstrations by, 480, 483
  strikes of, 15, 308, 440–41, 469, 487–88, 531
  and women, 486
Lafayette, marquis de, 46
Lakota Sioux, 106–7, 109–12, 127, 518–19
Lane, Joseph, 168
Lanier, Sidney, 514
Larkin, Thomas, 43
Latrobe, Osmun, 233
Lee, Light Horse Harry, 250
Lee, Robert E.:
  at Antietam, 256–60
  at Appomattox, 362–64
  and black troops, 355
  at Chancellorsville, 276, 277–78, 290
  as Confederate army commander, 250, 279, 283, 288, 326, 346, 360
  and desertions, 354
  at Fredericksburg, 263, 264–66, 374
  at Gettysburg, 283, 284–89
  and Harpers Ferry, 159
  home of, 219–20
  and Mexican War, 51, 216, 250, 284, 362
  military strategy of, 252–54, 255, 256, 278, 287–88, 328–30, 350
  personal traits of, 250–51, 252
  in postwar years, 422, 426
  at Richmond, 263–64
  and secession, 185, 251
  and Seven Days' Battles, 253–54, 255
  and surrender, 362–64
  at Wilderness, 326–27
Leon, Louis, 322
Lewis, Edmonia, 523
Liberal Republicans, 475–76, 477, 478
Liberty Party, 37, 38, 53, 54
Light Hair (Crazy Horse), 111–12, 127
Lincoln, Abraham, 4, 79, 92, 96
  cabinet of, 198–99, 214
  and Civil War, 8, 201–3, 205, 207, 215, 222, 225, 229, 235, 244, 254, 256, 257, 274, 278, 288–89, 295, 328, 333–36, 361
  and the Constitution, 8, 100, 183, 195–96, 197, 199–202, 214, 246, 248, 261
  death of, 365–69
  debates with Douglas, 7–8, 150–57, 164

and elections (1848), 52; (1856), 120, 122, 125; (1858), 150–57; (1860), 8, 166–72, 178–79, 306; (1864), 335–38, 340, 341–43
and emancipation, 9, 245, 248, 261–63, 267, 280, 334–37, 352
First Inaugural, 199–200
at Ford's Theater, 364–65
Gettysburg Address, 9, 293–94, 302, 358
global perspective of, 103, 207, 215, 343
"House Divided" speech, 8, 153
journey to D.C., 196–98
memories of, 245
messages to Congress, 215, 263, 380, 418, 487
in New York, 180–81, 197
patent held by, 303
political opponents of, 214, 266
political sense of, 151–52, 154, 214–15, 359, 495
and popular sovereignty, 102
and postwar plans, 418–19
and Republican Party, 120, 156, 164–66, 196, 245, 335
at Richmond, 361–62, 368
and rule of law, 6, 93, 196, 199
and secession, 195–97, 199
Second Inaugural, 10–11, 344, 356–59, 360, 367, 368, 371
and slavery, 84–85, 100–103, 117–18, 119, 155–56, 174, 245–46, 247–48, 262, 290, 333, 353, 359
and Union, 9, 84–85, 100, 119, 157, 173, 196, 200, 214–15, 246, 261
and Whig Party, 93, 101, 103, 119, 151, 178
Lincoln, Mary Todd, 121, 364–65
Lincoln, Robert, 288, 365
Lincoln, Tad, 365
Lincoln, Willie, 227, 235, 240–41
Little Big Horn, battle of, 518–19
Little Thunder, 111–12
Livermore, Mary, 527
Lodge, Henry Cabot, 529
Logan, John, 375
Long, John Dixon, 141
Longfellow, Henry Wadsworth, 121
Longstreet, James B., 255, 264, 285, 286, 311, 312, 313, 497
Louisiana:
  Battle of Liberty Place, 497
  Colfax massacre in, 493–94
  federal troops in, 500–501
  readmission of, 418, 419
  White League in, 496–97
Louisiana Purchase, 97
Louis Napoleon, 60, 114, 115
Lovejoy, Elijah, 161
Lovejoy, Owen, 303
Lowell, James Russell, 481
Lyman, Theodore, 320, 374
Lynch, John R., *The Facts of Reconstruction*, 529